W9-DFU-698

Glassware

1887 – 1982

Identification & Values

95 Years of Glassmaking

Frances Bones

COLLECTOR BOOKS

A Division of Schroeder Publishing Co., Inc.

On the Cover:

Front Cover:

Queen Anne – Colony 1103 Blue Lustre, $275.00 – 325.00.

2276 Blue Vanity, $190.00 – 220.00.

Legion 2440 Topaz Vase, $150.00 – 175.00.

Back Cover:

Homespun 4183 Teal Blue Tumbler, $35.00 – 40.00.

Needlepoint 4184 Gold Tumbler, $35.00 – 40.00.

Candy Jar 2250, Canary and Black Enamel, $55.00 – 65.00.

Cover design: Terri Stalions
Book design: Holly C. Long

Collector Books
P.O. Box 3009
Paducah, Kentucky 42002 – 3009

Printed in the U.S.A. by Image Graphics Inc., Paducah KY

Contents

About the Author

Frances Bones has collected original Fostoria catalogs and material since 1970. For years she has looked forward to the time when she could share this material with other collectors and dealers, but realizes that even with this publication, there is still a considerable amount of unidentified Fostoria in the market place. A dealer in both American silver and glass, in 1971 she published *Collectibles of the Depression* and in 1973 *The Book of Duncan Glass.* In the spring of 1998 she and Lee Roy Fisher published *The Standard Encyclopedia of American Silverplate.* Frances has made numerous radio and television appearances and is always eager to talk about her favorite subject, American glassware.

Acknowledgments

The compilation of this book would have been impossible without the help of fellow collectors, glass club members, and dealers. A great big thanks goes to Fostoria's Hugh Buzzard Sr. for permitting the research and copying of all available Fostoria archival material in 1970. The offices and halls of the Fostoria plant were decorated at that time with colored photographs of older pieces of glass. Hugh suggested we take these items off the wall and copy them also. One of the outstanding photographs featured a "Gone With the Wind Lamp" with a painted scene of a magnificent stag being stalked by a wolf. This item is typical of the outstanding merchandise that Fostoria produced around 1900.

Others who have supported this endeavor by loaning their Fostoria material and by sharing their knowledge are the late Norman Alford; Carol Bartholf; Max Miller; Lydia McNeil; and Linda Rippert. Special thanks goes to Bill Schroeder of Collector Books who shares our belief that original catalogs are the premier source for studying and understanding the products produced by Fostoria during their 95 years of manufacturing hand-made glass. Thanks also to Lisa Stroup and Billy Schroeder for their helpful suggestions.

How To Use This Book

This identification guide of the products of the former Fostoria Glass Company is easy to use. The glass presented here, as well as the suggested price guide, is divided alphabetically into 19 sections listed in the contents. Dinnerware was always the backbone of the Fostoria operations, so this category is the largest section. Fostoria dinnerware is divided into four categories: Cut, Etched, Needle Etched, and Pressed. Patterns within each of these four categories are presented alphabetically. In the classification Blown Stemware and Tumblers, the catalog pages are chronologically by line number. All these blown drinking vessels had line numbers; very few were given pattern names.

The Price Guide is presented only as a rough guide for Fostoria collectors. The prices are for items that are in excellent condition; no chips, scratches, or obvious wear. Gold, silver, or enamel decorations must be in mint condition. Prices reflect the market experience of the author at the time of publication and are subject to variation with time and by region.

Fostoria Glassware
1887 — 1992
95 Years of Glassmaking

Assembling a Fostoria collection is an adventure with many facets. Not only can we own beautiful glass to use and enjoy, but interest and desire are generated to learn more about all glassware manufactured in America. Our family's quest for Fostoria actually began at a Texas estate sale in 1969. We left that sale the proud owners of several pieces of honey-colored stemware. We did not know at the time that this was the pattern Vesper or that Fostoria was the maker. After looking through very limited available material showing Cambridge and Heisey glass, we thought perhaps our pattern might be a Fostoria product. It took a trip in 1970 to the Fostoria plant in Moundsville, West Virginia, to establish the correct identify. We were delighted when Hugh Buzzard Sr., the general sales manager, said those magic words, "Yes, that's ours, we made that a long time ago."

There is little doubt Fostoria was the most versatile of all the American glass manufacturers. Because of extensive advertising, Fostoria became a household word. When the company first opened its doors, the manufacturing of oil burning lamps was a major part of their business. Some of the more glamorous lamps were the opal decorated pieces sold as parlor lamps. Other interesting items that were also made in opal were miniature lamps, vases, and vanity items. Much of the early tableware was pressed glass with geometric designs. Some of these pressed patterns were made in colors of canary, emerald green, and opal, and various decorations such as gilding, ruby, and purple blushes. The early Fostoria years yielded carloads of jelly glasses plus bar and hotel wares. The jug and tankard lines were extensive, made by both the blown and pressed processes.

After 1900, blown stemware became very popular with the American housewife, and Fostoria became a leader in this field. This firm was a large producer of candlesticks, candelabra, and lustres, and by the 1920s, these items were illustrated in a separate catalog. In the mid-1920s, Fostoria began to concentrate on the bridal market and brought out colored stems. By 1927, these stems were more elaborate in design and made in three parts: bowl, stem, and foot.

The wonderful burgundy, regal blue, and ruby colors were marketed extensively starting around 1933, a trend away from the pink, amber, green, and azure of former years. The crystal etchings Navarre and Meadow Rose were introduced in 1936 and became instant successes. Several of the dinnerware patterns were greatly expanded in 1939 and 1940, but this period of expansion was cut short by the advent of World War II. Color was also severely limited during this period. In the 1950s, Fostoria turned to manufacturing milk glass, and this was a highly successful move. Animals, novelties, and dresser items were produced in milk-white in addition to pastel colors. Several new pressed patterns were introduced in color in the 1960s. In addition, the patterns American and Colony were still being made but were limited in size.

The 1970s brought renewed interest in the acid etched patterns Navarre and Meadow Rose, and these were made in two new pastel shades. By the late 1970s, Fostoria Glass Company realized that manufacturing methods would have to change; they were faced with rising production costs plus competition from imported glass.

In May of 1982, Fostoria announced that their production of hand-made glass would cease. They pledged to continue the production of lead crystal glassware. At the time this decision was reached, Fostoria was America's oldest producer of hand-made glass. In 1983 the Fostoria Glass Company was sold to the Lancaster Colony Corporation, and in 1986 the Moundsville, West Virginia plant was closed.

Bowls and Candlesticks

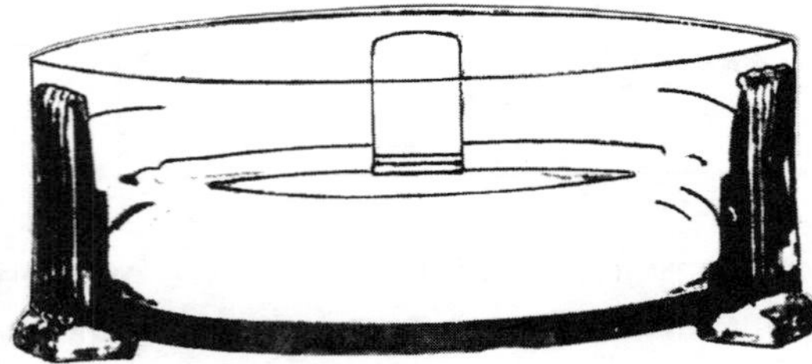

2445 Footed Bowl
Diameter, 8½", 1931 Catalog
Colors of Az-Gr-Amb-Tz-Ro
Also known in Ebony

2352 Candlestick
Height 5¾", 1927 Catalog
Colors of Amb-Bl-Gr

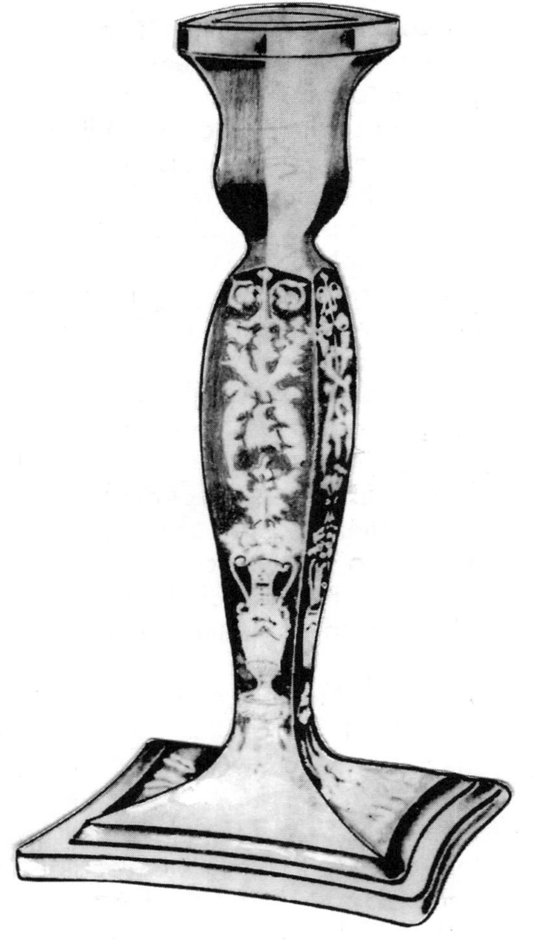

1965 Candlestick
Height 8", 1924 Catalog

1612 Candle
Height 5", 1914 Catalog

2432 Oval Bowl
Length 11", 1934 Catalog
Possibly made for only one or two years

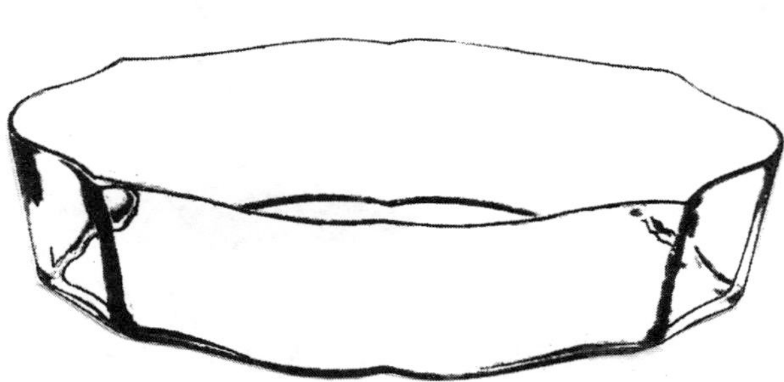

2426 Oval Bowl
Length 12", 1931 Catalog
Colors of RB-Bur-EG

2545 Lustre Flame
Height 7½", 1939 Catalog
Made in Cry-GT-Az

2383 Candle, 3-Light
1931 Catalog
Colors of Ro-Az-Gr-Amb-Eb-Tz

2244 Candlestick
Height 8", 1924 Catalog
Made in many enamel decorations
including Dresden Roses

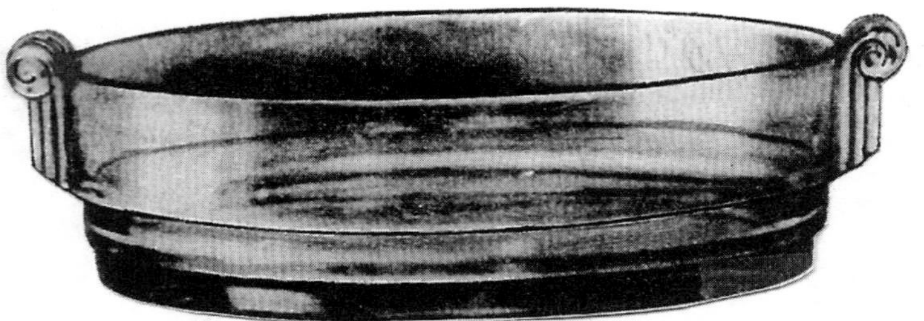

2443 Oval Bowl
Length 8½", 1936 Catalog

2443 Candlestick
Height 4", 1936 Catalog
Also made in 6" Ice Tub

2480 Handled Bowl
Length 10", 1931 Catalog
Colors of Gr-Amb-Tz
This bowl predates the Baroque pattern but was later incorporated into that line. The new Azure-Tint was introduced in 1936; it was not a successful color. Topaz was dropped when Gold-Tint was introduced in 1938.

2997 Candlestick
Height 6", 1927 Catalog
Made in Amb-Bl-Gr-Eb.
Made earlier in Canary

2550 Candle Lamp
Height 8½", 1940 Catalog
Spool pattern

2434 Bowl
Length 13", Introduced 1931
Colors of Gr-Amb, limited production

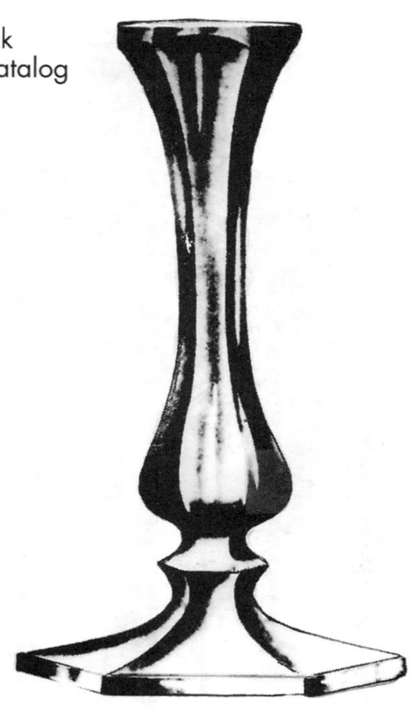

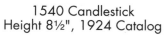

1540 Candlestick
Height 8½", 1924 Catalog

1192 Candlestick
Height 10½", 1902 Catalog

737 Candlestick
1901 Catalog

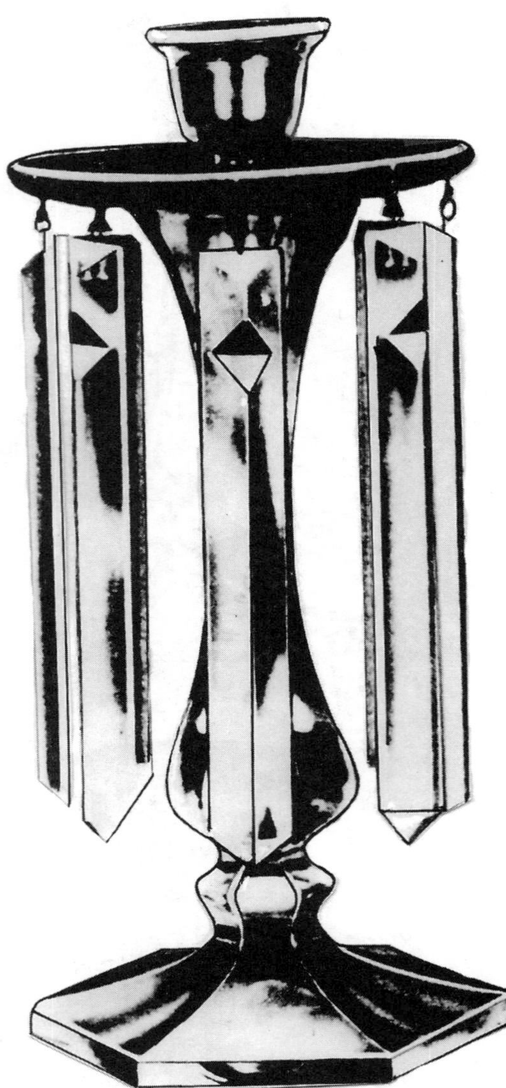

1640 Lustre
Height 11½", 1924 Catalog
Prisms 6"
Fostoria also made the prisms.

19 Saucer Candle
1904 Catalog

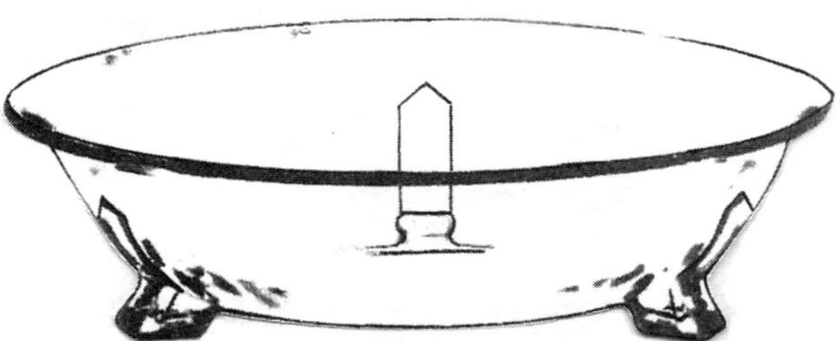

2458 Flared Bowl
Diameter 11½", 1931 Catalog
Colors of RB-Bur-EG, limited production

17 Candlestick
1904 Catalog

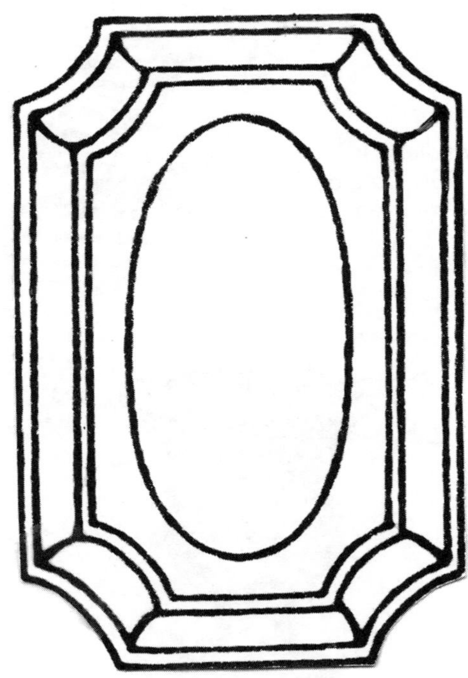

2466 Plateau
1932 Designer Drawing

2466 Candlestick
Height 3", 1932 Drawing

2424 Flared Bowl
Diameter 9", 1932 Designer Drawing
This bowl is known in Wisteria.

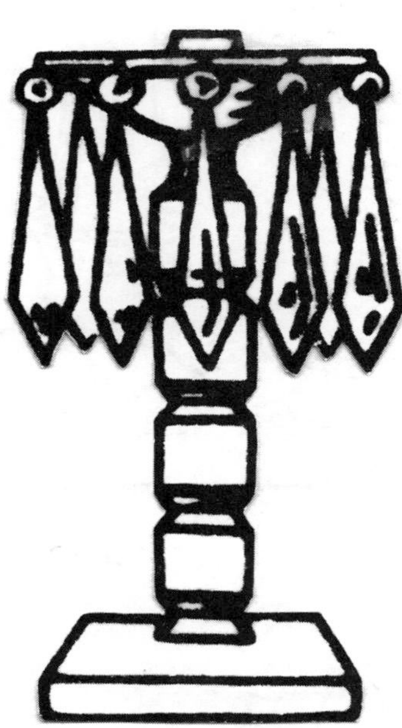

2453 Lustre
Height 7½", 1932 Drawing
Colors of Eb-Tz-Gr-Wisteria

2395 Candlestick
Height 3", 1930 Catalog
Colors of Ro-Az-Gr-Am-Eb

1801 Candlestick
Height 8", 1902 Catalog

1485 Candlestick
Height 8", 9½", 11½"
Cut Cattails, 1924 Catalog

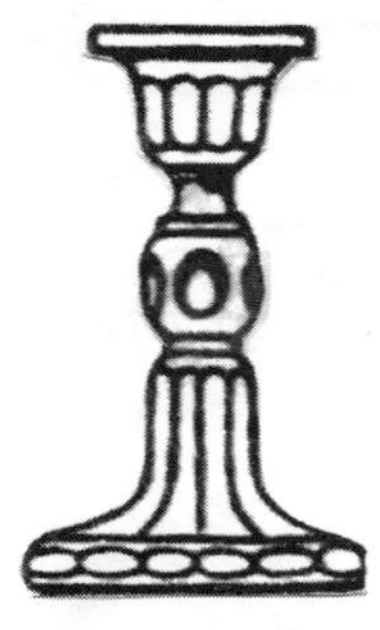
2449 Candlestick
Height 6", 1932 Designer
Drawing, Hermitage Pattern

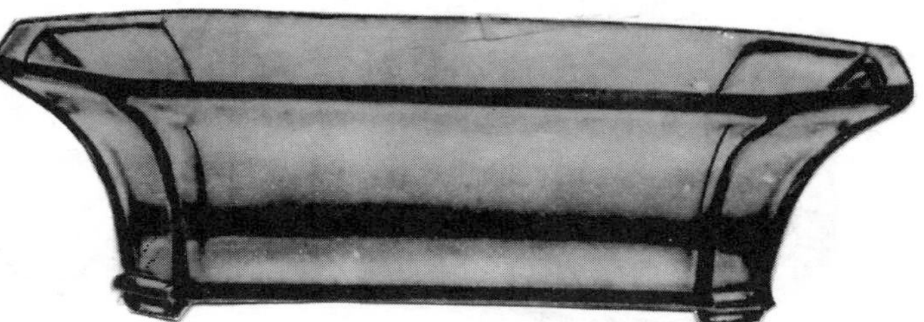

2481 Footed Oblong Bowl
Length 11", Introduced 1931
Used in 1933 for Midnight Rose
and Springtime etchings.

1064 Candlestick
Height 8", 1902 Catalog

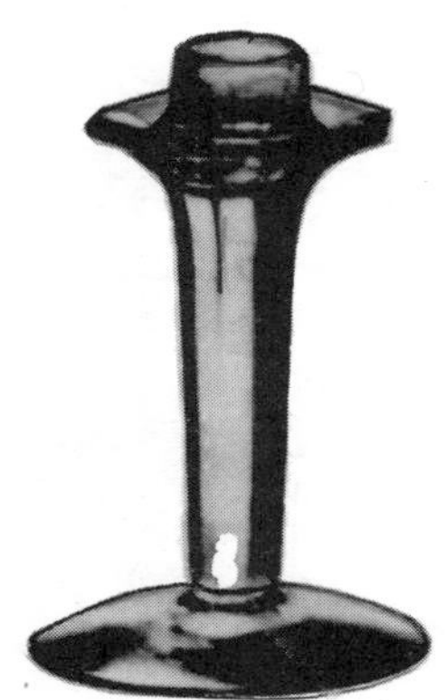

2481 Candlestick
Height 5", 1931 Catalog

2441 Footed Bowl
Diameter 12", 1931 Catalog
Colors of Ro-Az-Tz-Gr–Amb

2594 Trindle Candlestick
Height 8", 1941 Catalog

2574 Duo Candlestick
Height 5¼"

2324 Etched Candlestick
Height 9", 1924 Catalog
Colors of Canary, Bl-Gr–Amb
Made with many decorations including white enamel lines.

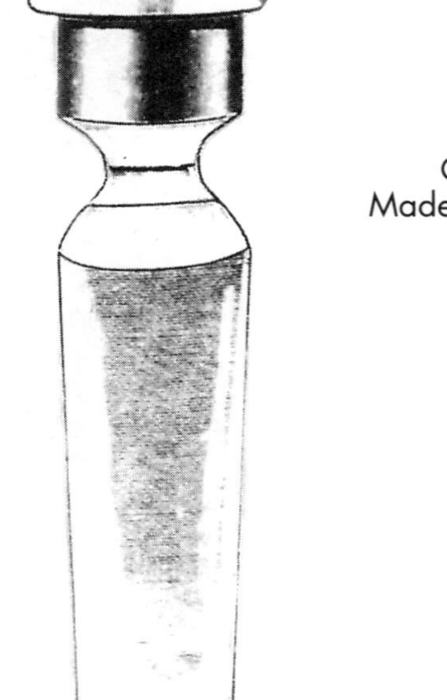

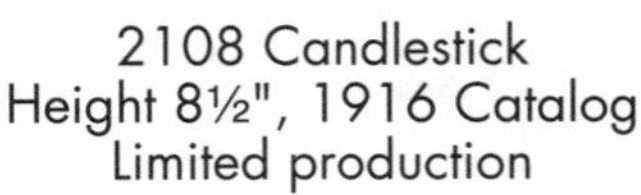

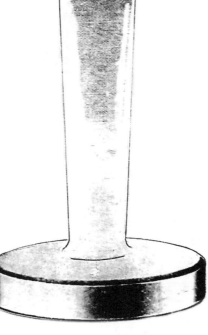

2108 Candlestick
Height 8½", 1916 Catalog
Limited production

2472 Duo Candlestick
Height 4⅞", 1939 Catalog

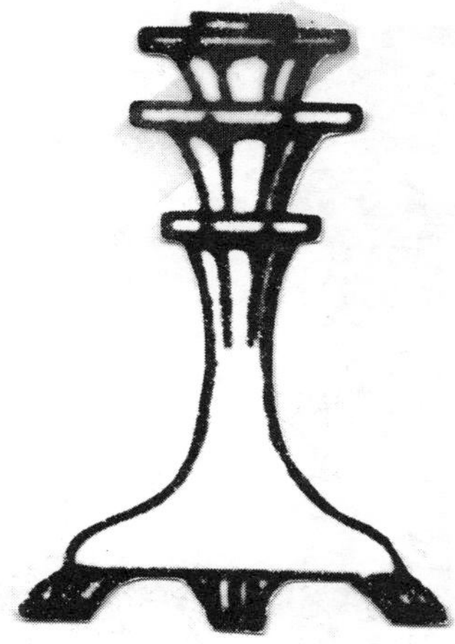

2470 Candlestick
Height 5½", 1932 Designer
Drawing, Hugh pattern

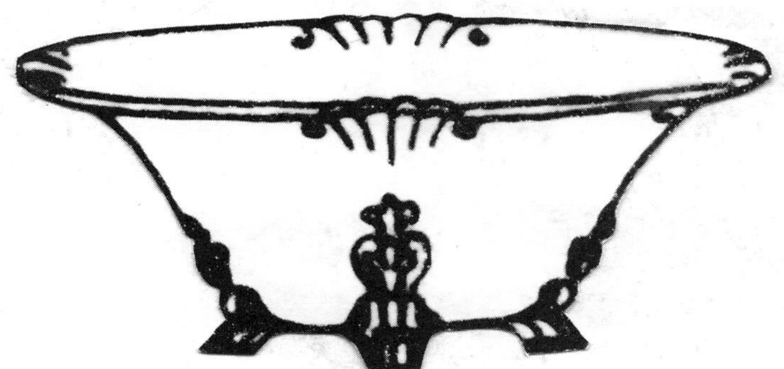

2470½" Footed Bowl
Diameter 10½", 1932 Designer
Drawing, Hugh pattern

2455 Footed Bowl
Diameter 11", 1932 Designer
Drawing, narrow optic,
limited production

2455 Candlestick
Height 6", 1932 Drawing
narrow optic, limited production

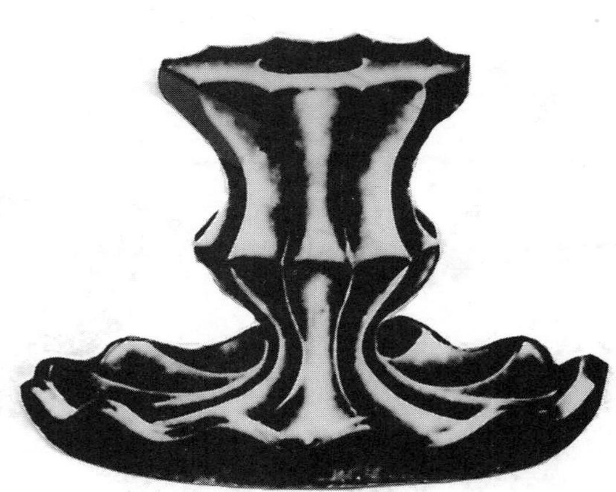

1513 Florence Saucer Candle
1907 Catalog

2245 Candlestick
Height 8½", 1921 Catalog
Also made in 6" size.
Colors of Gr-Amb

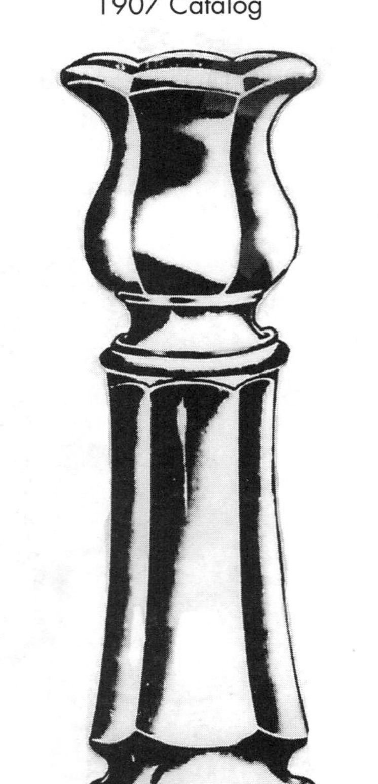

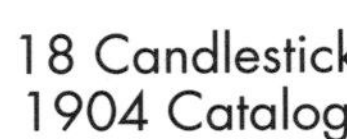

18 Candlestick
1904 Catalog

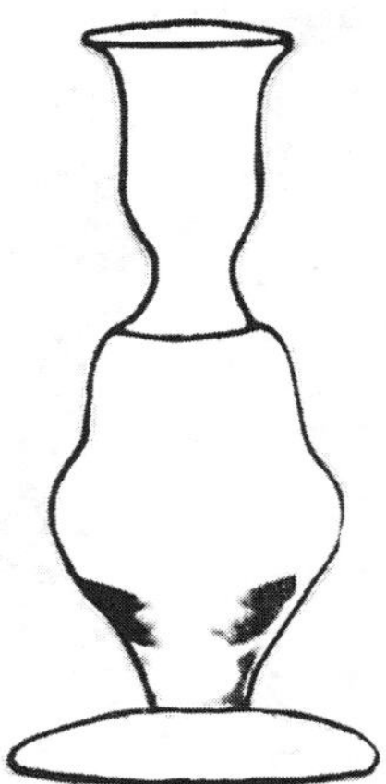

4113 Candlestick
Height 6", 1932 Designer
Drawing, Colors of RB-Bur-EG

BOWLS AND CANDLESTICKS

2364—13 in. Fruit Bowl
Height 2¾ in.

2364—10½ in. Salad Bowl
Height 4 in.

2364—12 in. Bowl, Flared
Height 2⅞ in.

6023—Duo Candlestick
Height 5½ in. Spread 6 in.
For use with any Plain Bowls

2570—9 in. Bowl
Height 4⅜ in.

2570—11½ in. Bowl
Height 3⅜ in.

Fostoria Glass Company, Moundsville, West Virginia, July 1, 1940

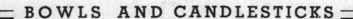

2364—12 in. Lily Pond
Height 2¼ in.

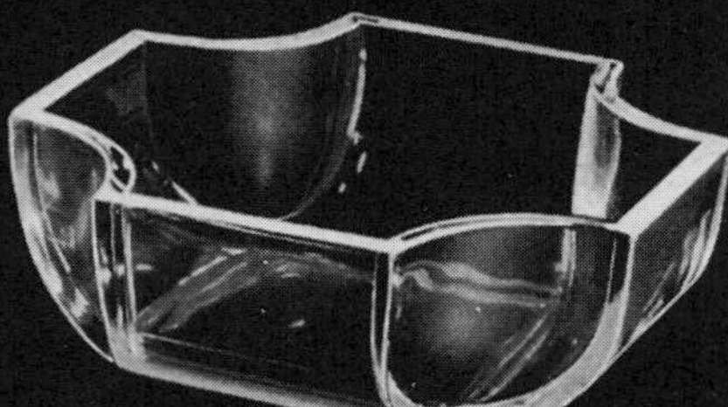

2596—7½ in. Square Bowl
Height 2½ in.

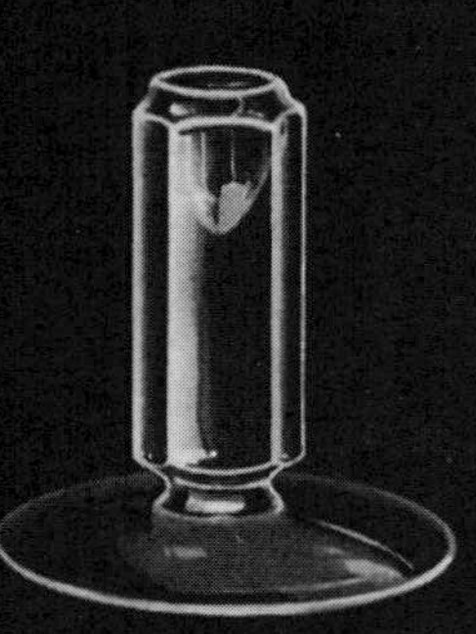

2596—5 in. Candlestick

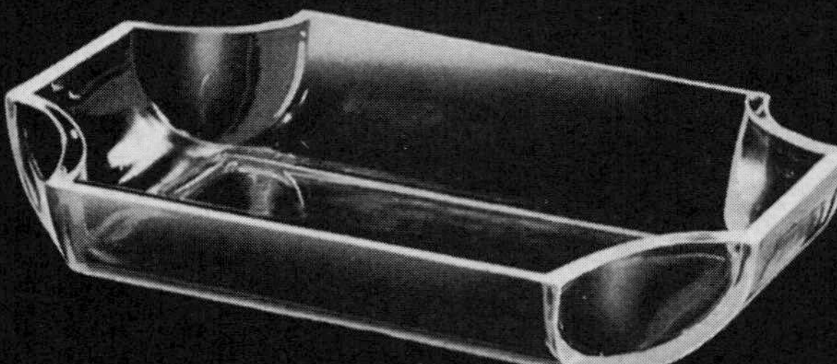

2596—11 in. Oblong Shallow Bowl
Height 2 in.

2598—11 in. Oval Bowl
Height 2¾ in.

2598—Duo Candlestick
Height 7½ in. Spread 7⅛ in.

Fostoria Glass Company, Moundsville, West Virginia, July 1, 1940

2594 Handled Bowl
Length 10", 1941 Catalog

1485 Candlestick
Height 11", Etched "B"
1914 Catalog

140 Saucer Candle
Handled, 1904 Catalog

2331 Lustre
Height 9", 1924 Catalog
Made in Gr-Amb with Fostoria
4" colored prisms.

BOWLS AND CANDLESTICKS
Fostoria Glass Company, Moundsville, West Virginia, January 1, 1941

2601—10½ in. Lyre, Oval Bowl
Height 2¾ in.
Width 8¼ in.

2601—Lyre Duo Candlestick
Height 8 in. Spread 5¾ in.

2600—Acanthus Trindle Candlestick
Height 10 in. Spread 8½ in.
2600—Acanthus 3 Lt. Candelabra
Same as above but using 2545 Bobache
and 18 U.D. Prisms

2600—9½ in. Acanthus Footed Bowl
Height 6 in.

BOWLS, CANDLESTICKS, CANDELABRA
and Other Miscellaneous

FOSTORIA GLASS COMPANY, MOUNDSVILLE, WEST VIRGINIA — 1953

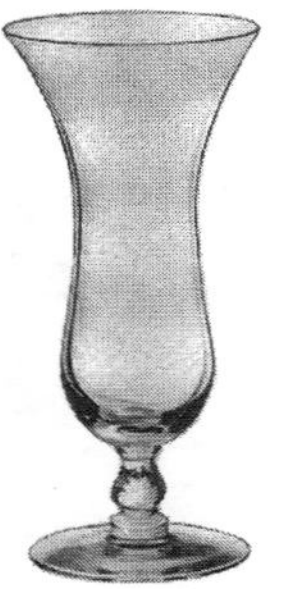

6047
Parfait
Height 6⅝ in.

2655
4 light Candelabra, 18 U.D.P.
(Illustrated)
Using 3 No. 2545 Bobaches
Height 11⅜ in.
Also 2655
4 Light Candelabra, 24 U.D.P.
Using 4 No. 2545 Bobaches
Height 11⅜ in.

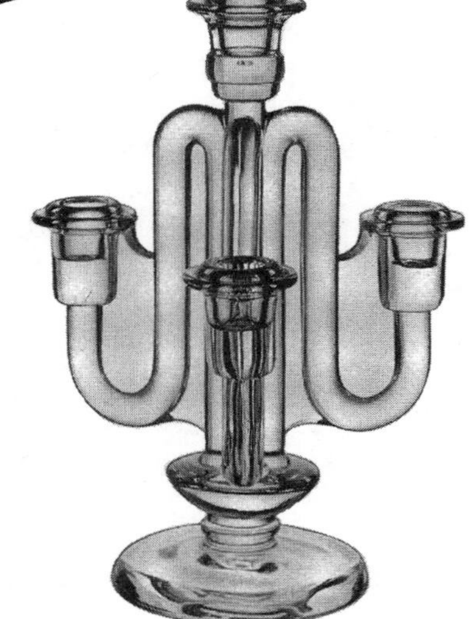

2655
4 Light Candlestick
Height 11⅜ in.

2636
"Plume" Book End
Height 9¼ in.

No. 2639
11 in. Ivy Bowl
Height 3¾ in.

No. 2651
11 in. Handled Bowl
Height 3-⅝ in.

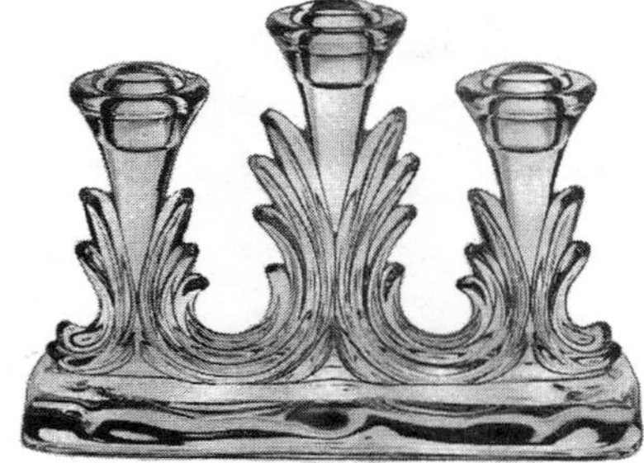

No. 2653
Trindle Candlestick
Height 6¼ in. Spread 9 in.

No. 2652
Trindle Candlestick
Height 5-¾ in. Spread 9 in.

No. 2652
13-½ in. Handled Bowl
Height 3-¼ in.

BOWLS, CANDLESTICKS HURRICANE LAMP, CANDLE LAMP and COMPORT

2667—6 in.
Candlestick

2667—9¼ in.
Footed Bowl
Height 5¾ in.

2667—2½ in.
Candlestick

2667—6 in.
Footed Comport
Height 4½ in.

2667—7 in.
Footed Bowl
Height 6½ in.

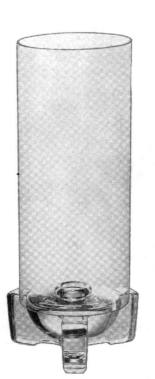

2668
Hurricane Lamp, Complete
Height 11¾ in.
Consisting of:
1/12 Doz. 2668—Candlestick
1/12 Doz. 2668 Hurricane Lamp
Chimney

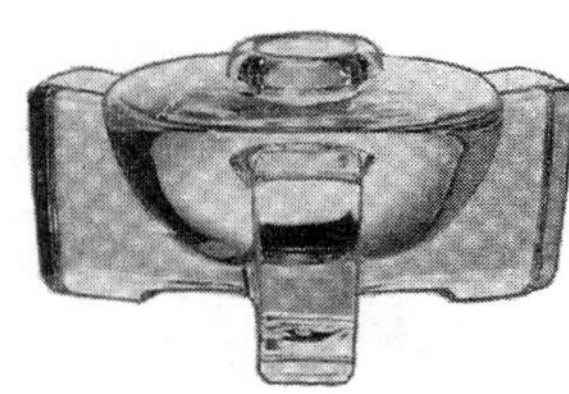

2668
Candlestick
Height 2½ in.

BOWLS, CANDLESTICKS AND CANDELABRA

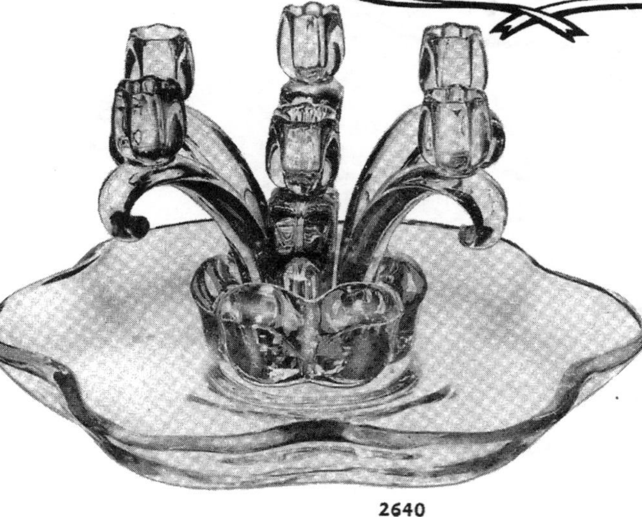

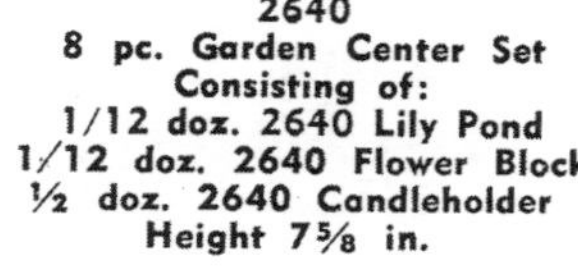
2640
8 pc. Garden Center Set
Consisting of:
1/12 doz. 2640 Lily Pond
1/12 doz. 2640 Flower Block
½ doz. 2640 Candleholder
Height 7⅝ in.

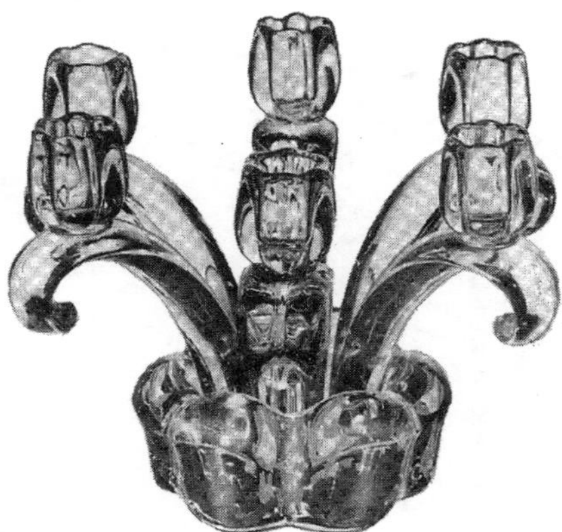

2640
Candleholder

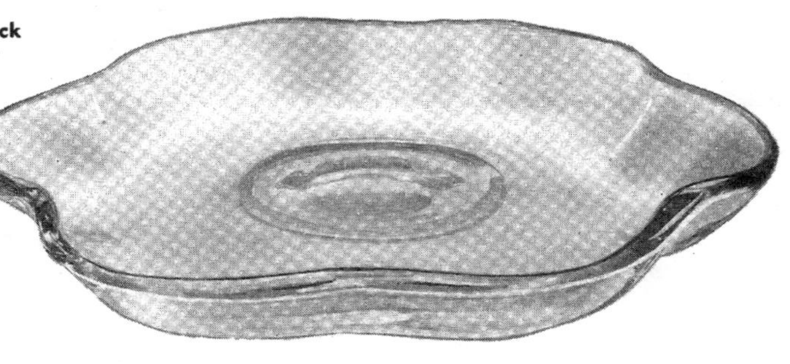

2640 — 14 in.
Lily Pond
Height 2 in.

2636
"Plume" Candlestick
Height 9-½ in.

2636
"Plume" Duo Candlestick
Height 9-½ in.
Spread 10 in.

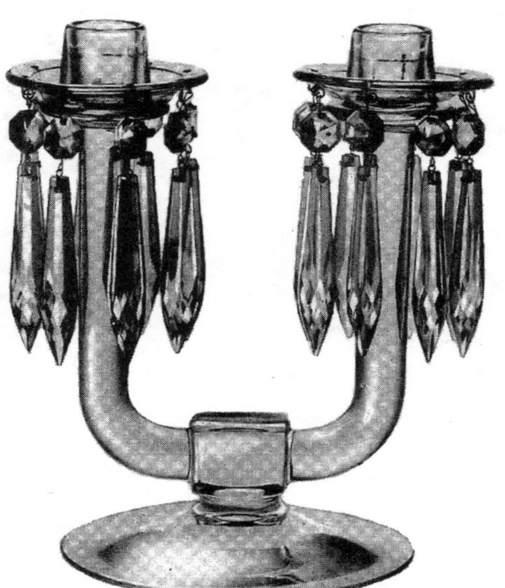

2527
2 light Candelabra, 16 U.D.P.
Using 2527 Bobache
Height 8-½ in.
Spread 7-½ in.

BOWLS, CANDLESTICKS AND CENTERPIECES

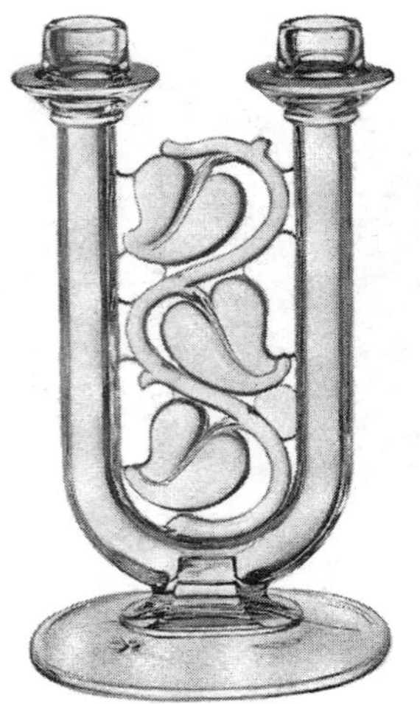

2639
Duo Candlestick
Height 9¾ in. Spread 5¾ in.

2639
Oval Bowl
Height 4 in. Length 13¼ in.

2634
Mermaid & Bowl Centerpiece
Height 11½ in. Diameter 13 in.

2635
Madonna
Height 10 in.

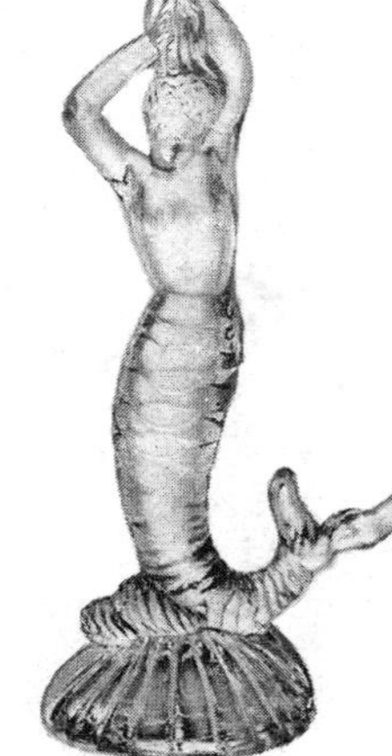

2634
Mermaid
Height 10⅛ in.

2634 — 13 in.
Floating Garden

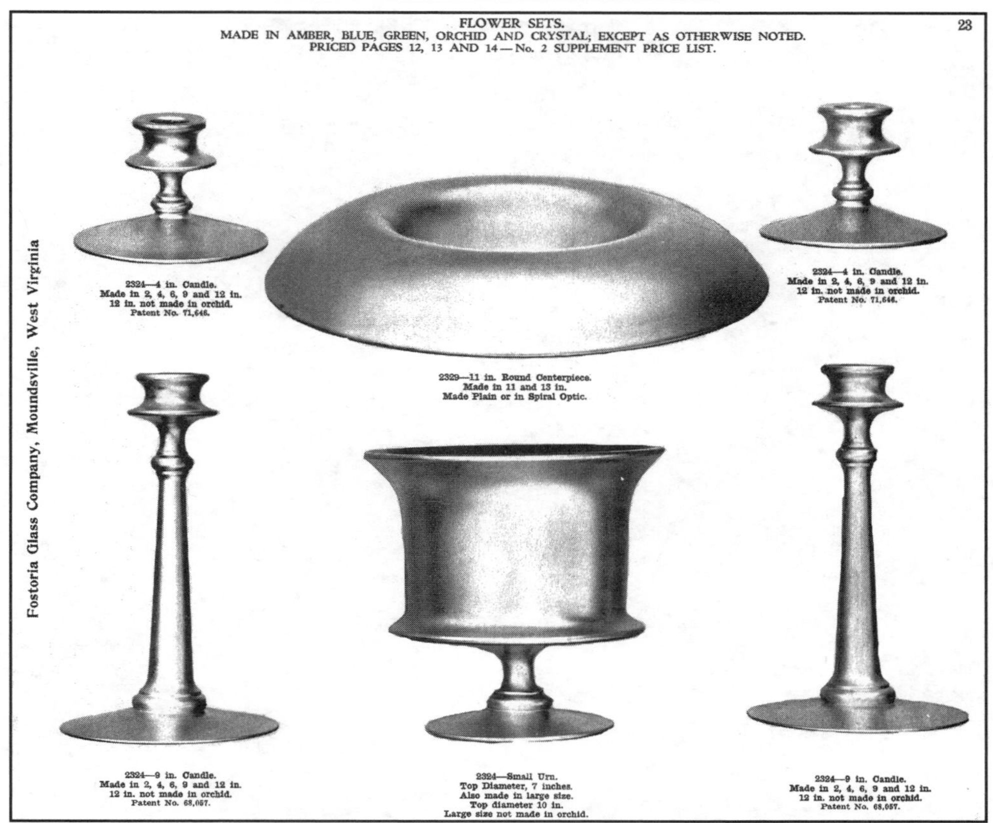
FLOWER SETS.
MADE IN AMBER, BLUE, GREEN, ORCHID AND CRYSTAL; EXCEPT AS OTHERWISE NOTED.
PRICED PAGES 12, 13 AND 14 — No. 2 SUPPLEMENT PRICE LIST.

23

2324—4 in. Candle.
Made in 2, 4, 6, 9 and 12 in.
12 in. not made in orchid.
Patent No. 71,646.

2329—11 in. Round Centerpiece.
Made in 11 and 13 in.
Made Plain or in Spiral Optic.

2324—4 in. Candle.
Made in 2, 4, 6, 9 and 12 in.
12 in. not made in orchid.
Patent No. 71,646.

2324—9 in. Candle.
Made in 2, 4, 6, 9 and 12 in.
12 in. not made in orchid.
Patent No. 68,057.

2324—Small Urn.
Top Diameter, 7 inches.
Also made in large size.
Top diameter 10 in.
Large size not made in orchid.

2324—9 in. Candle.
Made in 2, 4, 6, 9 and 12 in.
12 in. not made in orchid.
Patent No. 68,057.

Fostoria Glass Company, Moundsville, West Virginia

1927 Catalog

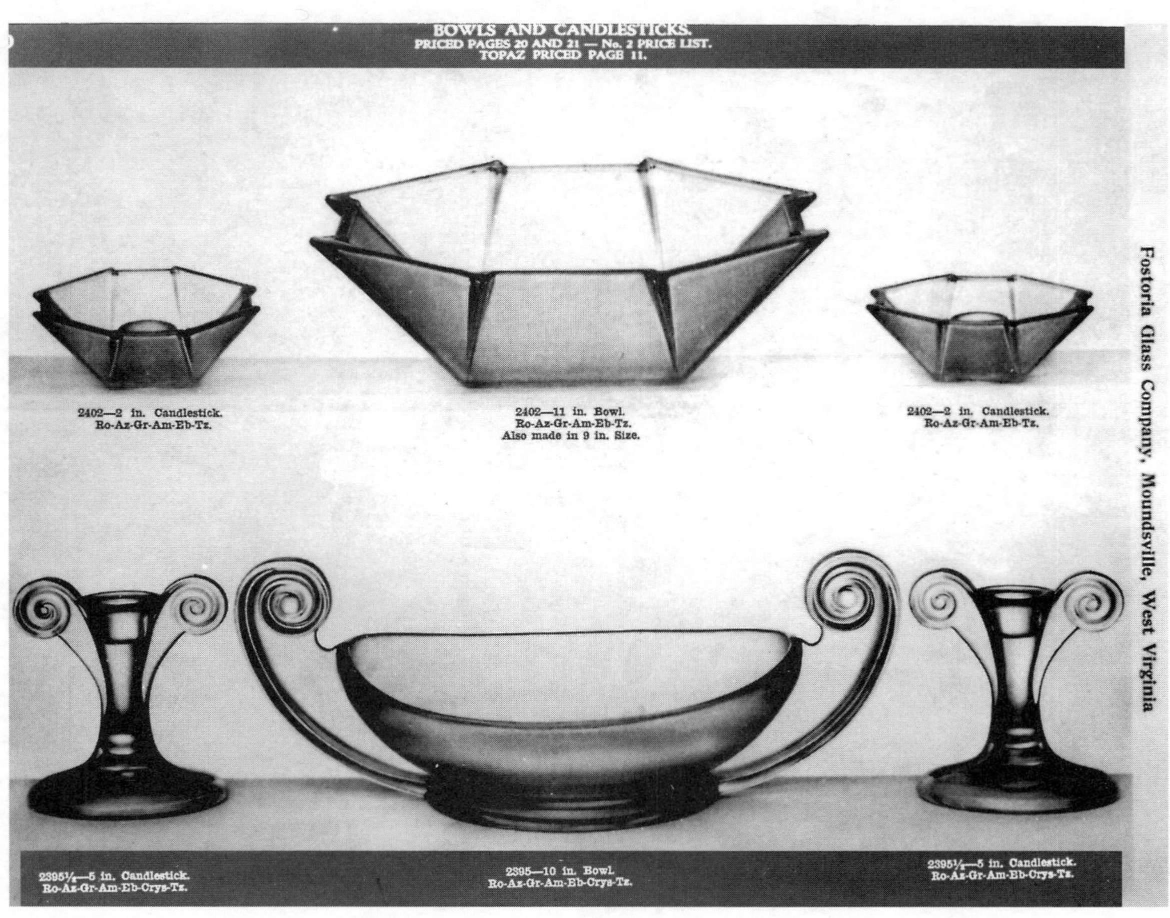
BOWLS AND CANDLESTICKS.
PRICED PAGES 20 AND 21 — No. 2 PRICE LIST.
TOPAZ PRICED PAGE 11.

2402—2 in. Candlestick.
Ro-Az-Gr-Am-Eb-Tz.

2402—11 in. Bowl.
Ro-Az-Gr-Am-Eb-Tz.
Also made in 9 in. Size.

2402—2 in. Candlestick.
Ro-Az-Gr-Am-Eb-Tz.

2395½—5 in. Candlestick.
Ro-Az-Gr-Am-Eb-Crys-Tz.

2395—10 in. Bowl.
Ro-Az-Gr-Am-Eb-Crys-Tz.

2395½—5 in. Candlestick.
Ro-Az-Gr-Am-Eb-Crys-Tz.

Fostoria Glass Company, Moundsville, West Virginia

BOWLS AND CANDLESTICKS

See Price List for Colors

2470½—5½ in. Candlestick

2470½—7 in. Bowl Height 3 in.
2470½—10½ in. Bowl Height 4 in.

2470½—5½ in. Candlestick

2394—2 in. Candlestick

2394—12 in. Bowl, A
Height 3¾ in.
2309—3¾ in.
Flower Block

2394—2 in. Candlestick

2324—6 in. Candlestick

6023—Footed Bowl, Blown
Height 4¼ in. Diameter 9¼ in.

2324—4 in. Candlestick

2563—4½ in. Viking Candlestick

2563—Handled Viking Bowl
Length 9½ in. Width 7⅜ in.
Height 3⅛ in.

FOSTORIA GLASS COMPANY, MOUNDSVILLE, WEST VIRGINIA – 1935

BOWLS AND CANDLESTICKS

See Price List For Colors

2536—9 in. Handled Bowl
Height 3¼ in.

2535
5½ in. Candlestick

2535—9 in. Bowl, Flared
Height 3⅝ in.

2535—7 in. Bowl, Cupped
Height 4⅛ in.

2533—Duo Candlestick
Height 6¼ in. Spread 6½ in.

2533—9 in. Handled Bowl
Height 4⅝ in.

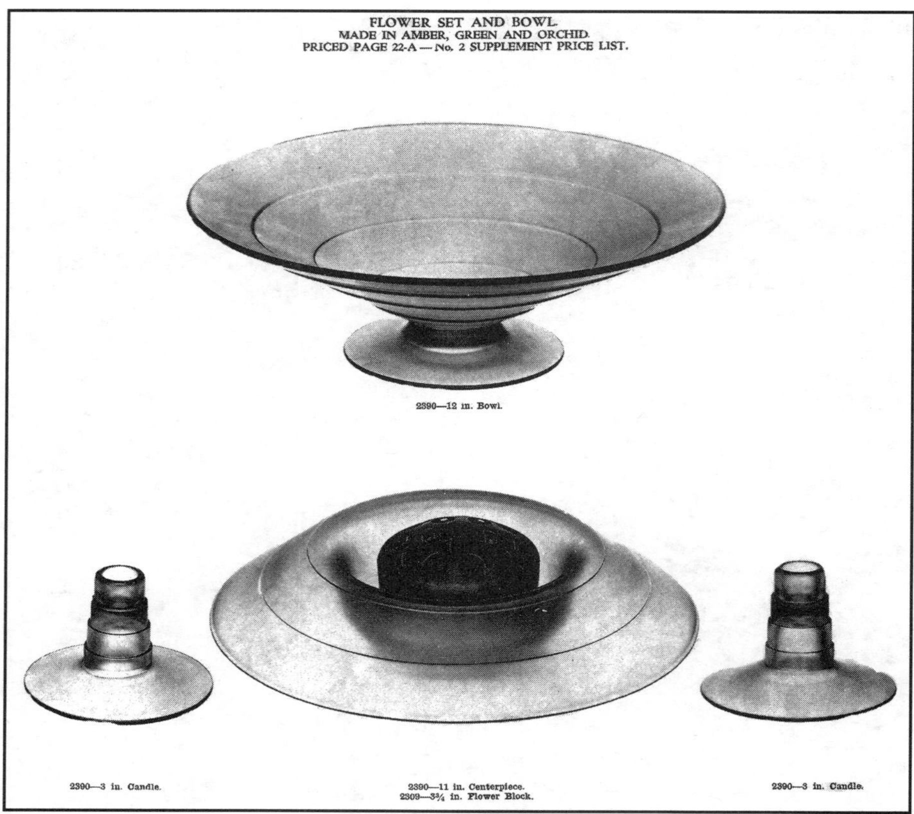
FLOWER SET AND BOWL.
MADE IN AMBER, GREEN AND ORCHID.
PRICED PAGE 22-A — No. 2 SUPPLEMENT PRICE LIST.

2390—12 in. Bowl.

2390—3 in. Candle.

2390—11 in. Centerpiece.
2309—3¾ in. Flower Block.

2390—3 in. Candle.

1927 Catalog

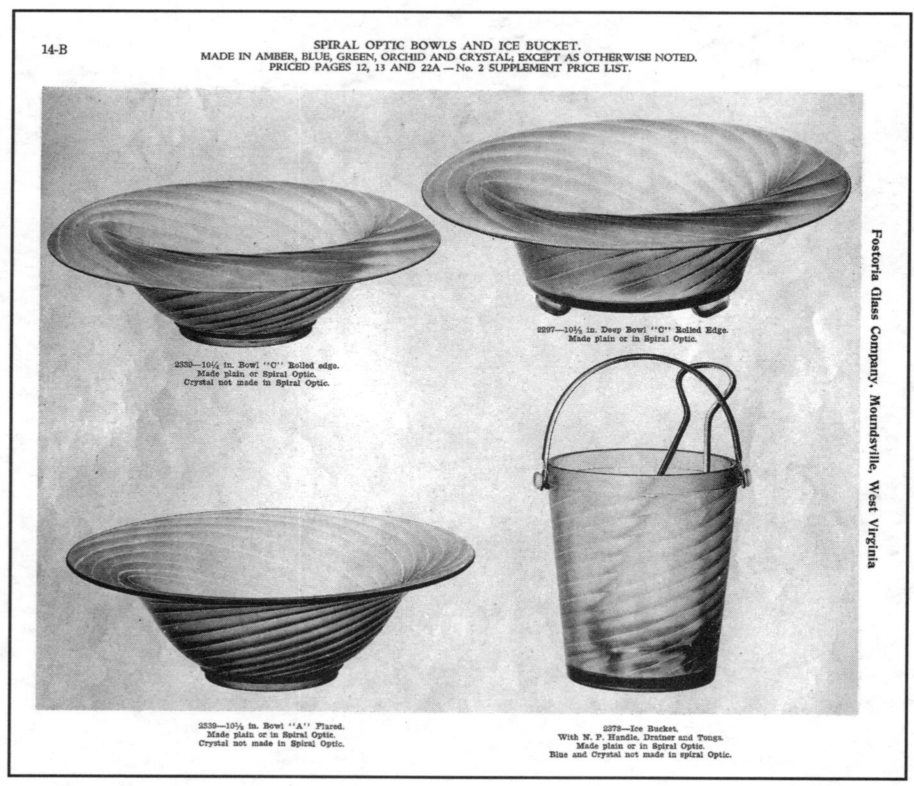
14-B

SPIRAL OPTIC BOWLS AND ICE BUCKET.
MADE IN AMBER, BLUE, GREEN, ORCHID AND CRYSTAL; EXCEPT AS OTHERWISE NOTED.
PRICED PAGES 12, 13 AND 22A — No. 2 SUPPLEMENT PRICE LIST.

2339—10½ in. Bowl "C" Rolled edge.
Made plain or Spiral Optic.
Crystal not made in Spiral Optic.

2297—10½ in. Deep Bowl "C" Rolled Edge.
Made plain or in Spiral Optic.

2339—10½ in. Bowl "A" Flared.
Made plain or in Spiral Optic.
Crystal not made in Spiral Optic.

2378—Ice Bucket.
With N. P. Handle, Drainer and Tongs.
Made plain or in Spiral Optic.
Blue and Crystal not made in spiral Optic.

Fostoria Glass Company, Moundsville, West Virginia

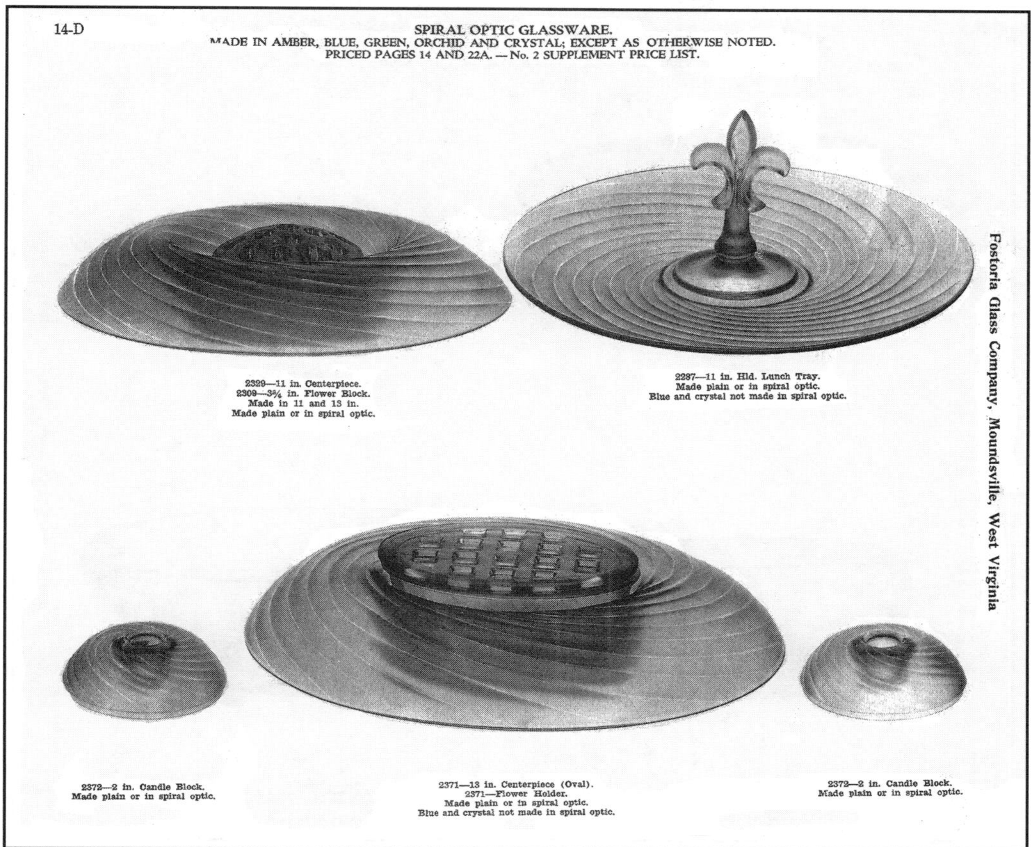

14-D

SPIRAL OPTIC GLASSWARE.
MADE IN AMBER, BLUE, GREEN, ORCHID AND CRYSTAL; EXCEPT AS OTHERWISE NOTED.
PRICED PAGES 14 AND 22A. — No. 2 SUPPLEMENT PRICE LIST.

2329—11 in. Centerpiece.
2309—3¾ in. Flower Block.
Made in 11 and 13 in.
Made plain or in spiral optic.

2287—11 in. Hld. Lunch Tray.
Made plain or in spiral optic.
Blue and crystal not made in spiral optic.

2372—2 in. Candle Block.
Made plain or in spiral optic.

2371—13 in. Centerpiece (Oval).
2371—Flower Holder.
Made plain or in spiral optic.
Blue and crystal not made in spiral optic.

2372—2 in. Candle Block.
Made plain or in spiral optic.

Fostoria Glass Company, Moundsville, West Virginia

1927 Catalog

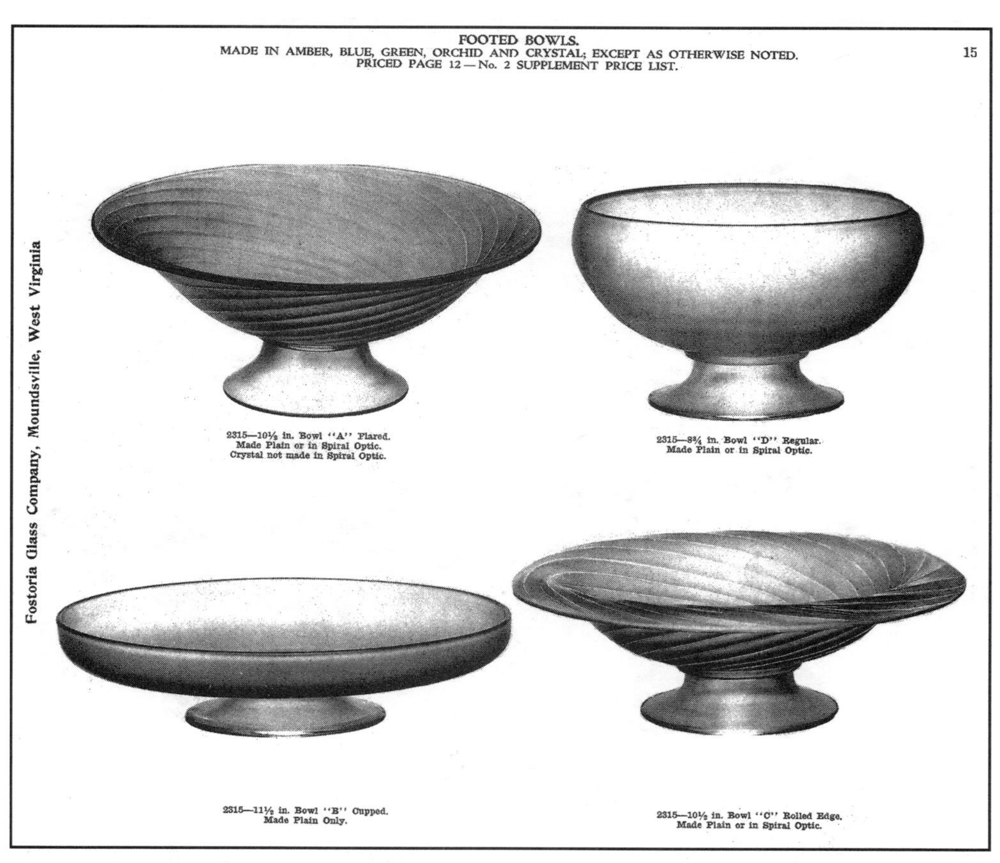

FOOTED BOWLS.
MADE IN AMBER, BLUE, GREEN, ORCHID AND CRYSTAL; EXCEPT AS OTHERWISE NOTED.
PRICED PAGE 12 — No. 2 SUPPLEMENT PRICE LIST.

15

Fostoria Glass Company, Moundsville, West Virginia

2315—10½ in. Bowl ''A'' Flared.
Made Plain or in Spiral Optic.
Crystal not made in Spiral Optic.

2315—8¾ in. Bowl ''D'' Regular.
Made Plain or in Spiral Optic.

2315—11½ in. Bowl ''B'' Cupped.
Made Plain Only.

2315—10½ in. Bowl ''C'' Rolled Edge.
Made Plain or in Spiral Optic.

16

LOW BOWLS.
MADE IN AMBER, BLUE, GREEN, ORCHID AND CRYSTAL; EXCEPT AS OTHERWISE NOTED.
SHALLOW BOWLS ARE NOT MADE IN ORCHID, OR IN SPIRAL OPTIC.
PRICED PAGE 12 — No. 2 SUPPLEMENT PRICE LIST.

2297—10½ in. Deep Bowl "C"
Rolled Edge.
Made Plain or in Spiral Optic.
Also made in Shallow Bowl.
Patent No. 69,664.

2297—10¼ in. Shallow Bowl "A"
Flared.
Also made in Deep Bowl.
Deep Bowl made Plain or in Spiral Optic.
Patent No. 69,667.

2297—7½ in. Shallow Bowl "D" Reg.
Also made in Deep Bowl.
Deep Bowl made in Spiral Optic,
except crystal.
Patent No. 69,666.

2297—10½ in. Deep Bowl "B" Cupped
Also made in Shallow Bowl.
Deep Bowl made in Spiral Optic,
except crystal.
Patent No. 69,665.

Fostoria Glass Company, Moundsville, West Virginia

1927 Catalog

LOW BOWLS.
MADE IN AMBER, BLUE, GREEN, ORCHID AND CRYSTAL; EXCEPT AS OTHERWISE NOTED.
PRICED PAGE 13 — No. 2 SUPPLEMENT PRICE LIST.

17

2339—7 in. Bowl "D" Regular.
Furnished with or without ebony base.

2339—10 in. Bowl "C" Rolled Edge.
Also made in Spiral optic except crystal.
Furnished with or without ebony base.

2339—10½ in. Bowl "A" Flared.
Also made in Spiral optic except crystal.
2314—3½ in. Base.
Base made in Ebony only.
Furnished with or without ebony base.

2339—10½ in. Bowl "B" Cupped.
2314—3½ in. Base.
Base made in Ebony only.
Furnished with or without ebony base.

Fostoria Glass Company, Moundsville, West Virginia

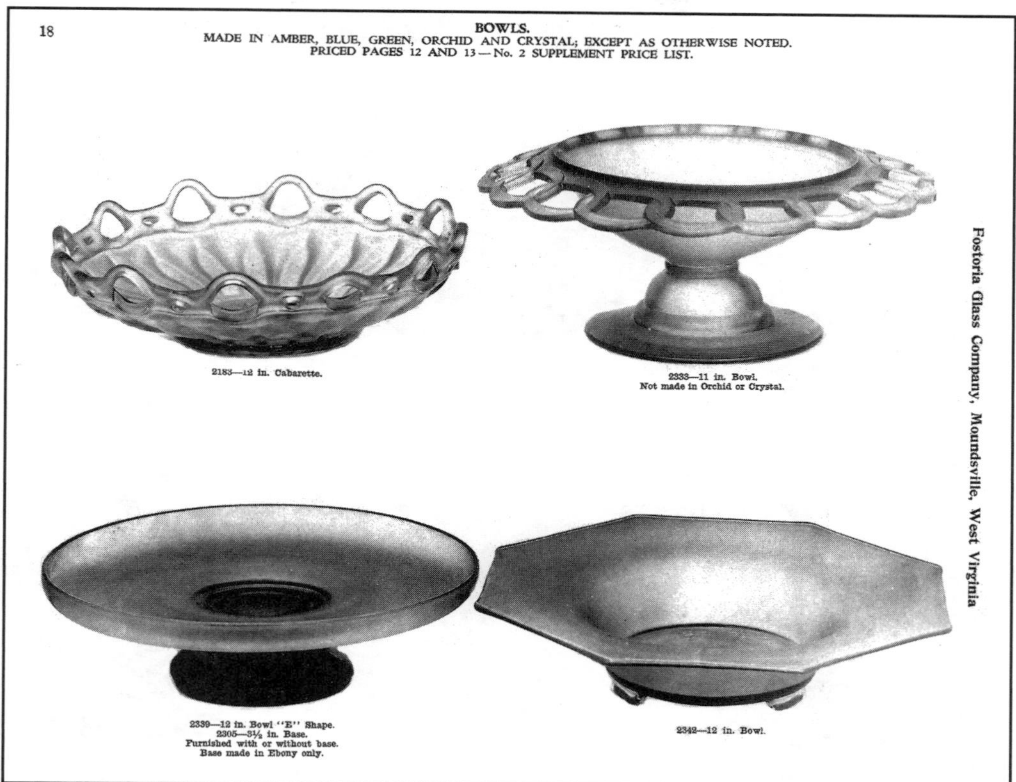
18

BOWLS.
MADE IN AMBER, BLUE, GREEN, ORCHID AND CRYSTAL; EXCEPT AS OTHERWISE NOTED.
PRICED PAGES 12 AND 13 — No. 2 SUPPLEMENT PRICE LIST.

2183—12 in. Cabarette.

2333—11 in. Bowl.
Not made in Orchid or Crystal.

2339—12 in. Bowl "E" Shape.
2305—3½ in. Base.
Furnished with or without base.
Base made in Ebony only.

2342—12 in. Bowl.

Fostoria Glass Company, Moundsville, West Virginia

1927 Catalog

BOWLS.
MADE IN AMBER, BLUE, GREEN, ORCHID AND CRYSTAL; EXCEPT AS OTHERWISE NOTED.
PRICED PAGES 12 AND 13 — No. 2 SUPPLEMENT PRICE LIST.

19

2320—11 in. Nap "A".
Also made in 12 in.
Not made in orchid.
Furnished with or without ebony base.

2320—10 in. Nap "B".
with 2305—3½ in. Base, Ebony only.
Also made in 11 in.
10 in. not made in orchid.
Furnished with or without ebony base.

2324—10 in. Bowl.
Also made in 13 in.
Patent No. 69,898.

2297—12 in. Deep Bowl "E."
Made plain or in Spiral Optic.
Crystal not made in Spiral Optic.

Fostoria Glass Company, Moundsville, West Virginia

CONSOLE SET AND BOWL.
MADE IN AMBER, BLUE, GREEN AND ORCHID; EXCEPT AS OTHERWISE NOTED.
PRICED PAGES 12 AND 13 — No. 2 SUPPLEMENT PRICE LIST.

21

Fostoria Glass Company, Moundsville, West Virginia

2342—12 in. Salad Bowl

2362—9 in. Candle.
Made in 3 and 9 in.
Patent No. 70,021.

2362—11 in. Comport.
Also made in crystal.
Patent Applied For.

2362—9 in. Candle.
Made in 3 and 9 in.
Patent No. 70,021.

1927 Catalog

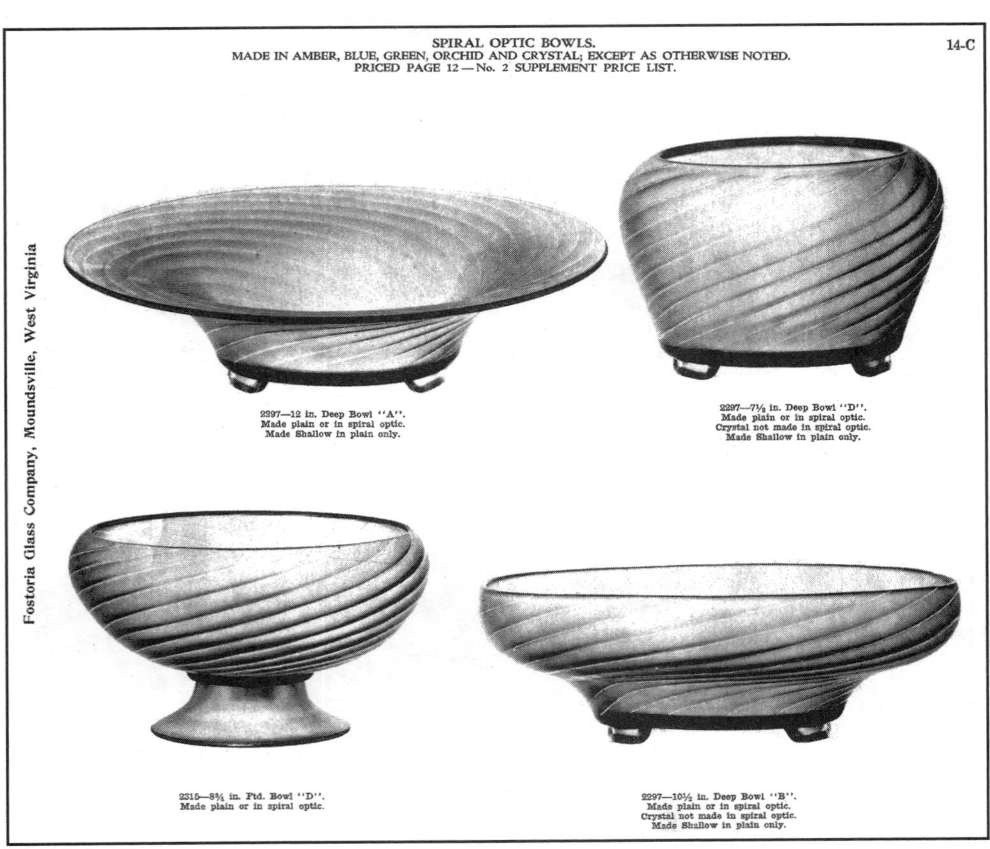

SPIRAL OPTIC BOWLS.
MADE IN AMBER, BLUE, GREEN, ORCHID AND CRYSTAL; EXCEPT AS OTHERWISE NOTED.
PRICED PAGE 12 — No. 2 SUPPLEMENT PRICE LIST.

14-C

Fostoria Glass Company, Moundsville, West Virginia

2297—12 in. Deep Bowl "A".
Made plain or in spiral optic.
Made Shallow in plain only.

2297—7½ in. Deep Bowl "D".
Made plain or in spiral optic.
Crystal not made in spiral optic.
Made Shallow in plain only.

2315—8¾ in. Ftd. Bowl "D".
Made plain or in spiral optic.

2297—10½ in. Deep Bowl "B".
Made plain or in spiral optic.
Crystal not made in spiral optic.
Made Shallow in plain only.

18-A

Miscellaneous Candlesticks.

PRICED PAGE 24, No. 1 PRICE LIST.

1856-8 in. Candle | 1962-9 in. Candle | 1963-9 in. Candle | 1964-9 in. Candle | 1965-8 in. Candle

1204-8 in. Candle | 1218-8 in. Candle | 1485-8 in. Candle | 1490-8 in. Candle | 1639-8 in. Candle

Fostoria Glass Company, Moundsville, West Virginia

1921 Catalog

56

Candlesticks Deep Etched.

No. 2245-6 in. Candle, Et. | No. 2268-6 in. Candle, Et.

No. 2244-6 in. Candle, Et. | No. 2269-6 in. Candle, Et. | No. 2275-9½ in. Candle, Et. | No. 1490-15 in. Candle, Et.

Fostoria Glass Company, Moundsville, West Virginia.

1921 Catalog

Brocades

No. 288 Cupid Brocade Pattern
Blue, Green, and Ebony

The Cupid Brocade Pattern was the second Fostoria brocaded type. The acid etching on Cupid is almost fuzzy in appearance and rough to the touch. Cupid is very scarce. It was produced only in 1927 and 1928. The dresser items and the clock sets were expensive; no doubt this accounts for their scarcity. Colors were blue, green, and ebony. Ebony pieces are especially attractive and will be found decorated in gold. An ebony clock set decorated with gold has to rank among the most collectible Fostoria items.

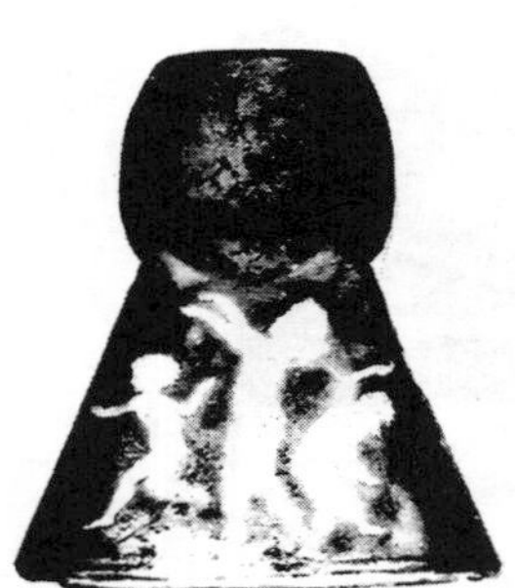

2298 Candle

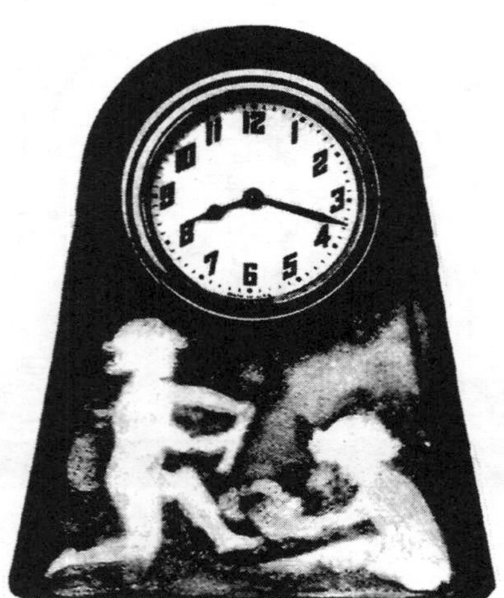

2298 Clock

2324–4" Candle

1927 Catalog

2329 – 11" Centerpiece
2309 – 3¾" Flower Block

No. 288 Cupid Brocade Pattern
Blue, Green, and Ebony

1928 Listing

2297	Deep Bowl "A"
2314	Candlestick, 4"
2329	Centerpiece, 11"
	Centerpiece, 13"
2276	Vanity Set
2359	Puff and Cover (2359½)
2322	Cologne
2298	Candle (St. Clair blank)
	Clock (St. Clair blank)
	Clock Set (includes clock and two candles)

2276 Vanity Set

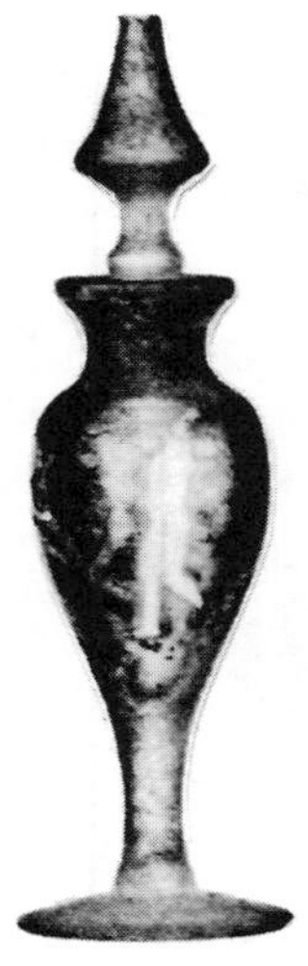

2322 Cologne

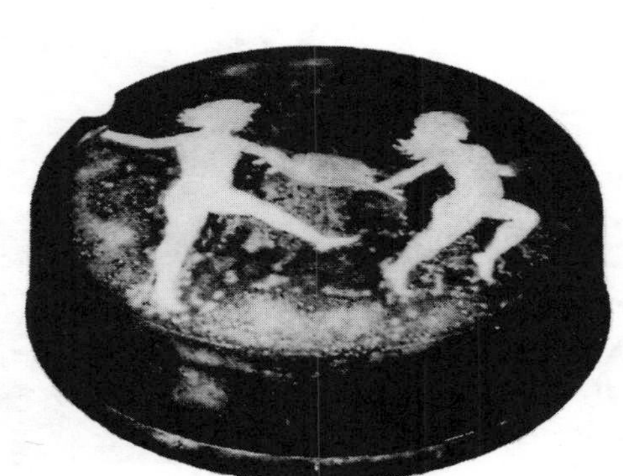

2359½ Puff and Cover

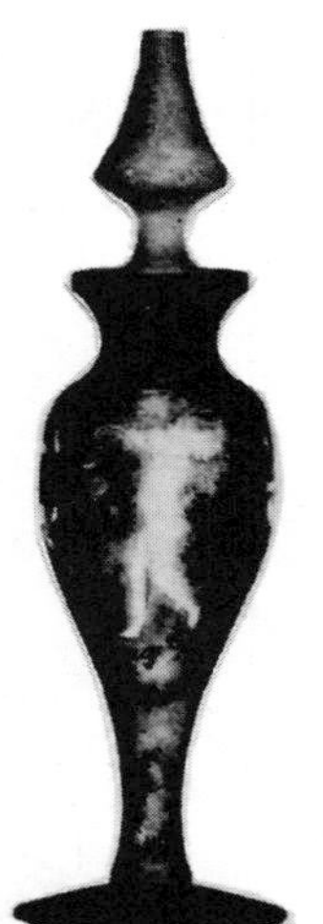

2322 Cologne

50

"GRAPE" PATTERN, PLATE ETCHING No. 287.
MADE IN BLUE, GREEN AND ORCHID.
PRICED PAGE 36 — No. 2 SUPPLEMENT PRICE LIST.

2362—11 in. Comport.

2331—3 Candy Box and Cover.

2342—12 in. Hld. Lunch Tray.

2369—7 in. Vase. Optic.

Fostoria Glass Company, Moundsville, West Virginia

1927 Catalog

50-A

"GRAPE" PATTERN, PLATE ETCHING No. 287.
MADE IN BLUE, GREEN AND ORCHID.
PRICED PAGE 36 — No. 2 SUPPLEMENT PRICE LIST.

Fostoria Glass Company, Moundsville, West Virginia

2327—7 in. Comport.

2297—10½ in. Deep Bowl "C."

2297—12 in. Deep Bowl "A."

2378—Ice Bucket.
With N. P. Handle, Drainer and Tongs.

2297—12½ in. Deep Bowl "E".

"GRAPE" PATTERN, PLATE ETCHING No. 287.
MADE IN BLUE, GREEN AND ORCHID.
PRICED PAGE 36 — No. 2 SUPPLEMENT PRICE LIST.

51

Fostoria Glass Company, Moundsville, West Virginia

2292—8 in. Vase.

4100—6 in. Vase.
Optic.

4103—5 in. Vase.
Optic.

1927 Catalog

50-B

"GRAPE" PATTERN, PLATE ETCHING No. 287.
MADE IN BLUE, GREEN AND ORCHID.
PRICED PAGE 36 — No. 2 SUPPLEMENT PRICE LIST.

2324—4 in. Candle.

2329—11 in. Centerpiece.
2309—3¾ in. Flower Block.

2324—4 in. Candle.

2287—11 in. Hld. Lunch Tray.

2339—7¼ in. Bowl "D."

2362—3 in. Candle.

2309—3¾ in. Flower Block.

2362—3 in. Candle.

Fostoria Glass Company, Moundsville, West Virginia

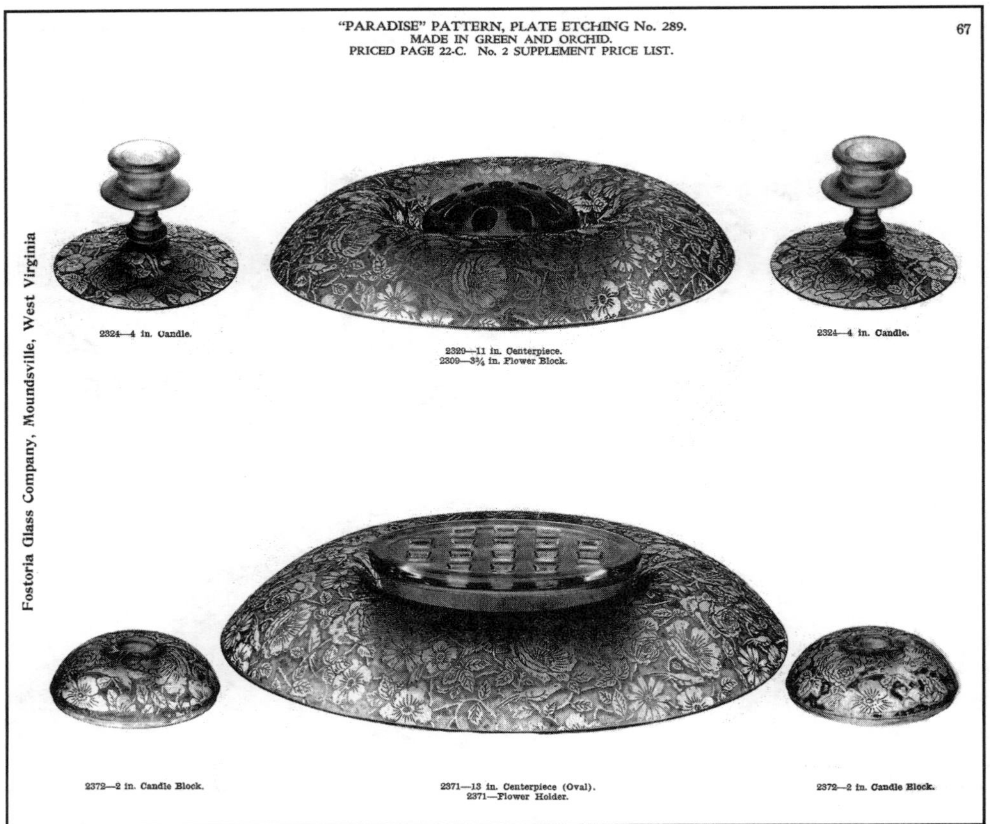

"PARADISE" PATTERN, PLATE ETCHING No. 289.
MADE IN GREEN AND ORCHID.
PRICED PAGE 22-C. No. 2 SUPPLEMENT PRICE LIST.

67

Fostoria Glass Company, Moundsville, West Virginia

2324—4 in. Candle.

2329—11 in. Centerpiece.
2309—3¾ in. Flower Block.

2324—4 in. Candle.

2372—2 in. Candle Block.

2371—13 in. Centerpiece (Oval).
2371—Flower Holder.

2372—2 in. Candle Block.

1927 Catalog

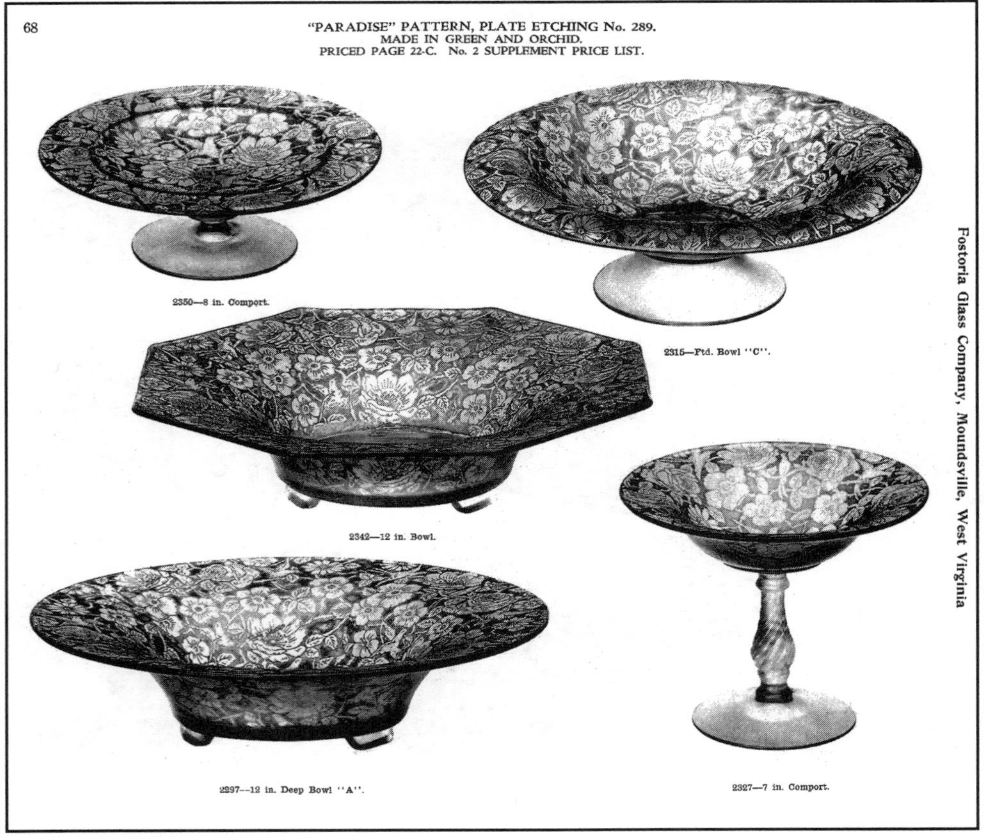

68

"PARADISE" PATTERN, PLATE ETCHING No. 289.
MADE IN GREEN AND ORCHID.
PRICED PAGE 22-C. No. 2 SUPPLEMENT PRICE LIST.

2350—8 in. Comport.

2315—Ftd. Bowl "C".

2342—12 in. Bowl.

2297—12 in. Deep Bowl "A".

2327—7 in. Comport.

Fostoria Glass Company, Moundsville, West Virginia

"PARADISE" PATTERN, PLATE ETCHING No. 289.
MADE IN GREEN AND ORCHID.
PRICED PAGE 22-C. No. 2 SUPPLEMENT PRICE LIST.

69

Fostoria Glass Company, Moundsville, West Virginia

2342—12 in. Lunch Tray.

2362—11 in. Comport.

2362—3 in. Candle.

2362—12 in. Bowl.
2309—3¾ in. Flower Block.

2362—3 in. Candle.

1927 Catalog

70

"PARADISE" PATTERN, PLATE ETCHING No. 289.
MADE IN GREEN AND ORCHID.
PRICED PAGE 22-C. No. 2 SUPPLEMENT PRICE LIST.

Fostoria Glass Company, Moundsville, West Virginia

4103—5 in. Vase.
Optic.

2380—Confection & Cover.

2378—Ice Bucket.
With N. P. Handle, Drainer & Tongs.

4100—8 in. Vase.
Optic.

2369—7 in. Vase.
Optic.

2331—3 Candy Box & Cover.

Candelabra

No. 13 Candelabra
Bobaches Wired for Prisms
Made in 4, 5, and 6 lights
Pink Holders, 1904 Catalog

18-C.

Candelabras.

PRICED PAGE 23, No. 1 PRICE LIST.

22-2 Light Candelabra
With U Drop Prisms
Height 20 in. Spread 15 in.

23-3 Light Candelabra
With Spearhead Prisms
Height, 22 in. Spread, 15 in.

1-4 Light Candelabra
With U drop Prisms
Height, 19 in. Spread, 12 in.

Fostoria Glass Company, Moundsville, West Virginia

1921 Catalog

No. 16 Candelabra
5 and 6 Light 1901 Catalog
Height 20" 6½" base diameter

No. 25 Candelabra, 5 Light
with Spearhead Prisms
Height 24" Spread 18"
8½" base diameter
This beautiful piece was re-introduced in the late 1950s as No. 25/342-5 Light.

Candy Boxes and Jars

Fostoria Glass Company, Moundsville, West Virginia

2395—Oval Confection and Cover.
Ro-Az-Gr-Am-Tz.

2380—Confection and Cover.
Ro-Az-Gr-Am.
2380—Confection and Cover, S/O.
Ro-Gr-Am.

2413—Urn and Cover.
Ro-Az-Gr-Am.

2394—½ lb. Candy Jar and Cover.
Ro-Az-Gr-Am-Crys-Tz.

2331—3 Candy Box and Cover.
Ro-Az-Gr-Am-Crys.

1930 Catalog

28 CANDY JARS, PRESSED AND BLOWN.
MADE IN AMBER, BLUE, GREEN AND CRYSTAL; EXCEPT AS OTHERWISE NOTED.
PRICED PAGE 9—No. 2 SUPPLEMENT PRICE LIST.

5084—Candy Jar and Cover.
Made Solid Amber, Blue, Green, Crystal in Reg. Optic.
Made Amber Foot, Loop Optic.
Made Green Foot, Spiral Optic.
Made Blue Foot, Regular Optic.

2219—½ lb. Candy Jar and Cover.

2380—Confection and Cover.
Made Plain or Spiral Optic.
Also made in orchid.
Patent Applied For

2331—3 Candy Box and Cover.
3 Partitions.
Also made in ebony and orchid.

2250—½ lb. Candy Jar and Cover.
Also made in ebony.

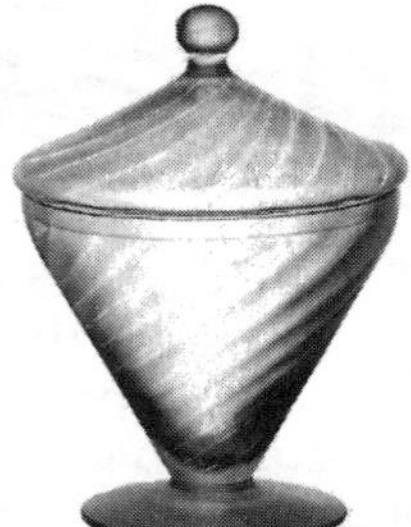

4095½—Candy Jar and Cover, Spiral Optic.
Made Spiral Opt. solid green, also green foot.
Made Loop Opt. solid amber, also amber foot.
Made Regular Opt. solid blue, also blue foot.

Fostoria Glass Company, Moundsville, West Virginia

1927 Catalog

Carvings

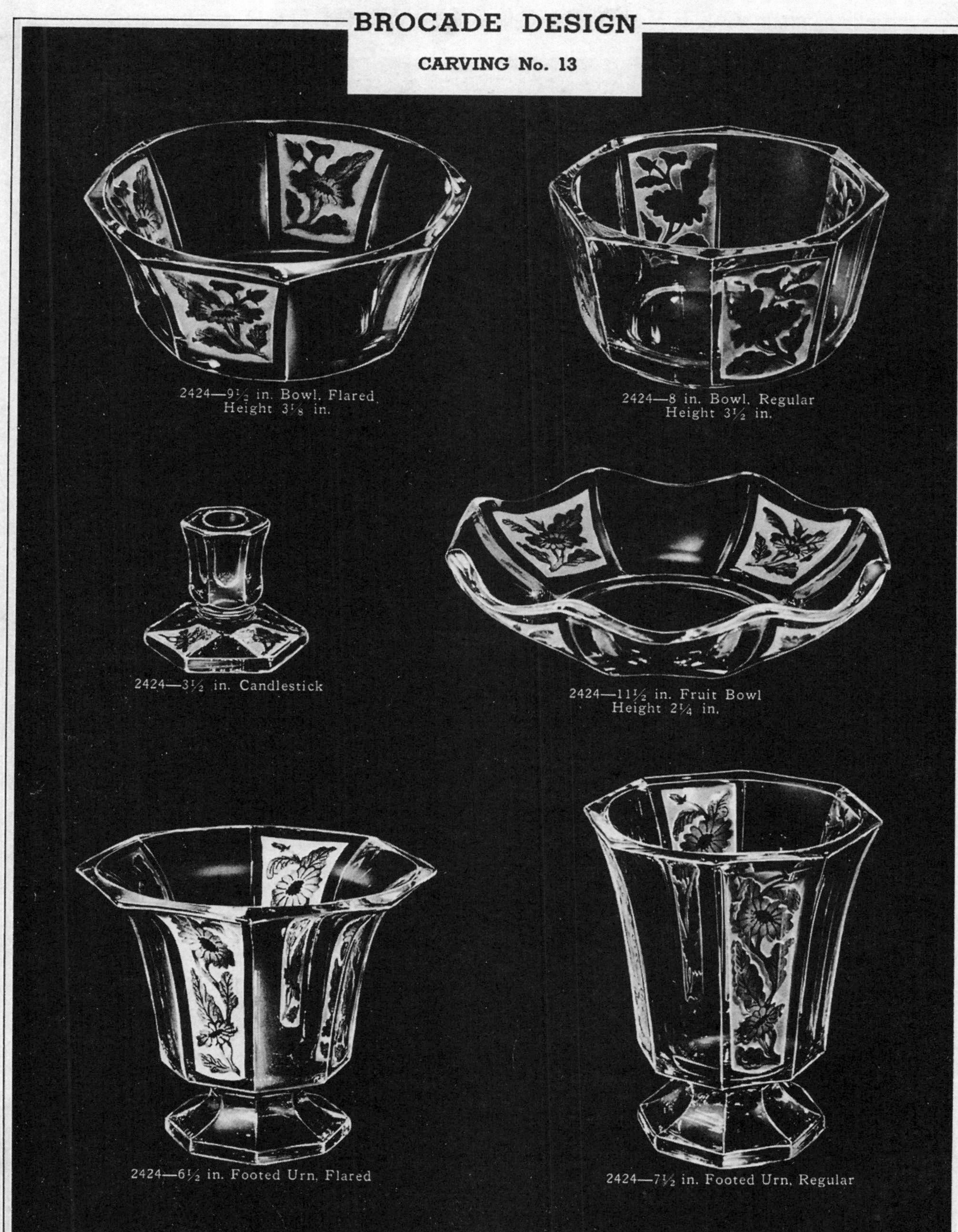

Fostoria Glass Company, Moundsville, West Virginia, July 1, 1939

Carved Decorative Group

CARVED DECORATIVE GROUP

4116½—5 in. Ball
Bubble Baby Carving 28

2577—5½ in. Wide Vase
Greyhounds Carving 25

315—9 in. Bowl
Archer Carving 24

2577—8½ in. Vase
Dolphin Carving 27

4132½—8 in. Vase
Three Geese Carving 26

Fostoria Glass Company, Moundsville, West Virginia, July 1, 1940

Carved Smoking Accessories

FOSTORIA GLASS COMPANY, MOUNDSVILLE, WEST VIRGINIA – 1940

4148—2¼ in.
Cigarette Holder
Blown
Horse Carving 35
Top Diameter 2 in.

4148—2½ in.
Ind. Ash Tray, Blown
Horse Carving 35

4148—2¼ in.
Cigarette Holder
Blown
Elephant Carving 36
Top Diameter 2 in.

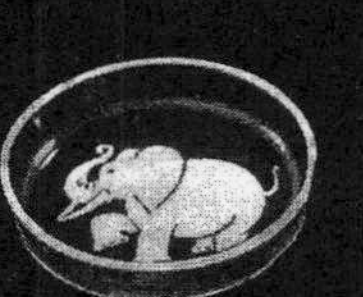

4148—2½ in.
Ind. Ash Tray, Blown
Elephant Carving 36

4148—2¼ in.
Cigarette Holder
Blown
Rooster Carving 37
Top Diameter 2 in.

4148—2½ in.
Ind. Ash Tray, Blown
Rooster Carving 37

2427—Oblong Cigarette Box and Cover
Snow Crystal Carving 42
Length 7 in.
Height 2¼ in. Width 3⅛ in.
Each side holds 35 Cigarettes

2427—Oblong Cigarette Box and Cover
Gros Point Carving 43
Length 7 in.
Height 2¼ in. Width 3⅛ in.
Each side holds 35 Cigarettes

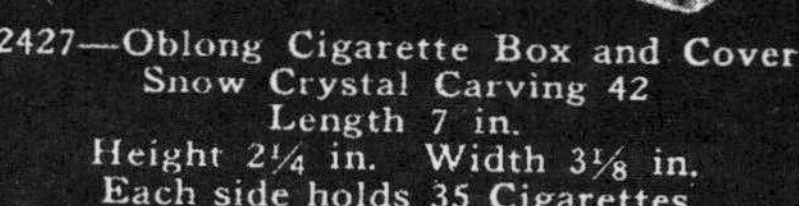

2427—Oblong Ash Tray
Snow Crystal Carving 42
Length 3½ in. Width 2¾ in.

2516—Ash Tray
Chanticleer Carving 41
Height 2⅛ in. Diameter 5 in.

2427—Oblong Ash Tray
Gros Point Carving 43
Length 3½ in. Width 2¾ in.

2427—Oblong Cigarette Box and Cover
Lyre Carving 30
Length 7 in. Height 2¼ in.
Width 3⅛ in.
Each side holds 35 Cigarettes

2427—Oblong Ash Tray
Lyre Carving 30
Length 3½ in.
Width 2¾ in.

2516—Ash Tray
Thoroughbred Carving 40
Height 2⅛ in. Diameter 5 in.

CARVINGS

Stallion Design
Carving No. 10
2567—7½ in. Vase

Colonial Design
Carving No. 5
26/1 Candle Lamp
with 2545—2 in. "Flame" Candlestick
Height 7 in.

Carnival Design
Carving No. 7
4128½—5 in. Vase

Skater Design
Carving No. 9
4132½—8 in. Vase

Yachting Design
Carving No. 8
4132½—8 in. Vase

Fostoria Glass Company, Moundsville, West Virginia, Jan. 1, 1939

Cornucopia
Carving No. 46

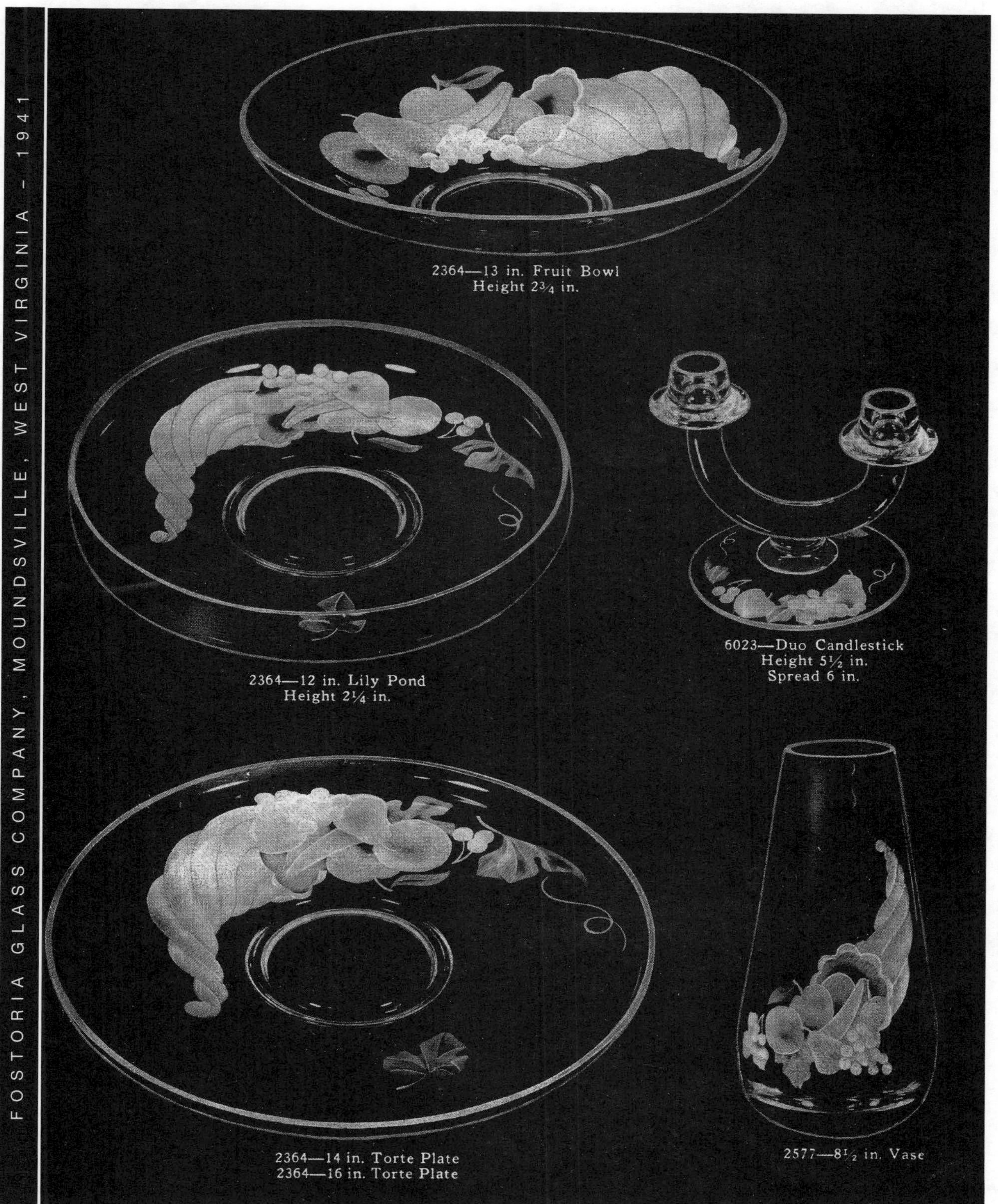

2364—13 in. Fruit Bowl
Height $2\frac{3}{4}$ in.

2364—12 in. Lily Pond
Height $2\frac{1}{4}$ in.

6023—Duo Candlestick
Height $5\frac{1}{2}$ in.
Spread 6 in.

2364—14 in. Torte Plate
2364—16 in. Torte Plate

2577—$8\frac{1}{2}$ in. Vase

Fostoria Glass Company, Moundsville, West Virginia, January 1, 1940

HOLLYHOCK DESIGN

CARVING No. 16

4126½—11 in. Vase

5100—10 in. Vase

1895½—10 in. Vase

NARCISSUS DESIGN

CARVING No. 17

4126½—11 in. Vase

4143½—6 in. Footed Vase
4143½—7½ in. Footed Vase

2577—6 in. Vase

LILY OF THE VALLEY DESIGN

CARVING No. 19

4143½—6 in. Footed Vase
4143½—7½ in. Footed Vase

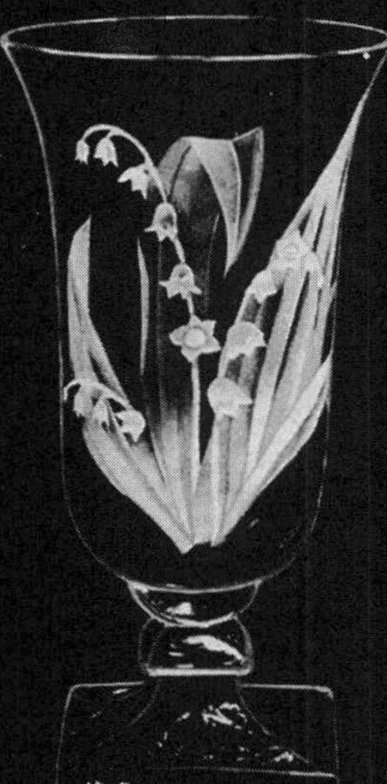

2568—9 in. Footed Vase

4132½—8 in. Vase

TIGER LILY DESIGN

CARVING No. 18

4132—5 in. Vase
(Ice Bowl)

2577—6 in. Vase

2577—5½ in. Wide Vase

Fostoria Glass Company, Moundsville, West Virginia, January 1, 1940

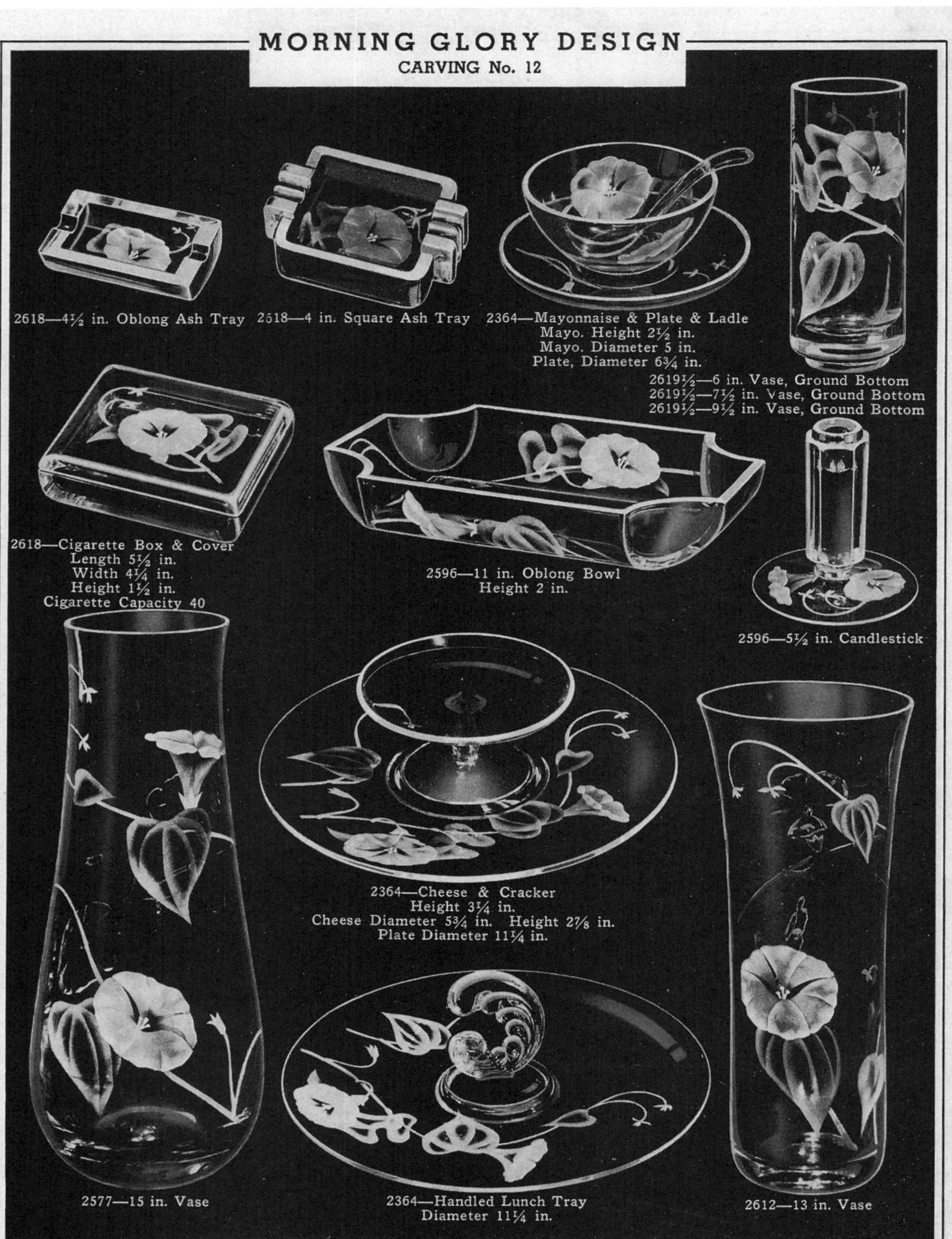

MORNING GLORY DESIGN

CARVING No. 12

2618—4½ in. Oblong Ash Tray

2518—4 in. Square Ash Tray

2364—Mayonnaise & Plate & Ladle
Mayo. Height 2½ in.
Mayo. Diameter 5 in.
Plate, Diameter 6¾ in.

2619½—6 in. Vase, Ground Bottom
2619½—7½ in. Vase, Ground Bottom
2619½—9½ in. Vase, Ground Bottom

2618—Cigarette Box & Cover
Length 5½ in.
Width 4¼ in.
Height 1½ in.
Cigarette Capacity 40

2596—11 in. Oblong Bowl
Height 2 in.

2596—5½ in. Candlestick

2364—Cheese & Cracker
Height 3¼ in.
Cheese Diameter 5¾ in. Height 2⅞ in.
Plate Diameter 11¼ in.

2577—15 in. Vase

2364—Handled Lunch Tray
Diameter 11¼ in.

2612—13 in. Vase

Fostoria Glass Company, Moundsville, West Virginia, January 1, 1942

MORNING GLORY DESIGN

Carving No. 12

2618—4½ in.
Oblong Ash Tray

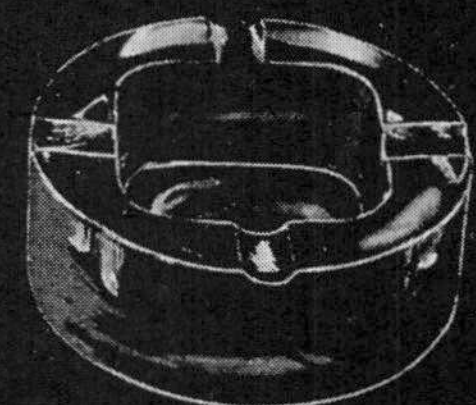

2516
Ash Tray

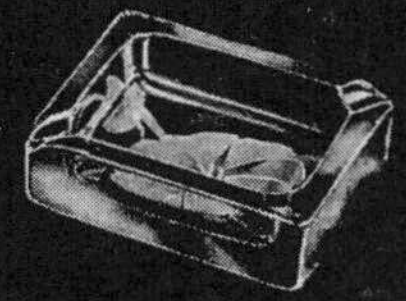

2427
Oblong Ash Tray
Length 3½ in. Width 2¾ in.

2618—4 in.
Square Ash Tray

2618
Cigarette Box and Cover
Length 5½ in. Width 4¼ in.
Height 1½ in.
Cigarette Capacity 40

2364—12 in.
Bowl, Flared
Height 2⅞ in.

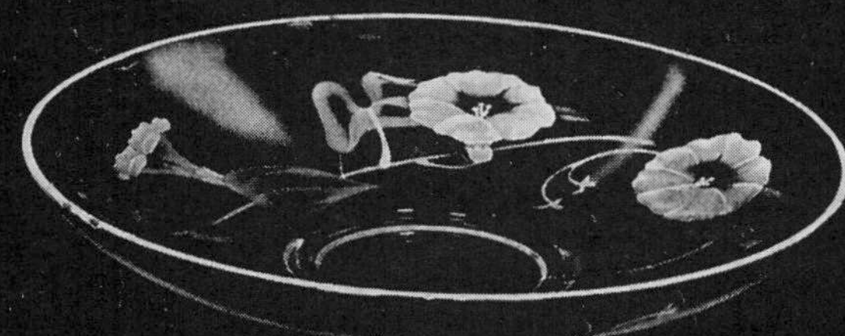

2364—13 in.
Fruit Bowl
Height 2¾ in.

2364—12 in.
Lily Pond
Height 2¼ in.

2324—6 in.
Candlestick

6023
Duo Candlestick
Height 5½ in. Spread 6 in.

Fostoria Glass Company, Moundsville, West Virginia, July 1, 1939

MORNING GLORY DESIGN

CARVING No. 12

2337—Plate
See Price List for Sizes

2419—Cake Plate, 2 Hdles.
Length 9½ in.

2364—16 in. Torte Plate

315—7 in. Bowl
315—9 in. Bowl

2427—Oblong Ash Tray
Length 3½ in.
Width 2¾ in.

2427—Oblong Cigarette Box and Cover
Length 7 in.
Height 2¼ in. Width 3⅛ in.
Each side holds 35 cigarettes.

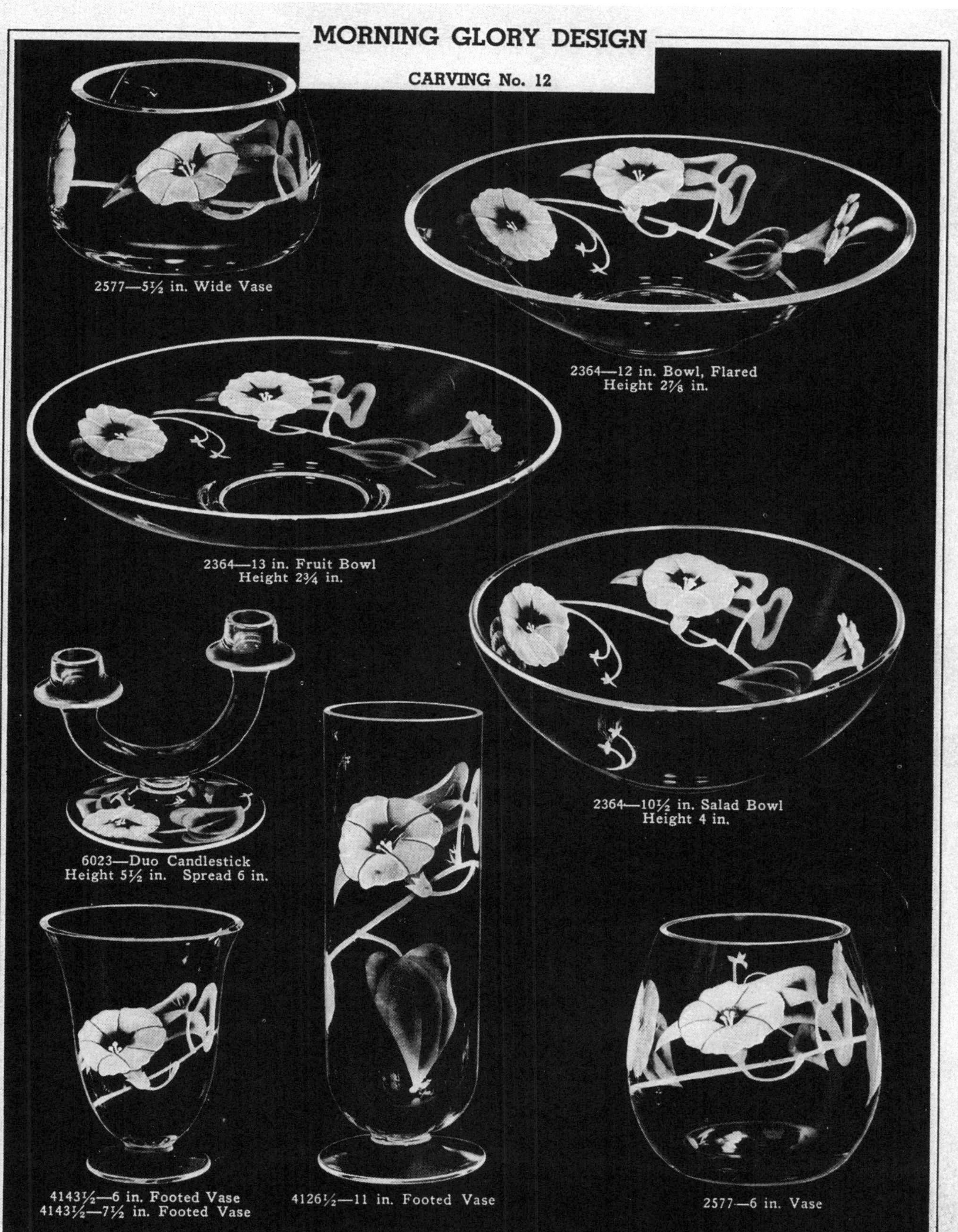

MORNING GLORY DESIGN

CARVING No. 12

2577—5½ in. Wide Vase

2364—12 in. Bowl, Flared
Height 2⅞ in.

2364—13 in. Fruit Bowl
Height 2¾ in.

2364—10½ in. Salad Bowl
Height 4 in.

6023—Duo Candlestick
Height 5½ in. Spread 6 in.

4143½—6 in. Footed Vase
4143½—7½ in. Footed Vase

4126½—11 in. Footed Vase

2577—6 in. Vase

Fostoria Glass Company, Moundsville, West Virginia, January 1, 1940

Fostoria Glass Company, Moundsville, West Virginia, July 1, 1940

MISCELLANEOUS CARVINGS

HUNT DESIGN

CARVING No. 34

4146—9 oz. Scotch & Soda
Height 3⅛ in.

4146—4 oz. Cocktail
Height 2½ in.

4146—1 oz. Cordial
Height 1½ in.

TOY DESIGN

DECORATION 620

Using Carving 33 with five different colors of Enamel

4146—9 oz. Scotch & Soda
Height 3⅛ in.

4146—4 oz. Cocktail
Height 2½ in.

4146—1 oz. Cordial
Height 1½ in.

2306—4 in. Ash Tray

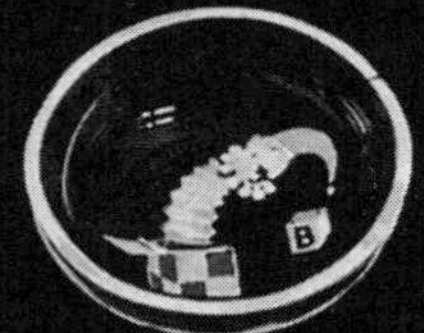

2306—3½ in. Ash Tray

2306—3 in. Ash Tray

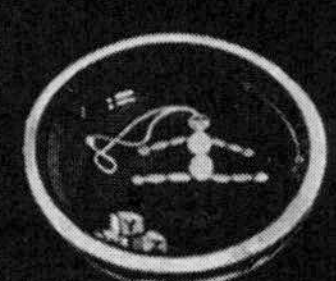

2306—2¾ in. Ash Tray

NIGHTMARE DESIGN

DECORATION 621 ·

Using Carving 39 with five different colors of Enamel

4146—9 oz. Scotch & Soda
Height 3⅛ in.

4146—4 oz. Cocktail
Height 2½ in.

4146—1 oz. Cordial
Height 1½ in.

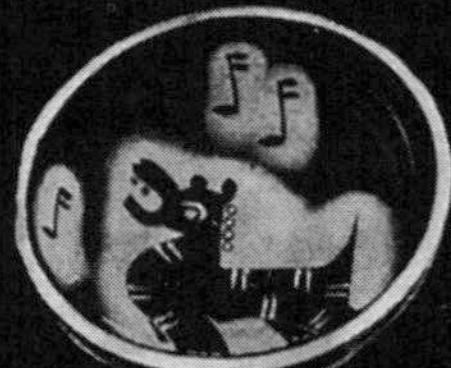

2306—4 in. Ash Tray

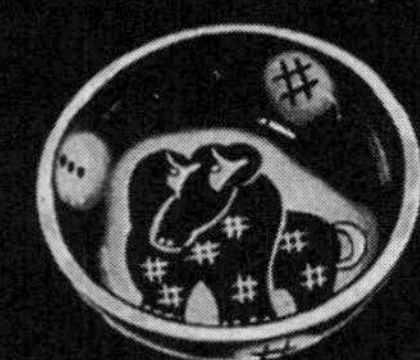

2306—3½ in. Ash Tray

2306—3 in. Ash Tray

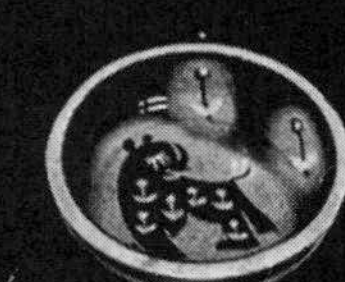

2306—2¾ in. Ash Tray

19TH HOLE DESIGN

CARVING No. 15

2391—Large Cigarette and Cover
Length 4¾ in. Width 3½ in.
(Driving)

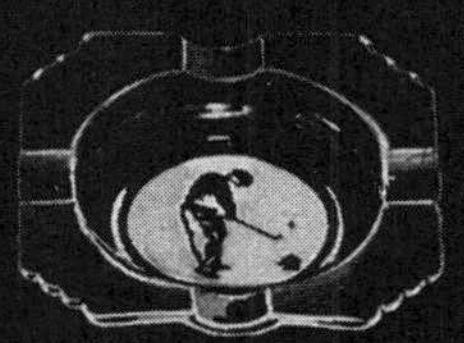

2419—Square Ash Tray
4 in. Square
(Approaching)

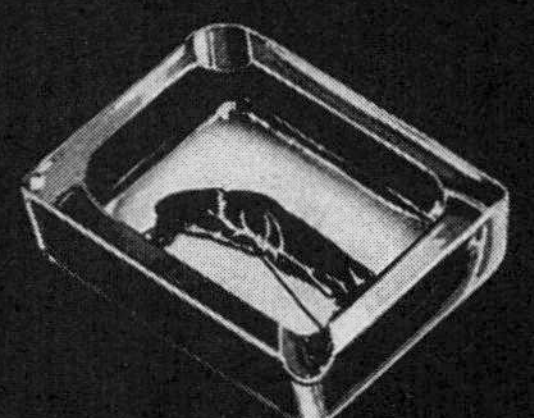

2427—Oblong Ash Tray
Length 3½ in. Width 2¾ in.
(Putting)

4132—7½ oz.
Old Fashioned Cocktail, Sham
Height 3⅛ in.
(Putting)

4132—Ice Bowl
Height 4¾ in.
(Putting)

4132—1½ oz. Whiskey, Sham
Height 2⅛ in.
(Approaching)

4132—5 oz. Tumbler, Sham
Height 3⅝ in.
(Exploding)

4132½—9 oz. Scotch & Soda, Sham
Height 4⅝ in.
(Exploding)

4132—12 oz. Tumbler, Sham
Height 4⅞ in.
(Driving)

4132—Decanter and Stopper
Capacity 24 oz.
Height 9¾ in.
(Driving)

Fostoria Glass Company, Moundsville, West Virginia, January 1, 1940

Fostoria Glass Company, Moundsville, West Virginia, January 1, 1941

ORCHID DESIGN

CARVING No. 48

An Orchid Carved in Crystal. It combines the traditions of an ancient craft with a modern technique.

892—11 oz. Goblet
Height 6½ in.

892—7 oz. Saucer Champagne
Height 5⅛ in.

892—6½ oz. Low Sherbet
Height 4 in.

892—4 oz. Cocktail
Height 4½ in.

892—4 oz. Claret
Height 4⅞ in.

892—3 oz. Wine
Height 4⅜ in.

892—5 oz. Footed Tumbler
Height 3⅞ in.

892—12 oz. Footed Tumbler
Height 5½ in.

892—4½ oz. Oyster Cocktail
Height 2⅞ in.

2337—Plate
See Price List for Sizes

1769—Finger Bowl
Height 2 in.
Diameter 4⅛ in.

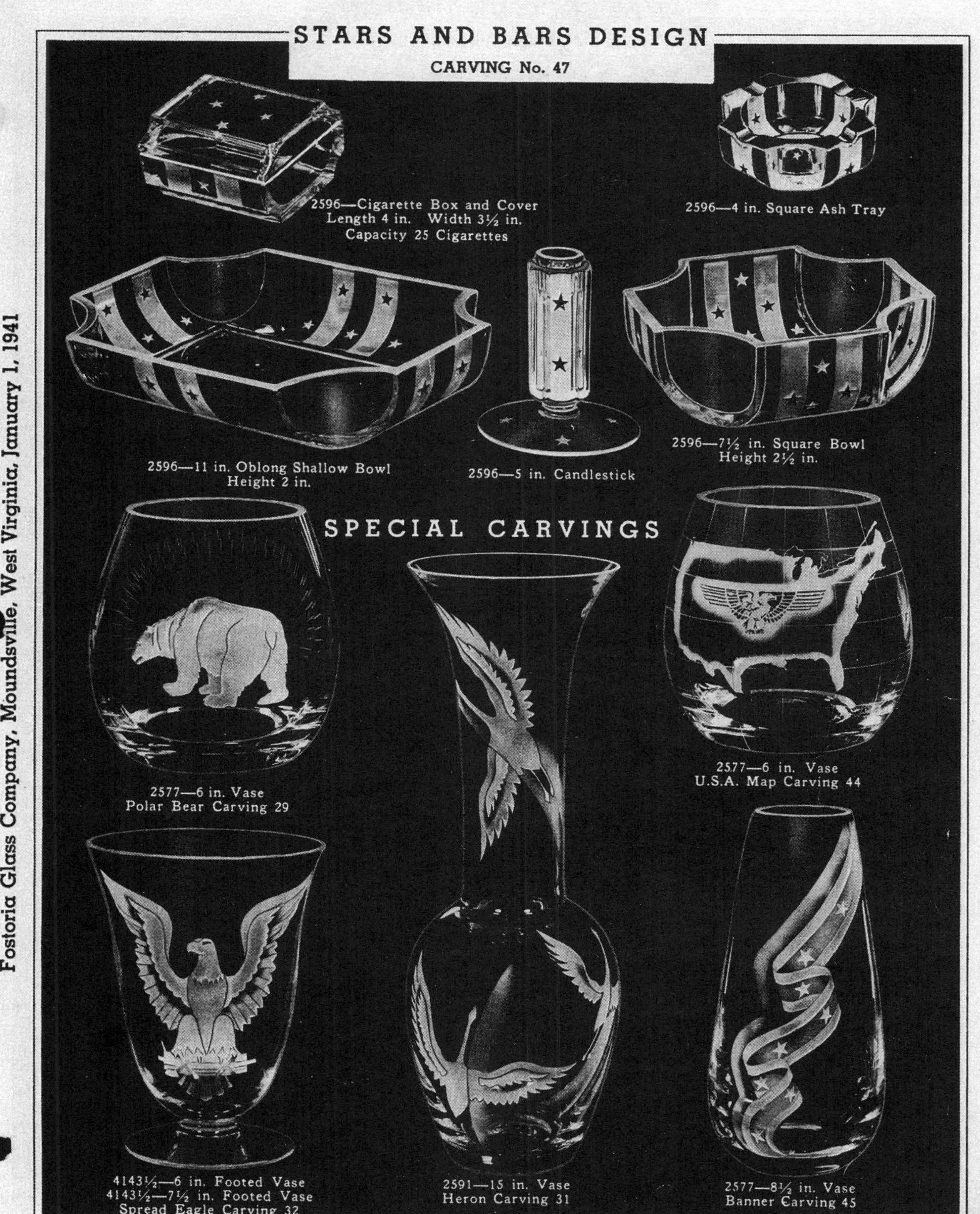

Fostoria Glass Company, Moundsville, West Virginia, January 1, 1941

WATERFOWL DESIGN

CARVING No. 1

4132—14 oz. Tumbler, Sham
Height 5 3/8 in.
4132—12 oz. Tumbler, Sham
Height 4 7/8 in.

4132½—9 oz. Scotch & Soda, Sham
Height 4 5/8 in.

4132—9 oz.
Tumbler, Sham
Height 3 3/4 in.

4132—5 oz.
Tumbler, Sham
Height 3 5/8 in.

2550—Round Ash Tray
Diameter 3 1/4 in.

4132—7½ oz.
Old Fashioned Cocktail, Sham
Height 3 1/8 in.

4132—Decanter and Stopper
Capacity 24 oz.
Height 9 3/4 in.

4132—Ice Bowl
Height 4 3/4 in.

2391—Large Cigarette and Cover
Length 4 3/4 in.—Width 3½ in.

4132—1½ oz.
Whiskey, Sham
Height 2 1/8 in.

SKI DESIGN

CARVING No. 2

4132—Decanter and Stopper
Capacity 24 oz.
Height 9 3/4 in.

4139—16 oz. Tumbler, Sham
Height 5 3/8 in.
4139—14 oz. Tumbler, Sham
Height 6 1/4 in.
4139—12 oz. Tumbler, Sham
Height 5 5/8 in.

4139—10 oz.
Tumbler, Sham
Height 5 1/4 in.
4139—5 oz.
Tumbler, Sham
Height 4 in.

4139—9 oz.
Water Tumbler, Sham
Height 3½ in.

4139—7 oz.
Old Fashioned
Cocktail, Sham
Height 2 3/4 in.

4139—1 3/4 oz.
Whiskey, Sham
Height 1 7/8 in.

2391—Large Cigarette and Cover
Length 4 3/4 in.—Width 3½ in.

2550—Round Ash Tray
Diameter 3 1/4 in.

4132—Ice Bowl
Height 4 3/4 in.

FOSTORIA GLASS COMPANY, MOUNDSVILLE, WEST VIRGINIA – Jan. 1, 1939

Clocks

St. Clair (rectangular) No. 2298
St. Alexis (oval) No. 2299

St. Alexis and St. Clair Clock Sets were listed in the old catalogs as "Vanity Dresser Novelties." Introduced mid-1924 and made through 1927, both patterns came packed in cartons containing one clock and two candlesticks. The most expensive of all the sets was the Ebony St. Clair decorated with encrusted gold. This set wholesaled for $13.70 in 1924. All the solid color undecorated clocks wholesaled for $3.35 each; the matching candlesticks were only 25 cents. It is interesting to note that Rose (pink-dawn) is not listed in any available records. Another oddity is the St. Clair clock, etched with the Cupid and made in 1927, the year Fostoria introduced Orchid (a delicate lavender) color, yet no records indicate clocks were produced in this color. The 1924 price list clearly shows that these clock sets had pattern names, yet by 1927 these names had been dropped. Canary and Ebony are the rarest of the clock sets. All clocks are hard to find and command a premium price.

Various decorations for St. Alexis and St. Clair

2299	St. Alexis, Decoration No. 25, dark or light blue enameled tints, Vase and Scroll design
2299	St. Alexis, Encrusted Gold Decoration No. 4
2298	St. Clair, White Enameled Edge, Decoration No. 1
2298	St. Clair, Encrusted Gold Decoration No. 2
2298	St. Clair, Decoration No. 25, dark or light blue enameled tints, Vase and Scroll design
2298	St. Clair, Encrusted Gold Decoration No. 37, Vase and Scroll design
2298	St. Clair, Encrusted Gold Decoration No. 3
2298	St. Clair, Encrusted Gold Decoration No. 67, Poinsetta Design
2298	St. Clair, Etched Brocade No. 288, Cupid Design
2298	St. Clair, Encrusted Yellow or White Gold

Colors of undecorated clocks	Introduced	Discontinued
Green	1924	1927
Canary	1924	1926
Amber	1924	1927
Ebony	mid-1924	1927
Crystal	1924	1927
Blue	1924	1927

26
VANITY DRESSER NOVELTIES.
MADE IN AMBER, BLUE, GREEN, EBONY AND CRYSTAL; EXCEPT AS OTHERWISE NOTED.
PRICED PAGES 10 AND 13 — No. 2 SUPPLEMENT PRICE LIST.
2298—Candle.
2298— Clock.
Clock Case Patented No. 67,532.
2298—Candle.
2306—Smoker Set.
4 Ash Trays Nested.
Not made in crystal.
2063—Candle.
Not made in ebony.
2276—Vanity Set.
Also made in Orchid.
Patent Nos. 65,367 and 1,478,026.
2297—7 in. Candle.
2352—Candle.
Also made in orchid.
Not made in ebony.
2299—Candle.
2299—Clock.
2299—Candle.
Fostoria Glass Company, Moundsville, West Virginia

1927 Catalog

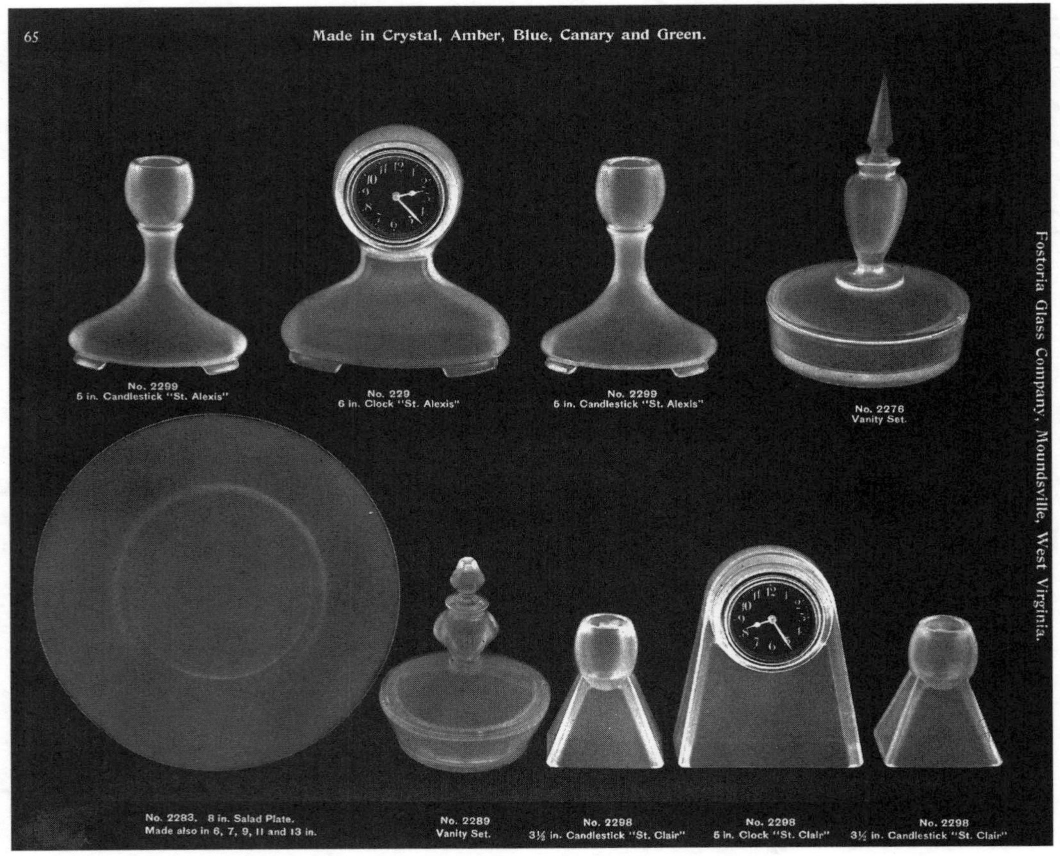

65
Made in Crystal, Amber, Blue, Canary and Green.
No. 2299
5 in. Candlestick "St. Alexis"
No. 229
6 in. Clock "St. Alexis"
No. 2299
5 in. Candlestick "St. Alexis"
No. 2276
Vanity Set.
No. 2283. 8 in. Salad Plate.
Made also in 6, 7, 9, 11 and 13 in.
No. 2289
Vanity Set.
No. 2298
3½ in. Candlestick "St. Clair"
No. 2298
5 in. Clock "St. Clair"
No. 2298
3½ in. Candlestick "St. Clair"
Fostoria Glass Company, Moundsville, West Virginia.

1925 Catalog

Decorations

Club Design A, Decoration No. 603
Square Base, Crystal with Gold Lines

4020	Goblet
4020	High Sherbet
4020	Low Sherbet, 7 oz.
4020	Low Sherbet, 4 oz.
4020	Cocktail, 3½ oz.
4020	Whiskey, 2 oz.
4020	Tumbler, 16 oz.
4020	Tumbler, 13 oz.
4020	Tumbler, 5 oz.
4120	Finger Bowl
2419	Plate, 8"
2350	Cream Soup
2419	Plate, 7"
2419	Plate, 6"
2350	Plate, 6"
2350	Plate, 7"
2350	Plate, 9"
2350	Footed Cup
2350	Saucer
2419	Saucer
2350	After Dinner Cup
2350	After Dinner Saucer
2419	After Dinner Saucer

Matching serving pieces would be Crystal with Gold Lines. This scarce design was made only in 1930. For some reason Fostoria decided not to make the Footed Jug and Footed Decanter in Club Design A.

Club Design B, Decoration No. 604
Square Ebony Base, Crystal Bowl and Gold Lines

4120	Goblet, 11 oz.
4120	High Sherbet, 7 oz.
4120	Low Sherbet, 7 oz.
4120	Low Sherbet, 5 oz.
4120	Cocktail, 3½ oz.
4120	Whiskey, 2 oz.
4120	Tumbler, 16 oz.
4120	Tumbler, 13 oz.
4120	Tumbler, 10 oz.
4120	Tumbler, 5 oz.
4121	Finger Bowl
2419	Plate, 8"
2419	Plate, 7"
2419	Plate, 6"
2350	Plate, 6"
2350	Plate, 7"
2350	Plate, 9"
2350	Cup, Footed (2350½)
2350	Saucer
2419	Saucer
2350	Cup, After Dinner
2419	Saucer, After Dinner
2350	Cream Soup
2350	Sugar, Footed (2350½)
2350	Cream, Footed (2350½)
2375	Lemon Dish
2375	Cake Plate, 10"
2297	Deep Bowl, "A", 12"
2324	Candlestick, 4"
2350	Ashtray, Large
2427	Cigarette Box, Covered
2400	Comport, 6"
2430	Bowl, 11"
2430	Candy Jar, Cov., ½ lb.
2430	Mint, 5½"
2430	Jelly, 7"
2430	Vase, 8"
2373	Window Vase, Cov., Lg.
2373	Window Vase, Cov., Sm.
2387	Vase, 8"
2404	Vase, 6"
2409	Vase, 7½"
2421	Vase, 10½"
4105	Vase, 8"

1930 Listing. The matching serving pieces are Ebony with Gold Lines, or Crystal with Gold Lines. Design B was made for only two or three years. Notice there is no wine this year.

Club Design C, Decoration No. 611
Square Base, Crystal with Green Enamel Lines

4020	Tumbler, Footed, 16 oz.
4020	Tumbler, Footed, 13 oz.
4020	Tumbler, Footed, 10 oz.
4020	Tumbler, Footed, 5 oz.
4020	Low Sherbet, 7 oz.
4020	Whiskey, 2 oz.
4020	Jug, Footed
4020	Decanter, Footed
2419	Plate, 7"

1931 Listing. Additional serving pieces would be Crystal with Green Enamel Lines. This is a rare decoration, possibly made for only two or three years. Club Design C is a pattern that is without stemmed pieces. It would be considered a bridge or luncheon set.

Polka-Dot Design, Decoration No. 607
Square Ebony Base with Crystal Bowl

4120	Goblet, 11 oz.
4120	High Sherbet, 7 oz.
4120	Low Sherbet, 5 oz.
4120	Cocktail, 3½ oz.
4120	Whiskey, 2 oz.
4120	Tumbler, Footed, 16 oz.
4120	Tumbler, Footed, 13 oz.
4120	Tumbler, Footed, 5 oz.
4121	Finger Bowl
4120	Jug, Footed
4120	Sugar, Footed
4120	Cream, Footed

Polka-Dot was introduced in 1931 and may have been produced through the year 1932. It is a scarce pattern and seldom shows up in the market place. The footed jug would be a fabulous Art Deco piece and the rarest of rare. Serving pieces should be undecorated Ebony.

Saturn Design, Decoration No. 605
Square Ebony Base, Crystal Bowl with Black Enamel Lines

4120	Goblet, 11 oz.
4120	High Sherbet, 7 oz.
4120	Low Sherbet, 5 oz.
4120	Cocktail, 3½ oz.
4120	Whiskey, 2 oz.
4121	Finger Bowl
4120	Tumbler, Footed, 16 oz.
4120	Tumbler, Footed, 13 oz.
4120	Tumbler, Footed, 10 oz.
4120	Tumbler, Footed, 5 oz.
2419	Plate, 8" (Crystal)
2419	Plate, 7" (Crystal)
2419	Plate, 6" (Crystal)
2350	Cup, Footed (Crystal)
2419	Saucer (Crystal)

If any serving pieces were made (other than the jug, cream, or sugar), they would be Crystal with Black Enamel Lines. Saturn was introduced in 1930; the list shown here is dated 1930. The footed jug, cream, and sugar were not made in the introductory year, and so, due to limited production, they will be harder to find than the tumblers. Consider the Saturn jug very rare.

Spanish Lustre Iridescent Decoration 1927 Catalog

877 Claret, 10 oz.
Cocktail, 3½ oz.
Cordial, ¾ oz.
Goblet, 10 oz.
Grapefruit with Liner
Oyster Cocktail, Ftd., 4½ oz.
Parfait, Ftd., 5½ oz.
Sherbet, High, 6 oz.
Sherbet, Low, 6 oz.
Tumbler, Ftd., 12 oz.
Tumbler, Ftd., 9 oz.
Tumbler, Ftd., 5 oz.
Tumbler, 2½ oz.
Wine, 2¾ oz.
2283 Plate, 6"
Plate, 7"
Plate, Salad, 8"
5100 Jug, 7-Pint

Spanish Lustre is seldom seen. Do not confuse this decoration with Mother-of-Pearl. The lustre was sprayed on crystal glass while still hot. Amber iridescent glass was a different Fostoria treatment. Stem No. 877 was made only in 1927 and 1928. Stem No. 660 (not illustrated) was continued through 1929. This treatment was introduced in 1917 on stem No. 766.

Autumn Glow Decoration 1925 Catalog

869 Goblet, 9 oz.
Saucer Champagne, 5½ oz.
Fruit, 5½ oz.
Parfait, 6 oz.
Cocktail, 3 oz.
Wine, 2¾ oz.
Cordial, 1 oz.
Oyster Cocktail (837)
Finger Bowl (766)
Table Tumbler
Tumbler, 12 oz.
Tumbler, 8 oz.
Tumbler, 5 oz.
Tumbler, 2 oz.
Ice Tea, Handled, 12 oz.
1236 Jug, 6-Pint
2283 Plate, 6"
Plate, Salad, 7"
Plate, Salad, 8"

Autumn Glow is an attractive and scarce decoration. The glass is solid amber with an all-over mother-of-pearl iridescence. There is more intense coloring than the regular mother-of-pearl sprayed on crystal.

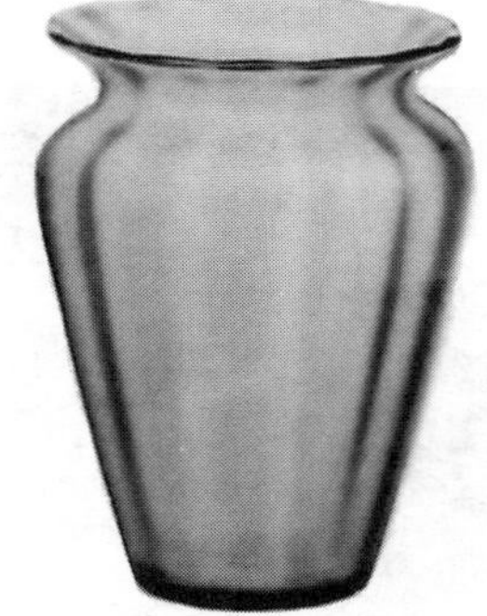

Solid Ebony Glass with Gold Lines
1931 Catalog

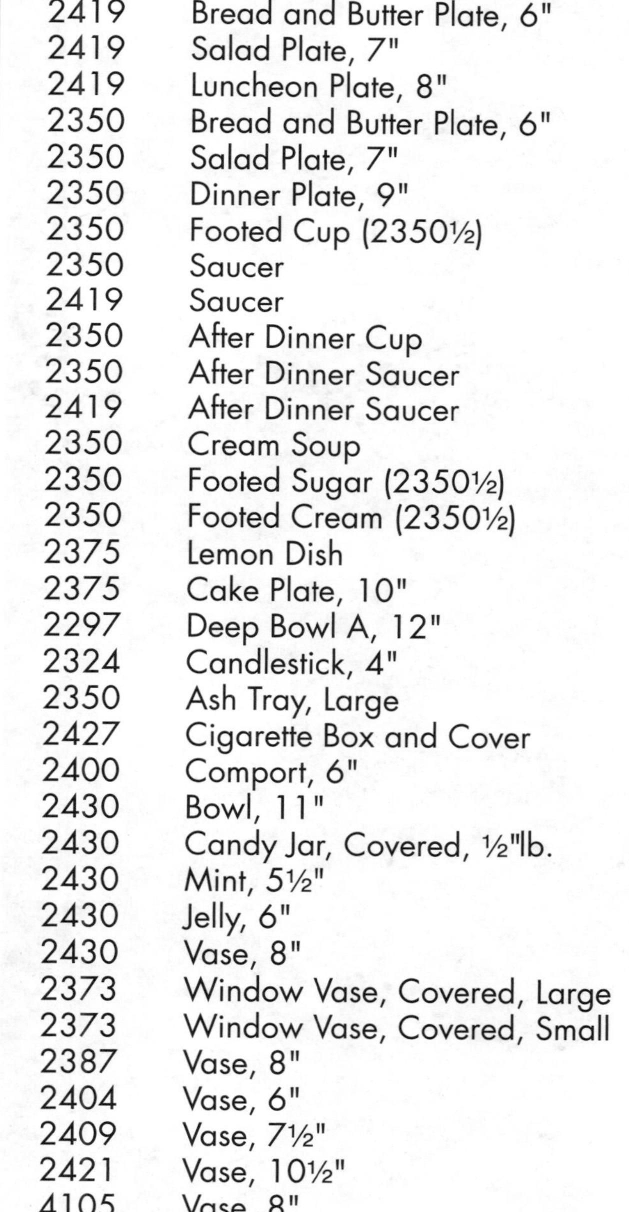

2419	Bread and Butter Plate, 6"
2419	Salad Plate, 7"
2419	Luncheon Plate, 8"
2350	Bread and Butter Plate, 6"
2350	Salad Plate, 7"
2350	Dinner Plate, 9"
2350	Footed Cup (2350½)
2350	Saucer
2419	Saucer
2350	After Dinner Cup
2350	After Dinner Saucer
2419	After Dinner Saucer
2350	Cream Soup
2350	Footed Sugar (2350½)
2350	Footed Cream (2350½)
2375	Lemon Dish
2375	Cake Plate, 10"
2297	Deep Bowl A, 12"
2324	Candlestick, 4"
2350	Ash Tray, Large
2427	Cigarette Box and Cover
2400	Comport, 6"
2430	Bowl, 11"
2430	Candy Jar, Covered, ½"lb.
2430	Mint, 5½"
2430	Jelly, 6"
2430	Vase, 8"
2373	Window Vase, Covered, Large
2373	Window Vase, Covered, Small
2387	Vase, 8"
2404	Vase, 6"
2409	Vase, 7½"
2421	Vase, 10½"
4105	Vase, 8"

"Onyx Lustre" on Ebony Glass

Onyx Lustre was a limited line of black opaque iridized glass that Fostoria made only in 1924 – 1925. The few pieces that have been seen show an intense iridescence with prominent shades of purple. *The Standard Encyclopedia of Carnival Glass, Fourth Edition*, published by Collector Books, pictures in color a pair of the No. 2324 Candlesticks and labels them as "Taffeta Lustre."

Onyx Lustre is highly sought after by collectors of American carnival glass. Other American glass firms also produced ebony iridized pieces, and each firm had wonderful exotic names for these wares. Diamond Glassware Co., Indiana, Pa., called their iridized ebony pieces "Egyptian Lustre." Fostoria pieces can be identified by the blanks (shapes). This 1925 list is from the Fostoria achives.

1681	Wall Vase
2269	Candle, 6"
2276	Vanity Set
2283	Plate, Cupped, 13"
2297	Bowl "A," Shallow, 10"
2297	Bowl, "A," Deep, 12"
2324	Candle, 4"
2327	Compote, 7"
2329	Bowl/Centerpiece, 11"
2329	Bowl/Centerpiece, 13"
2331	Candy Box, Cov., 3-Part
2367	Bowl, Bulb, 7"
2367	Bowl, Bulb, 8"

FOSTORIA GLASS COMPANY, MOUNDSVILLE, WEST VIRGINIA — 1948

DECORATIONS

MARDI GRAS DESIGN

Decoration No. 627

4116—6 in.
Vase

2618
Cigarette Box & Cover
Length 5 ½ in. Width 4 ¼ in.

2619—6 in.
Vase

2619—9 ½ in.
Vase

2666
Sweetmeat
Length 6 ¾ in.

2677
Ash Tray
Length 4 ¾ in. Width 3 ⅜ in.

2666
Tid Bit
Diameter 7 ½ in.

2666
Comport
Diameter 6 ⅞ in.

2666
Ribbon Bowl
Height 2 ¾ in.

HIGHLIGHTED BLUE SPRAY

Decoration No. 631

2513
Candy Jar & Cover
Height 6 ¼ in.

2519
Cologne & Stopper
Height 5 ½ in.

2519
Puff & Cover
Height 4 ½ in.

BURNISHED GOLD HIGHLIGHTS

Decoration No. 632

2513
Candy Jar & Cover
Height 6 ¼ in.

2519
Cologne & Stopper
Height 5 ½ in.

2519
Puff & Cover
Height 4 ½ in.

Dinnerware, Stems, and Tumblers, Cut

1930 Catalog

Athenian Design
Cutting No. 770

Beacon Design
Cutting No. 767
Rock Crystal

Aloha Design
Cutting No. 805

Brighton Design
Cutting No. 801, Rock Crystal

Chatteris Design, Polished Cutting No. 197
Made in Solid Crystal, Regular Optic

1930 Catalog

BRACELET DESIGN

Cutting No. 838

Rock Crystal

FOSTORIA GLASS COMPANY, MOUNDSVILLE, WEST VIRGINIA — 1954

6051
Goblet
Height 6 3/16 in.
Capacity 10½ oz.

6051
Sherbet
Height 4⅜ in.
Capacity 6½ oz.

6051
Cocktail
Height 3⅞ in.

6051
Claret-Wine
Height 4½ in.
Capacity 4 oz.

6051
Cordial
Height 3⅛ in.
Capacity 1¼ oz.

6051
Oyster Cocktail
Height 3¾ in.
Capacity 4¼ oz.

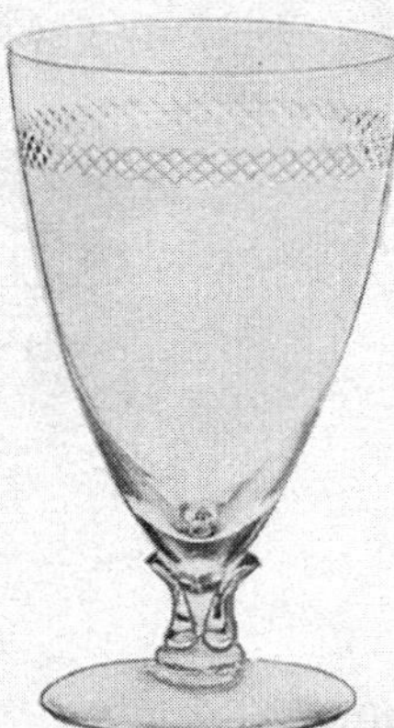

6051
Footed Ice Tea
Height 6⅛ in.
Capacity 12¼ oz.

6051
Footed Juice
Height 4 in.
Capacity 5 oz.

2337
7 in. Plate
2337
8 in. Plate

Cadence Design
Cutting No. 806, Rock Crystal

Christine Design
Cutting No. 798

Bordeaux Design
Cutting No. 758

Celebrity Design
Cutting No. 749, Rock Crystal

1939 Catalog

COVENTRY DESIGN

ROCK CRYSTAL CUTTING No. 807

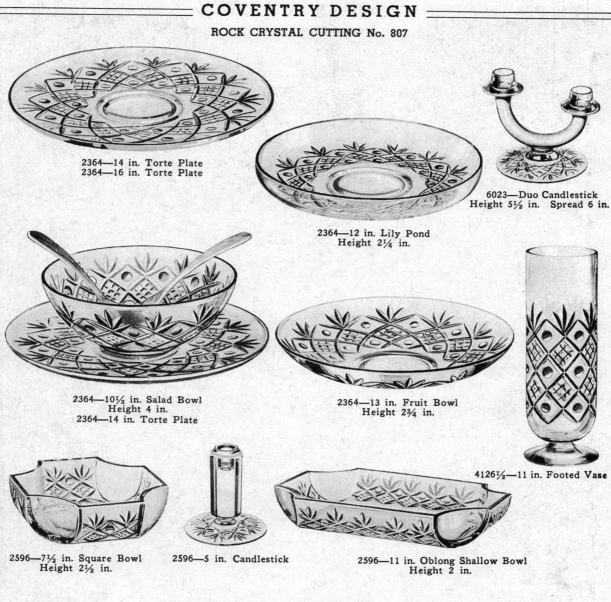

2364—14 in. Torte Plate
2364—16 in. Torte Plate

2364—12 in. Lily Pond
Height 2¼ in.

6023—Duo Candlestick
Height 5½ in. Spread 6 in.

2364—10½ in. Salad Bowl
Height 4 in.
2364—14 in. Torte Plate

2364—13 in. Fruit Bowl
Height 2¾ in.

4126½—11 in. Footed Vase

2596—7½ in. Square Bowl
Height 2½ in.

2596—5 in. Candlestick

2596—11 in. Oblong Shallow Bowl
Height 2 in.

2577—8½ in. Vase

4132½—8 in. Vase

4143½—6 in. Footed Vase
4143½—7½ in. Footed Vase

2577—6 in. Vase

2567—7½ in. Footed Vase
2567—8½ in. Footed Vase

Fostoria Glass Company, Moundsville, West Virginia, July 1, 1940

Fostoria Glass Company, Moundsville, West Virginia, Jan. 1, 1939

CRYSTAL CUTTINGS

CUTTING A

CUTTING B

CUTTING C

CUTTING D

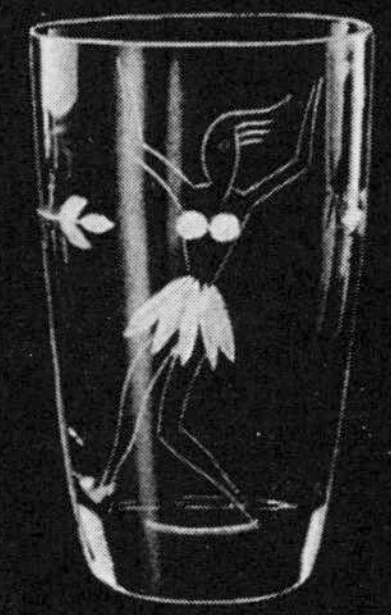

SOUTH SEAS DESIGN
CUTTING No. 779

SERENADE DESIGN
CUTTING No. 780

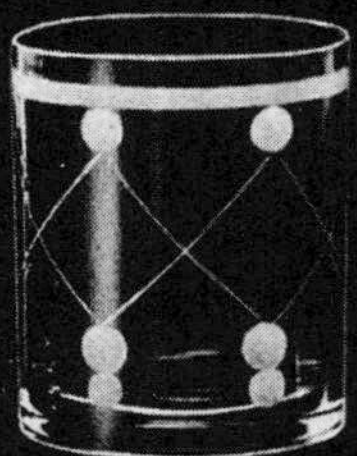

DRUM DESIGN
CUTTING No. 781

CHELSEA DESIGN
ROCK CRYSTAL
CUTTING No. 783

REGAL DESIGN
ROCK CRYSTAL
CUTTING No. 782

DRAPE DESIGN
CUTTING No. 784

CRYSTAL CUTTINGS

STAUNTON DESIGN
CUTTING No. 707

WATERBURY DESIGN
CUTTING No. 712

NATIONAL DESIGN
CUTTING No. 727

OXFORD DESIGN
CUTTING No. 714

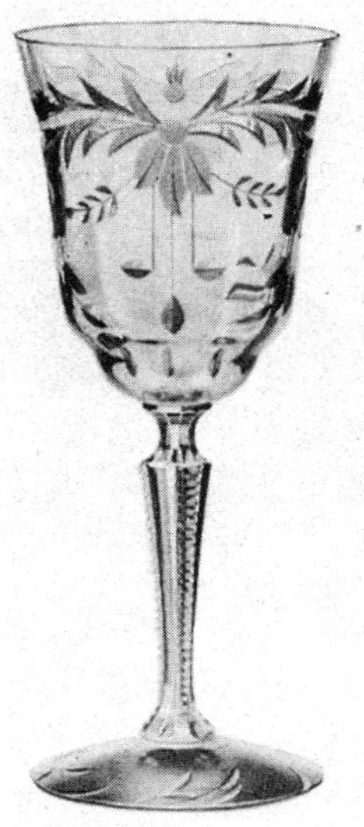

DONCASTER DESIGN
CUTTING No. 718

CIRCLET DESIGN

Cutting No. 840

Rock Crystal

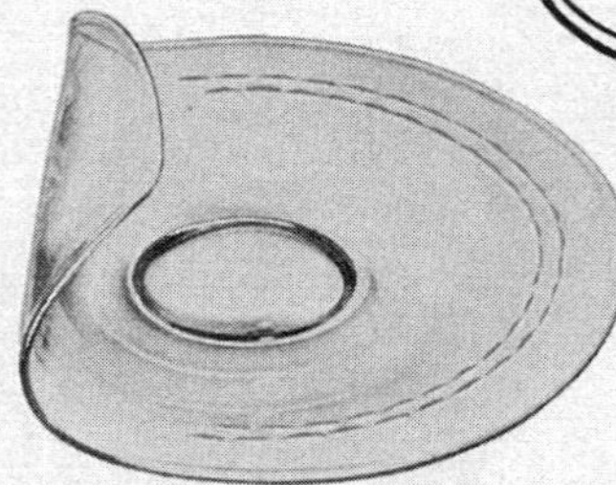

2666—10 in.
Snack Plate

2364—14 in.
Torte Plate

2666
Sugar
Height 2⅝ in.

2666
Cream
Height 3½ in.

2666—3 Piece
Individual Sugar & Cream & Tray
Consisting of:
1/12 Dz. 2666—S. & C. Tray (not cut)
1/12 Dz. 2666—Ind. Sugar
1/12 Dz. 2666—Ind. Cream

2364
2 Part Relish
Length 8¼ in.
Width 5 in.

2364
Mayonnaise and Plate and Ladle
Mayo. Height 2½ in.
Mayo. Diameter 5 in.
Plate Diameter 6¾ in.

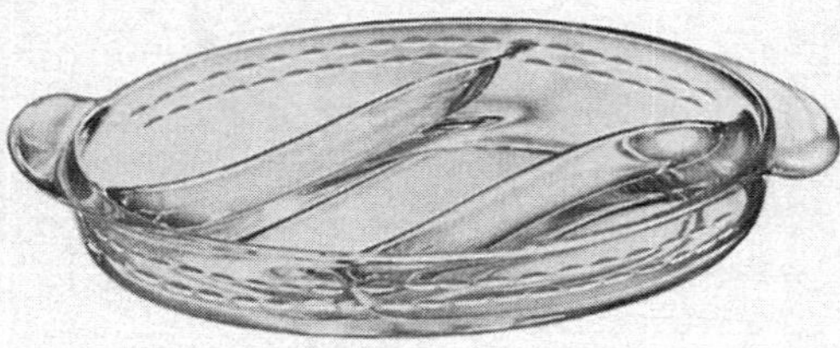

2364
3 Part Relish
Length 10 in.
Width 7¼ in.

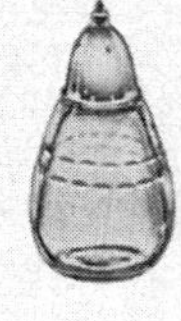

2364
Large Shaker
Chrome Top "B"
Height 3¼ in.

2666
Canape Plate
Diameter 7⅜ in.
Height 2 in.

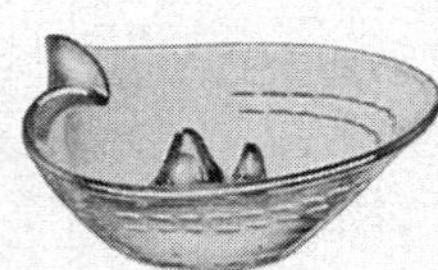

2666
Flora Candle
Diameter 6 in.

2666
Oval Bowl
Diameter 8¼ in.
Height 3¼ in.

CREST DESIGN

Cutting No. 843

Gray Cutting

6061
Goblet
Height 5⅛ in.
Capacity 11 oz.

6061
Sherbet
Height 4 in.
Capacity 7½ oz.

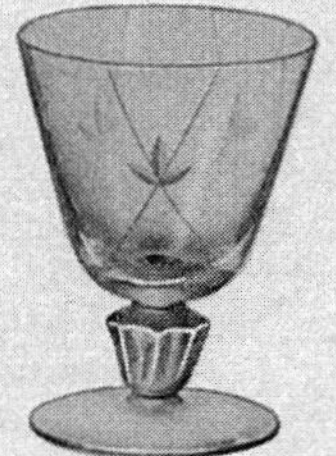

6061
Cocktail/Wine/Seafood
Height 3⅞ in.
Capacity 4 oz.

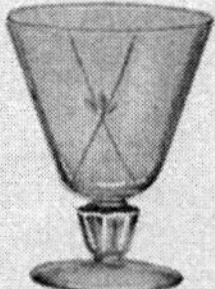

6061
Cordial
Height 2½ in.
Capacity 1 oz.

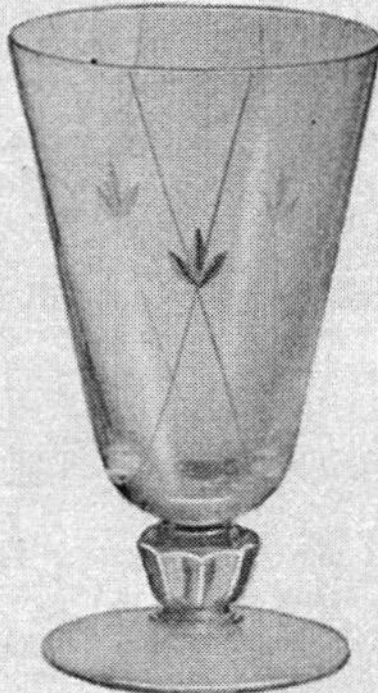

6061
Footed Ice Tea
Height 6 in.
Capacity 12 oz.

6061
Footed Juice
Height 4¾ in.
Capacity 6 oz.

2337
7 in. Plate
2337
8 in. Plate

FOSTORIA GLASS COMPANY, MOUNDSVILLE, WEST VIRGINIA — 1956

CYNTHIA DESIGN
CUTTING No. 785
6017—9 oz. Goblet
Height 7⅜ in.
6017
6 oz. Saucer Champagne
Height 5½ in.
6017
12 oz. Footed Tumbler
Height 6 in.
2560—Mayonnaise, Plate and Ladle
Height 3½ in.
2560—4 Part Relish
Length 10 in. Width 6¾ in.
2560—11½ in. Handled Lunch Tray
2560—Individual Cream
Height 3¼ in.
Capacity 4 oz.
2560—6¾ in. Olive
2560—8¾ in. Pickle
2560—11 in. Celery
2560—Sweetmeat, 2 Hdles.
Height 1½ in.
Diameter 5½ in.
2560—Individual Sugar
Height 3 in.
2560½—4 in. Candlestick
2560—11½ Bowl, Crimped
Height 3¼ in.
Fostoria Glass Company, Moundsville, West Virginia, Jan. 1, 1939

2560
Footed Cream
Height 4⅛ in.
Capacity 7 oz.

2560
Footed Sugar
Height 3½ in.

2560
8¾ in. Pickle

2560
3 Part Relish
Length 10 in. Width 7¾ in.

2560
11½ in. Handled Lunch Tray

2560
4½ in. Candlestick

2560
3 Toed Bon Bon
Diameter 7¼ in.
Height 2⅜ in.

2560
Mayonnaise and Plate and Ladle
Mayo. Height 3¼ in.
Mayo. Diameter 5½ in.
Plate Diameter 7⅛ in.

2560
11 in. Handled Bowl
Height 3¼ in.

2560
Duo Candlestick
Height 5⅛ in. Spread 9 in.

Gothic Design
Cutting No. 774, Rock Crystal

Federal Design
Cutting No. 771

Formal Garden
Cutting No. 700

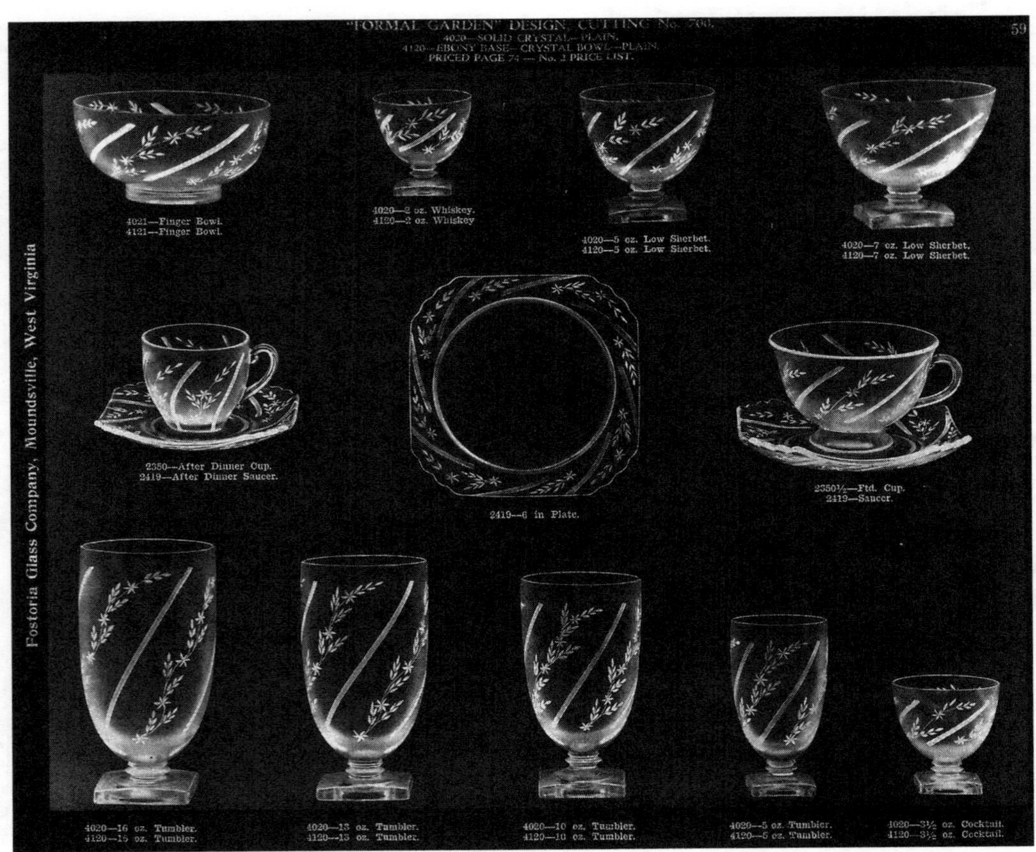

"FORMAL GARDEN" DESIGN, CUTTING No. 700.
4020—SOLID CRYSTAL—PLAIN.
4120—EBONY BASE—CRYSTAL BOWL—PLAIN.
PRICED PAGE 74 — No. 2 PRICE LIST.

59

Fostoria Glass Company, Moundsville, West Virginia

4021—Finger Bowl.
4121—Finger Bowl.

4020—2 oz. Whiskey.
4120—2 oz. Whiskey

4020—5 oz. Low Sherbet.
4120—5 oz. Low Sherbet.

4020—7 oz. Low Sherbet.
4120—7 oz. Low Sherbet.

2350—After Dinner Cup.
2419—After Dinner Saucer.

2419—6 in Plate.

2350½—Ftd. Cup.
2419—Saucer.

4020—16 oz. Tumbler.
4120—15 oz. Tumbler.

4020—13 oz. Tumbler.
4120—13 oz. Tumbler.

4020—10 oz. Tumbler.
4120—10 oz. Tumbler.

4020—5 oz. Tumbler.
4120—5 oz. Tumbler.

4020—3½ oz. Cocktail.
4120—3½ oz. Cocktail.

1930 Catalog

DAPHNE DESIGN
ROCK CRYSTAL
CUTTING No. 797

2424—8 in. Bowl Regular
Height 3½ in.

2424—9½ in. Bowl, Flared
Height 3⅞ in.

2424—3½ in. Candlestick

2424—11½ in. Fruit Bowl
Height 2¼ in.

2424—7½ in. Footed Urn, Regular

2424—6½ in. Footed Urn, Flared

Fostoria Glass Company, Moundsville, West Virginia, July 1, 1939

FOSTORIA GLASS COMPANY, MOUNDSVILLE, WEST VIRGINIA — 1953

FOSTORIA WHEAT DESIGN

Cutting No. 837

Combination Gray and Rock Crystal

6051
Goblet
Height 6-3/16 in.
Capacity 10½ oz.

6051
Sherbet
Height 4⅜ in.
Capacity 6½ oz.

6051
Cocktail
Height 3⅞ in.
Capacity 3¼ oz.

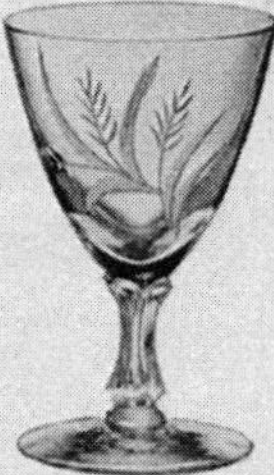

6051
Claret-Wine
Height 4½ in.
Capacity 4 oz.

6051
Cordial
Height 3⅛ in.
Capacity 1¼ oz.

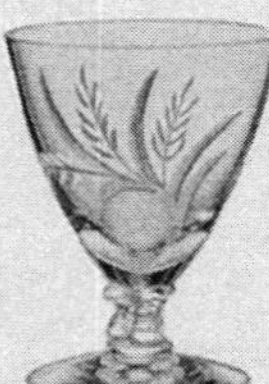

6051
Oyster Cocktail
Height 3¾ in.
Capacity 4¼ oz.

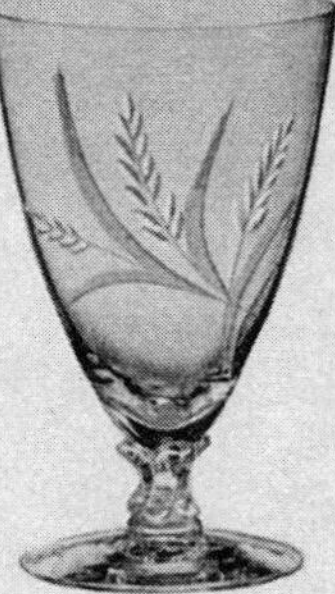

6051
Footed Ice Tea
Height 6⅛ in.
Capacity 12¼ oz.

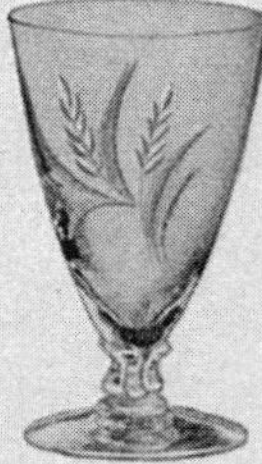

6051
Footed Juice
Height 4 in.
Capacity 5 oz.

2666
14 in. Serving Plate

2337
7 in. Plate
2337
8 in. Plate

FOSTORIA WHEAT DESIGN

Cutting No. 837

Combination Gray and Rock Crystal

2666
10 in. Snack Plate

2666
Cream
Height 3½ in.

2666
Sugar
Height 2⅝ in.

2666
2 Part Relish
Length 7⅜ in. Width 6 in.

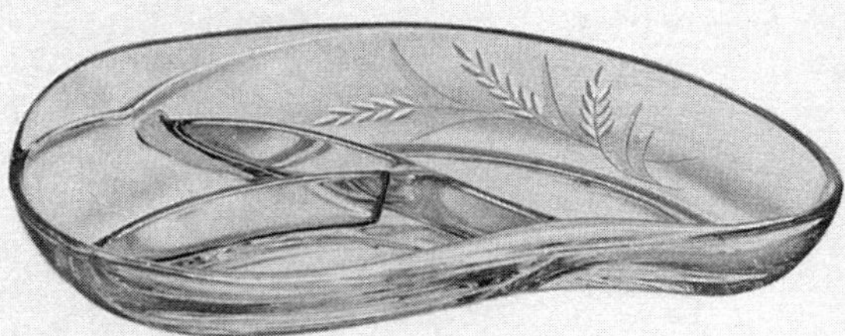

2666
3 Part Relish
Length 10¾ in.
Width 7⅞ in.

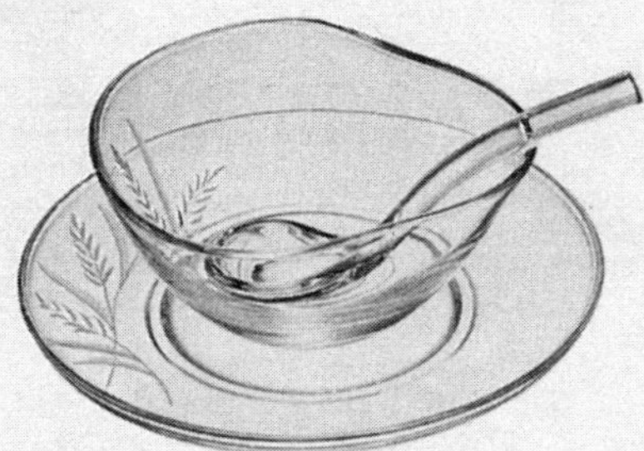

2666
Mayonnaise and Plate and Ladle
Height 3¼ in.

2364
Large Shaker
Chrome Top "B"
Height 3¼ in.

2666
Oval Bowl
Diameter 8¼ in.
Height 3¼ in.

2666
Flora-Candle
Diameter 6 in.

FOSTORIA GLASS COMPANY, MOUNDSVILLE, WEST VIRGINIA — 1953

FOSTORIA GLASS COMPANY, MOUNDSVILLE, WEST VIRGINIA — 1953

GADROON DESIGN

Cutting No. 816

Gray Cutting

6030
Goblet
Height 7⅞ in.
Capacity 10 oz.

6030
Low Goblet
Height 6⅜ in.
Capacity 10 oz.

6030
High Sherbet (Champagne)
Height 5⅝ in.
Capacity 6 oz.

6030
Low Sherbet
Height 4⅜ in.
Capacity 6 oz.

6030
Cocktail
Height 5¼ in.
Capacity 3½ oz.

6030
Claret-Wine
Height 6 in.
Capacity 3½ oz.

6030
Cordial
Height 3⅞ in.
Capacity 1 oz.

6030
Oyster Cocktail
Height 3¾ in.
Capacity 4 oz.

6030
Footed Ice Tea
Height 6 in.
Capacity 12 oz.

6030
Footed Juice
Height 4⅝ in.
Capacity 5 oz.

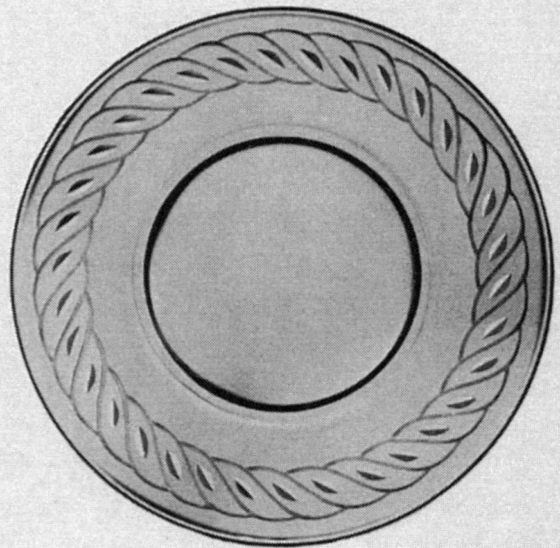

2337
6 in. Plate
2337
7 in. Plate
2337
8 in. Plate

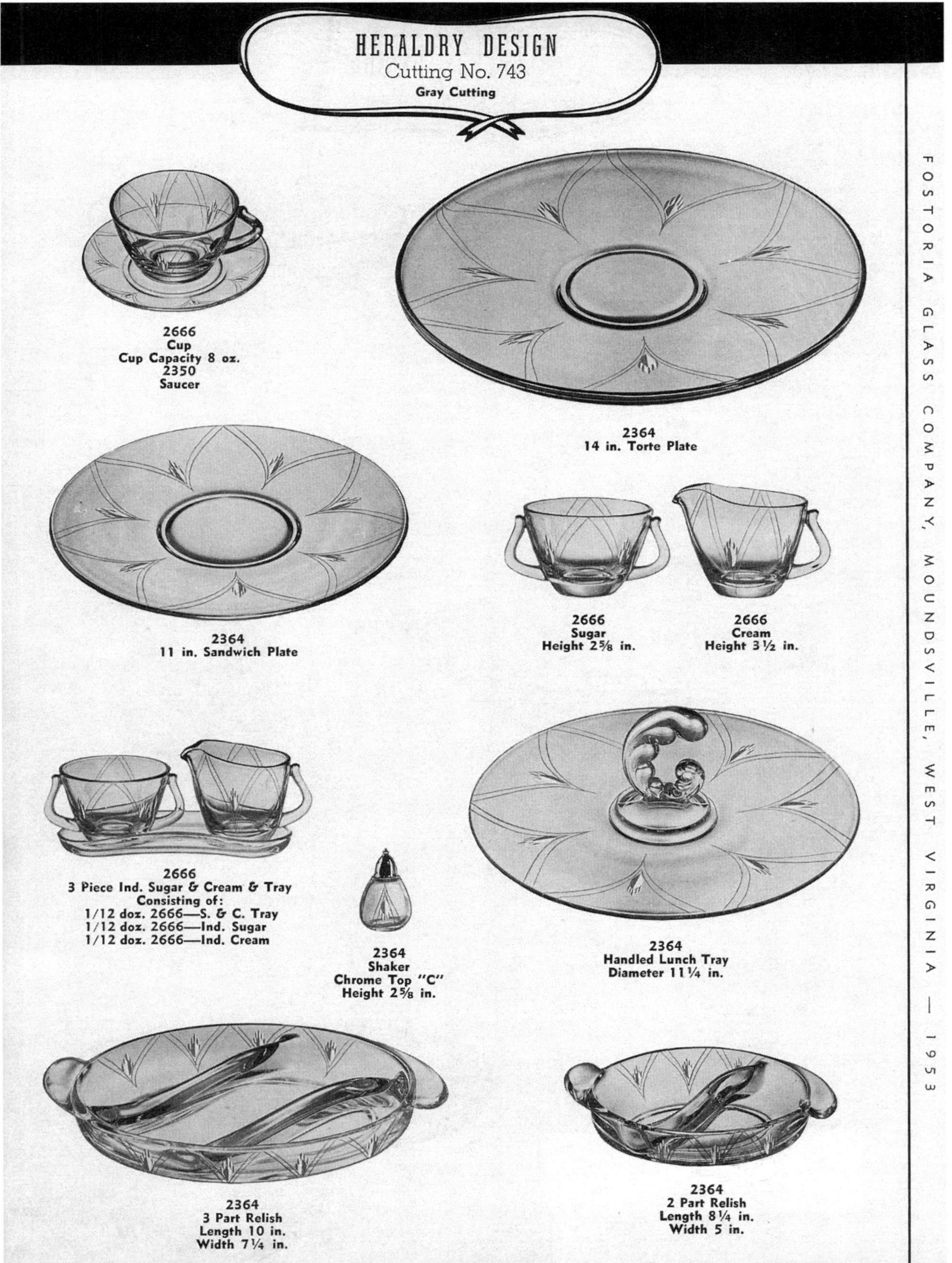

2666
Cup
Cup Capacity 8 oz.
2350
Saucer

2364
14 in. Torte Plate

2364
11 in. Sandwich Plate

2666
Sugar
Height 2⅝ in.

2666
Cream
Height 3½ in.

2666
3 Piece Ind. Sugar & Cream & Tray
Consisting of:
1/12 doz. 2666—S. & C. Tray
1/12 doz. 2666—Ind. Sugar
1/12 doz. 2666—Ind. Cream

2364
Shaker
Chrome Top "C"
Height 2⅝ in.

2364
Handled Lunch Tray
Diameter 11¼ in.

2364
3 Part Relish
Length 10 in.
Width 7¼ in.

2364
2 Part Relish
Length 8¼ in.
Width 5 in.

HERALDRY DESIGN

Cutting No. 743

Gray Cutting

2364
Mayonnaise and Plate and Ladle
Mayo. Diameter 5 in.
Height 2½ in.
Plate Diameter 6¾ in.

2364
9 in. Salad Bowl
Height 2⅝ in.

2364
12 in. Bowl, Flared
Height 2⅞ in.

6023
Duo Candlestick
Height 5½ in. Spread 6 in.

2324
4 in. Candlestick

2364
12 in. Lily Pond
Height 2¼ in.

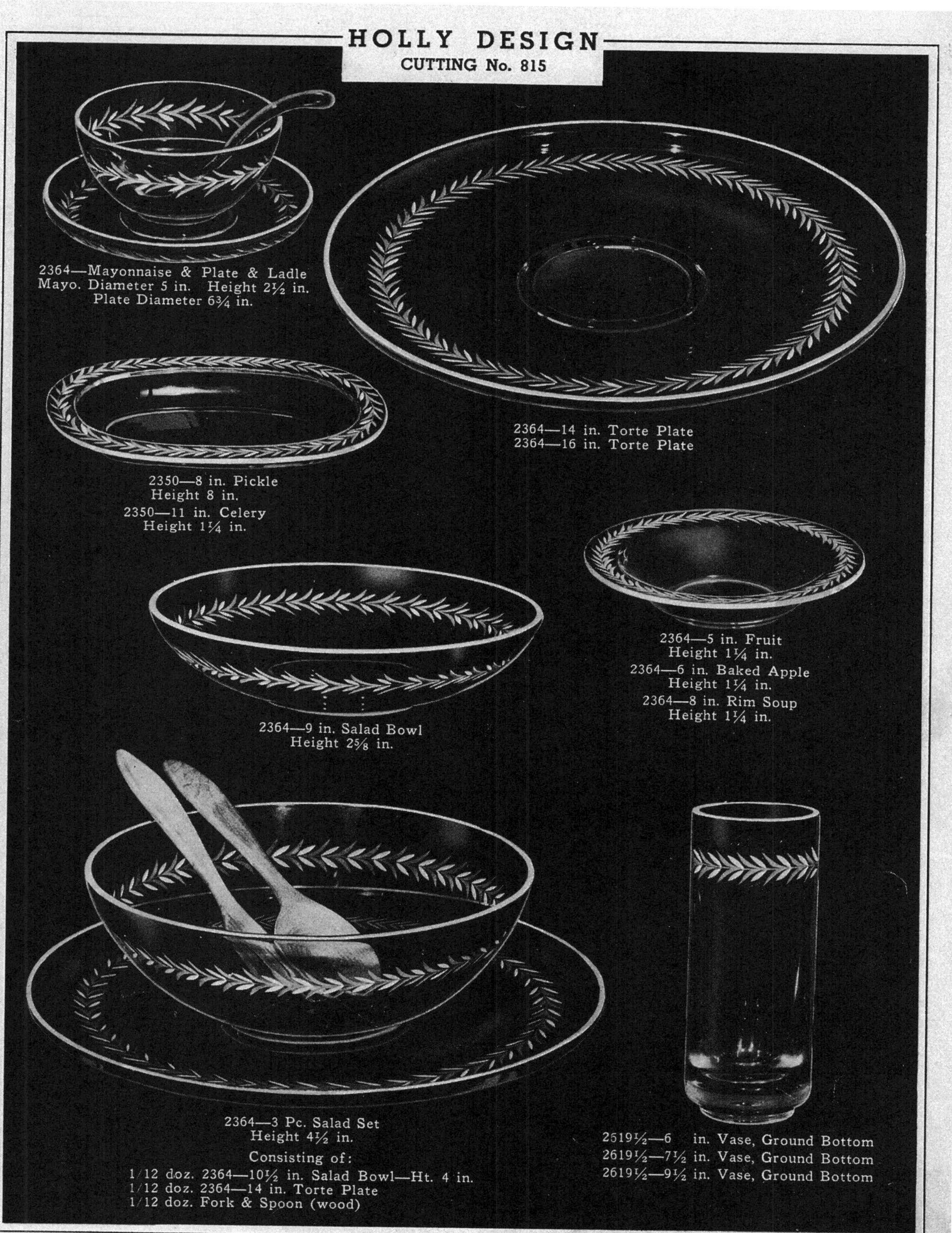

HOLLY DESIGN

CUTTING No. 815

2364—Mayonnaise & Plate & Ladle
Mayo. Diameter 5 in. Height 2½ in.
Plate Diameter 6¾ in.

2364—14 in. Torte Plate
2364—16 in. Torte Plate

2350—8 in. Pickle
Height 8 in.
2350—11 in. Celery
Height 1¼ in.

2364—5 in. Fruit
Height 1¼ in.
2364—6 in. Baked Apple
Height 1¼ in.
2364—8 in. Rim Soup
Height 1¼ in.

2364—9 in. Salad Bowl
Height 2⅝ in.

2364—3 Pc. Salad Set
Height 4½ in.
Consisting of:
1/12 doz. 2364—10½ in. Salad Bowl—Ht. 4 in.
1/12 doz. 2364—14 in. Torte Plate
1/12 doz. Fork & Spoon (wood)

2619½—6 in. Vase, Ground Bottom
2619½—7½ in. Vase, Ground Bottom
2619½—9½ in. Vase, Ground Bottom

Fostoria Glass Company, Moundsville, West Virginia, January 1, 1942

HOLLY DESIGN

CUTTING No. 815

6023—9 in. Footed Bowl
Height 4¼ in.

6023—Duo Candlestick
Height 5½ in. Spread 6 in.

2364—12 in. Bowl, Fld.
Height 2⅞ in.

2364—13 in. Fruit Bowl
Height 2¾ in.

2324—4 in. Candlestick

2364—12 in. Lily Pond
Height 2¼ in.

2364—6 in. Candlestick

Fostoria Glass Company, Moundsville, West Virginia, January 1, 1942

HOLLY DESIGN

CUTTING No. 815

6030—10 oz. Goblet
Height 7⅞ in.

6030—10 oz.
Low Goblet
Height 6⅜ in.

6030—6 oz.
Saucer Champagne
Height 5⅝ in.

6030—6 oz.
Low Sherbet
Height 4⅜ in.

6030—3½ oz.
Claret-Wine
Height 6 in.

6030—3½ oz.
Cocktail
Height 5¼ in.

6030—12 oz.
Footed Tumbler
Height 6 in.

6030—5 oz. Footed Tumbler
Height 4⅝ in.

6030—4 oz.
Oyster Cocktail
Height 3¾ in.

6030—1 oz. Cordial
Height 3⅞ in.

1769—Finger Bowl
Height 2 in.
Diameter 4⅛ in.

2364—Cigarette
Holder, Blown
Height 2 in.
Top Diameter 1⅝ in.
Cigarette Capacity 14

2364—Individual
Ash
Tray, Blown
Diameter 2⅝ in.

2350½—Footed Sugar
Height 3⅛ in.

2337—Plate

2350½—Footed Cream
Height 3¼ in.
Capacity 7 oz.

6011—Footed Jug
Capacity 53 oz.
Height 8⅞ in.

Fostoria Glass Company, Moundsville, West Virginia, January 1, 1942

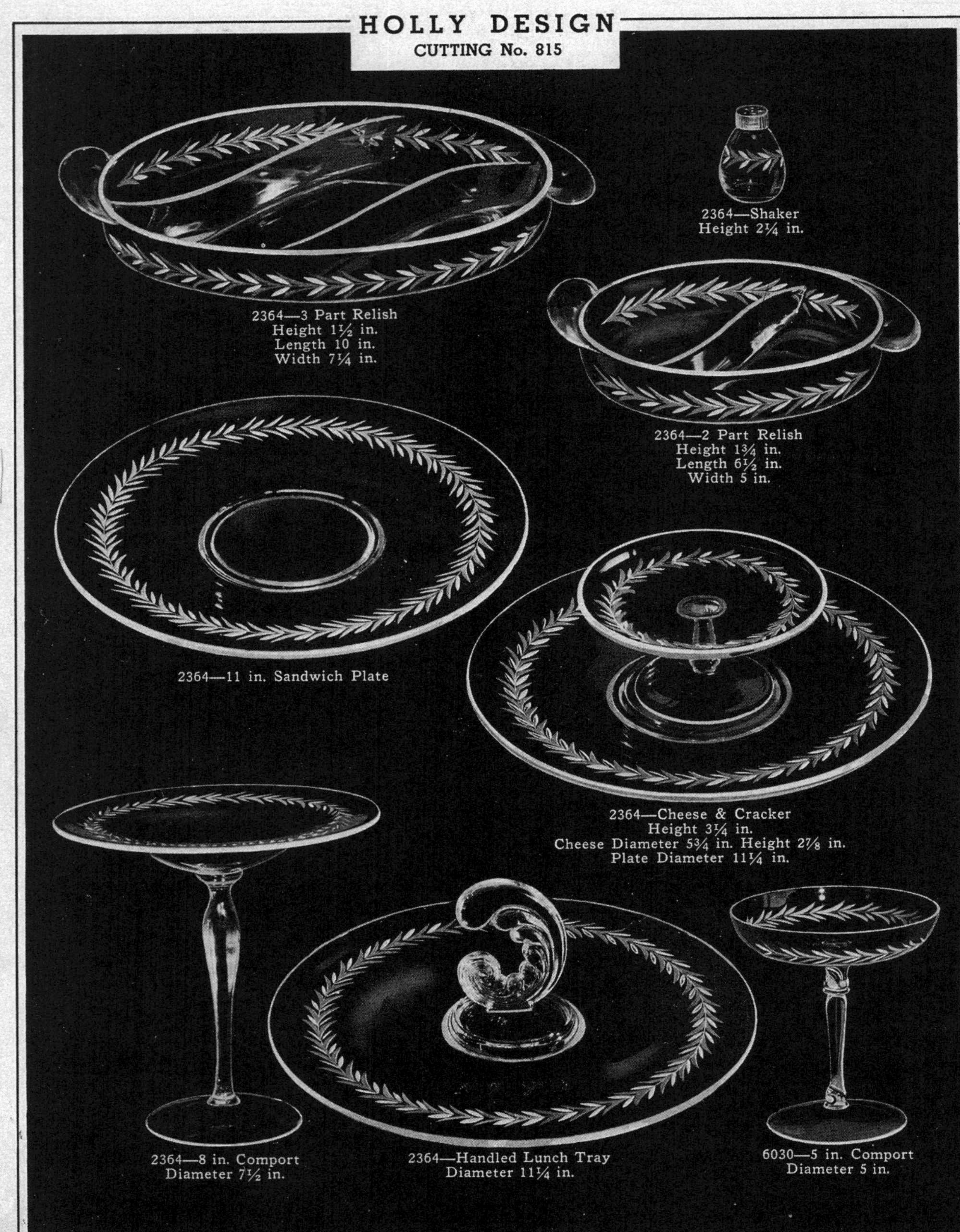

Fostoria Glass Company, Moundsville, West Virginia, January 1, 1942

FOSTORIA GLASS COMPANY, MOUNDSVILLE, WEST VIRGINIA — 1958

KIMBERLY DESIGN

Cutting No. 855

Rock Crystal

6071
Goblet
Height 6⅜ in.
Capacity 11½ oz.

6071
Sherbet
Height 4¾ in.
Capacity 7 oz.

6071
Cocktail/Wine/Seafood
Height 5 in.
Capacity 4½ oz.

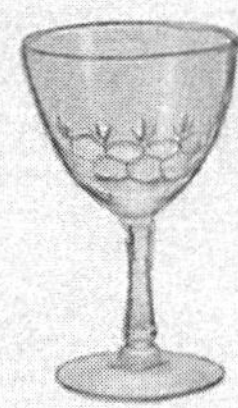

6071
Cordial
Height 3¼ in.
Capacity 1 oz.

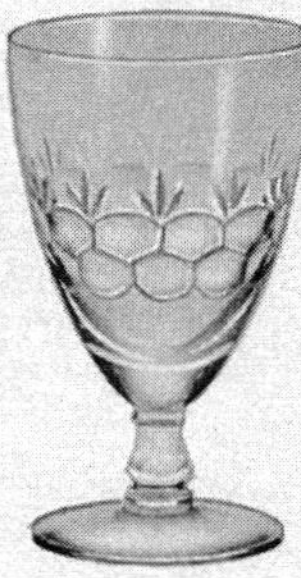

6071
Footed Juice
Height 4½ in.
Capacity 5¼ oz.

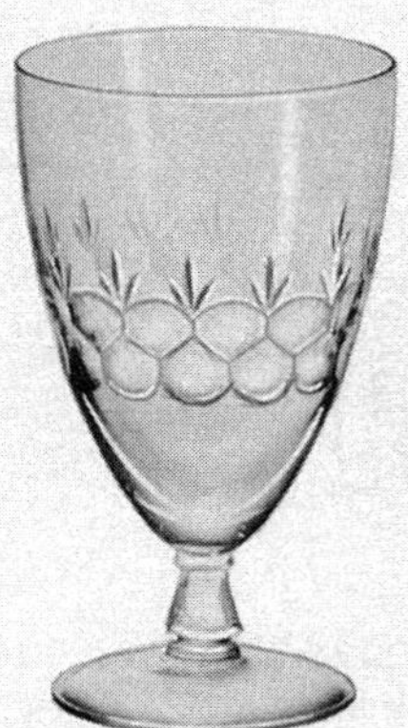

6071
Footed Ice Tea
Height 6 in .
Capacity 13 oz.

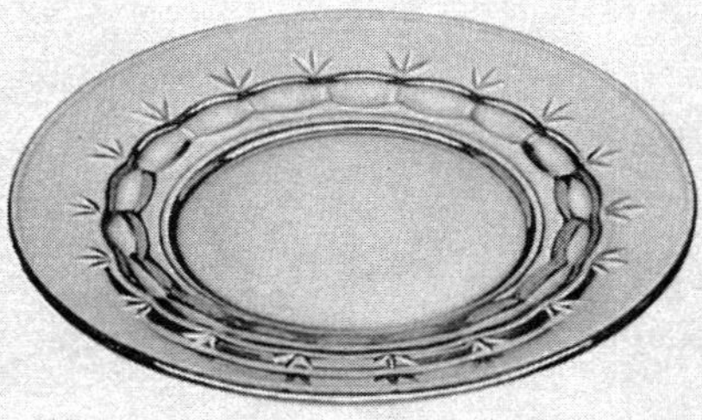

2574
7 in. Plate

2574
8 in. Plate

KIMBERLY DESIGN

Cutting No. 855

2574/567—14 in.
Torte Plate

2574/679
Footed Sugar
Height 3¾ in.

2574/681
Footed Cream
Height 4 in.
Capacity 7 oz.

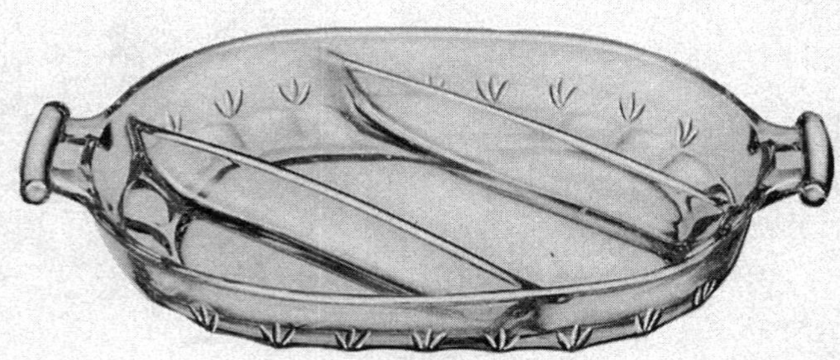

2574/622
3 Part Relish
Length 10 in. Width 7 in.
Height 1¾ in.

FOSTORIA GLASS COMPANY, MOUNDSVILLE, WEST VIRGINIA — 1958

Ivy Design
Cutting No. 745, Rock Crystal

Kimberley Design
Cutting No. 775, Rock Crystal

Millefleur Design No. 195

56

"MILLEFLEUR" DESIGN, CUTTING No. 195.
4020—SOLID CRYSTAL—PLAIN. 4120—EBONY BASE—CRYSTAL BOWL—PLAIN.
PRICED PAGE 71 — No. 2 PRICE LIST.
DESIGN PATENT No. 81,301

4020—16 oz. Tumbler.
4120—16 oz. Tumbler.

4020—13 oz. Tumbler.
4120—13 oz. Tumbler.

4020—10 oz. Tumbler.
4120—10 oz. Tumbler.

4020—5 oz. Tumbler.
4120—5 oz. Tumbler.

4020—3 oz. Cocktail.
4120—3 oz. Cocktail.

4021—Finger Bowl.
4121—Finger Bowl.

4020—2 oz. Whiskey.
4120—2 oz. Whiskey.

4020—5 oz. Sherbet.
4120—5 oz. Sherbet.

4020—7 oz. Sherbet.
4120—7 oz. Sherbet.

2350—After Dinner Cup.
2350—After Dinner Saucer.
Made in Crystal only.

2350—Cream Soup.
2350—9 in. Plate.
Made in Crystal only.

2350½—Footed Cup.
2350—Saucer.
Made in Crystal only.

Fostoria Glass Company, Moundsville, West Virginia

1930 Catalog

LAUREL DESIGN
Cutting No. 776
Gray Cutting

FOSTORIA GLASS COMPANY, MOUNDSVILLE, WEST VIRGINIA — 1953

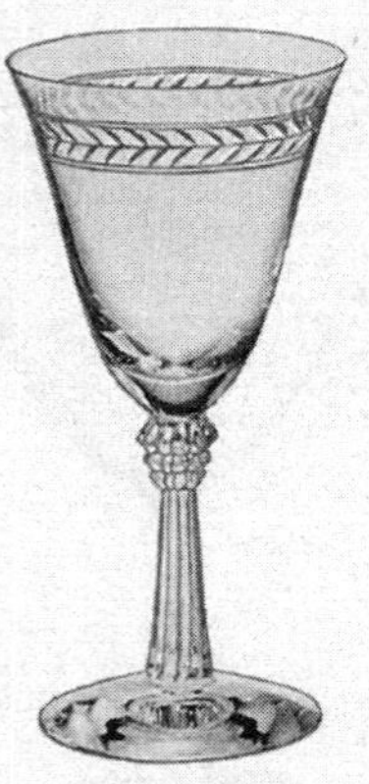
6017
Goblet
Height 7⅜ in.
Capacity 9 oz.

6017
High Sherbet (Champagne)
Height 5½ in.
Capacity 6 oz.

6017
Low Sherbet
Height 4½ in.
Capacity 6 oz.

6017
Cocktail
Height 4⅞ in.
Capacity 3½ oz.

6017
Claret
Height 5⅞ in.
Capacity 4 oz.

6017
Wine
Height 5½ in.
Capacity 3 oz.

6017
Cordial
Height 3⅞ in.
Capacity ¾ oz.

6017
Oyster Cocktail
Height 3⅝ in.
Capacity 4 oz.

6017
Footed Ice Tea
Height 6 in.
Capacity 12 oz.

6017
Footed Water
Height 5½ in.
Capacity 9 oz.

6017
Footed Juice
Height 4¾ in.
Capacity 5 oz.

2337
6 in. Plate
2337
7 in. Plate
2337
8 in. Plate

MARQUISE DESIGN

Cutting No. 831

Rock Crystal

6045
Goblet
Height 5⅞ in.
Capacity 15¾ oz.

6045
Sherbet
Height 3¾ in.
Capacity 9 oz.

6045
Cocktail
Height 3 in.
Capacity 4¾ oz.

6045
Claret-Wine
Height 4 in.
Capacity 4¾ oz.

6045
Cordial
Height 2⅝ in.
Capacity 1½ oz.

6045
Footed Ice Tea
Height 6⅛ in.
Capacity 16 oz.

6045
Footed Juice
Height 4⅝ in.
Capacity 7¼ oz.

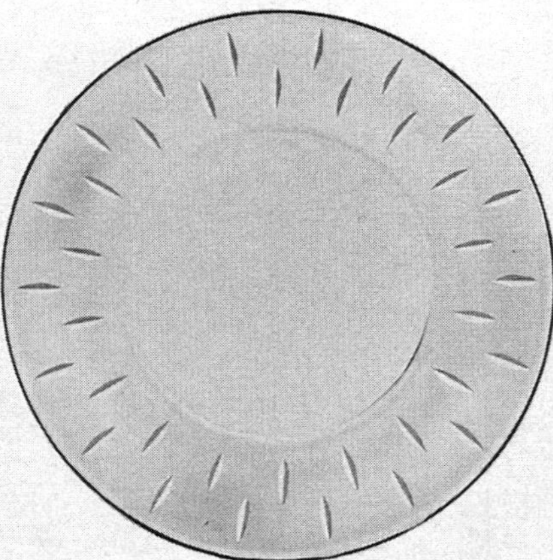

2337
8 in. Plate

FOSTORIA GLASS COMPANY, MOUNDSVILLE, WEST VIRGINIA — 1953

MOUNT VERNON DESIGN

Cutting No. 817

Gray Cutting

6031 Goblet Height 8⅛ in. Capacity 10 oz.

6031 Low Goblet Height 6¼ in. Capacity 10 oz.

6031 High Sherbet (Champagne) Height 5⅝ in. Capacity 6 oz.

6031 Low Sherbet Height 4¼ in. Capacity 6 oz.

6031 Cocktail Height 5¼ in. Capacity 3½ oz.

6031 Claret-Wine Height 6 in. Capacity 3½ oz.

6031 Cordial Height 3¾ in. Capacity 1 oz.

6031 Oyster Cocktail Height 3⅝ in. Capacity 4 oz.

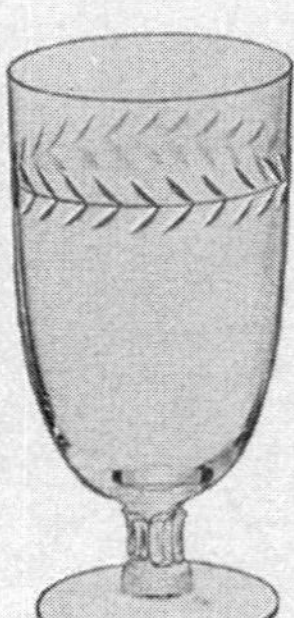

6031 Footed Ice Tea Height 5⅞ in. Capacity 12 oz.

6031 Footed Juice Height 4½ in. Capacity 5 oz.

2337 6 in. Plate 2337 7 in. Plate 2337 8 in. Plate

FOSTORIA GLASS COMPANY, MOUNDSVILLE, WEST VIRGINIA — 1953

FOSTORIA GLASS COMPANY, MOUNDSVILLE, WEST VIRGINIA — 1953

MULBERRY DESIGN

Cutting No. 799

Rock Crystal

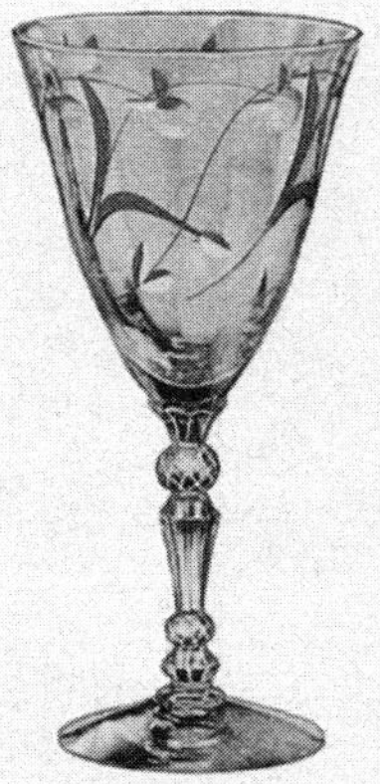

6026
Goblet
Height 7⅝ in.
Capacity 9 oz.

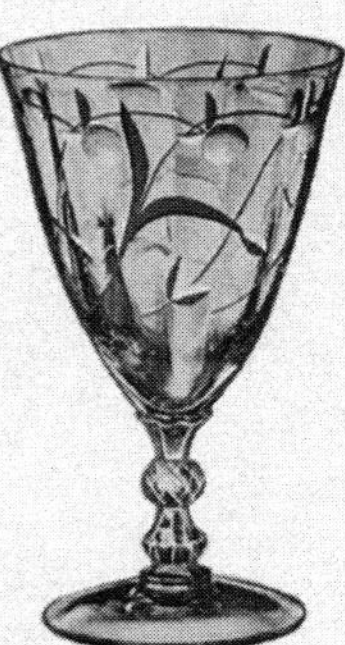

6026
Low Goblet
Height 6⅛ in.
Capacity 9 oz.

6026
High Sherbet (Champagne)
Height 5½ in.
Capacity 6 oz.

6026
Low Sherbet
Height 4⅜ in.
Capacity 6 oz.

6026
Cocktail
Height 5 in.
Capacity 4 oz.

6026
Claret-Wine
Height 5⅜ in.
Capacity 4½ oz.

6026
Cordial
Height 3⅞ in.
Capacity 1 oz.

6026
Oyster Cocktail
Height 3⅝ in.
Capacity 4 oz.

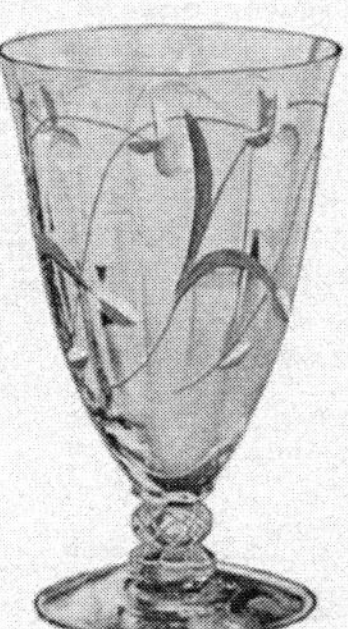

6026
Footed Ice Tea
Height 6 in.
Capacity 13 oz.

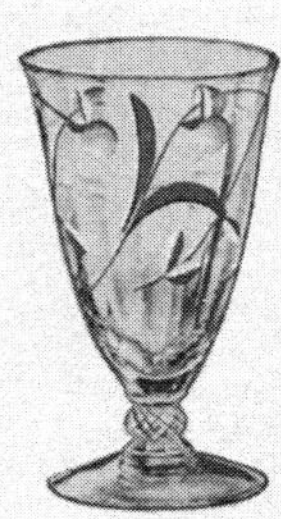

6026
Footed Juice
Height 3¾ in.
Capacity 5 oz.

2337
6 in. Plate
2337
7 in. Plate
2337
8 in. Plate

PLUME DESIGN

Cutting No. 839

Combination Gray and Rock Crystal

**2666—10 in.
Snack Plate**

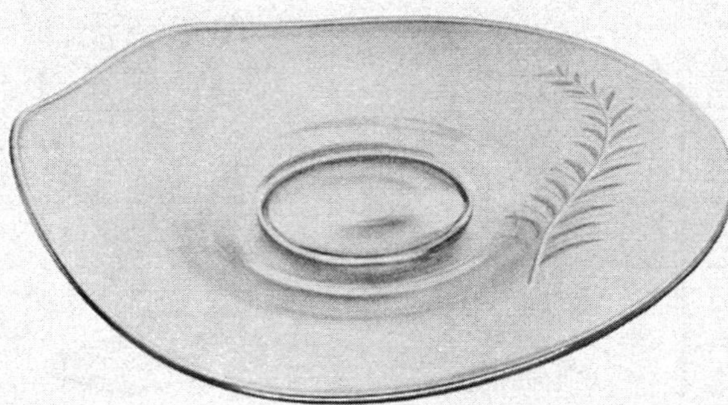

**2666—14 in.
Serving Plate**

**2666
Sugar
Height 2⅝ in.**

**2666
Cream
Height 3½ in.**

**2666—3 Piece
Individual Sugar & Cream & Tray
Consisting of:
1/12 Dz. 2666—S. & C. Tray (Not Cut)
1/12 Dz. 2666—Ind. Sugar
1/12 Dz. 2666—Ind. Cream**

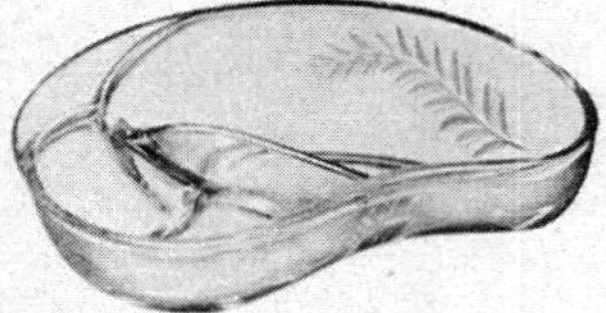

**2666
2 Part Relish
Length 7⅜ in. Width 6 in.**

**2666
Mayonnaise and Plate
and Ladle
Height 3¼ in.**

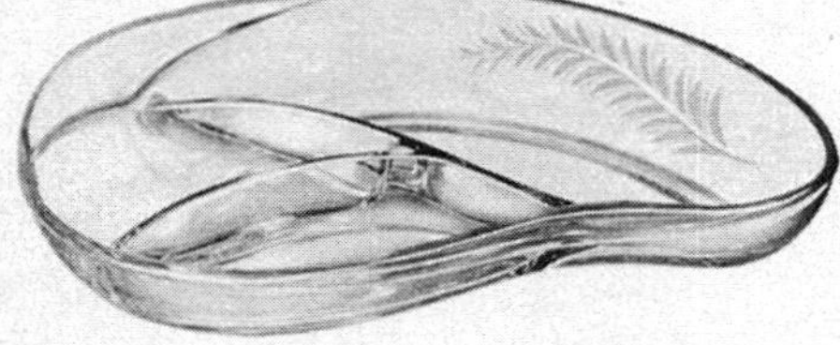

**2666
3 Part Relish
Length 10¾ in. Width 7⅜ in.**

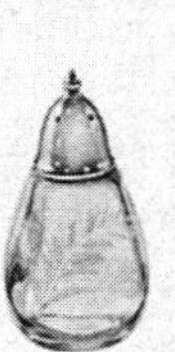

**2364
Large Shaker
Chrome Top "B"
Height 3¼ in.**

**2666
Canape Plate
Diameter 7⅜ in.
Height 2 in.**

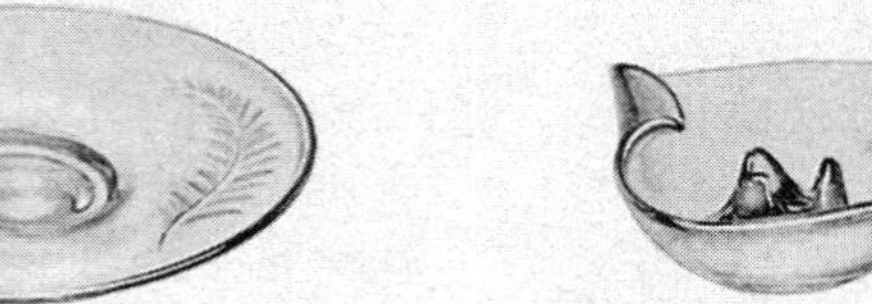

**2666
Flora Candle
Diameter 6 in.**

**2666
Oval Bowl
Diameter 8¼ in.
Height 3¼ in.**

REGAL DESIGN

Cutting No. 842

Gray Cutting

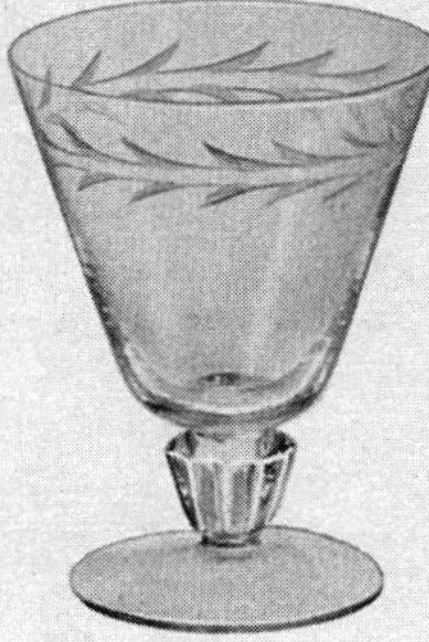

6061
Goblet
Height 5⅛ in.
Capacity 11 oz.

6061
Sherbet
Height 4 in.
Capacity 7½ oz.

6061
Cocktail/Wine/Seafood
Height 3⅞ in.
Capacity 4 oz.

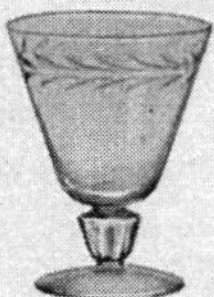

6061
Cordial
Height 2½ in.
Capacity 1 oz.

6061
Footed Ice Tea
Height 6 in.
Capacity 12 oz.

6061
Footed Juice
Height 4¾ in.
Capacity 6 oz.

2337
7 in. Plate

2337
8 in. Plate

Fostoria Glass Company, Moundsville, West Virginia, Jan. 1, 1939

REGENCY DESIGN

CUTTING No. 744

6012
10 oz. Goblet
Height 6⅞ in.

6012—5½ oz.
Saucer Champagne
Height 5 in.

6012—5½ oz.
Low Sherbet
Height 4 in.

6012
3 oz. Cocktail
Height 4⅝ in.

6012—4½ oz.
Rhine Wine
Height 5¾ in.

6012—4½ oz. Claret
Height 5¾ in.
6012—3 oz. Wine
Height 5¼ in.

6012
2 oz. Sherry
Height 4½ in.

6012—13 oz.
Footed Tumbler
Height 5¾ in.

6012—5 oz.
Footed Tumbler
Height 4¼ in.

6012—10 oz.
Footed Tumbler
Height 5⅜ in.

6012—2 oz.
Creme De Menthe
Height 4½ in.

6012
1 oz. Cordial
Height 3½ in.

6012—1 oz. Brandy
Height 4 in.

6012—4 oz.
Footed Cocktail
(Oyster)
Height 3½ in.

701—10 oz.
Tumbler, Sham, Plain
Height 4¾ in.
701—12 oz.
Tumbler, Sham, Plain
Height 5⅛ in.

1185—7 oz.
Old Fashioned
Cocktail, Sham
Height 3½ in.

1769—Finger Bowl

2337—Plate
See Price List for Sizes

6011—Footed Jug
Height 8⅞ in. Cap. 53 oz.

FOSTORIA GLASS COMPANY, MOUNDSVILLE, WEST VIRGINIA — 1953

RONDO DESIGN

Cutting No. 830

Rock Crystal

6045
Goblet
Height 5⅞ in.
Capacity 15¾ oz.

6045
Sherbet
Height 3¾ in.
Capacity 9 oz.

6045
Cocktail
Height 3 in.
Capacity 4¾ oz.

6045
Claret-Wine
Height 4 in.
Capacity 4¾ oz.

6045
Cordial
Height 2⅝ in.
Capacity 1½ oz.

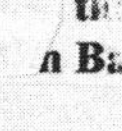

6045
Footed Ice Tea
Height 6⅛ in.
Capacity 16 oz.

6045
Footed Juice
Height 4⅝ in.
Capacity 7¼ oz.

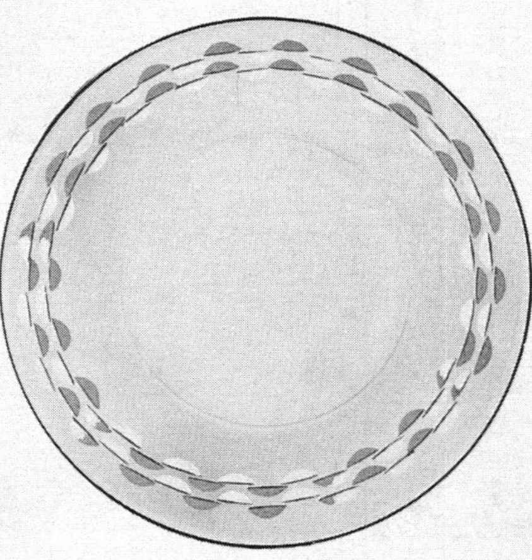

2337
8 in. Plate

Rheims Design
Cutting No. 803, Rock Crystal

Ripples Design
Cutting No. 766

1940 Catalog

Salon Design
Cutting No. 804

Selma Design
Cutting No. 800, Rock Crystal

Shooting Stars Design
Cutting No. 735

Tulip Design
Cutting No. 772, Rock Crystal

Tapestry Design
Cutting No. 701
Made in Solid Crystal, Plain

1930 Catalog

SPRAY DESIGN

Cutting No. 841

Combination Grey and Rock Crystal

6055
Goblet
Height 6⅛ in.
Capacity 10 oz.

6055
Sherbet
Height 4½ in.
Capacity 6 oz.

6055
Cocktail
Height 3⅞ in.
Capacity 3½ oz.

6055
Claret-Wine
Height 4⅝ in.
Capacity 4¼ oz.

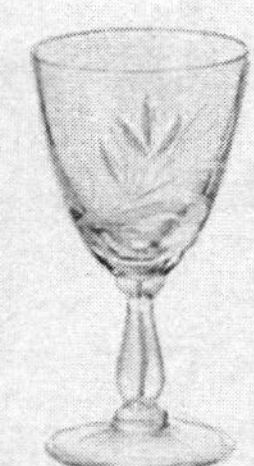

6055
Cordial
Height 3 5/16 in.
Capacity 1¼ oz.

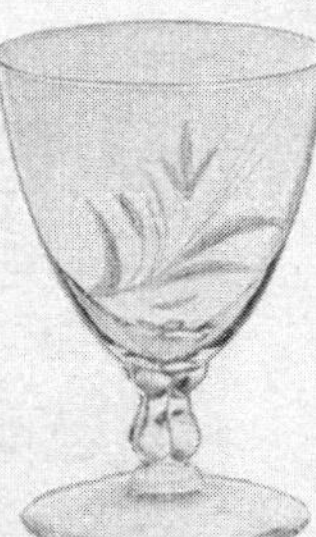

6055
Oyster Cocktail
Height 4 in.
Capacity 4¾ oz.

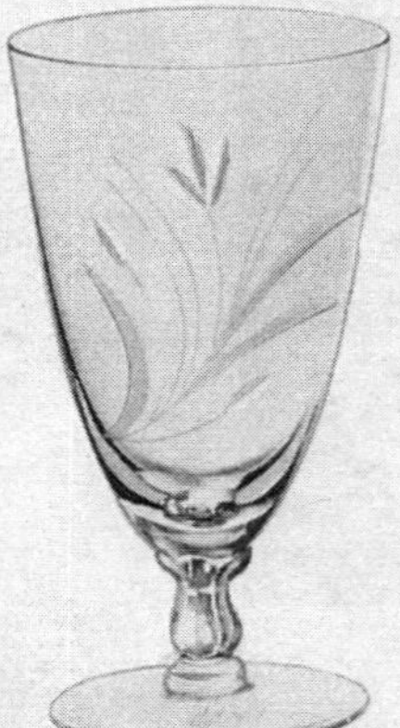

6055
Footed Ice Tea
Height 6⅛ in.
Capacity 12¼ oz.

6055
Footed Juice
Height 4⅞ in.
Capacity 5½ oz.

2337
7 in. Plate
2337
8 in. Plate

FOSTORIA GLASS COMPANY, MOUNDSVILLE, WEST VIRGINIA 1955

SPRING DESIGN
Cutting No. 844
Gray Cutting

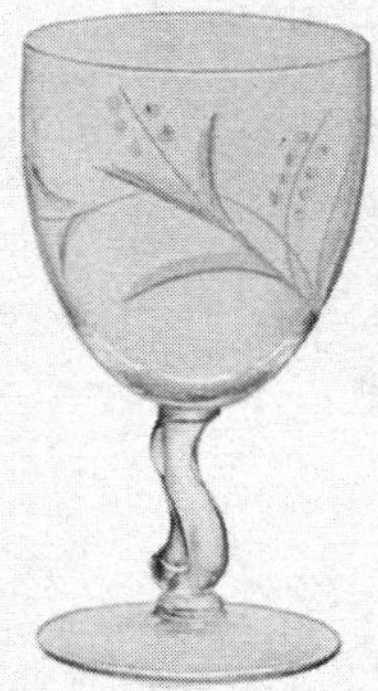

6060
Goblet
Height 5⅞ in.
Capacity 10½ oz.

6060
Sherbet
Height 4½ in.
Capacity 6½ oz.

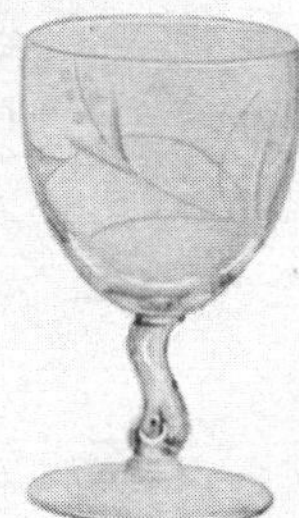

6060
Cocktail/Wine/Seafood
Height 4½ in.
Capacity 5 oz.

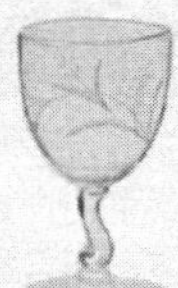

6060
Cordial
Height 2⅞ in.
Capacity 1 oz.

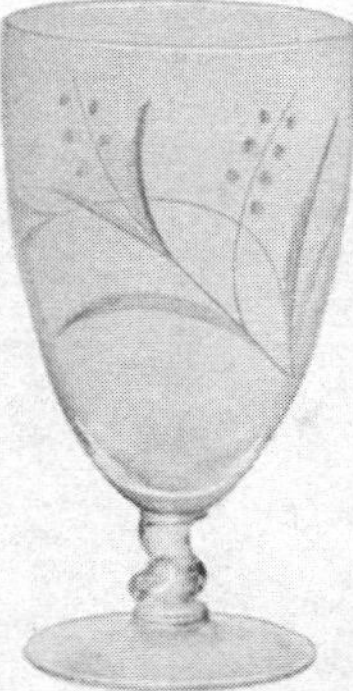

6060
Footed Ice Tea
Height 6¼ in.
Capacity 14 oz.

6060
Footed Juice
Height 4½ in.
Capacity 5½ oz.

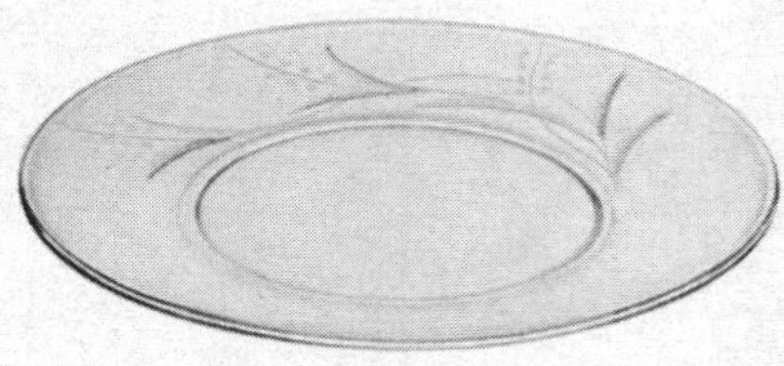

2337
7 in. Plate
2337
8 in. Plate

Dinnerware, Stems, and Tumblers, Cut

Watercress Design
Cutting No. 741
Rock Crystal

Warwick Design
Polished Cutting No. 198

1930 Catalog

Dinnerware, Stems, and Tumblers, Etched

Acanthus Design
Etching No. 282

"ACANTHUS" DESIGN, PLATE ETCHING No. 282.
MADE IN GREEN AND AMBER.
PRICED PAGES 59 AND 60 — No. 2 PRICE LIST.

5298—Goblet
5298—High Sherbet.
5298—Low Sherbet.
5298—Oyster Cocktail.
5298—5 oz. Ftd. Tumbler.
5298—9 oz. Ftd. Tumbler
5298—12 oz. Ftd. Tumbler.
5000—7 Ftd. Jug.

Fostoria Glass Company, Moundsville, West Virginia

84

"ACANTHUS" DESIGN, PLATE ETCHING No. 282.
MADE IN GREEN AND AMBER.
PRICED PAGES 59 AND 60 — No. 2 PRICE LIST.

2375—Cream Soup.
2375—Cream Soup Plate.
2430—½ lb. Candy Jar and Cover.
2375½—Footed Cup.
2375—Saucer.
2375—5 in. Fruit.
2375—9 in. Plate.
2375—8½ in. Relish.
2394—2 in. Candlestick.
2394—12 in. Bowl.
2309—3¾ in. Flower Block.
2394—2 in. Candlestick.

Fostoria Glass Company, Moundsville, West Virginia

1930 Catalog

Fostoria Glass Company, Moundsville, West Virginia, Jan. 1, 1939

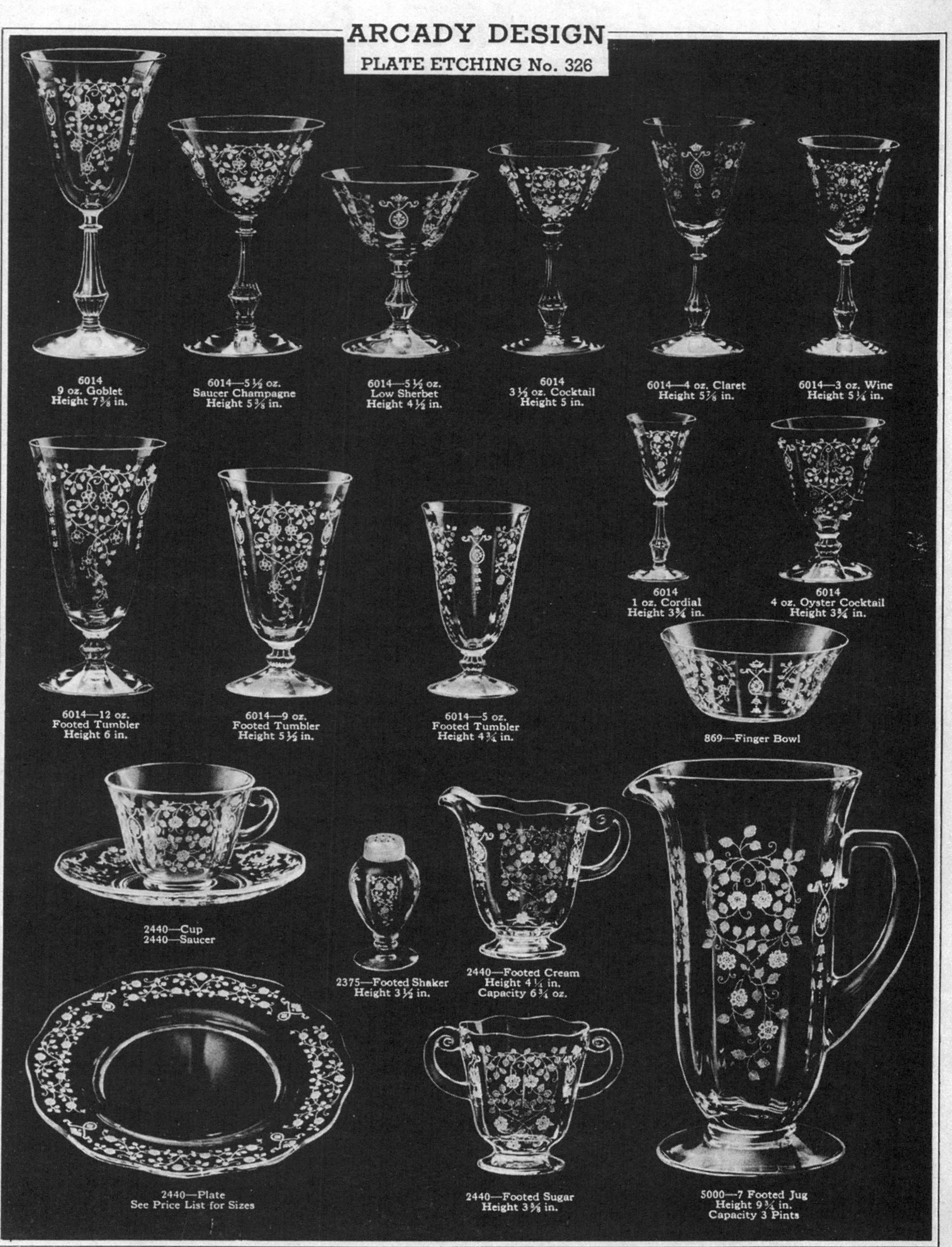

ARCADY DESIGN

PLATE ETCHING No. 326

6014
9 oz. Goblet
Height 7 3/8 in.

6014—5 1/2 oz.
Saucer Champagne
Height 5 3/8 in.

6014—5 1/2 oz.
Low Sherbet
Height 4 1/2 in.

6014
3 1/2 oz. Cocktail
Height 5 in.

6014—4 oz. Claret
Height 5 7/8 in.

6014—3 oz. Wine
Height 5 1/4 in.

6014—12 oz.
Footed Tumbler
Height 6 in.

6014—9 oz.
Footed Tumbler
Height 5 1/2 in.

6014—5 oz.
Footed Tumbler
Height 4 3/4 in.

6014
1 oz. Cordial
Height 3 3/4 in.

6014
4 oz. Oyster Cocktail
Height 3 3/4 in.

869—Finger Bowl

2440—Cup
2440—Saucer

2375—Footed Shaker
Height 3 1/2 in.

2440—Footed Cream
Height 4 1/4 in.
Capacity 6 3/4 oz.

2440—Plate
See Price List for Sizes

2440—Footed Sugar
Height 3 5/8 in.

5000—7 Footed Jug
Height 9 3/4 in.
Capacity 3 Pints

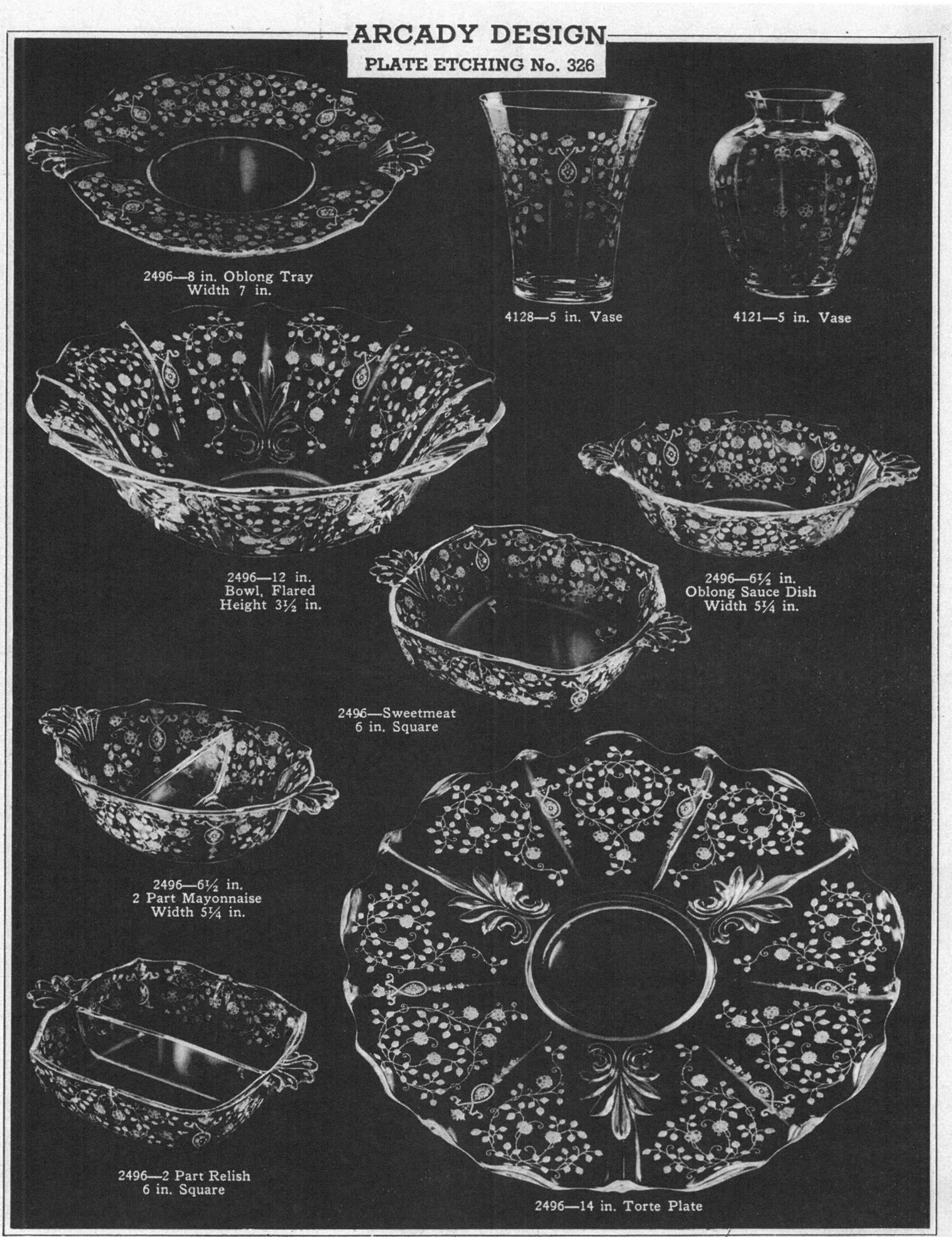
ARCADY DESIGN
PLATE ETCHING No. 326
Fostoria Glass Company, Moundsville, West Virginia, Jan. 1, 1939
2496—8 in. Oblong Tray
Width 7 in.
4128—5 in. Vase
4121—5 in. Vase
2496—12 in.
Bowl, Flared
Height 3½ in.
2496—6½ in.
Oblong Sauce Dish
Width 5¼ in.
2496—Sweetmeat
6 in. Square
2496—6½ in.
2 Part Mayonnaise
Width 5¼ in.
2496—2 Part Relish
6 in. Square
2496—14 in. Torte Plate

ARCADY DESIGN
PLATE ETCHING No. 326

2472—Duo Candlestick
Height 5 in. Spread 8¼ in.

2496—5½ in. Candlestick

2496—Duo Candlestick
Height 4½ in. Spread 8 in.

2470½—10½ in. Bowl
Height 4 in.

2496—10½ in. Handled Bowl
Height 3⅜ in.

2482—Trindle Candlestick
Height 6¾ in. Spread 8½ in.

2470—10 in. Vase

2496—Trindle Candlestick
Height 6 in. Spread 8¼ in.

Fostoria Glass Company, Moundsville, West Virginia, Jan. 1, 1939

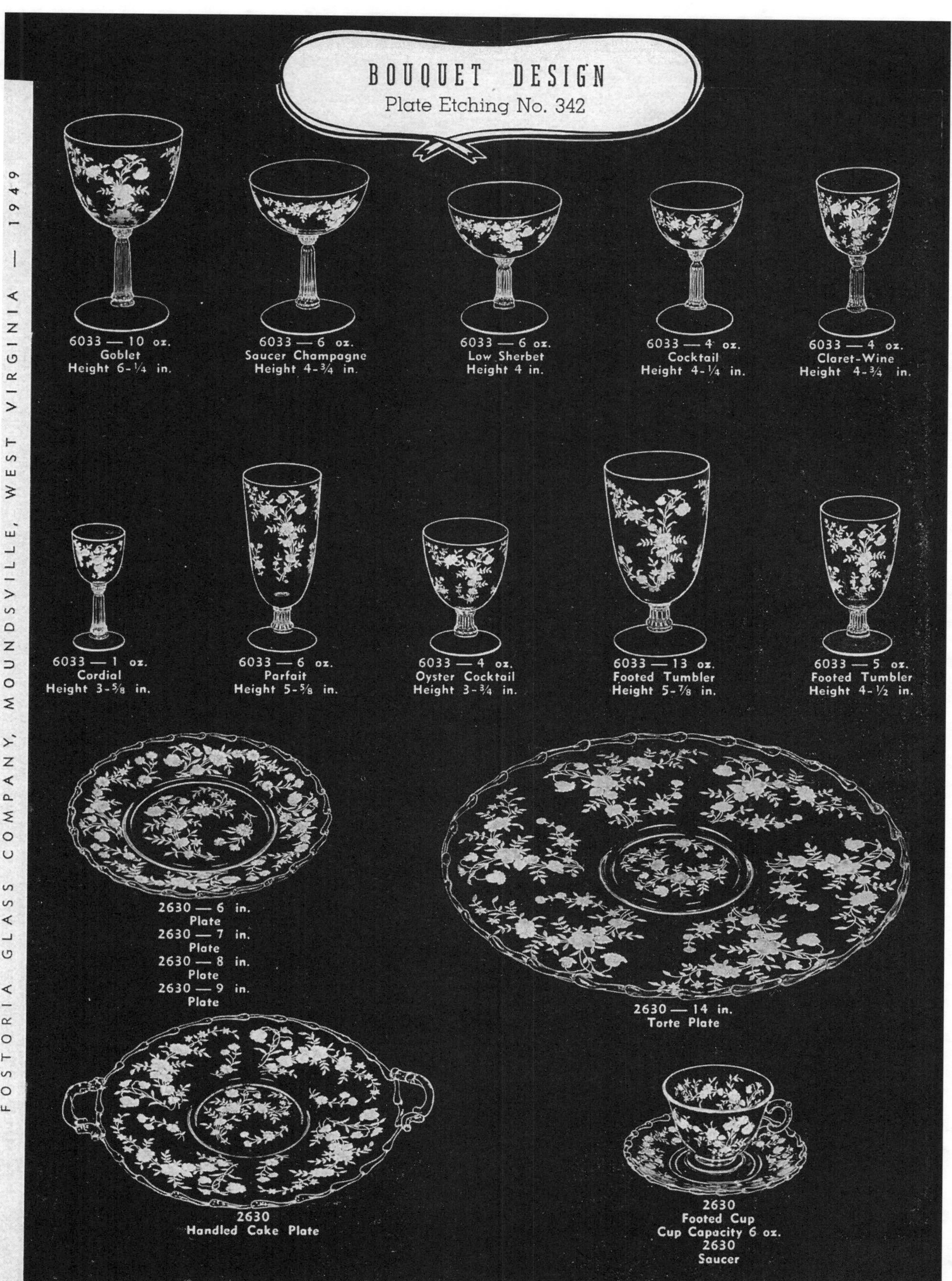

BOUQUET DESIGN
Plate Etching No. 342

6033 — 10 oz.
Goblet
Height 6-¼ in.

6033 — 6 oz.
Saucer Champagne
Height 4-¾ in.

6033 — 6 oz.
Low Sherbet
Height 4 in.

6033 — 4 oz.
Cocktail
Height 4-¼ in.

6033 — 4 oz.
Claret-Wine
Height 4-¾ in.

6033 — 1 oz.
Cordial
Height 3-⅝ in.

6033 — 6 oz.
Parfait
Height 5-⅝ in.

6033 — 4 oz.
Oyster Cocktail
Height 3-¾ in.

6033 — 13 oz.
Footed Tumbler
Height 5-⅞ in.

6033 — 5 oz.
Footed Tumbler
Height 4-½ in.

2630 — 6 in.
Plate
2630 — 7 in.
Plate
2630 — 8 in.
Plate
2630 — 9 in.
Plate

2630 — 14 in.
Torte Plate

2630
Handled Cake Plate

2630
Footed Cup
Cup Capacity 6 oz.
2630
Saucer

FOSTORIA GLASS COMPANY, MOUNDSVILLE, WEST VIRGINIA — 1949

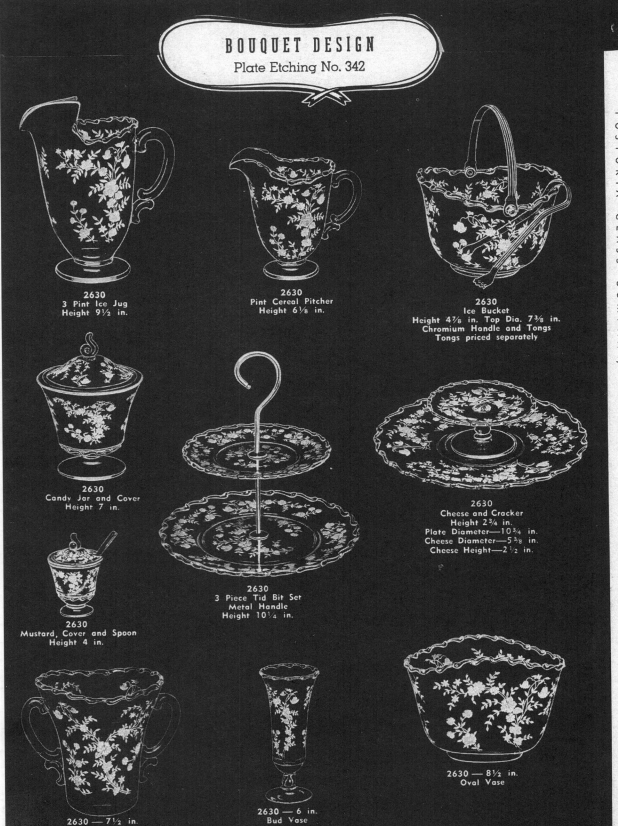

BOUQUET DESIGN

Plate Etching No. 342

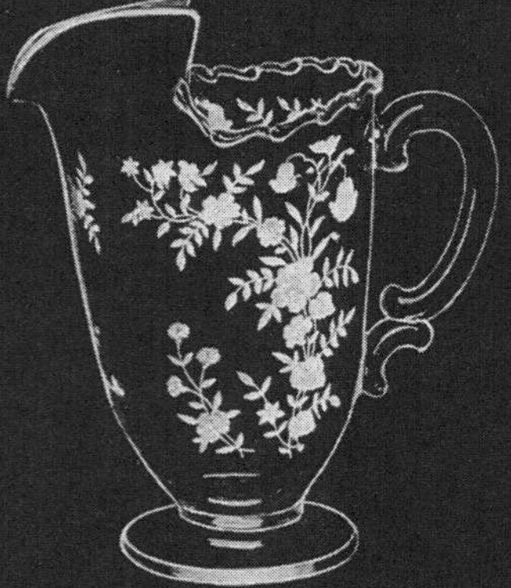

2630
3 Pint Ice Jug
Height 9½ in.

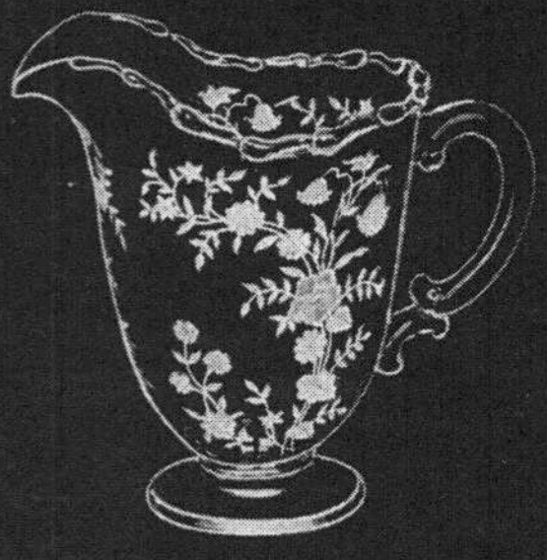

2630
Pint Cereal Pitcher
Height 6⅛ in.

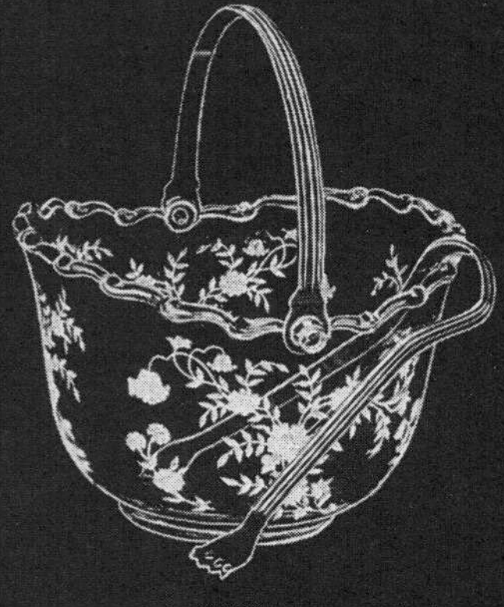

2630
Ice Bucket
Height 4⅞ in. Top Dia. 7⅜ in.
Chromium Handle and Tongs
Tongs priced separately

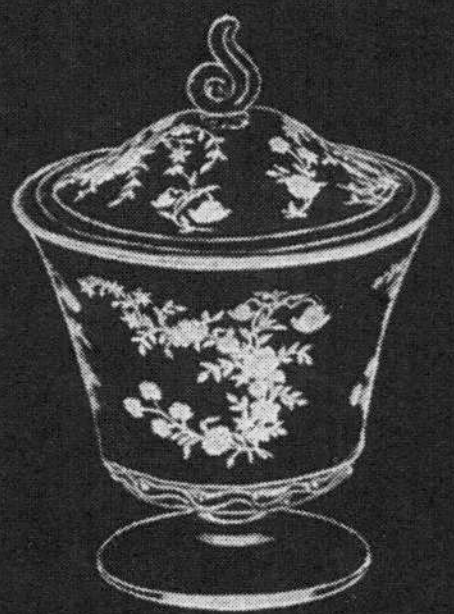

2630
Candy Jar and Cover
Height 7 in.

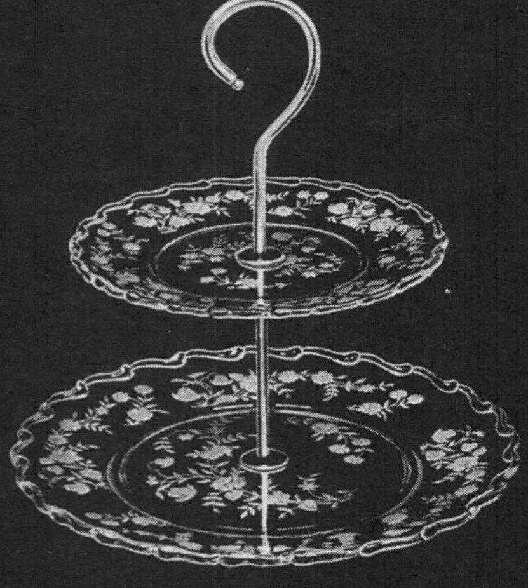

2630
3 Piece Tid Bit Set
Metal Handle
Height 10¼ in.

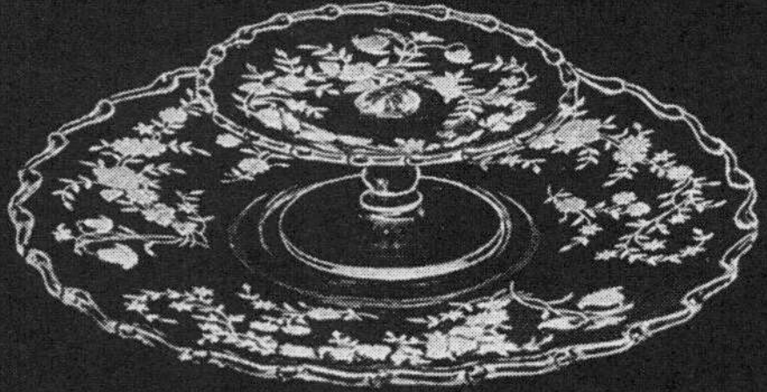

2630
Cheese and Cracker
Height 2¾ in.
Plate Diameter—10¾ in.
Cheese Diameter—5⅜ in.
Cheese Height—2½ in.

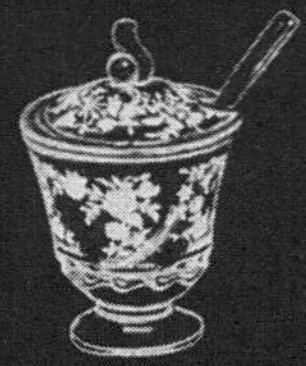

2630
Mustard, Cover and Spoon
Height 4 in.

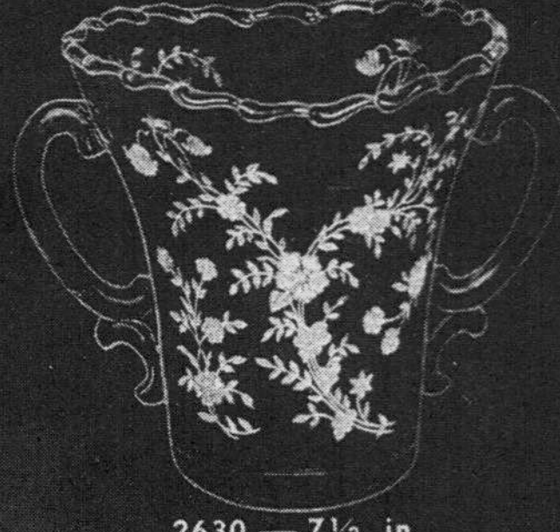

2630 — 7½ in.
Handled Vase

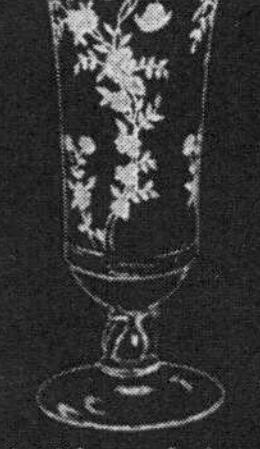

2630 — 6 in.
Bud Vase

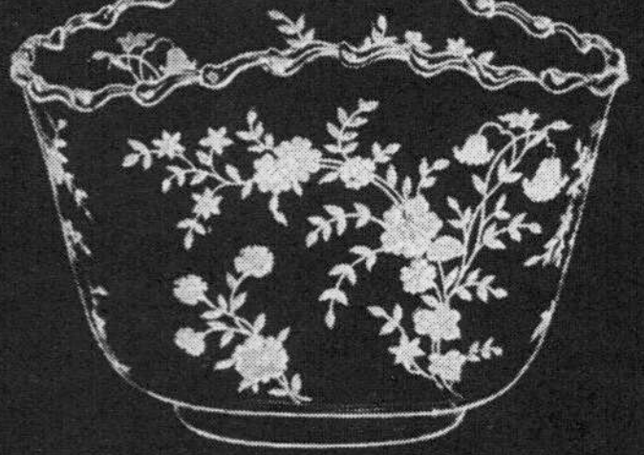

2630 — 8½ in.
Oval Vase

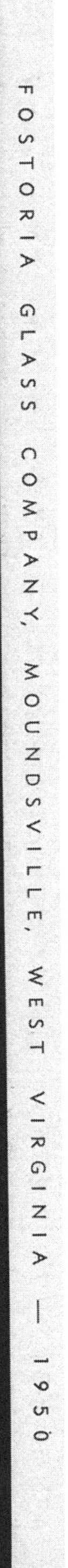

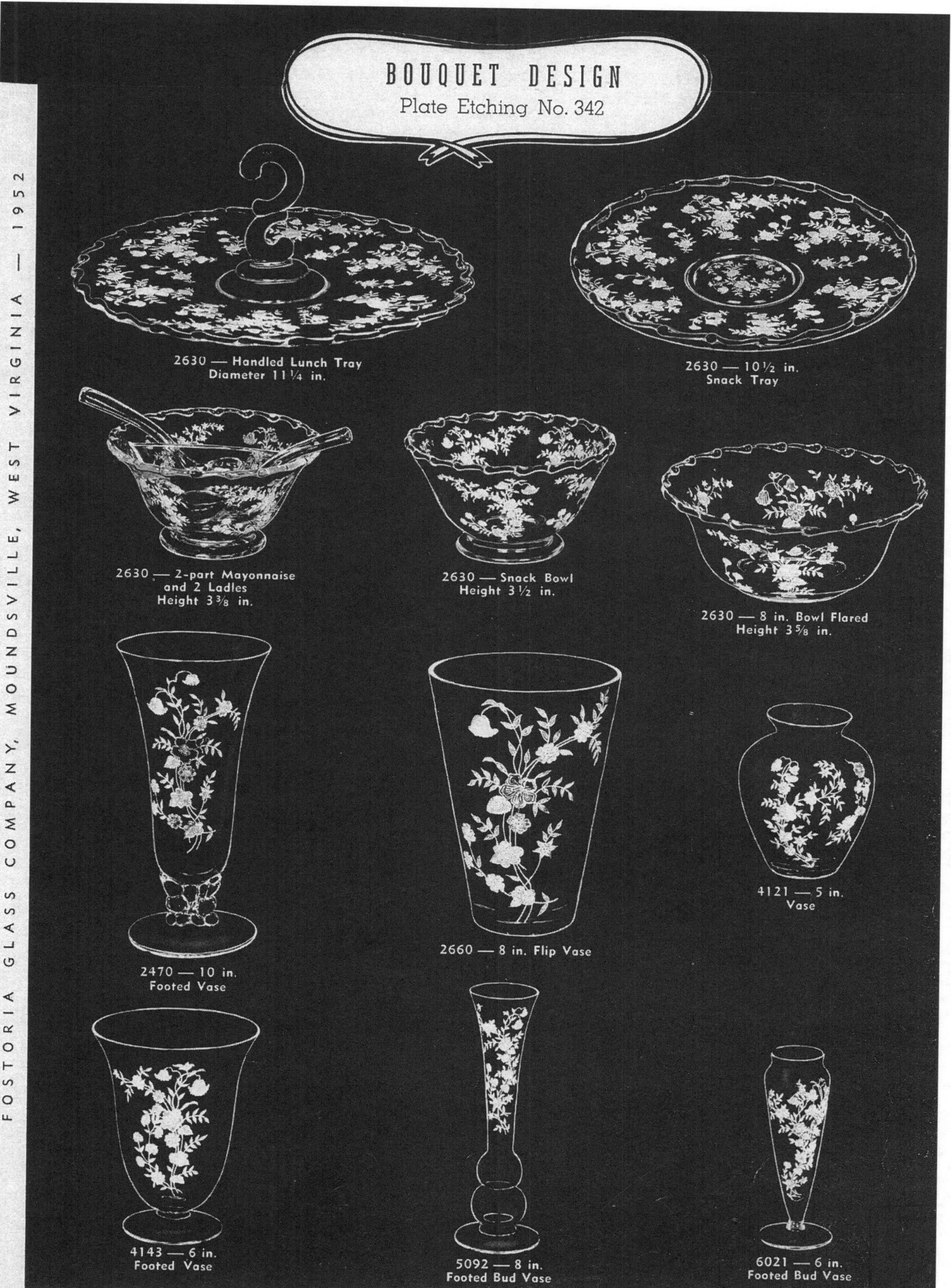
BOUQUET DESIGN
Plate Etching No. 342
FOSTORIA GLASS COMPANY, MOUNDSVILLE, WEST VIRGINIA — 1952
2630 — Handled Lunch Tray
Diameter 11¼ in.
2630 — 10½ in.
Snack Tray
2630 — 2-part Mayonnaise
and 2 Ladles
Height 3⅜ in.
2630 — Snack Bowl
Height 3½ in.
2630 — 8 in. Bowl Flared
Height 3⅝ in.
2470 — 10 in.
Footed Vase
2660 — 8 in. Flip Vase
4121 — 5 in.
Vase
4143 — 6 in.
Footed Vase
5092 — 8 in.
Footed Bud Vase
6021 — 6 in.
Footed Bud Vase

BUTTERCUP DESIGN
PLATE ETCHING No. 340
This Master Etching has been designed to harmonize with Spode's dinnerware and Gorham's silver of the same name.
6030—10 oz. Goblet Height 7⅞ in.
6030—10 oz. Low Goblet Height 6⅜ in.
6030—6 oz. Saucer Champagne Height 5⅝ in.
6030—6 oz. Low Sherbet Height 4⅜ in.
6030—3½ oz. Claret-Wine Height 6 in.
6030—3½ oz. Cocktail Height 5¼ in.
6030—12 oz. Footed Tumbler Height 6 in.
6030—5 oz. Footed Tumbler Height 4⅝ in.
6030—4 oz. Oyster Cocktail Height 3¾ in.
6030—1 oz. Cordial Height 3⅞ in.
1769—Finger Bowl Height 2 in. Diameter 4⅛ in.
2364—Individual Ash Tray, Blown Diameter 2⅝ in.
2364—Cigarette Holder, Blown Height 2 in. Top Diameter 1⅝ in.
2350½—Footed Sugar Height 3⅛ in.
2337—Plate See Price List for Sizes
2350½—Footed Cream Height 3¼ in. Capacity 7 oz.
6011—Footed Jug Capacity 53 oz. Height 8⅞ in.
Fostoria Glass Company, Moundsville, West Virginia, January 1, 1941

BUTTERCUP DESIGN
PLATE ETCHING No. 340
2350—8 in. Pickle
2350—11 in. Celery
2364—Cheese and Cracker
Height 3¼ in.
Plate Diameter 11¼ in. Cheese Diameter 5¾ in.
Cheese Height 2⅞ in.
2364—Crescent Salad Plate
Length 7¼ in. Width 4½ in.
2364—Mayonnaise and Plate and Ladle
Mayo. Height 2½ in.
Mayo. Diameter 5 in.
Plate Diameter 6¾ in.
2350½—Footed Cup
2350—Saucer
Cup Capacity 6 oz.
2364—14 in. Torte Plate
2364—16 in. Torte Plate
2364—Salad Set
10½ in. Set Consisting of:
1/12 Doz. 2364—10½ in. Salad Bowl—Height 4 in.
1/12 Doz. 2364—14 in. Torte Plate
9 in. Set Consisting of:
1/12 Doz. 2364—9 in. Salad Bowl—Height 2⅝ in.
1/12 Doz. 2364—11 in. Sandwich Plate

Fostoria Glass Company, Moundsville, West Virginia, January 1, 1941

BUTTERCUP DESIGN

PLATE ETCHING No. 340

2586—Sani-Cut Syrup
Height $5\frac{1}{2}$ in.
Capacity 9 oz.

2364—Candy Jar and Cover, Blown
Height with Cover 4 in.
Top Diameter $3\frac{3}{4}$ in.

2083—Salad Dressing Bottle
Height $6\frac{1}{2}$ in. Capacity 7 oz.

2324—6 in. Candlestick

2364—13 in. Fruit Bowl
Height $2\frac{3}{4}$ in.

2364—9 in. Salad Bowl
Height $2\frac{5}{8}$ in.
2364—$10\frac{1}{2}$ in. Salad Bowl
Height 4 in.

4143—6 in. Footed Vase
4143—$7\frac{1}{2}$ in. Footed Vase

2364—12 in. Bowl Flared
Height $2\frac{7}{8}$ in.

Fostoria Glass Company, Moundsville, West Virginia, January 1, 1941

BUTTERCUP DESIGN

PLATE ETCHING No. 340

2364—12 in. Lily Pond
Height 2¼ in.

2324—4 in. Candlestick

6023—Duo Candlestick
Height 5½ in. Spread 6 in.

6023—9 in. Footed Bowl
Height 4¼ in.

2594—10 in. Handled Bowl
Height 3 in.
Length Overall 13½ in.

2594—5½ in. Candlestick

Fostoria Glass Company, Moundsville, West Virginia, January 1, 1941

BUTTERCUP DESIGN

PLATE ETCHING No. 340

2364—3-Pt. Relish
Height 1½ in. Length 10 in.
Width 7¼ in.

2364—2-Pt. Relish
Height 1¾ in. Length 6½ in.
Width 5 in.

2364—Shaker
Height 2¼ in.

2364—6 in. Baked Apple
Height 1¼ in.

2364—8 in. Comport

2594—Trindle Candlestick
Height 8 in.
Spread 6½ in.

6030—5 in. Comport

2614—10 in. Vase

2364—Handled Lunch Tray
Diameter 11¼ in.

6021—6 in. Footed Vase

CAMELLIA DESIGN

Plate Etching No. 344

FOSTORIA GLASS COMPANY, MOUNDSVILLE, WEST VIRGINIA — 1952

6036 — 9½ oz. Goblet Height 6⅞ in.

6036 — 6 oz. High Sherbet (Champagne) Height 4¾ in.

6036 — 6 oz. Low Sherbet Height 4⅛ in.

6036 — 3½ oz. Cocktail Height 4⅛ in.

6036 — 3¼ oz. Claret-Wine Height 4¾ in.

6036 — 1 oz. Cordial Height 3¼ in.

6036 — 5½ oz. Parfait Height 5⅞ in.

6036 — 4 oz. Oyster Cocktail Height 3¾ in.

6036 — 12 oz. Footed Ice Tea Height 6⅛ in.

6036 — 5 oz. Footed Juice Height 4⅝ in.

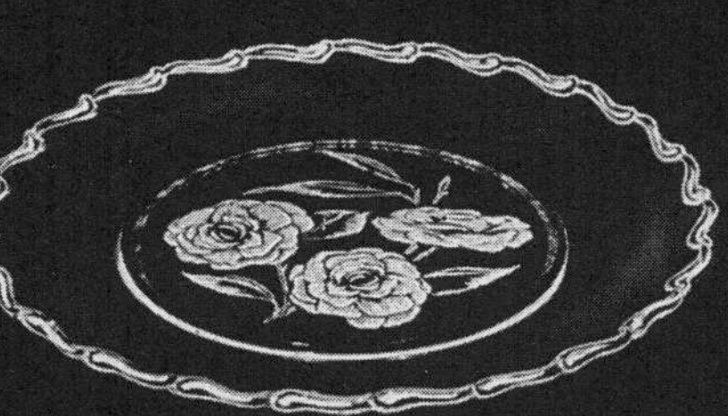
2630 — 6 in. Plate
2630 — 7 in. Plate
2630 — 8 in. Plate
2630 — 9 in. Plate
2630 — 10½ in. Dinner Plate

2630 — 14 in. Torte Plate
2630 — 16 in. Torte Plate

2630 Handled Cake Plate

2630 — Footed Cup
Cup Capacity 6 oz.
2630 — Saucer

CAMELLIA DESIGN

Plate Etching No. 344

2470 — 10 in.
Footed Vase

4143 — 6 in.
Footed Vase

2657 — 10½ in.
Footed Vase

5092 — 8 in.
Footed Bud Vase

2630 — 6 in.
Bud Vase

6021 — 6 in.
Footed Bud Vase

4121 — 5 in.
Vase

2630 — 8½ in.
Oval Vase

2660 — 8 in.
Flip Vase

2630 — 7½ in.
Handled Vase

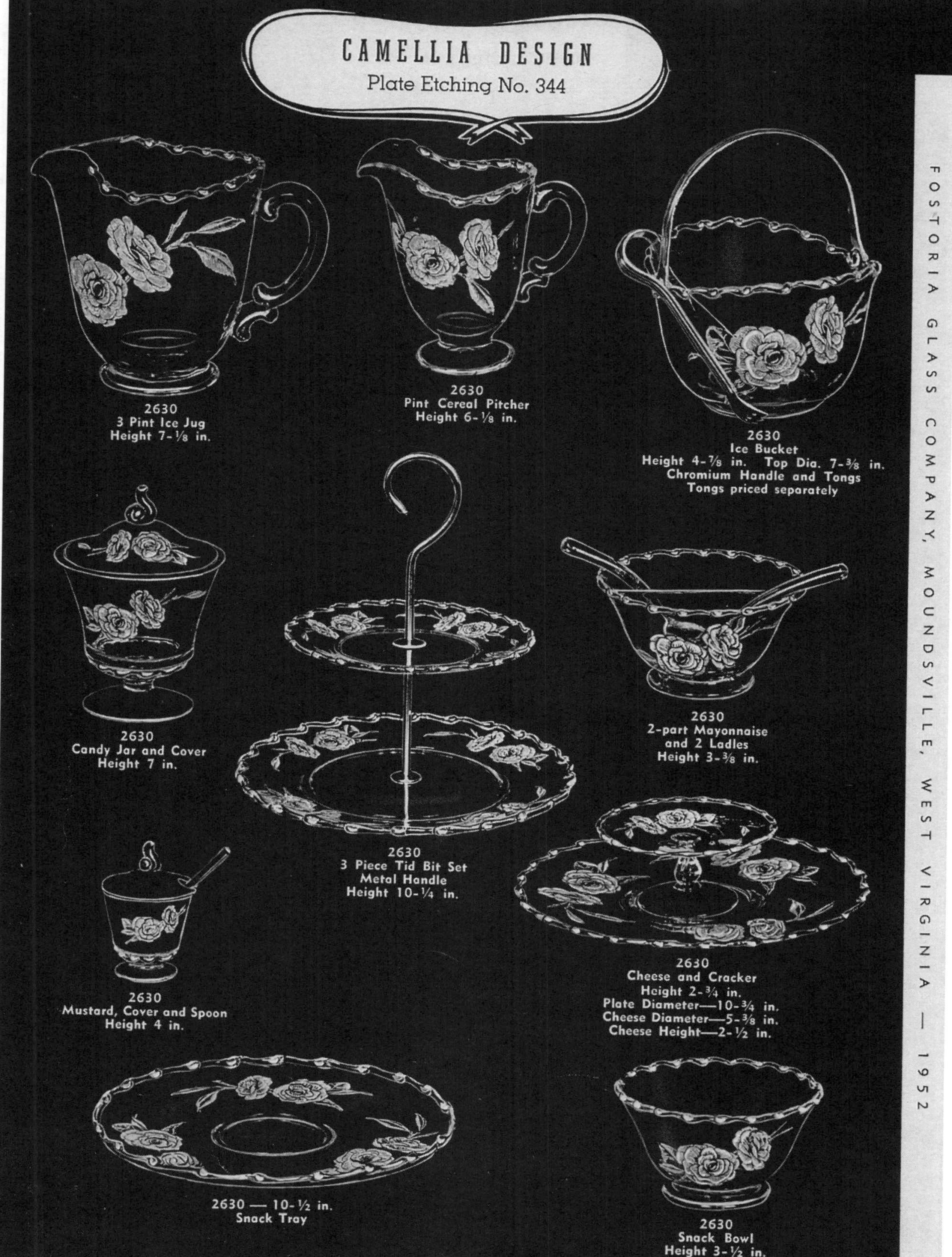
CAMELLIA DESIGN
Plate Etching No. 344
FOSTORIA GLASS COMPANY, MOUNDSVILLE, WEST VIRGINIA — 1952
2630
3 Pint Ice Jug
Height 7-1/8 in.
2630
Pint Cereal Pitcher
Height 6-1/8 in.
2630
Ice Bucket
Height 4-7/8 in. Top Dia. 7-3/8 in.
Chromium Handle and Tongs
Tongs priced separately
2630
Candy Jar and Cover
Height 7 in.
2630
3 Piece Tid Bit Set
Metal Handle
Height 10-1/4 in.
2630
2-part Mayonnaise
and 2 Ladles
Height 3-3/8 in.
2630
Mustard, Cover and Spoon
Height 4 in.
2630
Cheese and Cracker
Height 2-3/4 in.
Plate Diameter—10-3/4 in.
Cheese Diameter—5-3/8 in.
Cheese Height—2-1/2 in.
2630 — 10-1/2 in.
Snack Tray
2630
Snack Bowl
Height 3-1/2 in.

Fostoria Glass Company, Moundsville, West Virginia, January 1, 1940

CHINTZ DESIGN

PLATE ETCHING No. 338

6026—9 oz. Goblet
Height 7⅝ in.

6026—9 oz. Low Goblet
Height 6⅛ in.

6026—6 oz. Saucer Champagne
Height 5½ in.

6026—6 oz. Low Sherbet
Height 4⅜ in.

6026—4½ oz. Claret-Wine
Height 5⅜ in.

6026—1 oz. Cordial
Height 3⅞ in.

6026—4 oz. Footed Cocktail
Height 3⅝ in.

6026—4 oz. Cocktail
Height 5 in.

6026—13 oz. Footed Tumbler
Height 6 in.

6026—5 oz. Footed Tumbler
Height 4¾ in.

869—Finger Bowl
Height 2 in.
Diameter 4½ in.

2496—Footed Cup
2496—Saucer

2496—Footed Sugar
Height 3½ in.

2496—Footed Cream
Height 3¾ in.
Capacity 7½ oz.

2496—Plate
See Price List for Sizes

5000—Footed Jug
Height 9¾ in. Capacity 3 Pints

Fostoria Glass Company, Moundsville, West Virginia, January 1, 1940

CHINTZ DESIGN
PLATE ETCHING No. 338
6023—Duo Candlestick
Height 5½ in. Spread 6 in.
2496—5½ in. Candlestick
2496—Duo Candlestick
Height 4½ in. Spread 8 in.
2496—12 in. Bowl, Flared
Height 3½ in.
2496—Trindle Candlestick
Height 6 in. Spread 8¼ in.
2496—4 in. Candlestick
2484—10 in. Handled Bowl
Height 3½ in.
6023—9 in. Footed Bowl
Height 4⅛ in.
2496—10½ in. Handled Bowl
Height 3⅜ in.
Fostoria Glass Company, Moundsville, West Virginia, January 1, 1940

Fostoria Glass Company, Moundsville, West Virginia, January 1, 1940

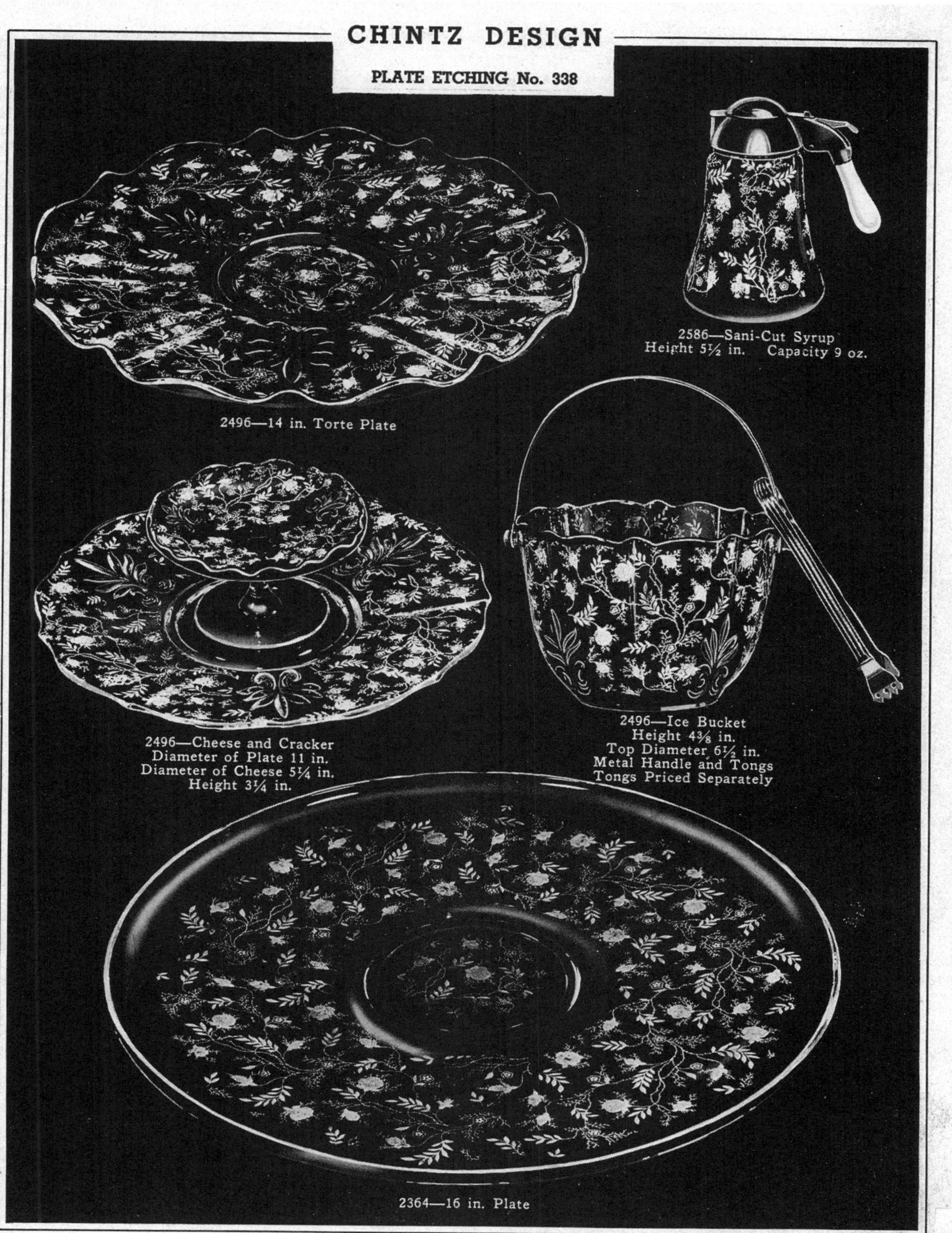

CHINTZ DESIGN

PLATE ETCHING No. 338

2586—Sani-Cut Syrup
Height $5\frac{1}{2}$ in. Capacity 9 oz.

2496—14 in. Torte Plate

2496—Cheese and Cracker
Diameter of Plate 11 in.
Diameter of Cheese $5\frac{1}{4}$ in.
Height $3\frac{1}{4}$ in.

2496—Ice Bucket
Height $4\frac{3}{8}$ in.
Top Diameter $6\frac{1}{2}$ in.
Metal Handle and Tongs
Tongs Priced Separately

2364—16 in. Plate

COLONIAL MIRROR DESIGN
PLATE ETCHING No. 334
6023—9 oz. Goblet Height 6⅜ in.
6023—6 oz. Saucer Champagne Height 4⅞ in.
6023—6 oz. Low Sherbet Height 4⅛ in.
6023—3¾ oz. Cocktail Height 4⅜ in.
6023—4 oz. Claret-Wine Height 4¾ in.
6023 12 oz. Footed Tumbler Height 5¾ in.
6023 9 oz. Footed Tumbler Height 5⅛ in.
6023 5 oz. Footed Tumbler Height 4½ in.
6023—1 oz. Cordial Height 3⅜ in.
6023—4 oz. Oyster Cocktail Height 3⅝ in.
766—Finger Bowl
2574—Individual Sugar Height 2⅞ in.
2574—Individual Cream Height 3½ in. Capacity 5¾ oz.
2574—Footed Sugar Height 3¾ in.
2574—Plate See Price List for Sizes
6011—Footed Jug Capacity 53 oz. Height 8⅞ in.
2574—Footed Cream Height 4 in. Capacity 6½ oz.
Fostoria Glass Company, Moundsville, West Virginia, Jan. 1, 1939

COLONIAL MIRROR DESIGN

PLATE ETCHING No. 334

2574—9½ in. Handled Bowl
Height 3⅜ in.

2574—5 in. Comport
Height 4⅞ in.

2574—4 in. Candlestick

2324—6 in. Candlestick

6023—Footed Bowl
Diameter 9¼ in.
Height 4¼ in.

Fostoria Glass Company, Moundsville, West Virginia, Jan. 1, 1939

DAISY DESIGN

PLATE ETCHING No. 324

CORSAGE DESIGN

PLATE ETCHING No. 325

FOSTORIA GLASS COMPANY, MOUNDSVILLE, WEST VIRGINIA – Jan. 1, 1939

Delphian Pattern Etching No. 272

1926 Catalog

Delphian Pattern, Plate Etching No. 272. Blue Stem and Foot.

Fostoria Glass Company, Moundsville, West Virginia

No. 4095-6 in. Nappy and Cover

No. 5082-6 oz. Parfait

No. 5082-2¾ oz. Wine

No. 5082-3 oz. Cocktail

No. 4095 Finger Bowl
No. 2283-6 in. Plate

No. 4095. Oyster Cocktail

No. 5082-5 oz. Fruit.

No. 5082-5 oz. Saucer Champagne.

No. 5082-9 oz. Goblet.

88

"FERN" DESIGN, PLATE ETCHING No. 305.
5098—SOLID CRYSTAL—REGULAR OPTIC.
5298—ROSE BOWL—CRYSTAL STEM—REGULAR OPTIC.
PRICED PAGES 65 AND 66 — No. 2 PRICE LIST.

369—Finger Bowl.
2283—6 in. Plate, R/O.

5098—5 oz. Ftd. Tumbler.
5298—5 oz. Ftd. Tumbler.

5098—9 oz. Ftd. Tumbler.
5298—9 oz. Ftd. Tumbler.

5098—12 oz. Ftd. Tumbler.
5298—12 oz. Ftd. Tumbler.

2375—Lemon Dish.

5098—Goblet.
5298—Goblet.

5098—High Sherbet.
5298—High Sherbet.

5098—Low Sherbet.
5298—Low Sherbet.

5098—Oyster Cocktail.
5298—Oyster Cocktail.

Fostoria Glass Company, Moundsville, West Virginia

Fern Design Etching No. 305

1930 Catalog

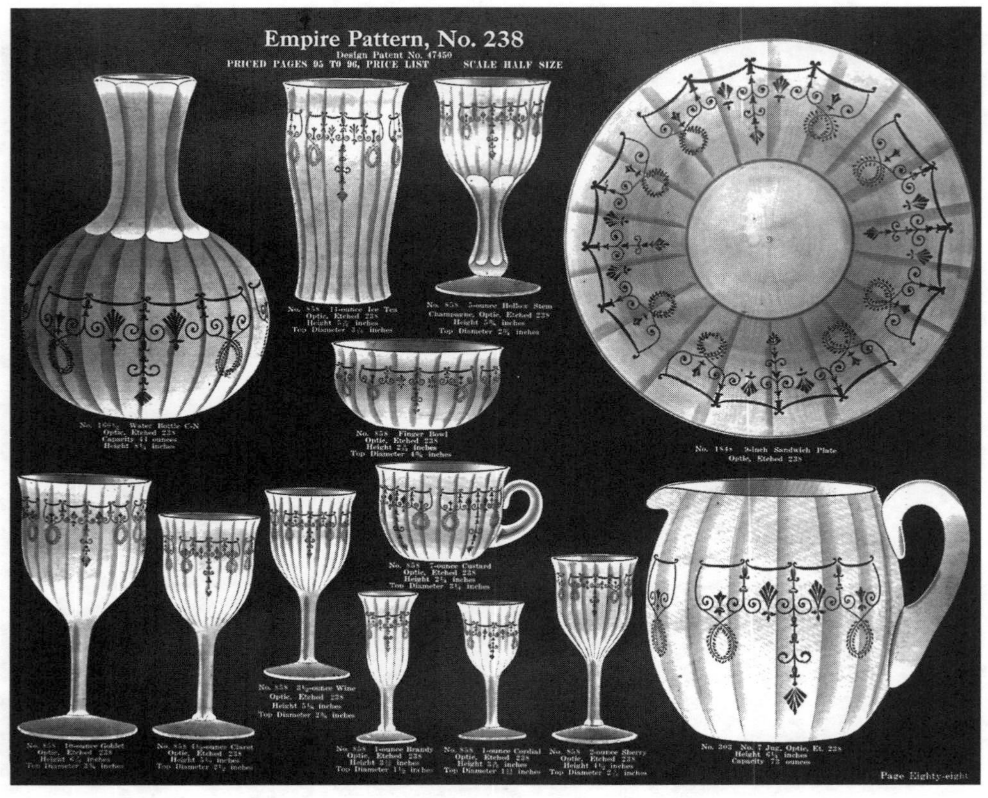

Empire Pattern No. 238

1925 Catalog

Fern Design No. 305

1930 Catalog

FUCHSIA DESIGN
PLATE ETCHING No 310

1939 Catalog

FLORENTINE DESIGN
PLATE ETCHING No. 311

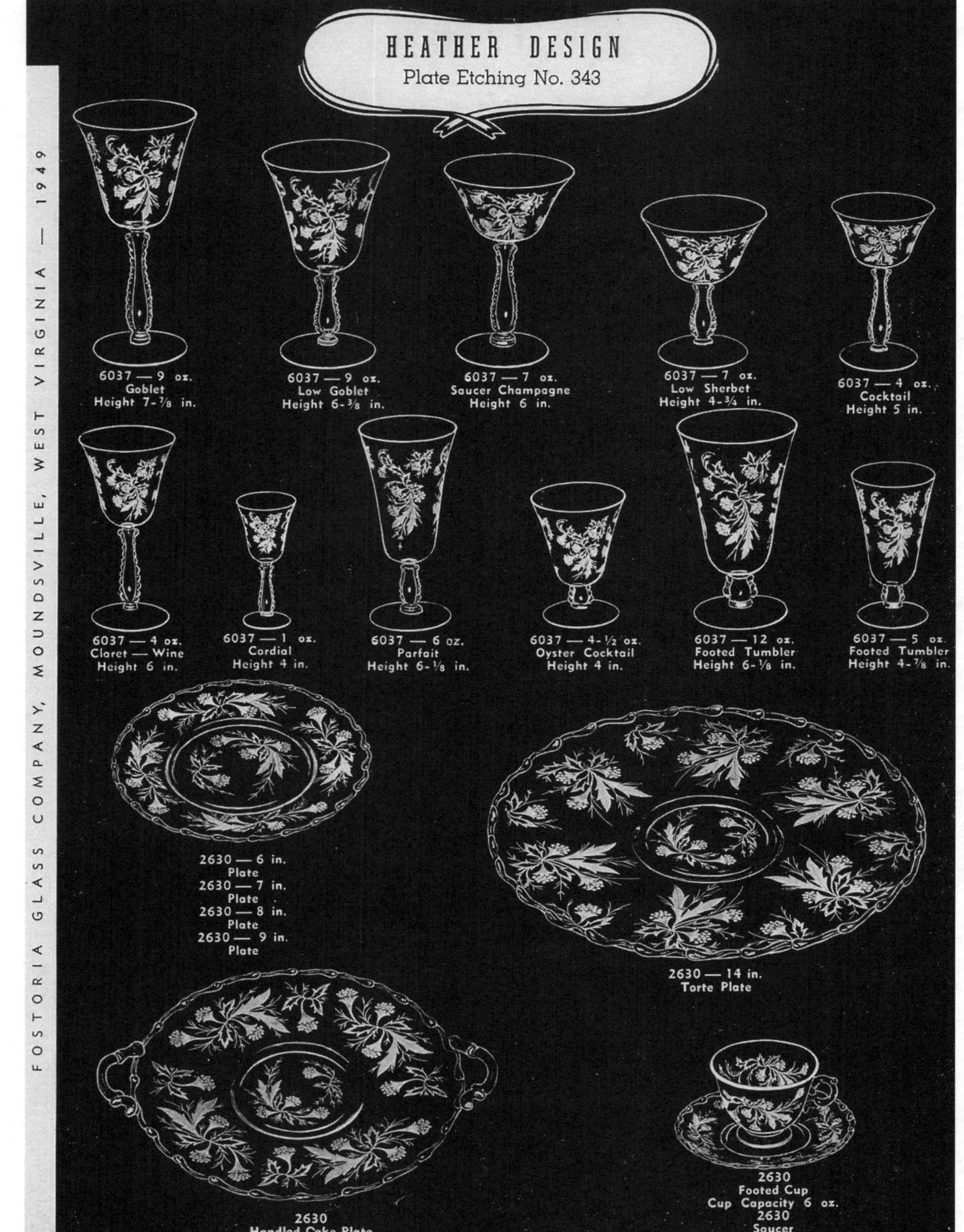
HEATHER DESIGN
Plate Etching No. 343
FOSTORIA GLASS COMPANY, MOUNDSVILLE, WEST VIRGINIA — 1949
6037 — 9 oz. Goblet Height 7-7/8 in.
6037 — 9 oz. Low Goblet Height 6-3/8 in.
6037 — 7 oz. Saucer Champagne Height 6 in.
6037 — 7 oz. Low Sherbet Height 4-3/4 in.
6037 — 4 oz. Cocktail Height 5 in.
6037 — 4 oz. Claret — Wine Height 6 in.
6037 — 1 oz. Cordial Height 4 in.
6037 — 6 oz. Parfait Height 6-1/8 in.
6037 — 4-1/2 oz. Oyster Cocktail Height 4 in.
6037 — 12 oz. Footed Tumbler Height 6-1/8 in.
6037 — 5 oz. Footed Tumbler Height 4-7/8 in.
2630 — 6 in. Plate
2630 — 7 in. Plate
2630 — 8 in. Plate
2630 — 9 in. Plate
2630 — 14 in. Torte Plate
2630 Handled Cake Plate
2630 Footed Cup Cup Capacity 6 oz.
2630 Saucer

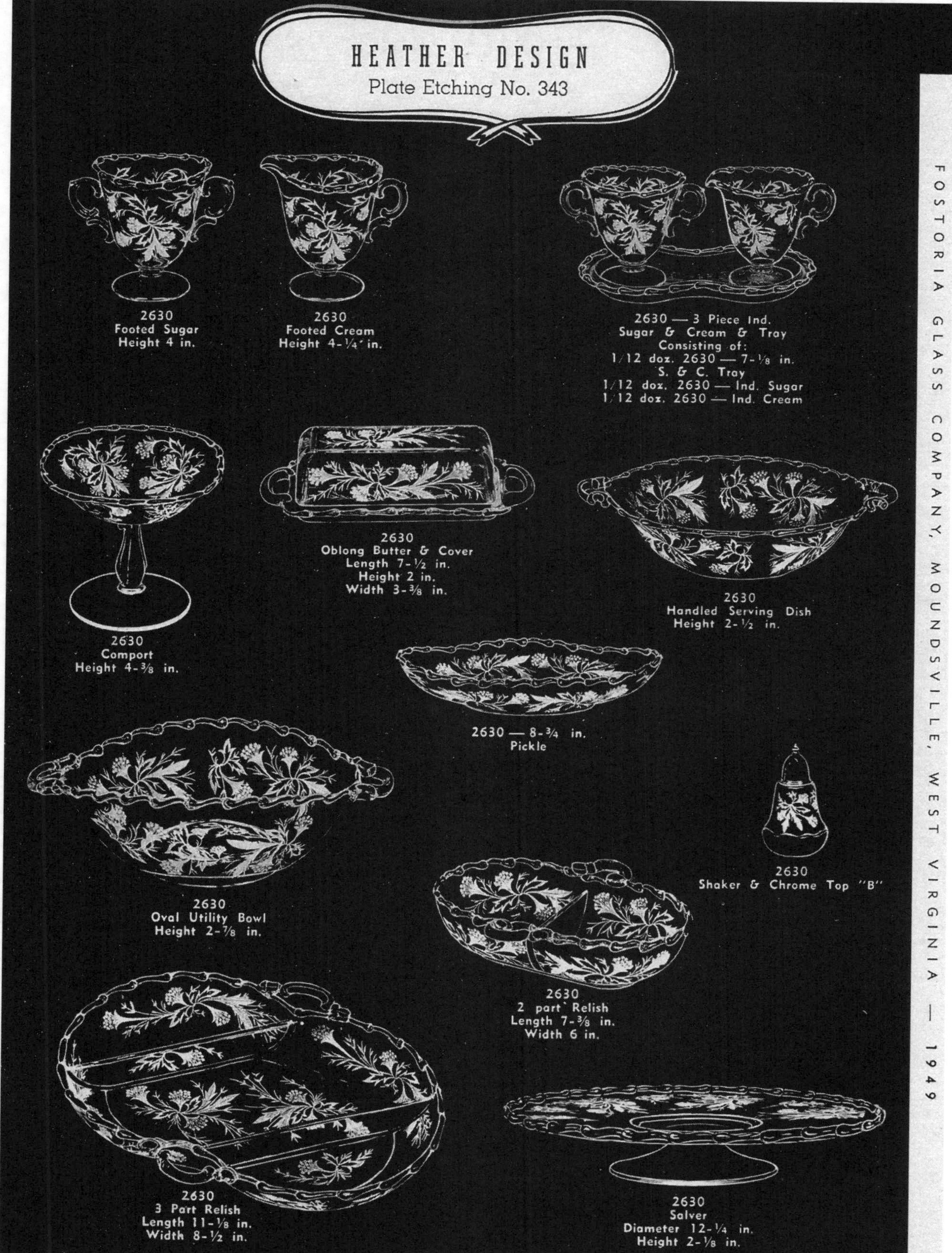

HEATHER DESIGN
Plate Etching No. 343

2630
Footed Sugar
Height 4 in.

2630
Footed Cream
Height 4-¼ in.

2630 — 3 Piece Ind.
Sugar & Cream & Tray
Consisting of:
1/12 doz. 2630 — 7-⅛ in.
S. & C. Tray
1/12 doz. 2630 — Ind. Sugar
1/12 doz. 2630 — Ind. Cream

2630
Comport
Height 4-⅜ in.

2630
Oblong Butter & Cover
Length 7-½ in.
Height 2 in.
Width 3-⅜ in.

2630
Handled Serving Dish
Height 2-½ in.

2630 — 8-¾ in.
Pickle

2630
Oval Utility Bowl
Height 2-⅞ in.

2630
Shaker & Chrome Top "B"

2630
2 part Relish
Length 7-⅜ in.
Width 6 in.

2630
3 Part Relish
Length 11-⅛ in.
Width 8-½ in.

2630
Salver
Diameter 12-¼ in.
Height 2-⅛ in.

FOSTORIA GLASS COMPANY, MOUNDSVILLE, WEST VIRGINIA — 1949

HEATHER DESIGN

Plate Etching No. 343

FOSTORIA GLASS COMPANY, MOUNDSVILLE, WEST VIRGINIA — 1952

2630
Handled Lunch Tray
Diameter 11¼ in.

2630 — 10½ in.
Snack Tray

2630
2-part Mayonnaise and 2 Ladles
Height 3⅜ in.

2630
Snack Bowl
Height 3½ in.

2630 — 8 in.
Bowl Flared
Height 3⅝ in.

2470 — 10 in.
Footed Vase

2660 — 8 in.
Flip Vase

4121 — 5 in.
Vase

4143 — 6 in.
Footed Vase

5092 — 8 in.
Footed Bud Vase

6021 — 6 in.
Footed Bud Vase

1930 Catalog

June Design No. 279

1930 Catalog

June Design No. 279

1930 Catalog

Kashmir Design No. 283

1930 Catalog

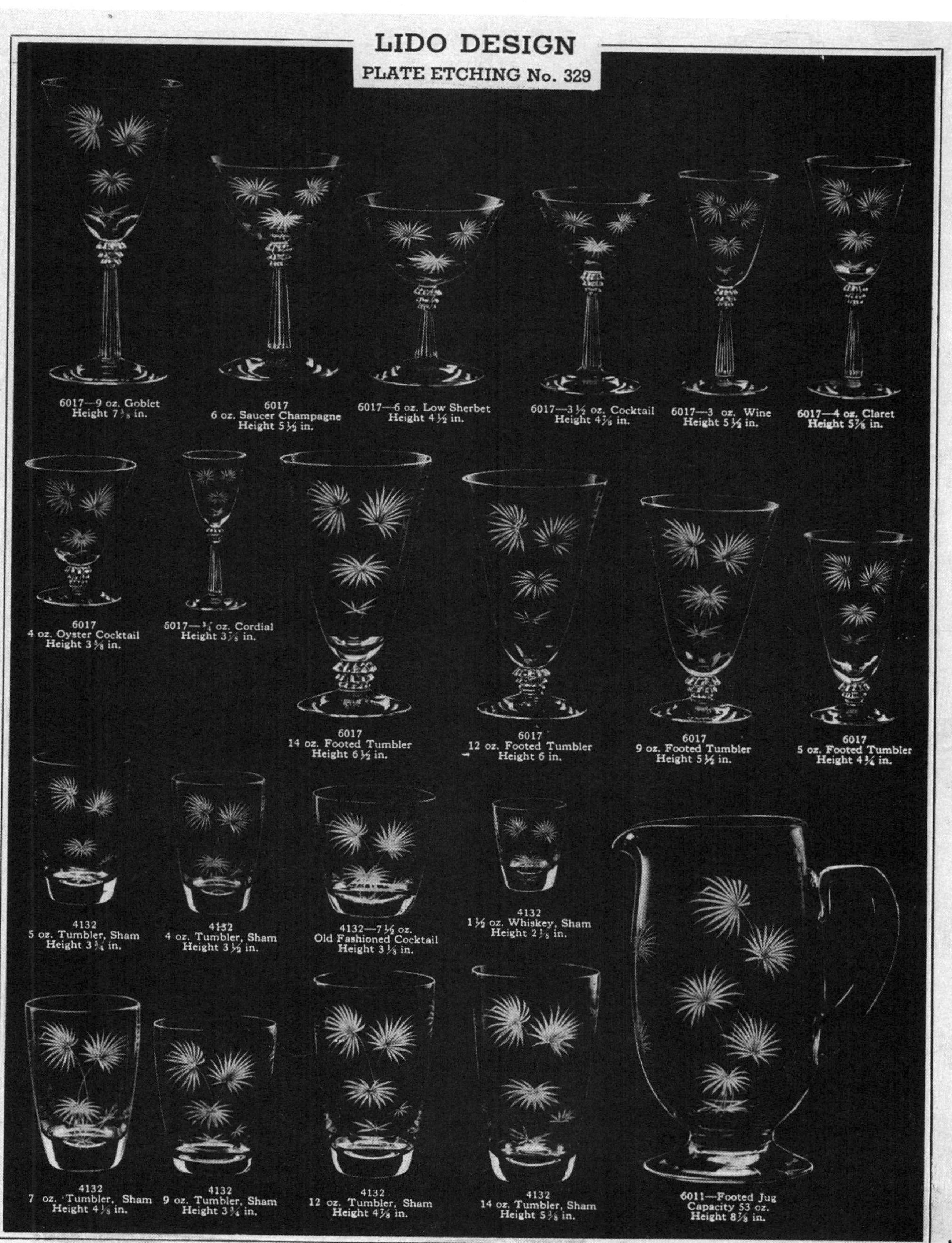
LIDO DESIGN
PLATE ETCHING No. 329
6017—9 oz. Goblet
Height 7⅜ in.
6017
6 oz. Saucer Champagne
Height 5½ in.
6017—6 oz. Low Sherbet
Height 4½ in.
6017—3½ oz. Cocktail
Height 4⅞ in.
6017—3 oz. Wine
Height 5½ in.
6017—4 oz. Claret
Height 5⅞ in.
6017
4 oz. Oyster Cocktail
Height 3⅝ in.
6017—¾ oz. Cordial
Height 3⅞ in.
6017
14 oz. Footed Tumbler
Height 6½ in.
6017
12 oz. Footed Tumbler
Height 6 in.
6017
9 oz. Footed Tumbler
Height 5½ in.
6017
5 oz. Footed Tumbler
Height 4¾ in.
4132
5 oz. Tumbler, Sham
Height 3¾ in.
4132
4 oz. Tumbler, Sham
Height 3½ in.
4132—7½ oz.
Old Fashioned Cocktail
Height 3⅛ in.
4132
1½ oz. Whiskey, Sham
Height 2⅕ in.
4132
7 oz. Tumbler, Sham
Height 4⅛ in.
4132
9 oz. Tumbler, Sham
Height 3¾ in.
4132
12 oz. Tumbler, Sham
Height 4⅞ in.
4132
14 oz. Tumbler, Sham
Height 5⅜ in.
6011—Footed Jug
Capacity 53 oz.
Height 8⅞ in.
Fostoria Glass Company, Moundsville, West Virginia, Jan. 1, 1939

LIDO DESIGN
PLATE ETCHING No. 329

766—Finger Bowl

2496—Plate
See Price List for Sizes

2496—Footed Cup
2496—Saucer

2496—Footed Sugar
Height 3½ in.

2496—Footed Cream
Height 3¾ in.
Capacity 7½ oz.

2496—Individual Sugar
Height 2⅞ in.

2496—Individual Cream
Height 3⅛ in.
Capacity 4 oz.

2496—8 in. Pickle

2496—Shaker
Height 2¾ in.

2496—6½ in. Sugar and Cream Tray
Width 3¾ in.

2496—11 in. Celery

2496½—Mayonnaise and
Plate and Ladle
Height 3½ in.

Fostoria Glass Company, Moundsville, West Virginia, Jan. 1, 1939

2470—10 in. Vase

2496—Duo Candlestick
Height 4½ in. Spread 8 in.

2496—4 in. Candlestick

2496—10½ in. Handled Bowl
Height 3⅜ in.

2496—5½ in. Candlestick

2496—12 in. Bowl, Flared
Height 3½ in.

2496—5½ in. Candlestick

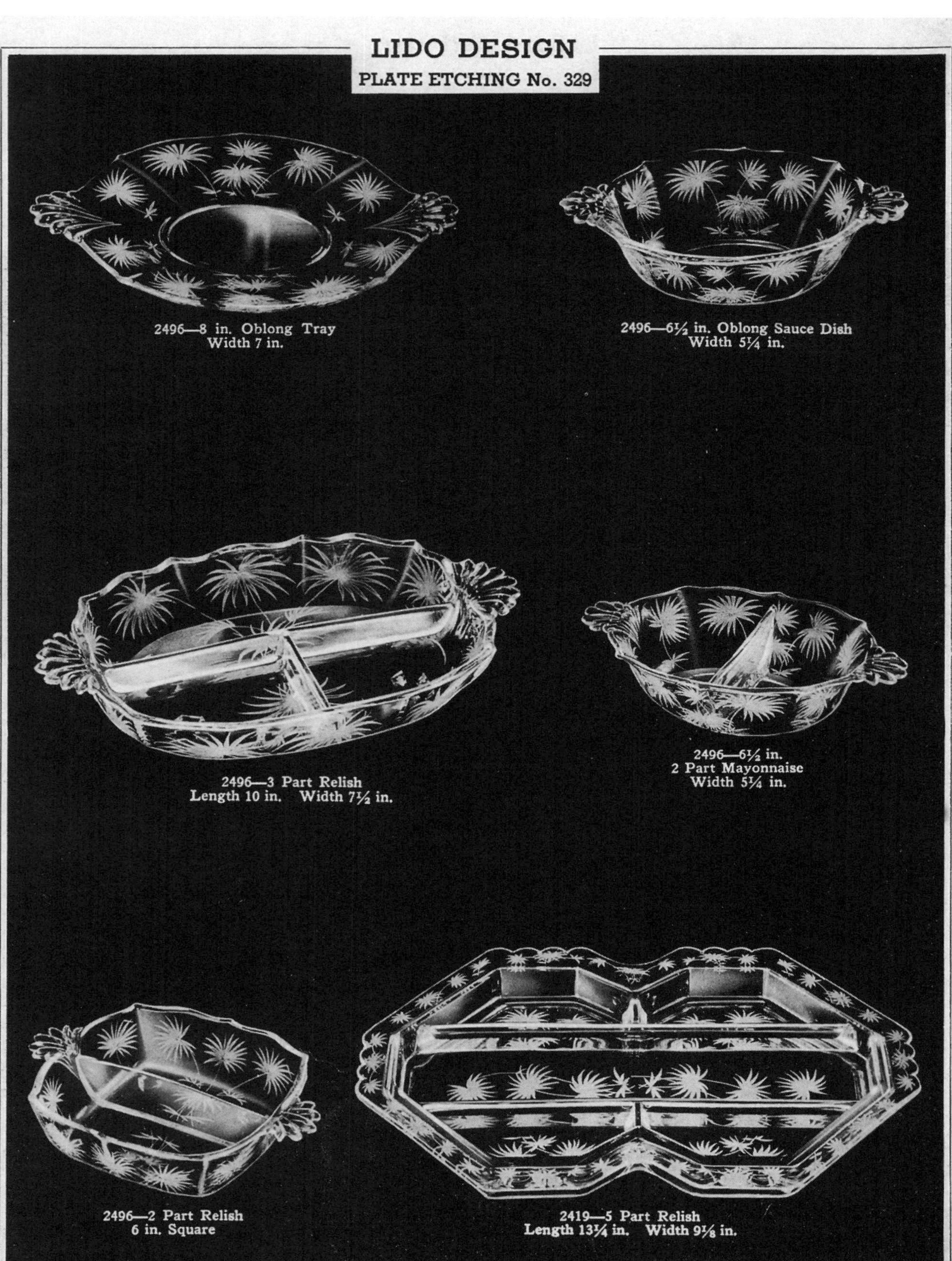

Fostoria Glass Company, Moundsville, West Virginia, Jan. 1, 1939

541

MAYFLOWER DESIGN

Plate Etching No. 332

FOSTORIA GLASS COMPANY, MOUNDSVILLE, WEST VIRGINIA — 1948

6020—9 oz. Goblet Height 7¼ in.

6020—6 oz. Saucer Champagne Height 5½ in.

6020—6 oz. Low Sherbet Height 4⅝ in.

6020—3½ oz. Cocktail Height 4⅞ in.

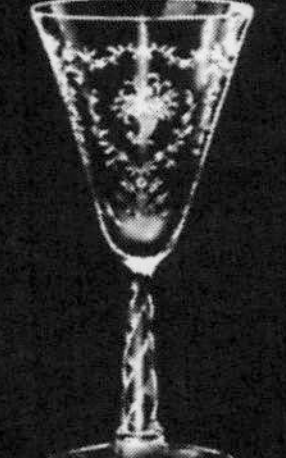

6020—4½ oz. Claret Height 5¾ in.

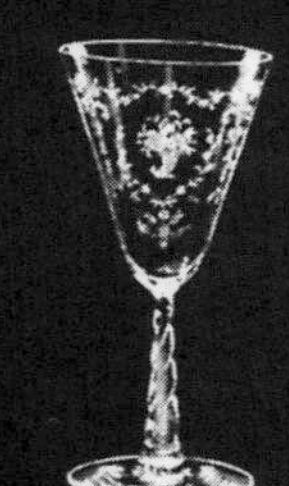

6020—3½ oz. Wine Height 5⅜ in.

6020—1 oz. Cordial Height 3¾ in.

6020—4 oz. Oyster Cocktail Height 3¾ in.

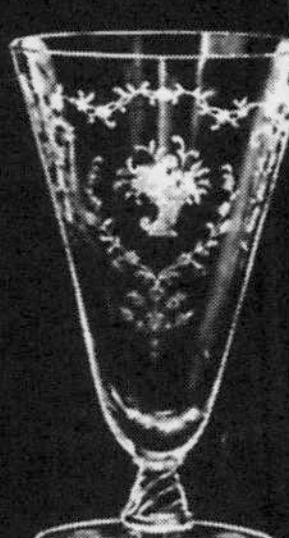

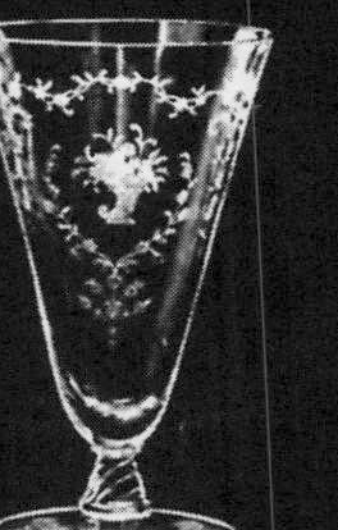

6020—12 oz. Footed Tumbler Height 6⅜ in.

6020—9 oz. Footed Tumbler Height 5¾ in.

6020—5 oz. Footed Tumbler Height 4⅞ in.

5000 Footed Jug Height 9¾ in. Capacity 3 Pints

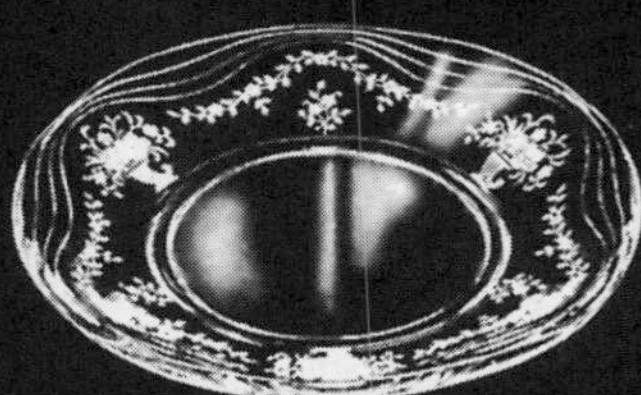

2560—6 in. Plate

2560—7 in. Plate

2560—8 in. Plate

2560—9 in. Plate

2560 Footed Cup

2560 Saucer

Mayflower is etched on the twist stem Melody. This stem and etching was introduced in 1938.

2560—3 Piece Ind. Sugar and Cream and Tray Consisting of:
1/12 Doz. 2560½—7½ in. Sugar and Cream Tray
1/12 Doz. 2560—Ind. Sugar
1/12 Doz. 2560—Ind. Cream

MAYFLOWER DESIGN

PLATE ETCHING No. 332

2560—5 in. Fruit
2560—6 in. Cereal

2560—Footed Shaker, F. G. T.
Height 2⅞ in.

2560—6¾ in. Olive
2560—8¾ in. Pickle
2560—11 in. Celery

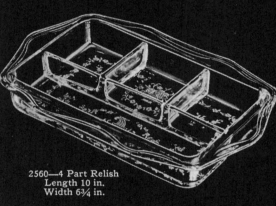

2560—4 Part Relish
Length 10 in.
Width 6¾ in.

2560½—4 in. Candlestick

2560—3 oz. Footed Oil & Stopper
Height 4½ in.

2560—2 Part Mayonnaise
with 2 Ladles
Height 3½ in.
Top Diameter 6¾ in.

2560—5 Part Relish
Length 13¼ in.
Width 9⅜ in.

Fostoria Glass Company, Moundsville, West Virginia, Jan. 1, 1939

MAYFLOWER DESIGN
PLATE ETCHING No. 332
2430—2 in. Candlestick
2430—11 in. Bowl
Height 3 in.
2430—2 in. Candlestick
2560—4½ in. Candlestick
2560—11 in. Handled Bowl
Height 3¼ in.
2560—4½ in. Candlestick
2496—10½ in. Handled Bowl
Height 3⅜ in.
2496—Duo Candlestick
Height 5 in. Spread 8¼ in.
Fostoria Glass Company, Moundsville, West Virginia, Jan. 1, 1939

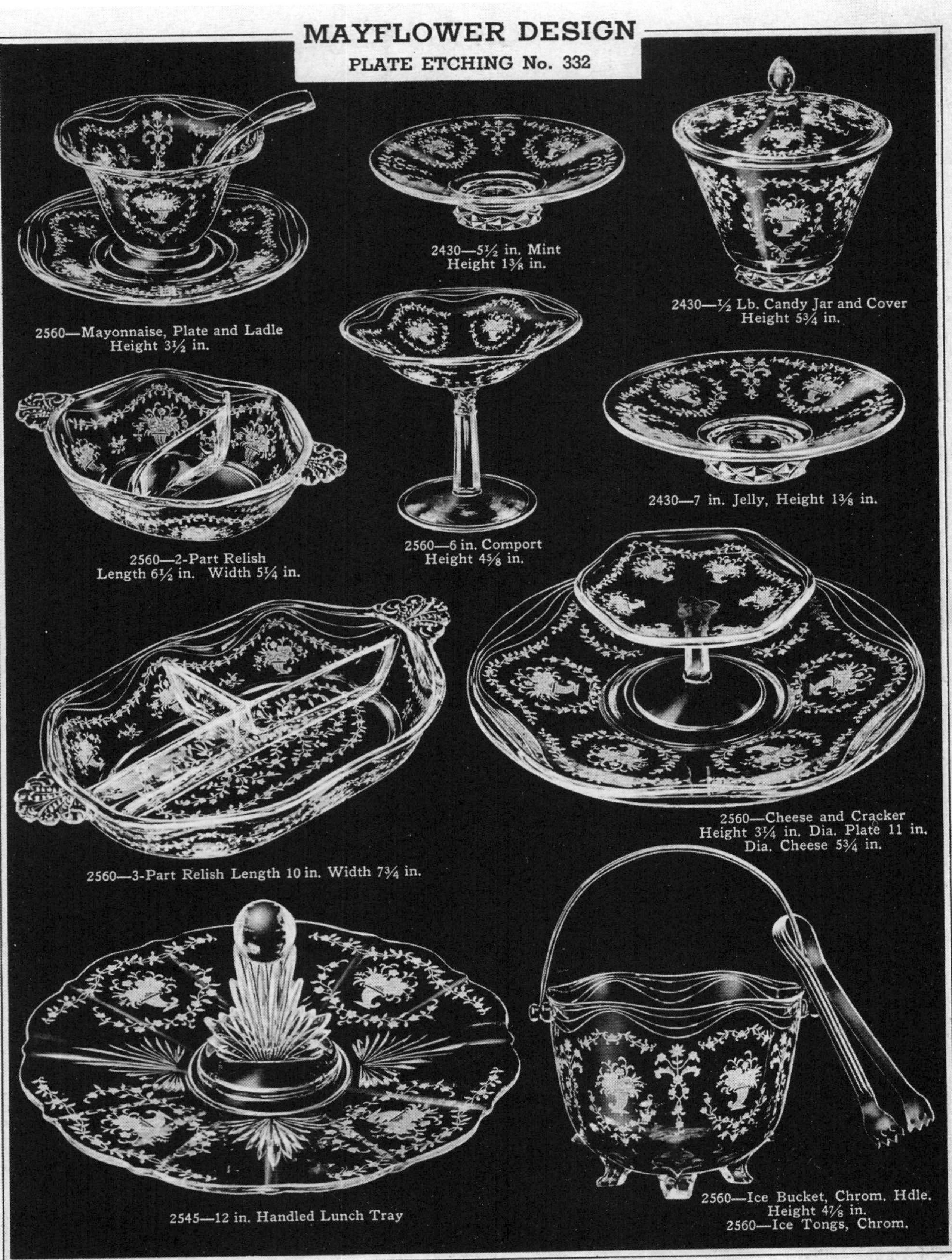

MAYFLOWER DESIGN

PLATE ETCHING No. 332

2560—Mayonnaise, Plate and Ladle
Height 3½ in.

2430—5½ in. Mint
Height 1⅜ in.

2430—½ Lb. Candy Jar and Cover
Height 5¾ in.

2560—2-Part Relish
Length 6½ in. Width 5¼ in.

2560—6 in. Comport
Height 4⅝ in.

2430—7 in. Jelly, Height 1⅜ in.

2560—3-Part Relish Length 10 in. Width 7¾ in.

2560—Cheese and Cracker
Height 3¼ in. Dia. Plate 11 in.
Dia. Cheese 5¾ in.

2545—12 in. Handled Lunch Tray

2560—Ice Bucket, Chrom. Hdle.
Height 4⅞ in.
2560—Ice Tongs, Chrom.

Fostoria Glass Company, Moundsville, West Virginia, Jan. 1, 1939

Fostoria Glass Company, Moundsville, West Virginia, Jan. 1, 1939

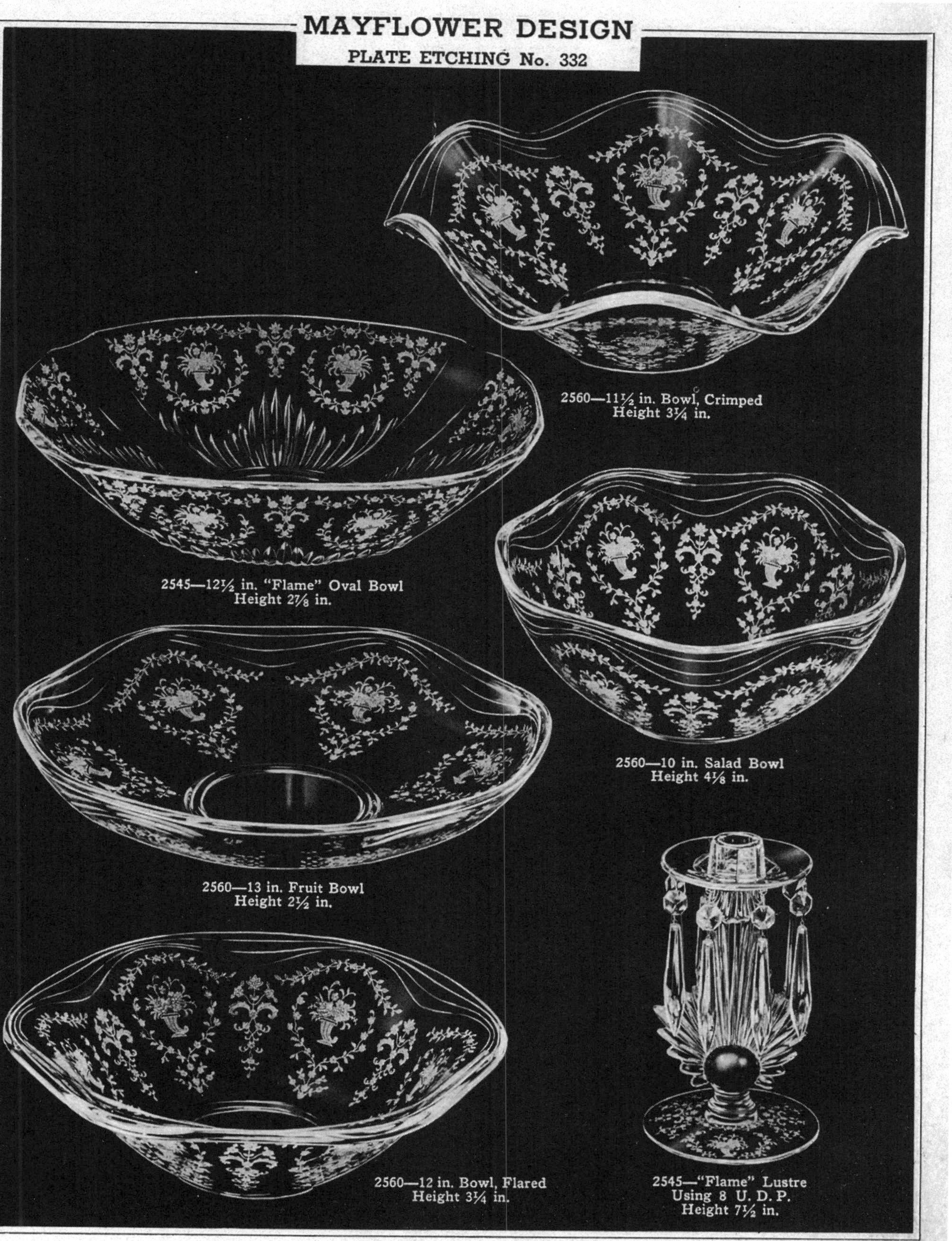

MAYFLOWER DESIGN

PLATE ETCHING No. 332

2560—11½ in. Bowl, Crimped
Height 3¼ in.

2545—12½ in. "Flame" Oval Bowl
Height 2⅞ in.

2560—10 in. Salad Bowl
Height 4⅛ in.

2560—13 in. Fruit Bowl
Height 2½ in.

2560—12 in. Bowl, Flared
Height 3¼ in.

2545—"Flame" Lustre
Using 8 U. D. P.
Height 7½ in.

2545—10 in. Vase

2545—"Flame" Duo Candlestick
Height 6¾ in. Spread 10¼ in.

2545—4½ in. Candlestick

2430—8 in. Vase

2430—3¾ in. Vase

2545—2-Light "Flame" Candelabra
Using 12 "B" Prisms
Height 6¾ in. Spread 11 in.

5100—10 in. Vase

MEADOW ROSE DESIGN

PLATE ETCHING No. 328

6016
10 oz. Goblet
Height 7⅝ in.

6016—6 oz.
Saucer Champagne
Height 5⅝ in.

6016
6 oz. Low Sherbet
Height 4⅜ in.

6016
3½ oz. Cocktail
Height 5¼ in.

6016
4½ oz. Claret
Height 6 in.

6016
3¼ oz. Wine
Height 5¼ in.

6016—13 oz.
Footed Tumbler
Height 5⅞ in.

6016—10 oz.
Footed Tumbler
Height 5⅜ in.

6016—5 oz.
Footed Tumbler
Height 4⅝ in.

6016—¾ oz.
Cordial
Height 3⅞ in.

6016—4 oz.
Oyster Cocktail
Height 3⅝ in.

869—Finger Bowl

2496—Footed Cup
2496—Saucer

2375
Footed Shaker
Height 3½ in.

2496—Footed Cream
Height 3¾ in.
Capacity 7½ oz.

2496—Plate

2496—Footed Sugar
Height 3½ in.

5000—7 Footed Jug
Height 9¾ in. Capacity 3 Pints

Fostoria Glass Company, Moundsville, West Virginia, Jan. 1, 1939

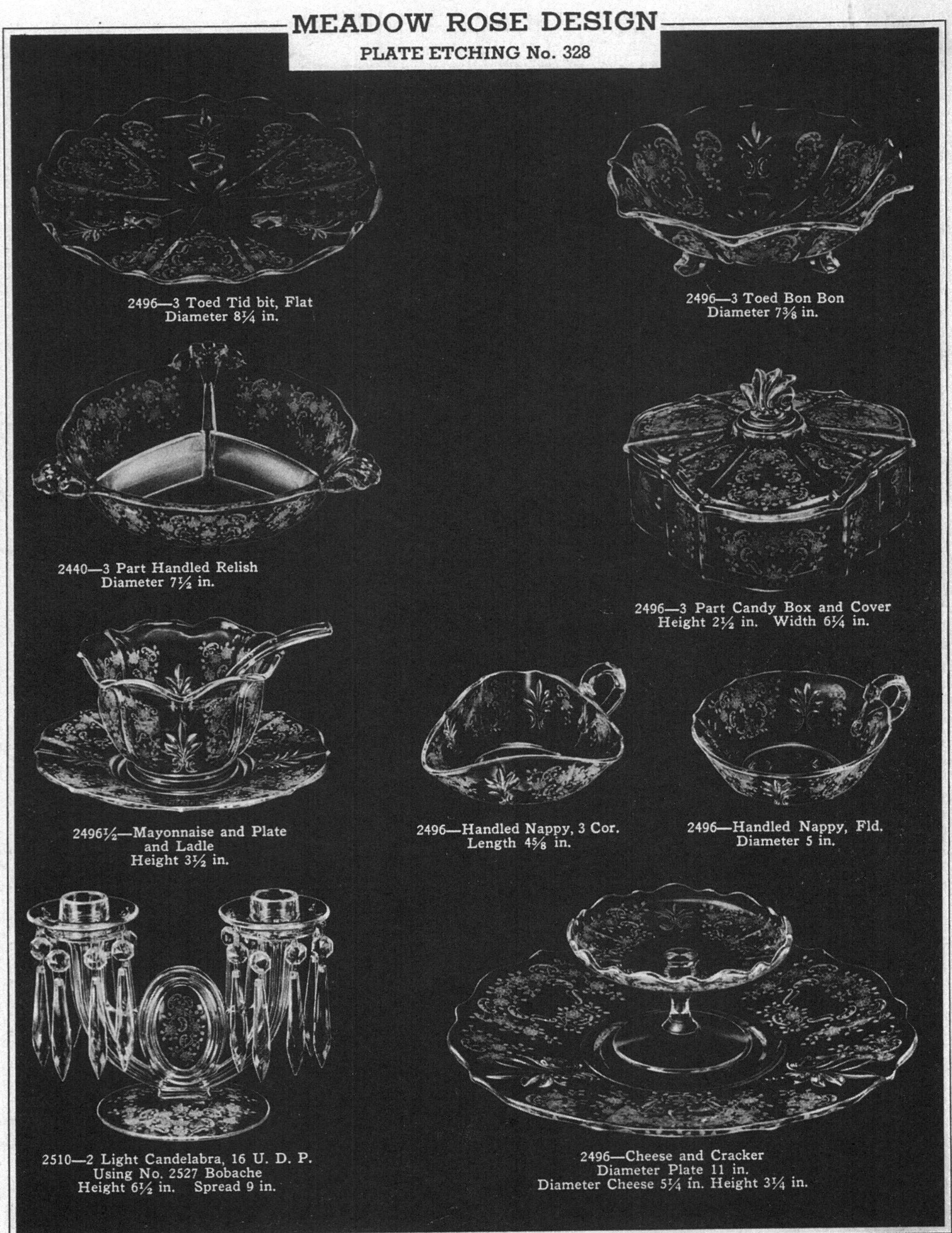

MEADOW ROSE DESIGN

PLATE ETCHING No. 328

2496—3 Toed Tid bit, Flat
Diameter 8¼ in.

2496—3 Toed Bon Bon
Diameter 7⅜ in.

2440—3 Part Handled Relish
Diameter 7½ in.

2496—3 Part Candy Box and Cover
Height 2½ in. Width 6¼ in.

2496½—Mayonnaise and Plate and Ladle
Height 3½ in.

2496—Handled Nappy, 3 Cor.
Length 4⅝ in.

2496—Handled Nappy, Fld.
Diameter 5 in.

2510—2 Light Candelabra, 16 U. D. P.
Using No. 2527 Bobache
Height 6½ in. Spread 9 in.

2496—Cheese and Cracker
Diameter Plate 11 in.
Diameter Cheese 5¼ in. Height 3¼ in.

Fostoria Glass Company, Moundsville, West Virginia, Jan. 1, 1939

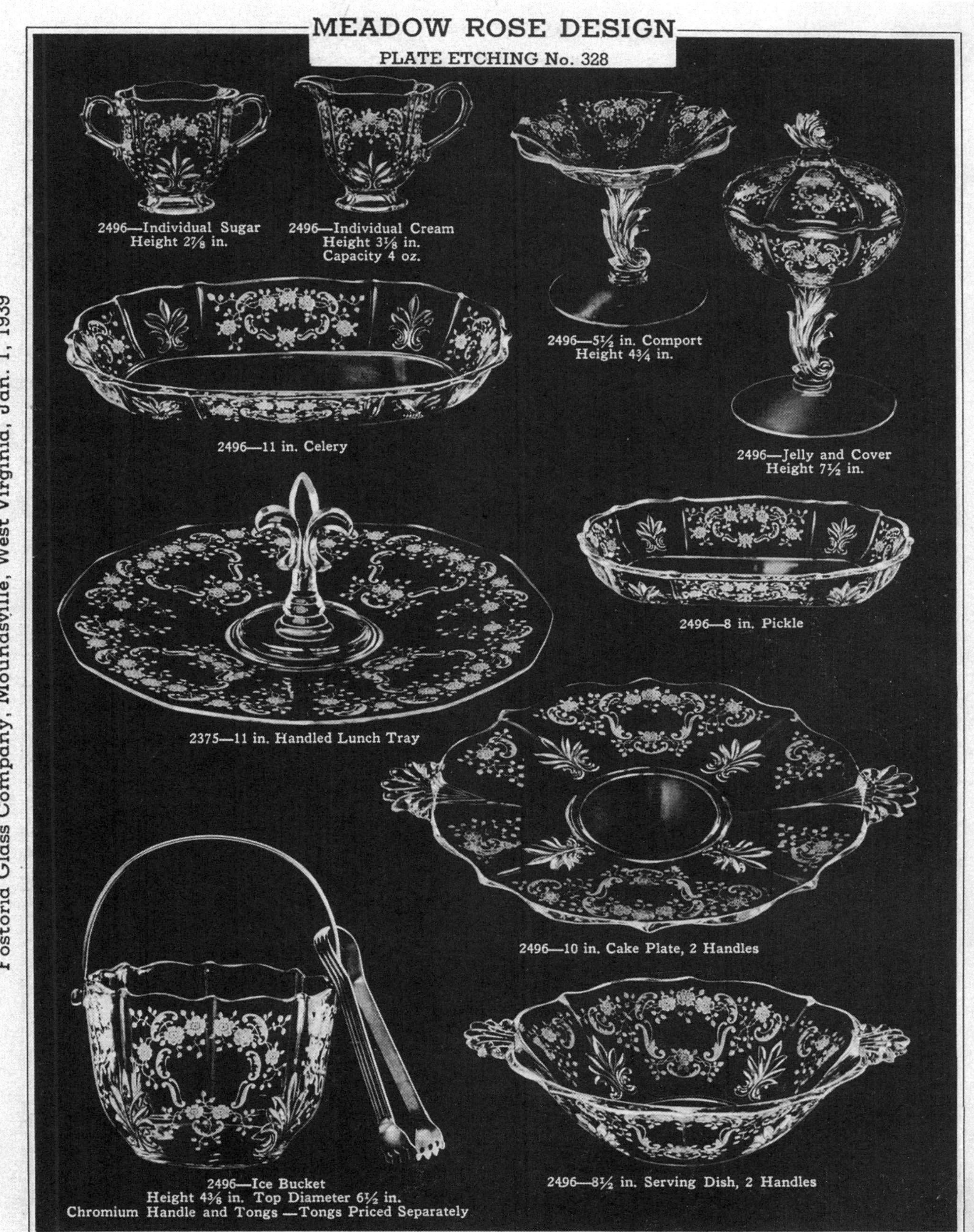

Fostoria Glass Company, Moundsville, West Virginia, Jan. 1, 1939

MEADOW ROSE DESIGN

PLATE ETCHING No. 328

2496—Individual Sugar
Height $2\frac{7}{8}$ in.

2496—Individual Cream
Height $3\frac{1}{8}$ in.
Capacity 4 oz.

2496—$5\frac{1}{2}$ in. Comport
Height $4\frac{3}{4}$ in.

2496—11 in. Celery

2496—Jelly and Cover
Height $7\frac{1}{2}$ in.

2496—8 in. Pickle

2375—11 in. Handled Lunch Tray

2496—10 in. Cake Plate, 2 Handles

2496—Ice Bucket
Height $4\frac{3}{8}$ in. Top Diameter $6\frac{1}{2}$ in.
Chromium Handle and Tongs —Tongs Priced Separately

2496—$8\frac{1}{2}$ in. Serving Dish, 2 Handles

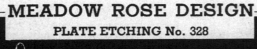

MEADOW ROSE DESIGN

PLATE ETCHING No. 328

2545—2 Light "Flame" Candelabra
Using 12 B Prisms
Height 6¾ in. Spread 11 in.

4128
5 in. Vase

2545
12½ in. "Flame" Oval Bowl
Height 2⅞ in.

2470
10 in. Vase

2545—"Flame" Duo Candlestick
Height 6¾ in. Spread 10¼ in.

Fostoria Glass Company, Moundsville, West Virginia, Jan. 1, 1939

MANOR DESIGN
PLATE ETCHING No. 286

1939 Catalog

MORNING GLORY DESIGN
PLATE ETCHING No. 313

NAVARRE DESIGN
PLATE ETCHING No. 327
6016
9 oz. Goblet
Height 7⅝ in.
6016—5½ oz.
Saucer Champagne
Height 5⅝ in.
6016—5½ oz.
Low Sherbet
Height 4⅜ in.
6016
3½ oz. Cocktail
Height 5¼ in.
6016—4 oz. Claret
Height 6 in.
6016—3 oz. Wine
Height 5½ in.
6016—13 oz.
Footed Tumbler
Height 5⅞ in.
6016—10 oz.
Footed Tumbler
Height 5⅜ in.
6016—5 oz.
Footed Tumbler
Height 4⅝ in.
6016
1 oz. Cordial
Height 3⅞ in.
6016
4 oz. Oyster Cocktail
Height 3⅝ in.
869—Finger Bowl
2440—Cup
2440—Saucer
2375—Footed Shaker
Height 3½ in.
2440—Footed Cream
Height 4¼ in.
Cap. 6¾ oz.
2440—Plate
2 440—Footed Sugar
Height 3⅝ in.
5000—7 Footed Jug
Height 9¾ in.
Capacity 3 Pints

Fostoria Glass Company, Moundsville, West Virginia, Jan. 1, 1939

NAVARRE DESIGN

PLATE ETCHING No. 327

2375—Ice Bucket with Tongs
Height 6 in. Top Dia. 5⅛ in.

2375—Mayonnaise
Top Dia. 5⅝ in.
2375—7 in. Mayonnaise Plate
2375—Ladle

2400—6 in. Comport
Height 4½ in.

2440—8½ in. Pickle

2440—11½ in. Celery

2496—3 Part Relish
Length 10 in. Width 7½ in.

2496—4 Part Relish
Length 10 in. Width 7½ in.

2440—Oval Cake Plate
2 Handles Length 10½ in.

2419—5 Part Relish
Length 13¼ in. Width 9⅛ in.

Fostoria Glass Company, Moundsville, West Virginia, Jan. 1, 1939

NAVARRE DESIGN
PLATE ETCHING No. 327
2472—Duo Candlestick
Height 5 in. Spread 8¼ in.
2496—5½ in. Candlestick
2496—Duo Candlestick
Height 4½ in. Spread 8 in.
2470½—10½ in. Bowl
Height 4 in.
2496—10½ in. Handled Bowl
Height 3⅜ in.
2482—Trindle Candlestick
Height 6¾ in. Spread 8½ in.
2470—10 in. Vase
2496—Trindle Candlestick
Height 6 in. Spread 8¼ in.
Fostoria Glass Company, Moundsville, West Virginia, Jan. 1, 1939

NAVARRE DESIGN

PLATE ETCHING No. 327

2496—8 in. Oblong Tray
Width 7 in.

4128—5 in. Vase

4121—5 in. Vase

2496—12 in.
Bowl, Flared
Height 3½ in.

2496—6½ in.
Oblong Sauce Dish
Width 5¼ in.

2496—Sweetmeat
6 in. Square

2496—6½ in.
2 Part Mayonnaise
Width 5¼ in.

2496—2 Part Relish
6 in. Square

2496—14 in. Torte Plate

Fostoria Glass Company, Moundsville, West Virginia, Jan. 1, 1939

Fostoria Glass Company, Moundsville, West Virginia, Jan. 1, 1939

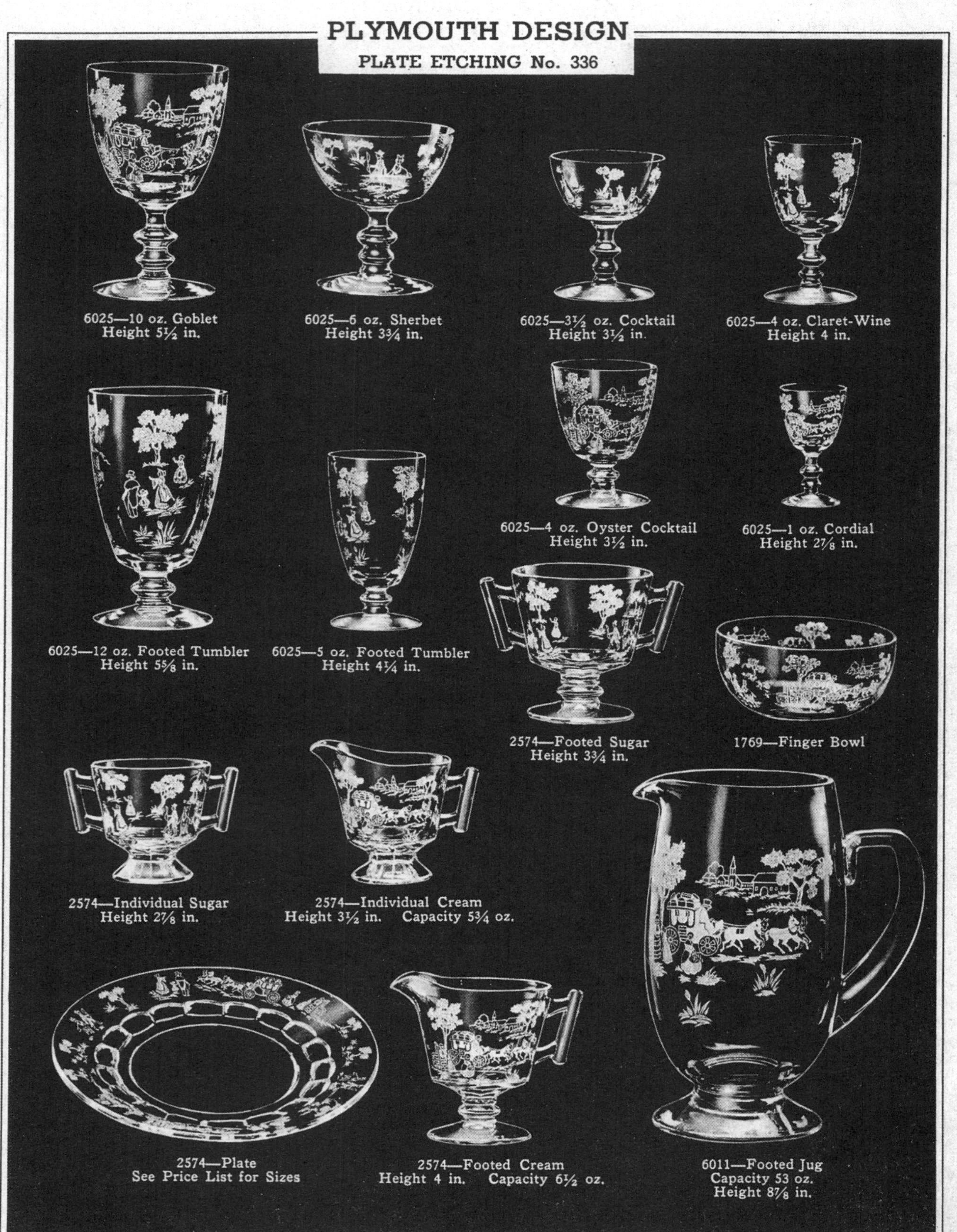

PLYMOUTH DESIGN

PLATE ETCHING No. 336

6025—10 oz. Goblet
Height 5½ in.

6025—6 oz. Sherbet
Height 3¾ in.

6025—3½ oz. Cocktail
Height 3½ in.

6025—4 oz. Claret-Wine
Height 4 in.

6025—4 oz. Oyster Cocktail
Height 3½ in.

6025—1 oz. Cordial
Height 2⅞ in.

6025—12 oz. Footed Tumbler
Height 5⅝ in.

6025—5 oz. Footed Tumbler
Height 4¼ in.

2574—Footed Sugar
Height 3¾ in.

1769—Finger Bowl

2574—Individual Sugar
Height 2⅞ in.

2574—Individual Cream
Height 3½ in. Capacity 5¾ oz.

2574—Plate
See Price List for Sizes

2574—Footed Cream
Height 4 in. Capacity 6½ oz.

6011—Footed Jug
Capacity 53 oz.
Height 8⅞ in.

PLYMOUTH DESIGN

PLATE ETCHING No. 336

2574—$9\frac{1}{2}$ in. Handled Bowl
Height $3\frac{3}{8}$ in.

2574—4 in. Candlestick

2574—5 in. Comport
Height $4\frac{7}{8}$ in.

6023—Footed Bowl
Diameter $9\frac{1}{4}$ in.
Height $4\frac{1}{4}$ in.

2324—6 in. Candlestick

Fostoria Glass Company, Moundsville, West Virginia, Jan. 1, 1939

ROMANCE DESIGN
Plate Etching No. 341

FOSTORIA GLASS COMPANY, MOUNDSVILLE, WEST VIRGINIA — 1948

6017—9 oz. Goblet Height 7 3/8 in.

6017—6 oz. Saucer Champagne Height 5 1/2 in.

6017—6 oz. Low Sherbet Height 4 1/2 in.

6017—3 1/2 oz. Cocktail Height 4 7/8 in.

6017—4 oz. Claret Height 5 7/8 in.

6017—3 oz. Wine Height 5 1/2 in.

6017—3/4 oz. Cordial Height 3 7/8 in.

6017—4 oz. Oyster Cocktail Height 3 5/8 in.

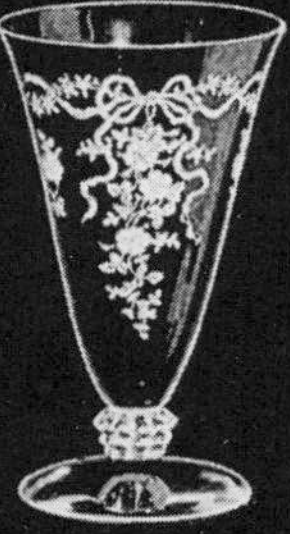
6017—12 oz. Footed Tumbler Height 6 in.

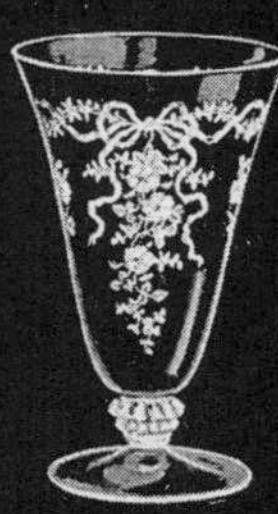
6017—9 oz. Footed Tumbler Height 5 1/2 in.

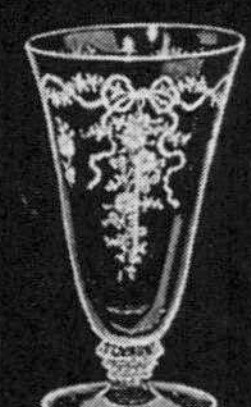
6017—5 oz. Footed Tumbler Height 4 3/4 in.

6011 Footed Jug Height 8 7/8 in. Capacity 53 oz.

2337—6 in. Plate

2337—7 in. Plate

2337—8 in. Plate

2337—9 in. Plate

2350 1/2 Footed Cup

2350 Saucer

2350 1/2 Footed Sugar Height 3 1/8 in.

2350 1/2 Footed Cream Height 3 1/4 in. Capacity 7 oz.

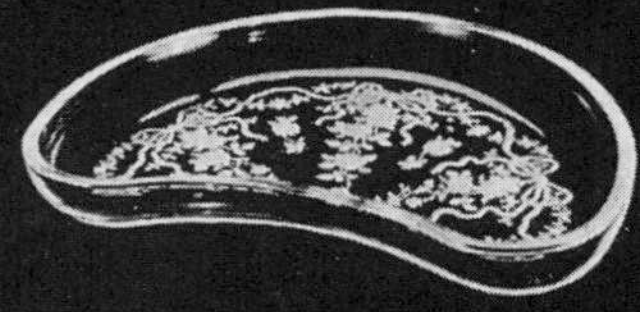
2364 Crescent Salad Plate

2364—13 in. Fruit Bowl
Height 2¾ in.

2596—11 in. Oblong Shallow Bowl
Height 2 in.

2364—12 in. Bowl, Fld.
Height 2⅞ in.

6023—Footed Bowl Blown
Height 4¼ in. Diameter 9¼ in.

2364—12 in. Lily Pond
Height 2¼ in.

2594—Trindle Candlestick
Height 8 in.
Spread 6½ in.

2594—10 in. Handled Bowl
Height 3 in.
Length Overall 13½ in.

2594—5½ in. Candlestick

6023—Duo Candlestick
Height 5½ in. Spread 6 in.

2596—5 in. Candlestick

2324—4 in. Candlestick

6021—6 in. Footed Bud Vase

2619½—6 in. Vase Ground Bottom
2619½—7½ in. Vase Ground Bottom
2619½—9½ in. Vase Ground Bottom

4121—5 in. Vase

2614—10 in. Vase

4143—6 in. Footed Vase
4143—7½ in. Footed Vase

2470—10 in. Vase

Fostoria Glass Company, Moundsville, West Virginia, January 1, 1942

Fostoria Glass Company, Moundsville, West Virginia, January 1, 1942

Queen Anne Pattern No. 306

1930 Catalog

Rogene Pattern No. 269

1925 Catalog

ROSEMARY DESIGN

PLATE ETCHING No. 339

892—11 oz. Goblet
Height 5½ in.

892—7 oz. Saucer
Champagne
Height 5⅝ in.

892—6½ oz. Low Sherbet
Height 4 in.

892—4 oz. Cocktail
Height 4½ in.

892—4 oz. Claret
Height 4⅞ in.

892—12 oz. Footed
Tumbler
Height 5½ in.

892—5 oz. Footed
Tumbler
Height 3⅞ in.

892—1 oz. Cordial
Height 3⅜ in.

892—4½ oz. Oyster
Cocktail
Height 2⅞ in.

892—3 oz. Wine
Height 4⅜ in.

1769—Finger Bowl
Height 2 in.
Diameter 4⅛ in.

2337—Plate
See Price List for Sizes

6011—Footed Jug
Height 8⅞ in.
Capacity 53 ozs.

Fostoria Glass Company, Moundsville, West Virginia, January 1, 1940

ROSEMARY DESIGN

PLATE ETCHING No. 339

2364—12 in. Bowl, Flared
Height 2⅞ in.

6023—9 in. Footed Bowl
Height 4⅛ in.

6023—Duo Candlestick
Height 5½ in. Spread 6 in.

2364—13 in. Fruit Bowl
Height 2¾ in.

4143—6 in. Footed Vase
4143—7½ in. Footed Vase

2364—10½ in. Salad Bowl
2364—14 in. Torte Plate
Salad Fork & Spoon—Wood

Fostoria Glass Company, Moundsville, West Virginia, January 1, 1940

54

"ROYAL" PATTERN, PLATE ETCHING No. 273.
MADE IN AMBER, BLUE, GREEN AND CRYSTAL.
PRICED PAGES 28 AND 29 — No. 2 SUPPLEMENT PRICE LIST.
Design Patent Nos. 68,424 and 68,425.

869—9 oz. Goblet Optic.

869—6 oz. Parfait. Optic.

869—5½ oz High Sherbet. Optic.

869—5½ oz. Low Sherbet. Optic.

5100—Ftd. Shaker. Optic. F. G. Top.

869—Finger Bowl.
2283—6 in. Finger Bowl Plate. Optic.

5100—9 oz. Ftd. Tumbler. Optic.

5100—5 oz. Ftd. Tumbler. Optic.

5100—2½ oz. Ftd. Tumbler. Optic.

869—Table Tumbler. Optic.

1236—No. 6 Jug. Optic.

Fostoria Glass Company, Moundsville, West Virginia

Royal No. 273

"ROYAL" PATTERN, PLATE ETCHING No. 273.
MADE IN AMBER, BLUE, GREEN AND CRYSTAL.
PRICED PAGES 28 AND 29 — No. 2 SUPPLEMENT PRICE LIST.
Design Patent Nos. 68,424 and 68,425.

55

2350—Pickle.

2315—Sugar.

2315½—Cream.

2350—Butter and Cover.

2350—Cream Soup.
2332—7 in. Cream Soup Plate.

2367—7 in. Bowl.

2350—6 in. Cereal.

2350½—Ftd. Tea Cup.
2350—Saucer.

1927 Catalog

SAMPLER DESIGN

PLATE ETCHING No. 337

6025—10 oz. Goblet
Height 5½ in.

6025—6 oz. Sherbet
Height 3¾ in.

6025—3½ oz. Cocktail
Height 3½ in.

6025—4 oz. Claret-Wine
Height 4 in.

6025—12 oz. Footed Tumbler
Height 5⅝ in.

6025—5 oz. Footed Tumbler
Height 4¼ in.

6025—4 oz. Oyster Cocktail
Height 3½ in.

6025—1 oz. Cordial
Height 2⅞ in.

2574—Footed Sugar
Height 3¾ in.

1769—Finger Bowl

2574—Individual Sugar
Height 2⅞ in.

2574—Individual Cream
Height 3½ in. Capacity 5¾ oz.

2574—Plate
See Price List for Sizes

2574—Footed Cream
Height 4 in. Capacity 6½ oz.

6011—Footed Jug
Capacity 53 oz.
Height 8⅞ in.

Fostoria Glass Company, Moundsville, West Virginia, Jan. 1, 1939

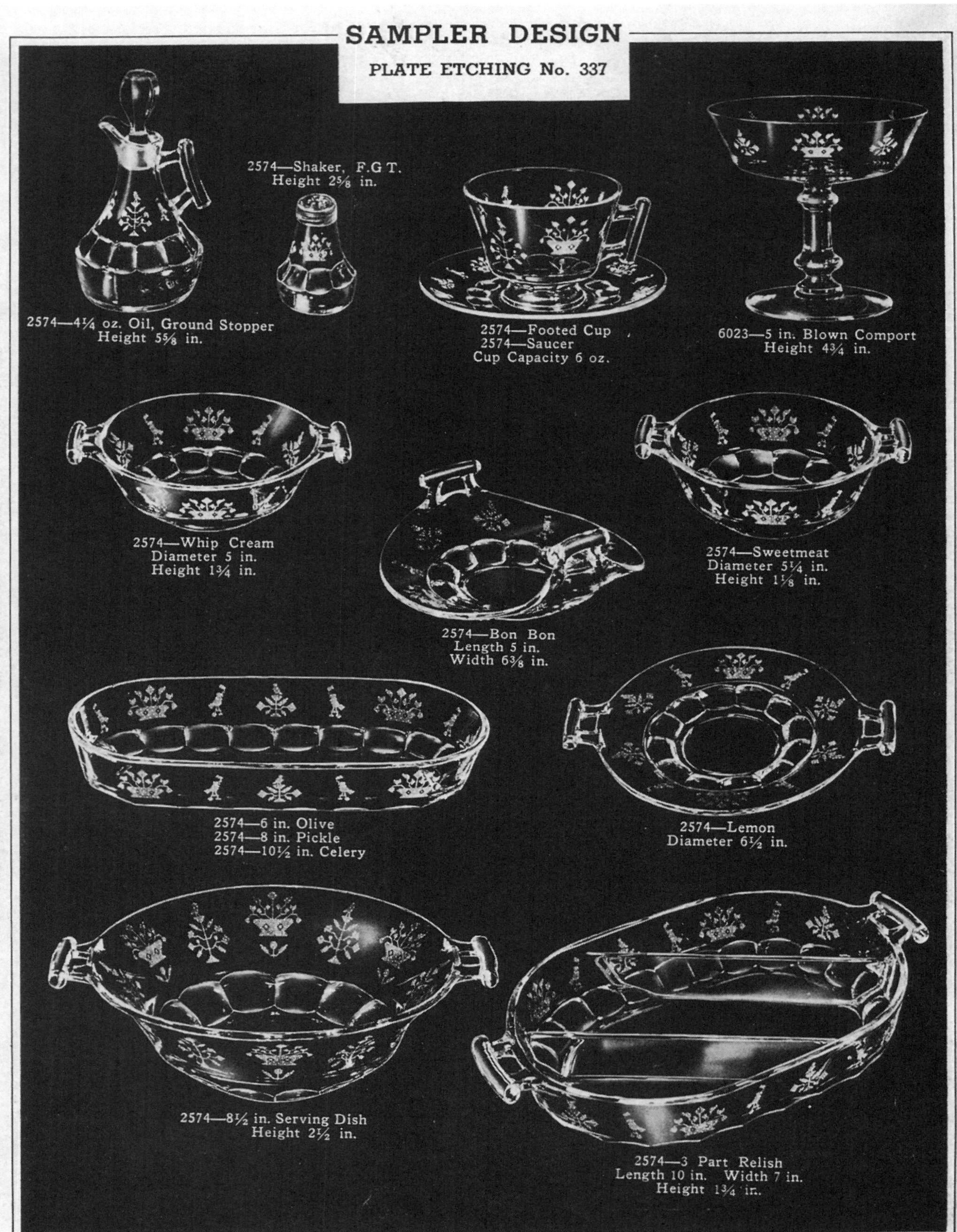
SAMPLER DESIGN
PLATE ETCHING No. 337
2574—Shaker, F.G.T.
Height 2⅝ in.
2574—4¼ oz. Oil, Ground Stopper
Height 5⅝ in.
2574—Footed Cup
2574—Saucer
Cup Capacity 6 oz.
6023—5 in. Blown Comport
Height 4¾ in.
2574—Whip Cream
Diameter 5 in.
Height 1¾ in.
2574—Sweetmeat
Diameter 5¼ in.
Height 1⅞ in.
2574—Bon Bon
Length 5 in.
Width 6⅜ in.
2574—6 in. Olive
2574—8 in. Pickle
2574—10½ in. Celery
2574—Lemon
Diameter 6½ in.
2574—8½ in. Serving Dish
Height 2½ in.
2574—3 Part Relish
Length 10 in. Width 7 in.
Height 1¾ in.

56
"SEVILLE" PATTERN, PLATE ETCHING No. 274.
MADE IN AMBER, GREEN AND CRYSTAL.
PRICED PAGES 30 AND 31 — No. 2 SUPPLEMENT PRICE LIST.
Design Patent Applied For.
5084—12 oz. Ftd. Tumbler, Optic.
5084—9 oz. Ftd. Tumbler, Optic.
5084—5 oz. Ftd. Tumbler, Optic.
945½—Grape Fruit.
945½—Grape Fruit Liner, Optic.
870—9 oz. Goblet, Optic.
870—5½ oz. High Sherbet, Optic.
870—5½ oz. Low Sherbet, Optic.
870—Oyster Cocktail, Optic.
Fostoria Glass Company, Moundsville, West Virginia

Seville No. 274

1927 Catalog

SHIRLEY DESIGN

PLATE ETCHING No. 331

DESIGN PATENT NO. 107837

6017—9 oz. Goblet
Height 7⅜ in.

6017
6 oz. Saucer Champagne
Height 5½ in.

6017—6 oz. Low Sherbet
Height 4½ in.

6017—3½ oz. Cocktail
Height 4⅞ in.

6017—4 oz. Claret
Height 5⅞ in.

6017—3 oz. Wine
Height 5½ in.

6017—¾ oz. Cordial
Height 3⅞ in.

6017
4 oz. Oyster Cocktail
Height 3⅝ in.

6017
14 oz. Footed Tumbler
Height 6½ in.

6017
12 oz. Footed Tumbler
Height 6 in.

6017
9 oz. Footed Tumbler
Height 5½ in.

6017
5 oz. Footed Tumbler
Height 4¾ in.

766—Finger Bowl

2350½—Footed Cup
2350 —Saucer

2496—Individual Cream
Height 3¼ in.
Capacity 4 oz.

2337—Plate
See Price List for Sizes

2496—Individual Sugar
Height 2⅞ in.

6011—Footed Jug
Capacity 53 oz.
Height 8⅞ in.

Fostoria Glass Company, Moundsville, West Virginia, Jan. 1, 1939

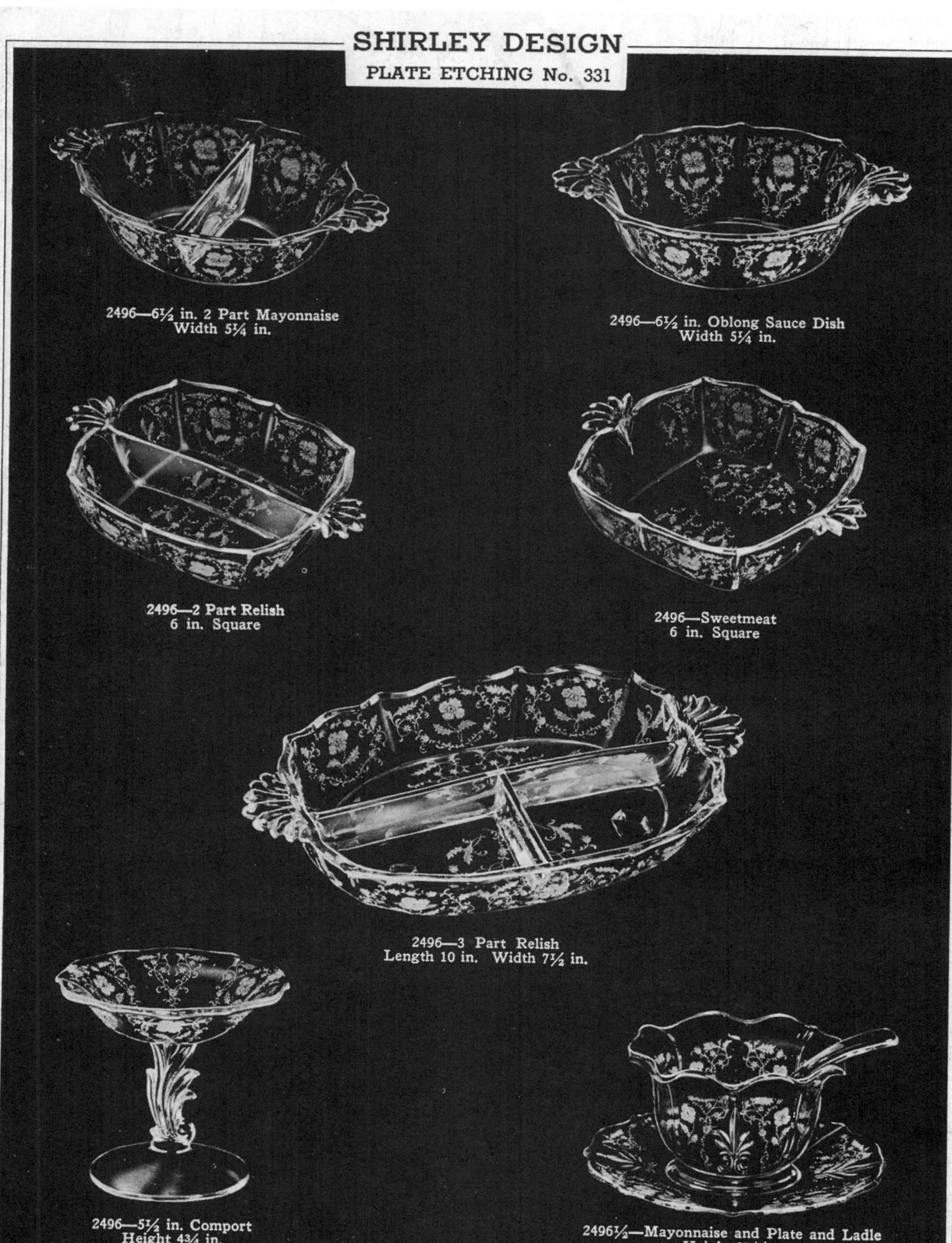
SHIRLEY DESIGN
PLATE ETCHING No. 331
2496—6½ in. 2 Part Mayonnaise
Width 5¼ in.
2496—6½ in. Oblong Sauce Dish
Width 5¼ in.
2496—2 Part Relish
6 in. Square
2496—Sweetmeat
6 in. Square
2496—3 Part Relish
Length 10 in. Width 7½ in.
2496—5½ in. Comport
Height 4¾ in.
2496½—Mayonnaise and Plate and Ladle
Height 3½ in.
Fostoria Glass Company, Moundsville, West Virginia, Jan. 1, 1939

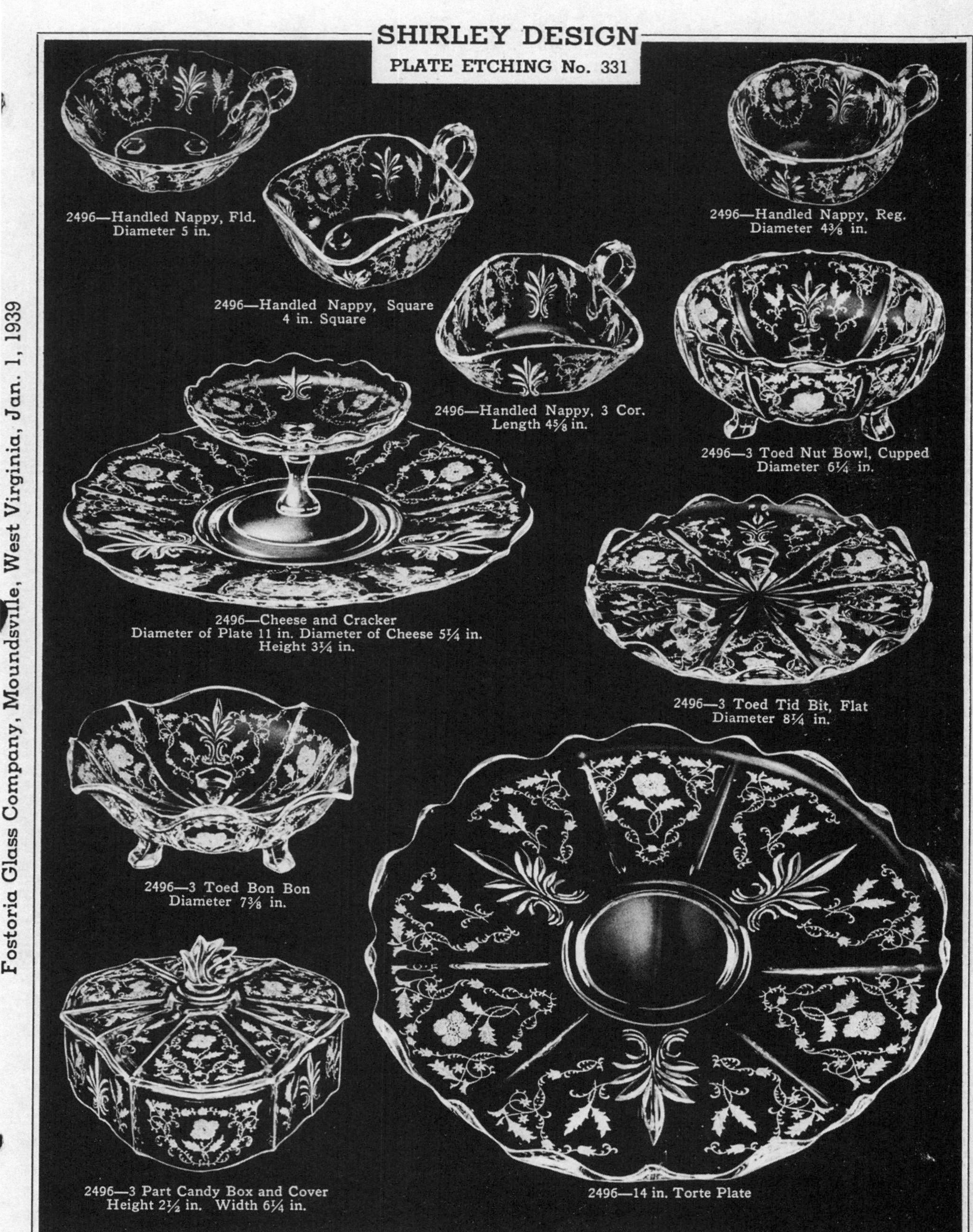
SHIRLEY DESIGN
PLATE ETCHING No. 331
Fostoria Glass Company, Moundsville, West Virginia, Jan. 1, 1939
2496—Handled Nappy, Fld. Diameter 5 in.
2496—Handled Nappy, Square 4 in. Square
2496—Handled Nappy, Reg. Diameter 4⅜ in.
2496—Handled Nappy, 3 Cor. Length 4⅝ in.
2496—3 Toed Nut Bowl, Cupped Diameter 6¼ in.
2496—Cheese and Cracker Diameter of Plate 11 in. Diameter of Cheese 5¼ in. Height 3¼ in.
2496—3 Toed Tid Bit, Flat Diameter 8¼ in.
2496—3 Toed Bon Bon Diameter 7⅜ in.
2496—3 Part Candy Box and Cover Height 2½ in. Width 6¼ in.
2496—14 in. Torte Plate

SHIRLEY DESIGN
PLATE ETCHING No. 331
2496—12 in. Bowl, Flared
Height 3½ in.
2496—4 in. Candlestick
2496—Duo Candlestick
Height 4½ in. Spread 8 in.
2496—5½ in. Candlestick
2496—10½ in. Handled Bowl
Height 3⅜ in.
Fostoria Glass Company, Moundsville, West Virginia, Jan. 1, 1939

2545—10 in. Vase

2545—"Flame" Duo Candlestick
Height 6¾ in. Spread 10¼ in

2545—4½ in. "Flame" Candlestick

2545—2 Light "Flame" Candelabra Using 12 "B" Prisms
Height 6¾ in. Spread 11 in.

2545—12½ in. "Flame" Oval Bowl
Height 2⅞ in.

2545—"Flame" Lustre
Using 8 U. D. P.
Height 7½ in.

STARFLOWER DESIGNS
Plate Etching No. 345
FOSTORIA GLASS COMPANY, MOUNDSVILLE, WEST VIRGINIA — 1952
6049 — 11¼ oz. Goblet Height 7 in.
6049 — 7¼ oz. High Sherbet (Champagne) Height 5¼ in.
6049 — 7¼ oz. Low Sherbet Height 4⅜ in.
6049 — 4 oz. Cocktail Height 4⅞ in.
6049 — 5 oz. Claret Height 5⅝ in.
6049 — 4 oz. Wine Height 5⅛ in.
6049 — 1¼ oz. Cordial Height 3½ in.
6049 — 6¾ oz. Parfait Height 6 in.
6049 — 4½ oz. Oyster Cocktail Height 4 in.
6049 — 15¼ oz. Footed Ice Tea Height 6¼ in.
6049 — 5¾ oz. Footed Juice Height 4⅞ in.
2630 — 14 in. Torte Plate
2630 — 16 in. Torte Plate
2630 — 6 in. Plate
2630 — 7 in. Plate
2630 — 8 in. Plate
2630 — 9 in. Plate
2630 — 10½ in. Dinner Plate
2630 Handled Cake Plate
2630 — Footed Cup Cup Capacity 6 oz.
2630 — Saucer

STARFLOWER DESIGNS
Plate Etching No. 345

2630
3 Pint Ice Jug
Height 7-1/8 in.

2630
Pint Cereal Pitcher
Height 6-1/8 in.

2630
Ice Bucket
Height 4-7/8 in. Top Dia. 7-3/8 in.
Chromium Handle and Tongs
Tongs priced separately

2630
Candy Jar and Cover
Height 7 in.

2630
3 Piece Tid Bit Set
Metal Handle
Height 10-1/4 in.

2630
2-part Mayonnaise
and 2 Ladles
Height 3-3/8 in.

2630
Mustard, Cover and Spoon
Height 4 in.

2630
Cheese and Cracker
Height 2-3/4 in.
Plate Diameter—10-3/4 in.
Cheese Diameter—5-3/8 in.
Cheese Height—2-1/2 in.

2630 — 10-1/2 in.
Snack Tray

2630
Snack Bowl
Height 3-1/2 in.

FOSTORIA GLASS COMPANY, MOUNDSVILLE, WEST VIRGINIA — 1952

STARFLOWER DESIGNS
Plate Etching No. 345
FOSTORIA GLASS COMPANY, MOUNDSVILLE, WEST VIRGINIA — 1952
2470 — 10 in. Footed Vase
4143 — 6 in. Footed Vase
2657 — 10½ in. Footed Vase
5092 — 8 in. Footed Bud Vase
2630 — 6 in. Bud Vase
6021 — 6 in. Footed Bud Vase
4121 — 5 in. Vase
2630 — 8½ in. Oval Vase
2660 — 8 in. Flip Vase
2630 — 7½ in. Handled Vase

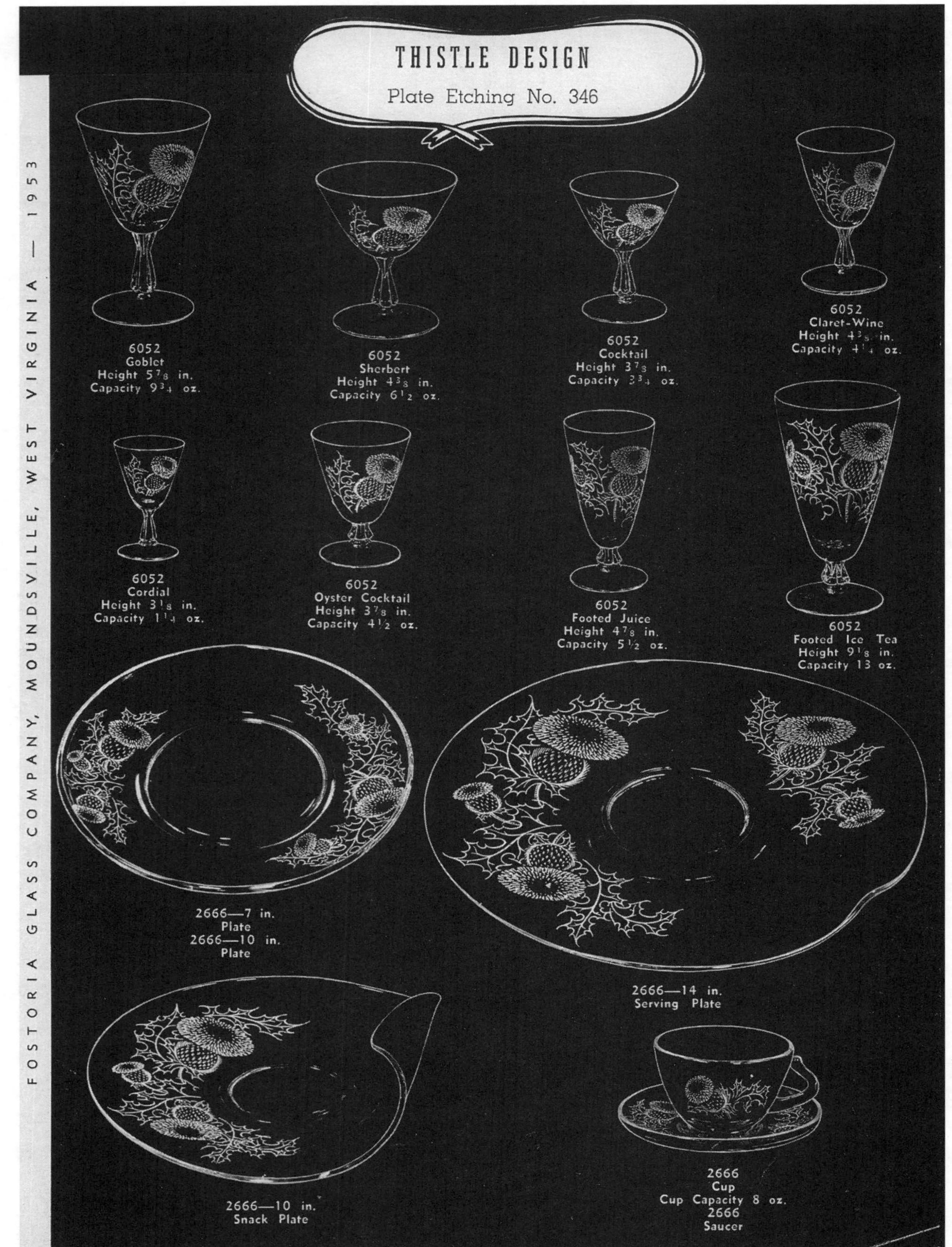

FOSTORIA GLASS COMPANY, MOUNDSVILLE, WEST VIRGINIA — 1953

THISTLE DESIGN

Plate Etching No. 346

6052 Goblet
Height 5 7/8 in.
Capacity 9 3/4 oz.

6052 Sherbert
Height 4 3/8 in.
Capacity 6 1/2 oz.

6052 Cocktail
Height 3 7/8 in.
Capacity 3 3/4 oz.

6052 Claret-Wine
Height 4 3/8 in.
Capacity 4 1/4 oz.

6052 Cordial
Height 3 1/8 in.
Capacity 1 1/4 oz.

6052 Oyster Cocktail
Height 3 7/8 in.
Capacity 4 1/2 oz.

6052 Footed Juice
Height 4 7/8 in.
Capacity 5 1/2 oz.

6052 Footed Ice Tea
Height 9 1/8 in.
Capacity 13 oz.

2666—7 in. Plate
2666—10 in. Plate

2666—14 in. Serving Plate

2666—10 in. Snack Plate

2666 Cup
Cup Capacity 8 oz.
2666 Saucer

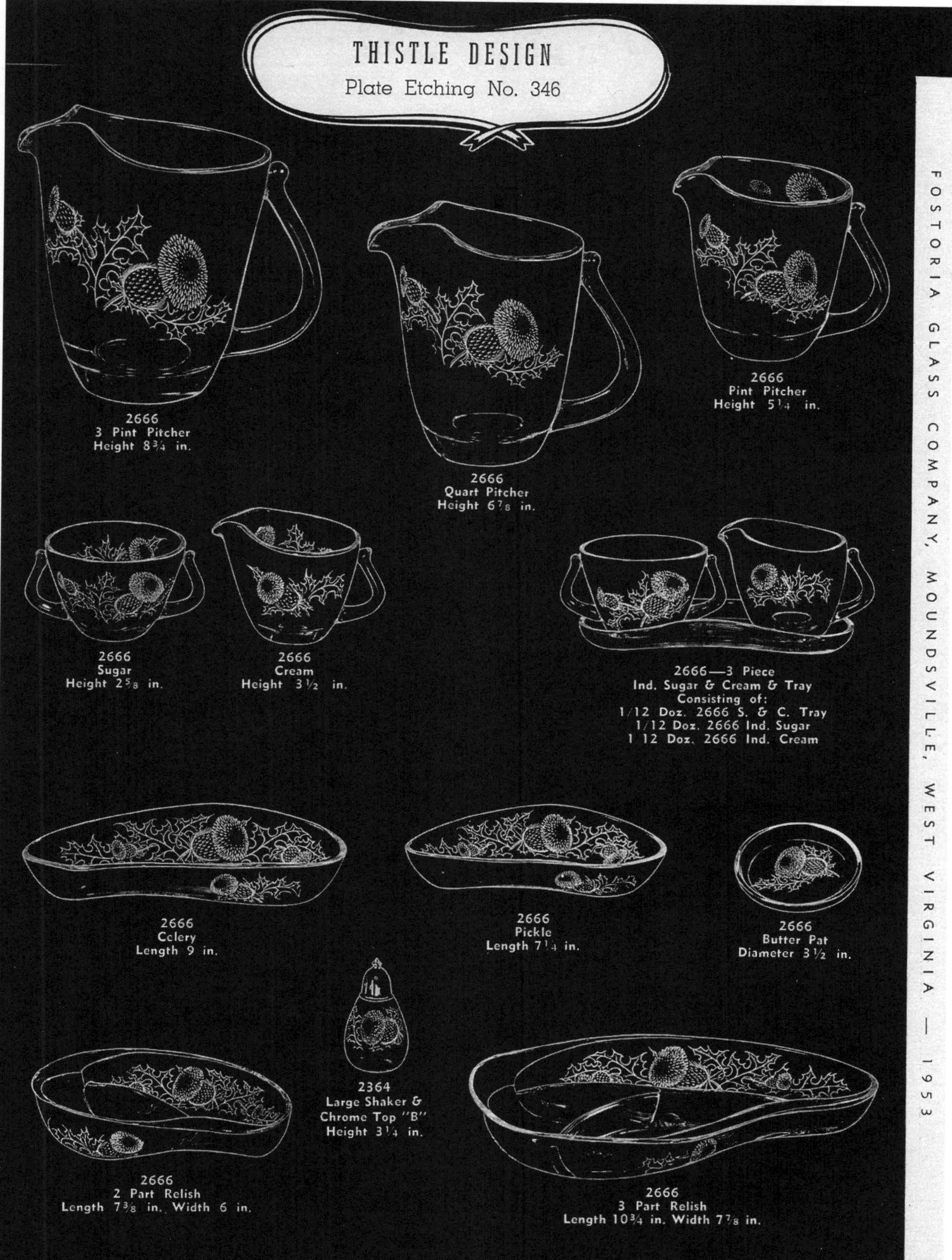
THISTLE DESIGN
Plate Etching No. 346
2666
3 Pint Pitcher
Height 8¾ in.
2666
Quart Pitcher
Height 6⅞ in.
2666
Pint Pitcher
Height 5¼ in.
2666
Sugar
Height 2⅝ in.
2666
Cream
Height 3½ in.
2666—3 Piece
Ind. Sugar & Cream & Tray
Consisting of:
1/12 Doz. 2666 S. & C. Tray
1/12 Doz. 2666 Ind. Sugar
1/12 Doz. 2666 Ind. Cream
2666
Celery
Length 9 in.
2666
Pickle
Length 7¼ in.
2666
Butter Pat
Diameter 3½ in.
2364
Large Shaker & Chrome Top "B"
Height 3¼ in.
2666
2 Part Relish
Length 7⅜ in. Width 6 in.
2666
3 Part Relish
Length 10¾ in. Width 7⅞ in.
FOSTORIA GLASS COMPANY, MOUNDSVILLE, WEST VIRGINIA — 1953

Trojan Design No. 280

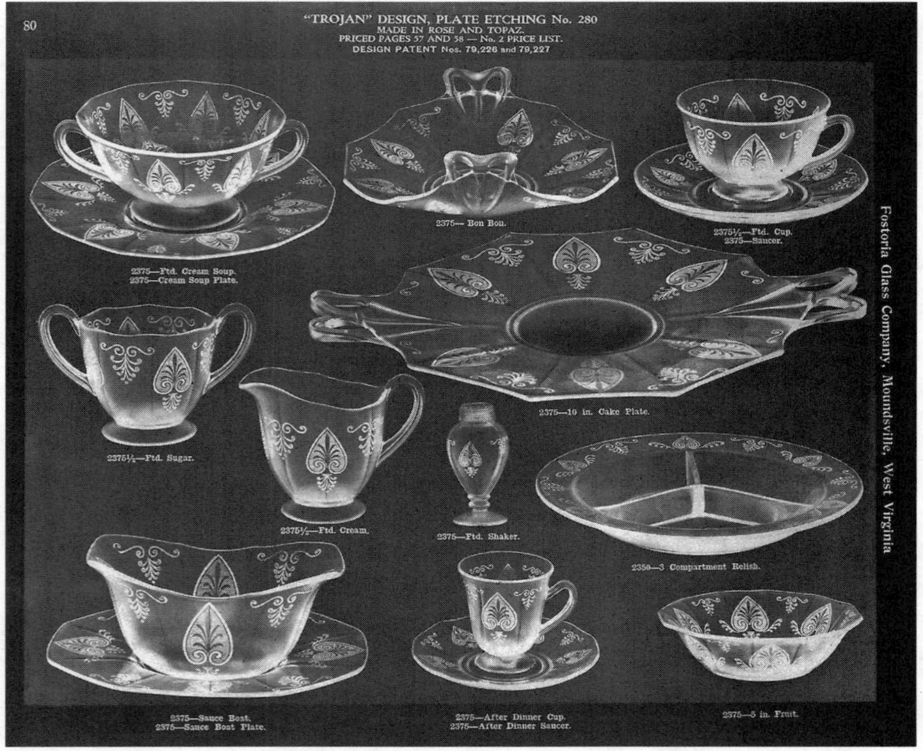

1930 Catalog

Trojan Design No. 280

1930 Catalog

Verona Design No. 281

1930 Catalog

Vernon Pattern, No. 277

1930 Catalog

Vesper Pattern, No. 275

1926 Catalog

58

"VESPER" PATTERN, PLATE ETCHING No. 275.
MADE IN AMBER, BLUE AND GREEN.
PRICED PAGES 32 AND 33—No. 2 SUPPLEMENT PRICE LIST.
Design Patent Nos. 70,356 and 70,357.

No. 5100—12 oz. Ftd. Tumbler, Optic.

No. 5100—9 oz. Ftd. Tumbler, Optic.

No. 5100—5 oz. Ftd. Tumbler, Optic.

No. 5082½—Grape Fruit.
No. 945½—G. F. Liner, Optic.

No. 869—Finger Bowl.
No. 2283—6 in. F. B. Plate, Optic.

No. 5093—9 oz. Goblet, Optic.

No. 5093—6 oz. Parfait, Optic.

No. 5093—5½ oz. High Sherbet, Optic.

No. 5093—5 oz. Low Sherbet, Optic.

No. 5093—Oyster Cocktail, Optic.

Fostoria Glass Company, Moundsville, West Virginia

Vesper Pattern, No. 275
1927 Catalog

"VESPER" PATTERN, PLATE ETCHING No. 275.
MADE IN AMBER, BLUE AND GREEN.
PRICED PAGES 32 AND 33—No. 2 SUPPLEMENT PRICE LIST.
Design Patent Nos. 70,356 and 70,357.

59

2350—7 in. Salad Plate.

2350—Cup.
2350—Saucer.

2350—7 in. Soup Plate.
2350—9 in. Dinner Plate.

2350—Cream Soup.

2350—Celery.

2368—Ftd. Cheese.
2368—11 in. Cracker Plate.

Fostoria Glass Company, Moundsville, West Virginia

72

"VERSAILLES" DESIGN, PLATE ETCHING No. 278.
MADE IN ROSE, AZURE, GREEN AND TOPAZ.
PRICED PAGES 49 AND 50 — No. 2 PRICE LIST — TOPAZ PRICED PAGES 51 AND 52.
DESIGN PATENT Nos. 76,372 and 76,454

5299—Goblet. Made in Topaz only.

5299—High Sherbet. Made in Topaz only.

5299—Low Sherbet. Made in Topaz only.

5299—9 oz. Ftd. Tumbler. Made in Topaz only.

2375½—Candlestick.

2375—12 in. Centerpiece.
2309—3¾ in. Flower Block.

2375½—Candlestick.

Fostoria Glass Company, Moundsville, West Virginia

Versailles Pattern No. 278

1930 Catalog

"VERSAILLES" DESIGN, PLATE ETCHING No. 278.
MADE IN ROSE, AZURE, GREEN AND TOPAZ.
PRICED PAGES 49 AND 50—No. 2 PRICE LIST—TOPAZ PRICED PAGES 51 AND 52.
DESIGN PATENT Nos. 76,372 and 76,464

73

2375—Ftd. Cream Soup.
2375—Cream Soup Plate.

2375—Ftd. Bouillon.
2375—Saucer.

2375—Ftd. Shaker.

2375½—Ftd. Sugar and Cover.

2375½—Ftd. Cream

2375½—Ftd. Cup.
2375—Saucer.

2375—6 in. Cereal.

2375—After Dinner Cup.
2375—After Dinner Saucer.

2375—Mayonnaise.
2375—Mayonnaise Plate.
2375—Mayonnaise Ladle.

Fostoria Glass Company, Moundsville, West Virginia

Versailles Design No. 278

1930 Catalog

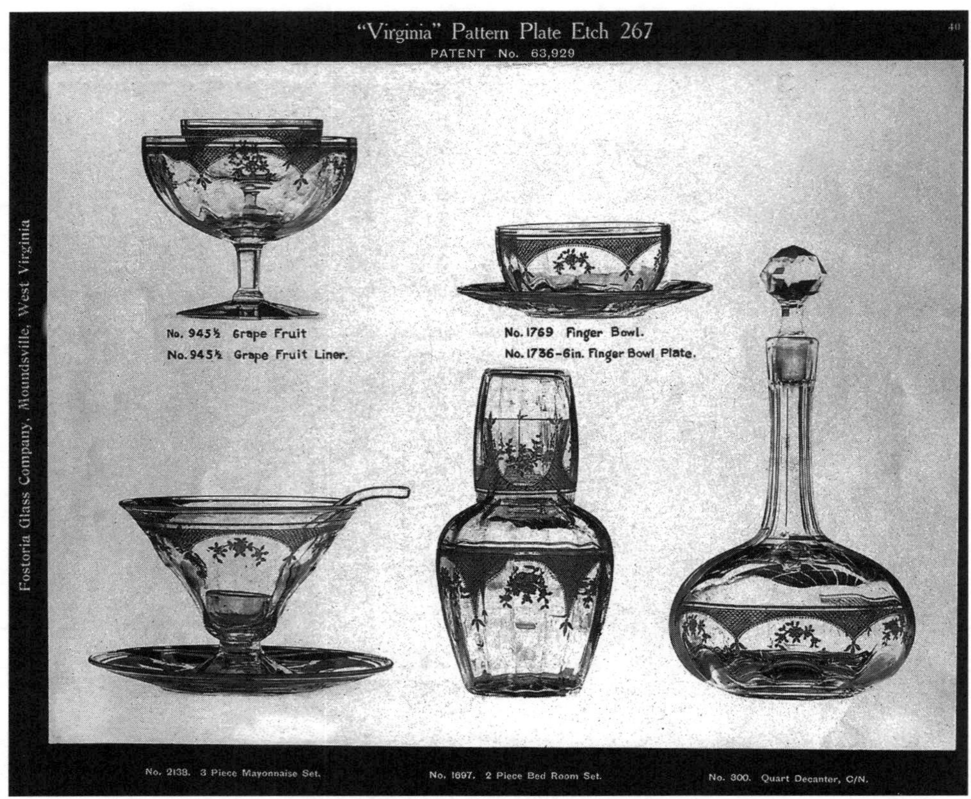

1926 Catalog

"Victory" Pattern, Plate Etching No. 257
PRICED PAGE 49, No. 1 PRICE List.
27-C
Fostoria Glass Company, Moundsville, West Virginia
766-4½ oz. Claret Optic
766-2¾ oz. Wine Optic
4011-5 oz. Tumbler Optic
4011-8 oz. Tumbler Optic
4011-12 oz. Tumbler Optic
766-¾ oz. Cordial Optic
837-4 oz. Oyster Cocktail Optic
4011-3 oz. Tumbler Optic
766-9 oz. Goblet Optic
766-5 oz. High Sherbet Optic
766-5 oz. Low Sherbet Optic
766-3 oz Cocktail Optic
763½-6 oz. Parfait Optic

1926 Catalog

Fostoria Glass Company, Moundsville, West Virginia, Jan. 1, 1939

WILLOW DESIGN
PLATE ETCHING No. 335
6023—9 oz. Goblet
Height 6⅜ in.
6023—6 oz.
Saucer Champagne
Height 4⅞ in.
6023—6 oz.
Low Sherbet
Height 4⅛ in.
6023—3¾ oz.
Cocktail
Height 4⅜ in.
6023—4 oz.
Claret-Wine
Height 4¾ in.
6023—12 oz.
Footed Tumbler
Height 5¾ in.
6023—9 oz.
Footed Tumbler
Height 5⅛ in.
6023—5 oz.
Footed Tumbler
Height 4½ in.
6023—1 oz. Cordial
Height 3⅜ in.
6023—4 oz.
Oyster Cocktail
Height 3⅝ in.
766—Finger Bowl
2574—Individual Sugar
Height 2⅞ in.
2574—Individual Cream
Height 3½ in. Capacity 5¾ oz.
2574—Footed Sugar
2574—Plate
See Price List For Sizes
6011—Footed Jug
Capacity 53 oz.
Height 8⅞ in.
2574—Footed Cream
Height 4 in. Capacity 6½ oz.

WILLOW DESIGN

PLATE ETCHING No. 335

2574—9½ in. Handled Bowl
Height 3⅜ in.

2574—5 in. Comport
Height 4⅞ in.

2574—4 in. Candlestick

2324—6 in. Candlestick

6023—Footed Bowl
Diameter 9¼ in.
Height 4¼ in.

Fostoria Glass Company, Moundsville, West Virginia, Jan. 1, 1939

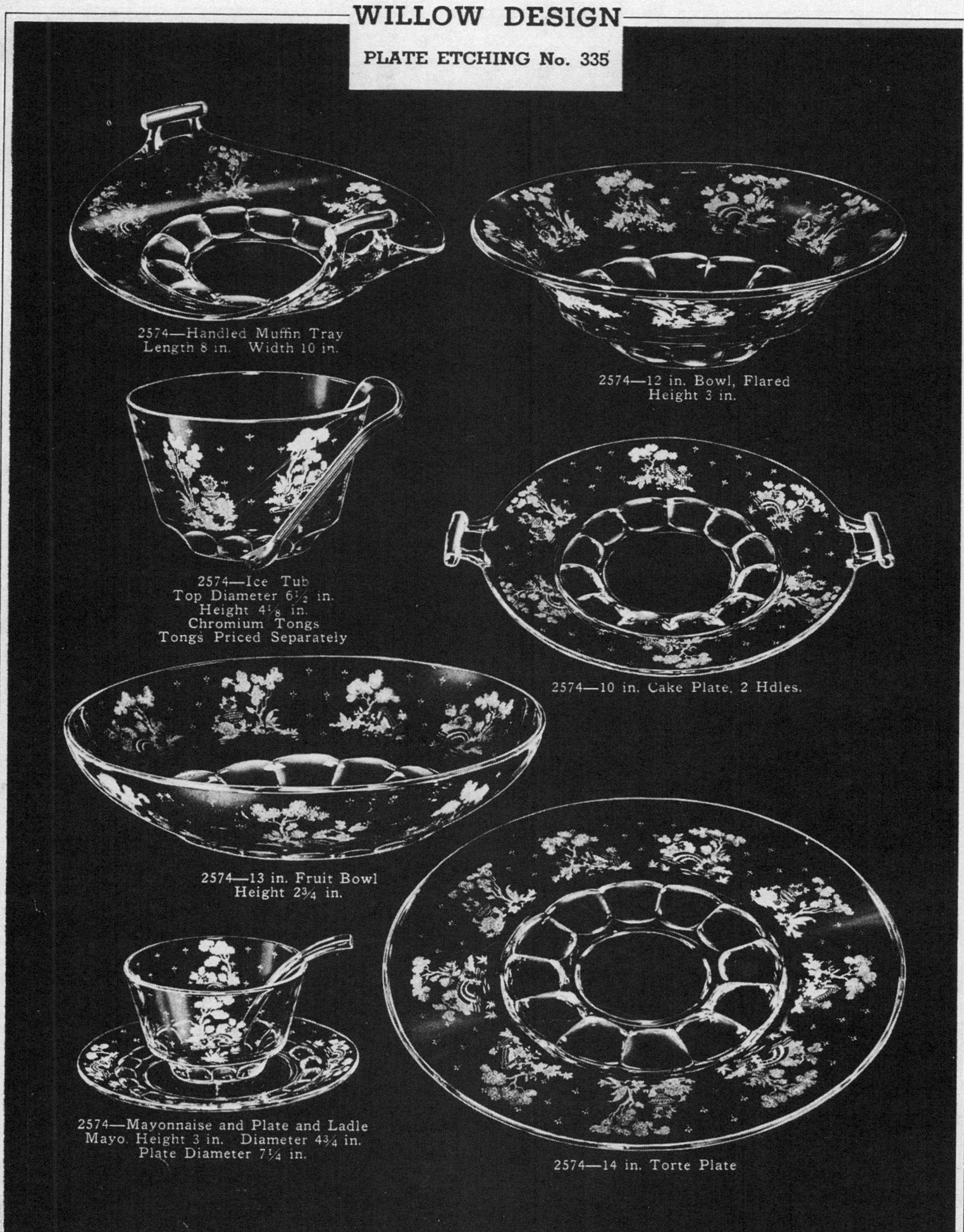

Fostoria Glass Company, Moundsville, West Virginia, July 1, 1939

WILLOWMERE DESIGN

PLATE ETCHING No. 333

6024—10 oz. Goblet
Height 7⅛ in.

6024—6 oz.
Saucer Champagne
Height 5⅝ in.

6024—6 oz.
Low Sherbet
Height 4¼ in.

6024—3½ oz.
Cocktail
Height 4¾ in.

6024—4 oz.
Claret
Height 5¾ in.

6024—3½ oz.
Wine
Height 5⅜ in.

6024—12 oz.
Footed Tumbler
Height 5¾ in.

6024—9 oz.
Footed Tumbler
Height 5¼ in.

6024—5 oz.
Footed Tumbler
Height 4⅝ in.

6024—1 oz.
Cordial
Height 3¾ in.

6024
4½ oz. Oyster Cocktail
Height 3½ in.

869—Finger Bowl

2560—Footed Cup
2560—Saucer
Cup Capacity 5½ oz.

2560
Footed Shaker
F. G. T.
Height 2⅞ in.

2560—Footed Cream
Height 4⅛ in.
Capacity 7 oz.

2560—Individual Sugar
Height 3 in.

2560—Individual Cream
Height 3¼ in.
Capacity 4 oz.

2560—Footed Sugar
Height 3½ in.

5000—7 Footed Jug
Height 9¾ in. Capacity 3 Pints

Fostoria Glass Company, Moundsville, West Virginia, Jan. 1, 1939

WILLOWMERE DESIGN

PLATE ETCHING No. 333

2560—11½ in. Bowl, Crimped
Height 3¼ in.

2560½—4 in. Candlestick

2560—Duo Candlestick
Height 5⅛ in.
Spread 9 in.

2560—11 in. Handled Bowl
Height 3¼ in.

2560—4½ in. Candlestick

2560—12 in. Bowl, Flared
Height 3¼ in.

Fostoria Glass Company, Moundsville, West Virginia, Jan. 1, 1939

Fostoria Glass Company, Moundsville, West Virginia, Jan. 1, 1939

WILLOWMERE DESIGN

PLATE ETCHING No. 333

2567—7½ in. Vase

2568—9 in. Vase

2470—10 in. Vase

5100—10 in. Vase

1926 Catalog

Crystal *or Clear Glass*

Crystal ware, the white or clear glass, like solid silver, fine linen, real lace, never goes out of fashion. It is ever the most aristocratic glassware, established by tradition and its own magic.

Delicately etched, handsomely cut, crystal tableware is perhaps the most formal sort of glassware. Its icy dazzle, its sparkling brilliance are in keeping with the most elegant table appointments.

Colored glassware is friendly, more appropriate for the informal table-settings and is permanently in the mode; yet for certain occasions many people prefer to have a service of crystal.

The complete Fostoria dinner service is made in crystal, intricately etched, engraved and plain. Fostoria crystal stemware—the goblets, the wine glasses, the sherbets, parfaits, and cocktail glasses as well as the more informal tumblers and iced-tea glasses are made in a great variety of designs and patterns. Some very fragile. Others in the new, more fanciful manner. Also the coin-gold-banded ware that is always correct.

Genuine Fostoria is also made in green, azure, dawn, amber, orchid and a very lovely iridescent ware. The finish of this is absolutely permanent and its delicate colors appeal to those who wish something at once formal and friendly, colorful in a conservative way.

10

The New Little Book About Glassware
Fostoria Glass Company, 1928

Dinnerware, Stems, and Tumblers, Needle Etched

"BRUNSWICK" PATTERN, NEEDLE ETCHING No. 79.
MADE IN CRYSTAL, AMBER, BLUE AND GREEN.
PRICED PAGE 25 — No. 2 SUPPLEMENT PRICE LIST.
Design Patent No. 70,366.

Fostoria Glass Company, Moundsville, West Virginia

No. 5084—9 oz. Ftd. Tumbler. Optic.

No. 869—Table Tumbler. Optic.

No. 869—5 oz. Tumbler. Optic.

No. 5084—5 oz. Ftd. Tumbler. Optic.

No. 870—9 oz. Goblet. Optic.

No. 870—5½ oz. High Sherbet. Optic.

No. 870—5½ oz. Low Sherbet. Optic.

No. 870—Oyster Cocktail. Optic.

Brunswick No. 79
1927 Catalog

Avalon No. 85

5200—12 oz. Ftd. Tumbler.

5200—9 oz. Ftd. Tumbler.

5200—5 oz. Ftd. Tumbler.

5282½—Grape Fruit.
945½—G. F. Liner.

869—Finger Bowl.
2283—6 in. Plate, R/O.

5293—Goblet.

5293—High Sherbet.

5293—Low Sherbet.

5200—Oyster Cocktail.

Fostoria Glass Company, Moundsville, West Virginia

44

"CORDELIA" PATTERN, NEEDLE ETCHING No. 82.
MADE IN GREEN AND ORCHID.
PRICED PAGE 22A—No. 2 SUPPLEMENT PRICE LIST.

877—4 oz. Claret. Optic.

877—3½ oz. Cocktail. Optic.

877—2¾ oz. Wine. Optic.

877—Grape Fruit.
877—G. F. Liner (945½).
Optic.

877—¾ oz. Cordial. Optic.

877—10 oz. Goblet. Optic.

877—6 oz. High Sherbet. Optic.

877—6 oz. Low Sherbet. Optic.

877—4½ oz. Oyster Cocktail. Optic.

Cordelia Pattern No. 82
1927 Catalog

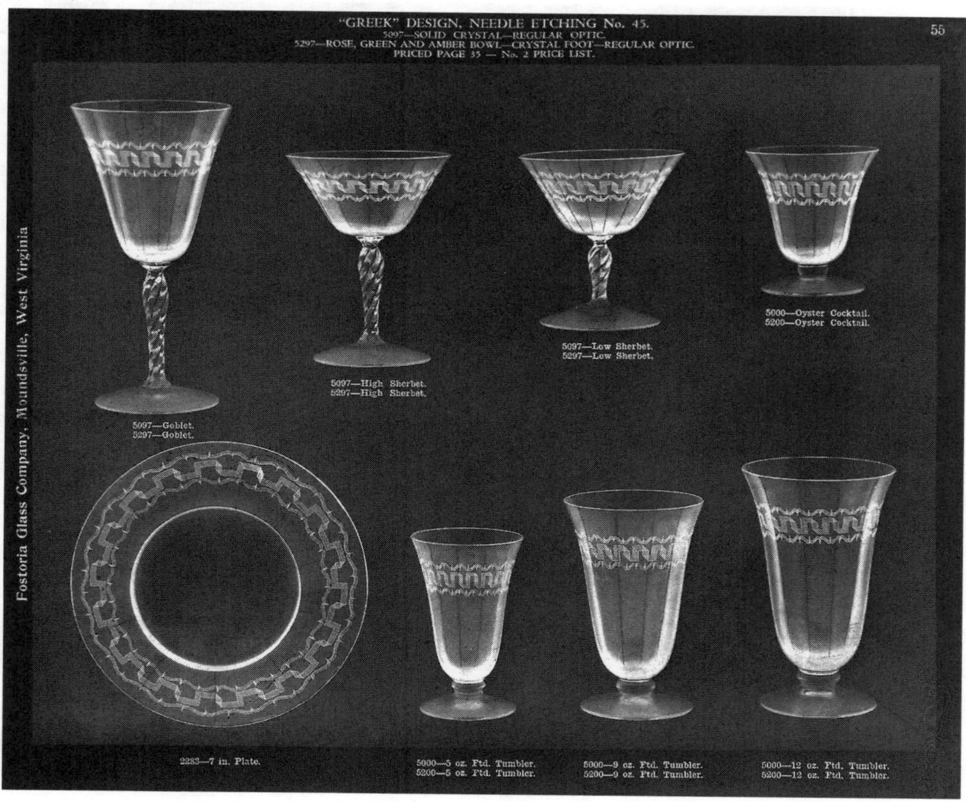

"GREEK" DESIGN, NEEDLE ETCHING No. 45.
5097—SOLID CRYSTAL—REGULAR OPTIC.
5297—ROSE, GREEN AND AMBER BOWL—CRYSTAL FOOT—REGULAR OPTIC.
PRICED PAGE 35 — No. 2 PRICE LIST.

55

5097—Goblet.
5297—Goblet.

5097—High Sherbet.
5297—High Sherbet.

5097—Low Sherbet.
5297—Low Sherbet.

5000—Oyster Cocktail.
5200—Oyster Cocktail.

2283—7 in. Plate.

5000—5 oz. Ftd. Tumbler.
5200—5 oz. Ftd. Tumbler.

5000—9 oz. Ftd. Tumbler.
5200—9 oz. Ftd. Tumbler.

5000—12 oz. Ftd. Tumbler.
5200—12 oz. Ftd. Tumbler.

Fostoria Glass Company, Moundsville, West Virginia

Greek Design No. 45
1930 Catalog

1926 Catalog

1926 Catalog

Spartan Pattern, Needle Etching No. 80

1927 Catalog

46

"SPARTAN" PATTERN, NEEDLE ETCHING No. 80.
MADE IN AMBER, GREEN AND ORCHID BOWL WITH CRYSTAL STEM AND FOOT; ALSO SOLID CRYSTAL.
PRICED PAGE 26 — No. 2 SUPPLEMENT PRICE LIST.
Patent Applied for.

No. 5297 5½ oz. Parfait. Optic.

No. 5297—3 oz. Cocktail. Optic.

No. 5297—2½ oz. Wine. Optic.

No. 5297½—Grape Fruit. No. 945½—Grape Fruit Liner. Optic.

No. 5297—9 oz. Goblet. Optic.

No. 5297—5½ oz. High Sherbet. Optic.

No. 5297—5½ oz. Low Sherbet. Optic.

No. 5200—Oyster Cocktail. Optic.

Fostoria Glass Company, Moundsville, West Virginia

"SPARTAN" PATTERN, NEEDLE ETCHING No. 80.
MADE IN AMBER, GREEN AND ORCHID BOWL WITH CRYSTAL STEM AND FOOT; ALSO SOLID CRYSTAL.
PRICED PAGE 26 — No. 2 SUPPLEMENT PRICE LIST.
Patent Applied for.

47

2283—7 in. Plate.

5200—2½ oz. Ftd. Tumbler. Optic.

869—Finger Bowl. 2283—6 in. Finger Bowl Plate. Optic.

5200—5 oz. Ftd. Tumbler. Optic.

5200—9 oz. Ftd. Tumbler. Optic.

5200—12 oz. Ftd. Tumbler. Optic.

5200—No. 7 Jug. Optic.

Fostoria Glass Company, Moundsville, West Virginia

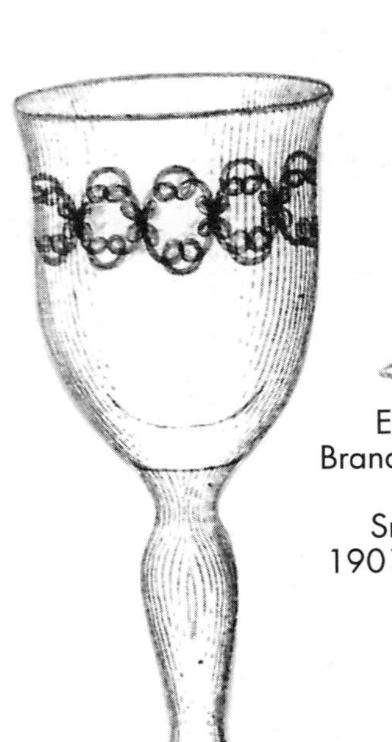

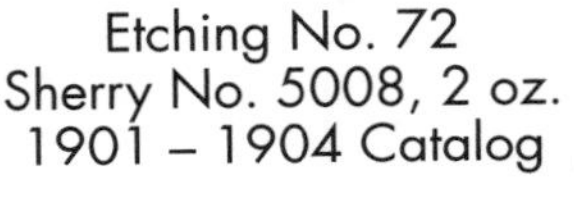

Etching No. 67
Brandy No. 810, 1 oz.
Blown
Small Cloverleaf
1901 – 1904 Catalog

Etching No. 72
Sherry No. 5008, 2 oz.
1901 – 1904 Catalog

Etching No. 48
Water Pitcher, No. 318
1898 Catalog

Etching No. 48
Covered Sugar, No. 315
1898 Catalog

Etching No. 48
Cream No. 315
1898 Catalog

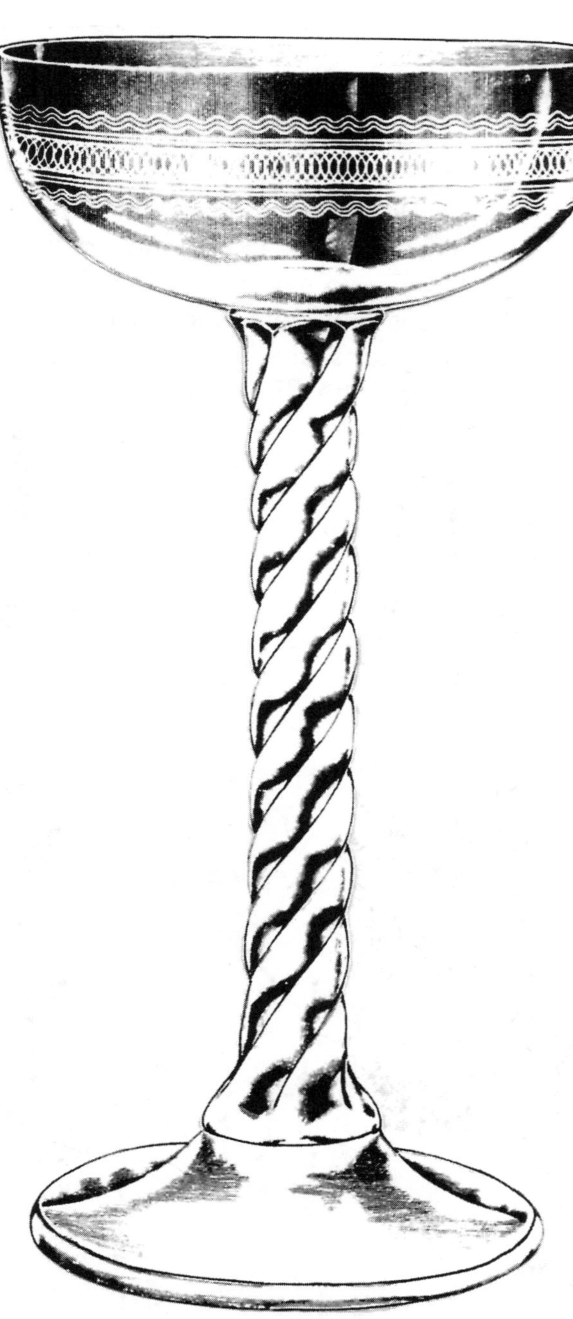

Etching No. 48
Roemer, Height 13½" – 14"
1898 Catalog

Etching No. 48
Hock No. 1402
Height 13", 1898 Catalog

Dinnerware, Pressed

Alexis Pattern
No. 1630 Line

Alexis is a highly collectible older Fostoria pressed pattern. It was introduced in 1909 and carried through the early 1920s. The line contains in excess of 75 different pieces. There are also a number of pieces that were sold with fitted metal lids or parts. Eight sizes of oils or catsups are known and at least five beverage pitchers were produced. The $3\frac{7}{8}$" tumblers shown are unique. The "Dripping Springs Whiskey" is etched and gilded. These are factory produced pieces.

American Pattern
Line No. 2056

The American line contains much more than just tableware. The vanity items that Fostoria designed add great interest to this pattern. At times the Fostoria catalogs listed vanity pieces as "Boudoir items." When this pattern was introduced in 1915, there was a boudoir jug that was part of the vanity line. This scare item has a large wide lip that differs in design from the regular quart pitcher that was also made this introductory year. The 1917 catalog showed 22 vanity items, the chiffonier was added in 1918, and these 23 items were continued into the 1920s. The Boudoir Set consisted of 10" tray, quart jug, candle, tumbler, and match box. Many dresser items that appear to be the Fostoria American pattern have been found in England. These items are also highly prized. The catalog page illustrated here is undated, but we feel 1925 would possibly be correct. Some American items from this period will be found in Blue, Green, Canary, and Amber.

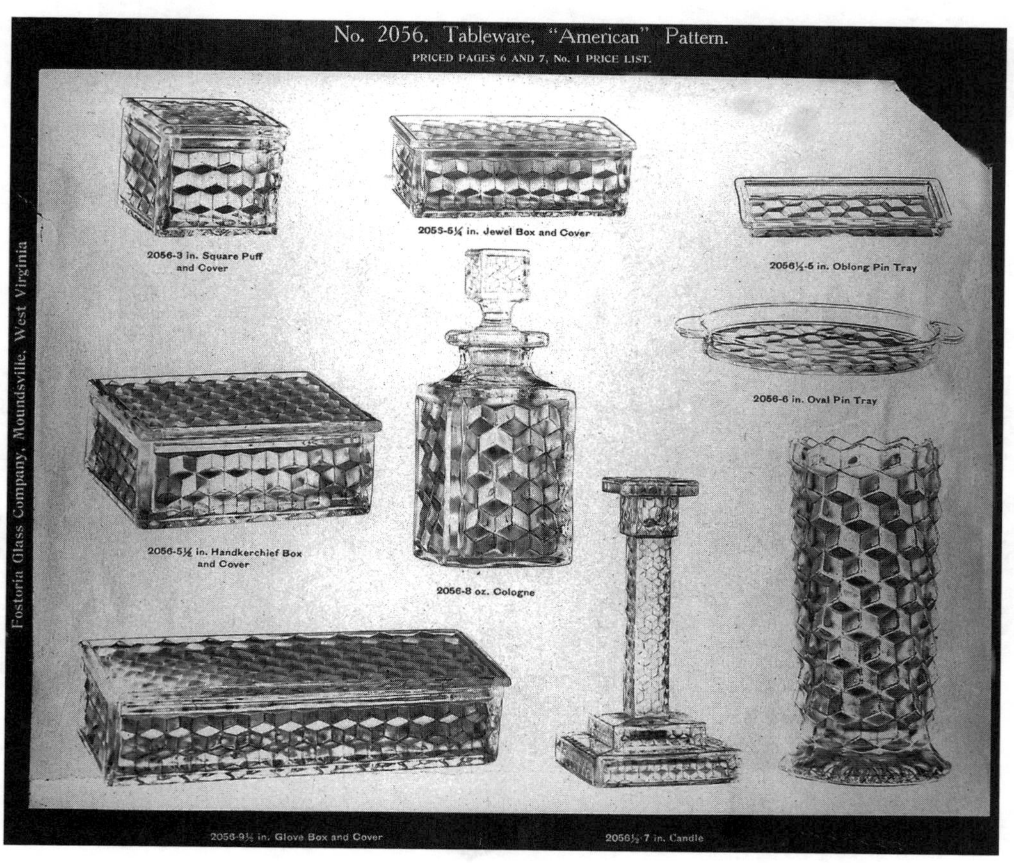

American Pattern
Line No. 2056

2056 Puff, Cov., Round
Height 2⅞", 1916 Catalog

2056 Hair Pin, Cov.
Length 3½", Width 1¾",
Height 1½"
1915 Catalog

2056 Jewel Box, Cov.
Length 5¼", Width 2¼"
1920 Catalog

2056 Pomade, Cov.
Square, 2"
1916 Catalog

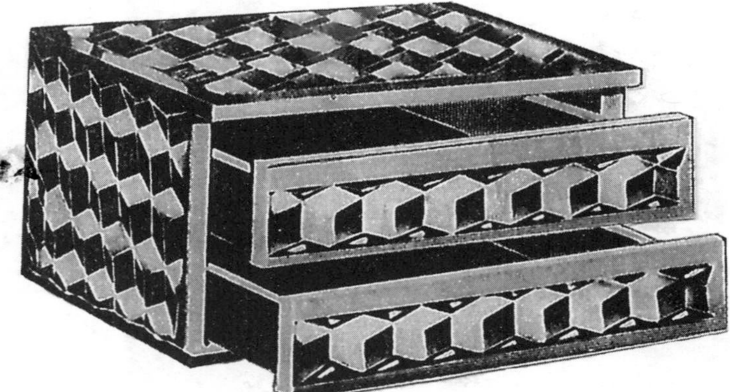
2056 Chiffonier
Height 2¼", Width 3¼"
Length 4¼"
1921 Catalog

2056 Hair Receiver, Cov.
Leight 3", Width 3", Height 2⅞"
1916 Catalog

AMERICAN PATTERN

No. 2056 Line

2056—10 oz.
Goblet
Hexagon Foot
Height 6⅞ in.

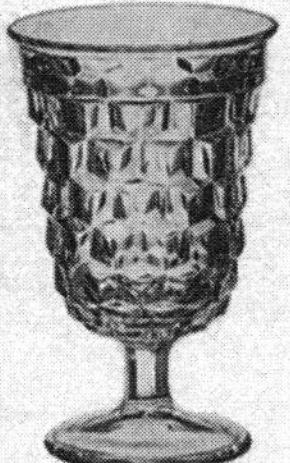
2056—9 oz.
Low Goblet
Height 5½ in.

2056—4½ oz.
Footed Dessert
Hexagon Foot
Height 4¾ in.

2056—4½ oz.
High Sherbet, Fld.
Height 4⅜ in.

2056½—4½ oz.
High Sherbet, Reg.
Height 4½ in.

2056—5 oz.
Low Sherbet, Fld.
Height 3¼ in.

2056½—5 oz.
Low Sherbet, Reg.
Height 3½ in.

2056—4½ oz.
Oyster Cocktail
Height 3½ in.

2056—6 oz.
Sundae
Height 3⅛ in.

2056—3 oz.
Footed Cocktail
Height 2⅞ in.

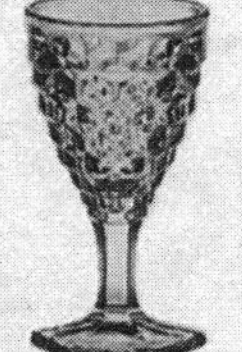
2056—2½ oz.
Wine
Hexagon Foot
Height 4⅜ in.

2056—6 oz.
Old Fashioned Cocktail
Height 3⅜ in.

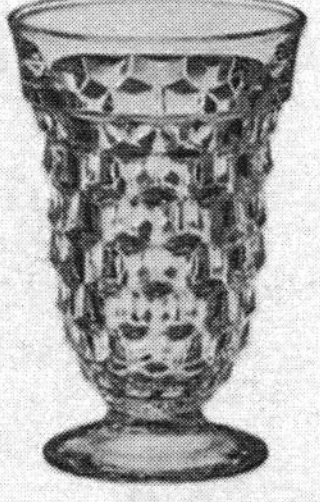
2056—12 oz.
Footed Ice Tea Fld.
Height 5¾ in.

2056—9 oz.
Footed Tumbler
Height 4⅜ in.

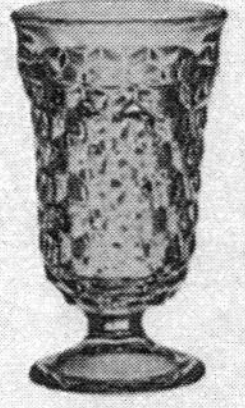
2056—5 oz.
Footed Tumbler
Height 4¾ in.

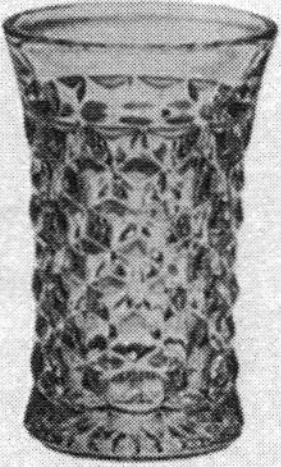
2056—12 oz.
Ice Tea, Fld.
Height 5¼ in.

2056—8 oz.
Table Tumbler, Fld.
Height 4⅛ in.

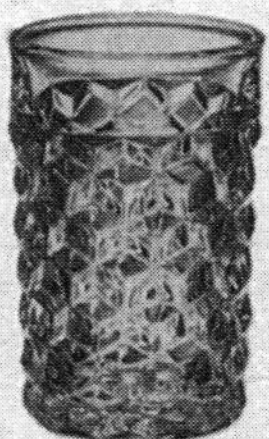
2056½—12 oz.
Ice Tea, Reg.
Height 5 in.

2056½—8 oz.
Table Tumbler, Reg.
Height 3⅞ in.

2056½—5 oz.
Tumbler, Reg.
Height 3⅝ in.

2056—2 oz.
Whiskey
Height 2½ in.

FOSTORIA GLASS COMPANY, MOUNDSVILLE, WEST VIRGINIA — 1949

AMERICAN PATTERN

No. 2056 LINE

Fostoria Glass Company, Moundsville, West Virginia, July 1, 1939

2056—Topper Ash Tray
Top Diameter 2⅛ in.

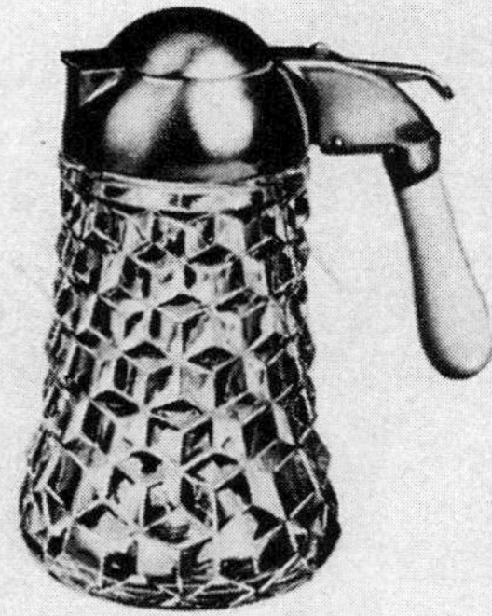

2056½—Sani-Cut Server
Height 5¼ in.
Capacity 6½ oz.

2056½—Tea Sugar
Height 2¼ in.

2056½—Tea Cream
Height 2⅜ in.
Capacity 3 oz.

2056—Hurricane Lamp Complete
Height 12 in.
Consisting of
Hurricane Lamp Base
Hurricane Lamp Chimney

Candle Not Included

2056½—4 Division Relish
Length 9 in. Width 6½ in.

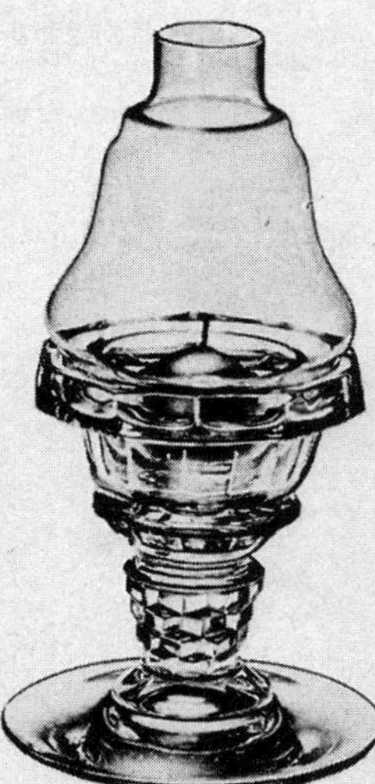

2056—3 in. Candle Lamp Complete
Height 8½ in.
Consisting of—
1/12 Doz. 26/1—3 Piece Candle Lamp
1/12 Doz. 2056—3 in. Candlestick
1/12 Doz. Wax Light

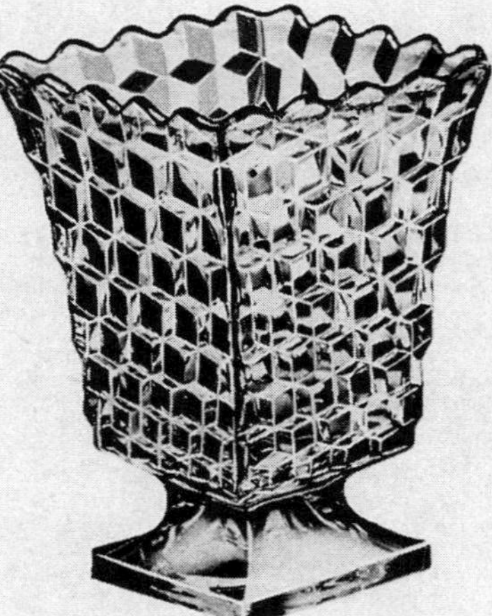

2056— 6 in. Square Urn
2056—7½ in. Square Urn

2056—12 in. Handled Lunch Tray

AMERICAN PATTERN

No. 2056 LINE

2056—Ice Dish
Tomato Juice Liner Illustrated
Patent No. 1858728

2451—4 oz. Crab
Meat Liner
Blown

2451—5 oz. Tomato
Juice Liner
Blown

2451—5 oz. Fruit
Cocktail Liner
Blown

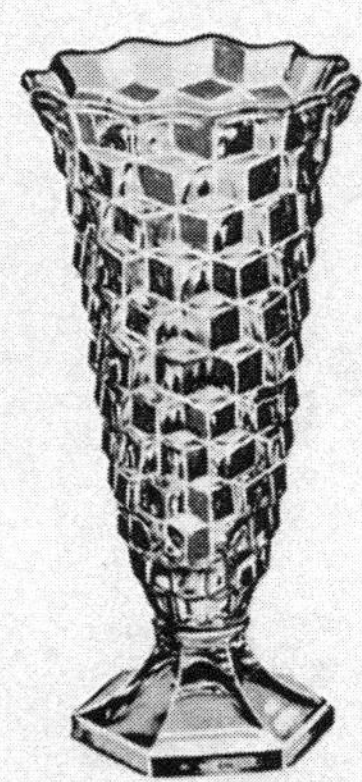

2056—6 in. Footed Bud Vase,
Flared

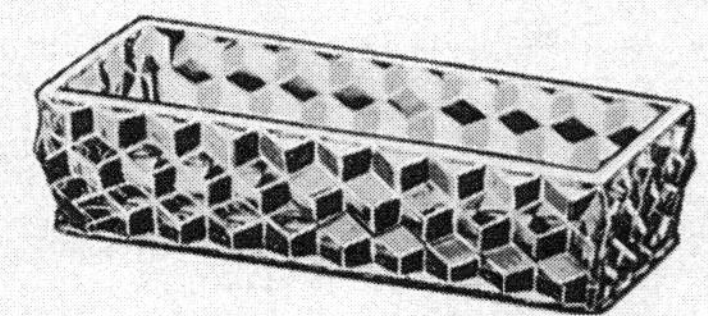

2056½—Flower Box (Butter Cover)
Length 5¾ in. Height 1½ in. Width 2¼ in.

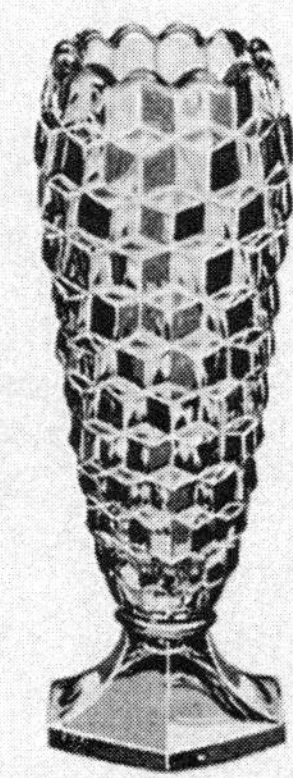

2056—6 in. Footed Bud Vase, Cupped

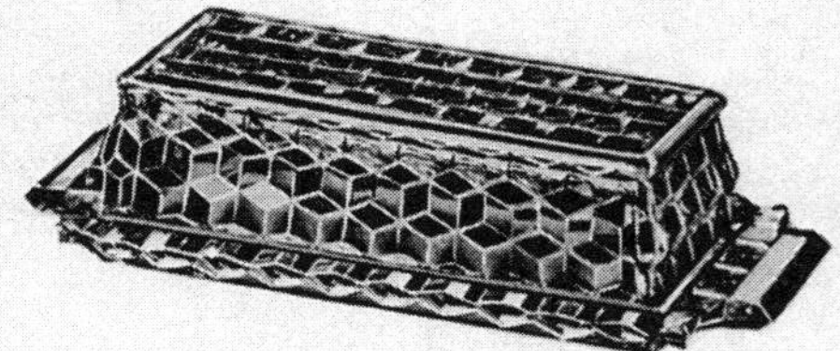

2056½—Oblong Butter and Cover
Length 7½ in. Height 2⅛ in. Width 3¼ in.

2056—2 Part Vegetable Dish
Length 10 in. Height 2⅛ in. Width 7 in.

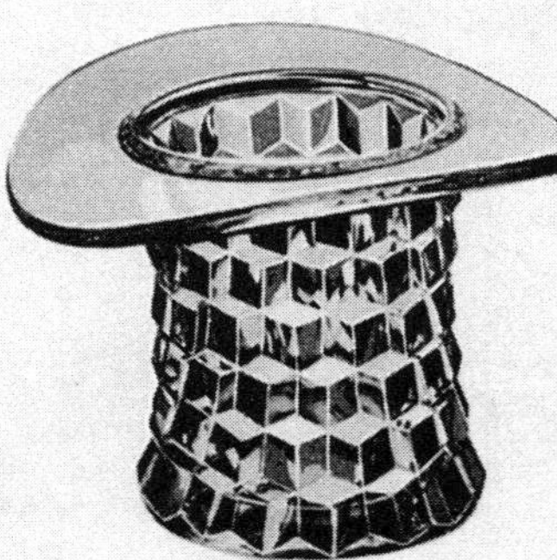

2056—4 in. Topper
Top Diameter 6 in.

Fostoria Glass Company, Moundsville, West Virginia, January 1, 1940

AMERICAN PATTERN

No. 2056 LINE

2056—Decanter and Stopper
Cap. 24-oz., Height 9¼ in.
2056—Cordial Bottle and Stopper
Cap. 9-oz., Height 7¼ in.

2056—8 Piece Decanter Set
Consisting of
1/12 Doz. 2056—Decanter and Stopper
1/2 Doz. 2056—2 oz. Whiskey
1/12 Doz. 2056—10½ in. Oblong Tray

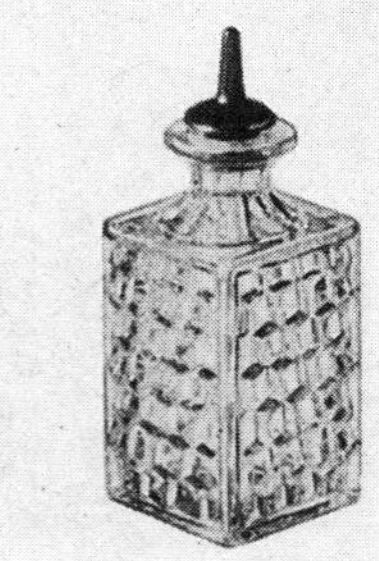

2056—2-oz. Whiskey
Height 2½ in.

2056
Bitters Bottle with Tube
Cap. 4½ oz. Height 5¾ in.

2056—2½ oz. Wine
Hexagon Foot
Height 4⅜ in.

2056—6-oz.
Old Fashioned Cocktail
Height 3⅜ in.

2056
3-oz. Footed Cocktail
Height 2⅞ in.

2056—Custard, Reg.

2056—14 in. Punch Bowl and High Foot (Illustrated)
Capacity 2 Gallons
2056—18 in. Punch Bowl
Capacity 3¾ Gallons
Low Foot is used with 18 in. Punch Bowl
Low Foot can also be furnished for 14 in. Punch Bowl

2056—Custard, Fld.

AMERICAN PATTERN

No. 2056 LINE

2056—Pretzel Jar and Cover
Height 8⅞ in.
Diameter 5¾ in.

2056—13 in. Shallow Fruit Bowl
Height 3 in.

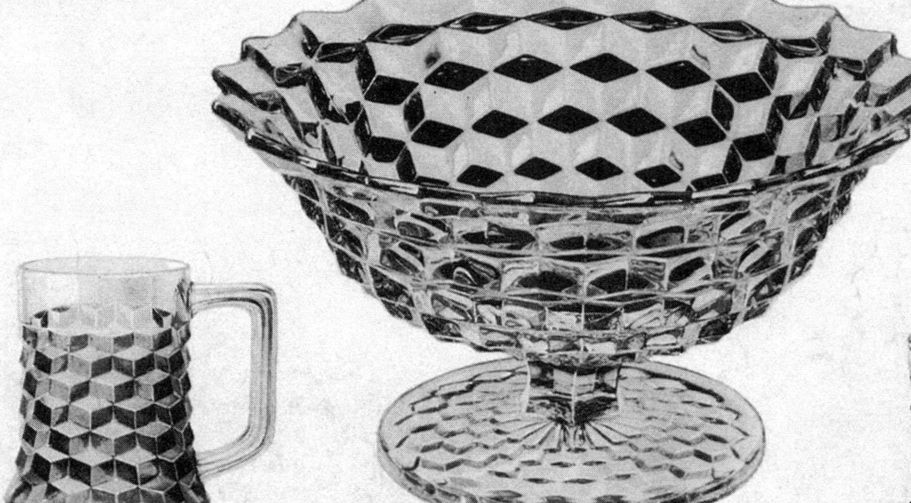

2056—12 oz. Beer Mug
Height 4½ in.

2056—12 in. Footed Fruit Bowl
Small Punch Bowl or Tom and Jerry Bowl
Capacity 1¾ gal. Height 7¼ in.

2056
Tom and Jerry Mug
Capacity 5½ oz.
Height 3¼ in.

Fostoria Glass Company, Moundsville, West Virginia, Jan. 1, 1939

AMERICAN PATTERN

No. 2056 LINE

Fostoria Glass Company, Moundsville, West Virginia, Jan. 1, 1939

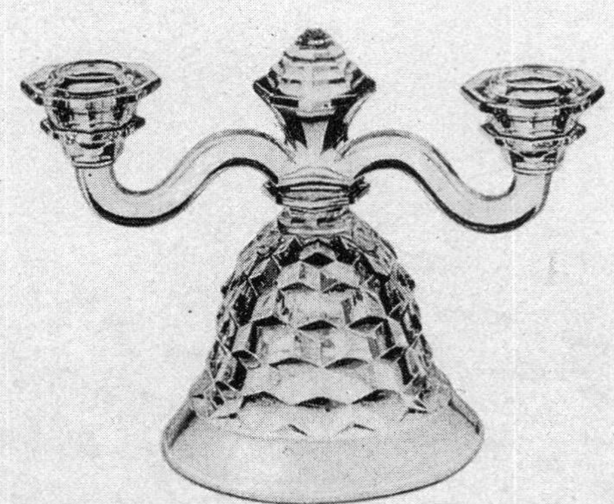

2056—Duo Candlestick
Height 6½ in.—Spread 8¼ in.

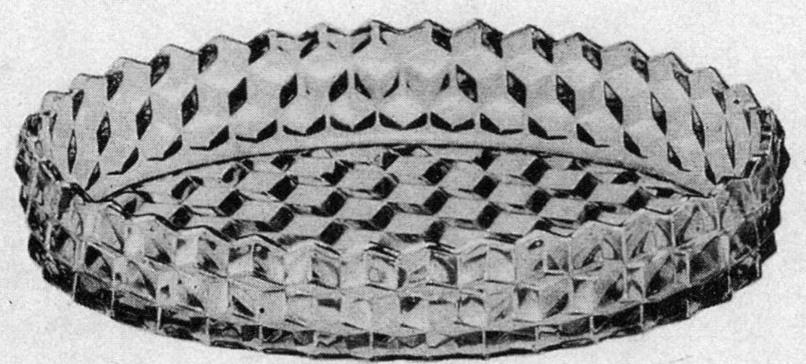

2056—10 in. Floating Garden
2056—11½ in. Floating Garden

2056
15 in. Centerpiece
Height 4¼ in.

2056
3 in. Candlestick

2056—2 Light Candelabra, 16 U. D. P.
Using No. 2527 Bobache
Height 6½ in. — Spread 9¼ in.

2056—9½ in. Centerpiece—Height 3⅝ in.
2056—11 in. Centerpiece—Height 4⅜ in.

AMERICAN PATTERN

No. 2056 LINE

2056—10½ in. Bowl, 3 Toes
Height 3½ in.

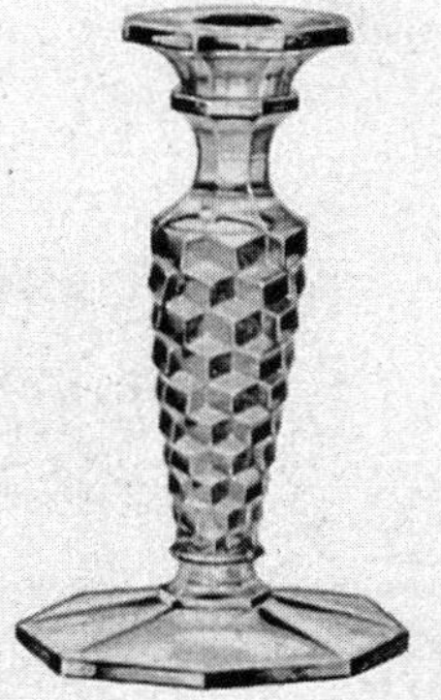

2056—6 in. Candlestick

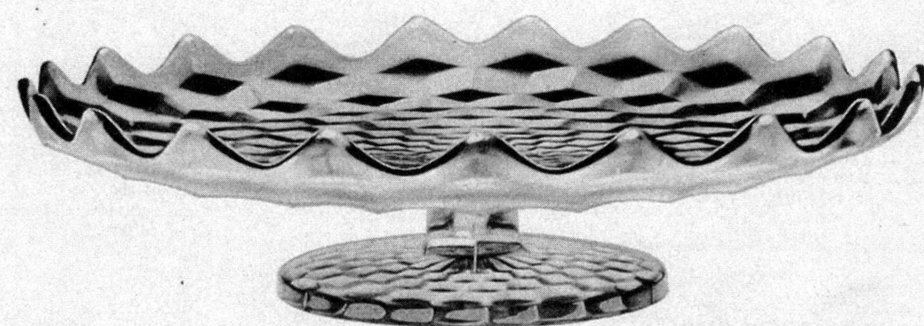

2056—16 in. Footed Fruit Bowl
Height 4¼ in.

2056—11¾ in. Oval Bowl
Height 2⅞ in.
Width 7½ in.

2056½—Twin Candlestick
Height 4⅜ in. Spread 8½ in.

Fostoria Glass Company, Moundsville, West Virginia, Jan. 1, 1939

BAROQUE PATTERN

No. 2496 LINE

2496—9 oz. Goblet
Height 6¾ in.
DESIGN PATENT NO. 102744

2496
5 oz. Sherbet
Height 3⅞ in.

2496—3½ oz.
Footed Cocktail
Height 3 in.

2496½—6½ oz.
Old Fashioned Cocktail
Height 3⅜ in.

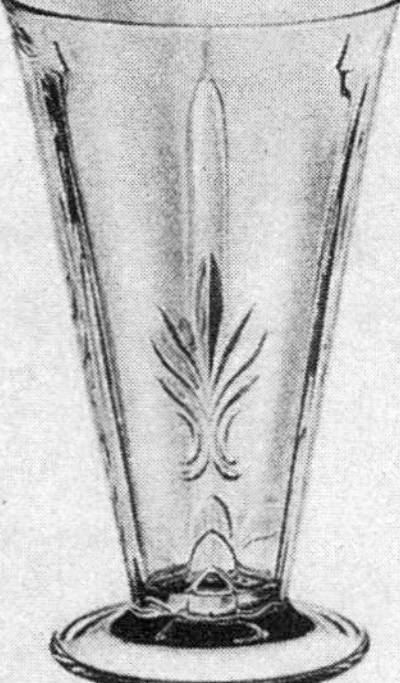

2496—9 oz.
Footed Tumbler
Height 5½ in.
2496—12 oz.
Footed Tumbler
Height 6 in.

2496—3 Piece Sugar and Cream Set
Consisting of:
1/12 Doz. 2496—Individual Sugar
1/12 Doz. 2496—Individual Cream
1/12 Doz. 2496—6½ in. Sugar and Cream Tray

2496—Footed Sugar
Height 3½ in.
2496—Individual Sugar
Height 2⅞ in.

2496—Footed Cream
Height 3¾ in.
Capacity 7½ oz.
2496—Individual Cream
Height 3⅛ in.
Capacity 4 oz.

2496—6½ in.
Sugar and Cream Tray
Width 3¾ in.

2496—Ice Jug
Capacity 3 Pint, Height 7 in.

2496½—5 oz. Tumbler
Height 3⅞ in.
2496½—9 oz. Tumbler
Height 4¼ in.
2496½—14 oz. Ice Tea
Height 5⅞ in.

2496—3 Pint Jug
Height 6½ in.

Fostoria Glass Company, Moundsville, West Virginia, Jan. 1, 1939

BAROQUE PATTERN
No. 2496 LINE
2496—Plate
See Price List for Sizes
DESIGN PATENT NO. 102742
2496½—Mayonnaise and Plate
and Ladle
Height 3½ in.
2496—Mustard and
Cover and Spoon
Height 3¾ in.
2496—Cream Soup
2496—Cream Soup Plate
2496—9½ in. Vegetable Dish
2496—Footed Cup
2496—Saucer
2496—8 in. Pickle
2496—11 in. Celery
2496—12 in. Oval Platter
2496—5 in. Fruit
2496—Shaker, F.G.T.
Height 2¾ in.
2496½—
Individual Shaker, F.G.T.
Height 2 in.
2496—6½ in. Oblong Sauce Dish
Width 5¼ in.
2496—8 in. Oblong Tray
Width 7 in.
2496—6½ in. 2 Part Mayonnaise
Width 5¼ in.
Fostoria Glass Company, Moundsville, West Virginia, Jan. 1, 1939
34

Fostoria Glass Company, Moundsville, West Virginia, Jan. 1, 1939

BAROQUE PATTERN

No. 2496 LINE

See Price List for Colors

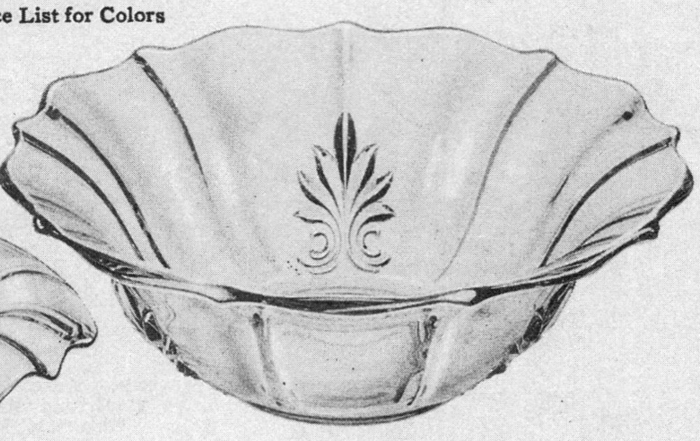

2496—12 in. Bowl, Flared
Height 3½ in.

2496—11 in. Bowl, Rolled Edge
Height 3⅜ in.

2484—10 in. Handled Bowl
Height 3⅛ in.
DESIGN PATENT NO. 91909

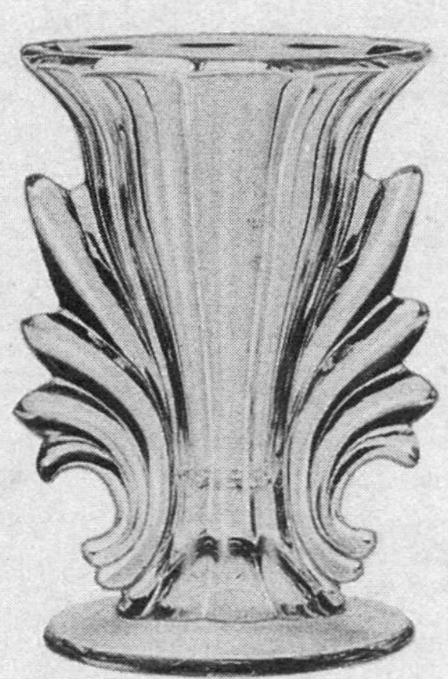

2484—7-in. Vase

2496—3½ in. Rose Bowl

2496—8 in. Vase

Fostoria Glass Company, Moundsville, West Virginia, Jan. 1, 1939

BAROQUE PATTERN

No. 2496 LINE

See Price List for Colors

2496—Jelly and Cover
Height 7½ in. including cover

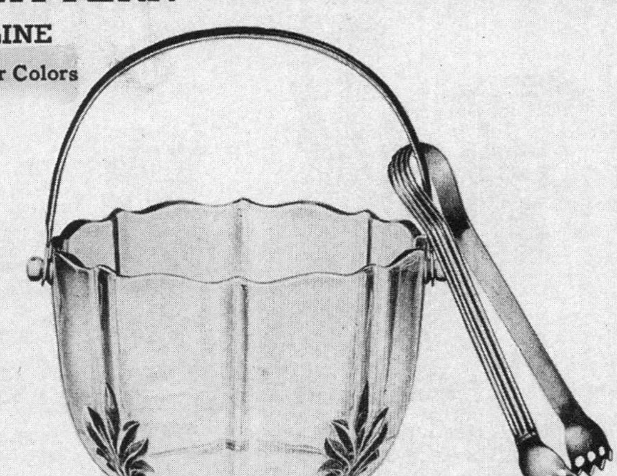

2496—Ice Bucket
Height 4⅜ in. Top Diameter 6½ in.
Chromium Handle and Tongs
Tongs priced separately

2496—5 Piece Smoker Set
Consisting of:
1/12 Doz. 2496—Cigarette Box and Cover
Length 5½ in. Width 3½ in.
1/3 Doz. 2496—Oblong Ash Tray
Length 3¾ in. Width 2¼ in.

2496—5½ in. Comport
Height 4¾ in.
2496—6½ in. Tall Comport
Height 5¾ in.

2496—Footed Punch Bowl
Capacity 1½ Gallon
Height 8¼ in. Top Diameter 13¼ in.
2496—6 oz. Punch Cups

BAROQUE PATTERN

No. 2496 LINE

See Price List for Colors

2496—Trindle Candlestick
Height 6 in. Spread 8¼ in.
DESIGN PATENT NO. 91687

2496—5½ in. Candlestick

2496—Duo Candlestick
Height 4½ in. Spread 8 in.

2496
4 in. Candlestick
DESIGN PATENT NO. 103058

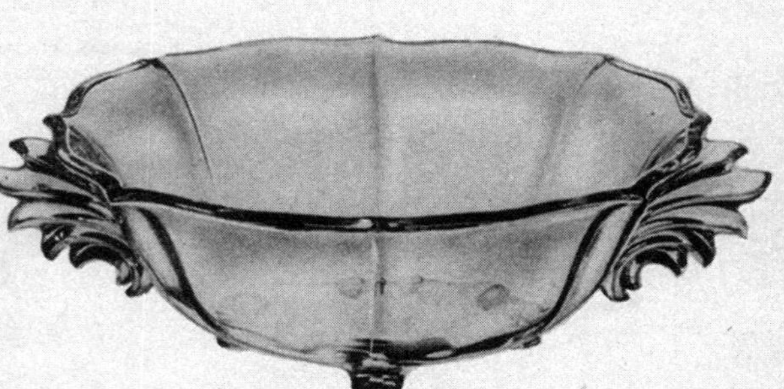

2496—10½ in. Handled Bowl
Height 3⅜ in.

2484—Lustre, 8 U. D. P.
Height 7¾ in.
DESIGN PATENT NO. 94442

2484—3 Light Candelabra, 24 U. D. P.
Using 2482 Bobache
Height 9½ in. Spread 12⅜ in.
DESIGN PATENT NO. 91688

2484—2 Light Candelabra, 16 U. D. P.
Using 2484 Bobache
Height 8¼ in. Spread 10 in.
DESIGN PATENT NO. 91686

Fostoria Glass Company, Moundsville, West Virginia, Jan. 1, 1939

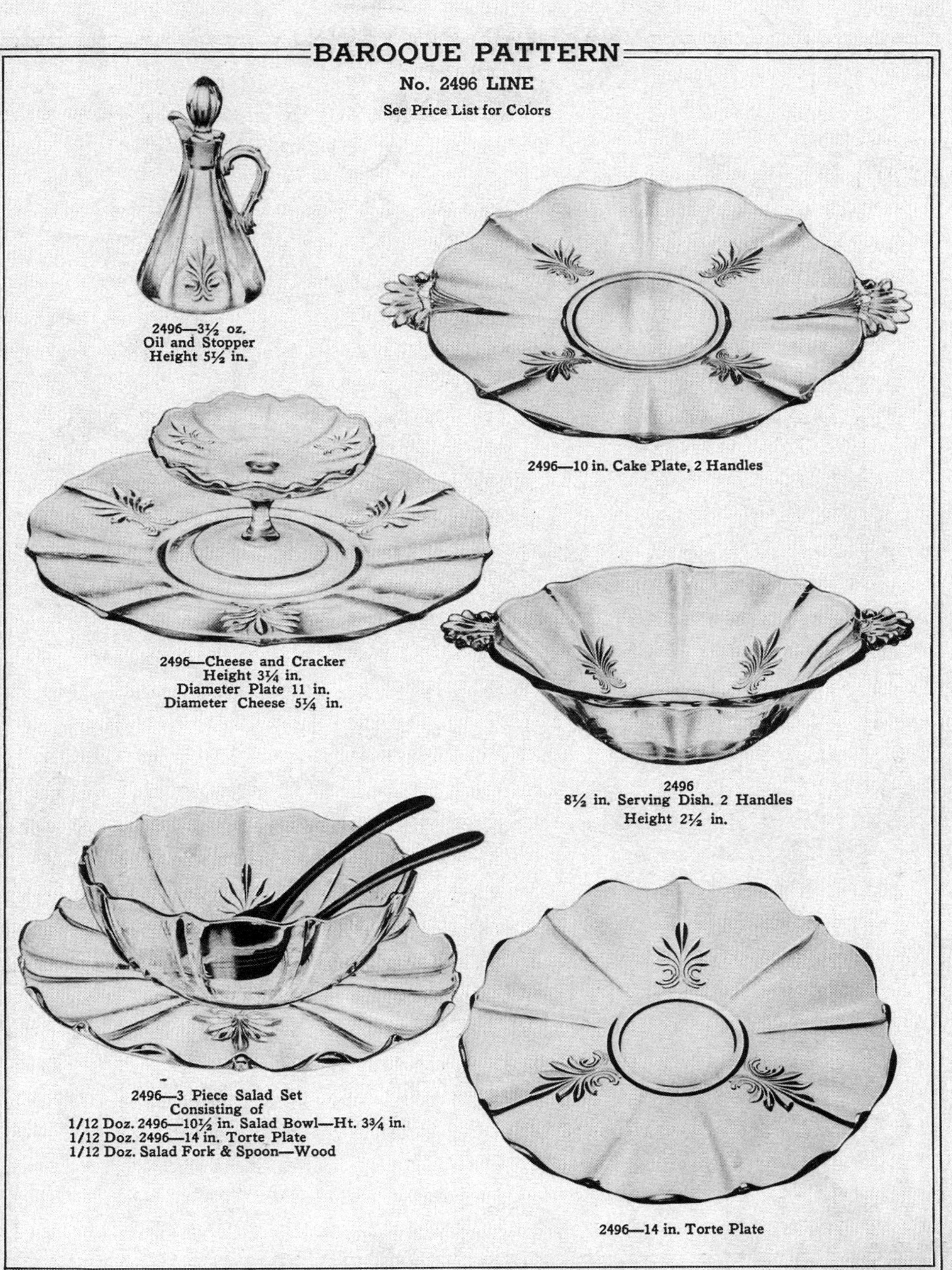

2496—3½ oz.
Oil and Stopper
Height 5½ in.

2496—10 in. Cake Plate, 2 Handles

2496—Cheese and Cracker
Height 3¼ in.
Diameter Plate 11 in.
Diameter Cheese 5¼ in.

2496
8½ in. Serving Dish. 2 Handles
Height 2½ in.

2496—3 Piece Salad Set
Consisting of
1/12 Doz. 2496—10½ in. Salad Bowl—Ht. 3¾ in.
1/12 Doz. 2496—14 in. Torte Plate
1/12 Doz. Salad Fork & Spoon—Wood

2496—14 in. Torte Plate

35

BAROQUE PATTERN

No. 2496 LINE

2496—Handled Mint
4 in. Square

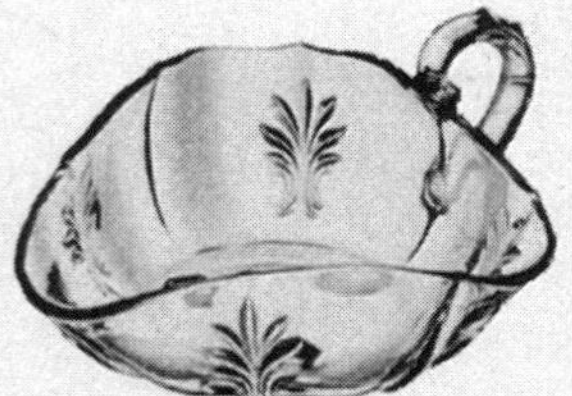
2496—Handled Nappy, 3 Cor.
Length 4⅝ in.

2496—Handled Nappy, Reg.
Diameter 4⅜ in.

2496—Sweetmeat
6 in. Square

2496—Handled Nappy, Square
4 in. Square

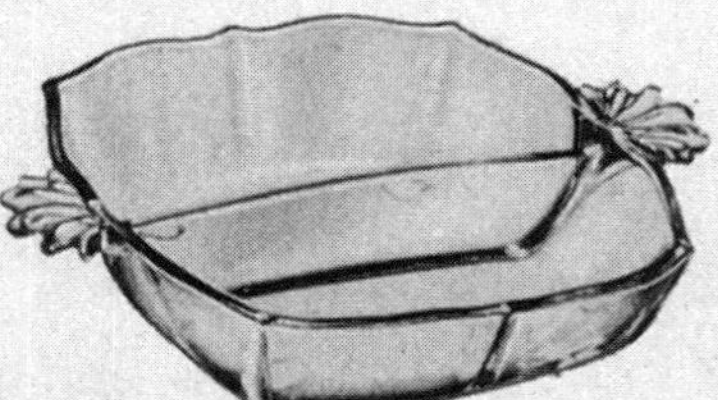
2496—2 Part Relish
6 in. Square

2496—3 Part Candy Box and Cover
Height 2½ in.—Width 6¼ in.

2496—Handled Nappy, Fld.
Diameter 5 in.

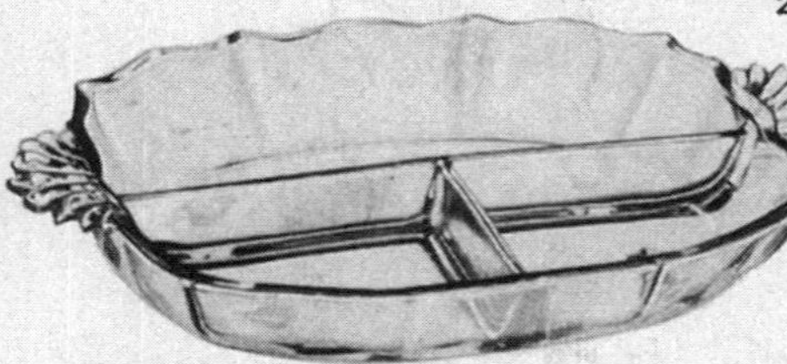
2496—3 Part Relish
Length 10 in. Width 7½ in.

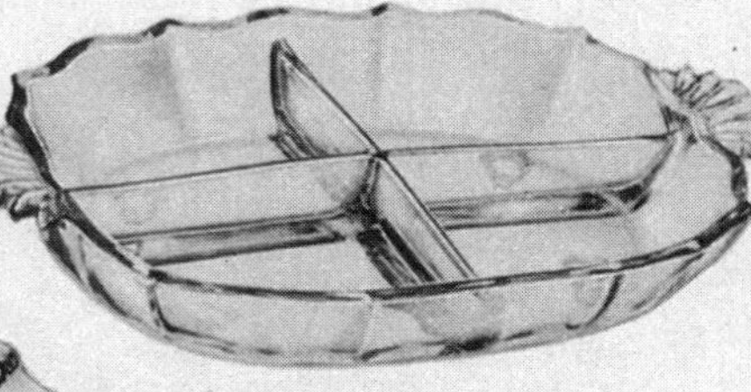
2496—4 Part Relish
Length 10 in. Width 7½ in.

2496—3 Toed Bon Bon
Diameter 7⅜ in.

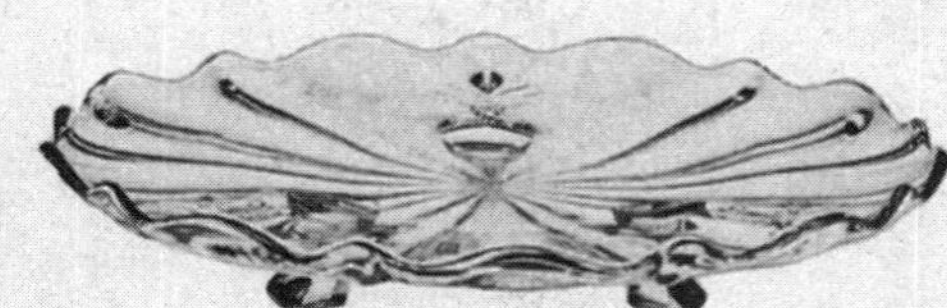
2496—3 Toed Tid Bit, Flat
Diameter 8¼ in.

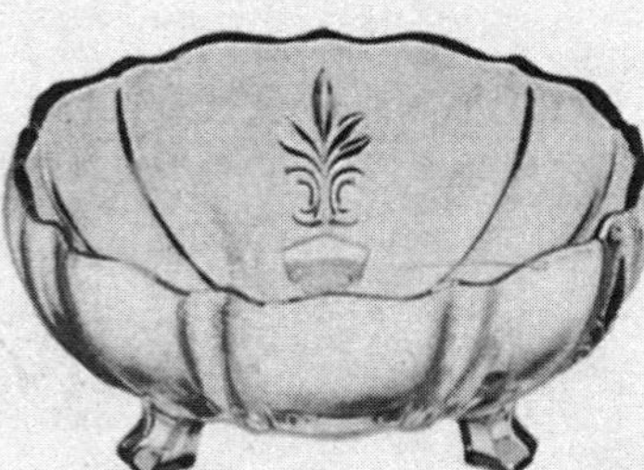
2496—3 Toed Nut Bowl, Cupped
Diameter 6¼ in.

Fostoria Glass Company, Moundsville, West Virginia, Jan. 1, 1939

ALL OUR WARE IS GOOD WEIGHT AND EXTRA FIRE POLISHED WITH NATURAL GAS, EXCEPT WHERE NOTED.
11
Brilliant Line, No. 1001.
8 inch Berry.
7 inch Berry.
Sugar.
Cream.
Spoon.
Butter.
4½ inch Nappy.
4 inch Nappy.
FOSTORIA GLASS CO., MOUNDSVILLE, W. VA.

1901 Catalog

1898 Catalog

Pattern No. 2222 Colonial was introduced in 1920. By the late 1920s, color was added and the line was promoted as hotel and tea room ware. 1930 Catalog

FOSTORIA GLASS COMPANY, MOUNDSVILLE, WEST VIRGINIA — 1950

CENTURY PATTERN

No. 2630 Line

2630—10½ oz.
Goblet
Height 5¾ in.

2630 — 5½ oz.
Sherbet
Height 4¼ in.

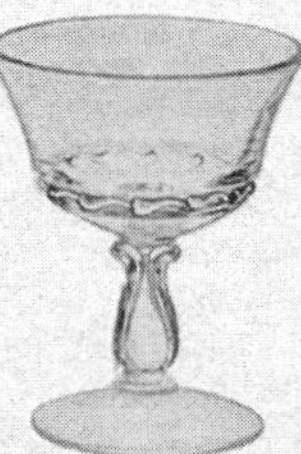

2630 — 3½ oz.
Cocktail
Height 4⅛ in.

2630 — 3½ oz.
Wine
Height 4½ in.

2630 — 4½ oz.
Oyster Cocktail
Height 3¾ in.

2630 — 12 oz.
Footed Tumbler
Height 5⅞ in.

2630 — 5 oz.
Footed Tumbler
Height 4¾ in.

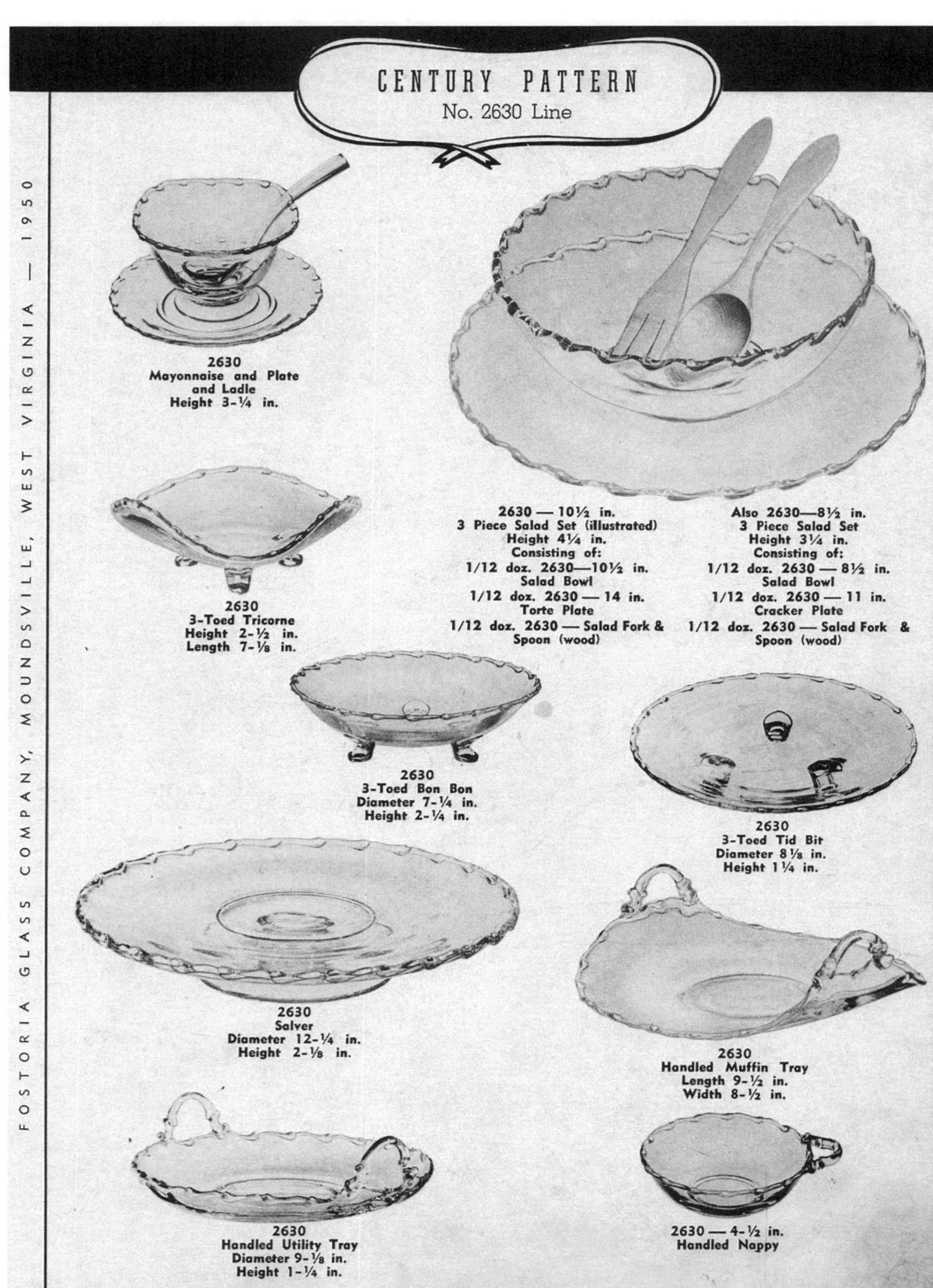
CENTURY PATTERN
No. 2630 Line
FOSTORIA GLASS COMPANY, MOUNDSVILLE, WEST VIRGINIA — 1950
2630
Mayonnaise and Plate
and Ladle
Height 3-¼ in.
2630 — 10½ in.
3 Piece Salad Set (illustrated)
Height 4¼ in.
Consisting of:
1/12 doz. 2630—10½ in.
Salad Bowl
1/12 doz. 2630 — 14 in.
Torte Plate
1/12 doz. 2630 — Salad Fork &
Spoon (wood)
Also 2630—8½ in.
3 Piece Salad Set
Height 3¼ in.
Consisting of:
1/12 doz. 2630 — 8½ in.
Salad Bowl
1/12 doz. 2630 — 11 in.
Cracker Plate
1/12 doz. 2630 — Salad Fork &
Spoon (wood)
2630
3-Toed Tricorne
Height 2-½ in.
Length 7-⅛ in.
2630
3-Toed Bon Bon
Diameter 7-¼ in.
Height 2-¼ in.
2630
3-Toed Tid Bit
Diameter 8⅛ in.
Height 1¼ in.
2630
Salver
Diameter 12-¼ in.
Height 2-⅛ in.
2630
Handled Muffin Tray
Length 9-½ in.
Width 8-½ in.
2630
Handled Utility Tray
Diameter 9-⅛ in.
Height 1-¼ in.
2630 — 4-½ in.
Handled Nappy

CENTURY PATTERN

No. 2630 Line

2630
3 Pint Ice Jug
Height 9½ in.

2630
Pint Cereal Pitcher
Height 6⅛ in.

2630
Ice Bucket
Height 4⅞ in. Top Dia. 7⅜ in.
Chromium Handle and Tongs
Tongs priced separately

2630
Candy Jar and Cover
Height 7 in.

2630
Mustard, Cover and Spoon
Height 4 in.

2630
3 Piece Tid Bit Set
Metal Handle
Height 10¼ in.

2630
Cheese and Cracker
Height 2¾ in.
Plate Diameter—10¾ in.
Cheese Diameter—5⅜ in.
Cheese Height—2½ in.

2630 — 7½ in.
Handled Vase

2630 — 6 in.
Bud Vase

2630 — 8½ in.
Oval Vase

FOSTORIA GLASS COMPANY, MOUNDSVILLE, WEST VIRGINIA — 1950

COIN GLASS PATTERN

No. 1372 Line

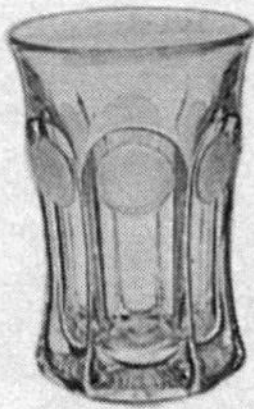

1372/64
Ice Tea/Highball
Height 5⅛ in.
Capacity 12 oz.

1372/73
Water Scotch & Soda
Height 4¼ in.
Capacity 9 oz.

1372/81
Juice/Old Fashioned
Height 3⅝ in.
Capacity 9 oz.

1372/114—7½ in.
Round Ash Tray

1372/115
Oblong Ash Tray
Length 4 in.

1372/124—10 in.
Ash Tray

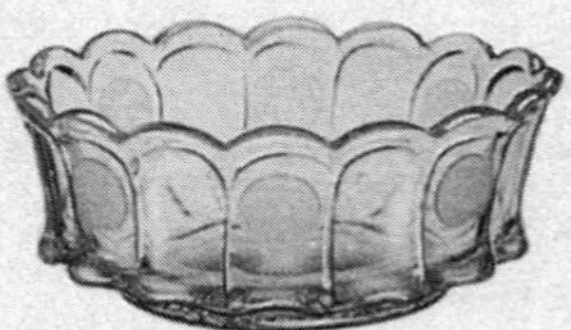

1372/179—8 in.
Bowl

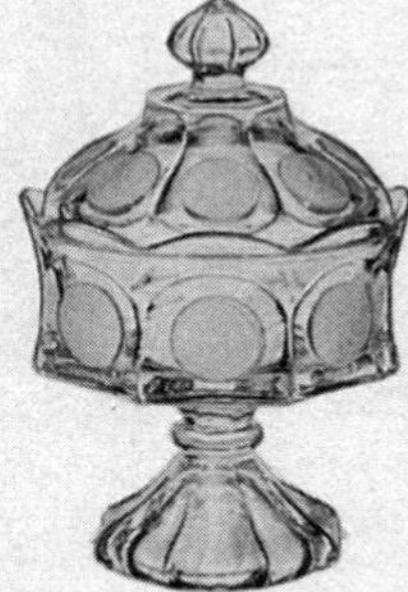

1372/162
Wedding Bowl and Cover
Height 8-3/16 in.

1372/189—9 in.
Oval Bowl

1372/316—4½ in.
Candleholder

1372/347
Candy Jar and Cover
Height 6-5/16 in.

1372/354
Candy Box and Cover
Diameter 6⅜ in.
Height 4⅛ in.

GOLD COIN PATTERN

No. 1372 Line

1372/374
Cigarette Box and Cover
Height 1¾ in.
Length 5¾ in. Width 4½ in.

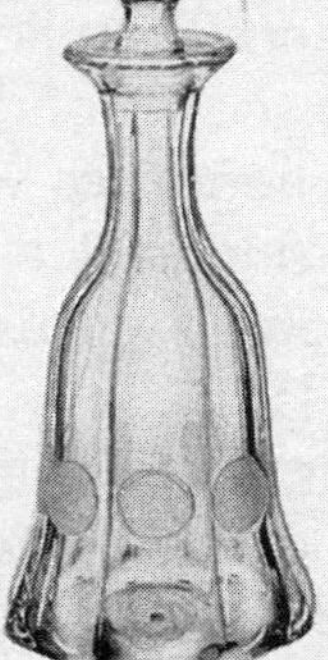

1372/400
Decanter and Stopper
Height 10-3/16 in.
Capacity 1 Pint

1372/448
Jelly

1372/453
Quart Pitcher
Height 6-9/16 in.

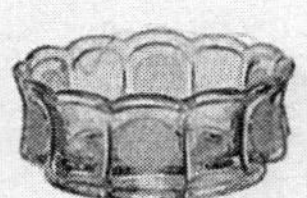

1372/495—4½ in.
Nappy
Height 3¾ in.

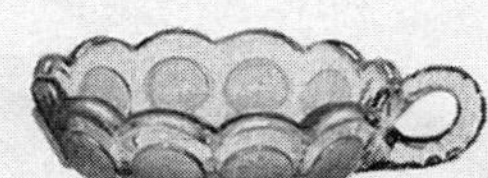

1372/499
Handled Nappy
Diameter 5⅜ in.

1372/673
Sugar & Cover
Height 5⅜ in.

1372/680
Cream
Height 3½ in.

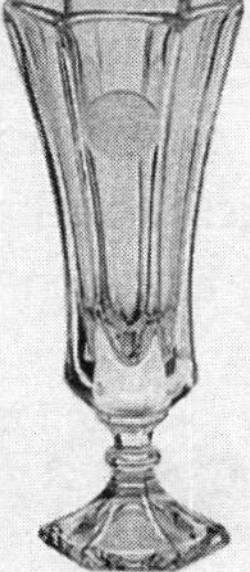

1372/799—8 in.
Bud Vase

GOLD COIN DESIGN

Decoration No. 646

Gold Decorated Coins

1372/162
Wedding Bowl and Cover
Height 8-3/16 in.
Length 5¾ in. Width 4½ in.

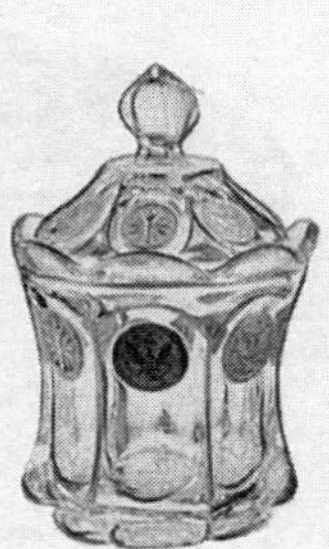

1372/347
Candy Jar and Cover
Height 6-5/16 in.

1372/400
Decanter and Stopper
Height 10-3/16 in.
Capacity 1 Pint

1372/374
Cigarette Box and Cover
Height 1¾ in.

FOSTORIA GLASS COMPANY, MOUNDSVILLE, WEST VIRGINIA — 1960

Colony Pattern
No. 2412 Line

The first catalog drawing of the pattern we now know as Colony was seen when the firm was still in Fostoria, Ohio. Most of the older swirl items carried the line No. 112, although some carried other numbers. Other available material indicates that the early name of this line was Cascade. By the mid-1920s this design had been assigned a new line number and name and appeared in catalogs as No. 2412 Queen Anne. Catalogs show Queen Anne as a line of occasional pieces that featured colors as well as crystal. All the colored pieces are scarce and highly collectible. The "swirls" of this pattern correctly go to the right, but some catalog negatives were inadvertently reversed and these will show the swirls going to the left. Possibly the strangest item made in this pattern is the little handled candle lamp that has slots in the glass for threading ribbons. In 1939 Colony became a major tableware line. The line was expanded in 1940 – 1941.

The curtailment of production during WWII resulted in some items being totally dropped. These pieces are especially hard to find now. The 1963 catalog showed 48 pieces of Colony; by 1966, the line had dropped to 40. In 1968, Colony sported 28 pieces but by 1972 contained only 23. Good news is that the Punch Bowl and Cups were still in production in 1972. The year 1982 brought some colored pieces of this design back into production. These pieces were machine made and advertised as Maypole Giftware; made in Ruby, Light Blue, Yellow (gold), and Peach (pink) were 6" bud vase, 9" candlestick, 3" candlestick, 13" torte plate, and a 9¾" salad bowl. There is a French Baccarat pattern that closely resembles Colony and the pieces were produced in both crystal and color. The colored pieces frequently seen are dresser items, but carafes, compotes, and relishes were also made. Many of these pieces will be found in Rose-Tiente color. The Baccarat lustres we have examined were much heavier than the Fostoria pieces because the former ones were made with a solid base that was completely ground and polished.

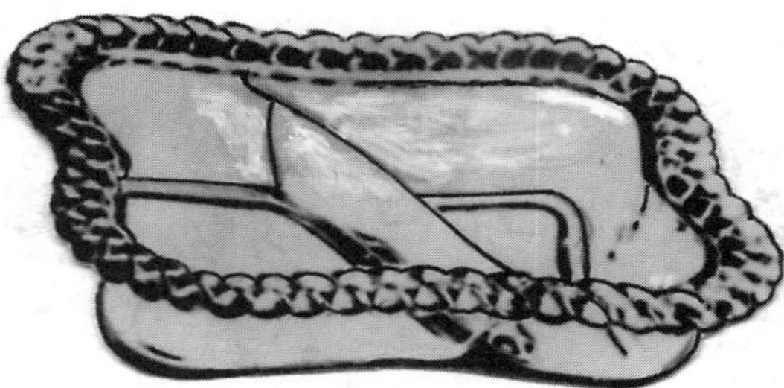

2412 Relish, 2-Part
Length 7¼", Width 5¼"
1940 Catalog

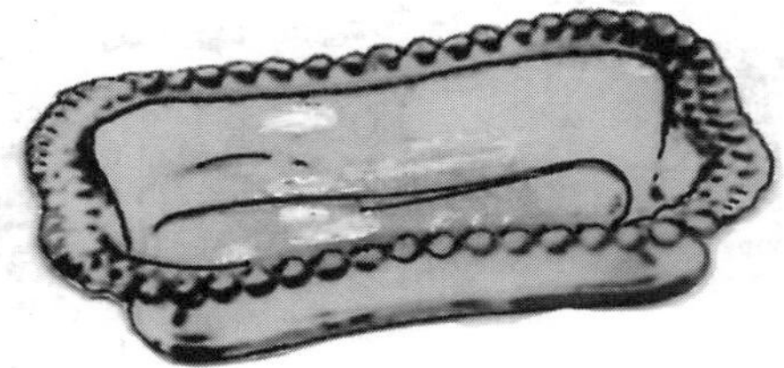

2412 Olive
Length 6½", 1940 Catalog

2412 Pickle
Length 8", 1940 Catalog

2412 Low Comport, Cov.
Height 6½", 1940 Catalog

Fostoria Glass Company, Moundsville, West Virginia, January 1, 1941

COLONY PATTERN

No. 2412 LINE

2412—9 oz. Goblet
Height 5⅛ in.

2412—5 oz. Sherbet
Height 3⅝ in.

2412—3½ oz. Cocktail
Height 4 in.

2412—3¼ oz. Wine
Height 4⅛ in.

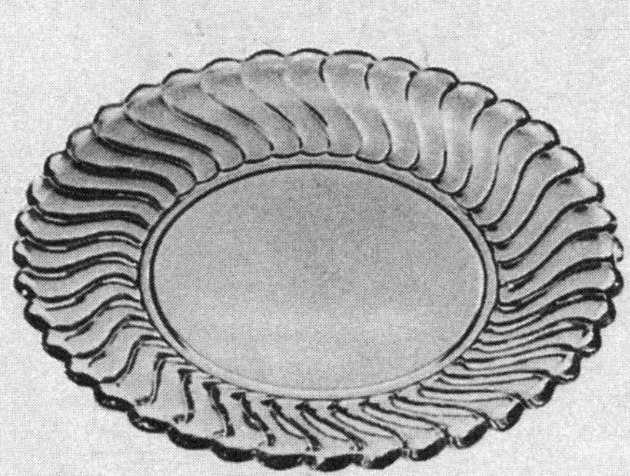
2412—Plate

2412—12 oz. Footed Tumbler
Height 5⅝ in.

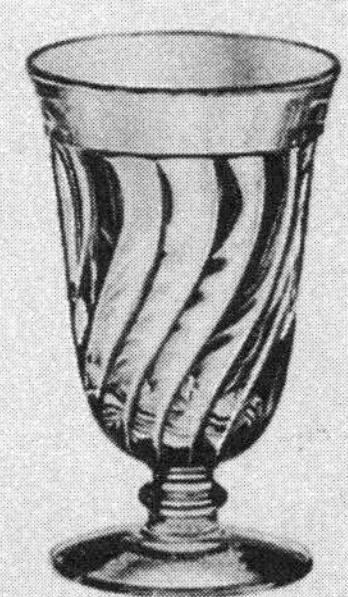
2412—5 oz. Footed Tumbler
Height 4½ in.

2412—4 oz. Oyster Cocktail
Height 3⅜ in.

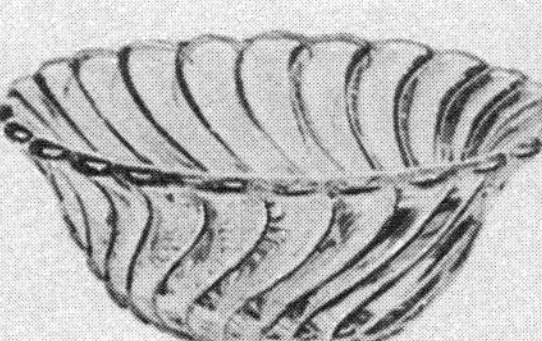

2412—Finger Bowl
Height 2 in.
Diameter 4¾ in.

2412½—5 oz. Tumbler
Height 3⅝ in.

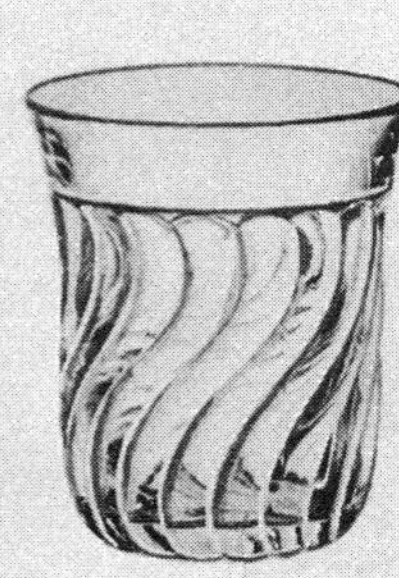
2412½—9 oz. Tumbler
Height 3⅞ in.

2412½—12 oz. Tumbler
Height 4⅞ in.

2412—2-Quart Ice Jug
Height 7¾ in.

COLONY PATTERN

No. 2412 LINE

2412—Footed Cup
2412—Saucer
Cup Capacity 6 oz.

2412—Cream Soup

2412—Mayonnaise and Plate and Ladle
Mayo. Height 3⅜ in. Mayo. Diameter 4⅝ in.
Plate Diameter 6¾ in.

2412—Individual Sugar
Height 2⅞ in.

2412—Individual Cream
Height 3¼ in.
Capacity 4¼ oz.

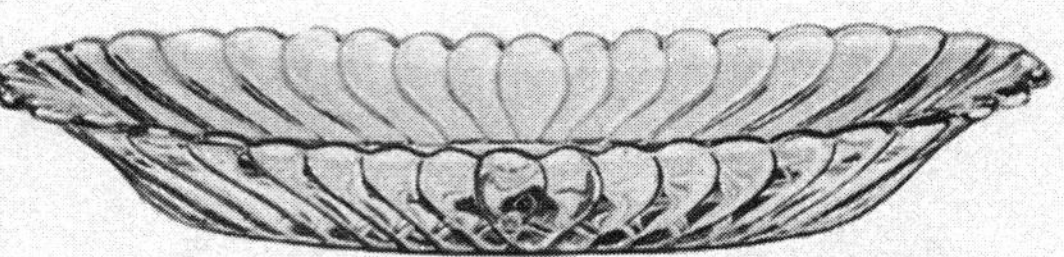

2412—7 in. Olive
2412—9½ in. Pickle
2412—11½ in. Celery

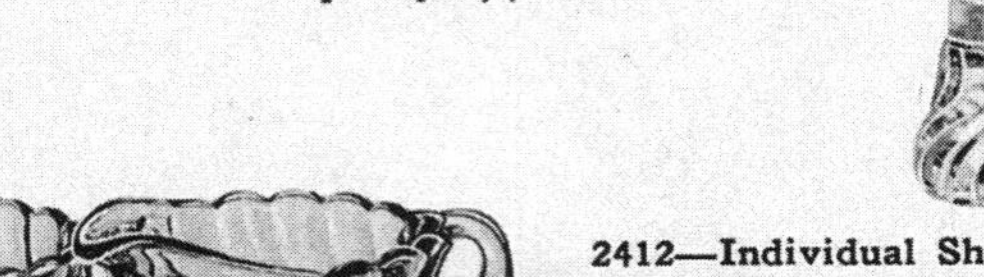

2412—Individual Shaker and E Top
Height 1⅞ in.

2412—3 Piece Ind. Shaker Set
Length 4½ in. Height 2¼ in.
Consisting of:
1/12 Doz. 2412—Ind. Shaker Tray
1/6 Doz. 2412—Ind. Shaker and E Top

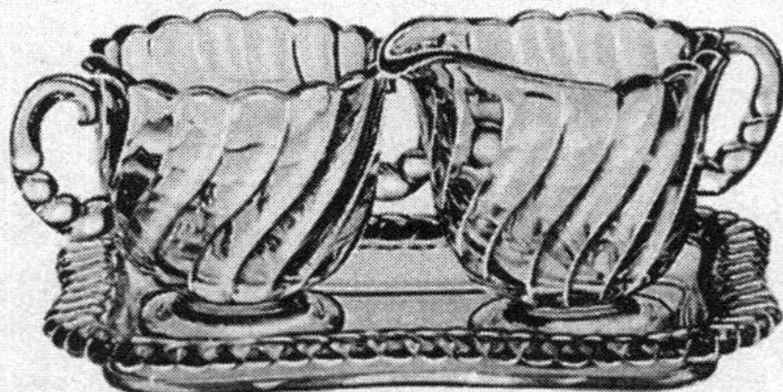

2412—Ind. Sugar and Cream and Tray
Height 3½ in.
Consisting of:
1/12 Doz. 2412—6¾ in. S. & C. Tray
1/12 Doz. 2412—Ind. Sugar
1/12 Doz. 2412—Ind. Cream

2412—Shaker and F Top
Height 2¾ in.

2412—Footed Sugar
Height 3⅜ in.

2412—Footed Cream
Height 3⅞ in.
Capacity 7 oz.

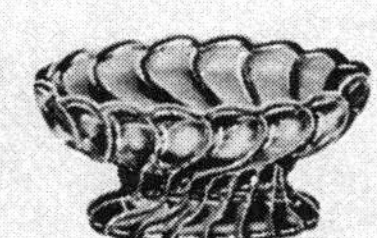

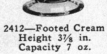

2412—Footed Almond
Height 1⅜ in.
Length 2¾ in.

2412—4 oz. Oil and Stopper
Ground Stopper
Height 5⅞ in.
Capacity 4½ oz.

Fostoria Glass Company, Moundsville, West Virginia, January 1, 1941

COLONY PATTERN

No. 2412 LINE

2412—Sweetmeat
Diameter 5 in.
Height 1½ in.

2412—Bon Bon
Length 5 in.
Width 6 in.

2412 Whip Cream
Diameter 4¾ in.
Height 1¾ in.

2412—Lemon
Diameter 6½ in.

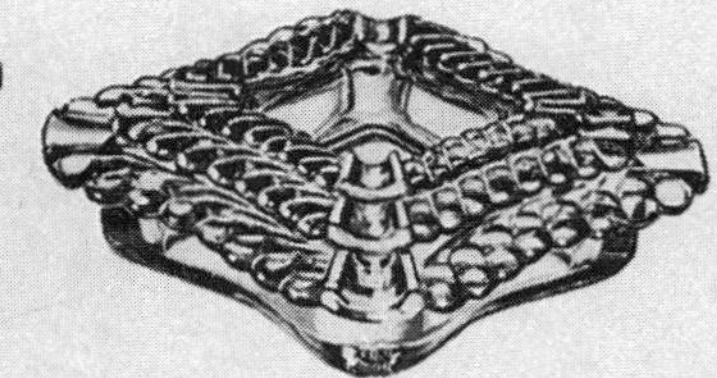

2412—3 Piece Ash Tray Set
Consisting of:
1/12 Doz. 2412—3 in. Ind. Ash Tray
1/12 Doz. 2412—3½ in. Small Ash Tray
1/12 Doz. 2412—4½ in. Large Ash Tray

2412—Oblong Cigarette Box and Cover
Length 6 in. Width 4¾ in.
Height 1⅜ in. Holds 38 Cigarettes

2412—3 in. Individual Ash Tray

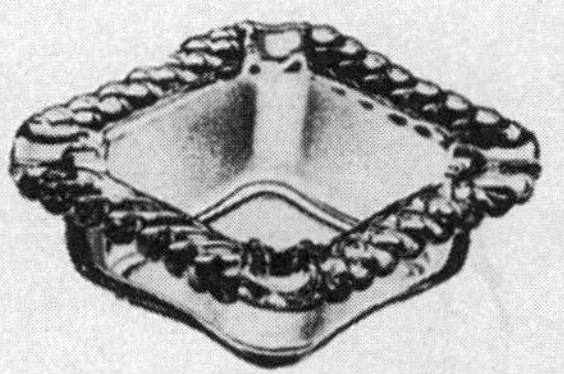

2412—3½ in. Small Ash Tray

2412—4½ in. Large Ash Tray

Fostoria Glass Company, Moundsville, West Virginia, January 1, 1941

COLONY PATTERN

No. 2412 LINE

2412—3 in. Candlestick

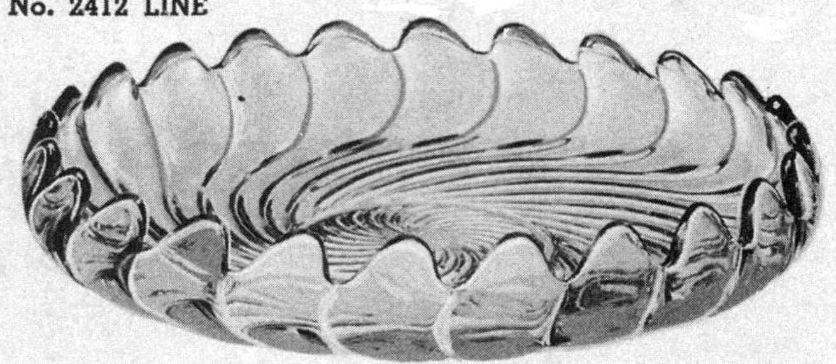

2412—10 in. Lily Pond
Height 2¼ in.

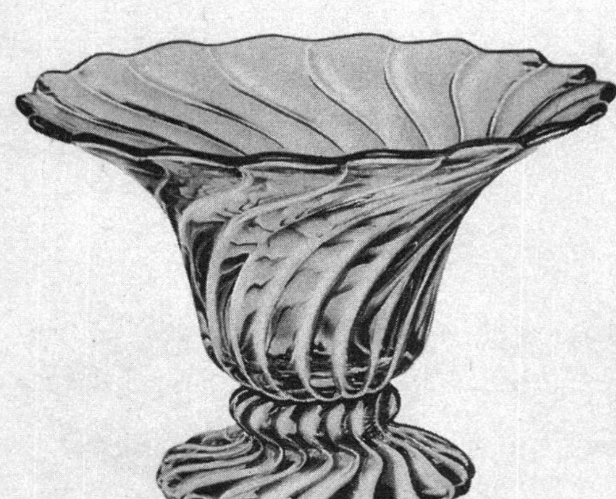

2412—7½ in Vase, Flared

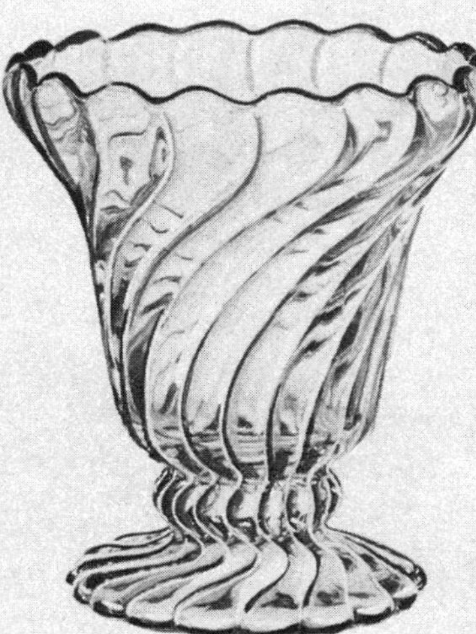

2412—7 in. Ftd. Vase, Cupped

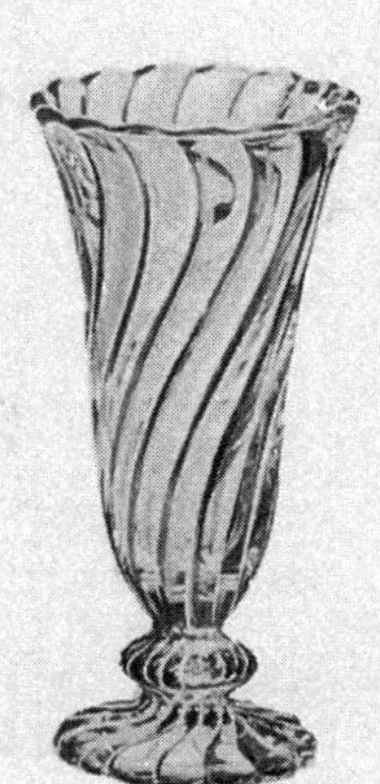

2412—6 in.
Footed Bud Vase, Flared

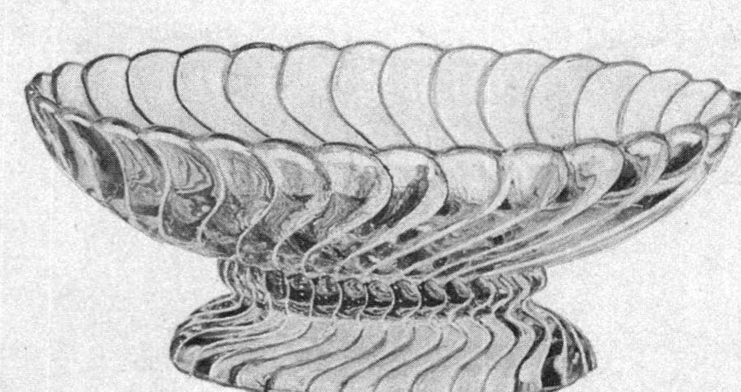

2412—11 in. Footed Oval Bowl
Height 4 in.

2412—Footed Urn No Cover
Height 6⅝ in.
2412—Footed Urn and Cover
Height 9 in.

Fostoria Glass Company, Moundsville, West Virginia, January 1, 1941

COLONY PATTERN

No. 2412 LINE

112 Ink #3
1901 Catalog

112 Salt, Indv.
1901 Catalog

121 Bobache
1901 Catalog

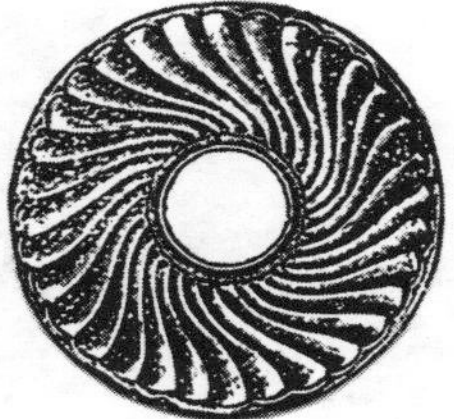

121 Bobache
Top View, 1901 Catalog

112 1/2 Water Bottle
1901 catalog

112 Sponge Cup
Diameter 3 in.
1901 Catalog

112 Ink & Tray
1 3/4 in., 1901 Catalog

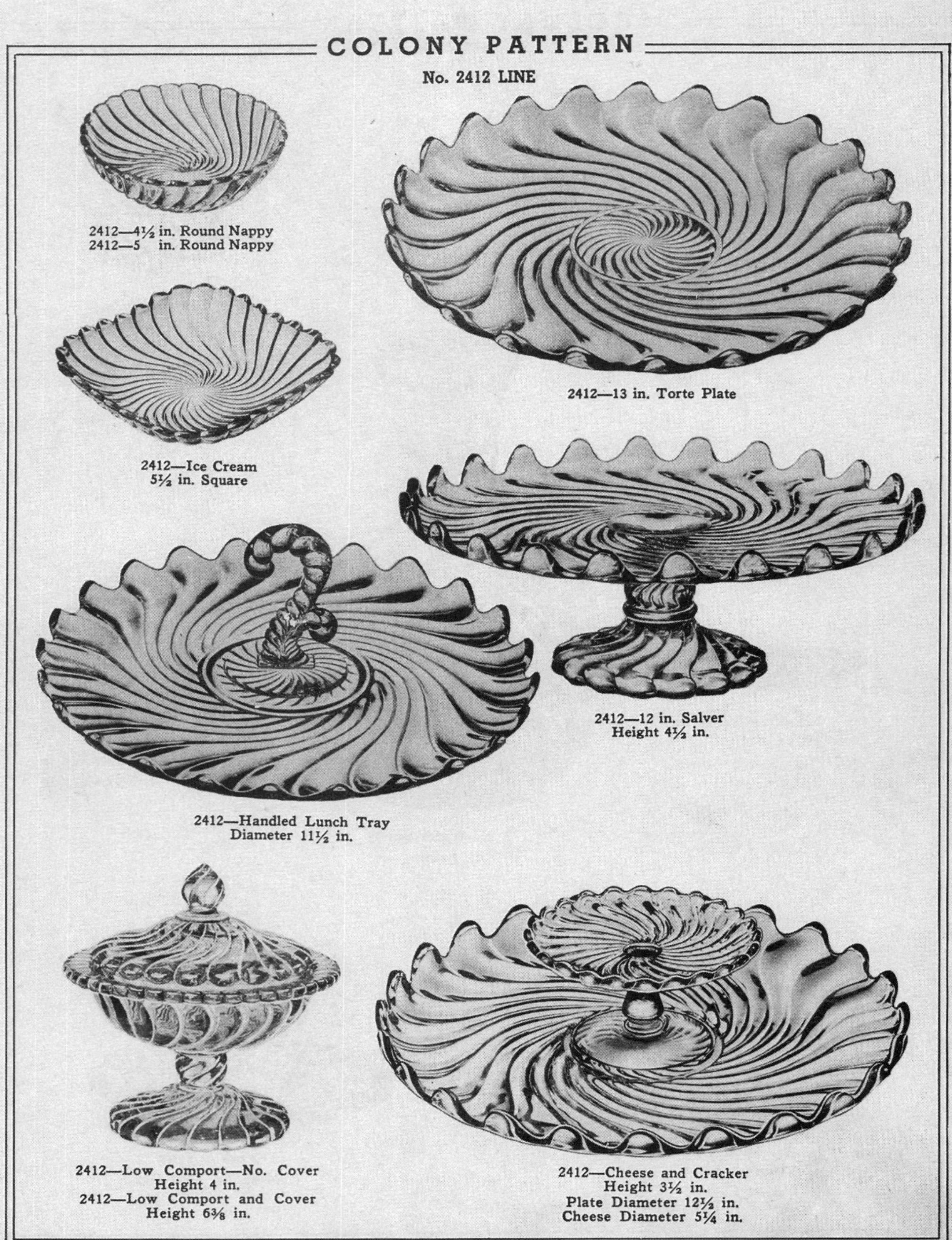

Fostoria Glass Company, Moundsville, West Virginia, January 1, 1941

COLONY PATTERN

No. 2412 LINE

2412—4½ in. Round Nappy
2412—5 in. Round Nappy

2412—13 in. Torte Plate

2412—Ice Cream
5½ in. Square

2412—12 in. Salver
Height 4½ in.

2412—Handled Lunch Tray
Diameter 11½ in.

2412—Low Comport—No. Cover
Height 4 in.
2412—Low Comport and Cover
Height 6⅜ in.

2412—Cheese and Cracker
Height 3½ in.
Plate Diameter 12½ in.
Cheese Diameter 5¼ in.

COLONY PATTERN

No. 2412 LINE

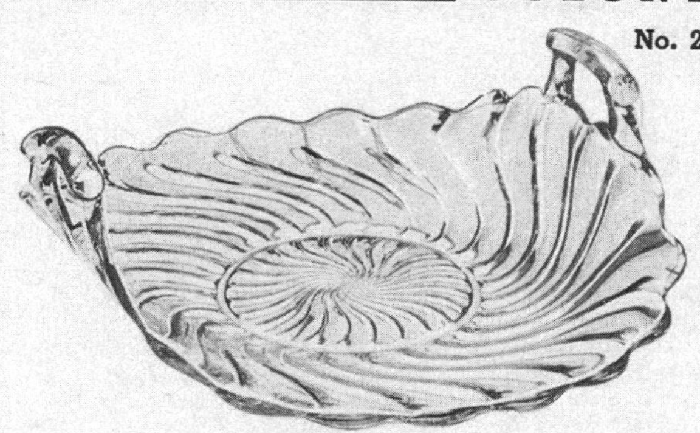

2412—Handled Muffin Tray
Length 8⅜ in. Width 9¾ in.

2412—7 in. Footed Tid Bit
Height 2⅞ in.

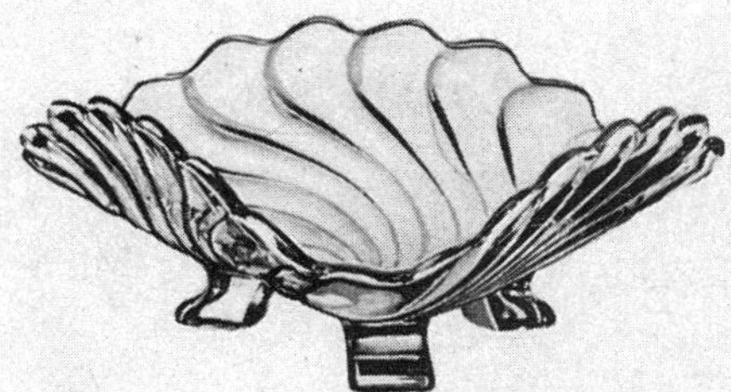

2412—3-Toed Tricorne
Length 7 in.
Height 2⅞ in.

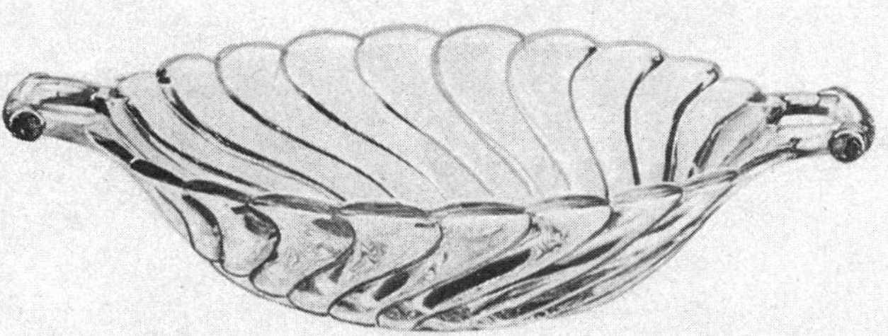

2412—8½ in. Serving Dish, 2 Handles
Height 2⅜ in.

2412—3-Toed Tid Bit
Diameter 7½ in.
Height 1⅜ in.

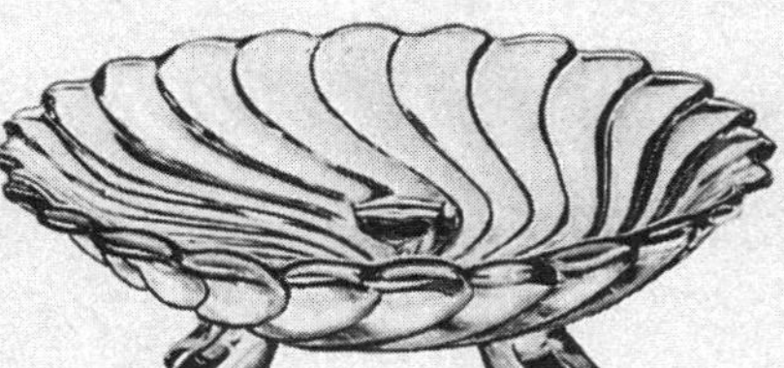

2412—3-Toed Bon Bon
Diameter 7 in.
Height 2 in.

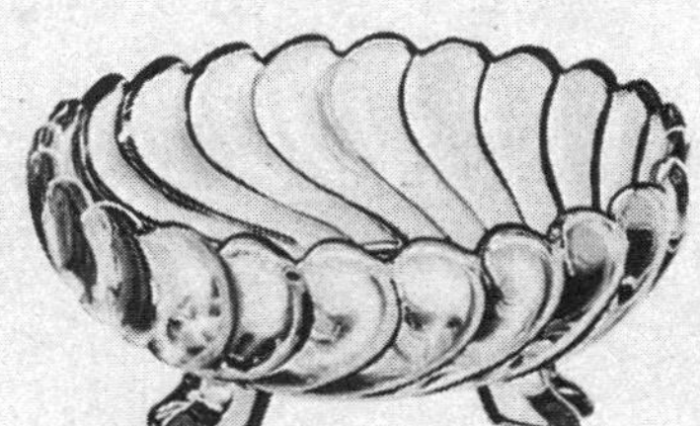

2412—3-Toed Nut Bowl
Diameter 5⅝ in.
Height 2⅝ in.

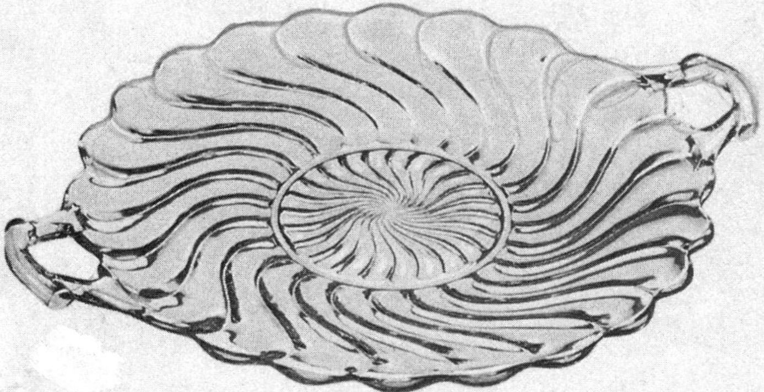

2412—10 in. Cake Plate, 2 Handles

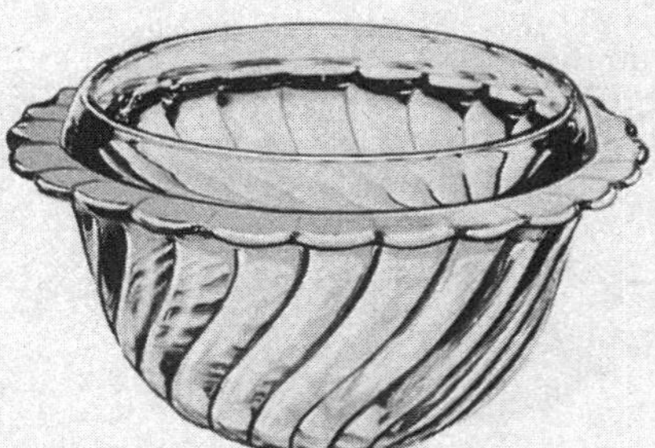

2412—Ice Bowl
Height 4 in.
Diameter 7¼ in.

Fostoria Glass Company, Moundsville, West Virginia, January 1, 1941

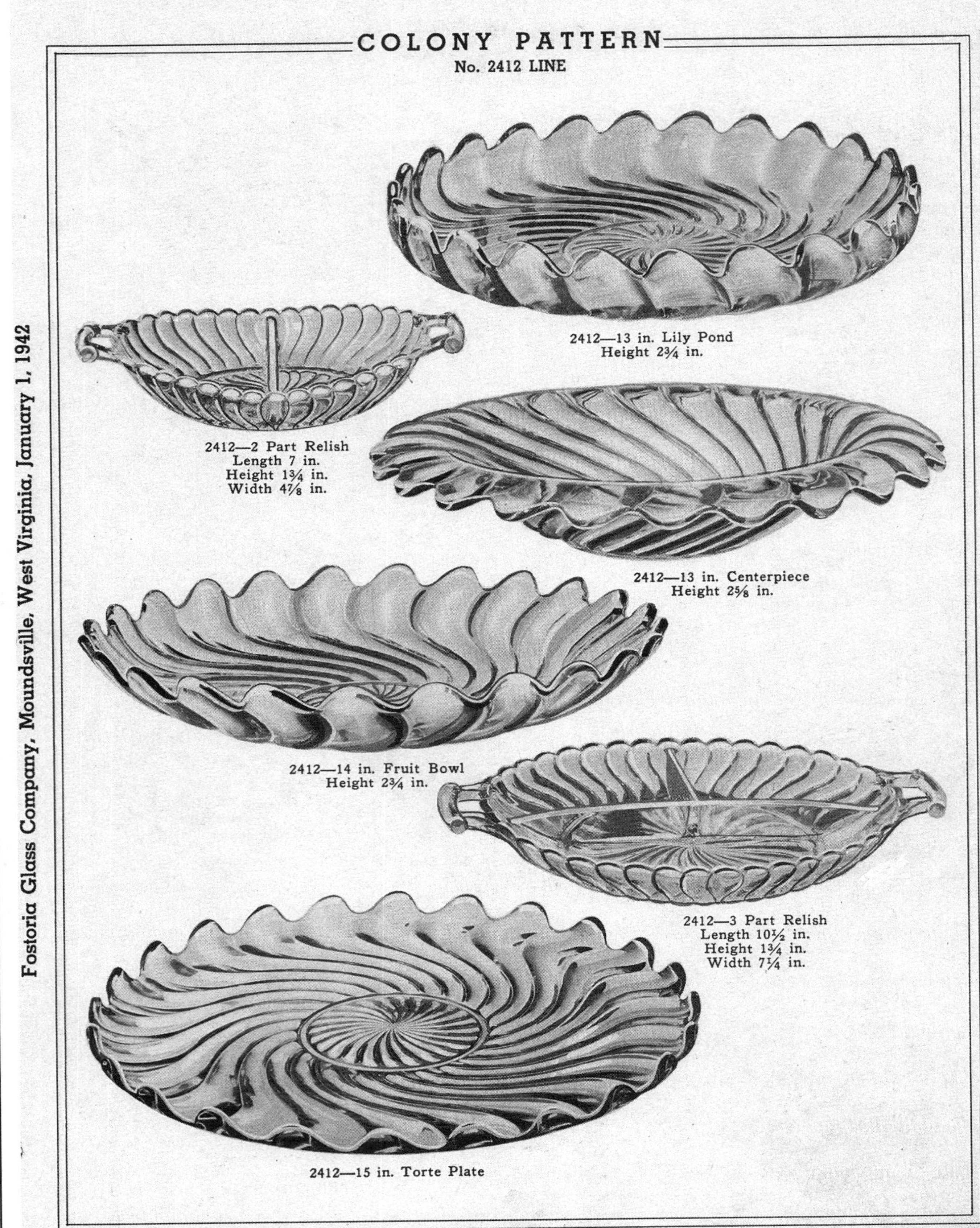

2412—13 in. Lily Pond
Height 2¾ in.

2412—2 Part Relish
Length 7 in.
Height 1¾ in.
Width 4⅞ in.

2412—13 in. Centerpiece
Height 2⅝ in.

2412—14 in. Fruit Bowl
Height 2¾ in.

2412—3 Part Relish
Length 10½ in.
Height 1¾ in.
Width 7¼ in.

2412—15 in. Torte Plate

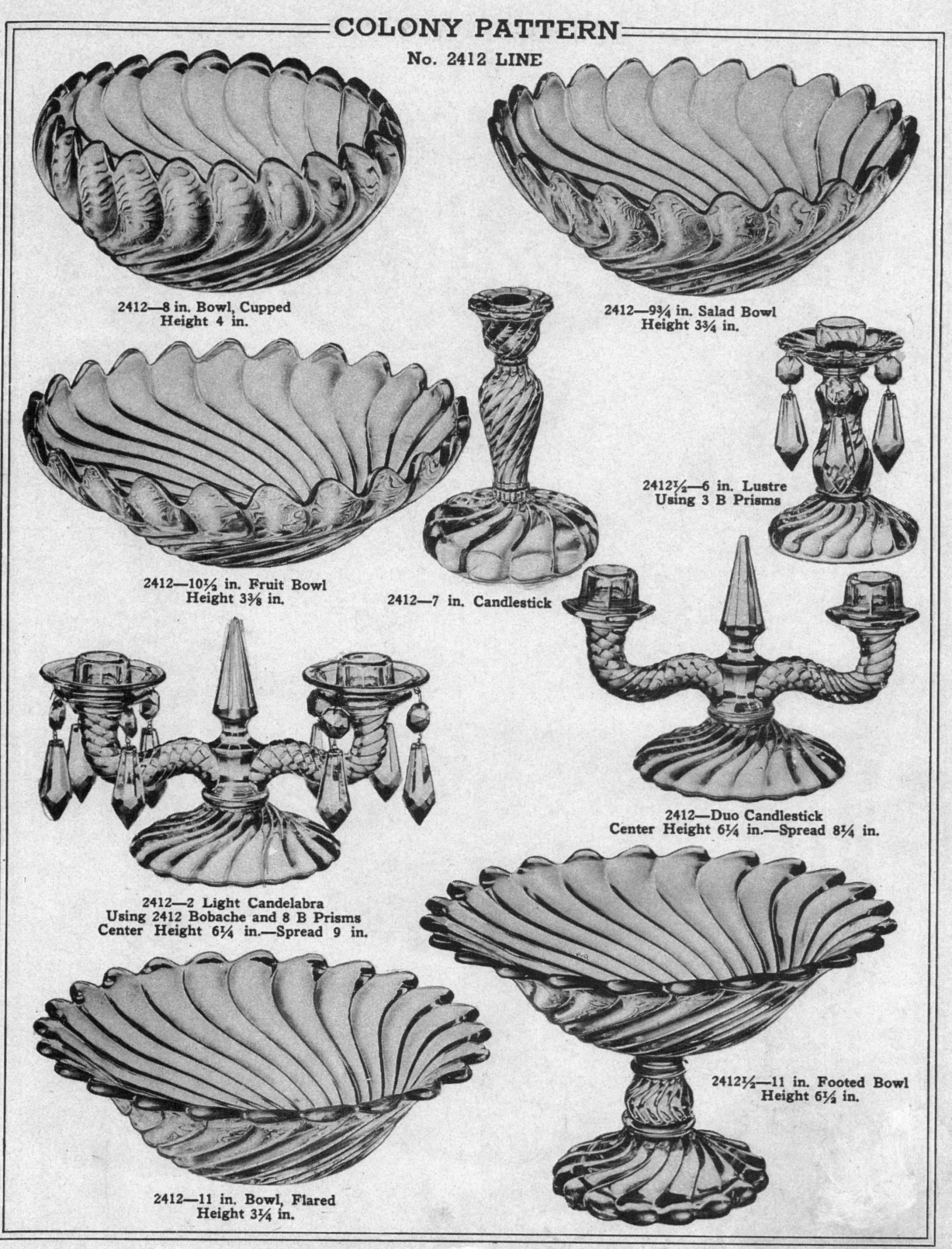
COLONY PATTERN
No. 2412 LINE
2412—8 in. Bowl, Cupped
Height 4 in.
2412—9¾ in. Salad Bowl
Height 3¾ in.
2412½—6 in. Lustre
Using 3 B Prisms
2412—10½ in. Fruit Bowl
Height 3⅜ in.
2412—7 in. Candlestick
2412—Duo Candlestick
Center Height 6¼ in.—Spread 8¼ in.
2412—2 Light Candelabra
Using 2412 Bobache and 8 B Prisms
Center Height 6¼ in.—Spread 9 in.
2412½—11 in. Footed Bowl
Height 6½ in.
2412—11 in. Bowl, Flared
Height 3¼ in.
Fostoria Glass Company, Moundsville, West Virginia, January 1, 1941

No. 4 Lustre (10 UDP)
Height 9¾ in.

2412—Low Foot Bowl
Diameter 10½ in. Height 5⅝ in.

2412—7½ in. Lustre
8 U Drop Prisms

2412—12 in. Vase
2412—14 in. Vase

2412—High Foot Bowl
Diameter 10½ in. Height 8¼ in.

1103—14½ in. Lustre
10 U Drop Prisms

Colony Pattern
No. 2412 Line

175½ Shaker
1901 Catalog

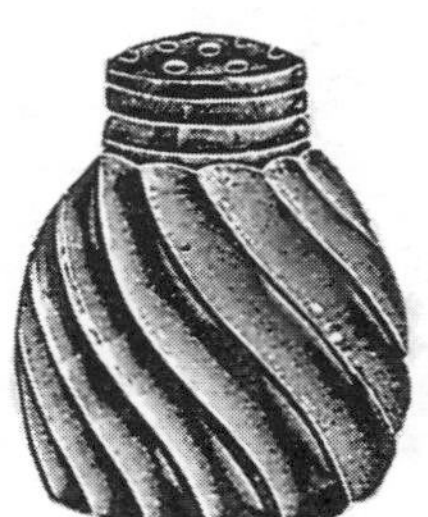

112 Shaker
1901 Catalog

112½ Shaker
1901 Catalog

Queen Anne Pattern
No. 2412
1927 Catalog

Colony Pattern
No. 2412 Line

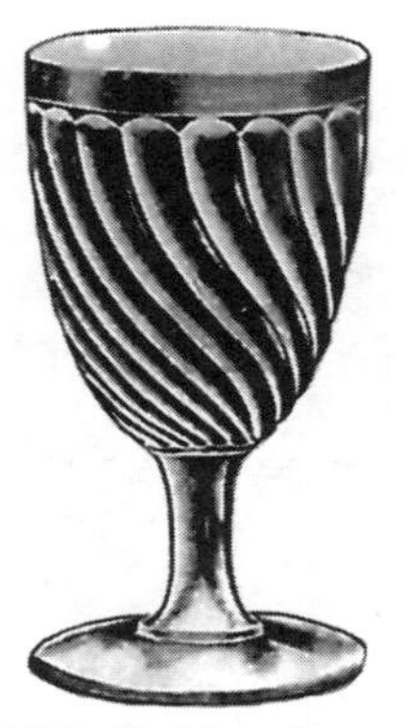

112 Goblet, 8 oz.
1904 Catalog

2412 Ftd. Bon Bon
1952 Catalog

2412 Indv. Shaker
3-Piece, 1952 Catalog

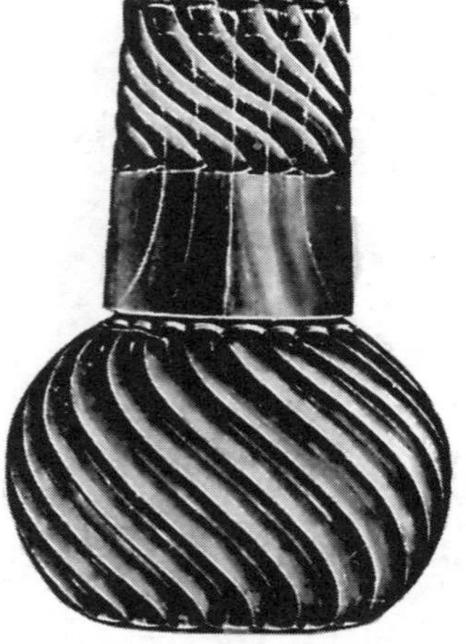

161 Water Bottle and Tumbler
Capacity 26 oz.
1901 Catalog

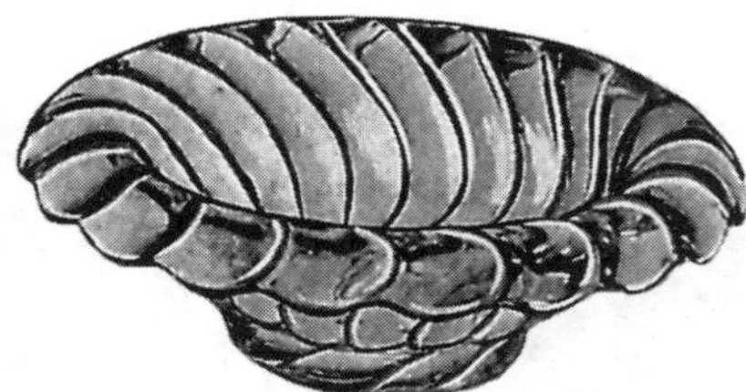

2412 Bowl, Rolled Edge
Diameter 9", 1952 Catalog

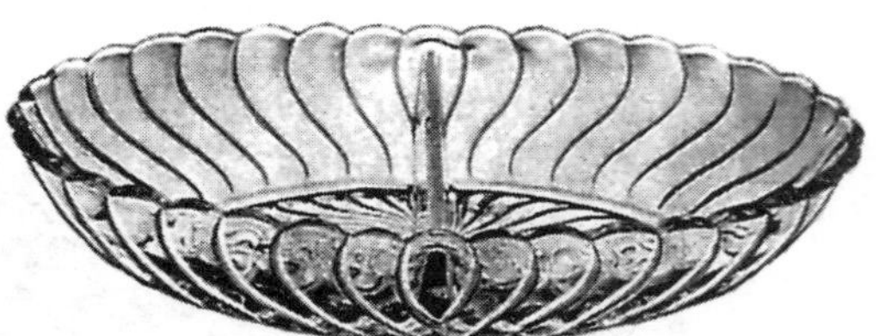

2412 Vegetable Dish
2-Part, 1952 Catalog

2412 Mayonnaise, Plate
and Ladle
1940 Catalog

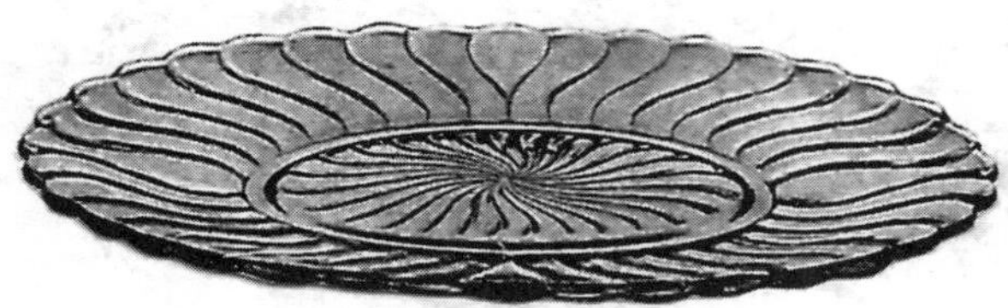

2412 Platter
Length 12½"
1952 Catalog

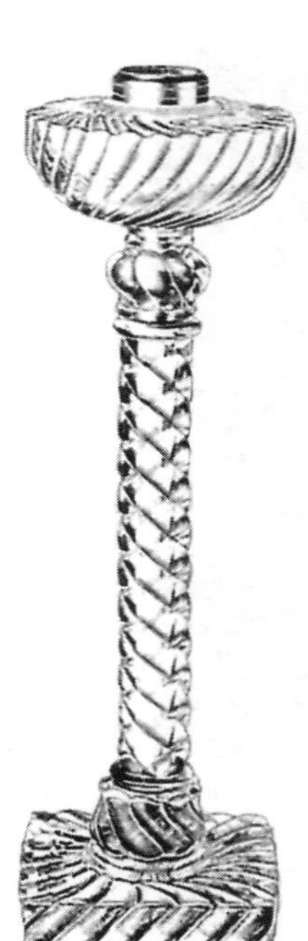

1 Banquet Lamp
Height 25", 1939 Catalog

2412 Candy Box and Cover
1952 Catalog

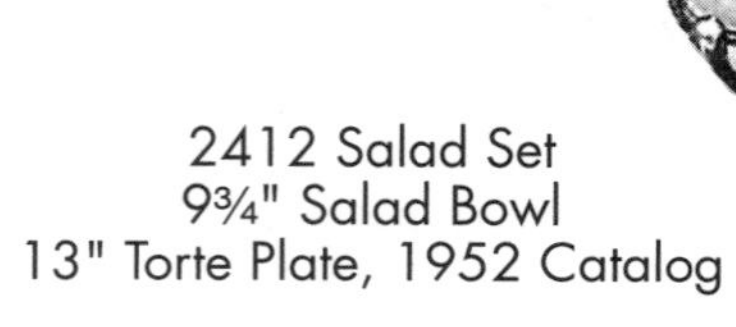

2412 Salad Set
9¾" Salad Bowl
13" Torte Plate, 1952 Catalog

Colony Pattern
No. 2412 Line

Fostoria made this wonderful banquet lamp for Quoizel Inc. Dating to around 1940, it was never marketed under the Fostoria name.

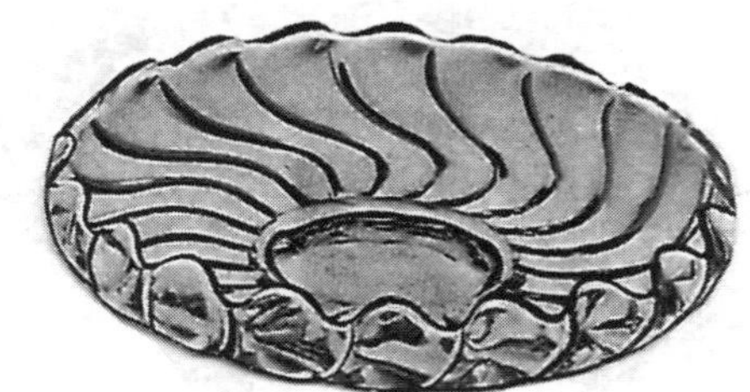

2412 Lily Pond
Diameter 9"
1952 Catalog

2412 Jelly and Cover
1952 Catalog

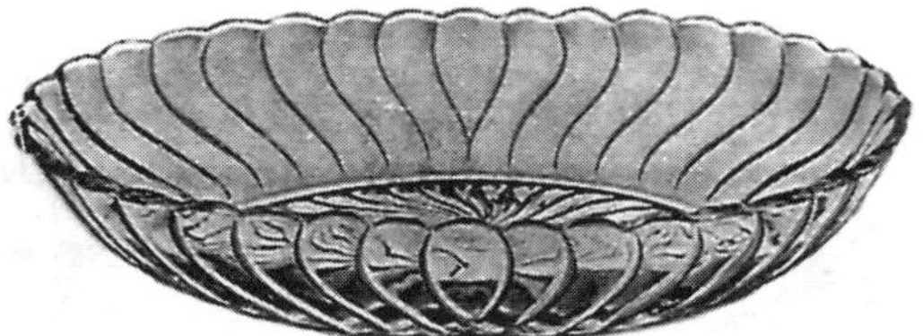

2412 Vegetable Dish
1952 Catalog

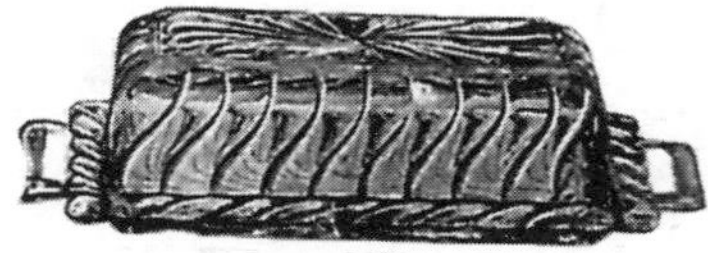

2412 Butter and Cover
1952 Catalog

4 Lustre with Prisms
1913 Catalog

2412 Cereal Pitcher
1-Pint, 1952 Catalog

2412 Ice Bowl
1952 Catalog

2 Banquet Lamp
Height 18", Capacity 32 oz.
1904 Catalog

Colony Pattern
No 2412 Line

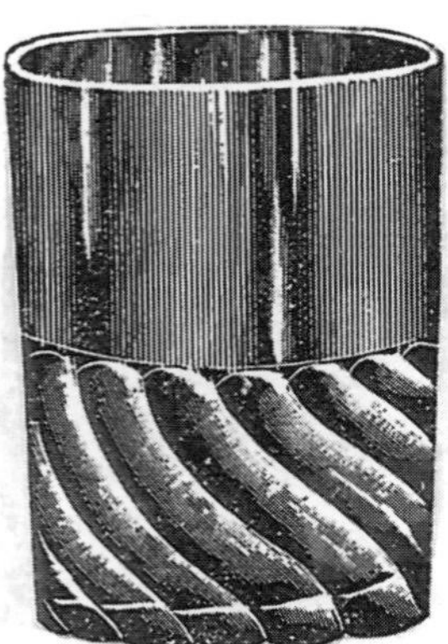

112 Tumbler
8½ oz., 1901 Catalog

161 Candle
Height 6½", 1914 Catalog

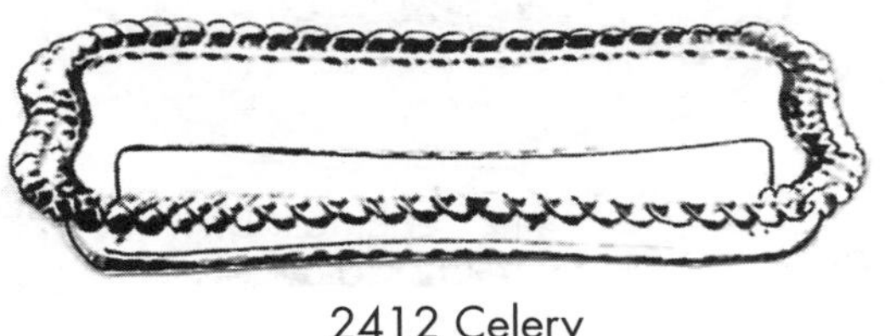

2412 Celery
Length 10½", 1940 Catalog

2412 Footed Urn and Cover
Height 9"
1940 Catalog

112 Jug, 3-Pint
1898 Catalog

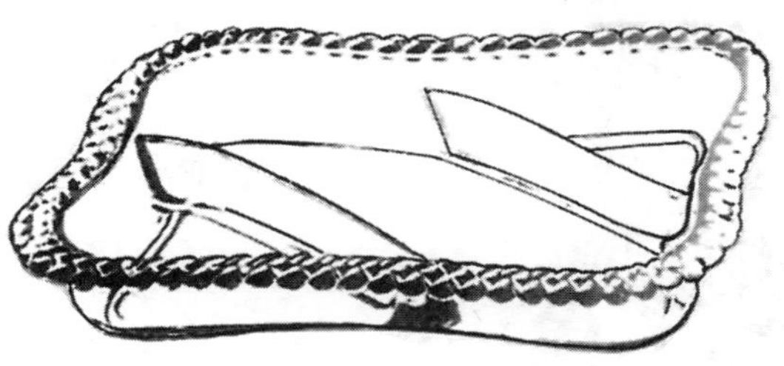

2412 Relish, 3-Part
Length 10", 1940 Catalog

Colony Pattern
No. 2412 Line

1 Candelabra, 3-Light
Bobaches wired ready for Prisms
Top Flower Vase, Height 7", 1905 Catalog

1103½ Shoe Plate and Stand
Heights 17", 24", 25", 1914 Catalog

Colony Pattern
No. 2412 Line

1952 Catalog

2412 Ice Jug
3-Pint, Height 8½"

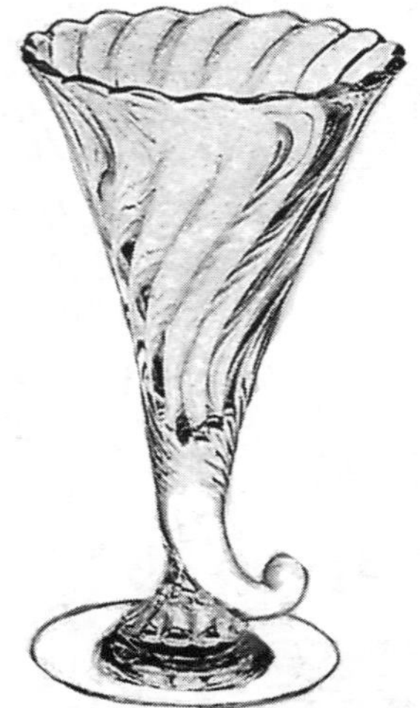

2412 Cornucopia Vase
Height 9¼"

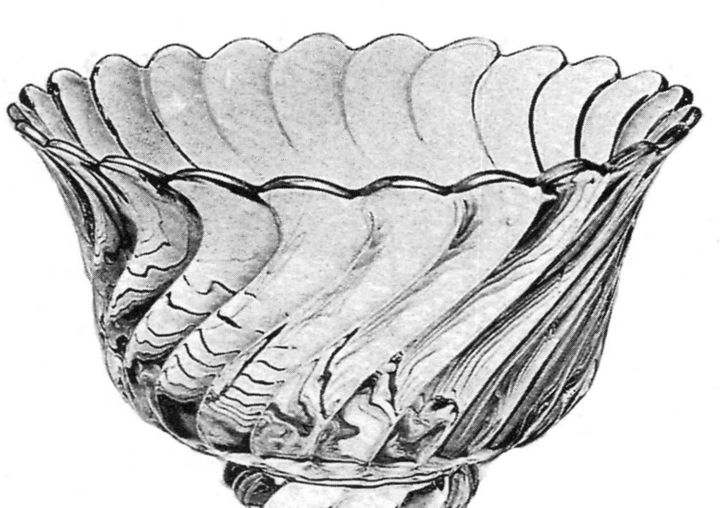

2412 Punch Bowl
2-Gal., Height 8⅛"

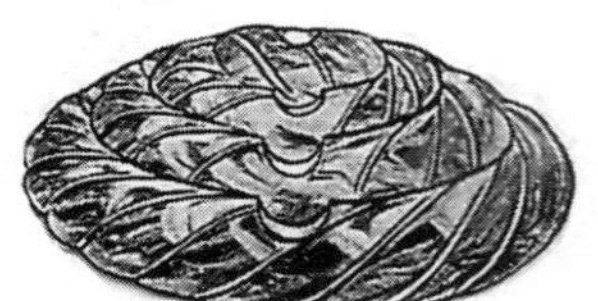

2412½ Ash Tray Set
3-Piece, 3", 4½", 6"

2412 Torte Plate
Diameter 18"

Colony Pattern
No. 2412 Line

5 Candle, Handled
1904 Catalog

Banquet Lamp, Peg Font
1904 Catalog

112 Candle
Height 9½", 9¾"
1904 Catalog

6 Candle, Ribboned
Assorted Colored Ribbon
1904 Catalog

CONTOUR PATTERN

No. 2666 Line

FOSTORIA GLASS COMPANY, MOUNDSVILLE, WEST VIRGINIA — 1955

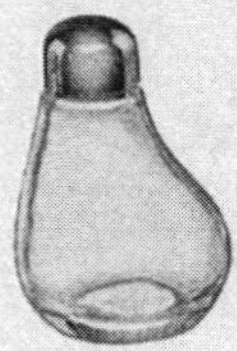

2666
Shaker
Chrome Top "E"
Height 2¾ in.

2666
Oil and Stopper
Height 5⅜ in.
Capacity 6 oz.

2666
Sauce Pitcher and Plate
Overall Length 8½ in.

2666
Sauce Pitcher
Length 8½ in.

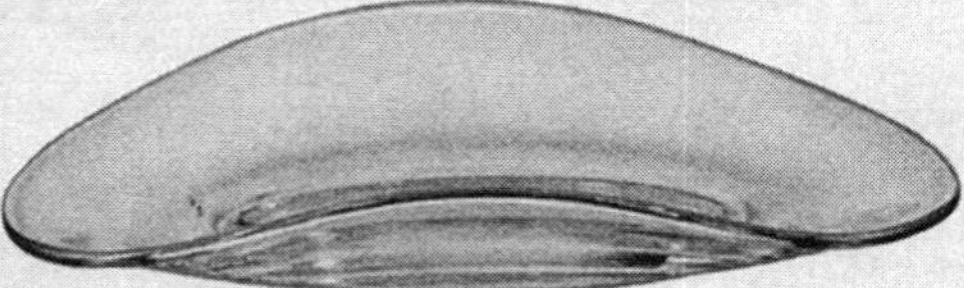

2666
Oval Plate
Length 8⅜ in. Width 5 in.

2666
Oblong Butter and Cover
Length 7 in. Height 2 in.

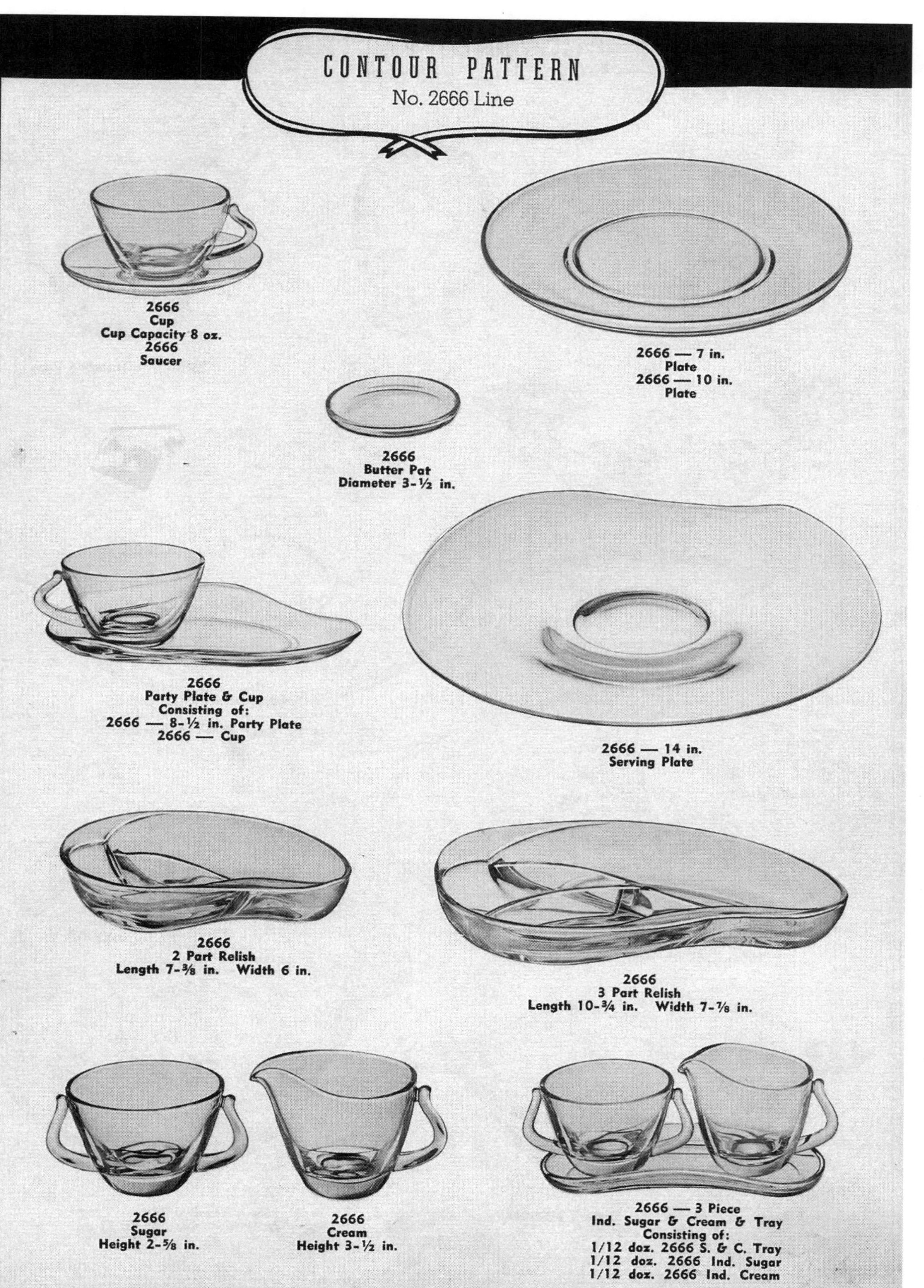
CONTOUR PATTERN
No. 2666 Line
FOSTORIA GLASS COMPANY, MOUNDSVILLE, WEST VIRGINIA — 1952
2666
Cup
Cup Capacity 8 oz.
2666
Saucer
2666 — 7 in.
Plate
2666 — 10 in.
Plate
2666
Butter Pat
Diameter 3-½ in.
2666
Party Plate & Cup
Consisting of:
2666 — 8-½ in. Party Plate
2666 — Cup
2666 — 14 in.
Serving Plate
2666
2 Part Relish
Length 7-⅜ in. Width 6 in.
2666
3 Part Relish
Length 10-¾ in. Width 7-⅞ in.
2666
Sugar
Height 2-⅝ in.
2666
Cream
Height 3-½ in.
2666 — 3 Piece
Ind. Sugar & Cream & Tray
Consisting of:
1/12 doz. 2666 S. & C. Tray
1/12 doz. 2666 Ind. Sugar
1/12 doz. 2666 Ind. Cream

CORONET PATTERN

No. 2560 LINE

2560½—4 in. Candlestick

2560
3¾ in. Pansy Vase

2560—6 in. Handled Vase

2560—Duo Candlestick
Height 5⅝ in.—Spread 9 in.

2560—10½ in. Cake Plate, 2 Handles

2560—11½ in. Handled Lunch Tray

2560—8½ in. Serving Dish, 2 Handles
Height 2⅜ in.

2560—Handled Muffin Tray
Length 8¼ in. Width 10 in.

Fostoria Glass Company, Moundsville, West Virginia, Jan. 1, 1939

29

DECORATOR PATTERN

No. 2691 Line

FOSTORIA GLASS COMPANY, MOUNDSVILLE, WEST VIRGINIA — 1956

2691
Cup
Capacity 7½ oz.
2691
Saucer

2691
Demitasse Cup
Capacity 2¼ oz.
2691
Demitasse Saucer

2691—7 in.
Plate

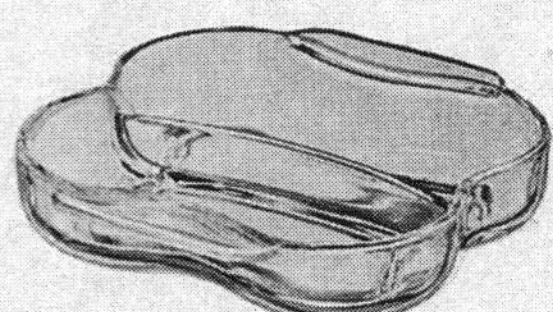

2691
2 Part Server
Height 1½ in. Width 6⅜ in.

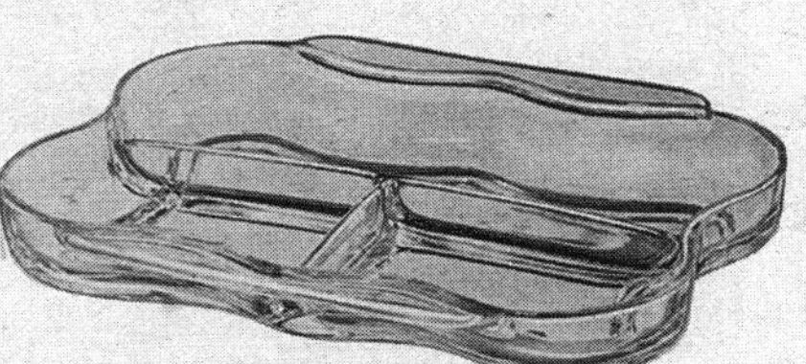

2691
3 Part Server
Length 9¾ in. Width 7½ in.
Height 1½ in.

2691
Sugar and Cream and Tray
Consisting of:
1/12 doz. 2691 Sugar and Cream and Tray
1/12 doz. 2691 Sugar and Cover
1/12 doz. 2691 Cream

2691
Sugar and Cover
Height 3¼ in.

2691
Cream
Height 3¼ in.

2691
Dessert
Diameter 4⅞ in.

2691
Soup
Diameter 4¾ in.

2691
Shaker and Chrome Top "A"
Height 3 in.

2691
Sauce Bowl and Plate and Ladle
Height 2¾ in.

2691
Handled Preserve
Width 4 in.

2691
Individual Cigarette Holder
Height 2½ in.

2691
Individual Ash Tray
Diameter 2⅝ in.

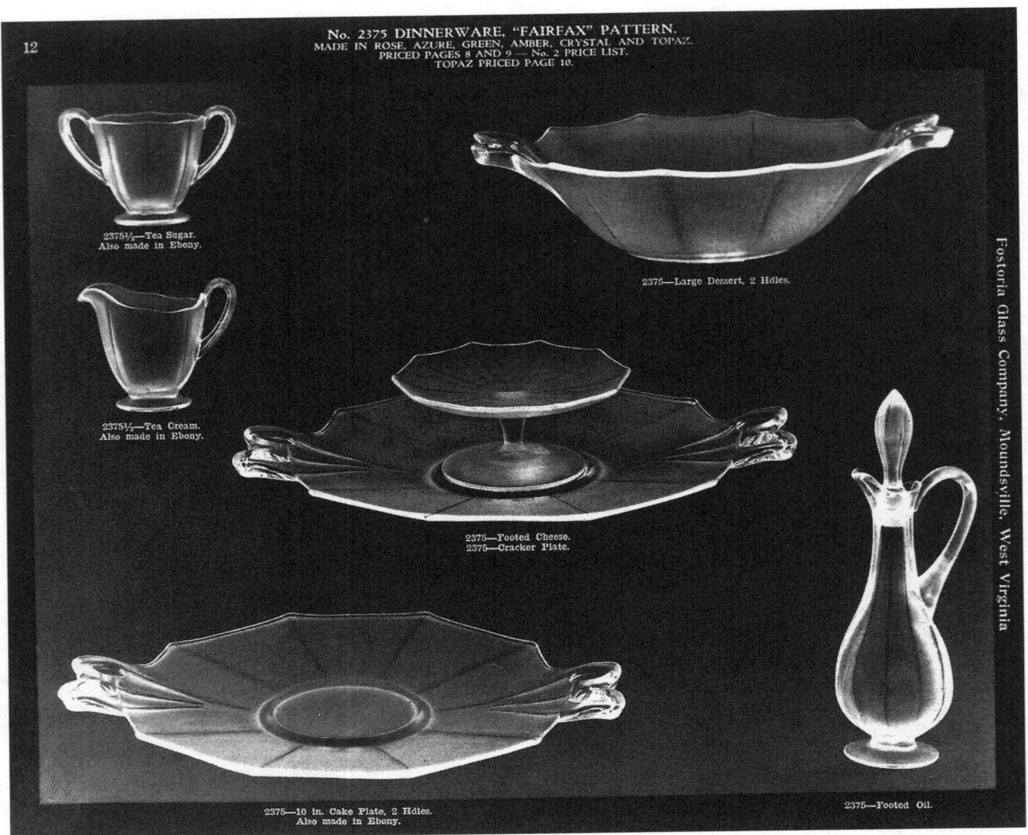
12

No. 2375 DINNERWARE, "FAIRFAX" PATTERN.
MADE IN ROSE, AZURE, GREEN, AMBER, CRYSTAL AND TOPAZ.
PRICED PAGES 8 AND 9 — No. 2 PRICE LIST.
TOPAZ PRICED PAGE 10.

2375½—Tea Sugar.
Also made in Ebony.

2375—Large Dessert, 2 Hdles.

2375½—Tea Cream.
Also made in Ebony.

2375—Footed Cheese.
2375—Cracker Plate.

2375—10 in. Cake Plate, 2 Hdles.
Also made in Ebony.

2375—Footed Oil.

Fostoria Glass Company, Moundsville, West Virginia

1930 Catalog

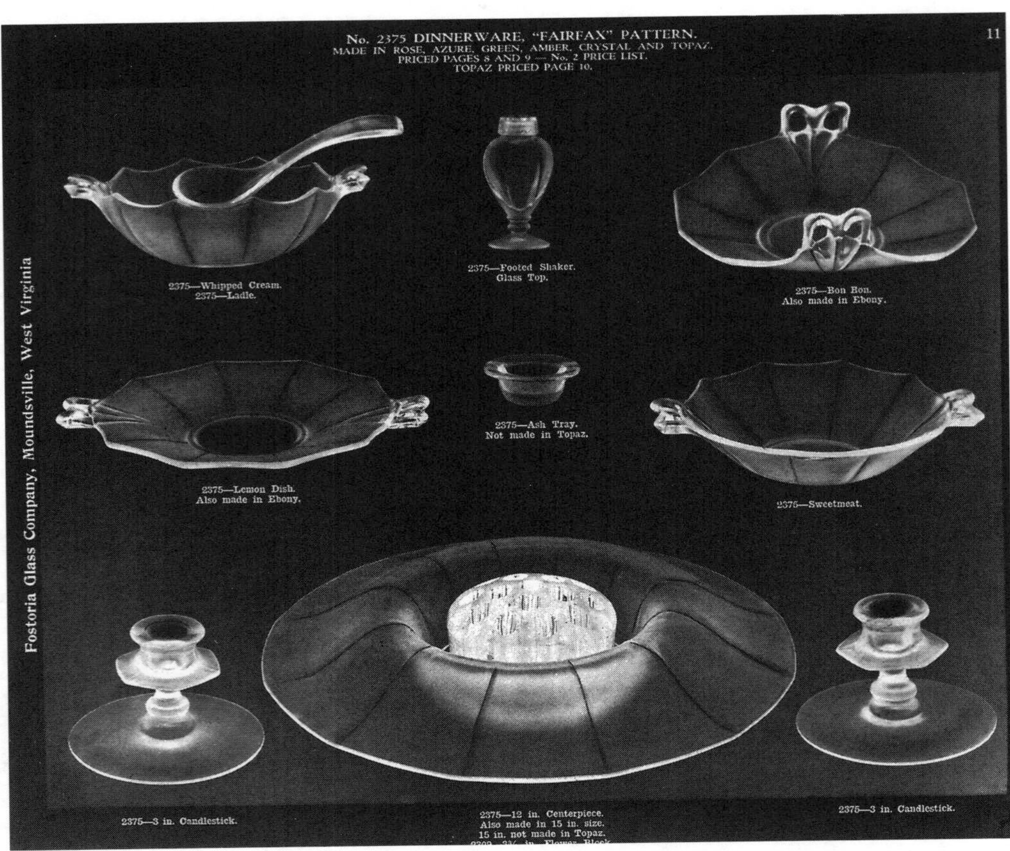
11

No. 2375 DINNERWARE, "FAIRFAX" PATTERN.
MADE IN ROSE, AZURE, GREEN, AMBER, CRYSTAL AND TOPAZ.
PRICED PAGES 8 AND 9 — No. 2 PRICE LIST.
TOPAZ PRICED PAGE 10.

Fostoria Glass Company, Moundsville, West Virginia

2375—Whipped Cream.
2375—Ladle.

2375—Footed Shaker.
Glass Top.

2375—Bon Bon.
Also made in Ebony.

2375—Lemon Dish.
Also made in Ebony.

2375—Ash Tray.
Not made in Topaz.

2375—Sweetmeat.

2375—3 in. Candlestick.

2375—12 in. Centerpiece.
Also made in 15 in. size.
15 in. not made in Topaz.

2375—3 in. Candlestick.

1930 Catalog

FAIRMONT PATTERN

No. 2718 Line

2718/2—10½ oz.
Goblet
Height 5⅞ in.

2718/7—6 oz.
Sherbet
Height—4⅜ in.

2718/63—13 oz.
Footed Ice Tea
Height—6⅜ in.

2718/421
Dessert
Diameter 5 in.

Made in Crystal, Blue, Green, and Amber
Other pieces added in 1963.

2718/550—8 in.
Plate

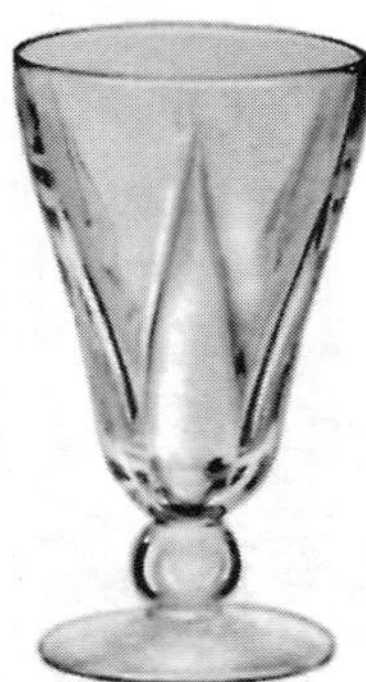

2718/88—5 oz.
Footed Juice
Height—5⅛ in.

Gov. Bradford Pattern
No. 1229 Line

1229 Cracker Jar, Covered
Silver Plated Lid, 1904 Catalog

1229 Swelled Syrup
Silver Plated Lid & Handle
1904 Catalog

1229 Syrup
Silver Plated Lid & Handle
1904 Catalog

1229 Swelled Shape Sugar
Silver Plated Lid, 1904 Catalog

Fostoria Glass Company, Moundsville, West Virginia, Jan. 1, 1939

HERMITAGE PATTERN

No. 2449 LINE

See Price List for Colors

2449—9 oz. Goblet
Height 5¼ in.

2449—5½ oz. High Sherbet
Height 3¼ in.

2449—7 oz. Low Sherbet
Height 3 in.

2449—5 oz. Fruit Cocktail
Height 2⅜ in.

2449—4 oz. Claret
Height 4⅝ in.

2449—5 oz.
Footed Tumbler
Height 4 in.

2449—9 oz. Footed Table Tumbler
Height 4⅛ in.

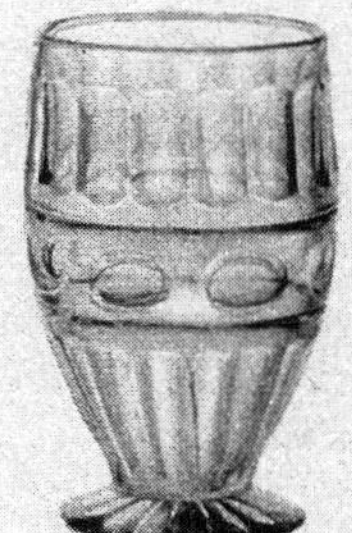
2449—12 oz. Footed Ice Tea
Height 5¼ in.

2449—2 oz. Footed Tumbler
Height 2½ in.

2449—4 oz. Cocktail
Height 3 in.

2449½—6 oz. Old Fashioned Cocktail
Height 3¼ in.

2449½—13 oz. Tumbler
Height 5⅞ in.

2449½—9 oz. Tumbler
Height 4¾ in.

2449½—5 oz. Tumbler
Height 3⅞ in.

2449½—2 oz. Tumbler
Height 2½ in.

HERMITAGE PATTERN

No. 2449 LINE

2449½—5 in. Fruit
2449½—6 in. Cereal

2449—Footed Cup
2449—Saucer

2449½—Plate, Snapped
2449 —Plate, Ground Bottom
See Price List for Sizes

2449½—6½ in. Coup Salad
2449½—7½ in. Coup Salad

2449—Footed Sugar
Height 3 in.

2449—Footed Cream
Height 4 in.
Capacity 6½ oz.

2449—3 Part Relish
Top Diameter 7¼ inches

2449—Ice Dish
2449—7 in. Ice Dish Plate
2451—T. J. Liner Illustrated

2449½—Finger Bowl
Top Diameter 4½ in.

2449—Ash Tray

2449—5 Piece Ash Tray Set
Height 3 in.
Consisting of
1/12 Doz. 2449—Holder
1/3 Doz. 2449—Ind. Ash Trays

2449—10 in. Bowl, Fld.

2449—6 in. Vase

Fostoria Glass Company, Moundsville, West Virginia, Jan. 1, 1939

FOSTORIA GLASS COMPANY, MOUNDSVILLE, WEST VIRGINIA — 1950

HOLIDAY PATTERN

No. 2643 Line

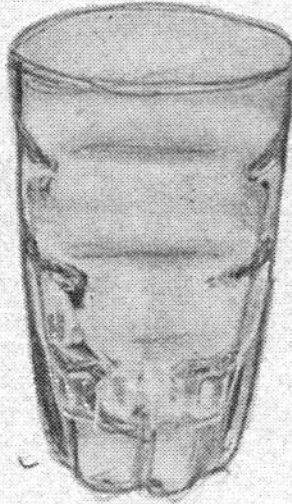

2643 — 12 oz.
Highball
Height 5-¼ in.

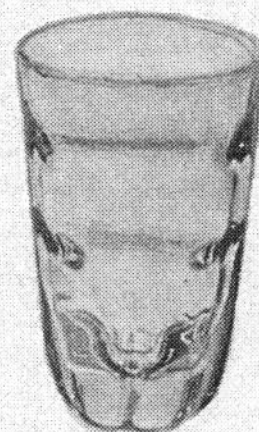

2643—9 oz.
Scotch & Soda
Height 4½ in.

2643—1½ oz.
Whiskey
Height 2⅛ in.

2643 — 6 oz.
Old Fashioned Cocktail
Height 3 in.

2643 — 12 oz.
Double Old Fashioned Cocktail
Height 3-¾ in.

2643 — 4 oz.
Cocktail
Height 2-½ in.

2643
20 oz. Cocktail Mixer
30 oz. Cocktail Mixer

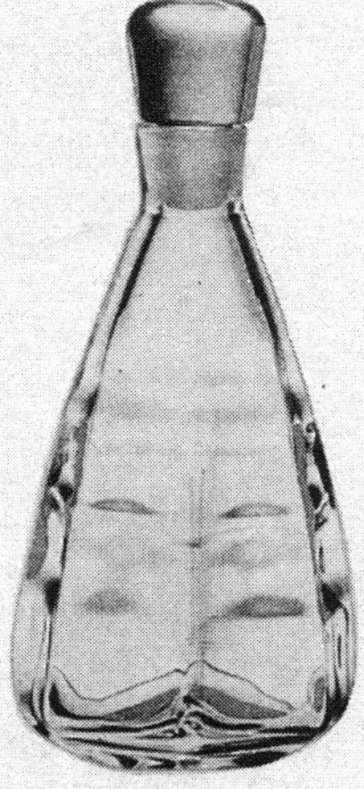

2643
Decanter & Stopper
Capacity 24 oz. Height 10¼ in.

2643
Coaster
Diameter 4 in.

2643
Ice Bowl
Height 5 in.
Diameter 6⅝ in.

HORIZON PATTERN

FOSTORIA GLASS COMPANY, MOUNDSVILLE, WEST VIRGINIA — 1951

HORIZON PATTERN
No. 5650 Line
Blown Lead Glass Duet-Tumblers

5650
Ice Tea/Highball
Height 6 in.

5650
Water/Scotch & Soda
Height 5 in.

5650
Sherbet/Old Fashioned
Height 3⅜ in.

5650
Juice/Cocktail
Height 3⅜ in.

5650
Dessert/Finger Bowl
Height 2⅞ in.

HORIZON PATTERN
No. 2650
Pressed Tableware

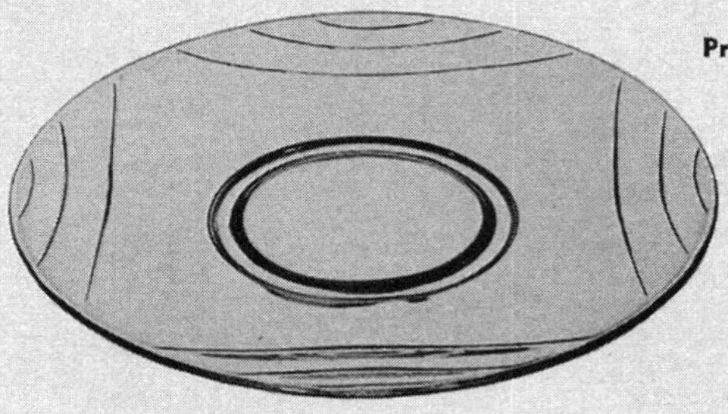

2650-11 in.
Sandwich Plate

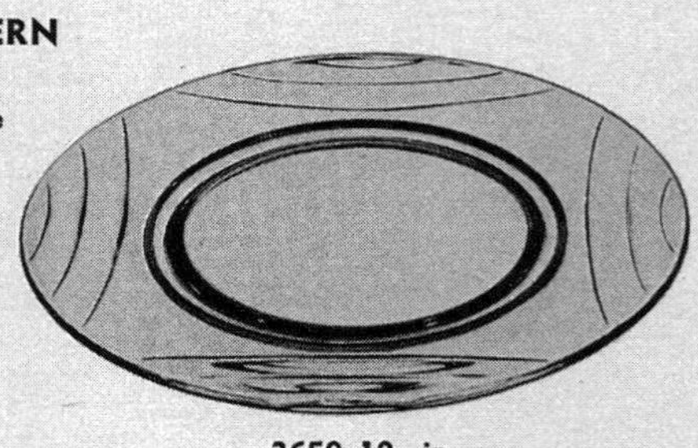

2650-10 in
Dinner Plate
2650-7 in.
Plate

2650
Sugar
Height 3-⅛ in.

2650
Cream
Height 3-½ in.

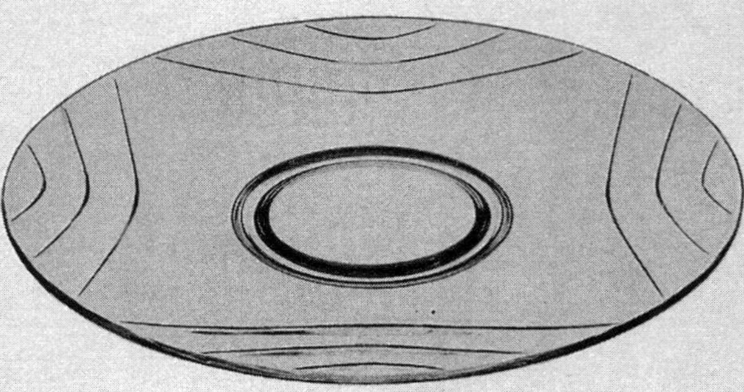

2650-14 in.
Torte Plate

2650-12 in.
Oval Platter

2650
Cup
Cup Capacity 8-½ oz.
2650
Saucer

Hugh Pattern
No. 2470 Dinnerware

Original Designer Drawings Shown Here Represent The 1932 "Hugh" Issue

2470-12" BOWL

2470-5½ CANDLESTICK

2470-6" LOW COMPORT

2470-BON-BON

2470-SWEET MEAT

2470-3-PART-RELISH DISH

2470-4-PART RELISH

2470-9" SERVICE DISH

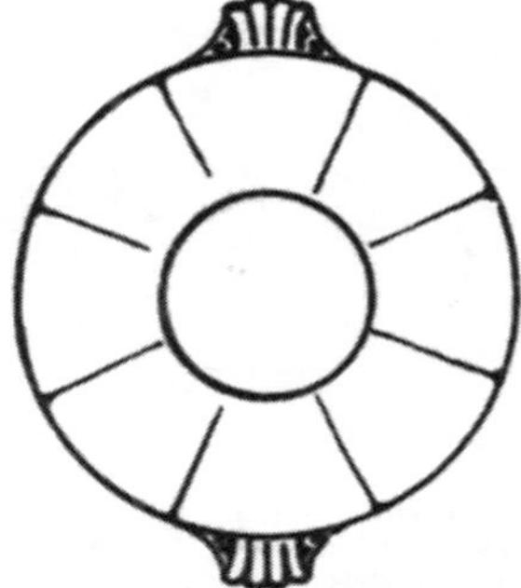

2470-10" CAKE PLATE

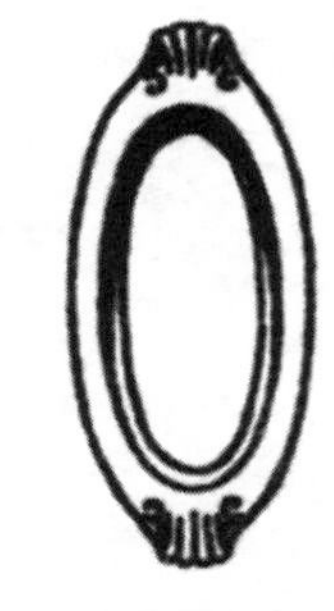

2470-SUGAR & CREAM TRAY

2470-LEMON-DISH

JAMESTOWN PATTERN

No. 2719 Line

2719/2—9½ oz. Goblet Height 5¾ in.

2719/7—6½ oz. Sherbet Height 4¼ in.

2719/26—4 oz. Wine Height 4 5/16 in.

2719/88—5 oz. Footed Juice Height 4 ¾ in.

2719/63—11 oz. Footed Ice Tea Height 6 in.

2719/64—12 oz. Tumbler Height 5⅛ in.

2719/73—9 oz. Tumbler Height 4¼ in.

2719/421 Dessert Diameter 4½ in. Height 2¼ in.

2719/550—8 in. Plate

2719/300 Oblong Butter & Cover Length 7 15/16 in. Height 2⅛ in. Width 3⅜ in.

2719/567—14 in. Torte Plate

2719/286 10 in. 4 Pc. Salad Set Height 4½ in.

Consisting of:
1 2719/211 10 in. Salad Bowl
1 2719/567 14 in. Torte Plate
1 2719/987 Salad Fork & Spoon (wood)

2719/306 Handled Cake Plate 9½ in. Diameter

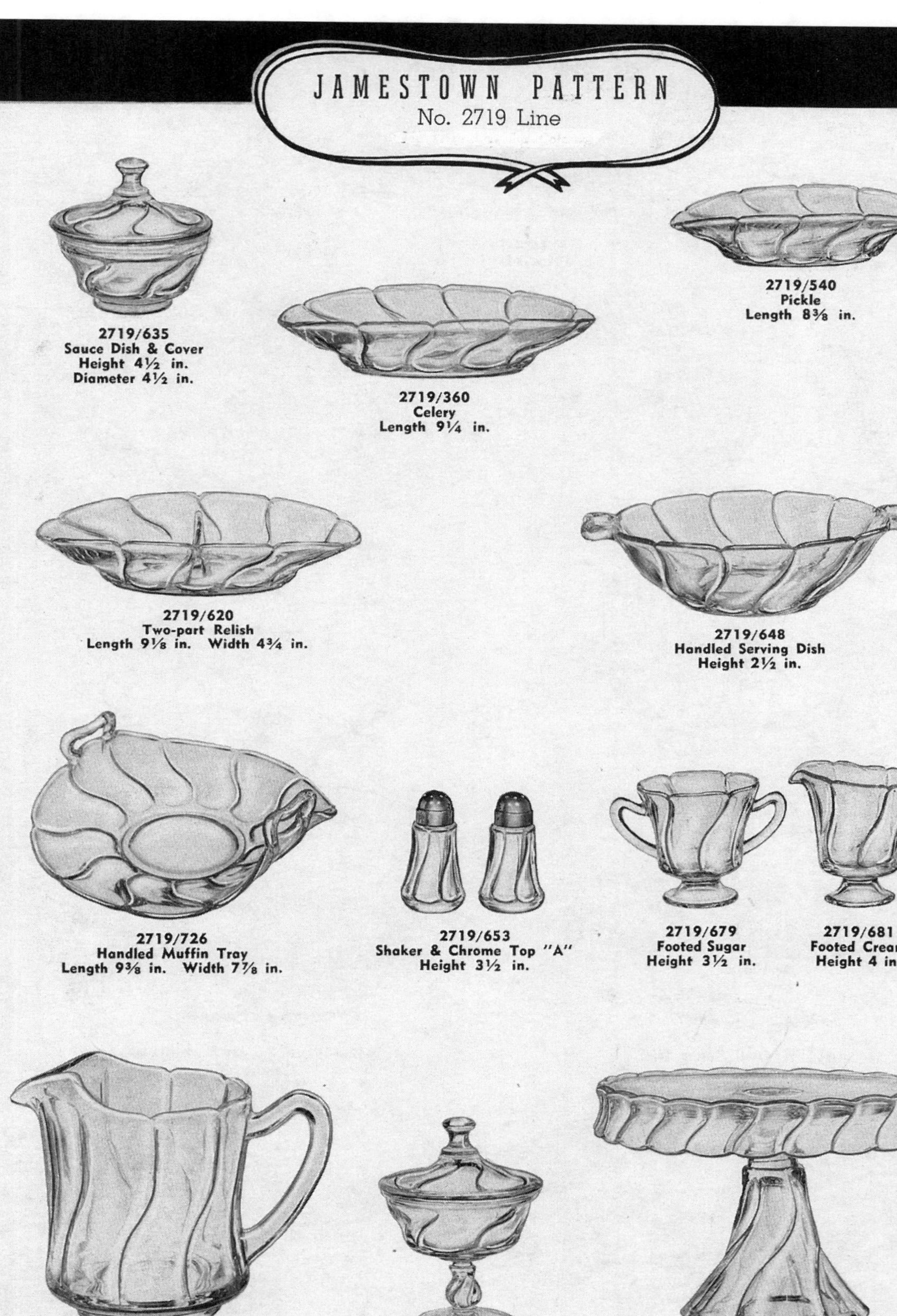
JAMESTOWN PATTERN
No. 2719 Line
2719/635
Sauce Dish & Cover
Height 4½ in.
Diameter 4½ in.
2719/360
Celery
Length 9¼ in.
2719/540
Pickle
Length 8⅜ in.
2719/620
Two-part Relish
Length 9⅛ in. Width 4¾ in.
2719/648
Handled Serving Dish
Height 2½ in.
2719/726
Handled Muffin Tray
Length 9⅜ in. Width 7⅞ in.
2719/653
Shaker & Chrome Top "A"
Height 3½ in.
2719/679
Footed Sugar
Height 3½ in.
2719/681
Footed Cream
Height 4 in.
2719/456—3 pt.
Ice Jug
Height 7 5/16 in.
2719/447
Jelly & Cover
Height 6⅛ in.
2719/630
Round Salver
Diameter 10 in. Height 7 in.
FOSTORIA GLASS COMPANY, MOUNDSVILLE, WEST VIRGINIA — 1959

LAFAYETTE PATTERN

No. 2440 DINNERWARE

2440—5 in. Fruit
2440—6 in. Cereal

2440—Plate
See Price List for Sizes

2440—Cup
2440—Saucer

2440—Footed Sugar
Height 3⅝ in.

2440—Footed Cream
Height 4¼ in.
Capacity 6¾ oz.

2440—Oval Cake Plate,
2 Hdles. Length 10½ in.

2440—3 Part Handled Relish
Diameter 7½ in.

2440—2 Part Handled Relish
Diameter 6½ in.

2440—6½ in. Oval Sauce Dish
Height 2 in.
Width 5¼ in.

2440—6½ in. 2 Part Mayonnaise
Height 2 in.
Width 5¼ in.

2440—13 in. Torte Plate

2440—6½ in. Olive
2440—8½ in. Pickle
2440—11½ in. Celery

Fostoria Glass Company, Moundsville, West Virginia, Jan. 1, 1939

50

MAYFAIR PATTERN

No. 2419 DINNERWARE

2419—Footed Cup
2419—Saucer

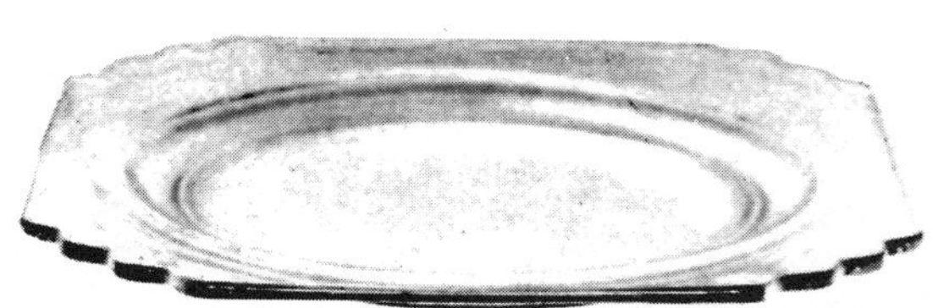

2419—Plate
See Price List for Sizes

2419—Shaker
Height 2⅞ in.

2419—Ash Tray
Diameter 4 in.

2419—Tea Sugar
Height 2¾ in.

2419—Tea Cream
Height 3¼ in.
Capacity 3¼ oz.

2419—5 Part Relish
Length 13¼ in.

2419—Syrup and Cover
2419—Syrup Saucer
Height 5½ in.

2419—4 Part Relish
Length 8½ in.

Fostoria Glass Company, Moundsville, West Virginia, Jan. 1, 1939

Moonstone Pattern
Line No. 2882

Moonstone was introduced January 1, 1974 in colors of Apple Green, Blue, and Pink. Yellow, Dark Blue, and Taupe were added later. Pieces available were Goblet, Dessert/Champagne, Wine, and Luncheon Goblet/Ice Tea. This is a machine-made pattern.

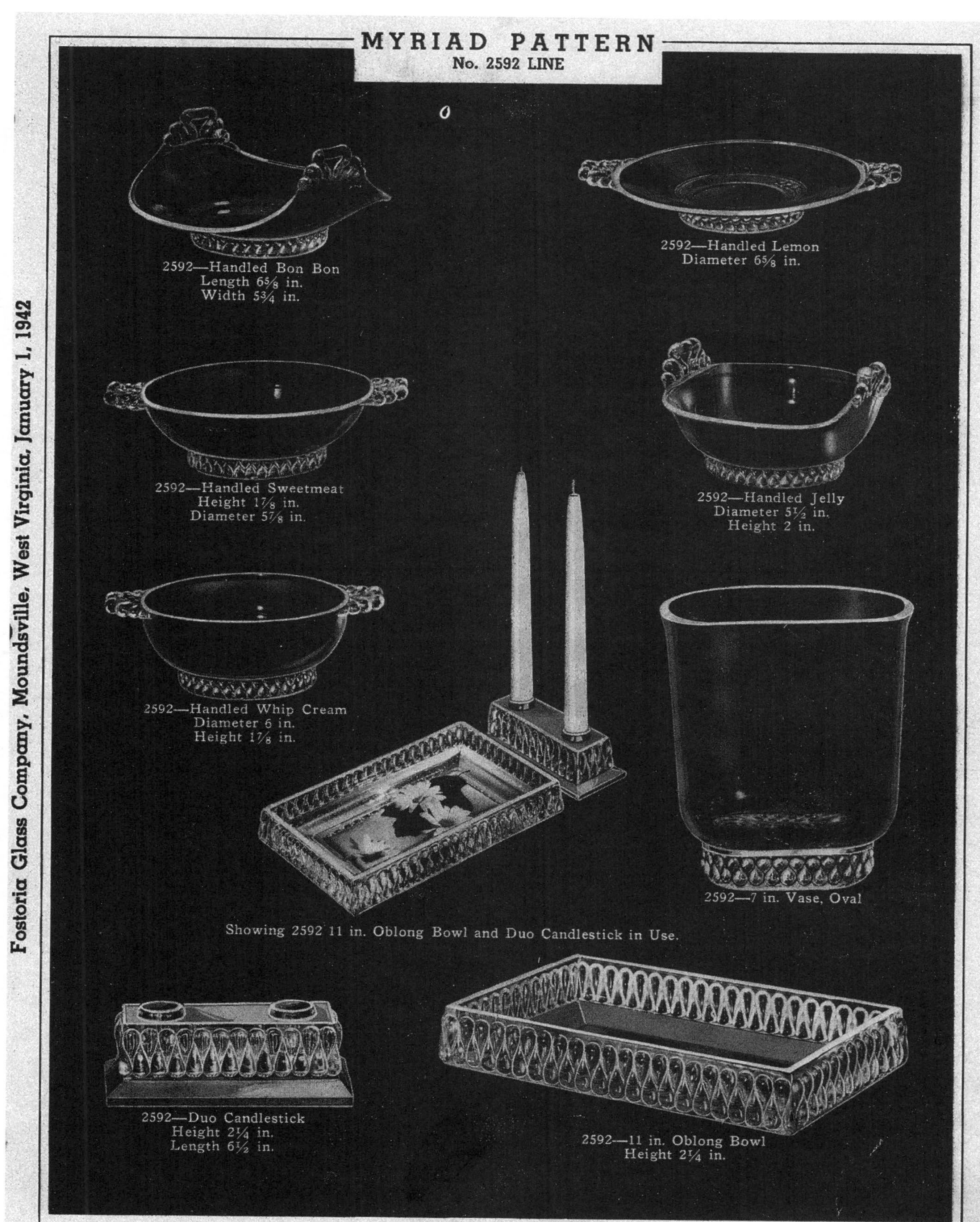
Fostoria Glass Company, Moundsville, West Virginia, January 1, 1942
MYRIAD PATTERN
No. 2592 LINE
2592—Handled Bon Bon
Length 6⅝ in.
Width 5¾ in.
2592—Handled Lemon
Diameter 6⅝ in.
2592—Handled Sweetmeat
Height 1⅞ in.
Diameter 5⅞ in.
2592—Handled Jelly
Diameter 5½ in.
Height 2 in.
2592—Handled Whip Cream
Diameter 6 in.
Height 1⅞ in.
2592—7 in. Vase, Oval
Showing 2592 11 in. Oblong Bowl and Duo Candlestick in Use.
2592—Duo Candlestick
Height 2¼ in.
Length 6½ in.
2592—11 in. Oblong Bowl
Height 2¼ in.
57

No. 2350 DINNERWARE, "PIONEER" DESIGN.
MADE IN AMBER, BLUE, GREEN AND CRYSTAL; EXCEPT AS OTHERWISE NOTED.
PRICED PAGES 4 AND 22A — No. 2 SUPPLEMENT PRICE LIST.
2350½—Ftd. Cream Soup
2350—Cream Soup Plate
Cream Soup not made in blue
2350—Ash Tray.
Not made in Blue.
Also made in Orchid
2350½—Ftd. Bouillon
2350—Saucer
Bouillon not made in Blue.
2350—8 in. Pickle.
2350—Egg Cup.
Not made in Blue.
2350—8 in. Comport
Also made in Orchid.
2350—11 in. Celery.
2350—10 in. Baker.
2350—Grape Fruit.

1927 Catalog

Priscilla No. 2321

1930 Catalog

FOSTORIA GLASS COMPANY, MOUNDSVILLE, WEST VIRGINIA — 1956

RADIANCE PATTERN

No. 2700 Line

2700—10 oz.
Beverage
Height 5¾ in.

2700—6 oz.
Sherbet
Height 3 in.

2700—5½ oz.
Juice
Height 4½ in.

2700
Cup
2700
Saucer

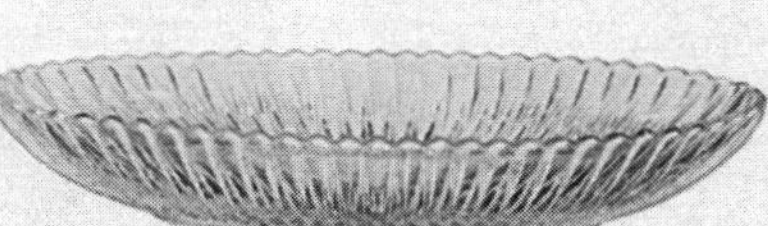

2700
Serving Dish
Length 11 in. Width 6 in.
Height 1¾ in.

2700—10 in.
Dinner Plate
2700—7 in.
Salad/Dessert Plate

2700—14 in.
Buffet Plate

2700—15 in.
Platter

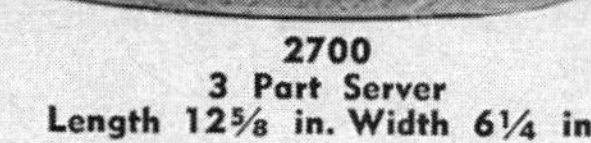

2700
3 Part Server
Length 12⅝ in. Width 6¼ in.

2700
Sauce Bowl and Plate and Ladle
Height 2¾ in.

2700
Shaker and Gold Top
Height 2½ in.

2700—12 in.
4 Piece Salad Set
Height 3 in.
Consisting of:
1/12 doz. 2700—12 in. Salad Bowl
1/12 doz. 2700—14 in. Buffet Plate
1/12 doz. 2700—Salad Fork & Spoon (Wood)

2700
Sugar
Height 2¾ in.

2700
Cream
Height 3¼ in.

2700
Individual Cereal/Dessert
Diameter 5½ in.

603 Robin Hood.
603 Can. Spun Nickel Top. Capacity 15 oz.
Packed 6 doz. in bbl.
Sugar and Cover.
Packed 5 doz. in bbl.
603 SET.
Packed 1½ doz. in bbl.
603 Tumbler.
Packed 15 doz. in bbl.
603 3-Pint Jug.
Packed 2 doz. in bbl.
Cream. Packed 8 doz. in bbl.
Spoon. Packed 9 doz. in bbl.
603, Shaker Salt.
2½ gro. in bbl.
Butter and Cover. Packed 4 doz. in bbl.
603 Pickle Dish. Packed 15 doz. in bbl.

No. 1704 Rosby Pattern
64
Véase lista de precios, páginas 21-22
No. 1704 Botella Para Aceite Y Vinagre
Capacidad 6 Oz.
Altura 6-½ pulgadas
No. 1704 Vaso
Capacidad 8 Oz.
Altura 4-½ pulgadas
No. 1704½ Salero:
Tapa de Cristal
F. G. T.
Altura 3 pulgadas
No. 1704 Salero,
Tapa de Cristal
F. G. T.
Altura 3 pulgadas
No. 1704 Jarro Para Galleticas Con Tapa
Altura 9 pulgadas
No. 1704 Jarro Para Encurtidos
Diametro 3½ pulgadas
Altura 4-¾ pulgadas
No. 1704 Jarro Para Leche Con Tapa de
Metal (E. N. T.)
Capacidad 9 Oz. Altura 5-¾ pulgadas
No. 1704 Jarro Para Agua
Capacidad ½ Galon
Altura 8 pulgadas

This catalog sheet was made for the Spanish speaking market.
Date is unknown.

SEASCAPE PATTERN

No. 2685 Line

See Price List For Colors

Made in 1955 – 1958
Opalescent Colors,
Blue, Pink, Yellow,
Seascape, Crystal

FOSTORIA GLASS COMPANY, MOUNDSVILLE, WEST VIRGINIA — 1955

2685—14 in.
Buffet Plate

2685
3 Part Relish
Length 11¾ in. Width 8½ in.

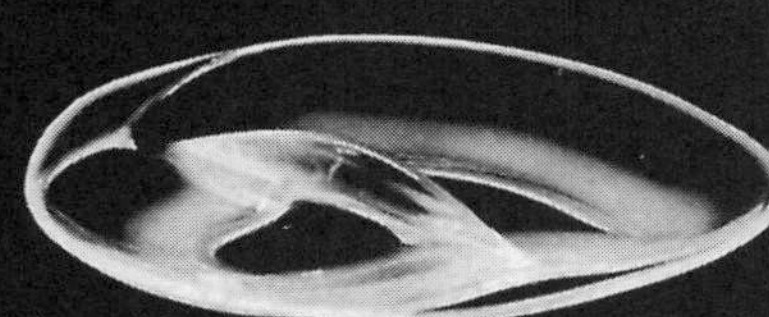

2685
2 Part Relish
Length 9 in. Width 6 in.

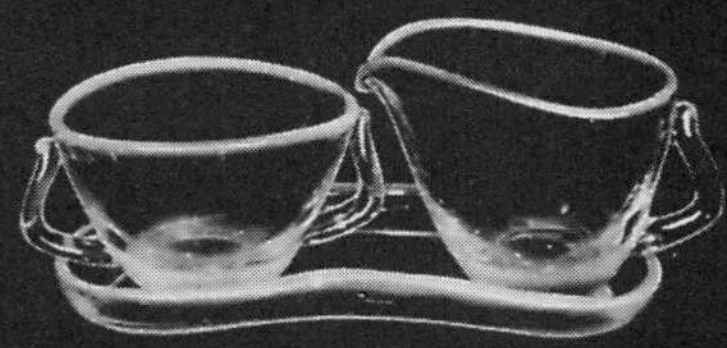

2685—3 Piece
Individual Sugar and Cream and Tray
Consisting of:
1/12 Dz. 2685—S. & C. Tray
1/12 Dz. 2685—Ind. Sugar
1/12 Dz. 2685—Ind. Cream

2685
Sugar
Height 2⅞ in.

2685
Cream
Height 3⅜ in.

2685—10 in.
Salad Bowl

2685
Mayonnaise and Plate
and Ladle
Height 2⅜ in.

2685
Handled Preserve
Length 6½ in.

SONATA PATTERN

No. 2364 LINE

2364—6 in. Baked Apple
Height 1¼ in.

2364—5 in. Fruit
Height 1¼ in.

2364—8 in. Comport

2364—Shaker E. Top
Height 2¼ in.

2364—11 in. Celery
Height 1¼ in.

2364—3 Pt. Relish
Height 1½ in. Length 10 in.
Width 7¼ in.

2364—8 in. Pickle
Height 1 in.

2364—2 Pt. Relish
Height 1¾ in. Length 6½ in.
Width 5 in.

2364—Handled Lunch Tray
Diameter 11¼ in.

58

Fostoria Glass Company, Moundsville, West Virginia, January 1, 1942

SUNRAY PATTERN

No. 2510 LINE

2510—9-oz. Goblet
Height 5¾ in.

2510—5½-oz. Low Sherbet
Height 3½ in.

2510—3½ oz. Fruit Cocktail
Height 3¼ in.

2510—4½ oz. Claret
Height 4⅞ in.

2510—4 oz. Footed Cocktail
Height 3 in.

2510
13-oz. Footed Tumbler
Height 5¼ in.

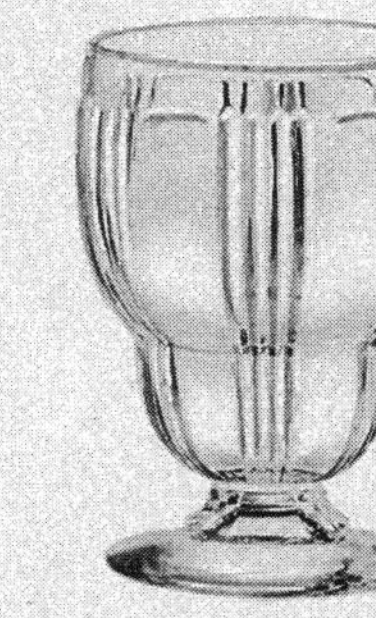

2510—Footed Table Tumbler
Height 4¾ in. Capacity 9 oz.

2510—5 oz.
Footed Tumbler
Height 4⅝ in.

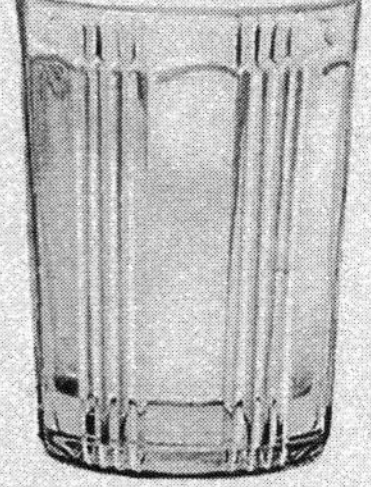

2510½—9-oz. Tumbler
Height 4⅛ in.

2510½
2-oz. Whiskey
Height 2¼ in.

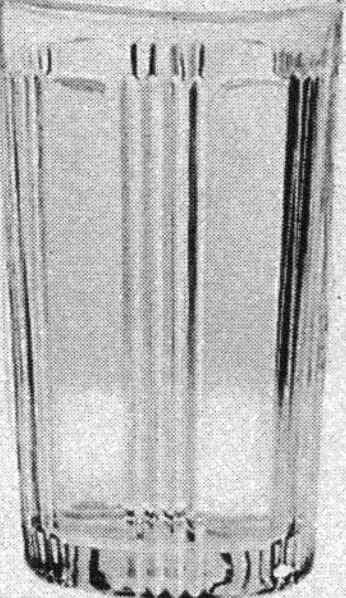

2510½—13-oz. Tumbler
Height 5⅛ in.

2510½
6-oz. Old Fashioned
Cocktail
Height 3½ in.

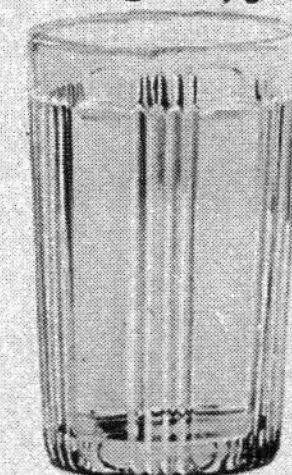

2510½—5-oz. Tumbler
Height 3½ in.

2510—2 Quart Jug
Height 8½ in.

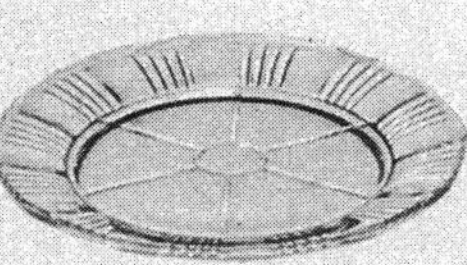

2510—Coaster
Diameter 4 in.

2510—Ice Jug
Capacity 2 Quarts Height 7½ in.

Fostoria Glass Company, Moundsville, West Virginia, Jan. 1, 1939

SUN RAY PATTERN
No. 2510 LINE
See Price List for Colors
2510½—Oblong Cigarette Box and Cover Length 4¾ in. Width 3⅜ in.
2510—Cheese and Cover or Butter and Cover Length 6 in. Width 3⅜ in.
2510 3 in. Candlestick
2510—8½ in. Condiment Tray
2510—5-Piece Condiment Set Consisting of:
1/6 Doz. 2510—3 oz. Oil, D/S
1/6 Doz. 2510—Mustard and Cover and Spoon
1/12 Doz. 2510—8½ in. Condiment Tray
2510½—8-Piece Decanter Set Consisting of:
1/12 Doz. 2510½—Oblong Decanter and Stopper
1/2 Doz. 2510½—2 oz. Whiskey
1/12 Doz. 2510 —10½ in. Oblong Tray
2510½—Oblong Decanter and Stopper Capacity 26 oz. Height 9⅛ in.
Fostoria Glass Company, Moundsville, West Virginia, July 1, 1936
18-1-A

SUNRAY PATTERN
No. 2510 LINE
2510
Shaker F.G.T.
Height 4 in.
2510½
Ind. Shaker F.G.T.
Height 2¼ in.
2510
Salt Dip
2510—Mustard and
Cover and Spoon
Height 3¾ in.
2510
3 oz. Oil and Stopper
Height 4¾ in.
2510—11 in. Torte Plate
2510—15 in. Torte Plate
2510—Mayonnaise and Plate and Ladle
Mayo Height 2⅞ in.
Mayo Diameter 5½ in.
Plate Diameter 7⅛ in.
2510—12 in. Sandwich Plate
2510—16 in. Flat Plate
2510—Ice Bucket
Height 4¼ in. Top Diameter 6⅛ in.
Chromium Handle and Tongs
Tongs Priced Separately
2510—2 Part Relish
Length 10 in.
2510—4 Part Relish
Diameter 8 in.
2510—3 Part Relish
Diameter 6½ in.
Fostoria Glass Company, Moundsville, West Virginia, Jan. 1, 1939
43

SUNRAY PATTERN

No. 2510 LINE

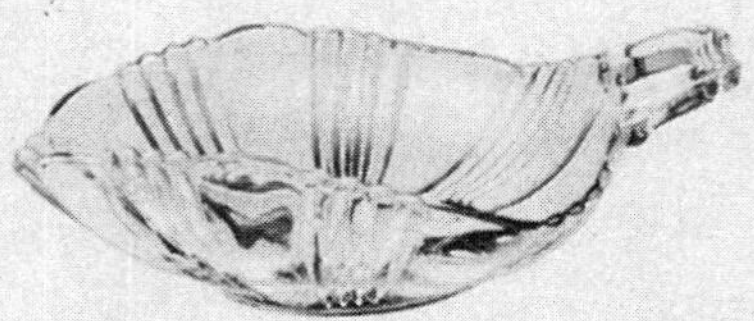

2510—Handled Nappy, 3 Cor.
Length 5 in.

2510—Handled Nappy, Fld.
Diameter 6 in.

2510—Handled Nappy, Square
5 in. Square

2510—Handled Nappy, Reg.
Diameter 5 in.

2510—6 in. Divided Sweetmeat
Width 4 in.

2510—5 in. Comport
Height 4 in.

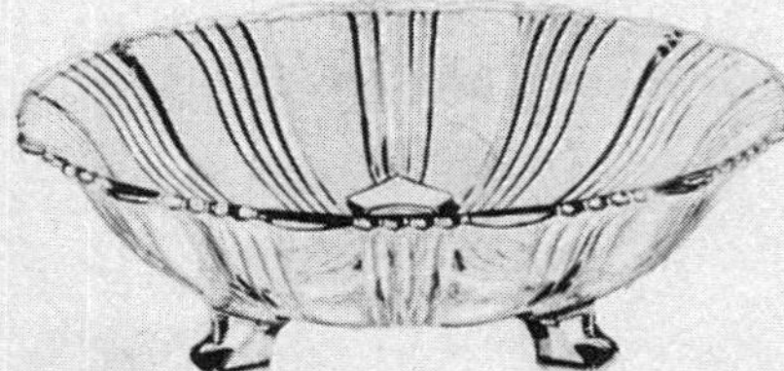

2510—3 Toed Bon Bon
Diameter 7 in.

2510
Footed Individual
Almond

2510½—Oblong Cigarette Box
and Cover
Length 4¾ in. Width 3⅜ in.

2510½—Oblong Decanter and Stopper
Capacity 26 oz.
Height 9⅛ in.

2510½
2-oz. Whiskey
Height 2¼ in.

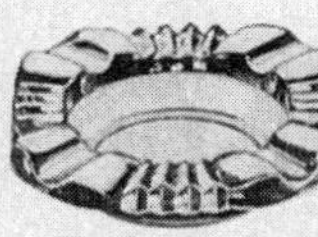

2510
Square Ash Tray
3 in. Square

2510½
Individual Ash Tray
Diameter 2½ in.

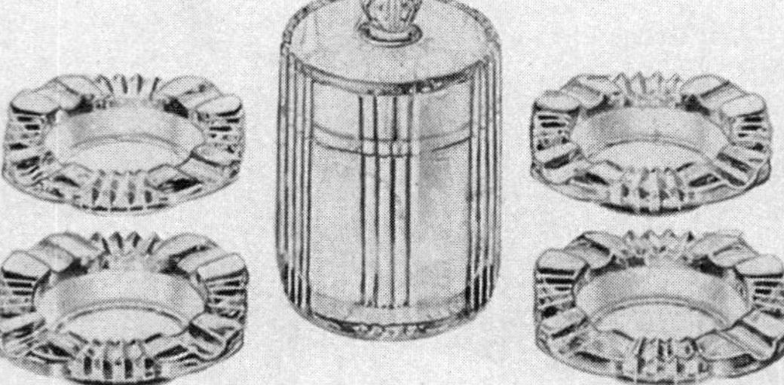

2510—5 Piece Smoker Set
Consisting of
1/12 Doz. 2510—Cigarette and Cover
1/3 Doz. 2510—Square Ash Trays

2510
Cigarette and Cover
Height 3⅞ in.

Fostoria Glass Company, Moundsville, West Virginia, Jan. 1, 1939

SUNRAY PATTERN

No. 2510 LINE

2510—10-in. Handled Bowl
Height 3⅛ in.

2510—Duo Candlestick
Height 6½ in.
Spread 7 in.

2510—5½ in. Candlestick

2510
3 in. Candlestick

2510—Rose Bowl
Height 3¼ in.

2510—7-in. Vase

2510—9 in. Square Footed Vase

Fostoria Glass Company, Moundsville, West Virginia, Jan. 1, 1939

No. 789 Wedding Bells Pattern

Introduced in 1900, production possibly only four years.

WISTAR PATTERN

No. 2620 LINE

2620—9 oz. Goblet
Height 5⅞ in.

2620—6 oz. High Sherbet
Height 4⅛ in.

2620—12 oz. Tumbler
Height 5½ in.

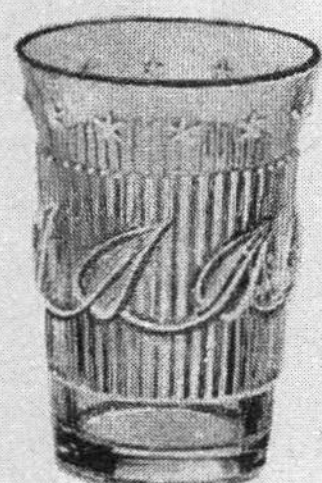
2620—5 oz. Tumbler
Height 3¾ in.

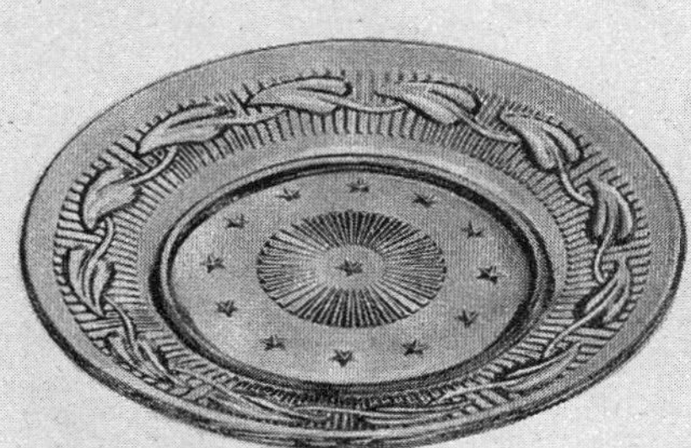
2620—7 in. Plate

2620—Mayonnaise & Plate & Ladle
Mayo. Height 2⅞ in.
Mayo. Diameter 5¼ in.
Plate Diameter 7 in.

2620—Footed Sugar
Height 3½ in.

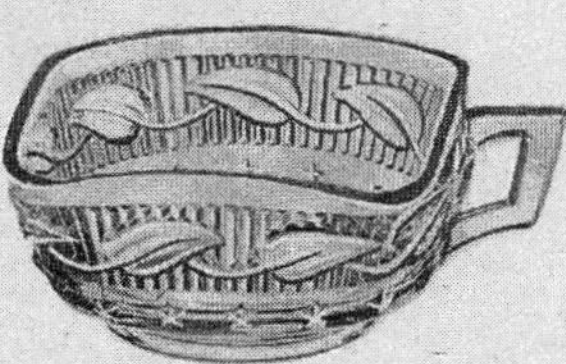
2620—Handled Nappy, Sq.
Width 4 in.
Height 2 in.

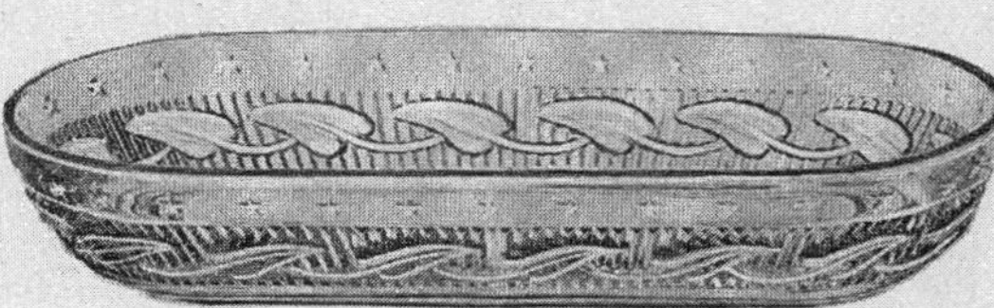
2620—9½ in. Celery

2620—Footed Cream
Height 4 in.
Capacity 7½ oz.

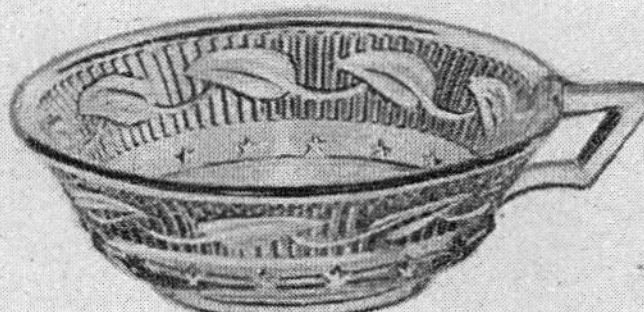
2620—Handled Nappy, Fld.
Diameter 5 in.
Height 1⅞ in.

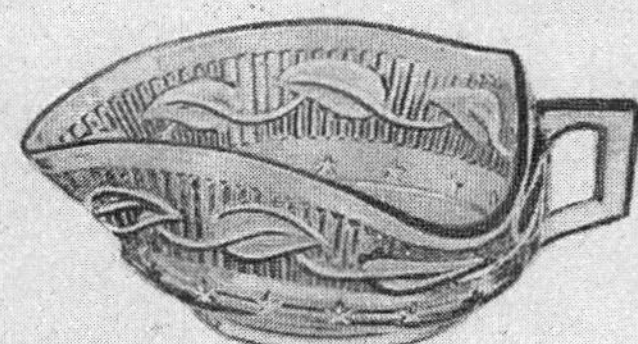
2620—Handled Nappy, 3 Cor.
Length 4½ in.
Height 2 in.

2620—Handled Nappy, Reg.
Diameter 4¼ in.
Height 2 in.

Fostoria Glass Company, Moundsville, West Virginia, January 1, 1942

Ebony

EBONY GLASS ITEMS
FOSTORIA GLASS COMPANY, MOUNDSVILLE, WEST VIRGINIA — 1954
2288—8½ in.
Tut Vase, Handled
2402—9 in.
Bowl
2402—2 in.
Candlestick
2404—6 in.
Vase
2409—7½ in.
Vase
2428—13 in.
Vase (ill.)
2428—9 in.
Vase
2428—6 in.
Vase
2428—7 in.
Round Bowl
2430
Candy Jar and Cover
Height 5¾ in.
2430—2 in.
Candlestick
2430—11 in.
Bowl

EBONY GLASS ITEMS

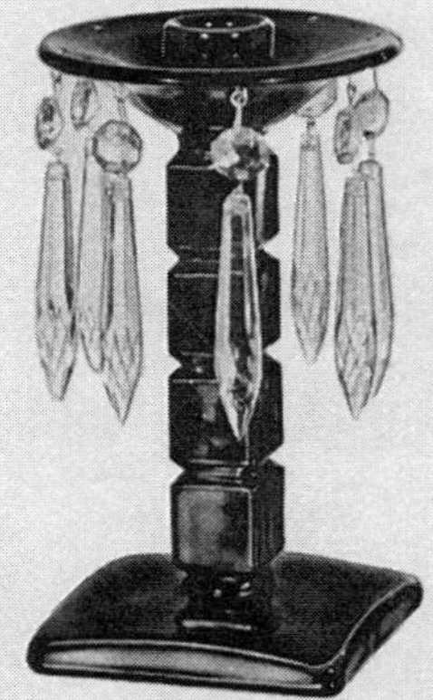
2453
Lustre
8 U. Drop Prisms
Height 7½ in.

2467—7½ in.
Vase

2496
5 Piece Smoker Set
Consisting of:
1/12 Doz. 2496 Cigarette Box & Cover (Cov. Cry.)
1/3 Doz. 2496 Oblong Ash Tray (Crystal)

2538
Place Card Holder
Height 2¾ in.

2567—7½ in.
Footed Vase

2545—2 in.
"Flame" Candlestick

2545
Candle Lamp, Complete
Consisting of:
1/12 Dz. 26 Candle Lamp Base (Crystal)
1/12 Dz. 26 Candle Lamp Chimney (Crystal)
1/12 Dz. 2545 2 in. Candlestick (Ebony)

2618
Cigarette Box and Cover
Length 5½ in. Width 4¼ in.

2592
Cigarette Box and Cover
Length 6 in. Width 3¼ in.

2592
Oblong Ash Tray
Length 3¾ in. Width 2¾ in.

EBONY GLASS ITEMS

FOSTORIA GLASS COMPANY, MOUNDSVILLE, WEST VIRGINIA — 1954

2629
Chanticleer
Height 10¾ in.

2636
"Plume" Book End
Height 9¼ in.

2638—4½ in.
Candlestick

2666
Mayonnaise and Plate
and Ladle
Height 3¼ in.

2666—9 in.
Salad Bowl
Height 2¾ in.

2666—11 in.
4 pc. Salad Set
Height 4⅞ in.
Consisting of:
1/12 doz. 2666 11 in. Salad Bowl (Ebony)
1/12 doz. 2666 14 in. Serving Plate (Crystal)
1/12 doz. Salad Fork & Spoon (Wood)

2666
Oval Bowl
Diameter 8¼ in.
Height 3¼ in.

2666
Flora-Candle
Diameter 6 in.

EBONY GLASS ITEMS

2667—5 in.
Ash Tray

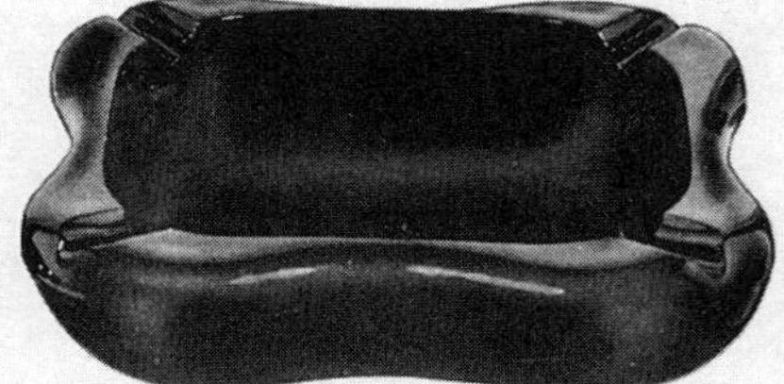

2667—9 in.
Ash Tray

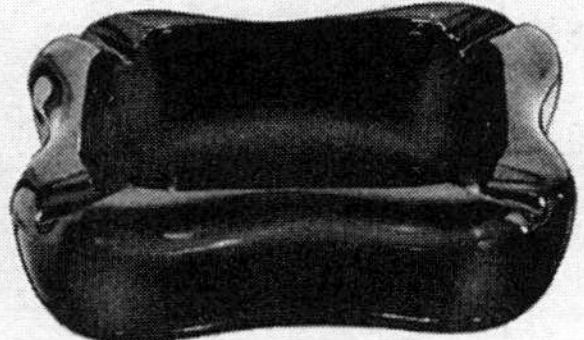

2667—7 in.
Ash Tray

2667
Cigarette Holder
Height 2¾ in.

2667—2½ in.
Candlestick

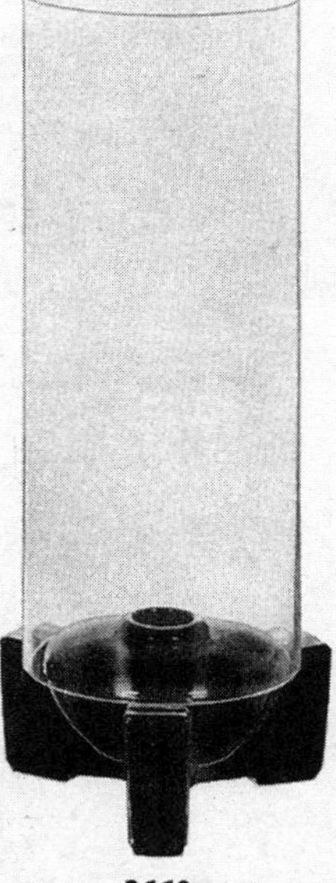

2668
Hurricane Lamp, Complete
Height 11¾ in.
Consisting of:
1/12 Doz. 2668—Candlestick (Ebony)
1/12 Doz. 2668 Hurricane Lamp
Chimney (Crystal)

2668
Candlestick
Height 2½ in.

Garden Center Items

GARDEN CENTER ITEMS

FOSTORIA GLASS COMPANY, MOUNDSVILLE, WEST VIRGINIA — 1960

All items made in Amber, Crystal, Milk Glass, Silver Mist, and Spruce.

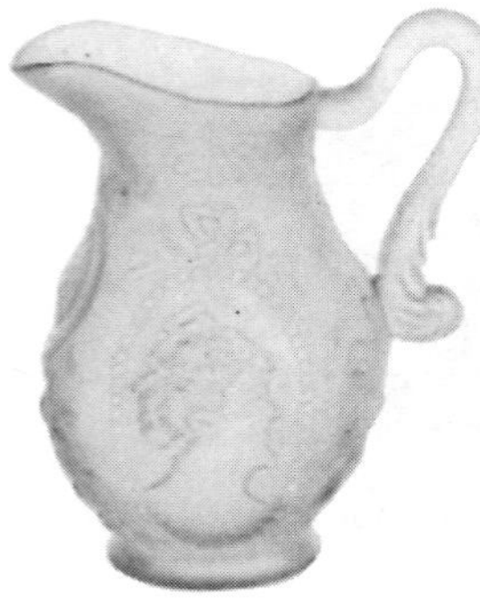

834/70
Jenny Lind Pitcher
Height 8¼ in.

1121/389—5¾ in.
Comport

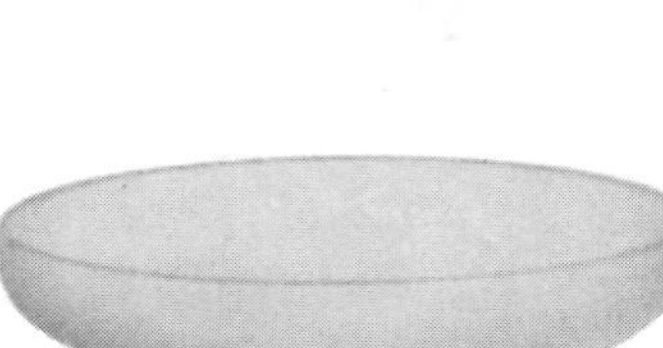

2364/197—9 in.
Lily Pond
Height 2 in.

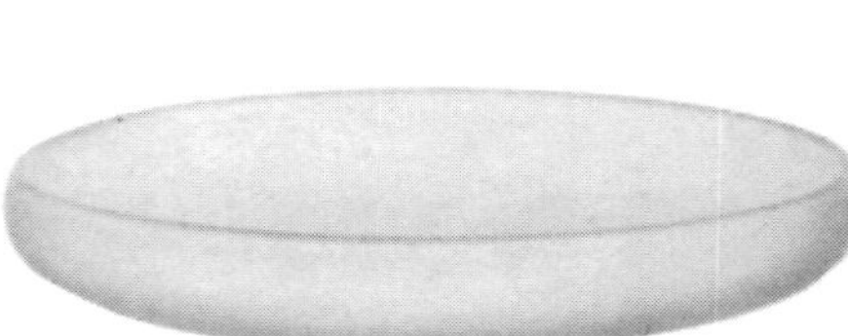

2364/251—12 in.
Lily Pond
Height 2¼ in.

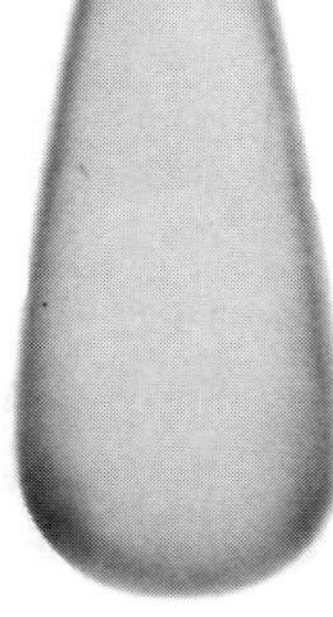

2577/792—8½ in.
Vase

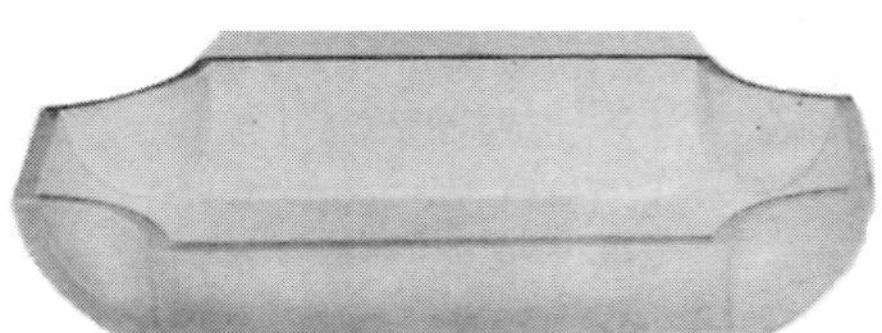

2596/215
Oblong Shallow Bowl
Length 11 in.
Height 2 in.

2638/220
10½" Oblong Bowl
Height 4½"

2666/189
Oval Bowl
Diameter 8¼ in.
Height 3¼ in.

2692/234—6½ in.
Fruit Bowl
Length 9¼ in. Height 5½ in.

GARDEN CENTER ITEMS

See Price List for Colors

All items made in Amber, Crystal, Milk Glass, Silver Mist, and Spruce.

2692/760—6 in.
Handled Urn
Height 6 in.

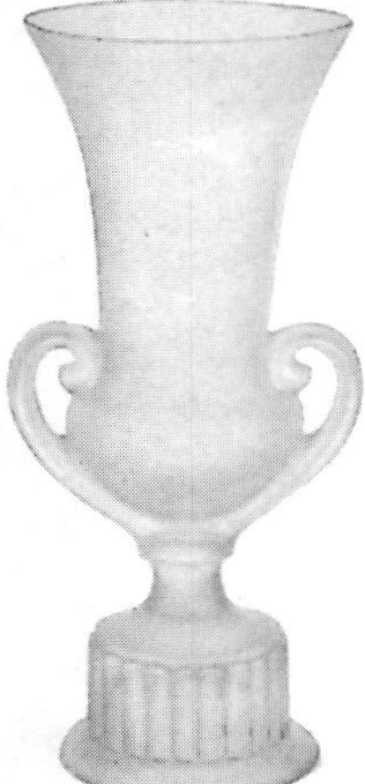

2692/828—12 in.
Handled Urn

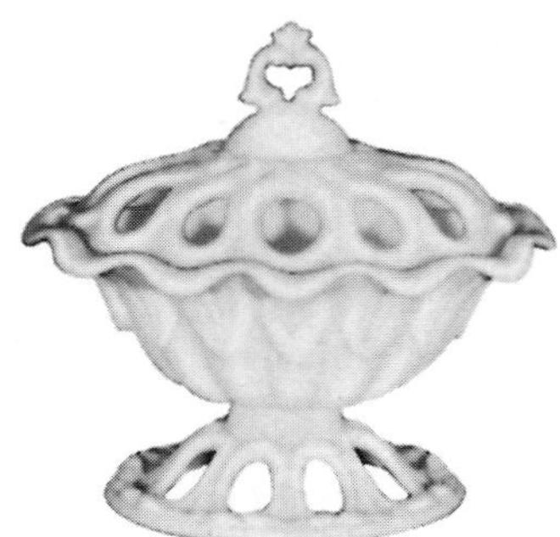

2693/162
Franklin Urn & Cover
Height 8½ in.

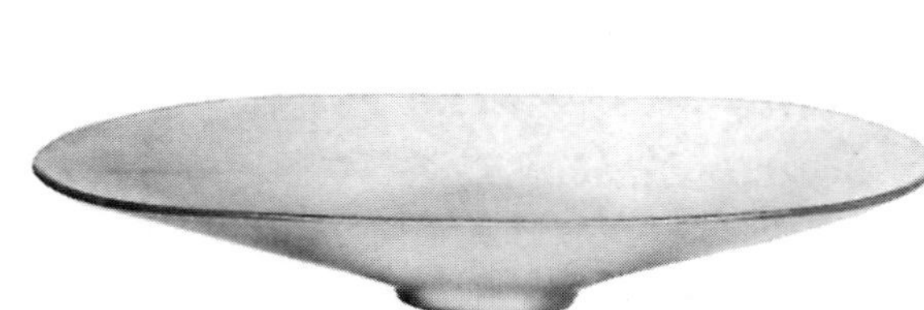

2703/189
Oblong Bowl
Length 14¾ in.
Width 10¼ in.

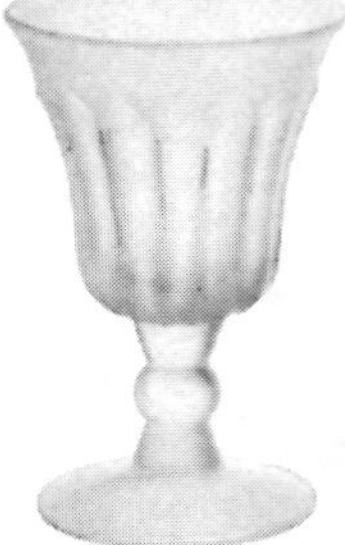

2724/779—7½ in.
Goblet Vase

2725/761
Handled Urn
Height 4⅜ in.
Diameter 5¾ in.

4152/751
Vase Bowl
Height 3⅞ in.

4166/151—5 in.
Footed Bowl
Height 5½ in.

4166/199—9 in.
Footed Bowl
Height 6¼ in.

4166/757—6 in.
Bud Vase

Victorian Pattern
4024 Line

This lamp was shown in a 1937 home magazine advertisement. It was marketed by Quoizel Inc. and listed in Empire Green. It is also known in Ruby and Regal Blue. The height is 15".

Daisy Pattern
Etching 324

This lamp is etched on a 5056 American Lady Pattern Lamp. The switch was on the fitting at the top, no hole was drilled through the glass. This item was possibly made for Quoizel Inc. around 1937. With proper cardboard or cloth shade, the height would be about 15".

26 Candle Lamp without Shade, 1911 Catalog

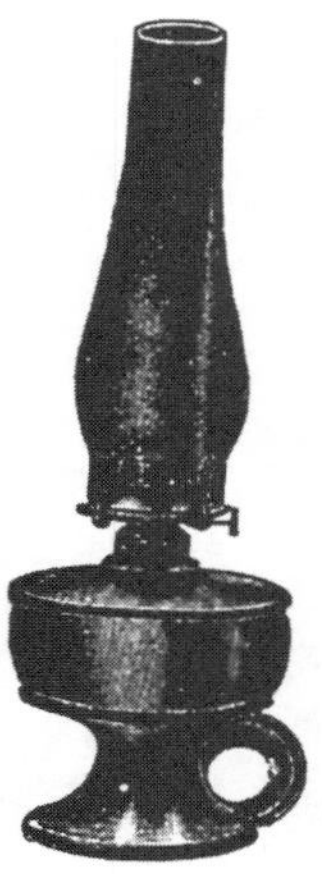
191 Squat Lamp with #1 Burner, 1901 Catalog

183 Fairy Lamp Made Crystal, Plain, and Etched on Crystal Bottom. Also available with Rose Glass Shade. Victoria Pattern, 1904 Catalog

183 Peg with Spring Socket, Silver Plated Burner and Trimmings, sold with or without Silk Shade and Holder. Victoria Pattern, 1904 Catalog

Screw-in Holder 1911 Catalog

191 Lamp, Squat #1 Burner and Chimney 1901 Catalog

26 Candle Lamp Base without Peg, 1904 Catalog

Candle Lamp Pot 1904 Catalog

26-1 Candle Lamp Base with Peg, 1904 Catalog

17 Banquet Lamp
Height 19", Capacity 40 oz.
1905 – 1911 Catalogs

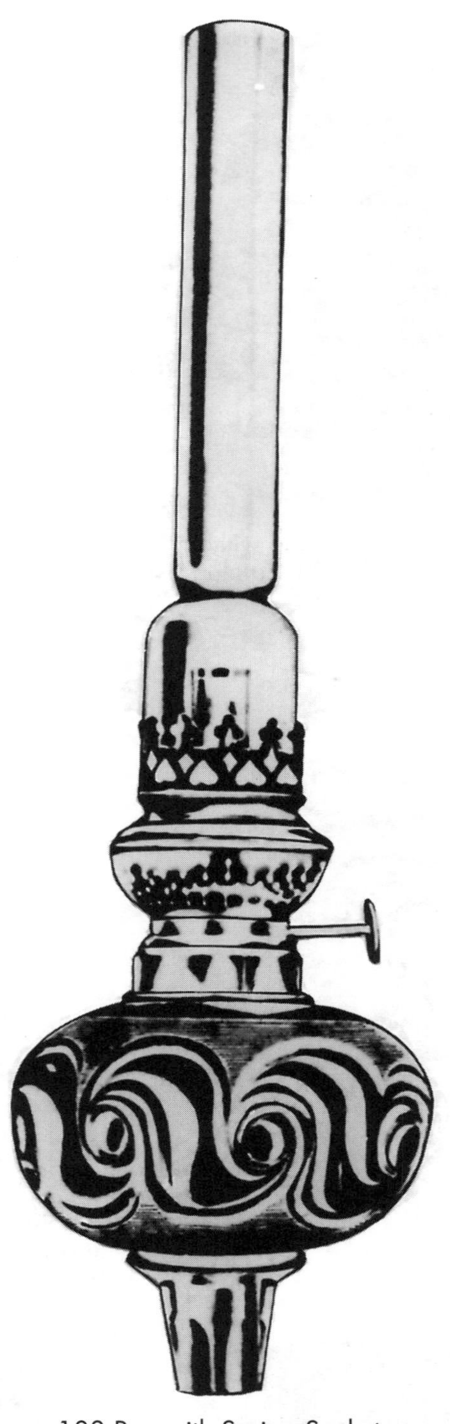

183 Peg with Spring Socket,
Silver Plated Burner and Trimmings,
sold with or without Silk Shade
and Holder
Victoria Pattern, 1904 Catalog

200 Lamp
Size "A," Height 9½"
Size "C," Height 10¼"
Size "D," Height 11"
1907 Catalog

1550 Lamp
Shrunk-On Collar
Size "B," Height 9½"
Size "C," Height 10"
1907 Catalog

Machine Made Lamps
Pressed and Blown
in One Operation

200 Footed Handled Lamp
Height 6½"
1907 Catalog

179 Lamp
Size "B," Height 9¾"
Size "C," Height 10¾"
1907 Catalog

Fostoria Candle Lamps

No. 1490 Candle Lamp Complete
Height 13½"
1911 Catalog

What it is

The Fostoria Candle Lamp is a compact little lamp, holding a special pot candle. It fits on any candlestick, glass, metal, or wood, and can be used with any style of shade. It overcomes all the nuisance of candles and makes them perfectly safe. It is being sold everywhere by all the leading dealers and is in great demand. Everyone who delights in candles for table decorations finds the Fostoria Candle lamp a great relief from the worry and care candles bring.

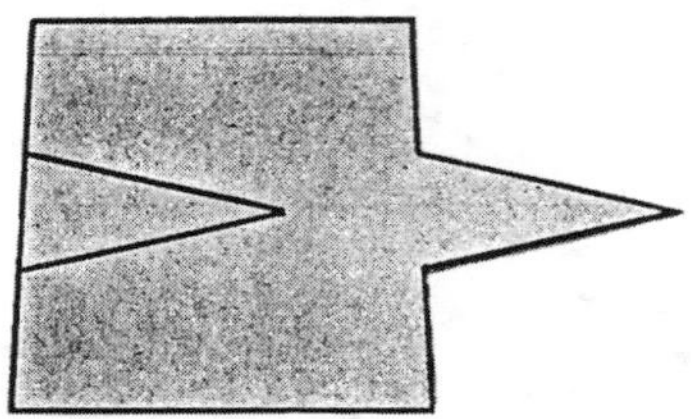

Actual Size

This is a ferrule that fits over the pot to make the Candle Lamp practical on other candlesticks than our own. These are furnished only when ordered at extra price.

What it Prevents

The Fostoria Candle Lamp has a glass chimney which shields the flame of the candle from the shade, so that the shade or the fringe cannot be set on fire.

The candle sets firmly in the little lamp pot so that it can't tip or wobble, and the wax can't drip down on the candlestick or the tablecloth. Then the shade sets firmly in place and doesn't spoil the effect by tipping sidewise at the least little jolt.

In short, the Fostoria Candle Lamp remedies all the disagreeable and provoking features of candles which nevertheless are so popular and add much charm to the table or mantle shelf.

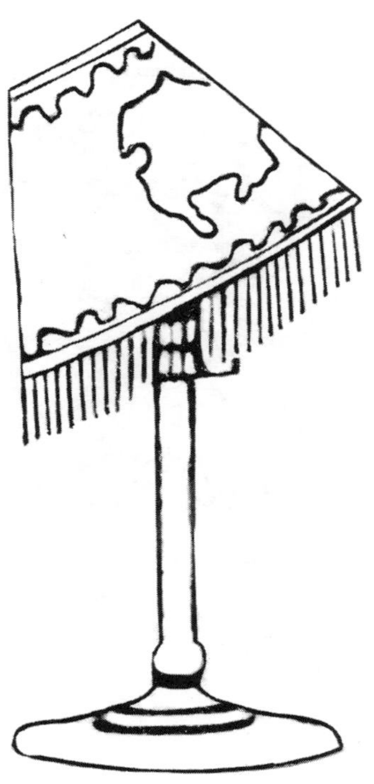

1911 Catalog

To the Lamp Trade

Shapes

All our shapes are new. We would not insult your good judgment and taste by asking you to buy last season's ideas. Our shapes are by the best designers and can be relied on as the very latest.

Trimmings

On our very cheapest grade Lamps, we use best quality Gold Plated Bases. On our finer grade Lamps we use Gold and Japan Bronze finished spelter bases. On all grades down to the very cheapest, we use best quality Brass Founts.

Our Center Draft Fount

Has all recent improvements such as ratchet wick lift and lighting lift. This fount is our special design and we guarantee it perfect. In burners we procure the very best manufactured regardless of cost. We guarantee trimmings satisfactory.

Chimneys

We manufacture our own and the chimney sent with our Lamps are just such as will produce best results.

Decorations

Our decorations are the result of careful, intelligent research and study. Our first effort is directed toward procuring a pleasing subject. Next, good workmanship and making on our own production such prices as will place them within the means of the masses. All this we think we have done and invite your judgment.

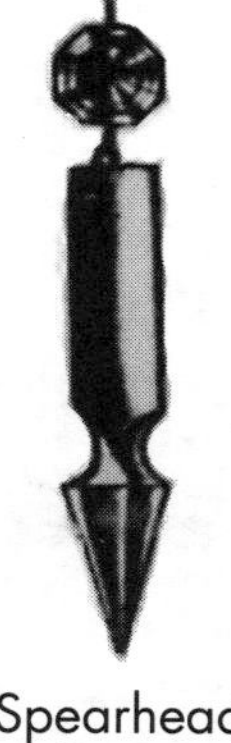

Spearhead Prism

U-Drop Prism

Lamp Post Night Lamp
1904 Catalog

No. 188 Bobache
Top view

No. 188 Bobache

No. 122 Bobache
Top view

No. 122 Bobache

Candle Lamp Chimney
1911 Catalog

1639 Candle Lamp Complete
Height 13½"
1911 Catalog

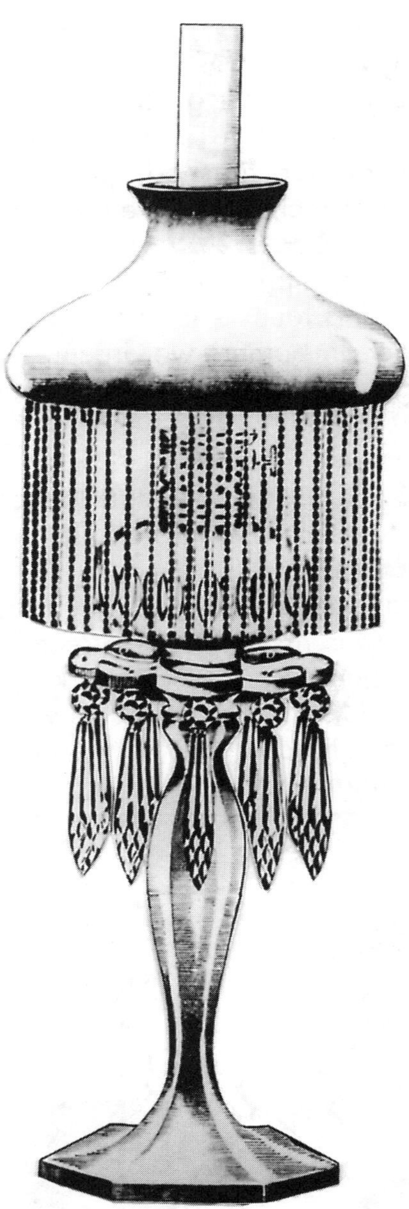

21 Princess Lamp
Height 20"
1911 Catalog

26 Candle Lamp
with Shade and Candle
1911 Catalog

1834 Tulip Lamp
Plaster Collar, Height 10"
1913 Catalog

Bobache
1911 Catalog

2325 Large Electric Boudoir Lamp
Standard-Ebony Glass
Height, including Shade, 15"
Stem hollow for wire
Also made 12" size
1921 Catalog

609 Filler Fount
1901 Catalog

191B Lamp
1901 Catalog

1592 Footed Handled Lamp
#1 Plaster Collar
1907 Catalog

1272 Sewing Lamp with Engraved Chimney, 1907 Catalog

Send for our colored catalog of decorated lamps
1901 Lamp Catalog

920 Filler Fount
1901 Catalog

803 Handled Fount
1901 Catalog

1273 Sewing Lamp Complete with Burner and Engraved Chimney, 1909 Catalog

Colonial Princess Lamp
Height 20"
1911 Catalog

734 Sewing Lamp
Priscilla with Flower
1901 Catalog

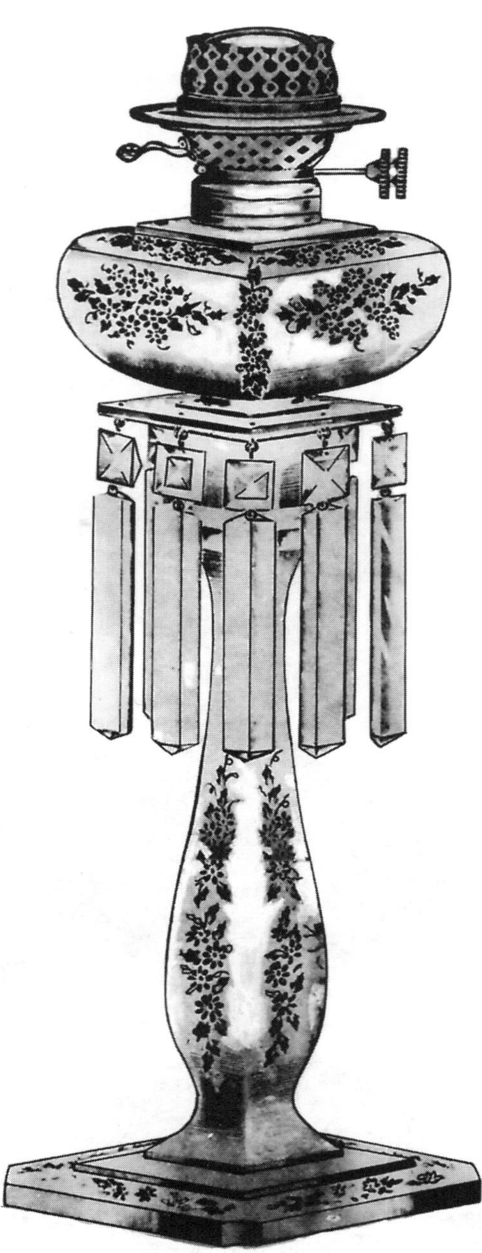

25½ Banquet Lamp, Etched, with Prisms
Height 19", 1911 Catalog

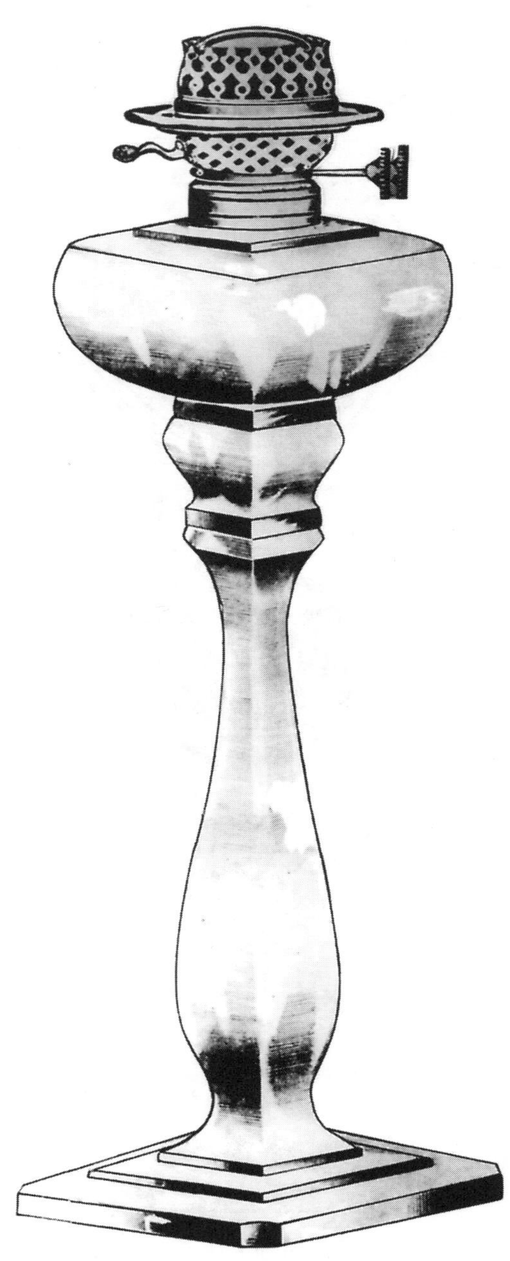

25 Banquet Lamp
Height 19"
1911 Catalog

Milk Glass

MILK GLASS

FOSTORIA GLASS COMPANY, MOUNDSVILLE, WEST VIRGINIA — 1959

2712/311
Flora-Candle
Height 2 5/16 in.

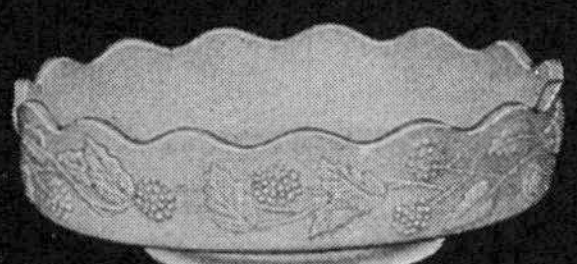

2712/355—6½ in.
Shallow Bowl

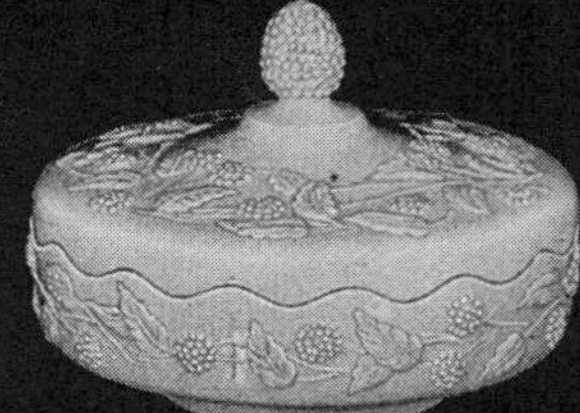

2712/354
Candy and Cover
Height 4¾ in.
Diameter 6¼ in.

2713/653
Shaker and Chrome Top "A"
Height 3½ in.

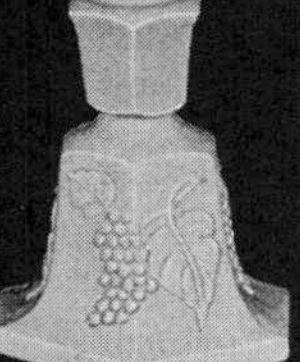

2713/315—4 in.
Candleholder

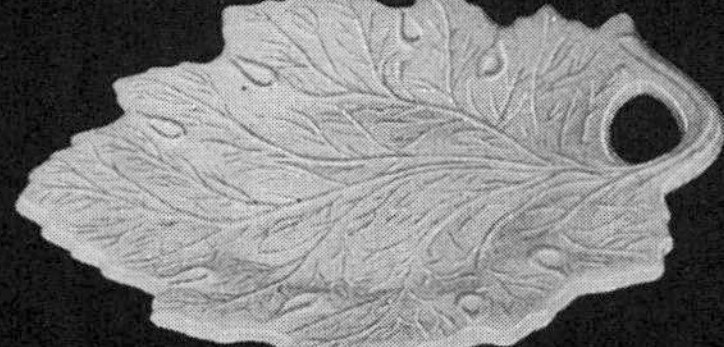

2713/720
Leaf Tray
Length 8⅜ in.
Width 7⅜ in.

2713/311
Leaf Candleholder
Height 1 9/16 in.

2713/162
Wedding Bowl and Cover
Height 7⅜ in.

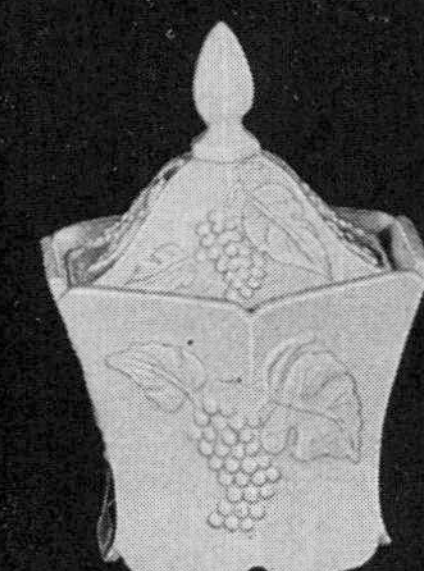

2713/347
Candy Jar and Cover
Height 6 3/16 in.

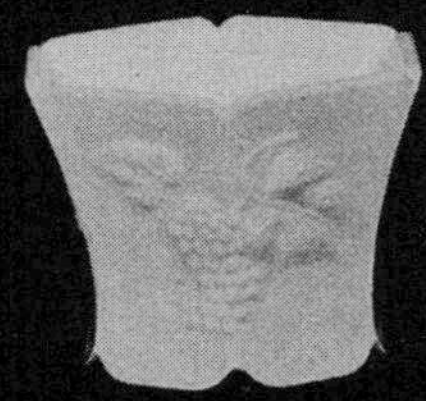

2713/348
Planter
Height 3½ in.

2720/718
Trivet
Height ¾ in.
Diameter 7¼ in.

FOSTORIA GLASS COMPANY, MOUNDSVILLE, WEST VIRGINIA — 1956

MILK GLASS ITEMS

1704—16 in.
Punch Bowl
Capacity 2¾ gal.
Height including foot—14 in.

1704—5½ oz.
Punch Cup
Height 2¼ in.
Top Diameter 3½ in.

2675—1½ in.
Candleholder

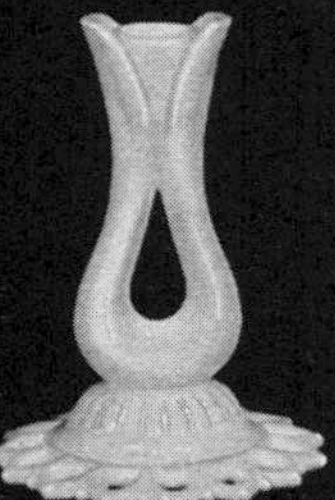

2675—6 in.
Candleholder

2675
Egg Plate
Length 12 in. Width 9½ in.

2675
Shaker & Chrome Top "A"
Height 3½ in.

834
Jenny Lind Pitcher
Height 8¼ in.

835
Jenny Lind Tumbler
Height 4½ in.

2675—10 in.
Shallow Footed Bowl

2693
Footed Urn & Cover
Height 8½ in.

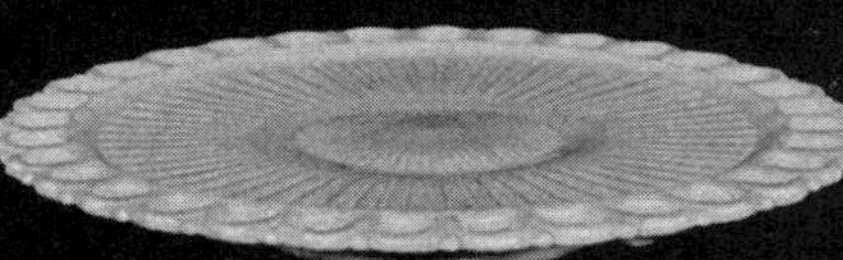

2675—12½ in.
Footed Buffet Plate

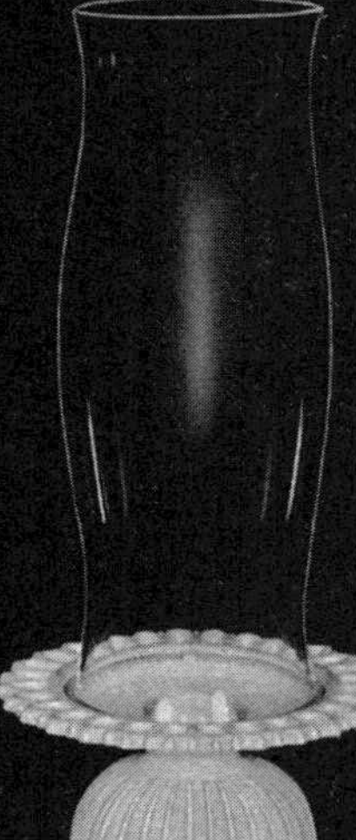

2675
Hurricane Lamp Complete
Height 14¾ in.
Consisting of:
1/12 doz. 2675
Hurricane Lamp Base
1/12 doz. 2675
Hurricane Lamp Chimney

FRUIT AND FLOWERS

Decoration No. 523
Enamel Decoration on Milk Glass

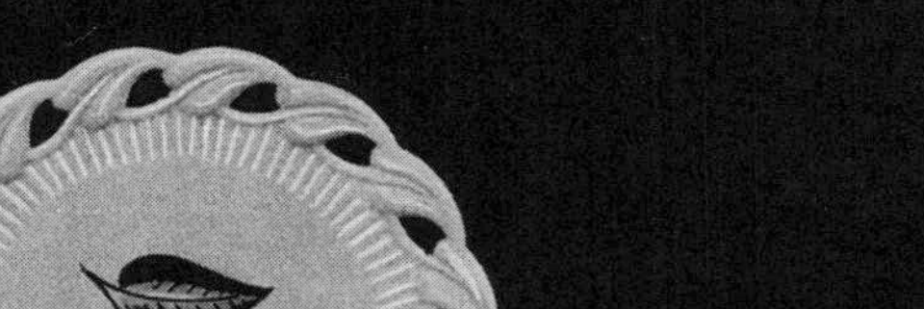

2620—8 in.
Plate
Apple

2620—8 in.
Plate
Grape

2620—8 in.
Plate
Peach

2620—8 in.
Plate
Pear

2620—8 in.
Plate
Raspberry

2620—8 in.
Plate
Cherry

1704
Pickle Jar and Cover
Daisey
Height 4¾ in.

1704
Pickle Jar and Cover
Redbud
Height 4¾ in.

FOSTORIA GLASS COMPANY, MOUNDSVILLE, WEST VIRGINIA — 1956

FOSTORIA GLASS COMPANY, MOUNDSVILLE, WEST VIRGINIA — 1954

MILK GLASS ITEMS

2620—8 in.
Plate

2620
Handled Nappy, 3 Cornered
Length 4½ in.

2620
Handled Nappy, Square
Width 4 in.

2620
Footed Sugar
Height 3¾ in.

2620
Footed Cream
Height 4 in.

2620—8½ in.
Bowl, Cupped

2620—10½ in.
Bowl, Flared

2620—10¾ in.
Fruit Bowl

2620—11½ in.
Basket

2620
Candlestick
Height 3 in.

2620
Hurricane Lamp, Complete
Height 9⅞ in.
Consisting of:
1/12 Dz. 2620 Candlestick
1/12 Dz. 2620 Hurricane Lamp Chimney

2675
Footed Preserve & Cover
Height 5⅝ in.

2675
Footed Urn & Cover
Height 8 in.

2675
Ash Tray
3½ in. square.

2675
Cigarette Box & Cover
Length 6⅜ in.
Width 4¾ in.

2676
Hen and Nest
Length 7¼ in.

2675—10 in.
Footed Bowl & Cover

2676
Hen and Nest (Decorated)
Length 7¼ in.

2678
Banana Bowl
Height 7 in.
Length 10¾ in.

2678
Salver
Height 4½ in.
Diameter 11¼ in.

2680
Stagecoach & Cover
Height 5⅜ in.

2679
Puff & Cover
Height 4⅝ in.

FOSTORIA GLASS COMPANY, MOUNDSVILLE, WEST VIRGINIA — 1958

MILK GLASS ITEMS

2694
7 in. Ash Tray
2694
9 in. Ash Tray

2694
Spoonholder and Cover
Height 7½ in.

2694
Comport Flared and Cover
Height 11½ in.

2694
Compote, Square
Height 9½ in.

2694
Compote, Belled
Height 8 in.

2694
Lace Bowl
Height 7 in.
Diameter 11½ in.

2694
Banana Stand
Height 7 in.
Width 13 in.

2694
Salver
Height 5 in.
Diameter 13½ in.

2694
Dripcut Syrup
Height 5¼ in.
Capacity 8½ oz.

2694
Mustard and Cover
and Spoon
Height 3¾ in.

2694
Marmalade and Cover
and Spoon
Height 5⅞ in.

2694
Salt Shaker
Height 5½ in.

2694
Pepper Mill
Height 6¼ in.

2694
Duo Candleholder
Height 5¼ in., Spread 8½ in.

2694
Oil and Stopper
Height 6⅝ in.
Capacity 5 oz.

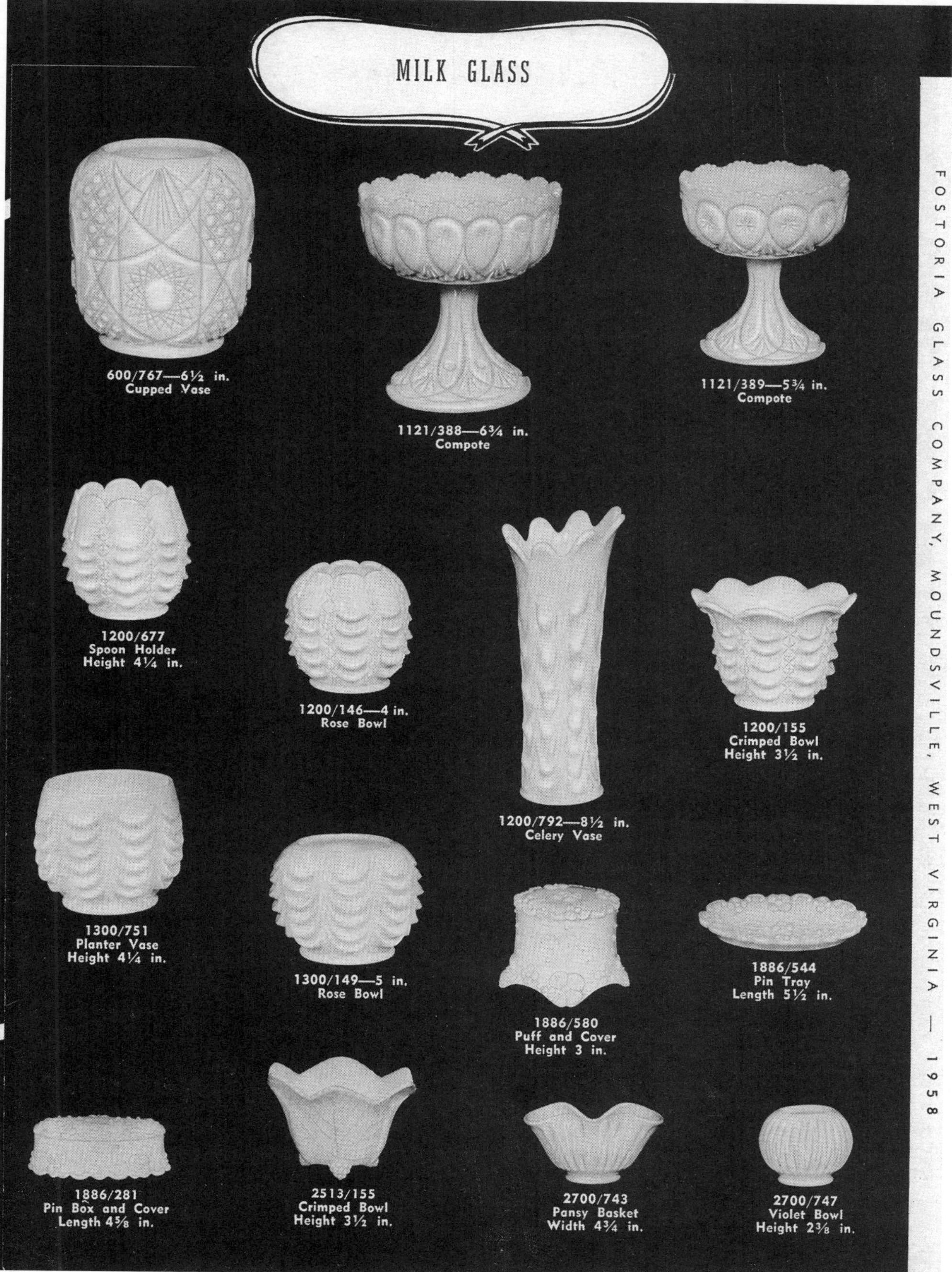

600/767—6½ in.
Cupped Vase

1121/388—6¾ in.
Compote

1121/389—5¾ in.
Compote

1200/677
Spoon Holder
Height 4¼ in.

1200/146—4 in.
Rose Bowl

1200/792—8½ in.
Celery Vase

1200/155
Crimped Bowl
Height 3½ in.

1300/751
Planter Vase
Height 4¼ in.

1300/149—5 in.
Rose Bowl

1886/580
Puff and Cover
Height 3 in.

1886/544
Pin Tray
Length 5½ in.

1886/281
Pin Box and Cover
Length 4⅝ in.

2513/155
Crimped Bowl
Height 3½ in.

2700/743
Pansy Basket
Width 4¾ in.

2700/747
Violet Bowl
Height 2⅜ in.

MILK GLASS ITEMS

FOSTORIA GLASS COMPANY, MOUNDSVILLE, WEST VIRGINIA — 1955

2183
Candleholder
Height 2¾ in.

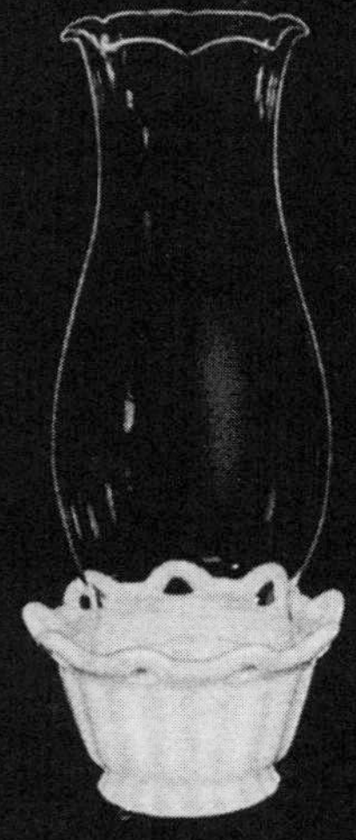

2493
Beer Mug
Height 5⅝ in.
Capacity 14 oz.

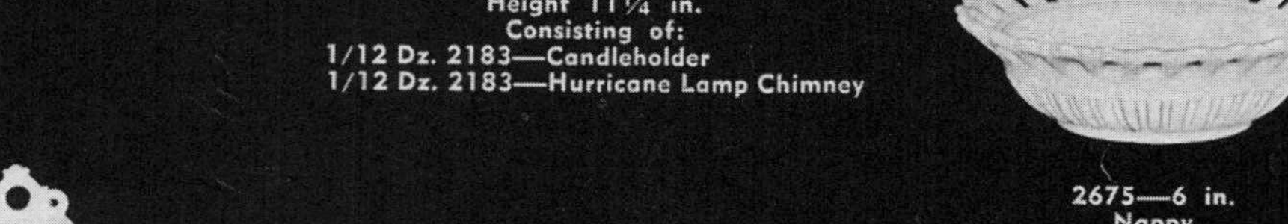

2183
Hurricane Lamp Complete
Height 11¼ in.
Consisting of:
1/12 Dz. 2183—Candleholder
1/12 Dz. 2183—Hurricane Lamp Chimney

2675—6 in.
Nappy

2675
Footed Sugar and Cover
Height 5¾ in.

2675
Footed Cream
Height 3⅝ in.

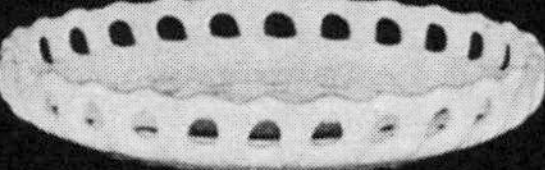

2675—7 in.
Tray

2675
Nappy, Cupped
Diameter 5⅜ in.

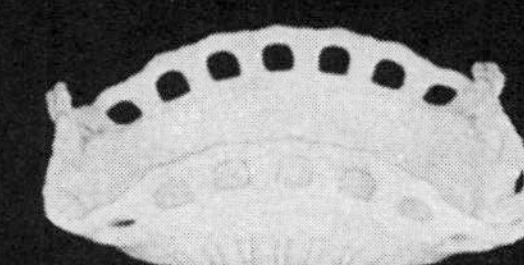

2675—6 in.
Nappy, Square

2675
Nappy, Oblong
Width 5 in.

2675
Egg Cup
Height 4½ in.

2675—9 in.
Plate

2675
Footed Cup
Cup Capacity 6 oz.

2675
Saucer

2675—9 oz.
Footed Tumbler
Height 5¼ in.

2678
Footed Fruit Bowl
Diameter 10 in.
Height 6½ in.

2678
Shallow Fruit Bowl
Length 10½ in. Width 7½ in.

2682
Fish Nappy
Length 9½ in.
Width 6 in.

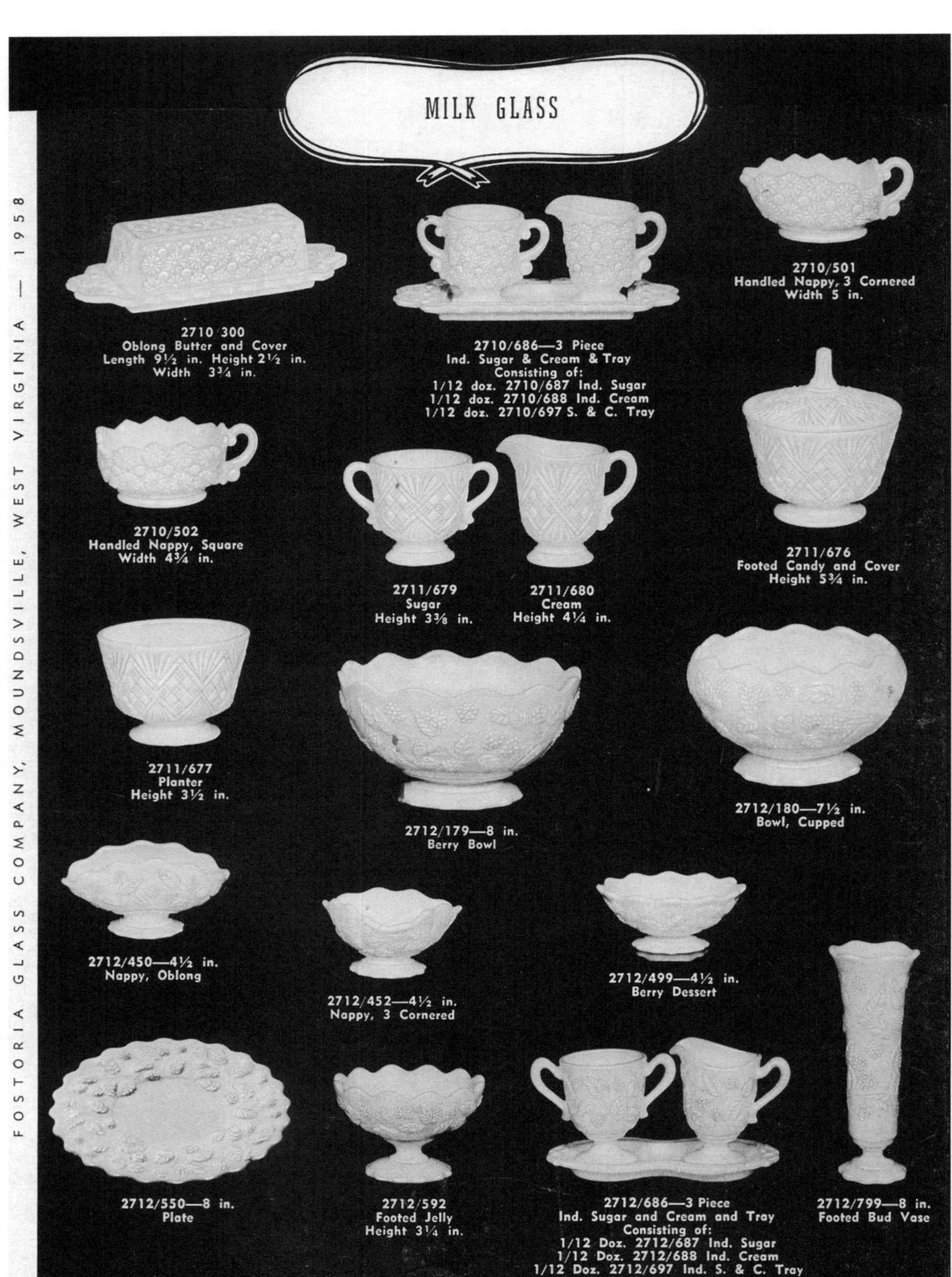

MILK GLASS

FOSTORIA GLASS COMPANY, MOUNDSVILLE, WEST VIRGINIA — 1958

2710/300
Oblong Butter and Cover
Length 9½ in. Height 2½ in.
Width 3¾ in.

2710/686—3 Piece
Ind. Sugar & Cream & Tray
Consisting of:
1/12 doz. 2710/687 Ind. Sugar
1/12 doz. 2710/688 Ind. Cream
1/12 doz. 2710/697 S. & C. Tray

2710/501
Handled Nappy, 3 Cornered
Width 5 in.

2710/502
Handled Nappy, Square
Width 4¾ in.

2711/679
Sugar
Height 3⅜ in.

2711/680
Cream
Height 4¼ in.

2711/676
Footed Candy and Cover
Height 5¾ in.

2711/677
Planter
Height 3½ in.

2712/179—8 in.
Berry Bowl

2712/180—7½ in.
Bowl, Cupped

2712/450—4½ in.
Nappy, Oblong

2712/452—4½ in.
Nappy, 3 Cornered

2712/499—4½ in.
Berry Dessert

2712/550—8 in.
Plate

2712/592
Footed Jelly
Height 3¼ in.

2712/686—3 Piece
Ind. Sugar and Cream and Tray
Consisting of:
1/12 Doz. 2712/687 Ind. Sugar
1/12 Doz. 2712/688 Ind. Cream
1/12 Doz. 2712/697 Ind. S. & C. Tray

2712/799—8 in.
Footed Bud Vase

MILK GLASS

FOSTORIA GLASS COMPANY, MOUNDSVILLE, WEST VIRGINIA — 1958

2713/2
Goblet
Height 6¼ in.
Capacity 11 oz.

2713/11
Sherbet
Height 4¾ in.
Capacity 7½ oz.

2713/63
Footed Ice Tea
Height 6¼ in.
Capacity 13 oz.

2713/179—8 in.
Berry Bowl

2713/180—8 in.
Bowl Crimped

2713/385
Bread Tray
Length 11 in.

2713/300
Oblong Butter and Cover
Length 8¼ in. Height 3 in.
Width 4 in.

2713/499—4½ in.
Berry Dessert

2713/500—4 in.
Nappy, Crimped

2713/502—4 in.
Nappy, Square

2713/550—8 in.
Plate

2713/686—3 piece
Ind. Sugar and Cream and Tray
Consisting of:
1/12 Doz. 2713/687 Ind. Sugar
1/12 Doz. 2713/688 Ind. Cream
1/12 Doz. 2713/697 Ind. S. & C. Tray

2714/287
Crocus Pot and Cover
Length 8½ in. Width 4 in.
Height 3¾ in.

MILK GLASS ITEMS

FOSTORIA GLASS COMPANY, MOUNDSVILLE, WEST VIRGINIA — 1954

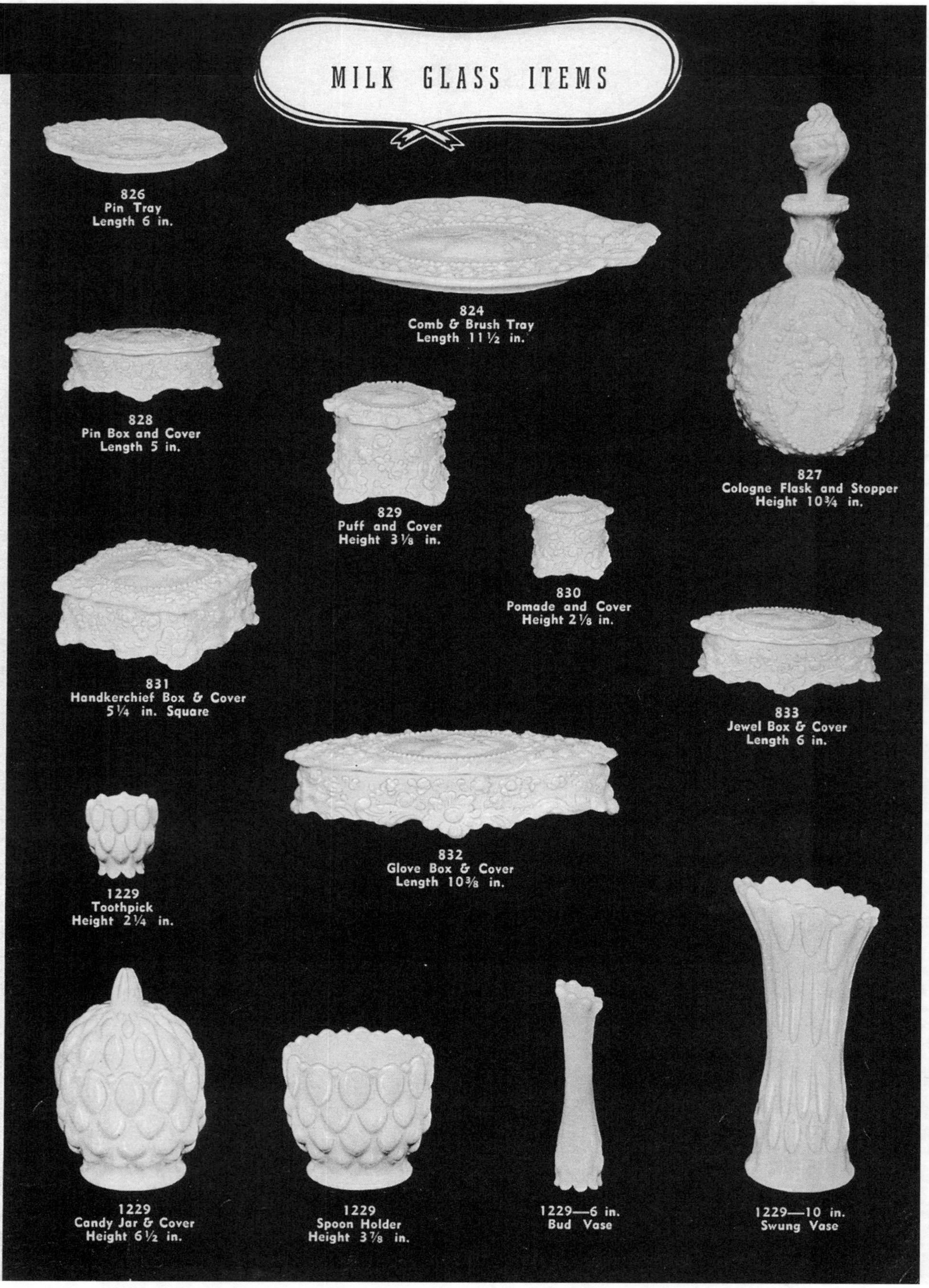

826
Pin Tray
Length 6 in.

824
Comb & Brush Tray
Length 11½ in.

827
Cologne Flask and Stopper
Height 10¾ in.

828
Pin Box and Cover
Length 5 in.

829
Puff and Cover
Height 3⅛ in.

830
Pomade and Cover
Height 2⅛ in.

831
Handkerchief Box & Cover
5¼ in. Square

833
Jewel Box & Cover
Length 6 in.

832
Glove Box & Cover
Length 10⅜ in.

1229
Toothpick
Height 2¼ in.

1229
Candy Jar & Cover
Height 6½ in.

1229
Spoon Holder
Height 3⅞ in.

1229—6 in.
Bud Vase

1229—10 in.
Swung Vase

MILK GLASS ITEMS

1704
½ Gallon Ice Jug
Height 8 in.

1704
Water (ill.)
Height 4⅜ in.
Capacity 7 oz.

1704
Ice Tea
Height 5¼ in.
Capacity 10½ oz.

1704
Cream
Height 4½ in.

1704
Sugar and Cover
Height 6⅞ in.

1704
Butter and Cover

1704
Cracker Jar and Cover
Height 8¾ in.

1704
Pickle Jar and Cover
Height 4¾ in.

1704
Handled Nappy, 3 Cornered

1704
Jelly, 3 Cornered
Height 3⅛ in.

1704
Handled Nappy, Square

1704
Jelly, Oblong
Height 4 in.

1704
Jelly, Square
Height 3¼ in.

FOSTORIA GLASS COMPANY, MOUNDSVILLE, WEST VIRGINIA — 1954

MILK GLASS ITEMS

FOSTORIA GLASS COMPANY, MOUNDSVILLE, WEST VIRGINIA — 1954

1704
Oil and Stopper
Height 6¼ in.
Capacity 6 oz.

1704
Shaker & Chrome Top "D"
Height 3 in.

1704
Shaker & Top, F.G.T.
Height 3 in.

2056—6½ in.
Wedding Bowl and Cover
Height 8 in.

2056—9 in.
Square Footed Vase

2056—8½ in.
Footed Bud Vase, Flared

2056—6 in.
Footed Bud Vase, Flared

2056
Topper Ash Tray
Top Diameter 2⅛ in.

2056—2½ in.
Topper
Top Diameter 3¾ in.

2056—3 in.
Topper
Top Diameter 4½ in.

2056—4 in.
Topper Vase
Top Diameter 6 in.

2183—12 in.
Shallow Bowl

2183—9 in.
Square Bowl

MILK GLASS ITEMS

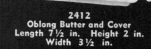

2412
Oblong Butter and Cover
Length 7½ in. Height 2 in.
Width 3½ in.

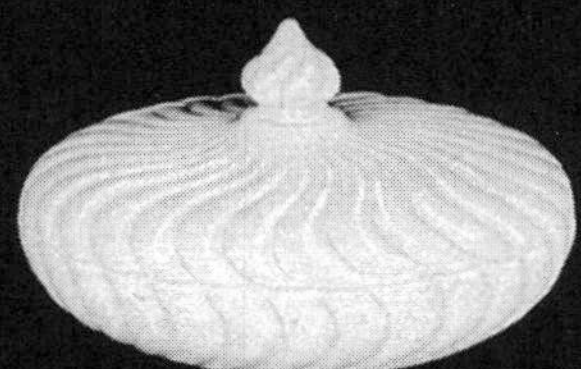

2412
Candy Box and Cover
Height 4 in. Diameter 6½ in.

2412
Low Comport and Cover
Height 6⅜ in.

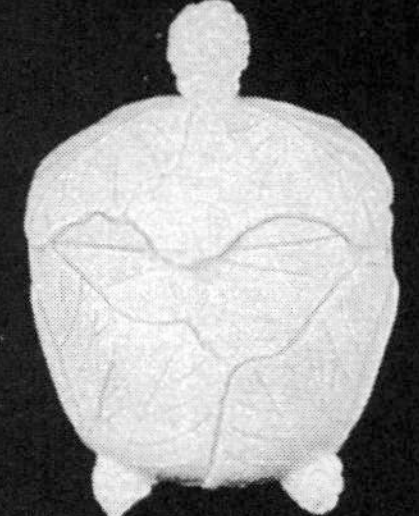

2513
Candy Jar and Cover
Height 6 in.

2519
Cologne and Stopper
Height 5½ in.

2519
Puff and Cover
Height 4⅜ in.

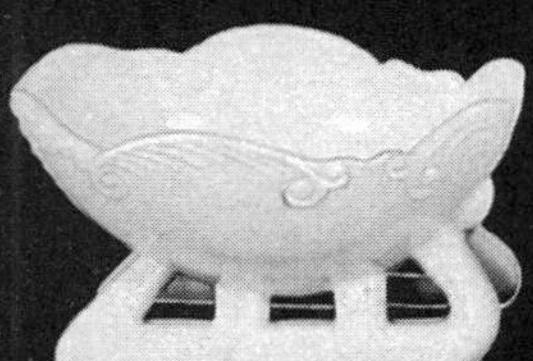

2595—3 in. Sleigh
Height 1¾ in. Width 2⅛ in.

2595—4¼ in. Sleigh
Height 2¼ in. Width 3⅛ in.

2595—6 in. Sleigh
Height 3⅜ in. Width 4⅜ in.

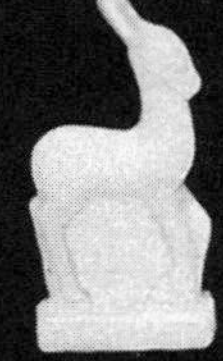

2589
Deer
Height 4⅜ in.

2589½
Deer
Height 2½ in.

2521
Bird

2620
Goblet
Height 6 in.
Capacity 9 oz.

2620
Sherbet
Height 4 in.
Capacity 4⅛ in.

2620
Ice Tea
Height 5¼ in.
Capacity 12 oz.

2620
Juice
Height 3⅝ in.
Capacity 5 oz.

FOSTORIA GLASS COMPANY, MOUNDSVILLE, WEST VIRGINIA — 1954

Stemware and Tumblers, Blown

BLOWN STEMWARE. 39

870—SOLID ROSE, GREEN, AMBER AND CRYSTAL, REGULAR OPTIC.
5084—SOLID ROSE, GREEN, AMBER AND CRYSTAL, REGULAR OPTIC.
PRICED PAGE 24 — No. 2 PRICE LIST.

870—9 oz. Goblet.

870—6 oz. High Sherbet.

870—6 oz. Low Sherbet.

5084—Oyster Cocktail.

5084—5 oz. Ftd. Tumbler.

5084—9 oz. Ftd. Tumbler.

5084—12 oz. Ftd. Tumbler.

5084—7 Ftd. Jug.

Fostoria Glass Company, Moundsville, West Virginia

1930 Catalog

32

BLOWN GLASSWARE.
MADE IN SOLID AMBER, BLUE, GREEN AND CRYSTAL, EXCEPT AS OTHERWISE NOTED.
PRICED PAGE 18 — No. 2 SUPPLEMENT PRICE LIST.

869—9 oz. Goblet, Optic.
Patent No. 69,184.

869—6 oz. Parfait, Optic.

869—5½ oz. High Sherbet, Optic.

869—5½ oz. Low Sherbet, Optic.

869—5 oz. Tumbler, Optic.
Also made in Orchid.

869—Table Tumbler, Optic.
Also made in Orchid.

869—12 oz. Tumbler, Optic.
Also made in Orchid.

1236—No. 6 Jug, Optic.

Fostoria Glass Company, Moundsville, West Virginia

1930 Catalog

1930 Catalog

1930 Catalog
This stem made in Burgundy, 1933

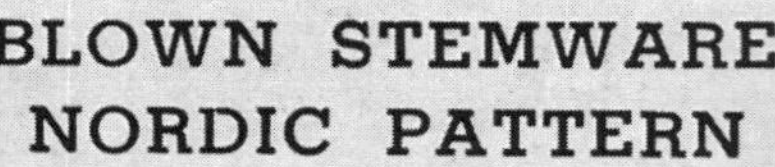

BLOWN STEMWARE
NORDIC PATTERN
No. 892 LINE—NO OPTIC

892—11 oz. Goblet
Height 6½ in.

892—7 oz. Saucer Champagne
Height 5⅛ in.

892—6½ oz. Low Sherbet
Height 4 in.

892—4 oz. Cocktail
Height 4½ in.

892—4 oz. Claret
Height 4⅞ in.

892—3 oz. Wine
Height 4⅜ in.

892—1 oz. Cordial
Height 3⅜ in.

892—4½ oz. Oyster Cocktail
Height 2⅞ in.

892—5 oz. Footed Tumbler
Height 3⅞ in.

892—13 oz. Footed Tumbler
Height 5½ in.

Fostoria Glass Company, Moundsville, West Virginia, July 1, 1939

402B

BLOWN STEMWARE

VICTORIAN PATTERN

No. 4024 LINE—NO OPTIC

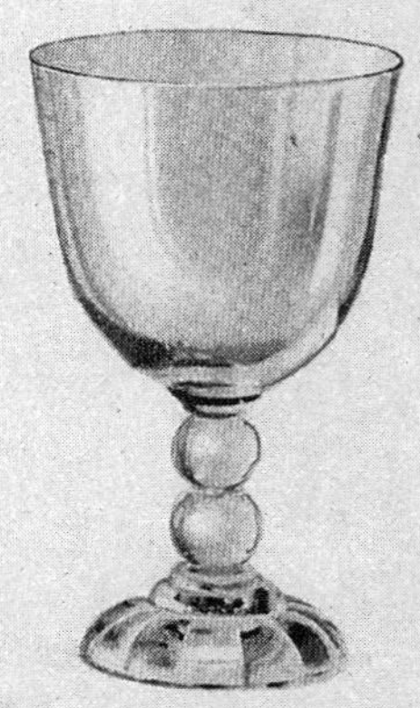

4024½—11 oz. Goblet
Height 6⅛ in.

4024—10 oz. Goblet
Height 5⅝ in.

4024—6½ oz.
Saucer Champagne
Height 4½ in.

4024—5½ oz.
Sherbet
Height 3⅞ in.

4024—4 oz.
Cocktail
Height 3⅝ in.

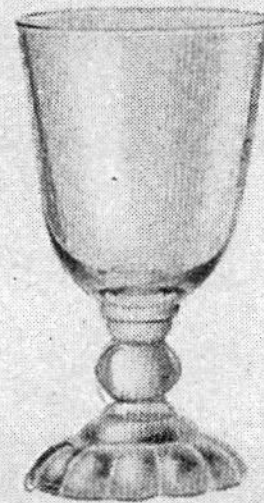

4024—3½ oz.
Claret-Wine
Height 4½ in.

4024—1 oz.
Cordial
Height 3⅛ in.

4024
1½ oz. Footed Whiskey
Height 2½ in.

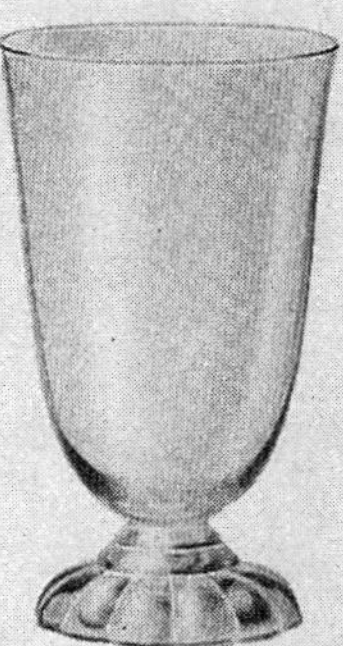

4024—12 oz.
Footed Tumbler
Height 5½ in.

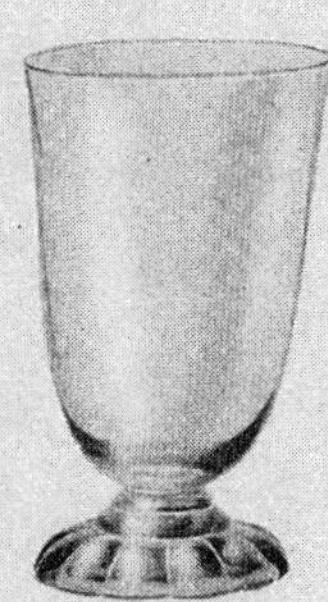

4024—8 oz.
Footed Tumbler
Height 4¾ in.

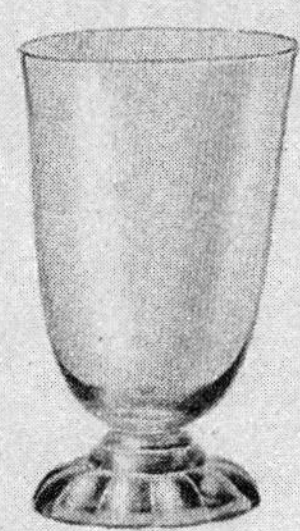

4024—5 oz.
Footed Tumbler
Height 4¼ in.

4024—4 oz.
Oyster Cocktail
Height 3⅜ in.

46

BLOWN STEMWARE.

5000—SOLID GREEN, AMBER AND CRYSTAL — REG. OPTIC. 5200—ROSE, AZURE, GREEN AND AMBER BOWL—CRYSTAL FOOT—REG. OPTIC.
5100—GREEN FOOT — CRYSTAL BOWL — SPIRAL OPTIC. 5100—AMBER FOOT — CRYSTAL BOWL — LOOP OPTIC.
PRICED PAGES 28, 29 AND 30 — No. 2 PRICE LIST.

5000—5 oz. Ftd. Tumbler.
5100—5 oz. Ftd. Tumbler.
5200—5 oz. Ftd. Tumbler.

5000—6 oz. Parfait.
Discontinued.

5000—4½ oz. Oyster Cocktail.
5100—4½ oz. Oyster Cocktail.
5200—4½ oz. Oyster Cocktail.

5000—6 oz. Sherbet.
Discontinued.

5000—2½ oz. Ftd. Tumbler.
5100—2½ oz. Ftd. Tumbler.
5200—2½ oz. Ftd. Tumbler.

5000—7 oz. Ftd. Tumbler.
Discontinued.

5000—9 oz. Ftd. Tumbler.
5100—9 oz. Ftd. Tumbler.
5200—9 oz. Ftd. Tumbler.

5000—12 oz. Ftd. Tumbler.
5100—12 oz. Ftd. Tumbler.
5200—12 oz. Ftd. Tumbler.

5000—7 Ftd. Jug.
Also made in Solid Rose, Azure and Topaz.
5100—7 Ftd. Jug.

Fostoria Glass Company, Moundsville, West Virginia

1930 Catalog

BLOWN STEMWARE.

4095—SOLID GREEN—SPIRAL OPTIC. 4195—AMBER FOOT—CRYSTAL BOWL—LOOP OPTIC.
4095—SOLID CRYSTAL—REGULAR OPTIC. 4195—GREEN FOOT—CRYSTAL BOWL—SPIRAL OPTIC.
4295—ROSE, AZURE, GREEN BOWL—CRYSTAL FOOT—REGULAR OPTIC.
PRICED PAGES 26 AND 27 — No. 2 PRICE LIST.

43

4095—6 oz. Parfait.
Discontinued.

4095—4 oz. Oyster Cocktail.
4195—4 oz. Oyster Cocktail.
4295—4 oz. Oyster Cocktail.

4095—2½ oz. Ftd. Tumbler.
4195—2½ oz. Ftd. Tumbler.
4295—2½ oz. Ftd. Tumbler.

4095—5 in. Nappy.
Discontinued.

4095—Ind. Almond.
4195—Ind. Almond.
4295—Ind. Almond.

4095—Ind. Salt.
4195—Ind. Salt.
4295—Ind. Salt.

4095—5 oz. Ftd. Tumbler.
4195—5 oz. Ftd. Tumbler.
4295—5 oz. Ftd. Tumbler.

4295—10 oz. Ftd. Tumbler.
4195—10 oz. Ftd. Tumbler.
4295—10 oz. Ftd. Tumbler.

4095—13 oz. Ftd. Tumbler.
4195—13 oz. Ftd. Tumbler.
4295—13 oz. Ftd. Tumbler.

4095—7 Ftd. Jug.
Also Solid Rose, Azure and Green.
4195—7 Ftd. Jug.

Fostoria Glass Company, Moundsville, West Virginia

1930 Catalog

AMERICAN LADY PATTERN

No. 5056 Line

Blown Lead Glass Stemware

See Price List For Color

FOSTORIA GLASS COMPANY, MOUNDSVILLE, WEST VIRGINIA — 1949

**5056—10 oz.
Goblet
Height 6⅛ in.**

**5056—5½ oz.
Sherbet
Height 4⅛ in.**

**5056—3½ oz.
Cocktail
Height 4 in.**

**5056—3½ oz
Claret
Height 4⅝ in.**

**5056—1 oz.
Cordial
Height 3⅛ in.**

**5056—4 oz.
Oyster Cocktail
Height 3½ in.**

**5056—12 oz.
Footed Tumbler
Height 5½ in.**

**5056—5 oz.
Footed Tumbler
Height 4⅛ in.**

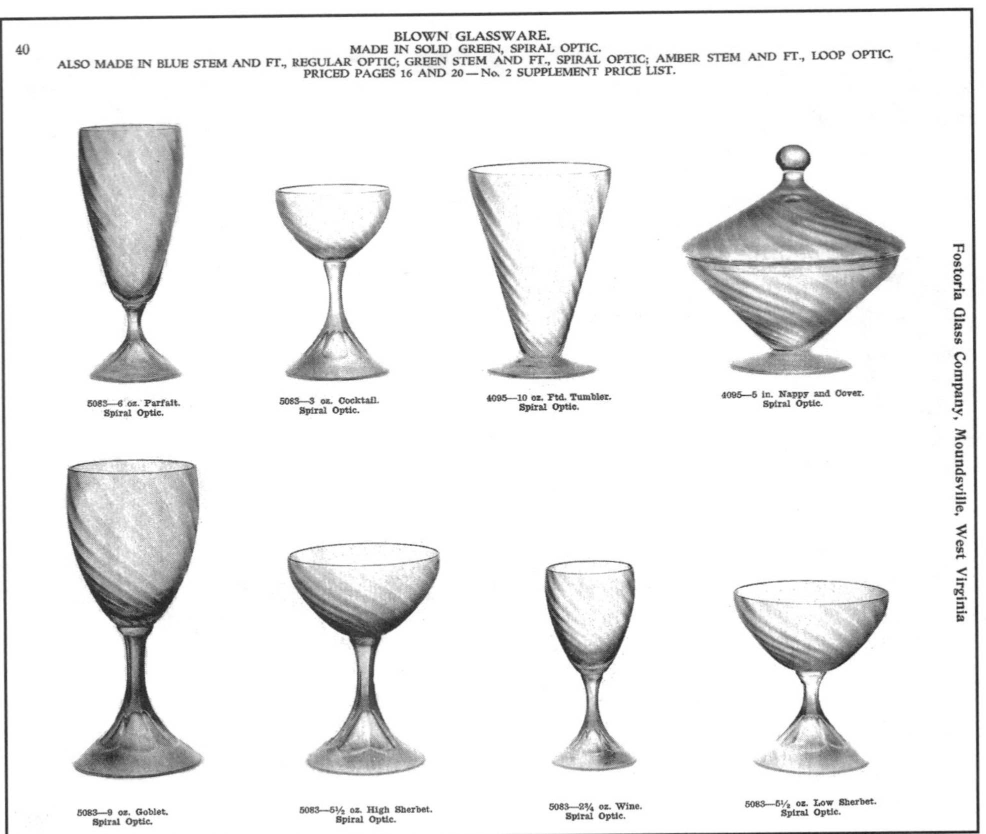

40

BLOWN GLASSWARE.
MADE IN SOLID GREEN, SPIRAL OPTIC.
ALSO MADE IN BLUE STEM AND FT., REGULAR OPTIC; GREEN STEM AND FT., SPIRAL OPTIC; AMBER STEM AND FT., LOOP OPTIC.
PRICED PAGES 16 AND 20 — No. 2 SUPPLEMENT PRICE LIST.

5083—6 oz. Parfait. Spiral Optic.

5083—3 oz. Cocktail. Spiral Optic.

4095—10 oz. Ftd. Tumbler. Spiral Optic.

4095—5 in. Nappy and Cover. Spiral Optic.

5083—9 oz. Goblet. Spiral Optic.

5083—5½ oz. High Sherbet. Spiral Optic.

5083—2¾ oz. Wine. Spiral Optic.

5083—5½ oz. Low Sherbet. Spiral Optic.

Fostoria Glass Company, Moundsville, West Virginia

1927 Catalog

42

BLOWN STEMWARE.
5082—SOLID GREEN—SPIRAL OPTIC. 5182—AMBER FOOT—CRYSTAL BOWL—LOOP OPTIC.
5082—SOLID CRYSTAL—REGULAR OPTIC. 5182—GREEN FOOT—CRYSTAL BOWL—SPIRAL OPTIC.
5282—ROSE, AZURE AND GREEN BOWL—CRYSTAL FOOT—REGULAR OPTIC.
PRICED PAGES 26 AND 27 — No. 2 PRICE LIST.
DESIGN PATENT No. 68,151

5082—6 oz. Parfait.
5182—6 oz. Parfait.
5282—6 oz. Parfait.

5082—4½ oz. Claret.
5182—4½ oz. Claret.
5282—4½ oz. Claret.

5082—2¾ oz. Wine.
5182—2¾ oz. Wine.
5282—2¾ oz. Wine.

5082—2½ oz. Cocktail. 5182—2½ oz. Cocktail.
5282—2½ oz. Cocktail.

5082—¾ oz. Cordial. 5182—¾ oz. Cordial.
5282—¾ oz. Cordial.

4095—4½ in. Nappy-Finger Bowl.
4195—4½ in. Nappy-Finger Bowl.
4295—4½ in. Nappy-Finger Bowl.
2283—6 in. Plate, R/O.

5082—9 oz. Goblet.
5182—9 oz. Goblet.
5282—9 oz. Goblet.

5082—5 oz. High Sherbet.
5182—5 oz. High Sherbet.
5282—5 oz. High Sherbet.

5082—5 oz. Low Sherbet.
5182—5 oz. Low Sherbet.
5282—5 oz. Low Sherbet.

5082½—Grape Fruit.
5182½—Grape Fruit.
5282½—Grape Fruit.
945½—G. F. Liner.

Fostoria Glass Company, Moundsville, West Virginia

1930 Catalog

1930 Catalog

1930 Catalog

BLOWN STEMWARE

No. 5099 LINE—12 RIB REGULAR OPTIC

See Price List for Colors

DESIGN PATENT NO. 79225

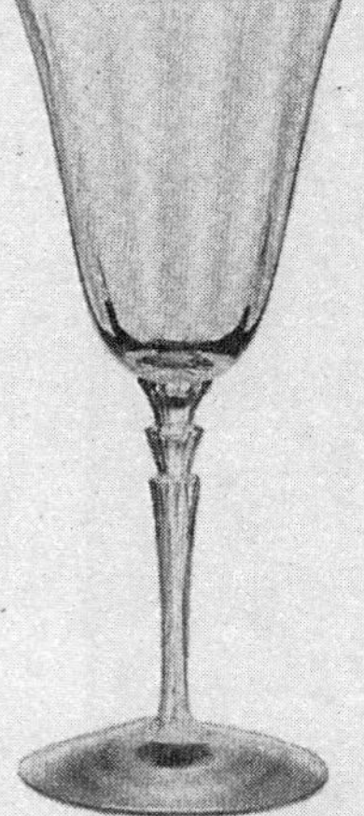

5099—9 oz. Goblet
Height 8¼ in.

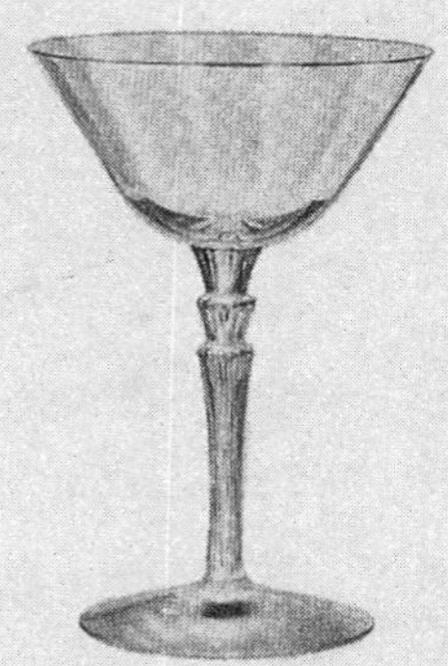

5099—6 oz. Saucer Champagne
Height 6⅝ in.

5099—6 oz. Low Sherbet
Height 4¼ in.

5099—3 oz. Cocktail
Height 5⅛ in.

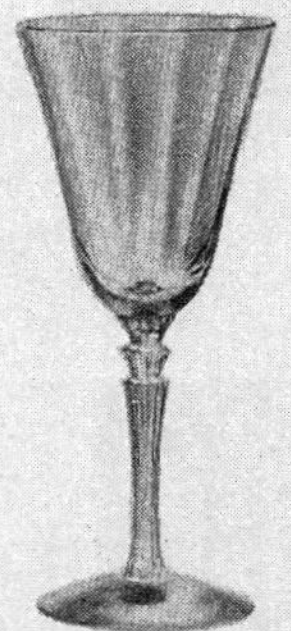

5099—4 oz. Claret
Height 6 in.

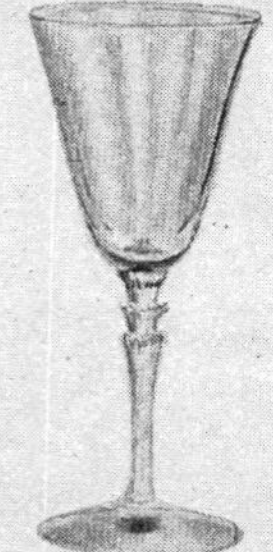

5099—2½ oz. Wine
Height 5½ in.

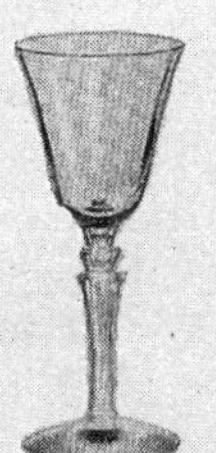

5099
¾ oz. Cordial
Height 3⅞ in.

5099—4½ oz. Oyster Cocktail
Height 3½ in.

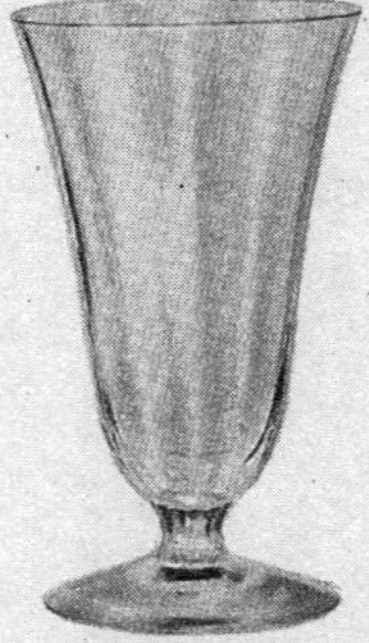

5099—12 oz. Footed Tumbler
Height 5⅞ in.

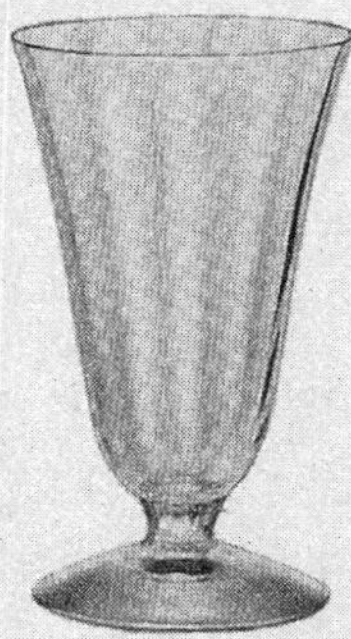

5099—9 oz. Footed Tumbler
Height 5⅜ in.

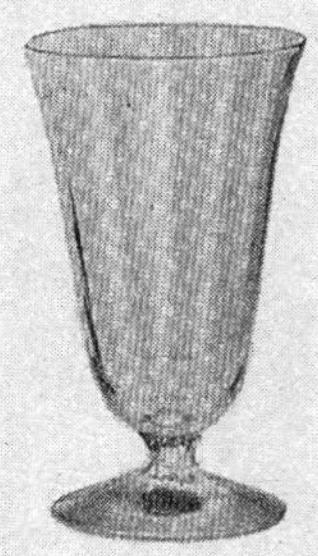

5099—5 oz. Footed Tumbler
Height 4½ in.

5099—2½ oz. Footed Tumbler
Height 3 in.

COLONIAL DAME PATTERN

No. 5412 Line

Blown Lead Glass Stemware

5412 — 11 oz. Goblet Height 6-3/8 in.

5412 — 6-1/2 oz. Sherbet Height 4-5/8 in.

5412 — 3-1/2 oz. Cocktail Height 4 in.

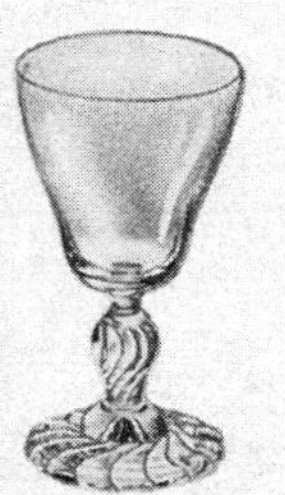

5412 — 3-3/4 oz. Claret-Wine Height 4-5/8 in.

5412 — 1 oz. Cordial Height 3-1/4 in.

5412 — 4-1/2 oz. Oyster Cocktail Height 3-7/8 in.

5412 — 12 oz. Footed Tumbler Height 6 in.

5412 — 5 oz. Footed Tumbler Height 4-5/8 in.

FOSTORIA GLASS COMPANY, MOUNDSVILLE, WEST VIRGINIA — 1949

Fostoria Glass Company, Moundsville, West Virginia, Jan. 1, 1939

BLOWN STEMWARE

No. 6004 LINE—16 RIB REGULAR OPTIC

See Price List for Colors and Optics

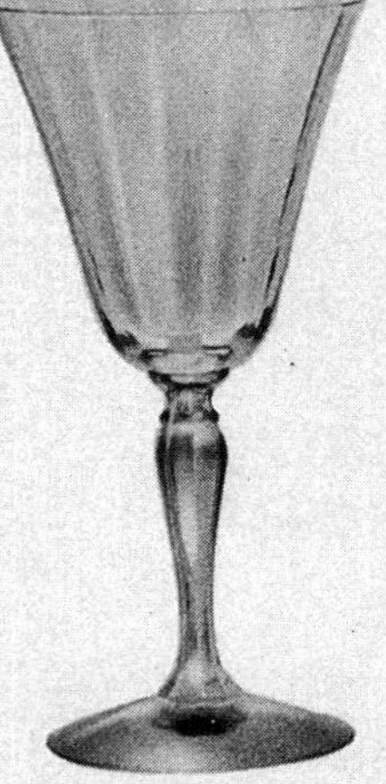

6004—9 oz. Goblet
Height 7⅜ in.

6004—5½ oz. Saucer Champagne
Height 5⅜ in.

6004—5½ oz. Low Sherbet
Height 4⅛ in.

6004—5½ oz. Parfait
Height 6 in.

6004—4 oz. Claret
Height 5⅝ in.

6004—2½ oz. Wine
Height 5 in.

6004—3 oz. Cocktail
Height 4¾ in.

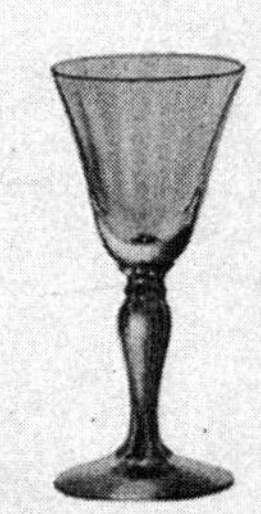

6004—¾ oz. Cordial
Height 3⅝ in.

6004—4½ oz. Oyster Cocktail. Height 3½ in.

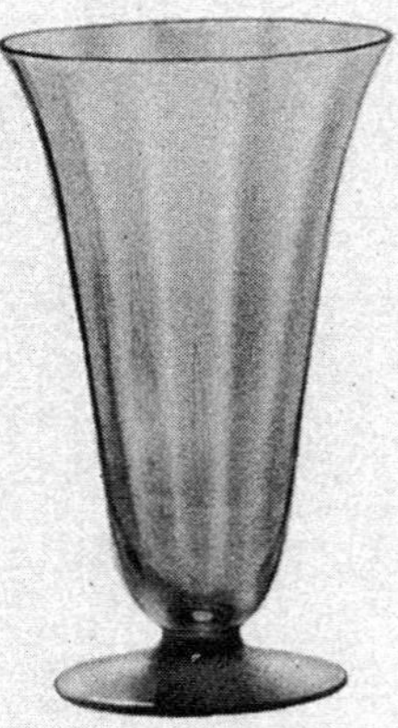

6004—12 oz. Footed Tumbler
Height 6 in.

6004—9 oz. Footed Tumbler
Height 5¼ in.

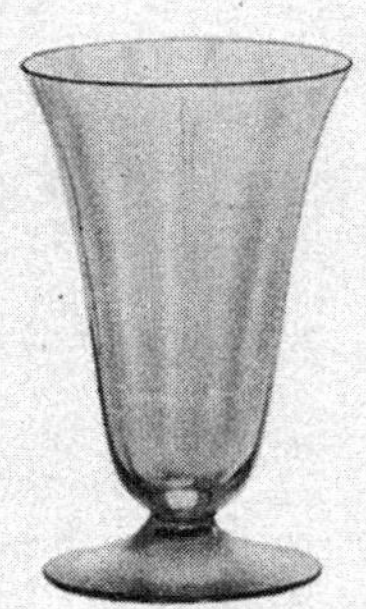

6004—5 oz. Footed Tumbler
Height 4¼ in.

6004—2½ oz. Footed Tumbler
Height 2¾ in.

BLOWN STEMWARE

No. 6007 LINE—16 RIB REGULAR OPTIC

See Price List for Colors and Optics

6007—10 oz. Goblet
Height 7½ in.

6007—5½ oz. Saucer Champagne
Height 5⅜ in.

6007—5½ oz. Low Sherbet
Height 4 in.

6007—3½ oz. Cocktail
Height 4⅝ in.

6007—4 oz. Claret
Height 5⅜ in.

6007—3 oz. Wine
Height 5 in.

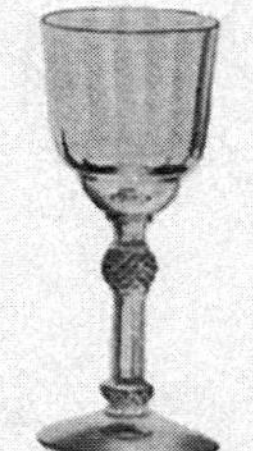
6007—1 oz. Cordial
Height 3⅝ in.

6007—4½ oz. Oyster Cocktail
Height 3⅛ in.

6007—12 oz. Footed Tumbler
Height 5⅝ in.

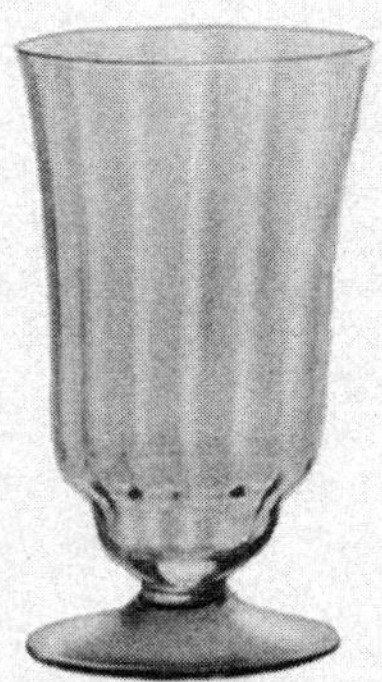
6007—9 oz. Footed Tumbler
Height 5⅛ in.

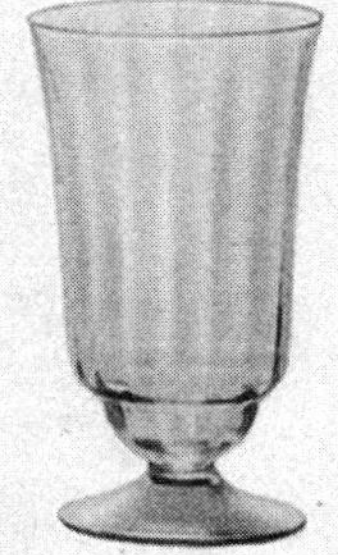
6007—5 oz. Footed Tumbler
Height 4¼ in.

6007—2 oz. Footed Tumbler
Height 2¾ in.

Fostoria Glass Company, Moundsville, West Virginia, Jan. 1, 1939

BLOWN STEMWARE

No. 6008 LINE—16 RIB REGULAR OPTIC

6008—10 oz. Goblet
Height 6⅝ in.

6008—5½ oz. Saucer Champagne
Height 5⅜ in.

6008—5½ oz. Low Sherbet
Height 4⅛ in.

6008—4 oz. Wine
Height 5 in.

6008—3¼ oz. Cocktail
Height 4¼ in.

6008—1 oz. Cordial
Height 3⅜ in.

6008—5 oz. Oyster Cocktail
Height 3½ in.

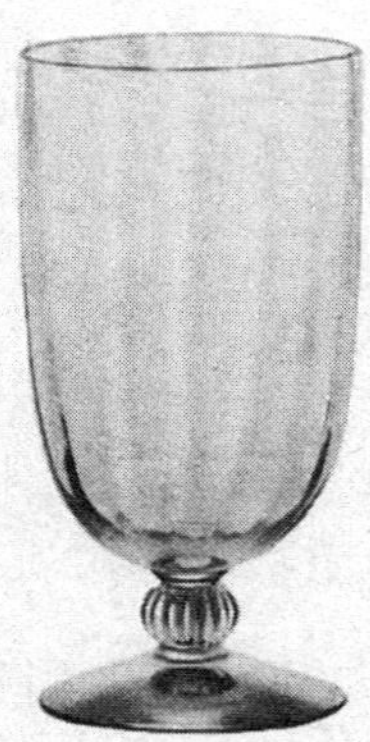

6008—12 oz. Footed Tumbler
Height 5¾ in.

6008—9 oz. Footed Tumbler
Height 5¼ in.

6008—5 oz. Footed Tumbler
Height 4½ in.

1769—Finger Bowl
Height 2 in. Diameter 4⅛ in.

Fostoria Glass Company, Moundsville, West Virginia, Jan. 1, 1939

BLOWN STEMWARE

No. 6009 LINE—12 RIB REGULAR OPTIC

6009—9 oz. Goblet
Height 7⅝ in.

6009—5½ oz. Saucer Champagne
Height 5⅝ in.

6009—5½ oz. Low Sherbet
Height 4⅜ in.

6009—3¾ oz. Claret-Wine
Height 5⅜ in.

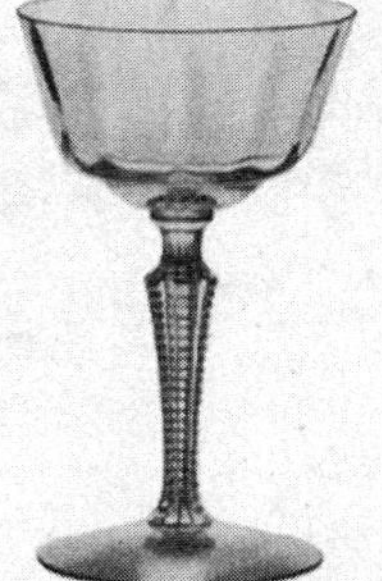
6009—3¾ oz. Cocktail
Height 4¾ in.

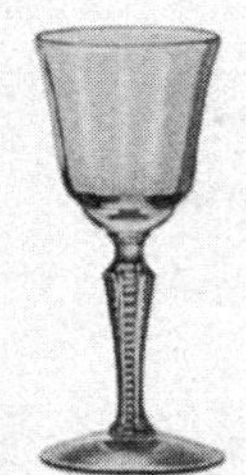
6009—1 oz. Cordial
Height 3¾ in.

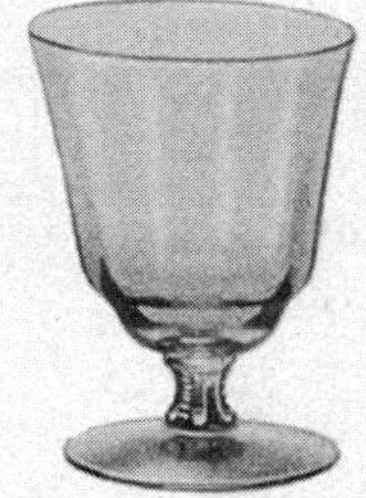
6009—4¾ oz. Oyster Cocktail
Height 3¾ in.

6009—12 oz. Footed Tumbler
Height 5⅞ in.

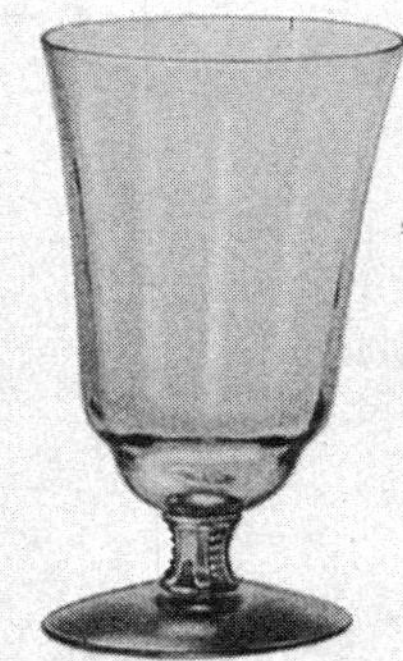
6009—9 oz. Footed Tumbler
Height 5¼ in.

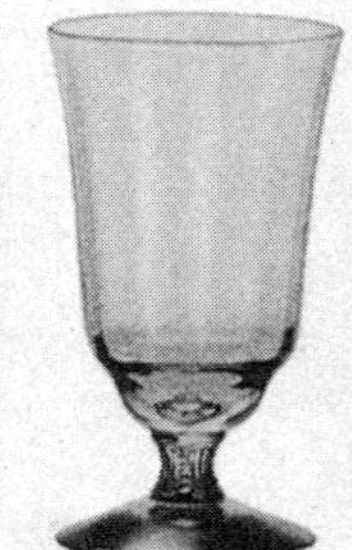
6009—5 oz. Footed Tumbler
Height 4⅜ in.

Fostoria Glass Company, Moundsville, West Virginia, Jan. 1, 1939

Fostoria Glass Company, Moundsville, West Virginia, Jan. 1, 1939

BLOWN STEMWARE

NEO CLASSIC PATTERN

No. 6011 LINE—NO OPTIC

[illegible] List for Colors

DESIGN PATENT NO. 92113

6011—10 oz. Goblet
Height 6⅜ in.

6011—5½ oz. Saucer Champagne
Height 4¾ in.

6011—5½ oz. Low Sherbet
Height 3¼ in.

6011—3 oz. Cocktail
Height 4⅝ in.

6011—4½ oz. Claret
Height 5⅝ in.

6011—3 oz. Wine
Height 5 in.

6011—2 oz. Sherry
Height 4⅝ in.

6011
2 oz. Creme de Menthe
Height 4½ in.

6011—1 oz. C[illegible]dial
Height 3¼ in.

6011—1 oz. Brandy
Height 4 in.

6011—4 oz. Oyster Cocktail
Height 3¼ in.

6011—2 oz. Whiskey
Height 2¾ in.

6011
13 oz. Footed Tumbler
Height 5⅜ in.

6011
10 oz. Footed Tumbler
Height 4½ in.

6011
5 oz. Footed Tumbler
Height 3⅞ in.

6011—Footed Jug
Cap. 53 oz. Height 8⅞ in.

BLOWN STEMWARE

WESTCHESTER PATTERN

No. 6012 LINE—NO OPTIC

DESIGN PATENT NO. 93380

6012—10 oz. Goblet
Height 6⅞ in.

6012—5½ oz. Saucer
Champagne—Height 5 in.

6012
5½ oz. Low Sherbet
Height 4 in.

6012
3 oz. Cocktail
Height 4⅝ in.

6012
4½ oz. Claret
Height 5¾ in.

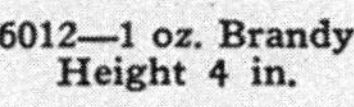

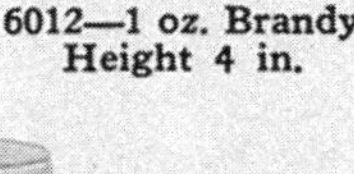

6012—1 oz. Brandy
Height 4 in.

6012—3 oz. Wine
Height 5¼ in.

6012
2 oz. Sherry
Height 4½ in.

6012—1 oz. Cordial
Height 3½ in.

6012—2 oz. Creme de Menthe
Height 4½ in.

6012—13 oz. Footed
Tumbler
Height 5¾ in.

6012—10 oz. Footed
Tumbler
Height 5⅜ in.

6012—5 oz. Footed
Tumbler
Height 4¼ in.

6012—4 oz. Footed
Cocktail (Oyster)
Height 3½ in.

Fostoria Glass Company, Moundsville, West Virginia, Jan. 1, 1939

BLOWN STEMWARE

No. 6013 LINE—30 RIB NARROW OPTIC

COLORS—NO OPTIC

6013—10 oz. Goblet
Height 7¾ in.

6013—9 oz. Low Goblet
Height 5¾ in.

6013
6 oz. Saucer Champagne
Height 5½ in.

6013
5 oz. Low Sherbet
Height 4⅛ in.

6013—4 oz. Claret
Height 6¼ in.

6013—3 oz. Wine
Height 5½ in.

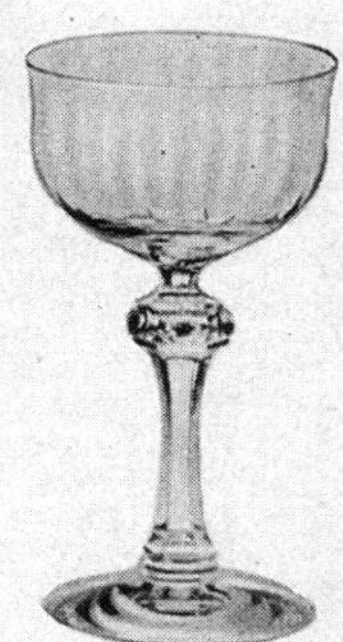

6013
3½ oz. Cocktail
Height 5½ in.

6013
13 oz. Footed Tumbler
Height 5½ in.

6013
5 oz. Footed Tumbler
Height 4½ in.

6013
4 oz. Oyster Cocktail
Height 3½ in.

6013
1 oz. Cordial
Height 4 in.

Fostoria Glass Company, Moundsville, West Virginia, Jan. 1, 1939

BLOWN STEMWARE

No. 6014 LINE

Made in Loop Optic and 16 Rib Regular Optic

In Loop Optic This Pattern is Called "Wave Crest"

"Wave Crest" Pattern
6014
9 oz. Goblet L/O
Height 7⅜ in.

Entire line also made in this Optic

6014
9 oz. Goblet
Height 7⅜ in.

6014
5½ oz. Saucer Champagne
Height 5⅜ in.

6014
5½ oz. Low Sherbet
Height 4½ in.

6014
3½ oz. Cocktail
Height 5 in.

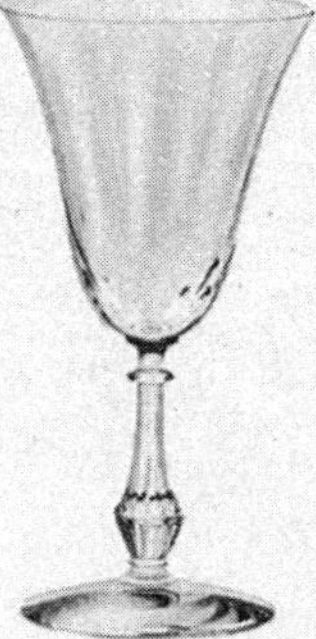

6014
4 oz. Claret
Height 5⅞ in.

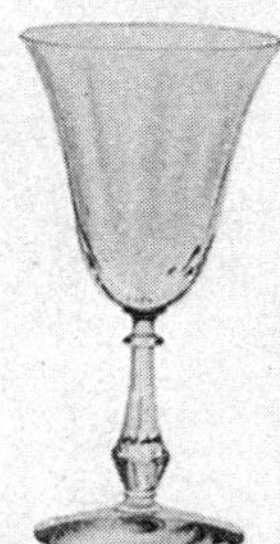

6014
3 oz. Wine
Height 5¼ in.

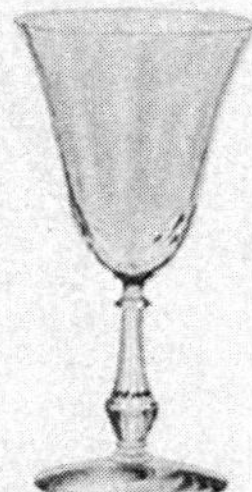

6014
1 oz. Cordial
Height 3¾ in.

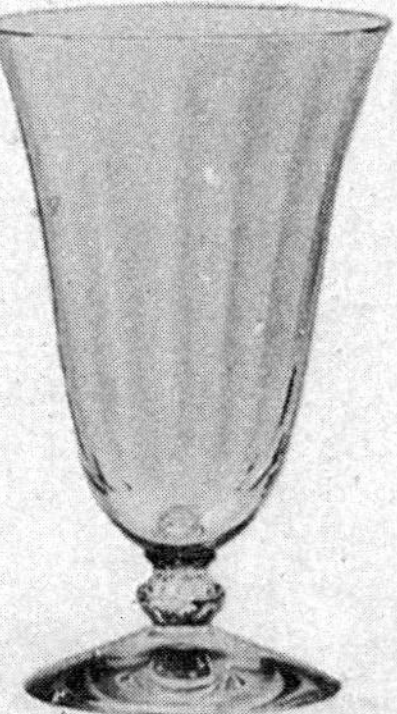

6014
12 oz. Footed Tumbler
Height 6 in.

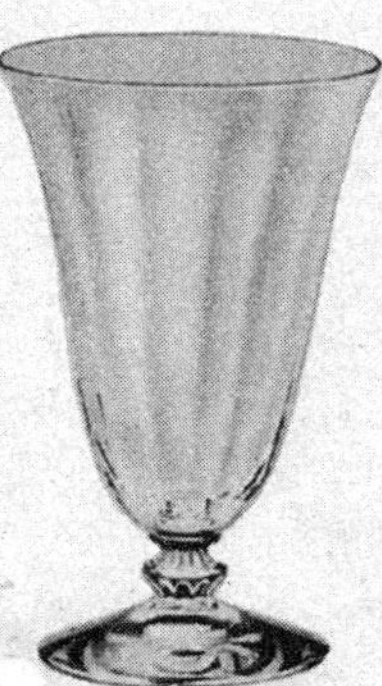

6014
9 oz. Footed Tumbler
Height 5½ in.

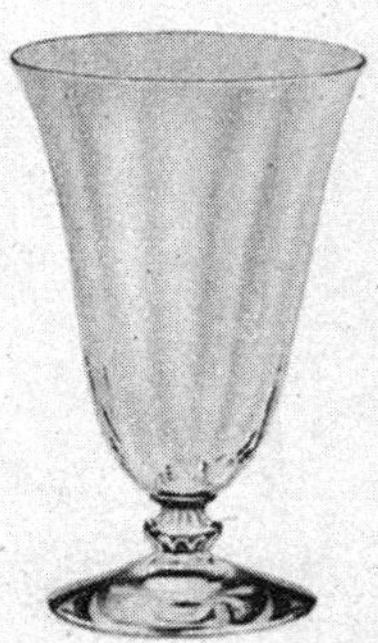

6014
5 oz. Footed Tumbler
Height 4¾ in.

6014
4 oz. Oyster Cocktail
Height 3¾ in.

Fostoria Glass Company, Moundsville, West Virginia, Jan. 1, 1939

Fostoria Glass Company, Moundsville, West Virginia, Jan. 1, 1939

BLOWN STEMWARE

No. 6016 LINE—16 RIB REGULAR OPTIC

See Price List for Colors

6016—10 oz. Goblet
Height 7⅝ in.

6016—6 oz. Saucer Champagne
Height 5⅝ in.

6016—6 oz. Low Sherbet
Height 4⅜ in.

6016—3½ oz. Cocktail
Height 5¼ in.

6016—4½ oz. Claret
Height 6 in.

6016—3¼ oz. Wine
Height 5¼ in.

6016—¾ oz. Cordial
Height 3⅞ in.

6016—4 oz. Oyster Cocktail
Height 3⅝ in.

6016—13 oz. Footed Tumbler
Height 5⅞ in.

6016—10 oz. Footed Tumbler
Height 5⅜ in.

6016—5 oz. Footed Tumbler
Height 4⅝ in.

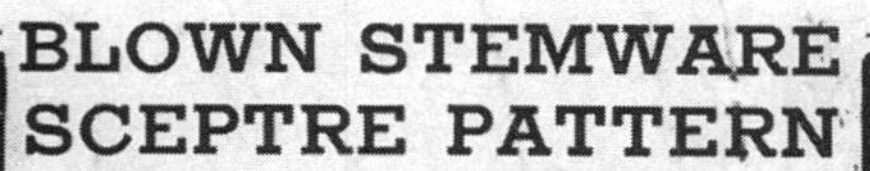
BLOWN STEMWARE SCEPTRE PATTERN

No. 6017 LINE—NO OPTIC

See Price List for Colors

DESIGN PATENT NO. 104703

6017—9 oz. Goblet
Height 7⅜ in.

6017
6 oz. Saucer Champagne
Height 5½ in.

6017—6 oz. Low Sherbet
Height 4½ in.

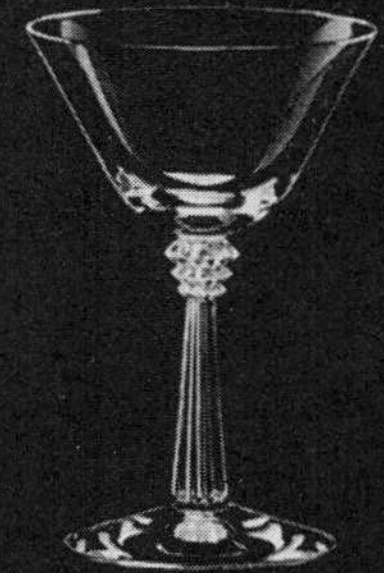
6017—3½ oz. Cocktail
Height 4⅞ in.

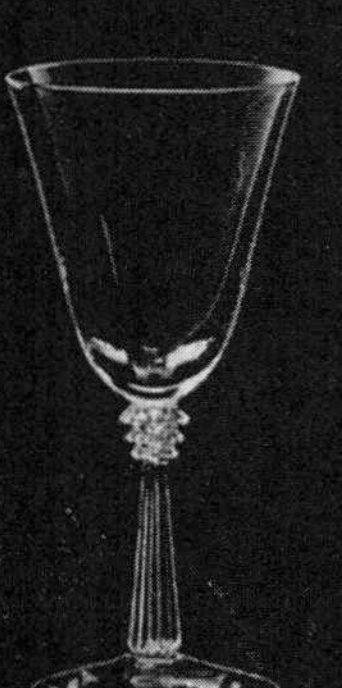
6017—4 oz. Claret
Height 5⅞ in.

6017—3 oz. Wine
Height 5½ in.

6017—¾ oz. Cordial
Height 3⅞ in.

6017
4 oz. Oyster Cocktail
Height 3⅝ in.

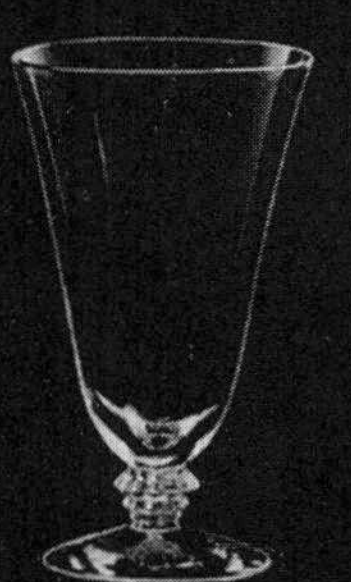
6017
5 oz. Footed Tumbler
Height 4¾ in.

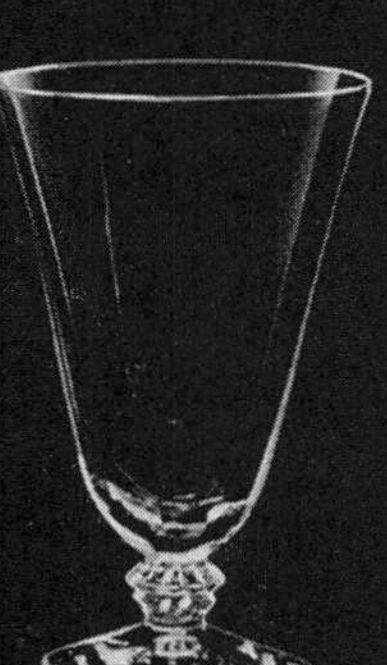
6017
9 oz. Footed Tumbler
Height 5½ in.

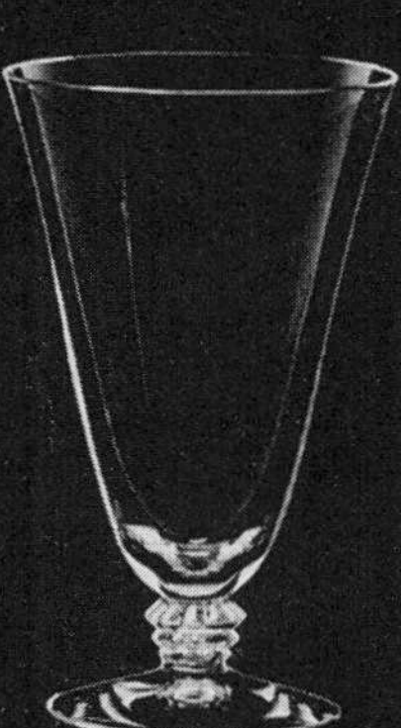
6017
12 oz. Footed Tumbler
Height 6 in.

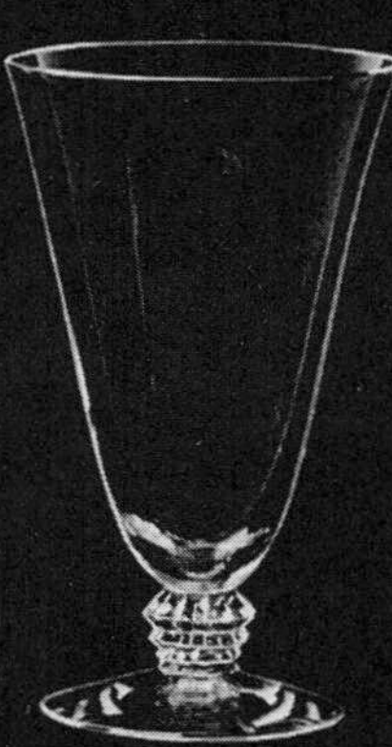
6017
14 oz. Footed Tumbler
Height 6½ in.

Fostoria Glass Company, Moundsville, West Virginia, Jan. 1, 1939

Fostoria Glass Company, Moundsville, West Virginia, Jan. 1, 1939

BLOWN STEMWARE
RONDEL PATTERN

No. 6019 LINE—NO OPTIC

See Price List for Colors

DESIGN PATENT NO. 108219

6019—10 oz. Goblet
Height 5⅞ in.

6019—6½ oz. Sherbet
Height 4⅛ in.

6019—3½ oz. Cocktail
Height 4 in.

6019—4½ oz. Claret
Height 4⅜ in.

6019—3½ oz. Wine
Height 4 in.

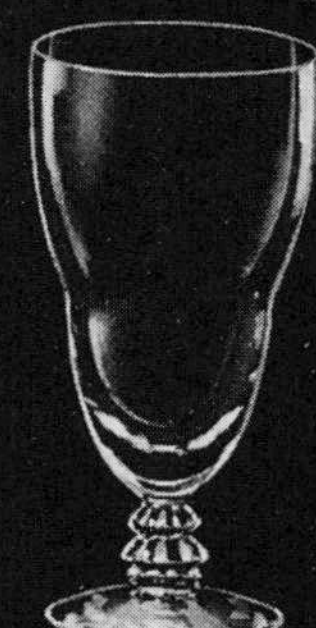

6019—6 oz. Parfait
Height 5¼ in.

6019—12 oz. Footed Tumbler
Height 5⅜ in.

6019—5 oz. Footed Tumbler
Height 3⅞ in.

6019—4¾ oz. Oyster Cocktail
Height 3½ in.

BLOWN STEMWARE
MELODY PATTERN

No. 6020 LINE

12 RIB REGULAR OPTIC

6020—9 oz. Goblet
Height 7¼ in.

6020—6 oz. Saucer Champagne
Height 5½ in.

6020—6 oz. Low Sherbet
Height 4⅝ in.

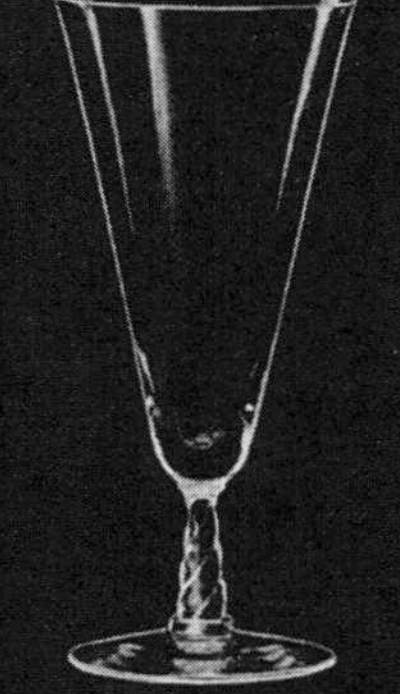

6020—5½ oz. Parfait
Height 6⅛ in.

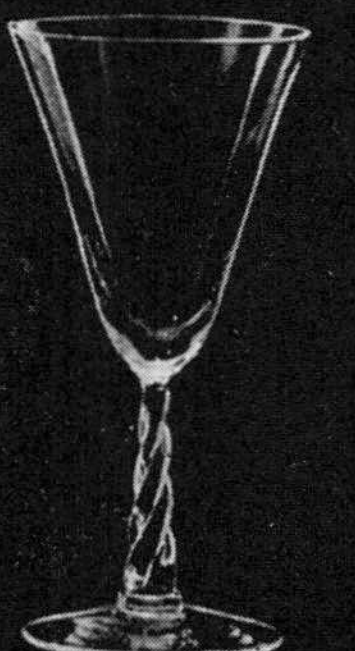

6020—4½ oz. Claret
Height 5¾ in.

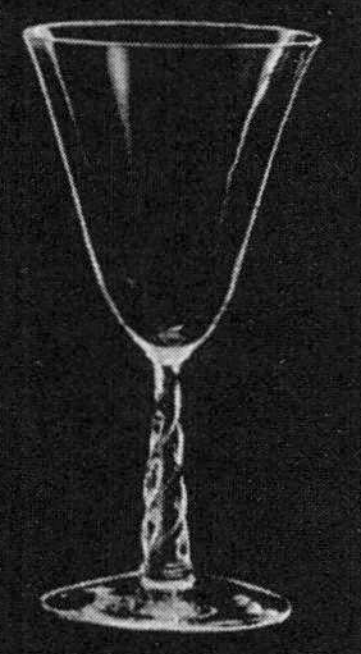

6020—3½ oz. Wine
Height 5⅜ in.

6020—3½ oz. Cocktail
Height 4⅞ in.

6020—1 oz. Cordial
Height 3¾ in.

6020—4 oz. Oyster Cocktail
Height 3¾ in.

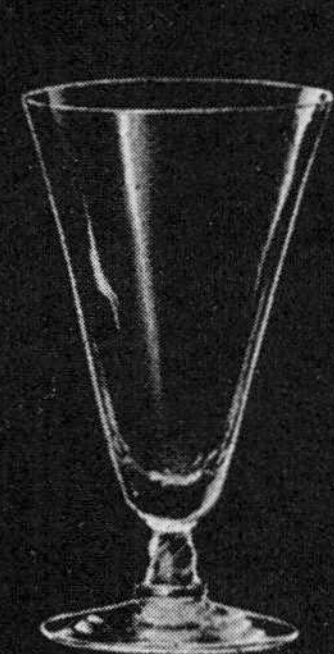

6020—5 oz. Footed Tumbler
Height 4⅞ in.

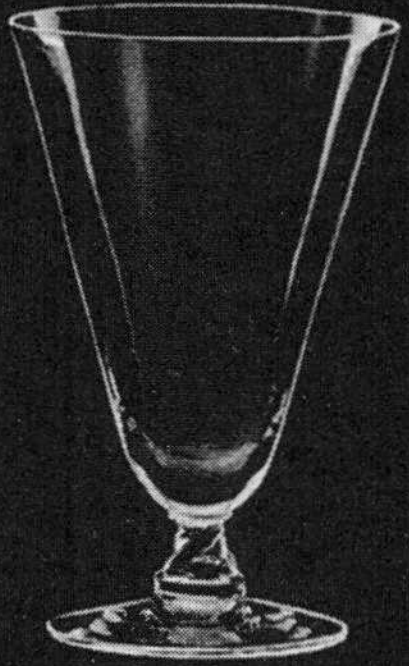

6020—9 oz. Footed Tumbler
Height 5¾ in.

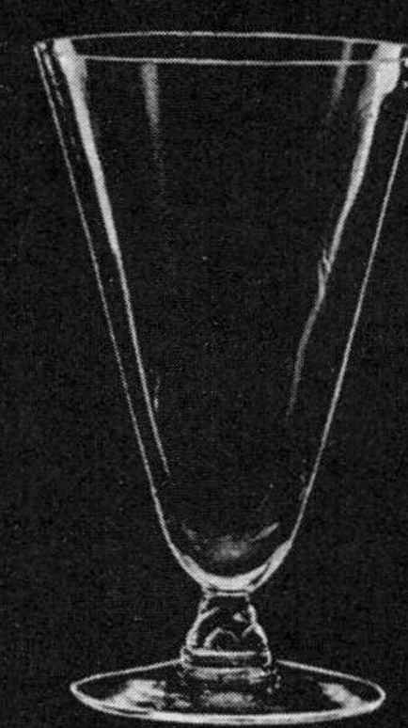

6020—12 oz. Footed Tumbler
Height 6⅜ in.

Fostoria Glass Company, Moundsville, West Virginia, Jan. 1, 1939

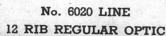

BLOWN STEMWARE COLFAX PATTERN

No. 6023 LINE—NO OPTIC

6023—9 oz. Goblet
Height 6⅜ in.

6023—6 oz. Saucer Champagne
Height 4⅞ in.

6023—6 oz. Low Sherbet
Height 4⅛ in.

6023—3¾ oz. Cocktail
Height 4⅜ in.

6023—4 oz. Claret-Wine
Height 4¾ in.

6023—1 oz. Cordial
Height 3⅜ in.

766—Finger Bowl
Height 2 in. Diameter 4½ in.

6023—12 oz. Footed Tumbler
Height 5¾ in.

6023—9 oz. Footed Tumbler
Height 5⅛ in.

6023—5 oz. Footed Tumbler
Height 4½ in.

6023—4 oz. Oyster Cocktail
Height 3⅝ in.

Fostoria Glass Company, Moundsville, West Virginia, Jan. 1, 1939

BLOWN STEMWARE CELLINI PATTERN
No. 6024 LINE
Made in
12 RIB REGULAR OPTIC and
LOOP OPTIC

6024—10 oz. Goblet R/O
Height 7⅛ in.
Entire Line also made in this Optic

6024—10 oz. Goblet L/O
Height 7⅛ in.

6024—6 oz. Saucer Champagne L/O
Height 5⅝ in.

6024—6 oz. Low Sherbet L/O
Height 4¼ in.

6024—3½ oz. Cocktail L/O
Height 4¾ in.

6024—4 oz. Claret L/O
Height 5¾ in.

6024—3½ oz. Wine L/O
Height 5⅜ in.

6024—1 oz. Cordial L/O
Height 3¾ in.

6024
12 oz. Footed Tumbler L/O
Height 5¾ in.

6024
9 oz. Footed Tumbler L/O
Height 5¼ in.

6024
5 oz. Footed Tumbler L/O
Height 4⅝ in.

6024
4½ oz. Oyster Cocktail L/O
Height 3½ in.

Fostoria Glass Company, Moundsville, West Virginia, Jan. 1, 1939

BLOWN STEMWARE
CABOT PATTERN
No. 6025 LINE—NO OPTIC

6025—10 oz. Goblet
Height 5½ in.

6025—6 oz. Sherbet
Height 3¾ in.

6025—3½ oz. Cocktail
Height 3½ in.

6025—4 oz. Claret-Wine
Height 4 in.

6025—1 oz. Cordial
Height 2⅞ in.

1769—Finger Bowl
Height 2 in. Diameter 4⅛ in.

6025—12 oz. Footed Tumbler
Height 5⅝ in.

6025—5 oz. Footed Tumbler
Height 4¼ in.

6025—4 oz. Oyster Cocktail
Height 3½ in.

BLOWN STEMWARE

No. 6025/1 LINE—DIMPLE OPTIC

6025/1—10 oz. Goblet
Height 5½ in.

6025/1—6 oz. Sherbet
Height 3¾ in.

6025/1—3½ oz. Cocktail
Height 3½ in.

6025/1—12 oz. Footed Tumbler
Height 5⅝ in.

6025/1—5 oz. Footed Tumbler
Height 4¼ in.

6025/1—4 oz. Claret-Wine
Height 4 in.

6025/1—1 oz. Cordial
Height 2⅞ in.

6025/1—4 oz. Oyster Cocktail
Height 3½ in.

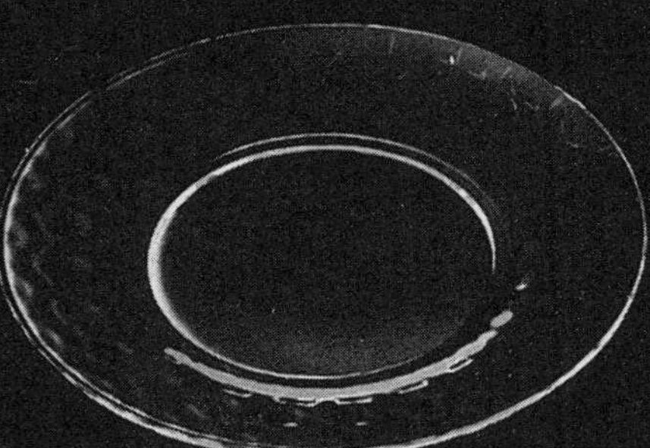
2337/1—Plate
See price list for sizes.

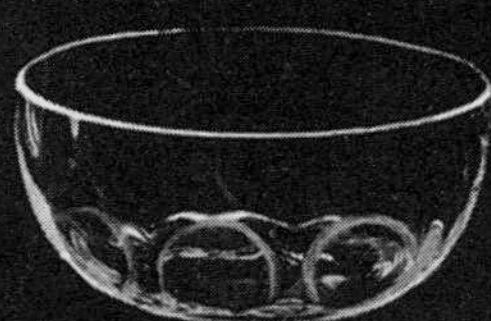
1769/1—Finger Bowl
Height 2 in.
Diameter 4⅛ in.

Fostoria Glass Company, Moundsville, West Virginia, January 1, 1940

Fostoria Glass Company, Moundsville, West Virginia, January 1, 1940

BLOWN STEMWARE
GREENBRIER PATTERN
No. 6026 LINE—16 RIB REGULAR OPTIC

6026—9 oz. Goblet
Height 7⅝ in.

6026—9 oz. Low Goblet
Height 6⅛ in.

6026—6 oz. Low Sherbet
Height 4⅜ in.

6026—6 oz. Saucer Champagne
Height 5½ in.

6026—4 oz. Cocktail
Height 5 in.

6026—4½ oz. Claret-Wine
Height 5⅜ in.

6026—1 oz. Cordial
Height 3⅞ in.

6026—13 oz. Footed Tumbler
Height 6 in.

6026—5 oz. Footed Tumbler
Height 4¾ in.

6026—4 oz. Footed Cocktail
Height 3⅝ in.

BLOWN STEMWARE
NIAGARA PATTERN

No. 6026/2 LINE

6026/2—9 oz. Goblet
Height 7⅝ in.

6026/2—9 oz. Low Goblet
Height 6⅛ in.

6026/2—6 oz. Saucer Champagne
Height 5½ in.

6026/2—6 oz. Low Sherbet
Height 4⅜ in.

6026/2—4½ oz. Claret-Wine
Height 5⅜ in.

6026/2—4 oz. Cocktail
Height 5 in.

6026/2—1 oz. Cordial
Height 3⅞ in.

6026/2—4 oz. Footed Cocktail
Height 3⅝ in.

869/2—Finger Bowl
Height 2 in.
Diameter 4½ in.

2337/2—7 in. Plate

6026/2—5 oz. Footed Tumbler
Height 4¾ in.

6026/2—13 oz. Footed
Tumbler Height 6 in.

Fostoria Glass Company, Moundsville, West Virginia, January 1, 1940

Fostoria Glass Company, Moundsville, West Virginia, July 1, 1940

BLOWN STEMWARE ENVOY PATTERN

No. 6027 LINE—NO OPTIC

6027—10 oz. Goblet
Height 5¼ in.

6027—5½ oz. Saucer Champagne
Height 4¼ in.

6027—6 oz. Low Sherbet
Height 3¼ in.

6027—3½ oz. Cocktail
Height 3⅞ in.

6027
4 oz. Wine
Height 4⅜ in.

6027—12 oz. Footed Tumbler
Height 5½ in.

6027—5 oz.
Footed Tumbler
Height 4 in.

6027—4 oz. Oyster or Fruit Cocktail
Height 3 in.

6027—1 oz. Cordial
Height 2¾ in.

HUMPTY DUMPTY PATTERN

No. 4146 LINE—NO OPTIC

4146—9 oz. Scotch & Soda
Height 3⅛ in.

4146—4 oz. Cocktail
Height 2½ in.

4146—1 oz. Cordial
Height 1½ in.

Fostoria Glass Company, Moundsville, West Virginia, January 1, 1941

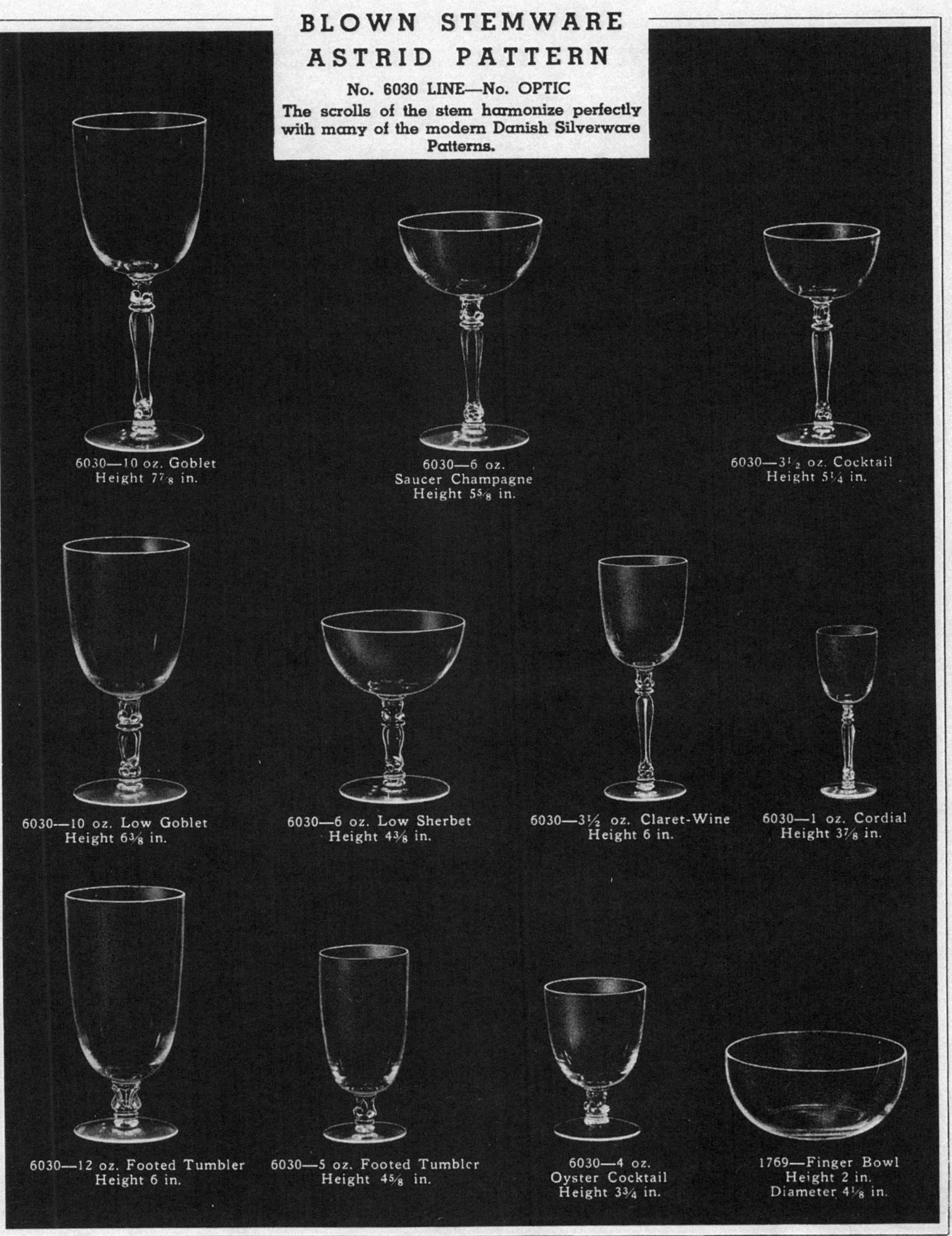

BLOWN STEMWARE
ASTRID PATTERN

No. 6030 LINE—No. OPTIC

The scrolls of the stem harmonize perfectly with many of the modern Danish Silverware Patterns.

6030—10 oz. Goblet
Height 7⅞ in.

6030—6 oz.
Saucer Champagne
Height 5⅝ in.

6030—3½ oz. Cocktail
Height 5¼ in.

6030—10 oz. Low Goblet
Height 6⅜ in.

6030—6 oz. Low Sherbet
Height 4⅜ in.

6030—3½ oz. Claret-Wine
Height 6 in.

6030—1 oz. Cordial
Height 3⅞ in.

6030—12 oz. Footed Tumbler
Height 6 in.

6030—5 oz. Footed Tumbler
Height 4⅝ in.

6030—4 oz.
Oyster Cocktail
Height 3¾ in.

1769—Finger Bowl
Height 2 in.
Diameter 4⅛ in.

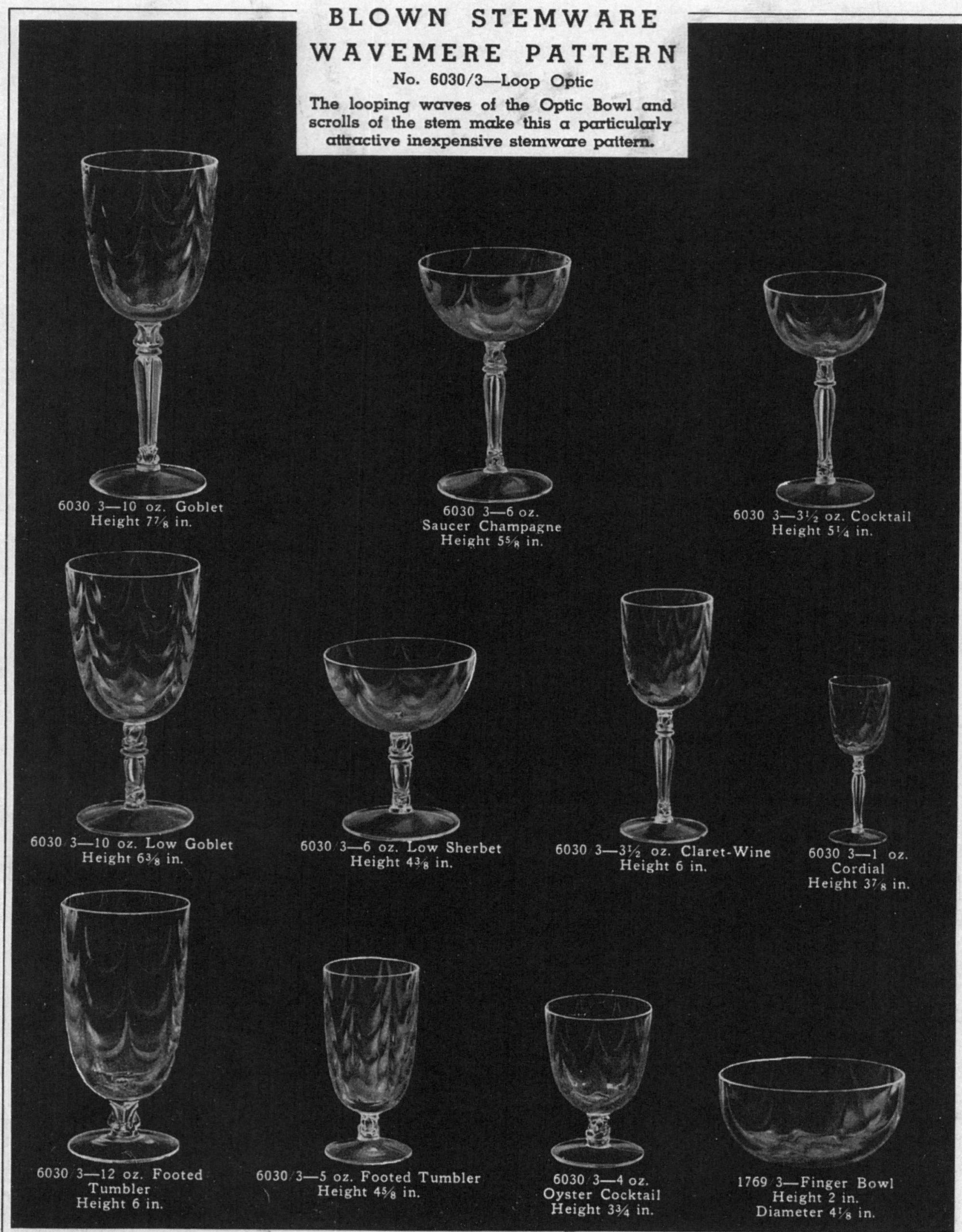

BLOWN STEMWARE WAVEMERE PATTERN

No. 6030/3—Loop Optic

The looping waves of the Optic Bowl and scrolls of the stem make this a particularly attractive inexpensive stemware pattern.

6030/3—10 oz. Goblet
Height 7 7/8 in.

6030/3—6 oz.
Saucer Champagne
Height 5 5/8 in.

6030/3—3 1/2 oz. Cocktail
Height 5 1/4 in.

6030/3—10 oz. Low Goblet
Height 6 3/8 in.

6030/3—6 oz. Low Sherbet
Height 4 3/8 in.

6030/3—3 1/2 oz. Claret-Wine
Height 6 in.

6030/3—1 oz.
Cordial
Height 3 7/8 in.

6030/3—12 oz. Footed
Tumbler
Height 6 in.

6030/3—5 oz. Footed Tumbler
Height 4 5/8 in.

6030/3—4 oz.
Oyster Cocktail
Height 3 3/4 in.

1769/3—Finger Bowl
Height 2 in.
Diameter 4 1/8 in.

Fostoria Glass Company, Moundsville, West Virginia, January 1, 1941

Fostoria Glass Company, Moundsville, West Virginia, January 1, 1942

6032—9 oz. Goblet
Height 7½ in.

6032—6 oz. Saucer Champagne
Height 5¾ in.

6032—6 oz. Low Sherbet
Height 4½ in.

6032—3½ oz. Cocktail
Height 5⅛ in.

6032—4½ oz. Claret
Height 5⅝ in.

6032—3½ oz. Wine
Height 5⅛ in.

6032—1 oz. Cordial
Height 3⅝ in.

6032—13 oz. Footed Tumbler
Height 5⅞ in.

6032—5 oz. Footed Tumbler
Height 4⅝ in.

6032—4 oz. Oyster Cocktail
Height 3½ in.

1769—Finger Bowl
Height 2 in.
Diameter 4⅛ in.

Fostoria Glass Company, Moundsville, West Virginia, January 1, 1942

SILVER FLUTES PATTERN

No. 6037 Line

Blown Lead Glass Stemware
Made in Crystal

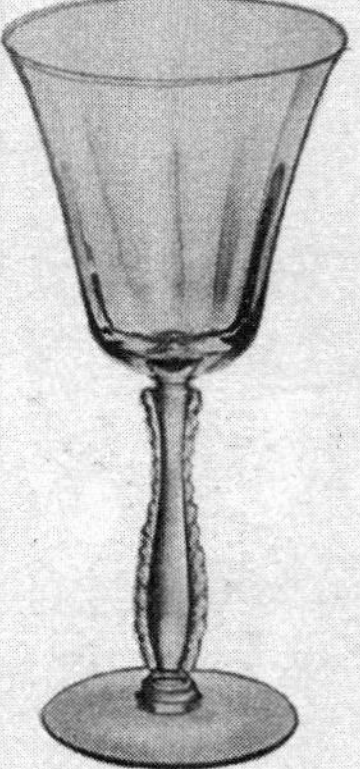

6037 — 9 oz.
Goblet
Height 7-7/8 in.

6037 — 9 oz.
Low Goblet
Height 6-3/8 in.

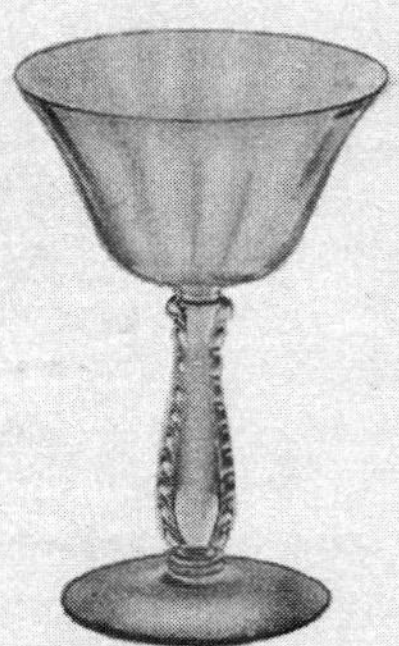

6037 — 7 oz.
Saucer Champagne
Height 6 in.

6037 — 7 oz.
Low Sherbet
Height 4-3/4 in.

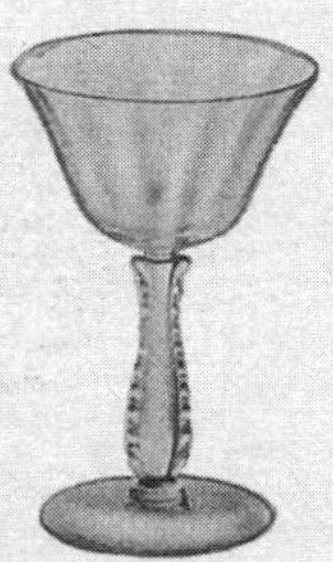

6037 — 4 oz.
Cocktail
Height 5 in.

6037 — 4 oz.
Claret — Wine
Height 6 in.

6037 — 1 oz.
Cordial
Height 4 in.

6037 — 6 oz.
Parfait
Height 6-1/8 in.

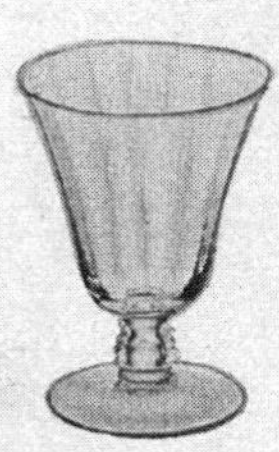

6037 — 4-1/2 oz.
Oyster Cocktail
Height 4 in.

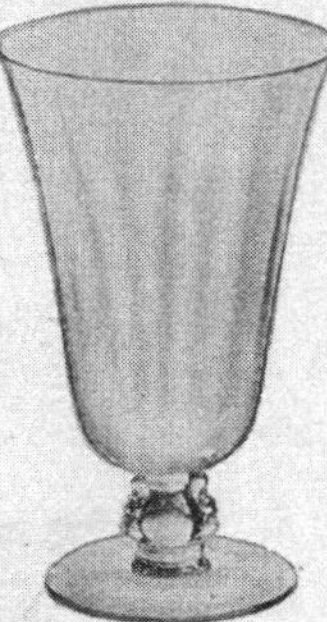

6037 — 12 oz.
Footed Tumbler
Height 6-1/8 in.

6037 — 5 oz.
Footed Tumbler
Height 4-7/8 in.

FOSTORIA GLASS COMPANY, MOUNDSVILLE, WEST VIRGINIA — 1949

CHALICE PATTERN

No. 6059 Line

Blown Lead Glass Stemware
See Price List For Colors

Crystal with Ebony Stem

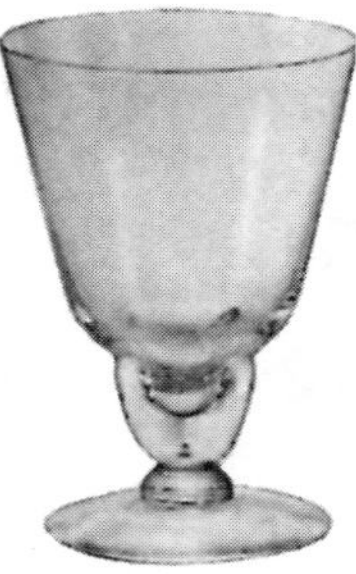

6059
Goblet
Height 5⅜ in.
Capacity 11 oz.

6059
Sherbet
Height 3½ in.
Capacity 7 oz.

6059
Cocktail/Wine/Seafood
Height 3¾ in.
Capacity 4½ oz.

6059
Cordial
Height 2½ in.
Capacity 1 oz.

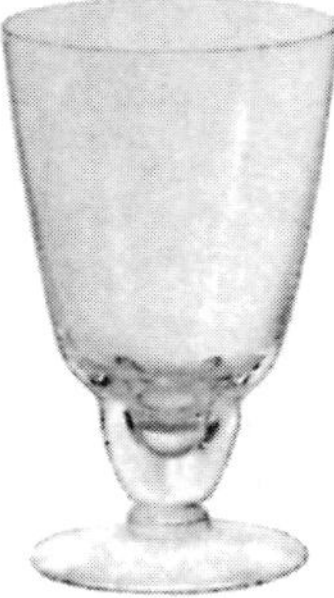

6059
Footed Ice Tea
Height 5⅞ in.
Capacity 14 oz.

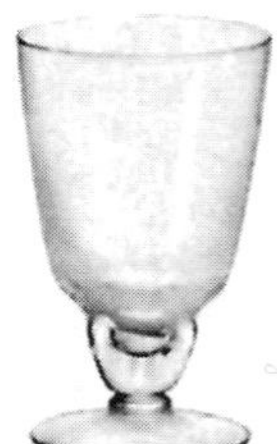

6059
Footed Juice
Height 4½ in.
Capacity 5½ oz.

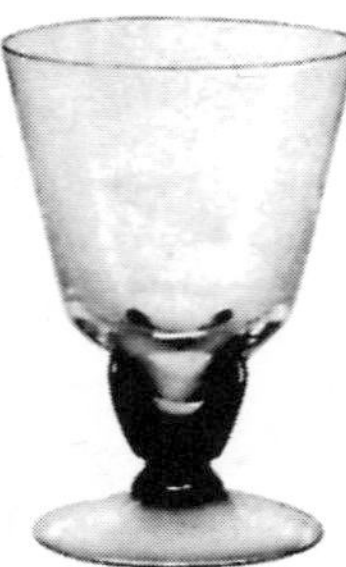

6059
Goblet
Height 5⅜ in.
Capacity 11 oz.

6059
Sherbet
Height 3½ in.
Capacity 7 oz.

6059
Cocktail/Wine/Seafood
Height 3¾ in.
Capacity 4½ oz.

6059
Cordial
Height 2½ in.
Capacity 1 oz.

6059
Footed Ice Tea
Height 5⅞ in.
Capacity 14 oz.

6059
Footed Juice
Height 4½ in.
Capacity 5½ oz.

FOSTORIA GLASS COMPANY, MOUNDSVILLE, WEST VIRGINIA — 1955

FOSTORIA GLASS COMPANY, MOUNDSVILLE, WEST VIRGINIA 1956

Contour Pattern
No. 6060 Line

6060
Goblet
Height 5⅞ in.
Capacity 10½ oz.

6060
Sherbet
Height 4½ in.
Capacity 6½ oz.

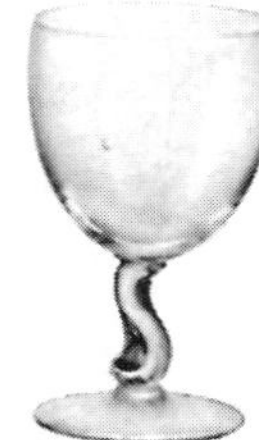

6060
Cocktail/Wine/Seafood
Height 4½ in.
Capacity 5 oz.

6060
Cordial
Height 2⅞ in.
Capacity 1 oz.

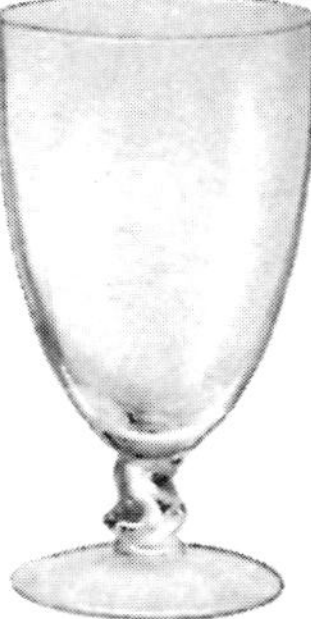

6060
Footed Ice Tea
Height 6¼ in.
Capacity 14 oz.

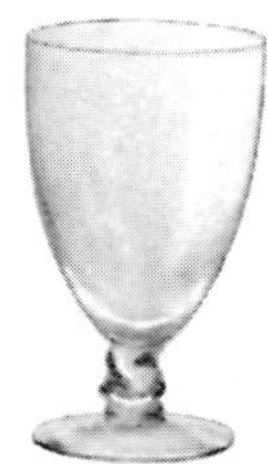

6060
Footed Juice
Height 4½ in.
Capacity 5½ oz.

Lyric Pattern
No. 6061 Line

6061
Goblet
Height 5⅛ in.
Capacity 11 oz.

6061
Sherbet
Height 4 in.
Capacity 7½ oz.

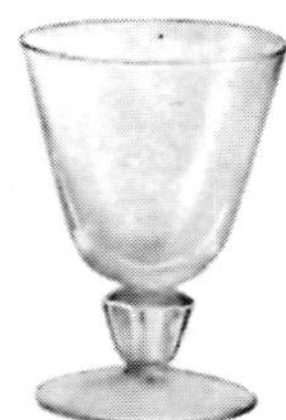

6061
Cocktail/Wine/Seafood
Height 3⅞ in.
Capacity 4 oz.

6061
Cordial
Height 2½ in.
Capacity 1 oz.

6061
Footed Ice Tea
Height 6 in.
Capacity 12 oz.

6061
Footed Juice
Height 4¾ in.
Capacity 6 oz.

BLOWN LEAD GLASS DUET-TUMBLERS

HORIZON PATTERN
No. 5650 Line

Chartreuse, Spruce and Cinnamon

5650
Ice Tea/Highball
Height 6 in.

5650
Water/Scotch & Soda
Height 5 in.

5650
Sherbet/Old Fashioned
Height 3⅜ in.

5650
Juice/Cocktail
Height 3⅜ in.

5650
Dessert/Finger Bowl
Height 2⅞ in.

TIARA PATTERN
No. 6044 Line

6044
Ice Tea/Highball
Height 5⅞ in.

6044
Water/Scotch & Soda
Height 4⅝ in.

6044
Sherbet/Old Fashioned
Height 3¼ in.

6044
Juice/Cocktail
Height 3¼ in.

6044
Dessert/Finger Bowl
Height 2¾ in.

CATALINA PATTERN
No. 6046 Line

6046
Ice Tea/Highball
Height 5 in.

6046
Water/Scotch & Soda
Height 4⅜ in.

6046
Sherbet/Old Fashioned
Height 3 in.

6046
Juice/Cocktail
Height 3¼ in.

6046
Dessert/Finger Bowl
Height 2¼ in.

FOSTORIA GLASS COMPANY, MOUNDSVILLE, WEST VIRGINIA — 1952

HOMESPUN PATTERN

No. 4183 Line

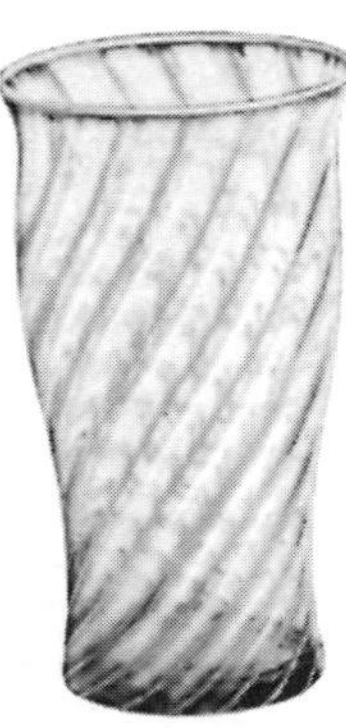

4183/58—15 oz.
Ice Tea/Highball
Height 5-11/16 in.

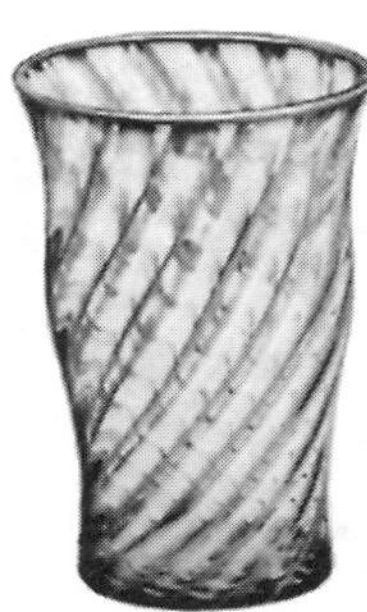

4183/64—11½ oz.
Water/Scotch and Soda
Height 4-11/16 in.

4183/84—9 oz.
Juice/Old Fashioned
Height 3-5/16 in.

Homespun and Needlepoint blown tumblers were made in colors of Gold, Moss Green, and Teal Blue. In addition to the colors there are White Opaque (struck) lines. These pieces are beautiful and very collectible.

NEEDLEPOINT PATTERN

No. 4184 Line

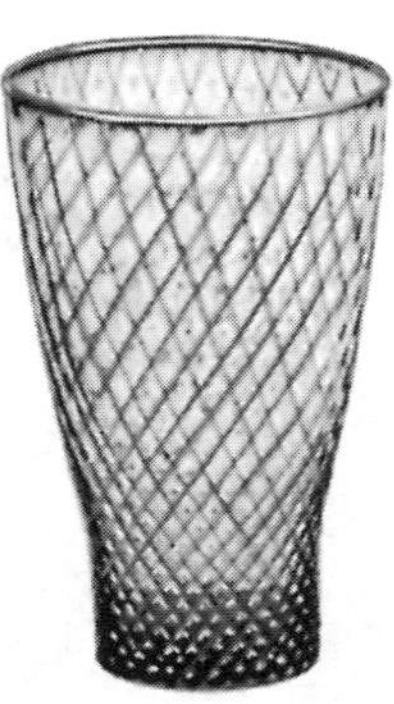

4184/58—16½ oz.
Ice Tea/Highball
Height 5½ in.

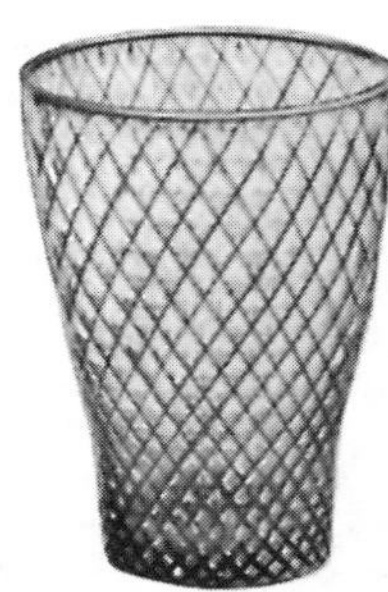

4184/64—12¼ oz.
Water/Scotch and Soda
Height 4½ in.

4184/84—8 oz.
Juice/Old Fashioned
Height 3-1/16 in.

MODERN PRIMITIVE TUMBLERS

Made in Pink, Smoke, Marine, Crystal, and Amber

Karnak Pattern
No. 4161 Line

4161
Cooler
Height 6¾ in.
Capacity 21 oz.

4161
Beverage
Height 5 in.
Capacity 14 oz.

4161
Juice
Height 3¾ in.
Capacity 6 oz.

4161
Dessert
Capacity 12 oz.

4161—7⅜ in.
Salad/Dessert Plate

Congo Pattern
No. 4162 Line

4162
Cooler
Height 6¾ in.
Capacity 21 oz.

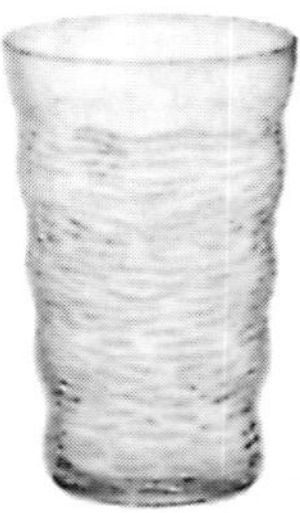

4162
Beverage
Height 5 in.
Capacity 14 oz.

4162
Juice
Height 3¾ in.
Capacity 6 oz.

4162
Dessert
Capacity 10 oz.

4162—7⅜ in.
Salad/Dessert Plate

Inca Pattern
No. 4163 Line

4163
Cooler
Height 6¾ in.
Capacity 21 oz.

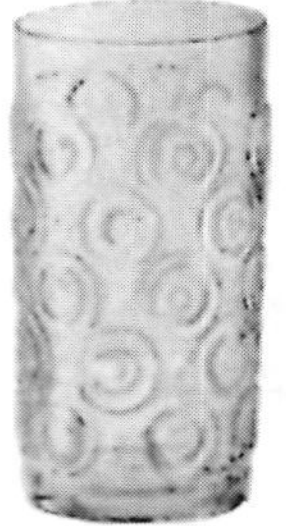

4163
Beverage
Height 5½ in.
Capacity 14 oz.

4163
Juice 3⅞ in.
Capacity 6 oz.

4163
Dessert
Capacity 12 oz.

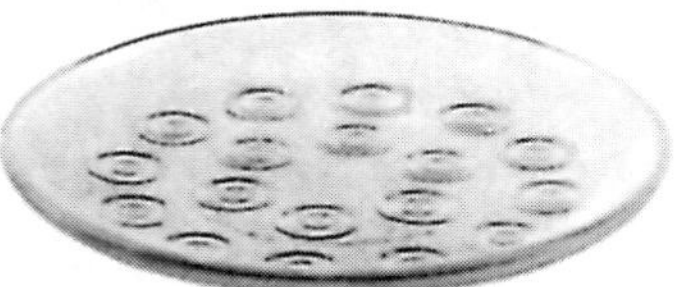

4163—7⅜ in.
Salad/Dessert Plate

Vanity Dresser Items

2276 Vanity, Cutting No. 174
Height 7¼", Diameter 4½"
1924 Catalog

2289 Vanity, Engraved "C"
Height 5¼", Diameter 4"
1924 Catalog

Fostoria vanity items were introduced in mid-1924 and continued through 1928. A Fostoria vanity is a round box with an affixed cologne. The cologne has a separate drip stopper. The 2276 shape was by far the more popular shape. "Tint decorations" are the result of enamel color being applied and fired for permanency. Tints will be found on both crystal and colors. The introductory vanity colors were Amber, Canary, Green, and Ebony. Blue was added in 1925. A vanity decorated with the etched Brocade treatment is possibly the hardest to locate.

2286 Comb & Brush Tray
Ebony with Encrusted Gold
No. 44 Rivera Pattern
1924 – 1925 Catalog

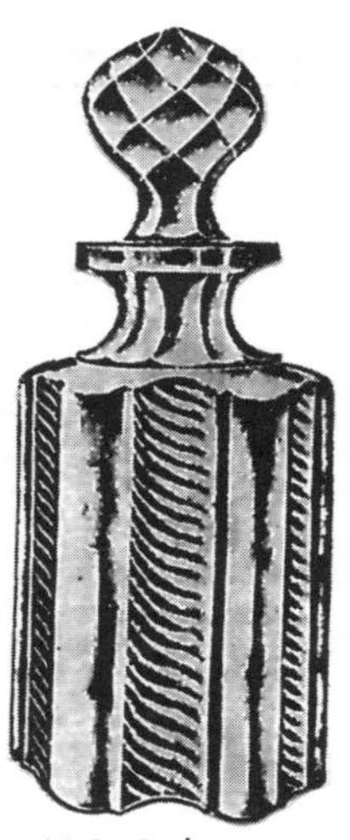
482 Cologne
8 oz., 1901 Catalog

2242 Cologne
Engraved 14
1924 – 1925 Catalog

2135 Puff, Cov.,
5", Cut 112, Plume
1913 Catalog

2118 Cologne
Cut 138, Apple Blossom
Pattern, 1913 Catalog

1666 Puff, Cov.
3¾", Etched 221
1913 Catalog

605 Cologne
8 oz., 1901 Catalog

2243 Cologne
Etched 253
1924 – 1925

2243 Cologne
Engraved "B"
1924 – 1925 Catalog

Vases

In 1928 Fostoria introduced a line of Art Deco vases. It is doubtful that any of these vases was ever shown in a catalog. They were not listed in the Jan. 1, 1928 No. 2 Price List. This was a booklet that listed (but did not illustrate) Pressed, Blown, Needle Etchings, Plate Etchings, Cuttings, and Decorations. These are known Fostoria pieces because of this advertisement and also the illustration in *The New Little Book About Glassware* published by Fostoria in 1928. All of these vases are acid etched on the No. 4100 8" (optic) blank and are found in the usual pastel colors made in this time period. Among the decorations known are Fish, Pirate, Sailor, Snowflake, and Trees.

Fostoria Glass Company
Moundsville W.Va.

1928 Fostoria Promotion

Window-Gardens in Glass

One of the very loveliest new ideas in interior decoration is the glass-garden, or window-garden.

As a way to display an interesting collection of glass or as a method of displaying flowers, it is both unique and attractive. Furthermore, it is simple to arrange and not expensive

You can almost capture the rainbow, so many colors are at your disposal. You can keep summer all winter in your breakfast room, or bring the country to the city.

Shelves are adjusted across the window – or windows you choose to decorate. Two, three, or four, according to the height of the window and the effect you wish to have.

Different colored vases, bowls, glasses, plates, cups, candlesticks, in a variety of shapes and sizes, are then arranged on the shelves, so that the light can shine through them – bringing a new brightness to a room that may have been a bit dull.

Gay flowers or plants that grow in water turn your glass-garden into a miniature conservatory.

If you are interested in further details of making a window-garden in glass, write us for more information!

The "Window-Gardens in Glass" is from *The New Little Book About Glassware.* Note the unusual deco vase on the bottom shelf. Something else interesting on this shelf is the diamond optic footed vase. We know of no catalog that shows this interesting piece. Unlike A.H. Heisey and Company, Tiffin Glass Company or Fenton Art Glass, Fostoria was not big into diamond optic designs. On the middle shelf note the No. 2390 footed bowl and candlesticks. At best these items were produced for two or three years.

Crystal Glass Blown Bouquet Holders

These blown vases on this page were made in crystal as well as Satin Pearl. This particular treatment was an all-over acid etched design on the inside of the vases. This resulted in a frosted dull look on the inside. The etched floral designs were applied on the outside of the vases. The Fostoria listing of this treatment shows only 10" vases numbered 2009 through 2012 as being used. These items were trimmed with the Encrusted Gold Decoration No. 31 Laurel, and Encrusted Gold Decoration No. 32 Regent. Some of these vases may be iridized and some may be decorated in enameled colors. This treatment was done around 1919 – 1920 and may not have been a successful line. Fostoria made scores of blown vases that have not been documented.

2211 Etched Vase
Height 10", 1901 Catalog

2210 Etched Vase
Height 10½", 1901 Catalog

2212 Etched Vase
Height 10", 1901 Catalog

2209 Etched Vase
Height 9", 1901 Catalog

Fostoria Glass Company, Moundsville, West Virginia, July 1, 1940

VASES

4144—3 in. Vase

4145—3 in. Vase

2577—5½ in. Wide Vase

4126½—11 in. Footed Vase, Heavy

4143—6 in. Footed Vase
4143½—6 in. Footed Vase, Heavy

2577—6 in. Vase

4143—7½ in. Footed Vase
4143½—7½ in. Footed Vase, Heavy

VASES

2600—7 in. Acanthus Vase

2579—6 in. Cornucopia

2577—8½ in. Vase, Heavy

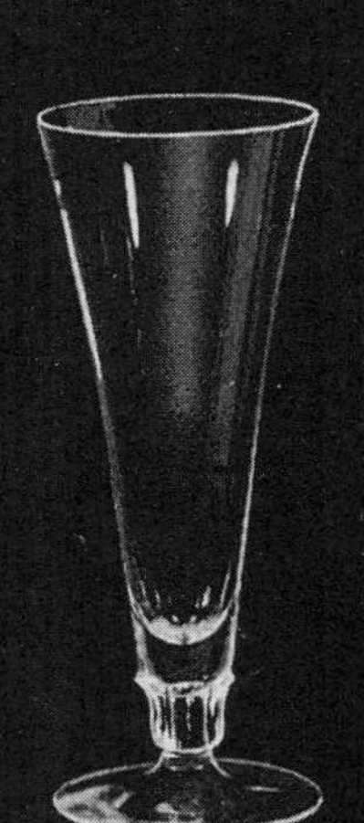
5300—7 in. Footed Bud Vase

2591—15 in. Vase, Heavy

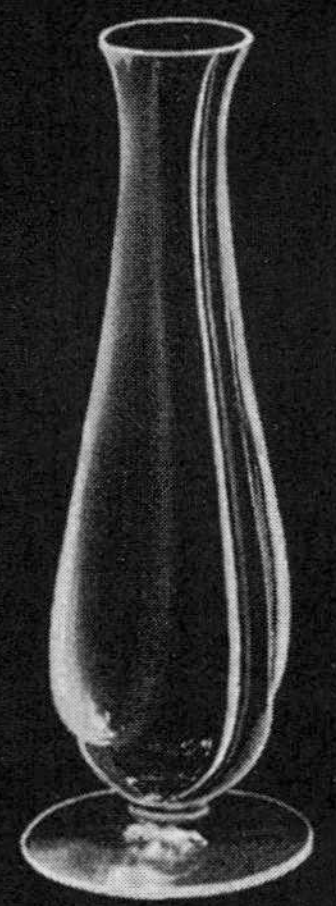
5301—8 in. Footed Bud Vase

Fostoria Glass Company, Moundsville, West Virginia, July 1, 1940

No. 1948 12 1-2 in. Vase
Cut and Engraved No. 5.
Price, 12 1-2 in. $3.00 each.
Price, 10 in. 2.20 each.
Price, 8 in. 1.50 each.
Price, 5 1-2 in. 1.10 each.
No. 1948 10 in. Vase
Cut and Engraved No. 5.
Also No. 1948 8 in. Vase
No. 1948 5 1-2 in. Vase
No. 760 12 in. Vase
Cut and Engraved No. 5.
Price, $3.00 each.
No. 1799 1-2 7 1-4 in. Vase
Cut and Engraved No. 5.
Price, $1.50 each.
FOSTORIA GLASS COMPANY, MOUNDSVILLE, WEST VIRGINIA, U. S. A.
30

1921 Catalog

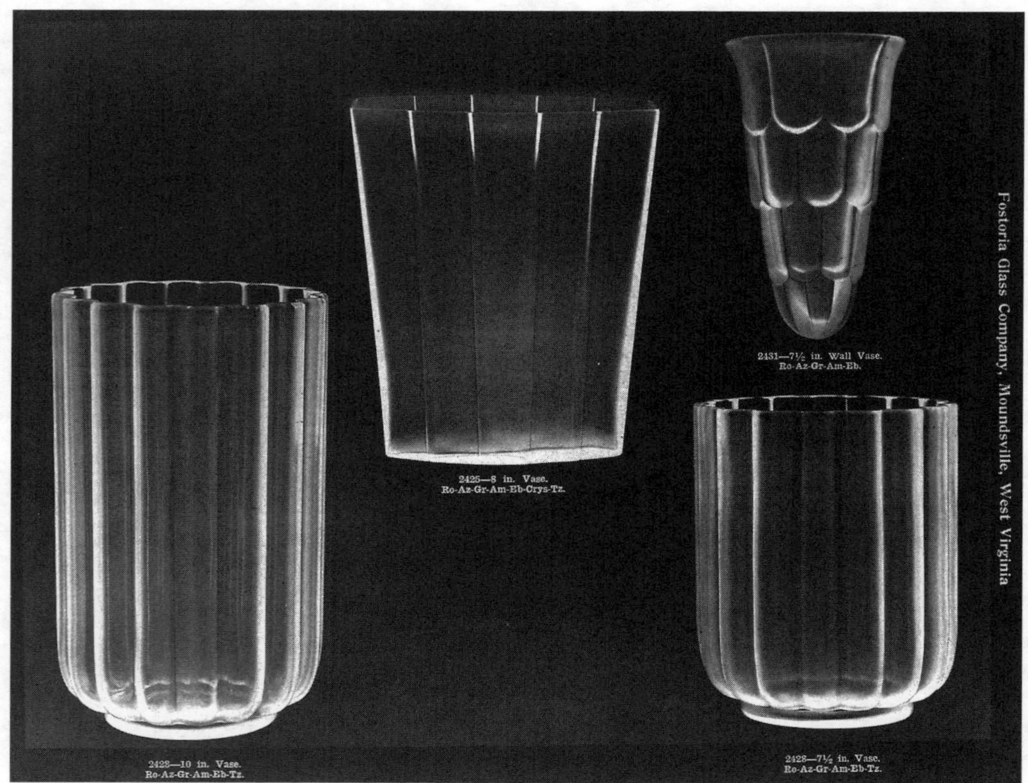

1930 Catalog

VASES

Fostoria Glass Company, Moundsville, West Virginia, Jan. 1, 1939

2470—8 in. Vase
2470—10 in Vase
2470—11½ in. Vase

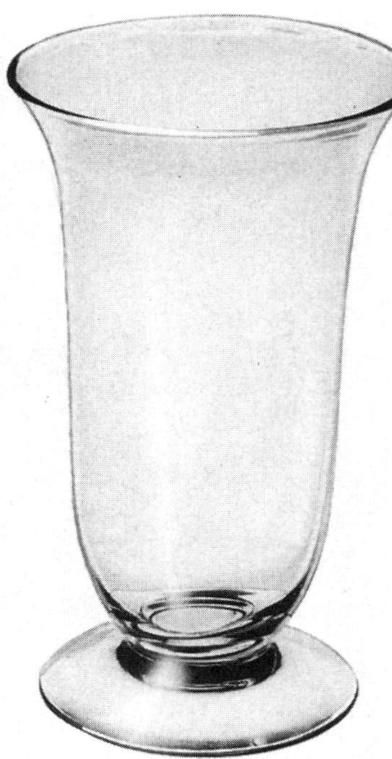

5100—10 in. Vase, Plain

2545—10 in. Vase

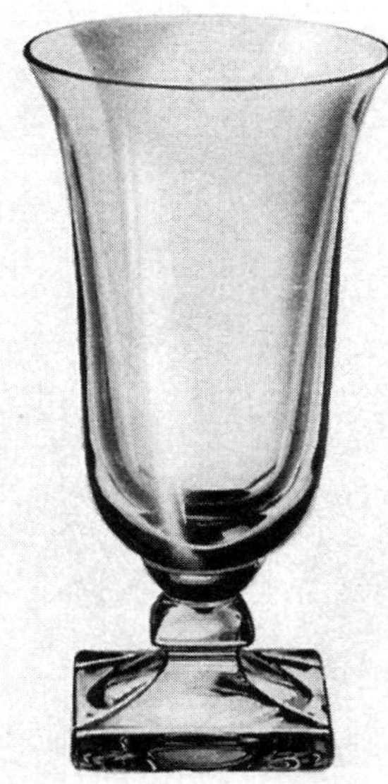

2568—9 in. Footed Vase, Heavy

2567—6 in. Footed Vase, Heavy
2567—7½ in. Footed Vase, Heavy
2567—8½ in. Footed Vase, Heavy

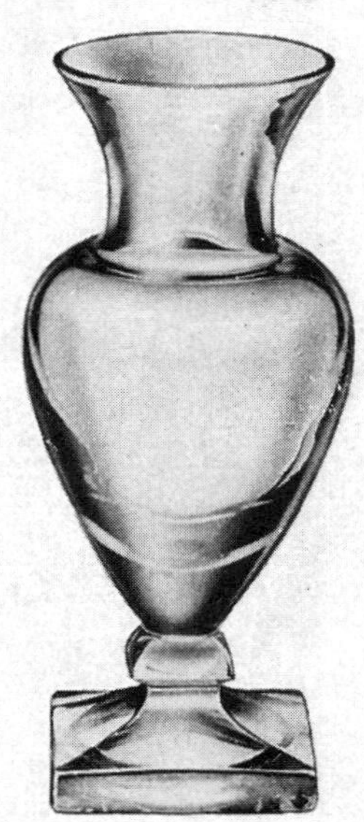

2569—9 in. Footed Vase, Heavy

VASES

2387—8 in. Vase

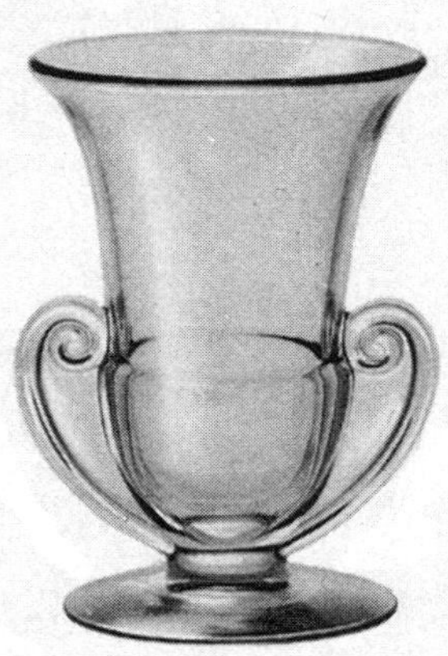

2467—7½ in. Vase

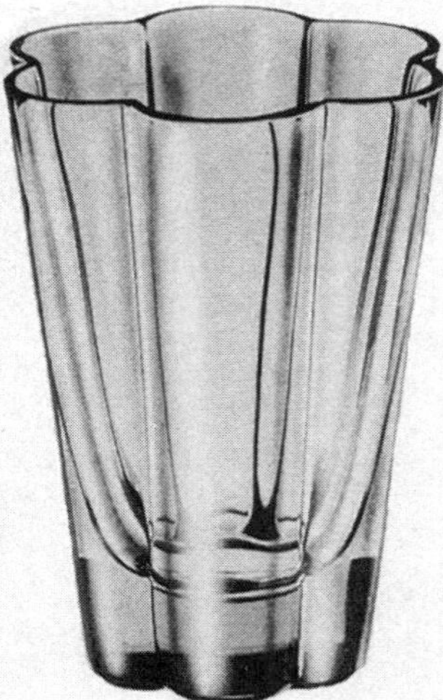

2387½—8 in. Vase, Heavy

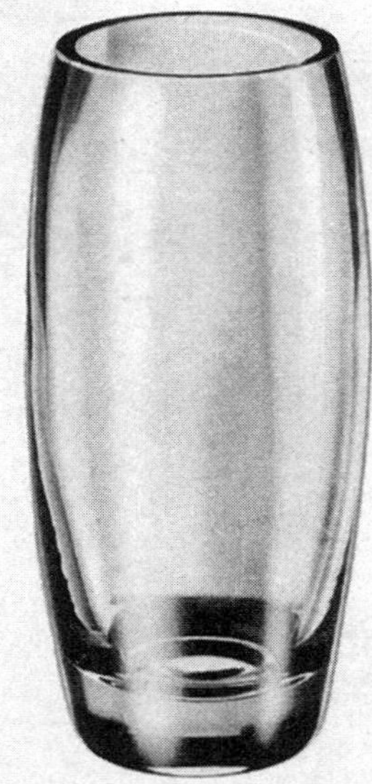

1895½—10 in. Vase, Heavy

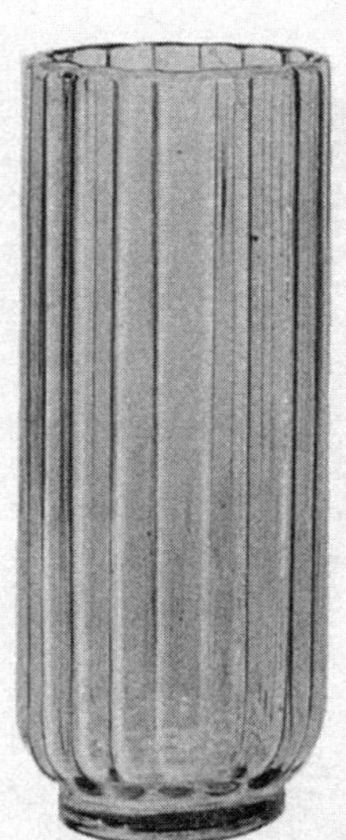

2428—13 in. Vase, Narrow
Diameter 5 in.

4132½—8 in. Vase, Heavy

Fostoria Glass Company, Moundsville, West Virginia, Jan. 1, 1939

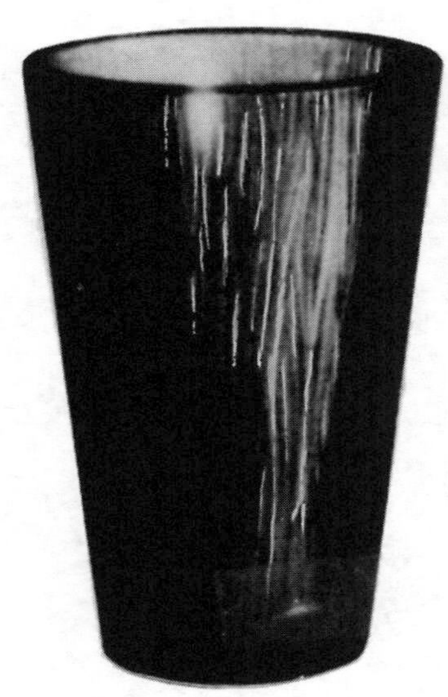

2522 Vase, Silver Mist
Height 8", 1934 Catalog

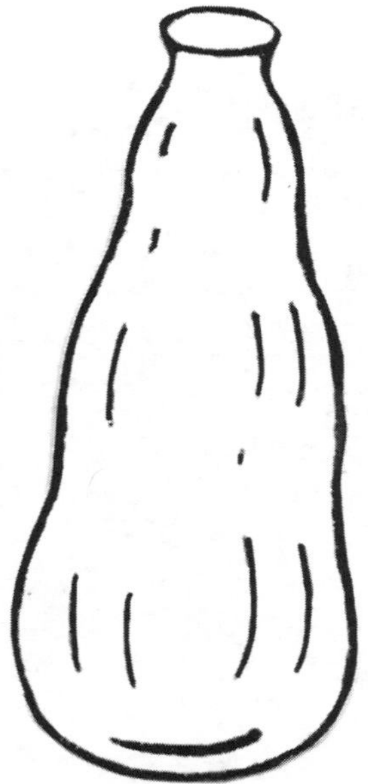

2468 Vase
Fostoria Drawing, 1934,
Blown rib optic, Height 5½"
Colors include Topaz

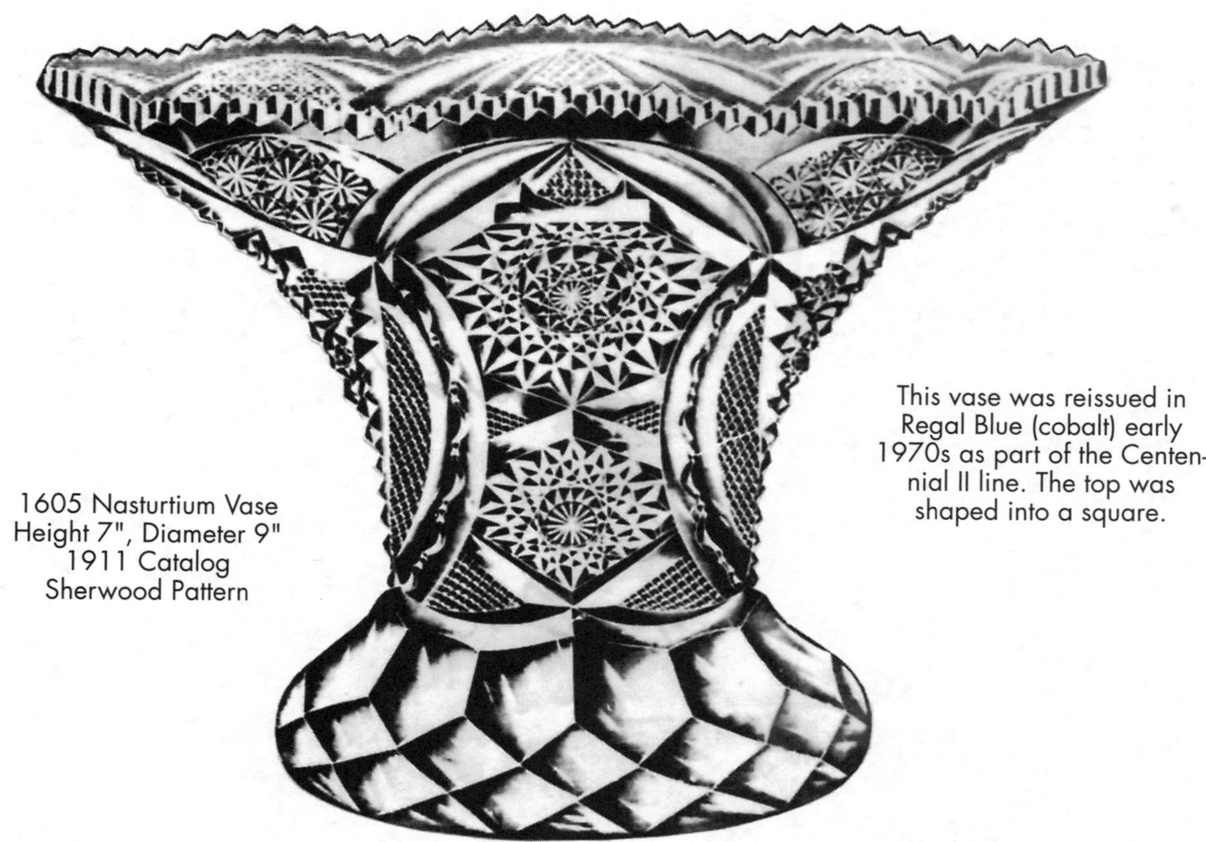

1605 Nasturtium Vase
Height 7", Diameter 9"
1911 Catalog
Sherwood Pattern

This vase was reissued in Regal Blue (cobalt) early 1970s as part of the Centennial II line. The top was shaped into a square.

2614—10 in. Vase

2619½—6 in. Vase Ground Bottom

2619½—7½ in. Vase Ground Bottom

2619½—9½ in. Vase Ground Bottom

2577—15 in. Vase

2612—13 in. Vase

2611—14 in. Vase

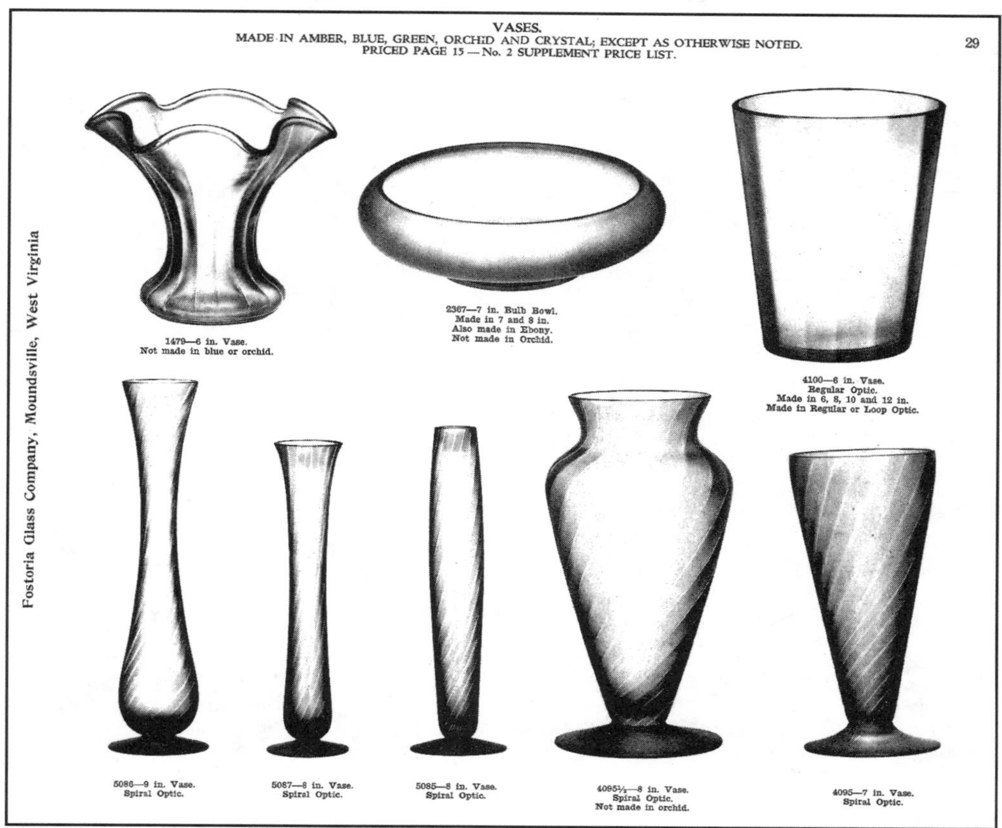

VASES.
MADE IN AMBER, BLUE, GREEN, ORCHID AND CRYSTAL; EXCEPT AS OTHERWISE NOTED.
PRICED PAGE 15 — No. 2 SUPPLEMENT PRICE LIST.

29

Fostoria Glass Company, Moundsville, West Virginia

1479—6 in. Vase.
Not made in blue or orchid.

2367—7 in. Bulb Bowl.
Made in 7 and 8 in.
Also made in Ebony.
Not made in Orchid.

4100—6 in. Vase.
Regular Optic.
Made in 6, 8, 10 and 12 in.
Made in Regular or Loop Optic.

5086—9 in. Vase.
Spiral Optic.

5087—8 in. Vase.
Spiral Optic.

5085—8 in. Vase.
Spiral Optic.

4095½—8 in. Vase.
Spiral Optic.
Not made in orchid.

4095—7 in. Vase.
Spiral Optic.

1927 Catalog

VASES.
MADE IN AMBER, BLUE, GREEN, ORCHID AND CRYSTAL, EXCEPT AS OTHERWISE NOTED.
PRICED PAGE 15 — No. 2 SUPPLEMENT PRICE LIST.

31

Fostoria Glass Company, Moundsville, West Virginia

4103—3 in. Vase.
Optic.
Made in 3, 4, 5 and 6 in.

4103—5 in. Vase.
Optic.

5100—10 in. Vase, Optic.
Not made in Blue or Crystal.

1120—15 in. Vase, Loop Optic.
Made in 12 and 15 in.
Not made in Blue or Orchid.

4100—8 in. Vase, Loop Optic.
Made in 6, 8, 10 and 12 in.
Made in Regular and Loop Optic.

VASES

Ruby-Cry-RB-
Bur-EG- Topaz

4123—Pansy Vase
Height 3¼ in.

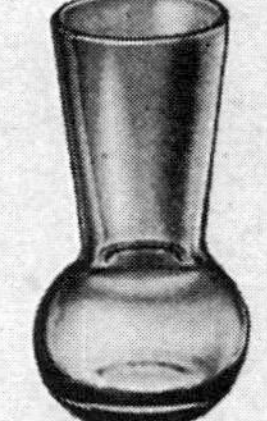

4137
3¾ in. Vase
Plain

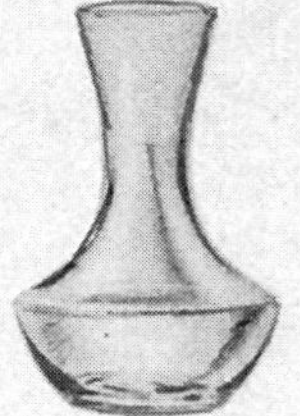

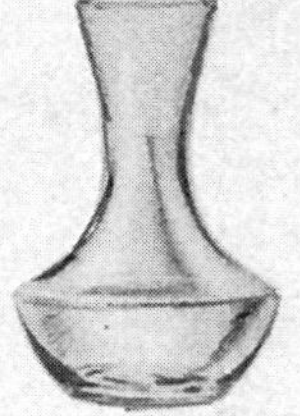

4130—Violet Base
Height 3⅝ in.
RB-EG-Bur
Cry-Az-Ruby

poss. intro. 1939
limited production

4138
3½ in. Vase
Plain

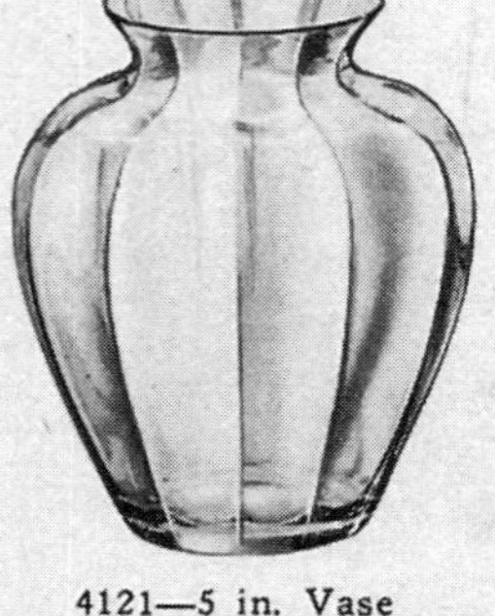

4121—5 in. Vase
Reg.Optic, Cry-Az
No Optic, RB-Bur-EG

4124—4½ in. Vase
Reg. Optic, Cry-Az

4128½—5 in. Vase, Heavy

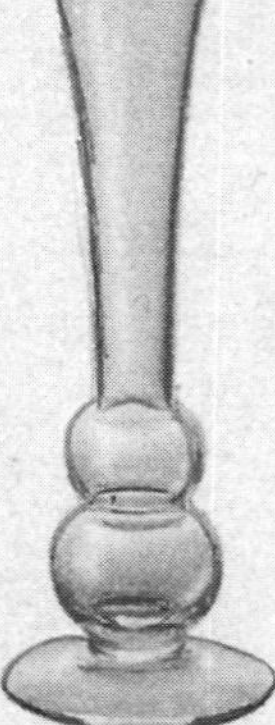

5092
8 in. Bud Vase
EG-RB-Bur top
w/cry base

6021
6 in. Ftd. Bud Vase
Plain
9 in. Footed Bud Vase
Plain

Cry w/Cry base
Cry base w/top
RB-Bur-EG

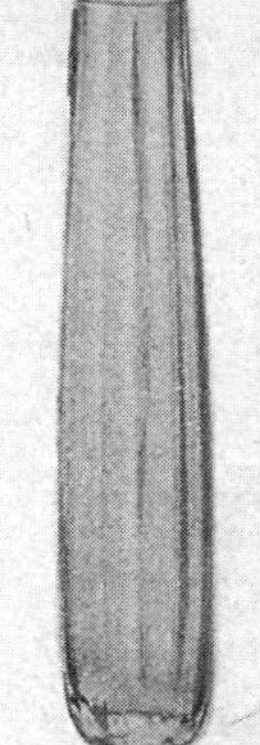

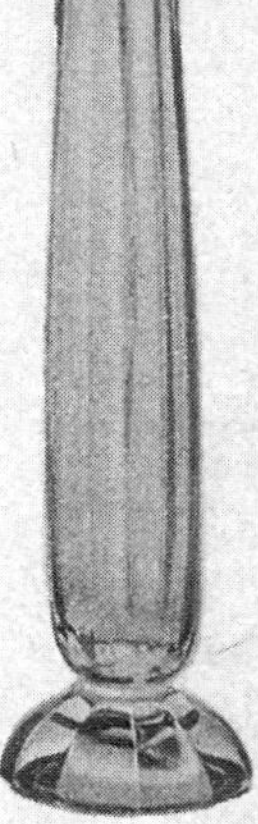

5088
8 in. Bud Vase
5" size not
in Burgundy

4128—5 in. Vase
Reg. Optic, Cry-Az-1938
No Optic, RB-EG-Bur

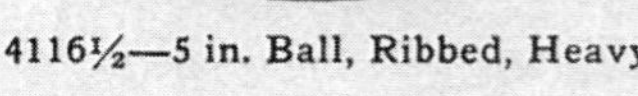

4116½—5 in. Ball, Ribbed, Heavy

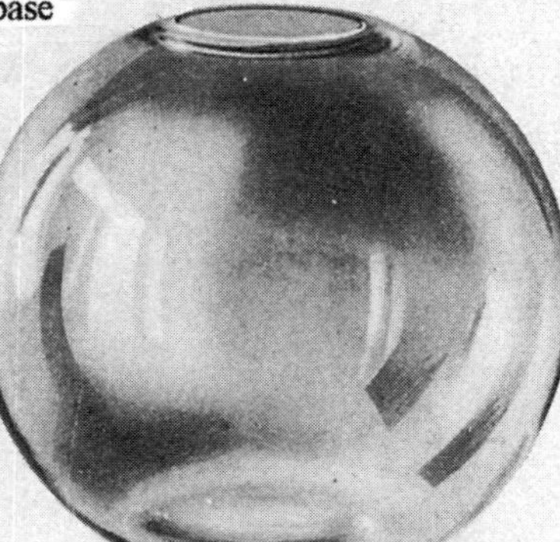

4116—Bubble Ball
Silver Mist, Mother of
Pearl-Ruby-RB-EG-Tz

4103½—5 in. Vase, Ribbed, Heavy

Fostoria Glass Company, Moundsville, West Virginia, Jan. 1, 1939

VASES

B4116—4 in. Ball, Bubbles
B4116—5 in. Ball, Bubbles
B4116—6 in. Ball, Bubbles

B4128—5 in. Vase, Bubbles

B4103—3 in. Vase, Bubbles
B4103—4 in. Vase, Bubbles
B4103—5 in. Vase, Bubbles

B4100—6 in. Vase, Bubbles
B4100—8 in. Vase, Bubbles

2570—6¾ in. Vase, Flared

2570—7 in. Vase, Regular

Fostoria Glass Company, Moundsville, West Virginia, July 1, 1939

VASES

BUBBLES GROUP

B-2577—6 in. Vase, Bubbles

B-4132—5 in. Vase, Bubbles (Ice Bowl)

B-4121—5 in. Vase, Bubbles

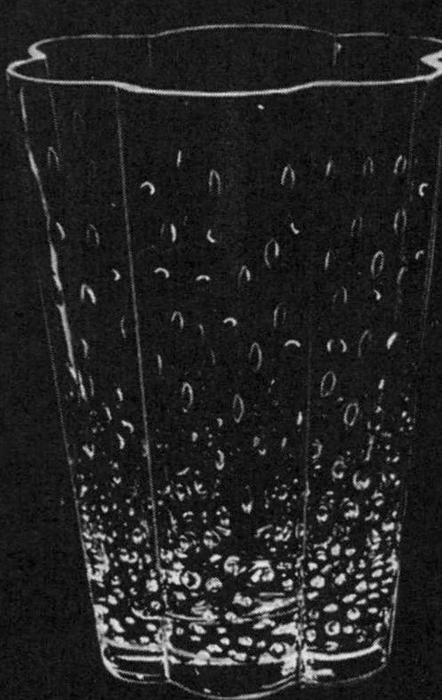
B-2387½—8 in. Vase, Bubbles

B-4124—4½ in. Vase, Bubbles

B-2577—5½ in. Vase, Bubbles

B-4125—7 in. Vase, Bubbles

Fostoria Glass Company, Moundsville, West Virginia, January 1, 1940

VASES

HAMMERED GROUP

H-4116—Ball, Hammered
See Price List for Sizes

H-2577—5½ in. Wide Vase, Hammered

H-4124—4½ in. Vase, Hammered

H-4100—Vase, Hammered
See Price List for Sizes

H-4121—5 in. Vase, Hammered

H-4125—7 in. Vase, Hammered

H-2577—6 in. Vase Hammered

Fostoria Glass Company, Moundsville, West Virginia, January 1, 1940

The Hammered Design is in the mold, these are not air bubbles.

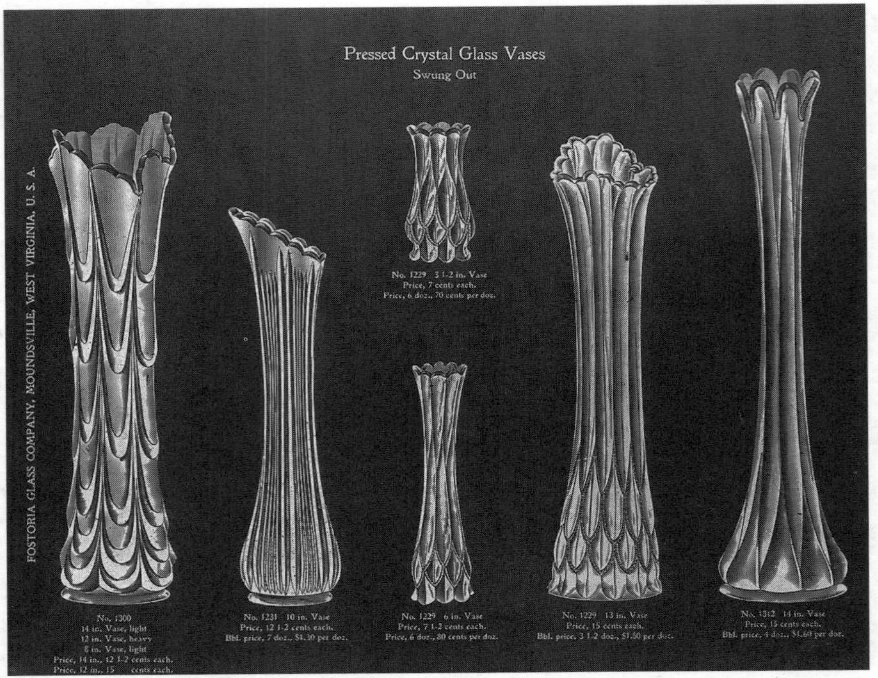

Pressed Crystal Glass Vases
Swung Out
FOSTORIA GLASS COMPANY, MOUNDSVILLE, WEST VIRGINIA, U. S. A.
No. 1229 3 1-2 in. Vase
Price, 7 cents each.
Price, 6 doz., 70 cents per doz.
No. 1300
14 in. Vase, light
12 in. Vase, heavy
8 in. Vase, light
Price, 14 in., 12 1-2 cents each.
Price, 12 in., 15 cents each.
No. 1231 10 in. Vase
Price, 12 1-2 cents each.
Bbl. price, 7 doz., $1.30 per doz.
No. 1229 6 in. Vase
Price, 7 1-2 cents each.
Price, 6 doz., 80 cents per doz.
No. 1229 13 in. Vase
Price, 15 cents each.
Bbl. price, 3 1-2 doz., $1.50 per doz.
No. 1312 14 in. Vase
Price, 15 cents each.
Bbl. price, 4 doz., $1.60 per doz.

1921 Catalog

Blown Crystal Glass Vases
FOSTORIA GLASS COMPANY, MOUNDSVILLE, WEST VIRGINIA, U. S. A.
No. 1798 9 in. Vase
Deep Etched Daisy and
Fern Design.
Price, 75 cents each.
No. 763 9 in. Vase
Deep Etched Daisy and
Fern Design.
Price, 75 cents each.
No. 764 8 in. Vase
Deep Etched Daffodil
Design.
Price 65 cents each.
No. 762 8 in. Vase
Deep Etched Oriental
Design.
Price, 65 cents each.
No. 1799 1-2 7 1-4 in. Vase
Deep Etched Poppy
Design.
Price, $1.00 each.

1921 Catalog

Bouquet Vases

2081 Engraved Vase
Engraving No. 17
Height 12", 1921 Catalog

2072 Engraved Vase
Engraving No. 16
Height 10", 1921 Catalog

VASES
CINNAMON-SPRUCE-CHARTREUSE EBONY and CRYSTAL

FOSTORIA GLASS COMPANY, MOUNDSVILLE, WEST VIRGINIA – 1952

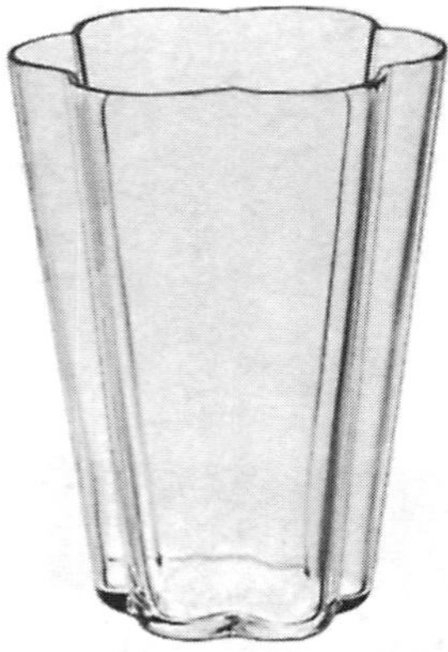

2387 — 8 in. Vase

2591 — 15 in. Vase
2591 — 11½ in. Vase
2591 — 8½ in. Vase

2470 — 10 in.
Footed Vase
"Hugh" RB-EG-Bur-Ruby with Cry ft., early to mid 1930's

2654 — 9½ in.
Footed Vase

2567 — 7½ in.
Footed Vase

2656 — 10 in.
Footed Vase

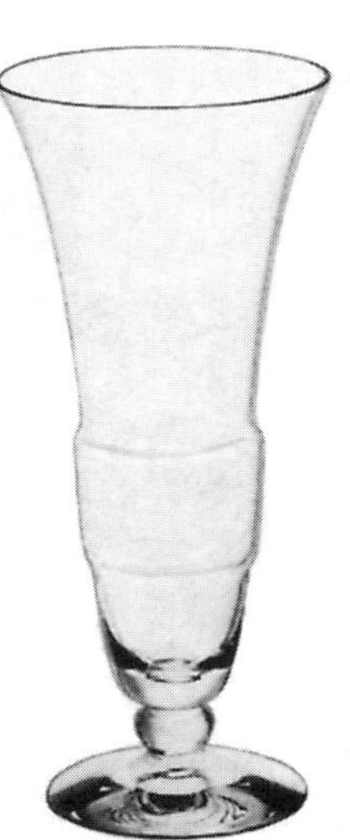

2658 — 10½ in.
Footed Vase

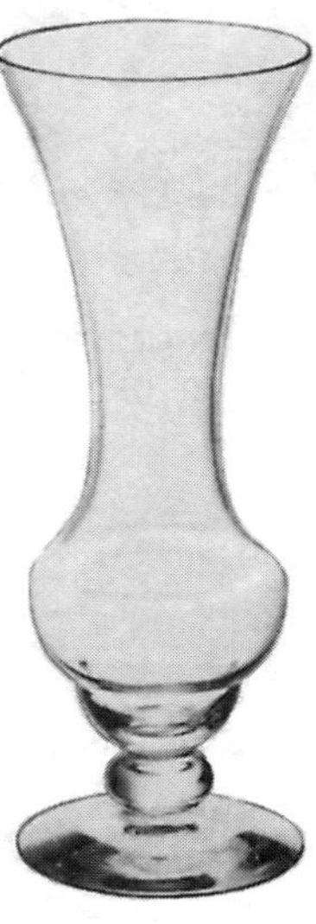

2657 — 10½ in.
Footed Vase

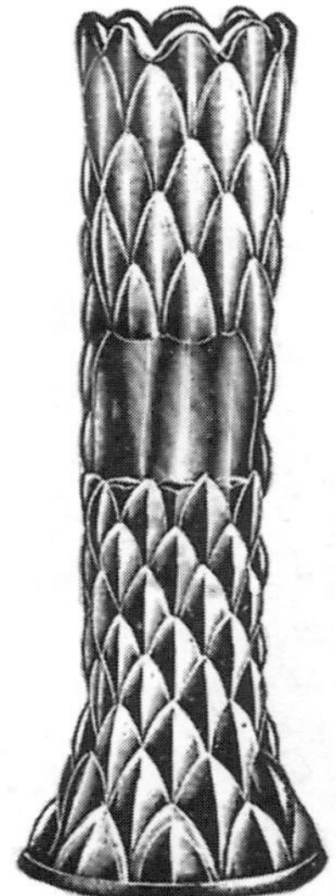

184 Vase for Engraving
Height 9", 1901 Catalog

2972 Bouquet Holder
Height 12", 1921 Catalog
Blown Crystal

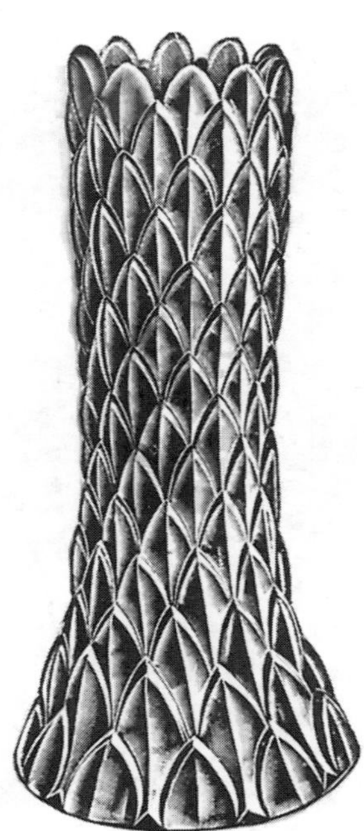

184 Vase
Height 11", 1901 Catalog

4105 Vase, Loop Optic
Height 10", 1930 Catalog

272 Vase
Height 5½", 1901 Catalog

195 Vase
Height 5", 1901 Catalog

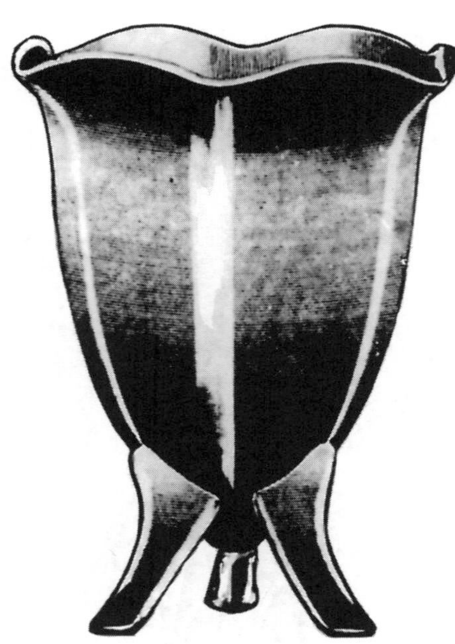

2218 Sweetpea Vase
Height 5", 1921 Catalog

2109 Vase
Height 9½", 1916 Catalog

4105 Vase, Reg. Optic
Height 8", 1930 Catalog

600 Pressed Vase
Height 11", 1901 Catalog
Brazilian Pattern

4134 Vase
Height 6", 1937 Catalog

2454 Tri-Pod Vase
Height 8", 1934 Fostoria drawing

2053 Handled Vase
Height 8", 1934 Catalog
Colors uncertain, the darkness of this vase indicates RB-EG or Ruby.

725 Vase, Etched or Plain
1901 Catalog. This blown vase was made both Crystal and with an acid finished body, leaving the flowers in bright relief.

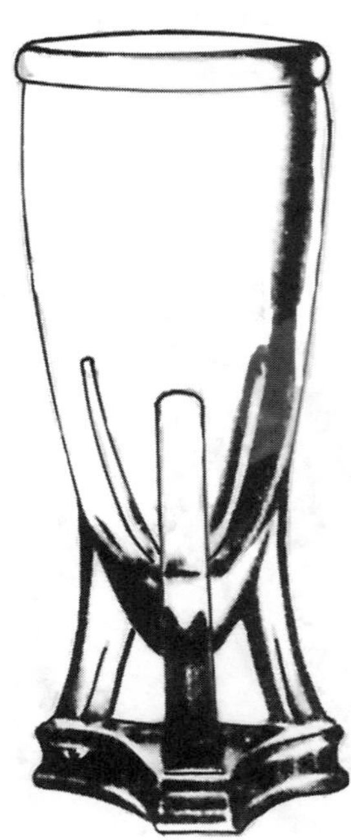

2454 Tri-Pod Vase
1936 Catalog, colors of RB-EG-Ruby.
1938 colors were Ro-Gr-Eb.

Opal Vases
Easter Vase Assortment
Hand Painted
These vases in colors and designs to suit the most fastidious

1154 Vase
Height 5"
1902 Catalog

989 Vase
Height 10"
Catalog ca. 1900

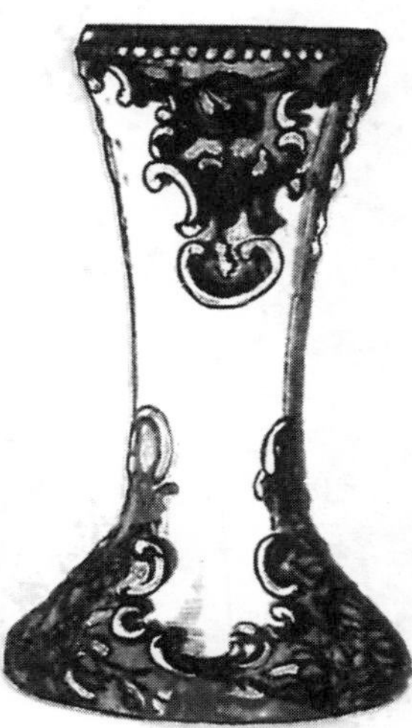

946 Vase
Height 7"
Catalog ca. 1900

950 Vase
Height 9"
Catalog ca.1900

Made in various sizes, the dark areas represent colors of Yellow and Pink. The daisies are Blue and Pink. Others of this type were painted in tones of Brown and Green. Many of these vases were trimmed in Gold.

1150 Vase
Height 15"

Artistic Opal Vases, Hand Painted Assorted Colors, Fired Decorations

1155 Vase
Height 6"
1902 Catalog

990 Vase
Height 12"
1902 Catalog

Vases with enameled roses were part of the American Beauty Rose series and the various decorations were numbered. Indian portraits, tavern scenes, etc. were also made.

Crystal Blown Vases
FOSTORIA GLASS COMPANY, MOUNDSVILLE, WEST VIRGINIA, U. S. A.
No. 761 10 in. Vase
Cut and Engraved No. 5.
Price, $2.85 each.
No. 1798 9 in. Vase
Cut and Engraved No. 5.
Price, $1.45 each.
No. 762 8 in. Vase
Cut and Engraved No. 5.
Price, $1.00 each.
No. 764 8 in. Vase
Cut 119.
Price, 70 cents each.
No. 763 9 in. Vase
Cut 117.
Price, $1.15 each.

1921 Catalog

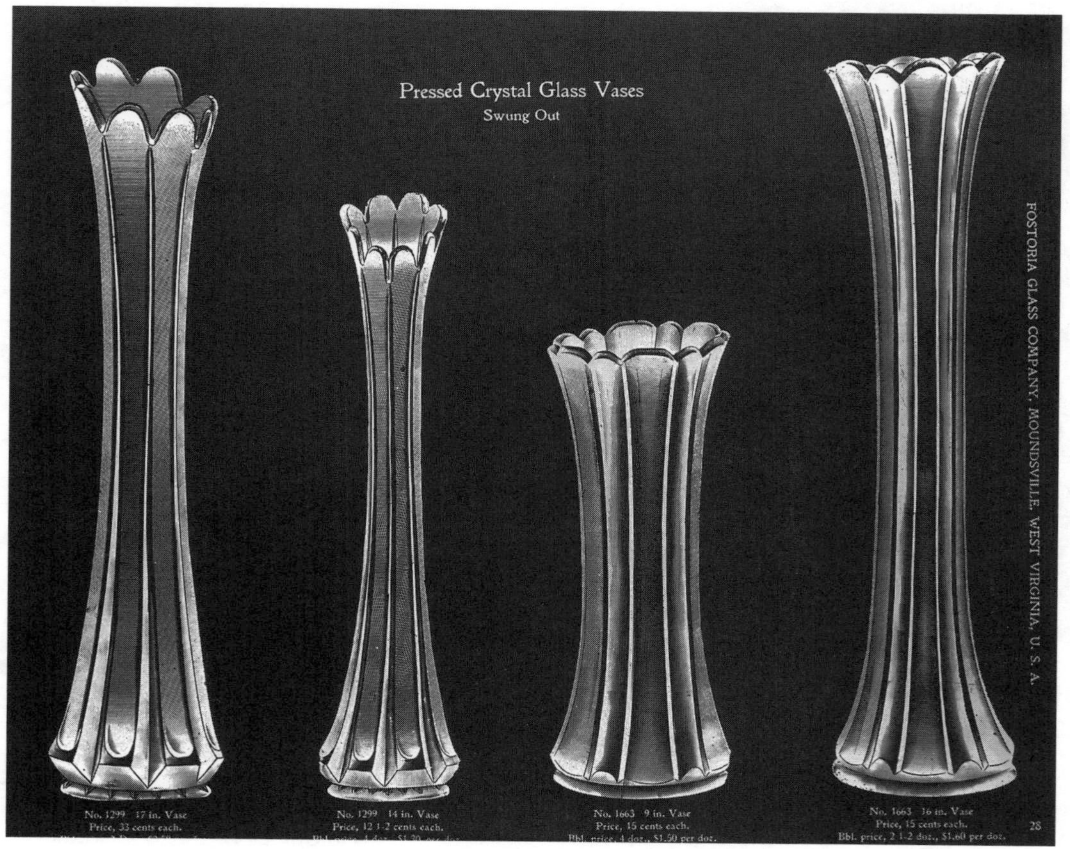

1921 Catalog

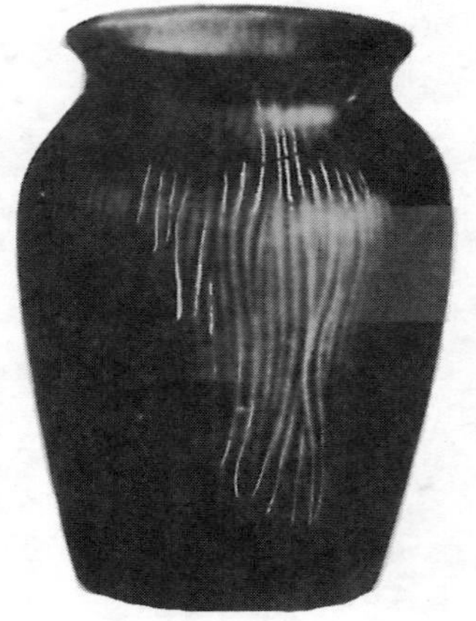

2523 Vase, Silver Mist
Height 6½", 1934 Catalog

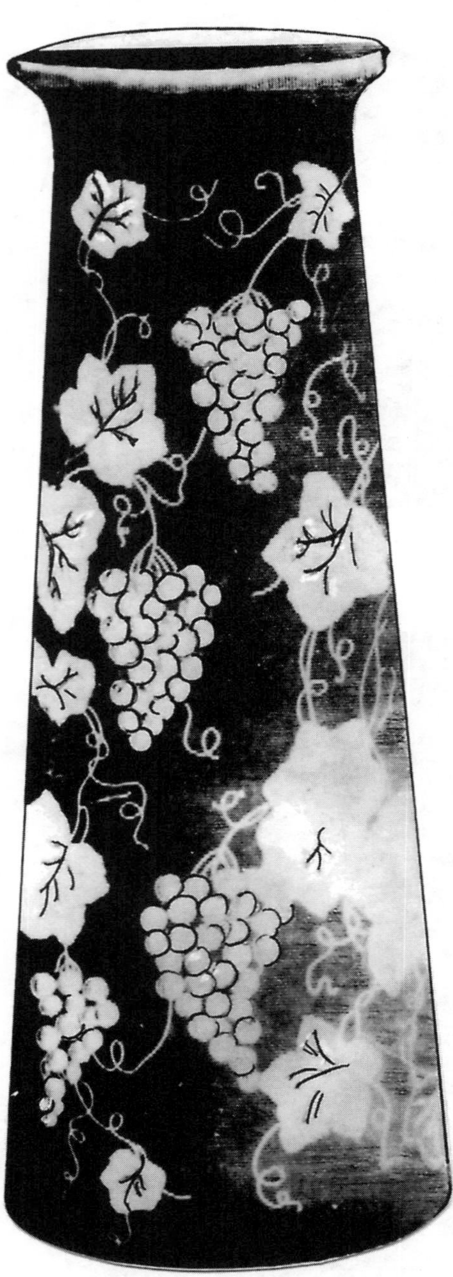

300 Vase, Deep Etched 227
Height 12", New Vintage Pattern

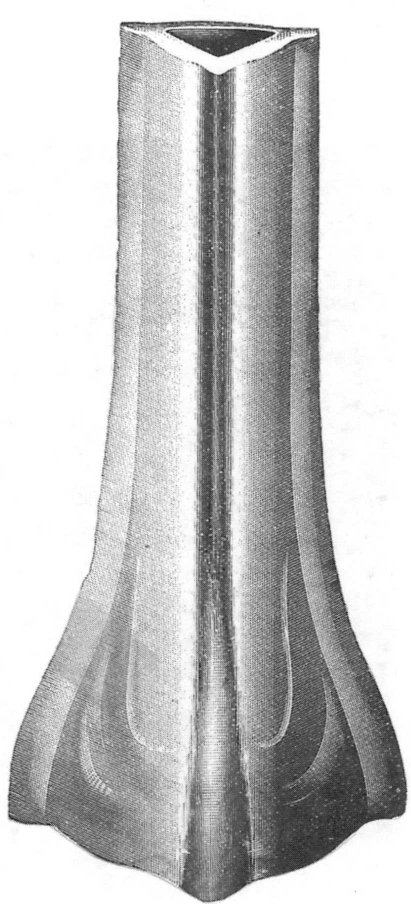

914 Vase, Blown
Height 11½", 1901 Catalog

466 Vase
Height 5", 1901 Catalog

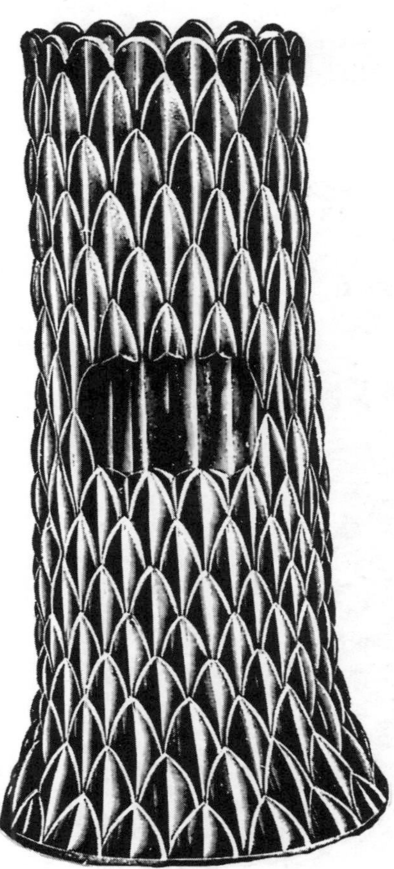
184 Vase
Height 14", 1901 Catalog

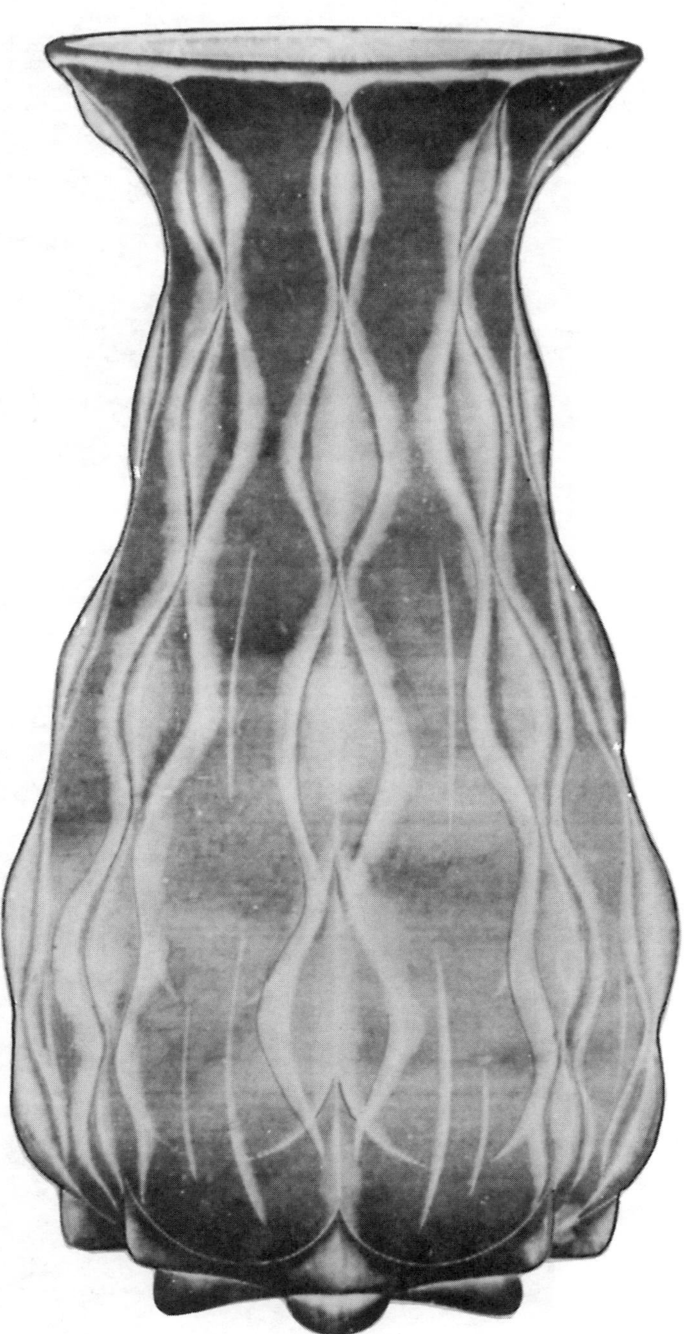
1752 Vase, Blown
Height 13", 1920 Catalog

Fostoria Glass Company, Moundsville, West Virginia
2421—10½ in. Vase, Ftd., Reg. Opt.
Ro-Az-Gr-Am-Eb.
2360—10 in. Vase, Reg. Opt.
Ebony.
5100—10 in. Vase, Ftd., Reg. Opt.
Gr-Am.

1930 Catalog

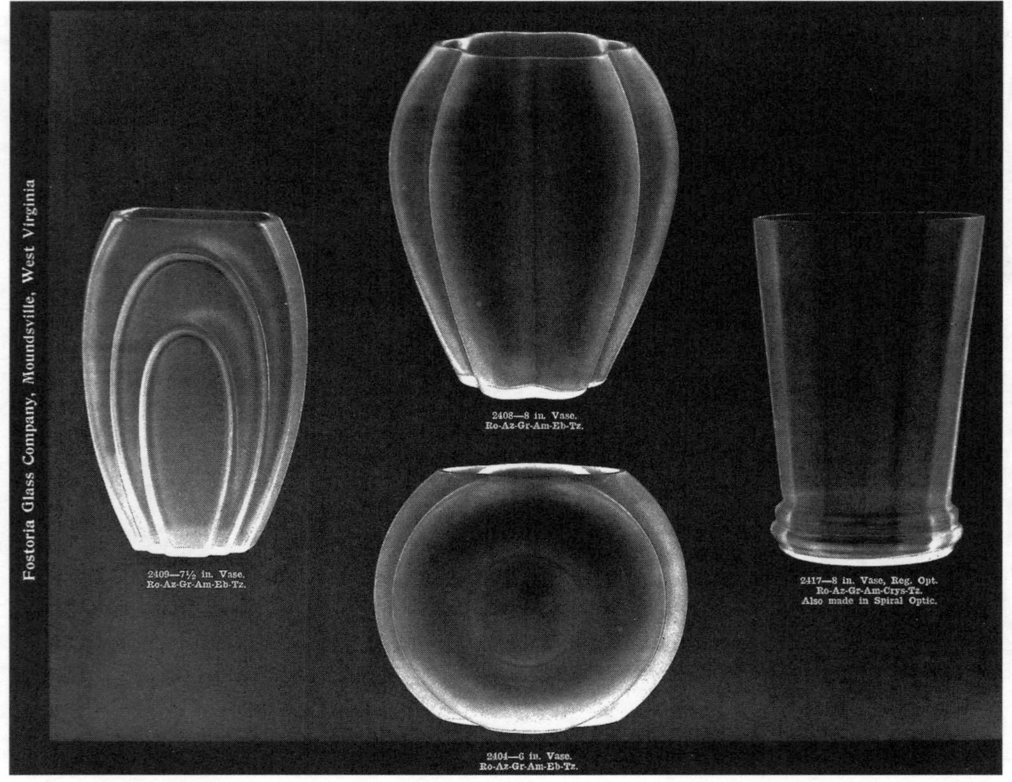
Fostoria Glass Company, Moundsville, West Virginia
2409—7½ in. Vase.
Ro-Az-Gr-Am-Eb-Tz.
2408—8 in. Vase.
Ro-Az-Gr-Am-Eb-Tz.
2404—6 in. Vase.
Ro-Az-Gr-Am-Eb-Tz.
2417—8 in. Vase, Reg. Opt.
Ro-Az-Gr-Am-Crys-Tz.
Also made in Spiral Optic.

1930 Catalog

30
VASES.
MADE IN AMBER, BLUE, GREEN, ORCHID AND CRYSTAL; EXCEPT AS OTHERWISE NOTED.
PRICED PAGE 15 — No. 2 SUPPLEMENT PRICE LIST.
2369—5 in. Vase, Optic. Made in 5, 7, 9 and 11 in. 5 and 11 in. Not made in crystal.
1681—8 in. Wall Vase. Made in ebony; Not made in orchid.
2292—8 in. Vase. Spiral Optic. Made plain or Spiral Optic. Made in ebony and crystal—Plain only.
Fostoria Glass Company, Moundsville, West Virginia
2360—8 in. Vase, Optic. Made in 8 and 10 in. Not made in crystal.
4095—8 in. Vase, Spiral Optic. Made in 8, 9 and 10 in. Not made in Orchid.
2369—7 in. Vase, Optic. Made in 5, 7, 9 and 11 in. 5 and 11 in. Not made in crystal.

1927 Catalog

Blown Crystal Glass Vases
No. 1948, Hollow to Foot
FOSTORIA GLASS COMPANY, MOUNDSVILLE, WEST VIRGINIA, U. S. A.
No. 1948 12 1-2 in. Vase Deep Etched Poppy Design. Price, $2.50 each.
No. 1948 10 in. Vase Deep Etched Poppy Design. Price, $1.75 each.
No. 1948 8 in. Vase Deep Etched Poppy Design. Price, $1.10 each.
No. 1948 5 1-2 in. Vase Deep Etched Poppy Design. Price, 75 cents each.
No. 760 12 in. Vase Deep Etched Poppy Design. Price, $2.00 each.

1921 Catalog

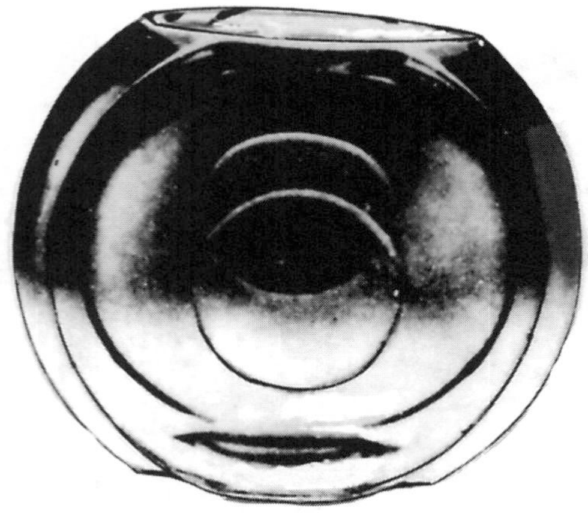

2404 Nautilus Vase
Height 6", 1936 Catalog
Also made 8" size in Rose, Azure, Green, Amber, Topaz, and Ebony.

4133 Vase
Height 4"
1937 Catalog

736 Vase, Etched or Plain
1901 Catalog. This blown vase made both in crystal and with an acid finished body, leaving the flowers in bright relief.

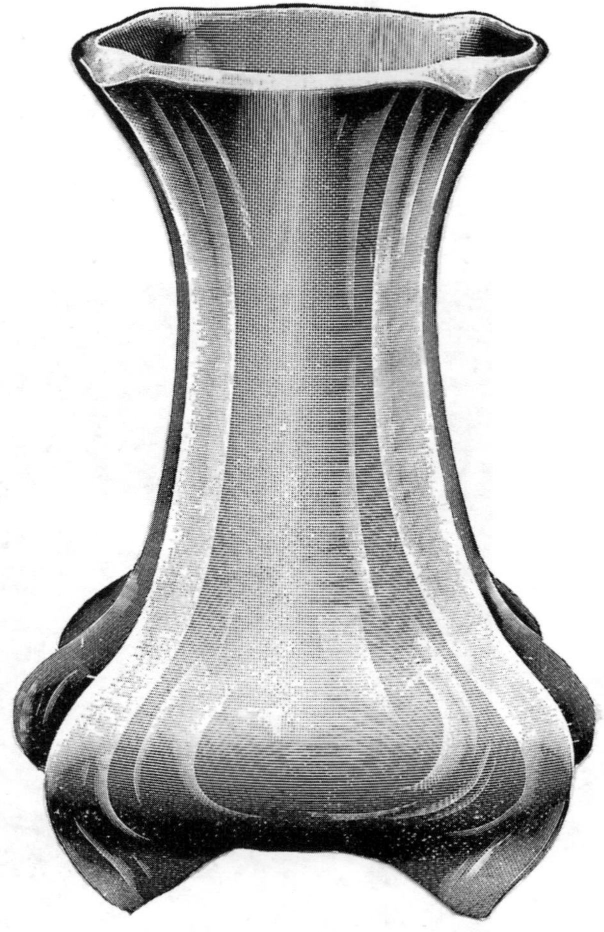

912 Blown Vase
Height 9", 1901 Catalog

Miscellaneous

No. 493 Boston Measuring Cup
1901 Catalog

No. 4095 Footed Jug
72 oz.
Height $10\frac{3}{4}$", also made
$8\frac{1}{2}$" and $9\frac{1}{2}$"
1924 Catalog

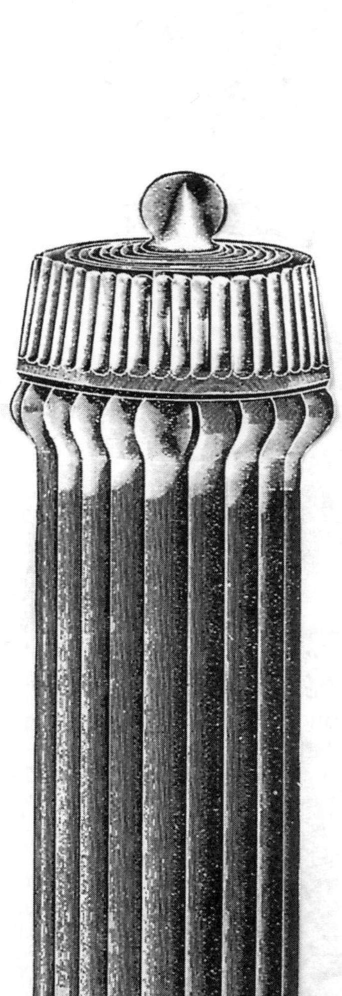

Covered Straw Jar
Optic, 1901 Catalog

No. 1062 Shaker
1902 Catalog

No. 820 Tumbler
Deep Etched No. 203
Persian Scroll Pattern
1902 Catalog

No. 1857 Hotel Cream
1913 Catalog

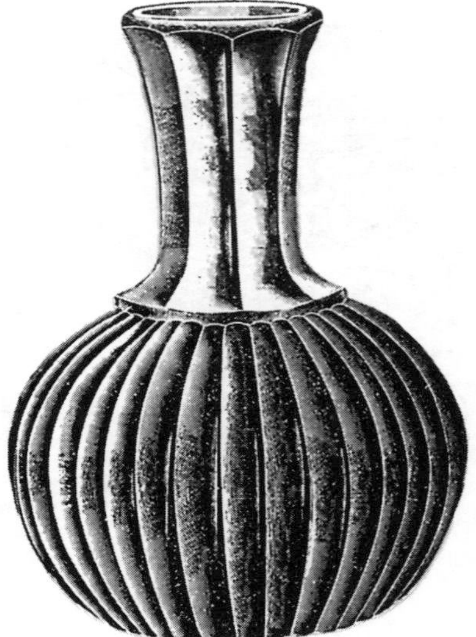

No. 581 Water Bottle
1-Quart, 1901 Catalog

No. 1857 Hotel Sugar
1913 Catalog

No. 4095 Ftd. Salt, Optic
Solid Colors or Colored Foot
1927 Catalog

No. 601 Spooner
1901 Catalog
Diana Pattern

No. 952 Jug, 3-Pint
1901 Catalog

No. 601 Butter and Cover
1901 Catalog
Diana Pattern

No. 402 Tantalus Set
Valkyrie Pattern, mold blown
with cut stoppers, 1898 Catalog

No. 2283

- 4" Ice Tea Plate
- 5" Ice Tea Plate
- 6" Bread and Butter, Finger Bowl or Sherbet Plate
- 7" Salad Plate
- 8" Salad Plate
- 9" Sandwich Plate
- 10" Sandwich Plate
- 11" Service Plate
- 12" Service Plate
- 13" Service Plate

Miscellaneous Plates
Made in Cry-Gr–Am-Canary, 1924 Catalog

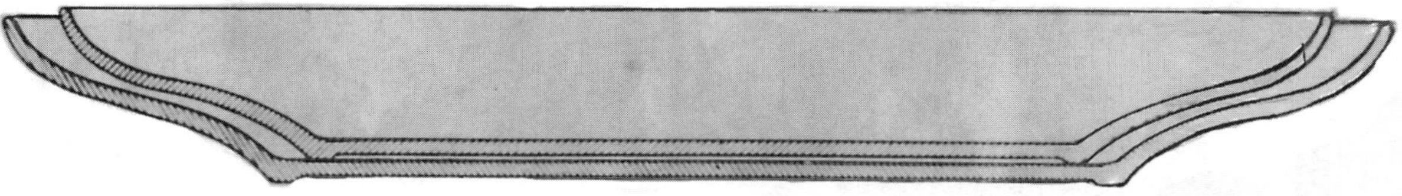

No. 2290 Deep Salad Plates
7", 8", and 13"

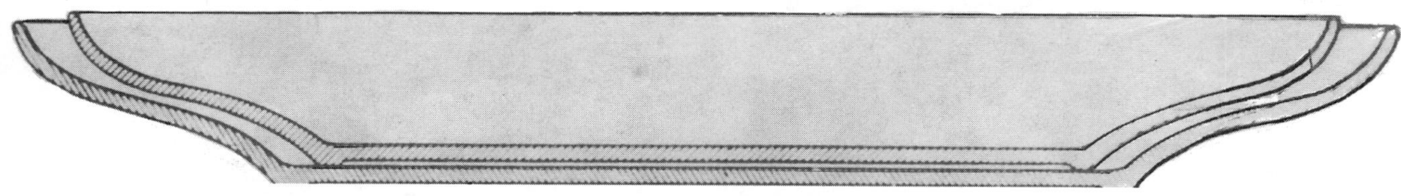

No. 2283 Service Plates
11", 12", and 13"

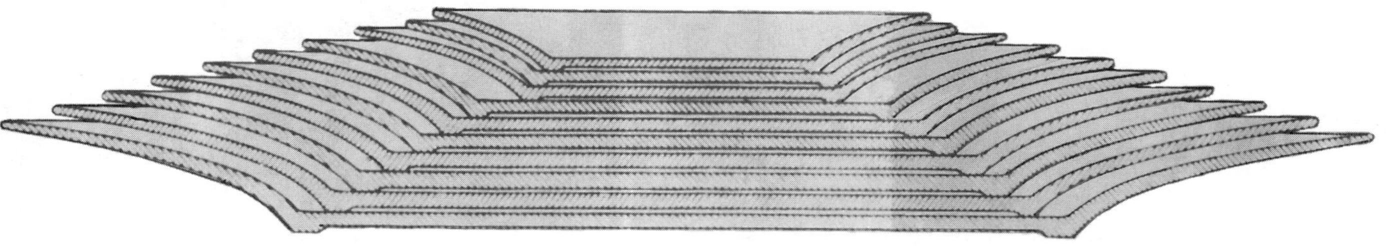

No. 2283 Plates

No. 576 Custard
Edgewood Pattern
1901 Catalog

No. 726 Can
1901 Catalog

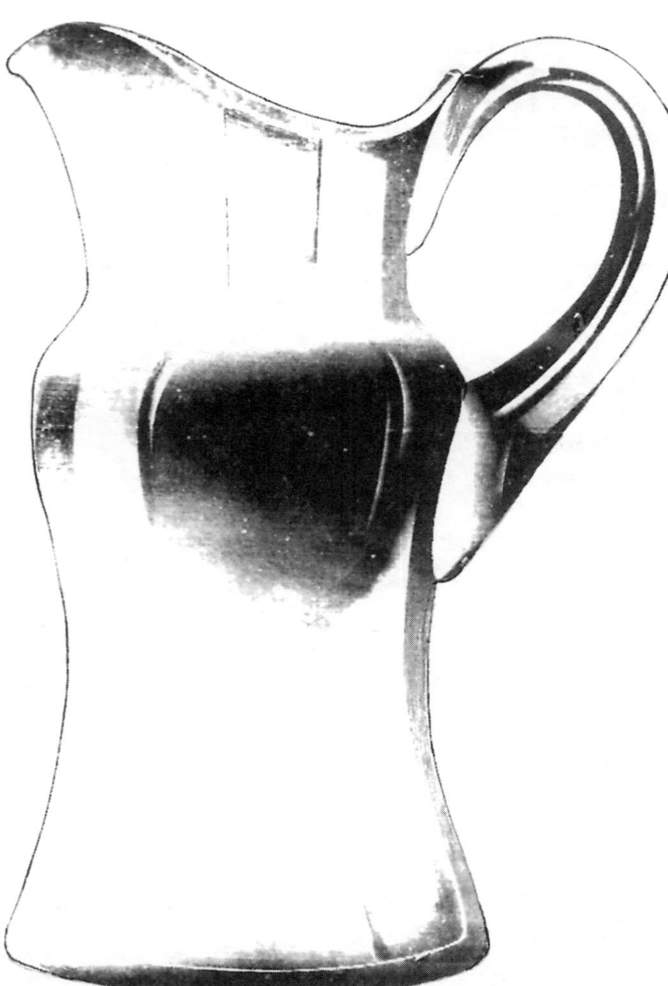

No. 1760 Jug
Blown, 1916 Catalog

No. 2111 Shaker
Glass Top, 1927 Catalog

No. 582 Mucilage Cup
and Brush, 1901 Catalog

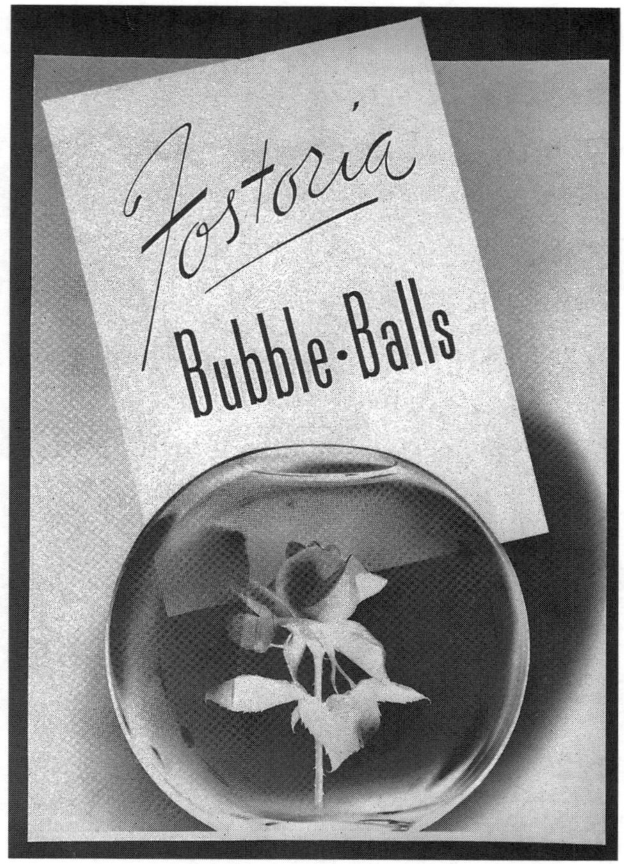

Bubble Balls	1938 Colors
4129 Bubble Ball, 2½"	Cry-RB-Bur-EG-Ruby
4116 Bubble Ball, 4"	Cry-RB-Bur-EG-Ruby
4116 Bubble Ball, 5"	Cry-RB-Bur-EG-Ruby
4116 Bubble Ball, 6"	Cry-RB-Bur-EG-Ruby
4116 Bubble Ball, 7"	Cry-RB-Bur-EG-Ruby
4116 Bubble Ball, 8"	Cry-RB-Bur-EG-Ruby
4116 Bubble Ball, 9"	Cry-RB-Bur-Ruby

Silver Mist, 1938	Decorations 516 & 517
4116 Bubble Ball, 4"	4116 Bubble Ball, 4"
4116 Bubble Ball, 5"	4116 Bubble Ball, 5"
4116 Bubble Ball, 6"	4116 Bubble Ball, 6"
4116 Bubble Ball, 7"	4116 Bubble Ball, 7"
4116 Bubble Ball, 8"	

Note: Decoration 516 Apple Blossom was used for some sizes of bubble balls. This decoration is White Enamel on Regal Blue glass. Decoration 517 Grapes was also used on Regal Blue. It is believed that these decorations date around 1933. Was this an attempt to compete with the Japonica line of the Cambridge Glass Company?

No. 465
1901 Catalog

No. 676½ Small
Shaker, Priscilla Pattern
1901 Catalog

No. 1697 Bedroom Set, 2-Piece
Etched 264, 7⅞" Height

No. 2321 Mah Jongg Set
1927 Catalog

No. 93 Salt
1901 Catalog

No. 302 Water Set
Etched No. 39

No. 302 Tumbler

Opal Castor Set
Decorated, Line Number Unknown
1901 Catalog

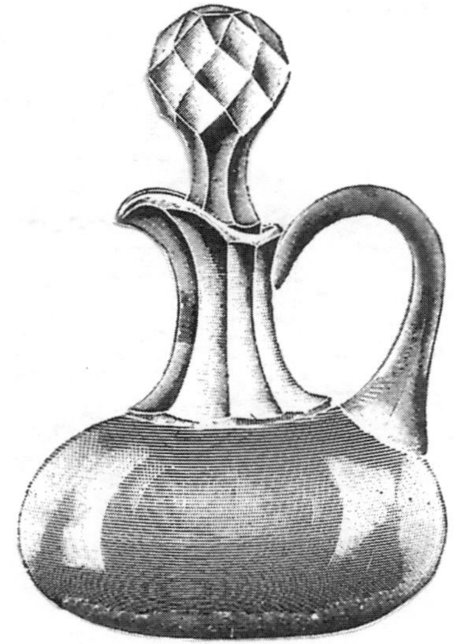

No. 795 Vinegar
Pressed Fluted Neck
Cut Stopper, 1901 Catalog

No. 136 Shaker
1901 Catalog

No. 137 Shaker
1901 Catalog

No. 300½ Water Set
Etched 38, 1898 Catalog

BUFFET SERVING ITEMS

and Other Miscellaneous

FOSTORIA GLASS COMPANY, MOUNDSVILLE, WEST VIRGINIA — 1953

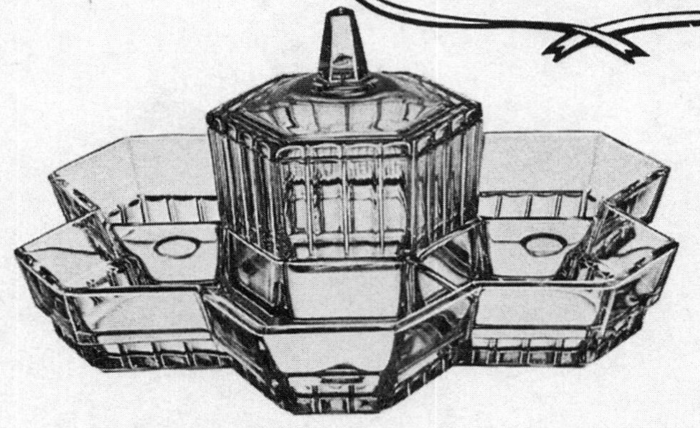

2661
3 Pc. Buffet Set
Consisting of:
1/12 Dz. 2661 5 Part Server
1/12 Dz. 2661 Sauce Dish & Cover
Height 6¼ in. Diameter 12¼ in.

2661
Sauce Dish & Cover
Height 4⅝ in.

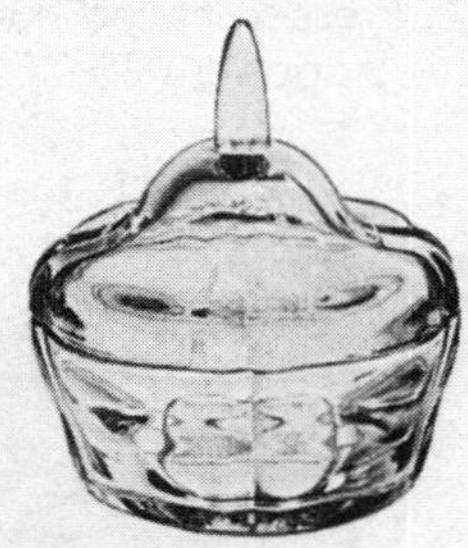

2662
Sauce Dish & Cover
Height 5¼ in.

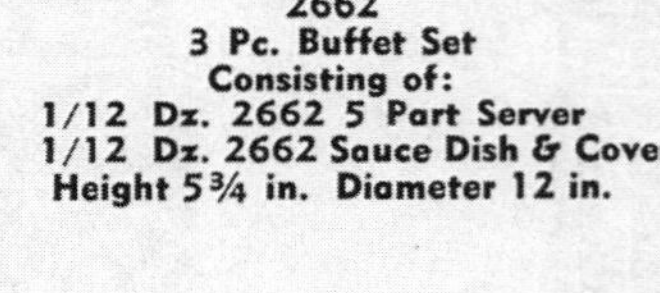

2662
3 Pc. Buffet Set
Consisting of:
1/12 Dz. 2662 5 Part Server
1/12 Dz. 2662 Sauce Dish & Cover
Height 5¾ in. Diameter 12 in.

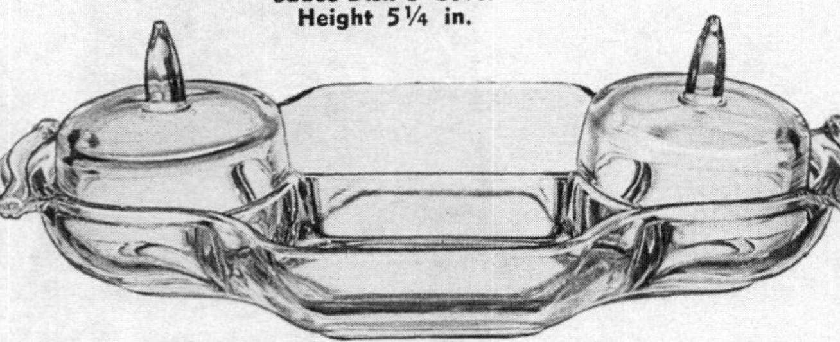

2663
3 Pc. Buffet Set
Consisting of:
1/12 Dz. 2663 4-Part Server
1/6 Dz. 2663 Cover
Height 4¼ in. Length 13¼ in.

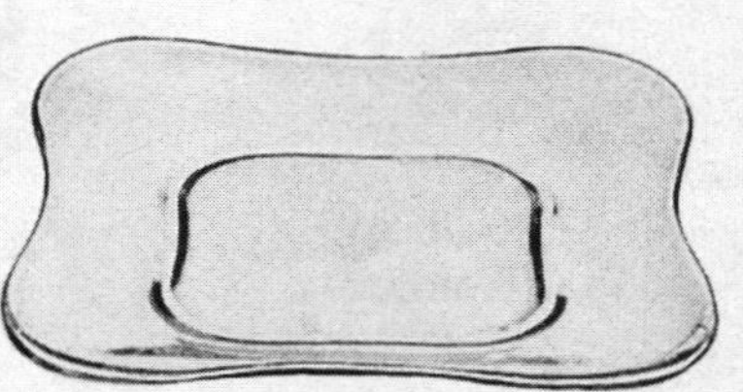

2665 — 7 in. Plate
2665 — 8 in. Plate

4152 — Snack Bowl
See price list for colors
Height 3⅞ in.

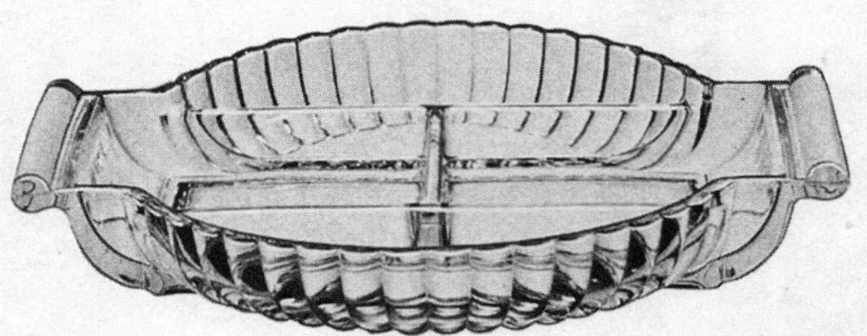

2664
4-Part Server
Length 12½ in. Width 10 in.

Crystal Glass Fixtures

Like the A.H. Heisey firm, Fostoria made "Candle Columns," or "Pedestal Columns." The ones used for hats had pedestal tops (tops not flattened). These ranged in height from 7" to 18". The flat top columns were glass shelf supports. Both styles were available with or without a candle hole.

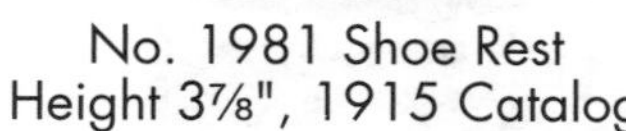

No. 1981 Shoe Rest
Height 3⅞", 1915 Catalog

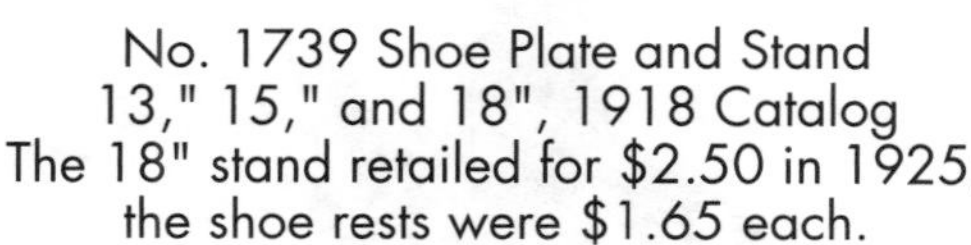

No. 1739 Shoe Plate and Stand
13," 15," and 18", 1918 Catalog
The 18" stand retailed for $2.50 in 1925;
the shoe rests were $1.65 each.

No. 1981½ Shoe Rest
Height 3¼", 1915 Catalog

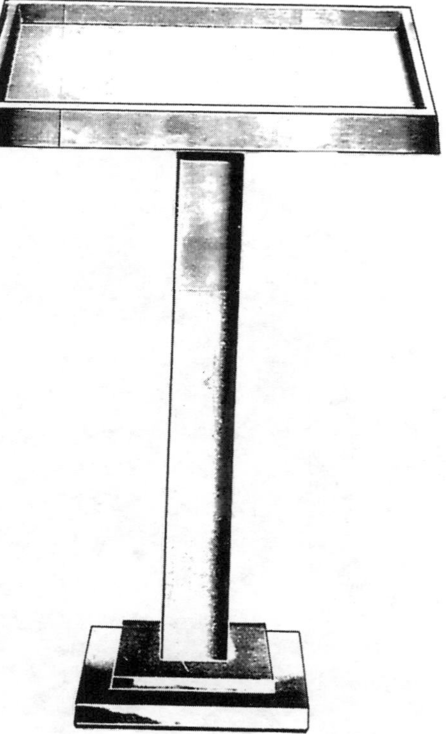

No. 1738 Show Window Plate and Stand
Made in 10½", 13", 16" Heights
For Jewelry Display, 1918 Catalog

No. 1515 Crushed Ice and Plate
Lucere Pattern, 1909 Catalog

No. 982 Jelly Glass
1901 Catalog

No. 97 Oil or Vinegar
6 oz. Capacity, 1901 Catalog

No. 5032 Blown Cocktail
3½ oz., 1901 – 1904 Catalog

No. 585 Salt
1901 Catalog

No. 300½ Small Cruet
Height 5½", Cut 132
Clover Pattern, 1924 Catalog

Covered Cheese and Plate, Cut "B,"
1924 Catalog
Line Number Unknown, Possibly Covered
Cheese No. 1590 with No. 2050 Plate

No. 329 Jug, 2-Quart
1901 Catalog

No. 4118 Tumbler
12 oz., Height 5"

No. 4118 Jug, 60 oz.
Height 8½", 1935 Catalog
Colors of RB-EG-Bur-Ruby

No. 2464 Ice Jug
Fostoria Drawing Jan. 1, 1932
Made in colors, part of the
"Repeal Ware" line.

No. 2464 Tumbler,
Blown

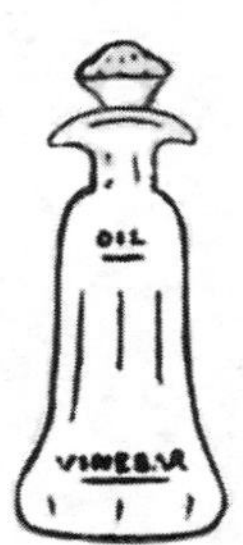

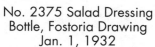

No. 2375 Salad Dressing
Bottle, Fostoria Drawing
Jan. 1, 1932

No. 2222 Footed Salt
Colonial Pattern
1927 Catalog

No. 2456 Candy Jar and Cover
Fostoria Drawing, Jan. 1, 1932
Colors unknown but has been
seen in Ebony. Limited production.

Fostoria Trade Mark
1911 Catalog

No. 910 Jug, 2-Quart
1901 Catalog

Fostoria Glass Company, Moundsville, West Virginia, Jan. 1, 1939

BATH BOTTLES

W. M. Means Wide Mouth

2561—Bath Bottle
Height 5¼ in.
Capacity 6¾ oz.

2561½—Bath Bottle, W.M.
Height 5¼ in.
Capacity 6¾ oz.

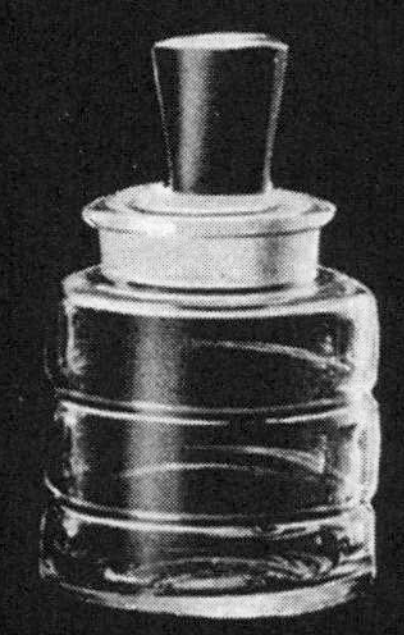

2562½—Bath Bottle, W.M.
Height 5 in.
Capacity 6½ oz.

2562—Bath Bottle
Height 5 in.
Capacity 6½ oz.

Gold Band Decoration
2562—Bath Bottle
2562½—Bath Bottle, W.M.

Silver Mist Decoration
2562—Bath Bottle
2562½—Bath Bottle, W.M.

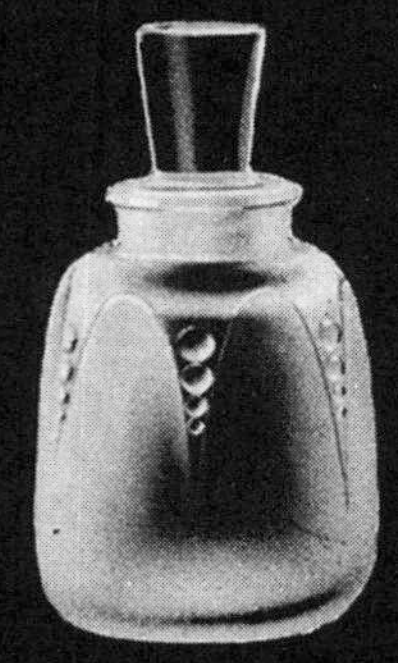

Silver Mist Decoration
2561—Bath Bottle
2561½—Bath Bottle, W.M.

Carved Decoration
2561—Bath Bottle
2561½—Bath Bottle, W.M.

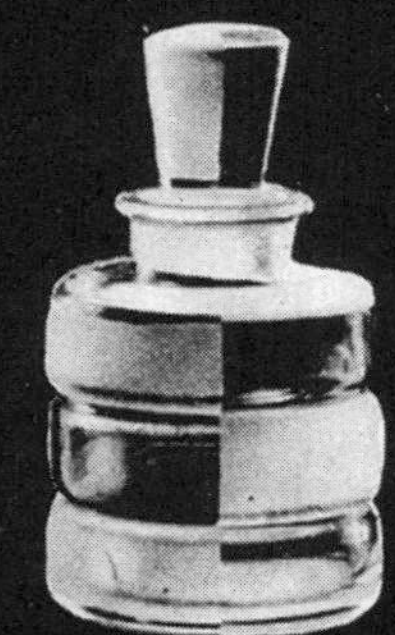

Carved Decoration
2562—Bath Bottle
2562½—Bath Bottle, W.M.

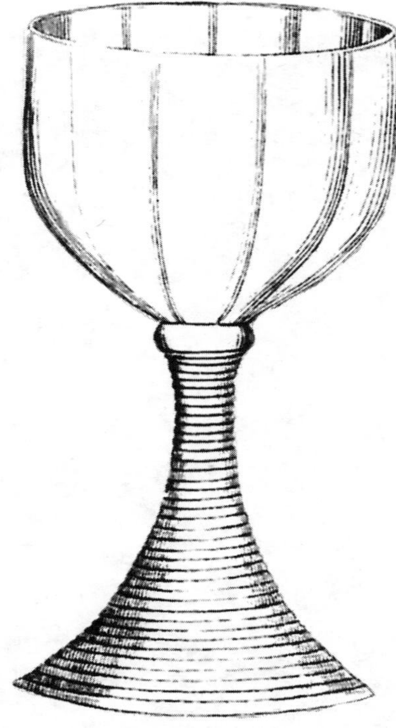

No. 5066 Schoeppen, Optic
7 oz., 1902 Catalog

No. 95 Salt, Indv.
1901 Catalog

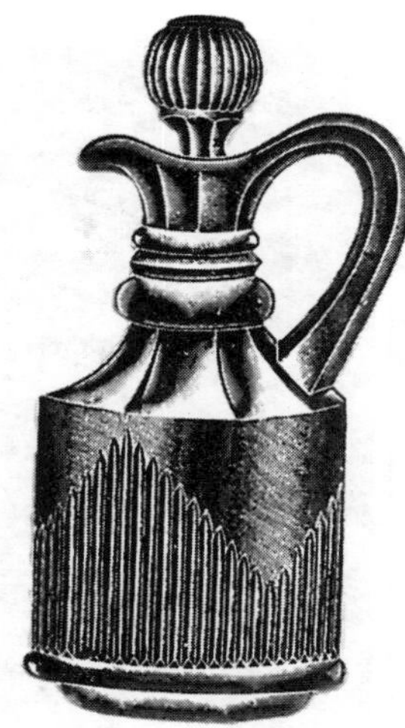

No. 152 Vinegar
1901 Catalog

No. 794 Nappy
4½", 1901 Catalog

Crystal Dipper, 1901 Catalog
Most Perfect Dipper Made

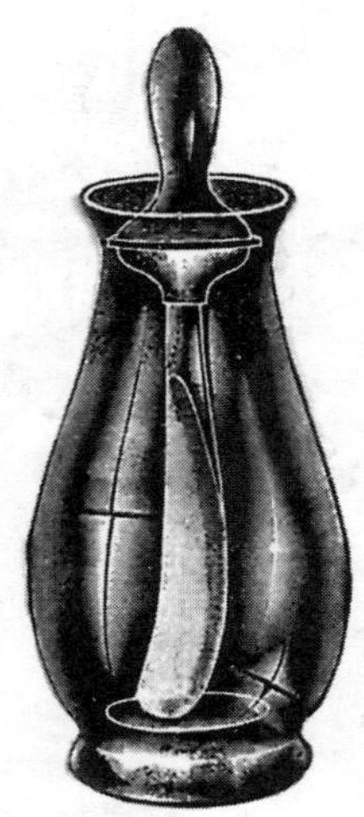

No. 456 Horseradish with No. 10 Glass Spoon, 1901 Catalog. A Mustard, Highball, and Ice Tea Glass Spoon are also listed.

No. 740 Berry Bowl
Diameter 9", 1901 Catalog

MISCELLANEOUS

2589½—Colt
Height 2¼ in.
Length 2¾ in.

2589—Colt
Height 3⅞ in.
Length 2½ in.

2531—Pelican
Height 3⅞ in. Length 4½ in.

2589—Deer
Height 4 in.
Length 2 in.

2585—Eagle Book End
Height 7½ in. Width 5 in.

2531—Seal
Height 3⅞ in.
Length 3¾ in.

2589½—Deer
Height 2⅜ in.
Length 2 in.

2531—Polar Bear
Height 4⅝ in. Length 4 in.

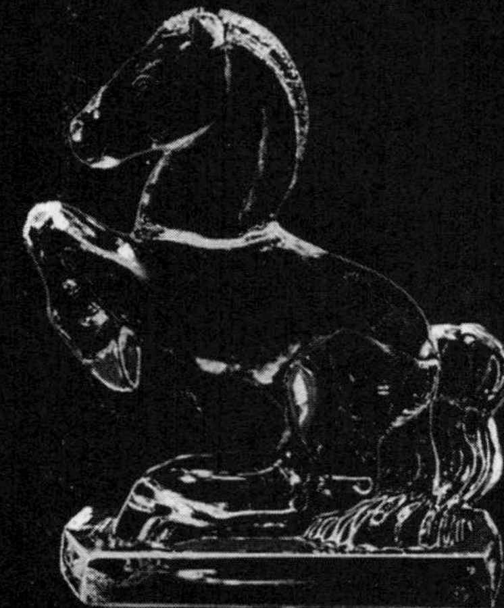
2564—Horse Book End
Height 5¼ in. Length 7⅜ in.

2580—Elephant Book End
Height 6½ in. Length 7¼ in.

2531—Penguin
Height 4⅝ in.

Fostoria Glass Company, Moundsville, West Virginia, January 1, 1940

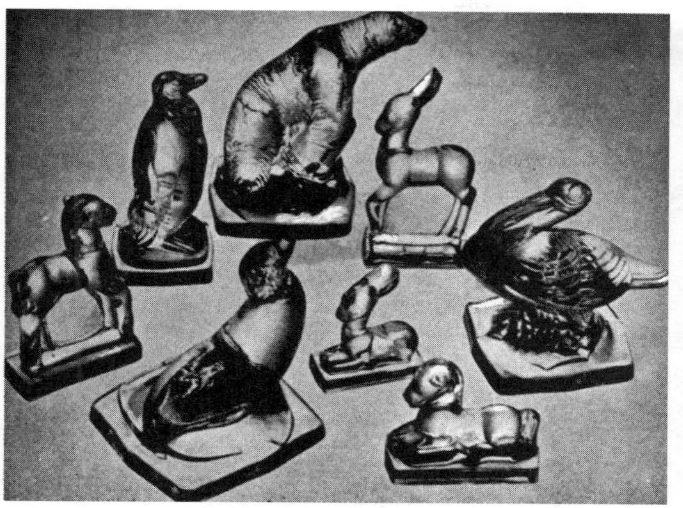

In 1938 only the Penguin, Pelican, Seal, and Polar Bear were available and these four were made in Crystal, Gold-Tint and Silver Mist (etched satin finish). Any Gold-Tint piece is rare. The Elephant, Owl, Eagle, and Rearing Horse are bookends, not table ornaments. The large and impressive Chinese Lotus Figures are highly collectible. The 10" Madonna and 13½" St. Francis were both made for several years and produced in Crystal and Silver Mist. A separate lighted base was designed for these two items. Also made in the 1950s were Chanticleer, Fish "A" Vertical, and Fish "B" Horizontal (not illustrated). The wholesale price for Chanticleer was around $7.00.

Made in Clear and Silver Mist Colors of Amber and Olive Green.

2-Piece Squirrel Set
Squirrel (sitting), 3⅛" Height
Squirrel (running), 2⅝" Height
Mama Duck, 4" Height
4-Piece Duckling Set
Duckling (head back), 2½" Height
Duckling (walking), 2⅜" Height
Duckling (head down), 1½" Height
1963 Catalog

Made in Clear and Silver Mist Colors of Crystal, Lemon, and Olive Green.

Stork, 2" Height
Cat, 2¾" Height
Dolphin, 4¾" Height
Frog, 1⅞" Height
Lady Bug, 1¼" Height
Owl, 2¾" Height
Baby Rabbit, 1¼" Height
Mama Rabbit, 2⅛" Height
1963 Catalog

MISCELLANEOUS

FOSTORIA GLASS COMPANY, MOUNDSVILLE, WEST VIRGINIA — 1957

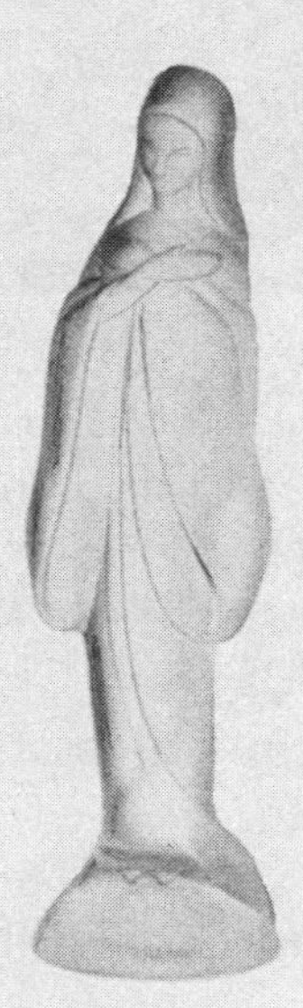

2635
Madonna
Decoration No. 525 Silver Mist
Height 10 in.

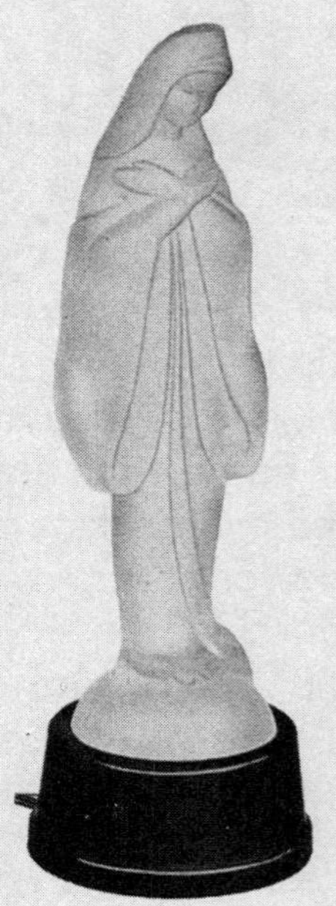

2635
Madonna with Base (Lighted)
Decoration No. 525 Silver Mist
Height 11¾ in.

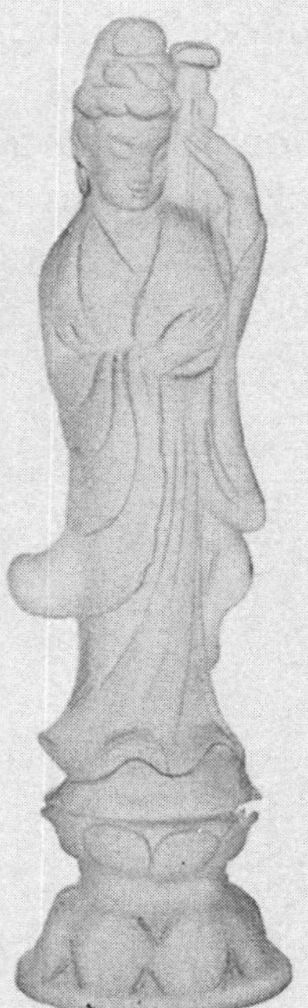

2626
Chinese Lotus
Decoration No. 525 Silver Mist
Height 12¼ in.

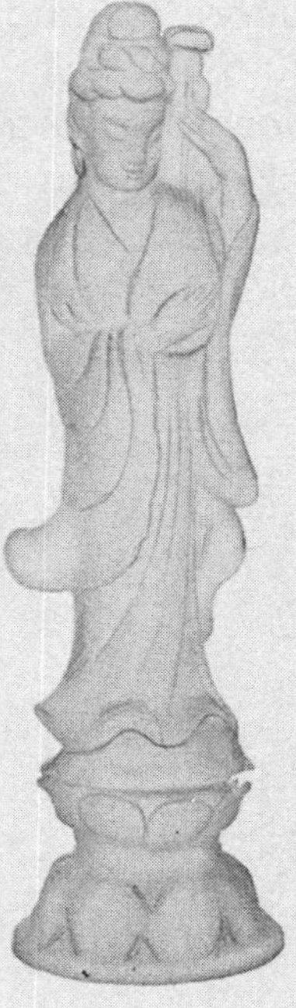

2626
Chinese Lute
Decoration No. 525 Silver Mist
Height 12¼ in.

2675
Egg Plate
Length 12 in. Width 9½ in.

2697
Bowl Flared, Wood Base,
Ebony Finish
Height 4½ in. Width 14 in.

2697
Floating Bowl, Wood Base,
Ebony Finish
Height 4¼ in. Width 13 in.

2697
Salad Bowl, Wood Base,
Ebony Finish
Height 6 in. Width 11 in.

2702
9½ in. Candleholder/Vase,
Brass

2702
8 in. Candleholder/Vase,
Brass

2702
6¾ in. Candleholder/Vase,
Brass

4171
10¼ in. Bowl, Wood Stand,
Ebony Finish
Height 6 in.

2705
Snack Set
Consisting of:
1/6 Doz. 2705 Snack Bowl
1/12 Doz. Wood Tray,
Ebony Finish
Height 6½ in. Width 13¾ in.

2706
Salad/Punch Bowl, Wood Base,
Ebony Finish
Height 7¼ in. Width 14 in.
Capacity 7 quarts

2706
Punch Cup

2708
8 in. Candleholder/Brass

2708
Shallow Comport & Base/Brass
Height 8⅜ in. Diameter 8⅞ in.

2708
Duo Candleholder & Base/Brass
Height 10 in.

2708
Deep Comport & Base/Brass
Height 9⅛ in. Diameter 7½ in.

Undated Catalog, Possibly 1919
Items available in Crystal, Dark Blue, and Green with Silver Deposit
These items were very expensive. The No. 135 Jug, 64 oz., sold for $25.00.

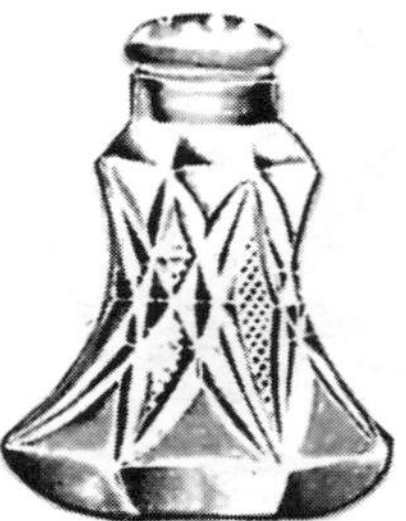

No. 728 Shaker
1902 Catalog

No. 2493 Beer Mug, Tavern Scene
14 oz., Height 5½"
1934 Catalog
Made in Cry-Amb-Tz

No. 1063 Pressed Tumbler
1901 – 1913 Production Years

No. 675 Vinegar, 8 oz.
Edgewood Pattern
1901 Catalog

No. 691 Shaker
1901 Catalog

No. 675 Salt Shaker
Edgewood Pattern
1901 Catalog

No. 2128 Shaker
Glass Top, 1927 Catalog

No. 140 Orange Bowl
1901 Catalog

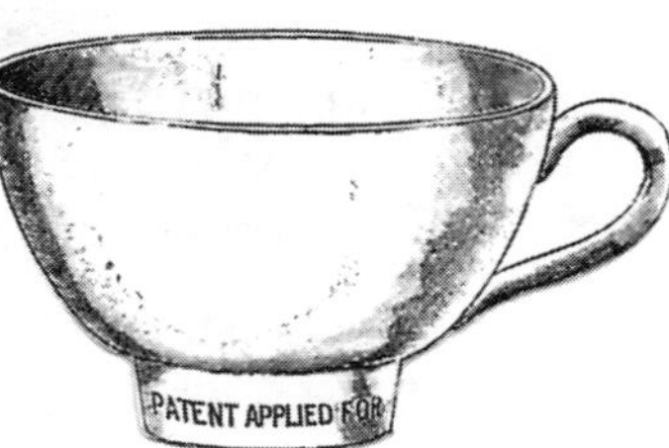

Fruit Jar Filler
1901 Catalog

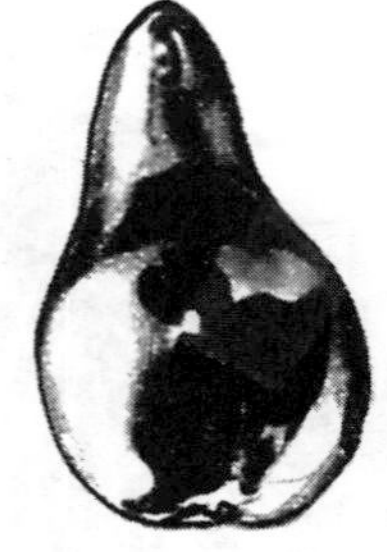

No. 2512 Pear, Hollow
1934 Catalog
Made in Colors

No. 2512 Banana, Hollow
1934 Catalog, Made in Colors

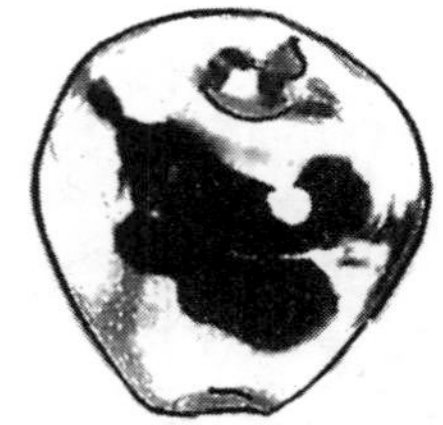

No. 2512 Apple, Hollow
1934 Catalog
Made in Colors

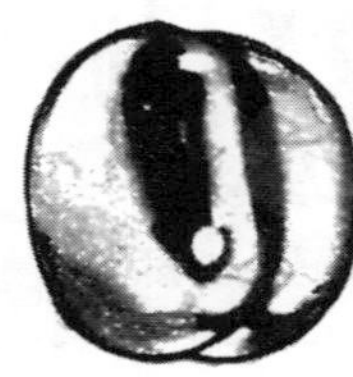

No. 2512 Peach, Hollow
1934 Catalog
Made in Colors

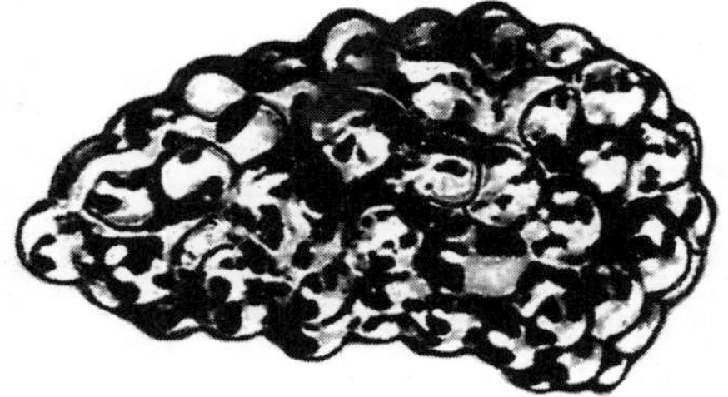

No. 2512 Grapes, Hollow
1934 Catalog
Made in Colors

No. 2512 Orange, Hollow
1934 Catalog
Made in Colors

No. 2519 Cologne and Stopper
Made in Silver Mist Only
Height 5½", 1934 Catalog

No. 2519 Puff and Cover
Made in Silver Mist Only
Height 5½", 1934 Catalog

1921 Catalog

18
COMPORTS AND JELLIES.
PRICED PAGE 17 — No. 2 PRICE LIST.
TOPAZ PRICED PAGE 12.
Fostoria Glass Company, Moundsville, West Virginia
2400—6 in. Comport. Ro-Az-Gr-Am-Eb-Crys-Tz.
1861½—Jelly. Ro-Az-Gr-Am-Crys.
5298—5 in. Comport. Ro-Az-Gr-Am-Crys-Tz.
2327—7 in. Comport. Ro-Gr-Am-Crys.
2400— 8 in. Comport. Ro-Az-Gr-Am-Crys.
5299—6 in. Comport. Ro-Az-Gr-Tz.

1930 Catalog

No. 1762 Covered Butter
1913 Catalog

No. 175½ Oil
4½ oz., 1901 Catalog

Victorian Pattern, Combination of Silver Mist and Crystal

No. 4024 Footed Bowl
10½", 1935 Catalog

No. 114 Egg Cup
1901 Catalog

No. 971 Berry Bowl
8", 1901 Catalog

4117 Bubble Candy Jar, Covered. Made RB-Ruby. 1933 Catalog

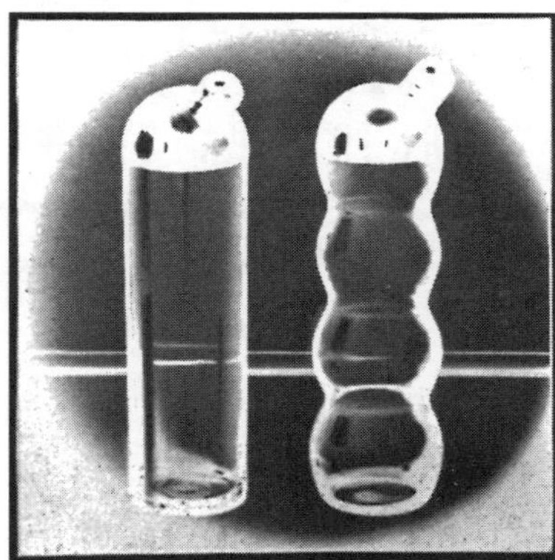

Right: 2525 Cocktail Shaker Top of Gold. Made RB-Bur-Ruby-Cry-Silver Mist. 1933 Catalog. Left: 2518 Cocktail Shaker, Made RB-Cry-Bur-EG-Ruby-Silver Mist. 1933 Catalog.

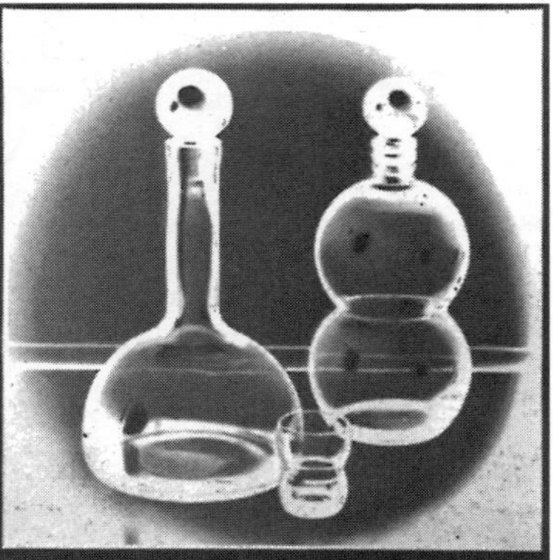

Right: 2518 Quart Decanter Made Cry-Azure w/Cry Stopper, 1933 Catalog. Left: 2525 Decanter, Stopper Made RB-Ruby-EG-Bur 1933 Catalog

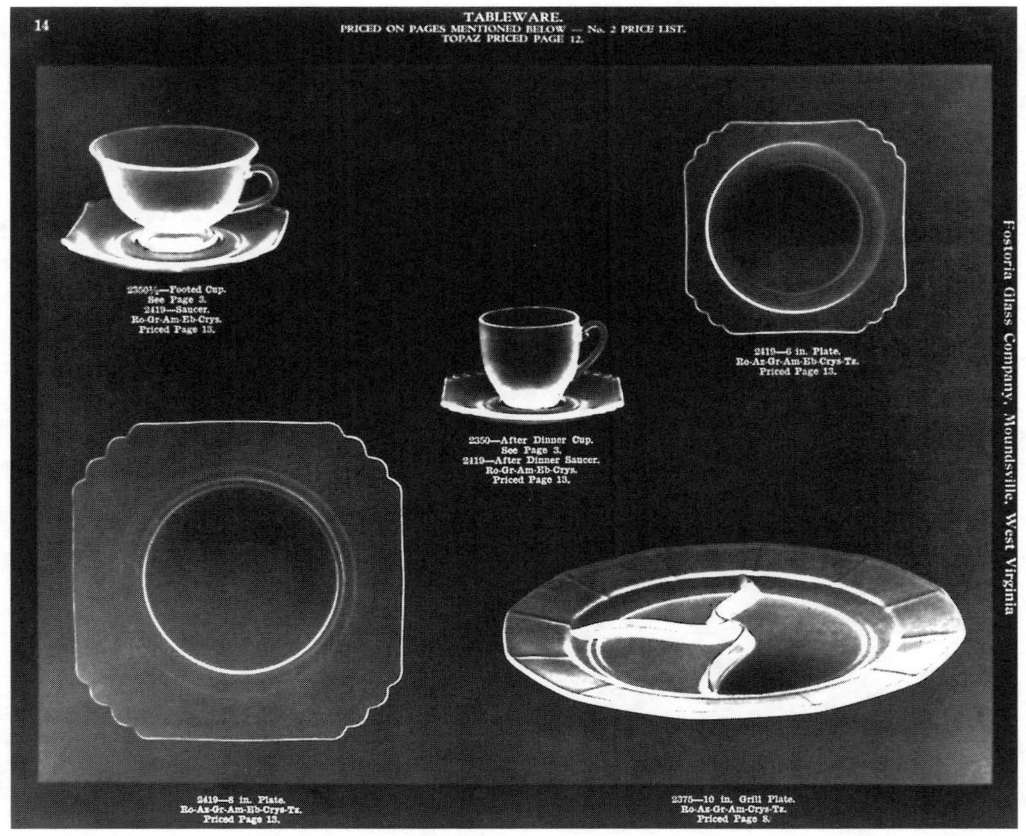

1930 Catalog

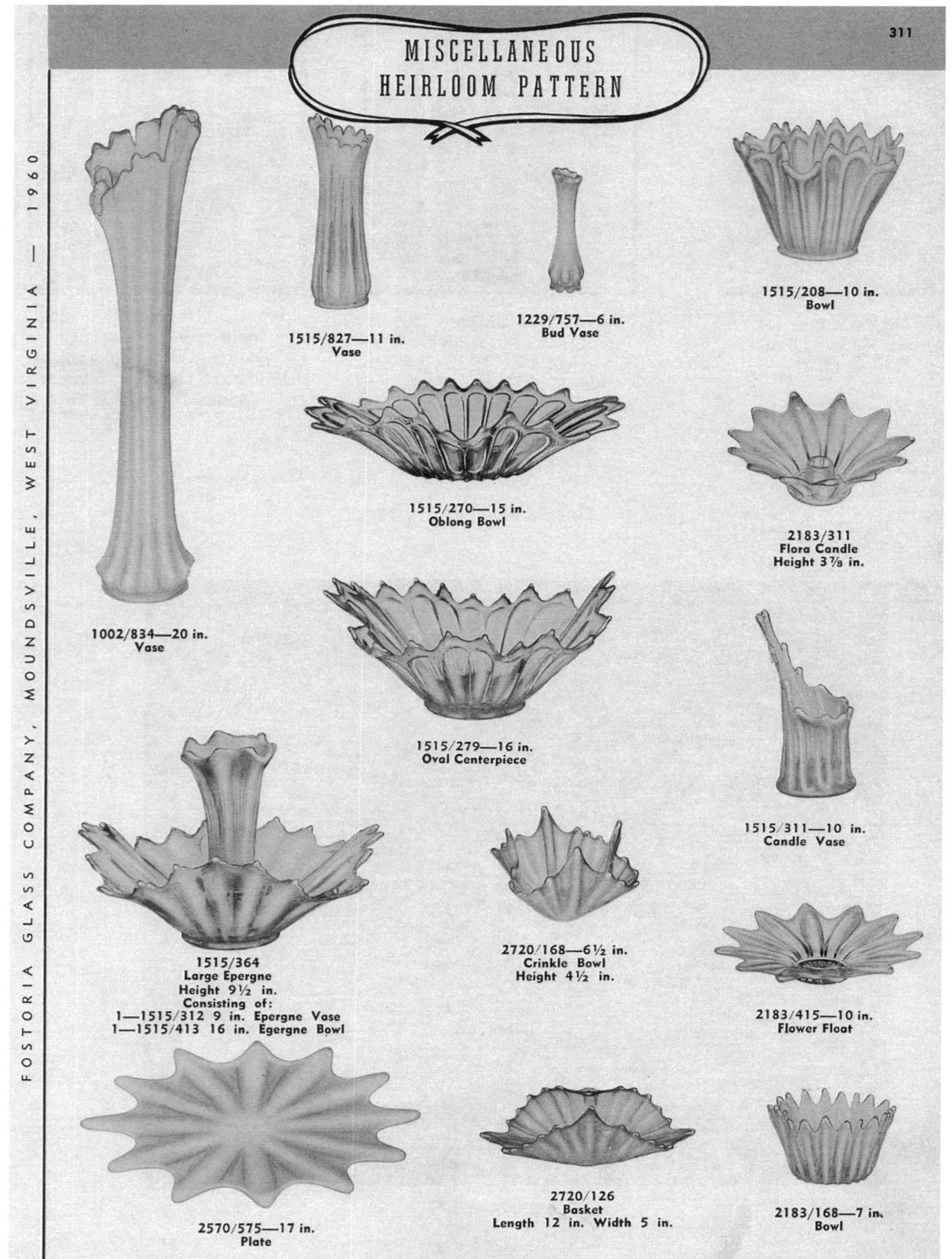

311

MISCELLANEOUS
HEIRLOOM PATTERN

FOSTORIA GLASS COMPANY, MOUNDSVILLE, WEST VIRGINIA — 1960

1002/834—20 in.
Vase

1515/827—11 in.
Vase

1229/757—6 in.
Bud Vase

1515/208—10 in.
Bowl

1515/270—15 in.
Oblong Bowl

2183/311
Flora Candle
Height 3⅞ in.

1515/279—16 in.
Oval Centerpiece

1515/311—10 in.
Candle Vase

1515/364
Large Epergne
Height 9½ in.
Consisting of:
1—1515/312 9 in. Epergne Vase
1—1515/413 16 in. Egergne Bowl

2720/168—6½ in.
Crinkle Bowl
Height 4½ in.

2183/415—10 in.
Flower Float

2570/575—17 in.
Plate

2720/126
Basket
Length 12 in. Width 5 in.

2183/168—7 in.
Bowl

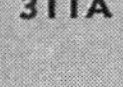

311A

MISCELLANEOUS HEIRLOOM PATTERN

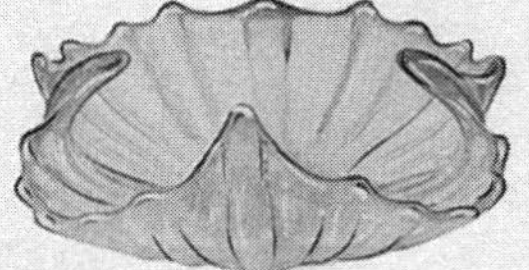

2720/170
Square Florette
Width 5⅜ in. Height 3½ in.

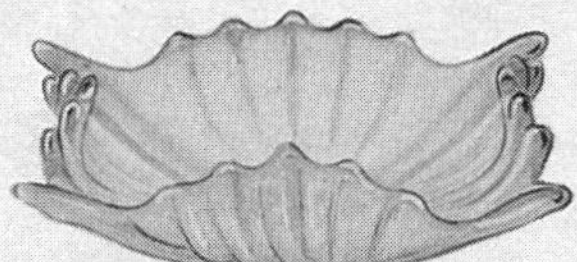

2720/191—8½ in.
Star Bowl
Width 8¼ in. Height 2¾ in.

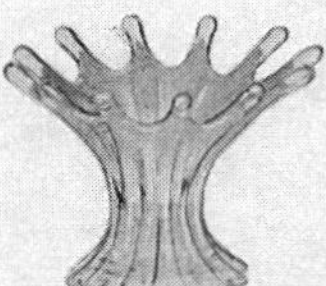

2726/311
Candleholder
Height 3½ in.

2727/202—9 in.
Square Bowl
Height 3⅝ in.

2727/231—11 in.
Shallow Bowl
Height 2 in.

2727/557—11 in.
Plate

2727/239—11 in.
Bowl Crimped
Height 2½ in.

2727/550—8 in.
Plate

2727/152—6 in.
Hanky Bowl
Height 2½ in.

FOSTORIA GLASS COMPANY, MOUNDSVILLE, WEST VIRGINIA — 1960

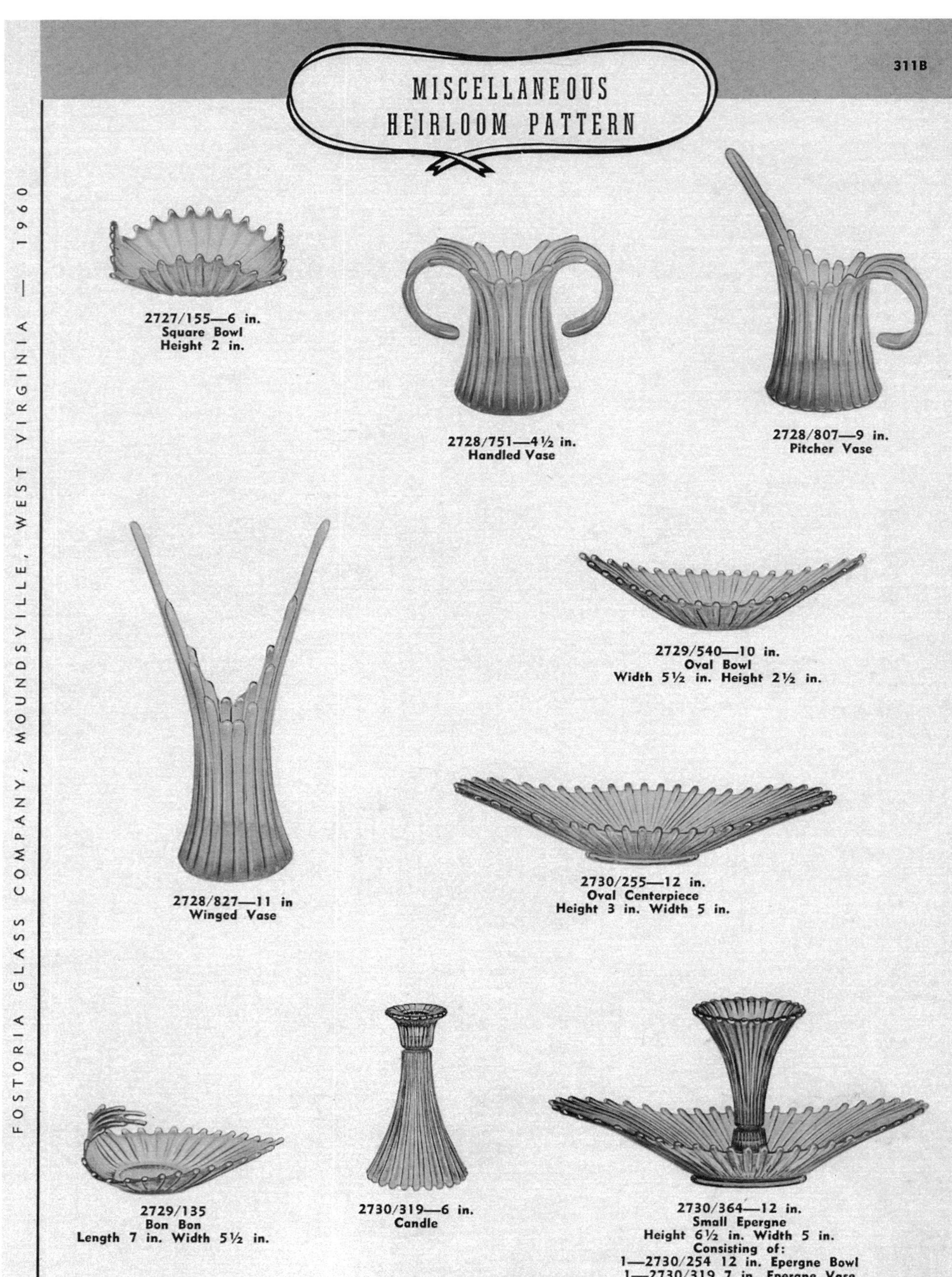

311B

MISCELLANEOUS
HEIRLOOM PATTERN

FOSTORIA GLASS COMPANY, MOUNDSVILLE, WEST VIRGINIA — 1960

2727/155—6 in.
Square Bowl
Height 2 in.

2728/751—4½ in.
Handled Vase

2728/807—9 in.
Pitcher Vase

2729/540—10 in.
Oval Bowl
Width 5½ in. Height 2½ in.

2728/827—11 in
Winged Vase

2730/255—12 in.
Oval Centerpiece
Height 3 in. Width 5 in.

2729/135
Bon Bon
Length 7 in. Width 5½ in.

2730/319—6 in.
Candle

2730/364—12 in.
Small Epergne
Height 6½ in. Width 5 in.
Consisting of:
1—2730/254 12 in. Epergne Bowl
1—2730/319 7 in. Epergne Vase

No. 1626 Individual Creamer
2⅜", 1914 Catalog

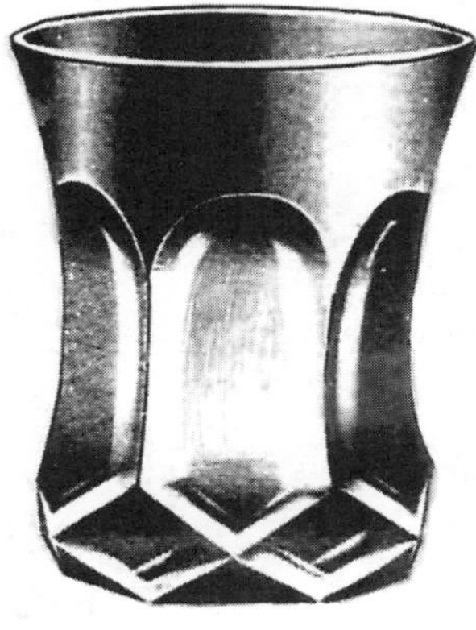

No. 1990 Table Tumbler
8½", 1914 Catalog

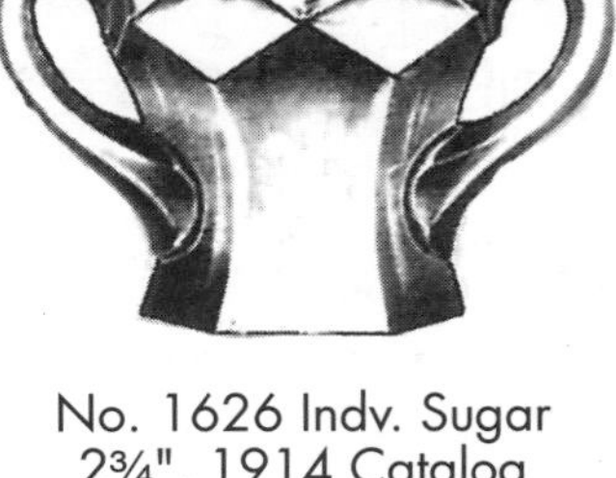

No. 1626 Indv. Sugar
2¾", 1914 Catalog

No. 1913 Sherry, 2 oz.
Height 3⅞", 1913
Catalog, Flemish Pattern

No. 5100 Footed Shaker
Optic, Glass Top
Also made in Orchid
1927 Catalog

No. 193 Shaker #1
1913 Catalog, Flemish Pattern

No. 2106 Coaster
3⅜" Diameter

No. 486 Safety Ink
1901 Catalog

No. 584 Sherbet, Handled
1901 Catalog

No. 1931 Covered Sugar
5 oz. Capacity, 1910 Catalog

No. 1712 Sugar Lid
Replacement, 1901 Catalog

No. 1931 Covered Cream
5 oz. Capacity, 1910 Catalog

Consider the Gift of Fostoria and think of these things

Footed tumblers
Cocktail glasses
Goblets
Iced-tea glasses
Teacups
A pair of compotes for candies and nuts
A cake plate
A sandwich tray
Salad plates and a salad bowl
Bread and butter plates
Salt and pepper shakers
A platter
Finger-bowls
Four low candlesticks and a flower bowl

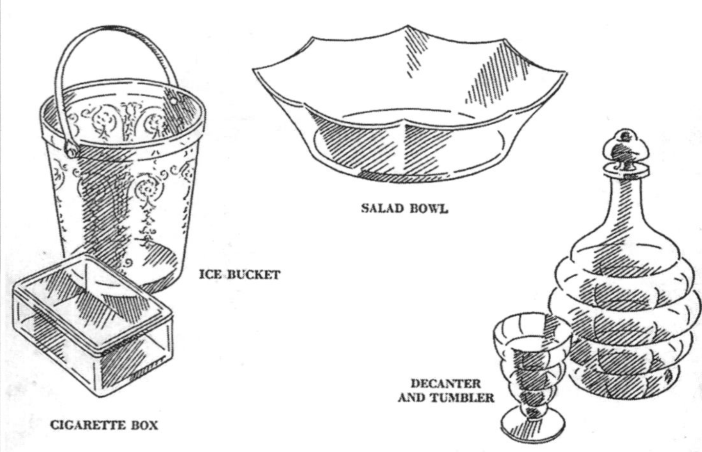

From *The New Little Book about Glassware,* a Fostoria promotional dated 1928. The footed Bath Salts Jar is shown in the 1927 Catalog as a Candy Jar. This is a blown item and possibly produced for only two years. The optic Night Set, No. 1697 was dropped after 1928. This item was also marketed as a Bedroom Set and a Carafe and Tumbler Set. It dates to at least 1917.

The Fan Vase was introduced in 1928 and was produced through 1930. Colors are Rose (Dawn), Azure, Green, and Ebony. It was used for some of the Brocades, as well as the etchings June and Versailles. The rectangular Bathroom Bottles are rare. The Powder Jar is listed in the 1927 Catalog as No. 2347 Puff and Cover. The No. 2342 Salad Bowl is 12" in diameter and possibly made only in 1927 – 1928. Colors include Orchid.

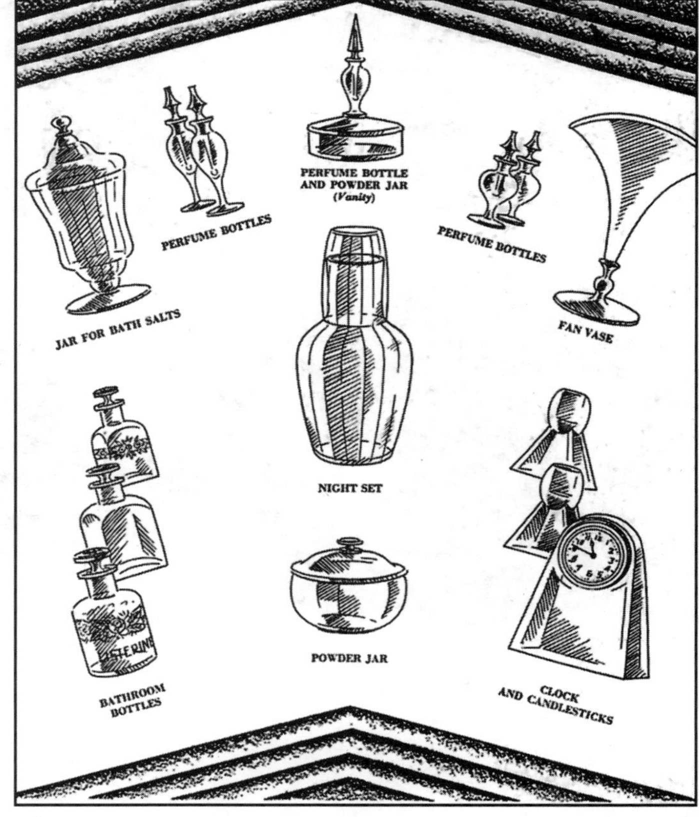

No. 598 Molasses Can
15 oz., Tin Top, 1901 Catalog

No. 417 Syrup, Silver Plated Top, Handle, 1901 Catalog

No. 597 Molasses Can
16 oz., Tin Top, 1901 Catalog

No. 16 Sponge Cup
Diameter 4", 1901 Catalog

No. 921 Syrup, Glass Lip
16 oz., 1901 Catalog

No. 300½" Jug
1901 Catalog

No. 1904 Bon Bon & Cover
Etched No. 221, 1913 Catalog

MISCELLANEOUS

Fostoria Glass Company, Moundsville, West Virginia, January 1, 1942

2594—Trindle Candlestick
Height 8 in. Spread 6½ in.

4147—7 oz. Jam Pot and Cover
Height including cover 3¾ in.
Top Diameter 3 in.
Capacity 7 oz.

4147—3 Piece Jam Set
Consisting of:
1/6 Doz. 4147 Jam Pot and Cover
1/12 Doz. 4147—7½ in. Oblong Tray

2616—Oval Candy Box & Cover
Height 3¼ in.
Width 4¾ in.

2593—Individual Salt
Height ¾ in. 1½ in. Square

2595—3 in. Sleigh
Height 1¾ in. Width 2⅛ in.

2595—4¼ in. Sleigh
Height 2¼ in. Width 3⅛ in.

2595—6 in. Sleigh
Height 3⅜ in. Width 4⅜ in.

6030—5 in. Comport
Blown Bowl

2615—Owl Book End
Height 7½ in.

2601—Lyre Book End
Height 7 in. Width 5½ in.

No.162 Jug
1901 Catalog
This pattern was first produced in Fostoria, Ohio.

No. 1723 Sundae, Tri-Pod Stem, 6 oz., 1911 Catalog

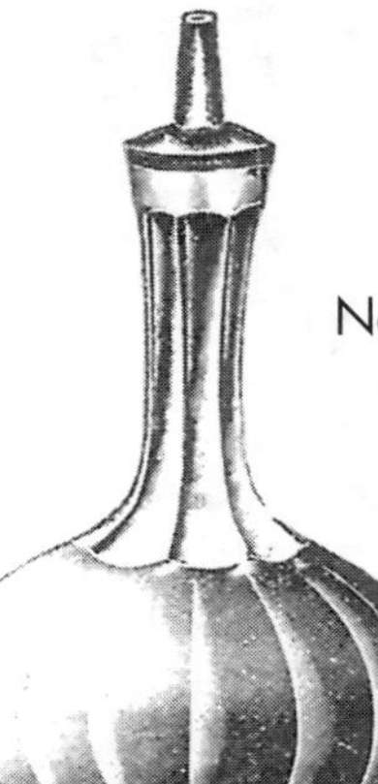

No. 315 Bitter Bottle, Optic Cut Neck, 11½ oz., 1901 Catalog

No. 2077 Muffin Cover, Pressed 6", ca.1910 Catalog

No. 2098 Pie Cover
Diameter 10½", Height 4½"
1916 Catalog

No. 444 Handled Custard
Pressed Handle
1901 Catalog
Czarina Pattern

No. 308 Government Ink
Made in 1¾", 2", 2¼", 2½", 3", 3½"

No. 1497 Comport
Diameter 8", 1906 Catalog

No. 1810 Cov. Jug
1913 Catalog

No. 1269 Sherbet
1906 Catalog

No. 1751 Indv. Cream and Plate
3" Cream, 4½" Plate
1910 Catalog

No. 597 Molasses Can
16 oz., 1901 Catalog

No. 583 Soap Dish, Opal
1902 Catalog

No. 675 Syrup, 8 oz.
Brit. Top, 1901 Catalog

No. 1549 Jug, 1-Quart
1907 Catalog

No. 2106½ Sugar Server
Height 6⅜"
Vogue Pattern

No. 459 Berry Bowl
Diameter 9", 1901 Catalog

No. 1333 Quart Decanter
1905 Catalog, Sydney Pattern

No. 305 Water Bottle
1898 Catalog

No. 2106 Ash Tray
Length 6¼"
1922 Catalog

No. 2378 Ice Bucket
Drainer and Tongs, 1927 Catalog

No. 317 Jug, Cut Neck and Star, 1901 Catalog

No. 828 Tumbler, Pressed Decoration 9, 1903 Catalog

No. 972 Berry Bowl Diameter 8", 1901 Catalog

No. 1166 Jug, Pressed Handle Panel D, 1904 Catalog

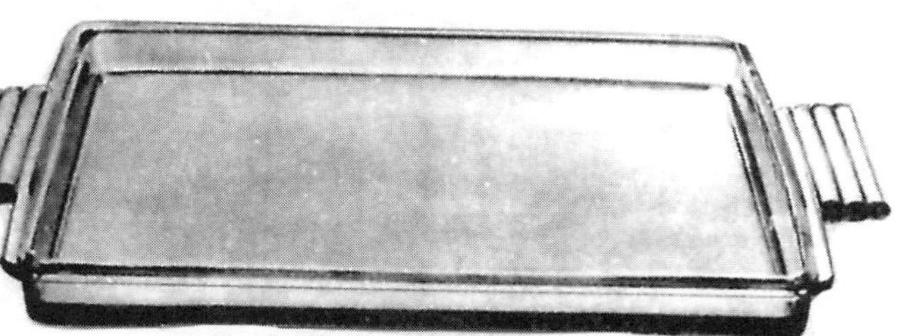

No. 2528 Cocktail Tray
11¾" x 10¾"
1935 Catalog
Made in colors

No. 551 Cream
Not Fire Polished
1898 Catalog

No. 551 Covered Butter
Not Fire Polished
1898 Catalog

No. 2228 Cov. Candy
Cutting No. 143, 4" Top
Diameter, ½ pound,
1921 Catalog

No. 1743 Jug, 5-Pint, 41 oz.
Also made 7-Pint, 59 oz.
1913 Catalog

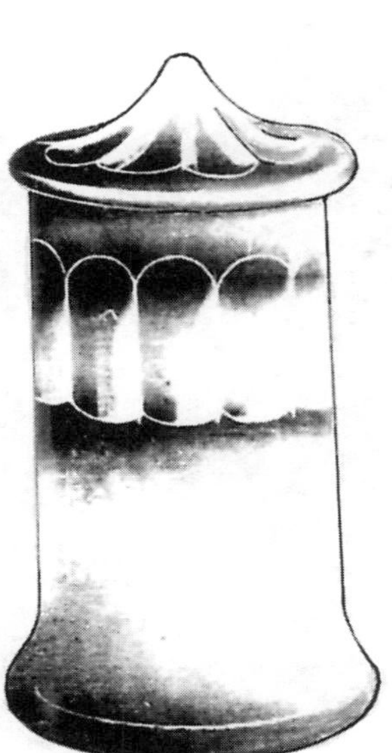

No. 1918 Small Straw Jar
Cut Neck and Cover, Height 6¼"
1900 Catalog

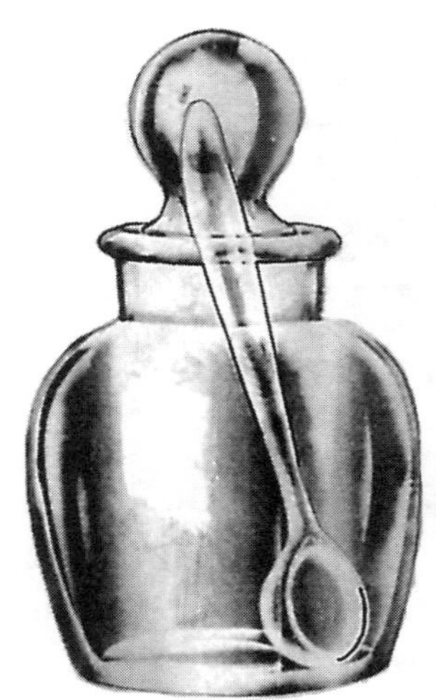

No. 1132 Bottle, Squat, 10 oz.
1902 Catalog

No. 1918 Olive Jar
Cut Stopper, Height 7"
1900 Catalog

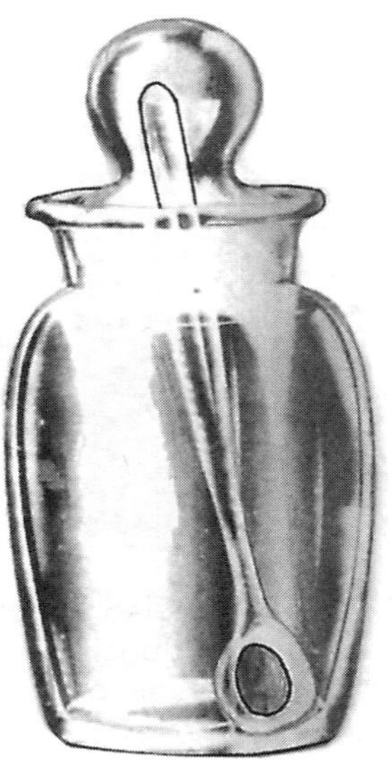

No. 963 Bottle with Glass
Spoon, 1902 Catalog

No. 1166 Jug, Pressed Handle
Panel A, 1904 Catalog

No. 2000 Condiment Tray
with No. 1913½ Indv. Salt
1927 Catalog

No. 2348 Plate, Diameter 8"
Laurel Ribbed, 1927 Catalog
Colors of Am-Gr-Bl-Orchid, also
known in Regal Blue.

No. 127 Handled Tumbler
8 oz. Capacity,
1901 Catalog

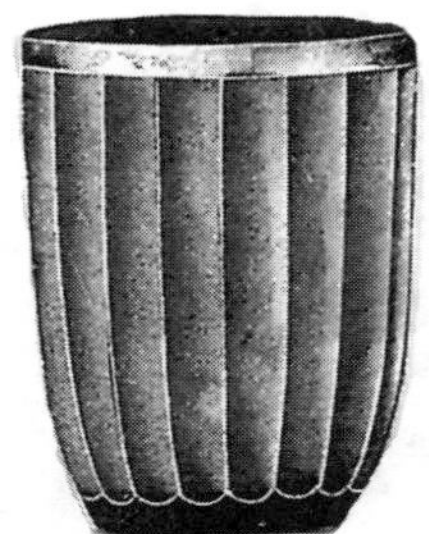

No. 900 Jelly Glass
½-Pint, 1901 Catalog

No. 476 Bitter Bottle
1901 Catalog

No. 1918 Cherry Jar
Cut Neck and Stopper
1900 Catalog

No. 1918 Rock and Rye
Cut Neck and Stopper
30 oz., Height 11¼"
1900 Catalog

No. 1461 Nappy
4½", 1907 Catalog

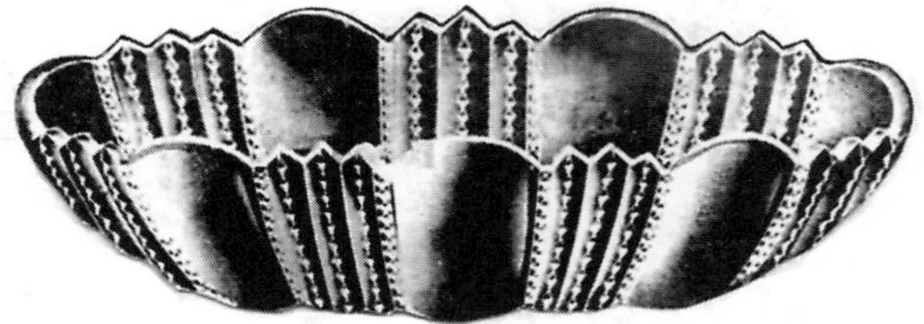

No. 954 Pickle Dish
1911 Catalog

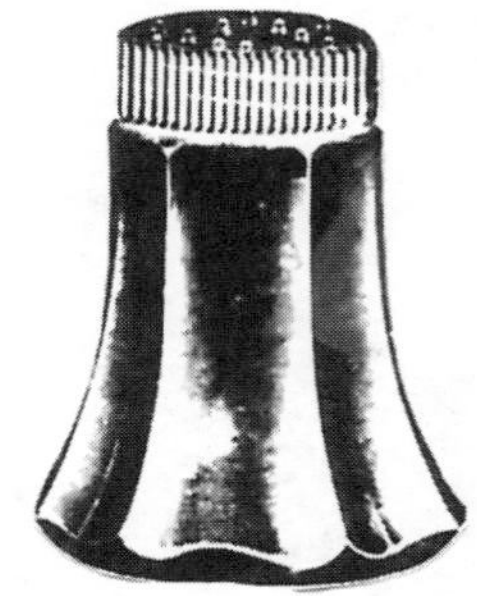
No. 1611 Shaker
Pressed, 1904 Catalog

No. 1800 Safety Ink
1901 Catalog

No. 93 Jug
3-Pint, 1901 Catalog

No. 14 Ink & Cover
1902 Catalog

Toothpick
1901 Catalog

No. 1793 Jug, Rib Optic
Blown, 75 oz. Capacity
1916 Catalog

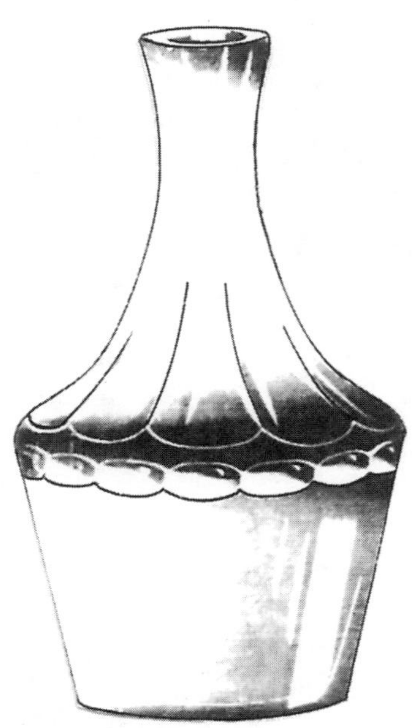
No. 1678 Bar Bottle
12 oz. Capacity
1900 Catalog

MISCELLANEOUS

FOSTORIA GLASS COMPANY, MOUNDSVILLE, WEST VIRGINIA — 1959

2056/259
Shrimp Bowl
Diameter 12¼"

24/341
4 Light Candelabra
With 40 spearhead prisms
Height 21" Spread 14"
Diameter of Base 6½"

25/342
5 Light Candelabra
With 50 spearhead prisms
Height 24" Spread 18"
Diameter of Base 8½"

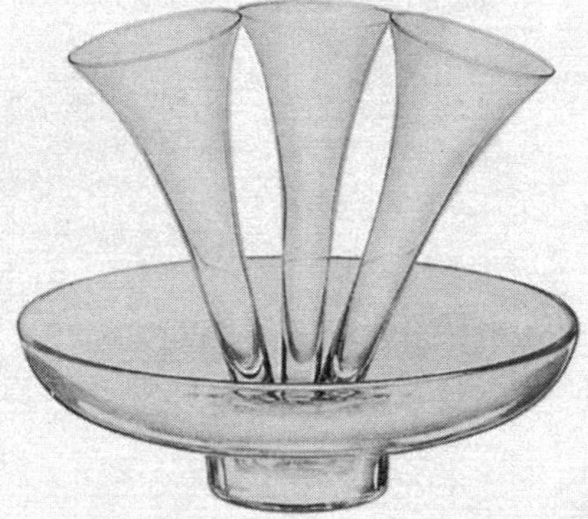

2723/364
Epergne Consisting of:
1 2723/208—10" Bowl

3 2723/312—8" Trumpet Vase

MISCELLANEOUS TABLE CHARMS

Made in Yellow, Blue, Pink, Green and Crystal Opalescent

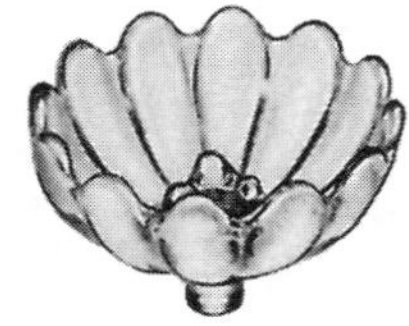

2722/460
Flora Candle/Snack Bowl
Height 3" Spread 5"

2722/334
Trindle Candle Arm
Height 2¼" Spread 7½"

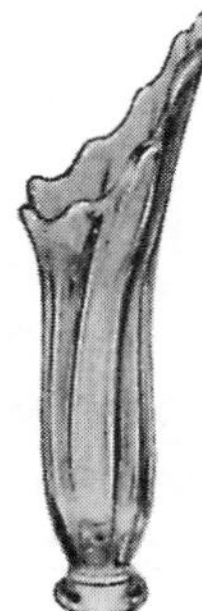

2722/312
Peg Vase
Height 8"

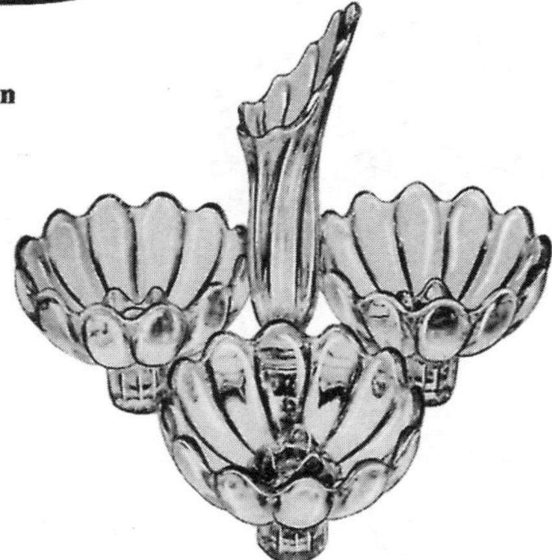

2722/364
Table Charms, Set No. 1
Consisting of:

1 2722/334 Trindle Candle Arm
1 2722/312 Peg Vase
3 2722/460 Flora Candle/Snack Bowl
Height 10" Spread 11"

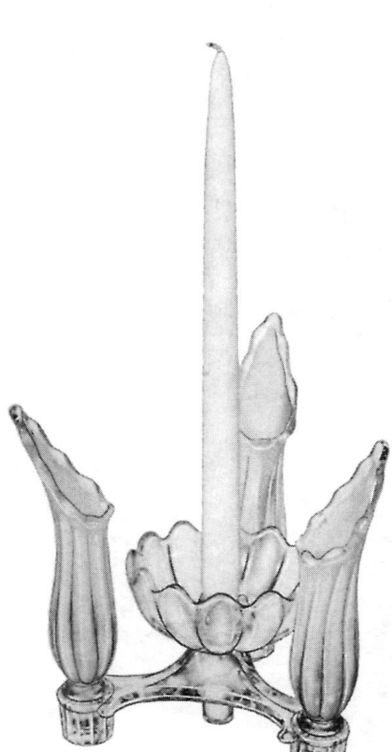

2722/364
Table Charms, Set No. 2
Consisting of:

1 2722/334 Trindle Candle Arm
3 2722/312 Peg Vase
1 2722/460 Flora Candle/Snack Bowl
Height 10" Spread 9"

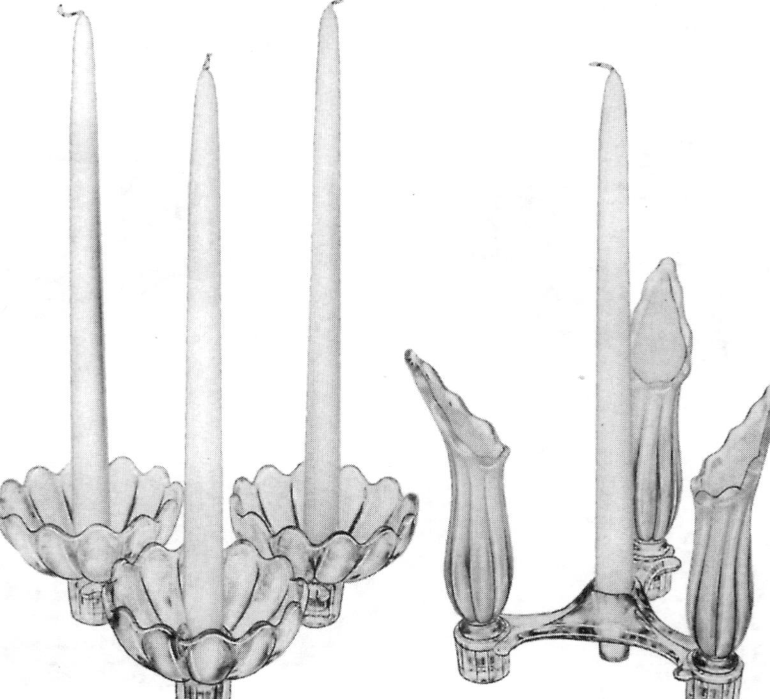

2722/364
Table Charms, Set No. 3
Consisting of:

1 2722/334 Trindle Candle Arm
3 2722/460 Flora Candle/Snack Bowl
Height 10" Spread 11"

2722/364
Table Charms, Set No. 4
Consisting of:

1 2722/334 Trindle Candle Arm
3 2722/312 Peg Vase
Height 10" Spread 9"

FOSTORIA GLASS COMPANY, MOUNDSVILLE, WEST VIRGINIA — 1959

Opal Bride Assortment Decorated Ware
All Hand Decorations and Catchy Designs in Color

No. 831 Handkerchief Box

Items made for Heininger Unger and Company
Ca. 1900

824¼	Comb and Brush Tray	831¼	Handkerchief, Cov.
825¼	Pen Tray	832¼	Glove and Cover
826¼	Pin Tray	833¼	Jewel and Cover
828¼	Hair Pin and Cover	1048	Sugar and Cover
829¼	Puff and Cover	1049	Cream
830¼	Pomade and Cover		Clock Case

No. 829½ Puff Box
Height 3½"

Fostoria made countless opal items around the turn of the century. Some were of limited production and may have never been illustrated in a catalog. The pieces that Fostoria hand decorated in the factory carried the 800½ line numbers. Note the 800 "¼" pieces that were made exclusively for the Unger firm. The 500 series denotes undecorated opal or crystal acidized pieces sold to firms other than Unger. Around 1954 Fostoria reused some of the old 800½ molds and these items were produced in Milk Glass (opaque white) and other opaques. At this time the mold number "½" was dropped.

No. 826½ Pin Tray

No. 828½ Hair Pin Box
Length 5"

No. 830½ Pomade Box

No. 832½ Glove Box
Length 10⅔"

MISCELLANEOUS

Made in Amber and Gold-Tint

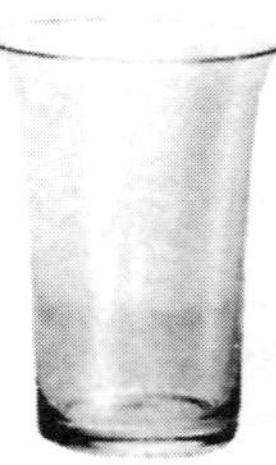

2451—5 oz. Tomato Juice Liner Blown

2451—Ice Dish
2451—7 in. Ice Dish Plate
Tomato Juice Liner Illustrated

DESIGN PATENT NO. 1858728

2451—4 oz. Crab Meat Liner Blown

2451—5 oz. Fruit Cocktail Liner Blown

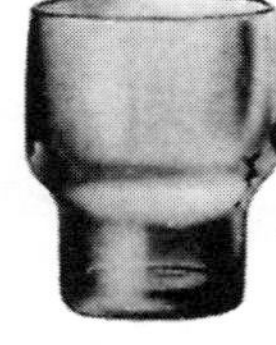

2479—5 oz. Tomato Juice Liner Pressed

2479—4 oz. Fruit Cocktail Liner Pressed

2479—4 oz. Crab Meat Liner Pressed

2272—Coaster
Diameter 4¼ in.

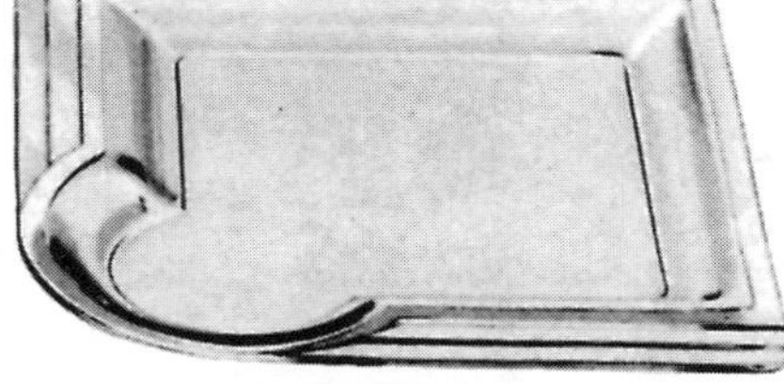

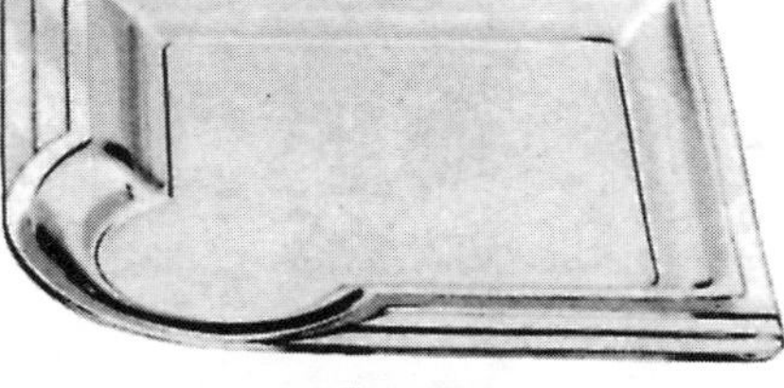

2541—Snack Plate
6¾ in. Square

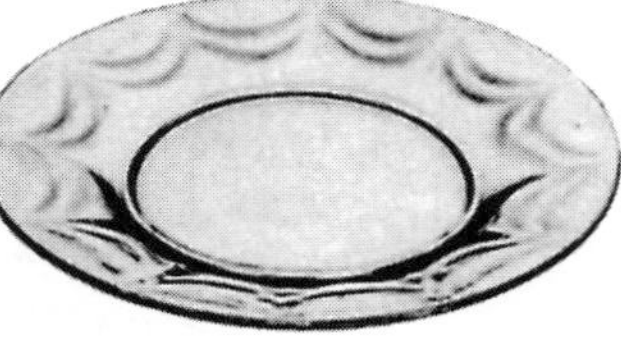

2337—Plate, Loop Optic

2442—Coaster
Diameter 4 in.

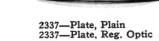

2337—Plate, Plain
2337—Plate, Reg. Optic

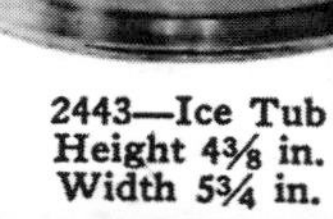

2443—Ice Tub
Height 4⅜ in.
Width 5¾ in.

2283—Plate, Plain
2283—Plate, Reg. Optic

2364—16 in. Plate

MISCELLANEOUS

FOSTORIA GLASS COMPANY, MOUNDSVILLE, WEST VIRGINIA — 1958

4168
Beverage Set
Consisting of:
½ Doz. 4168 Tumbler
Capacity 10½ oz.

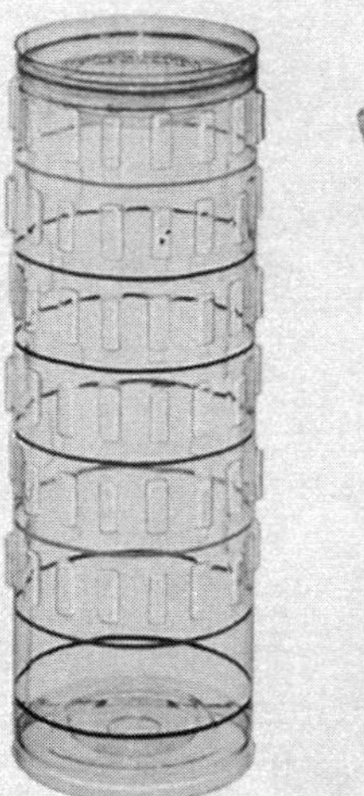

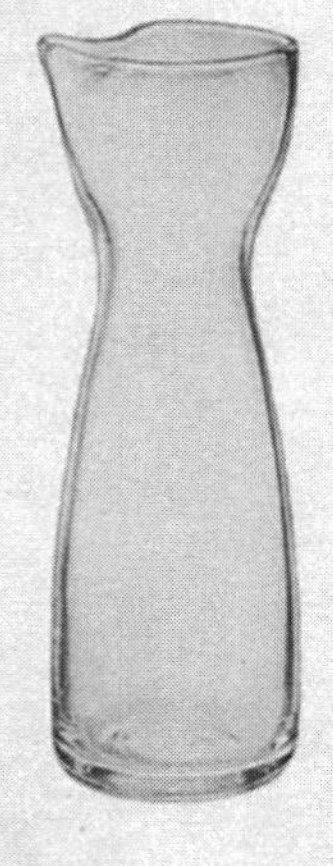

4169
Cocktail Mixer
Height 10¼ in. Capacity 28 oz.

Powder Room and Decorative Accessories

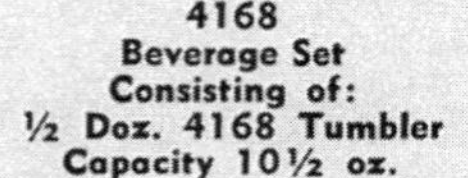

2698
Small Cologne and Cover
Height 5¼ in.

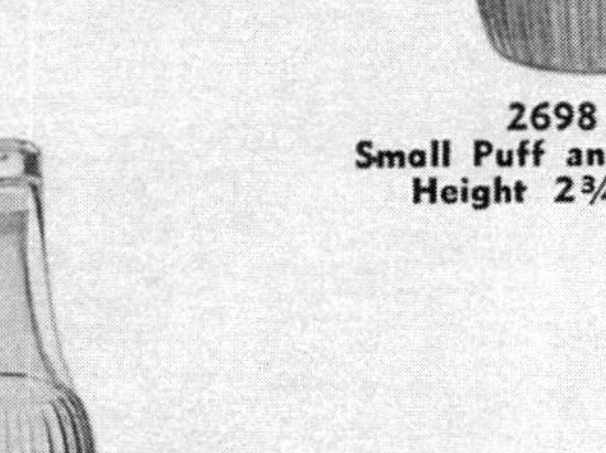

2698
Small Puff and Cover
Height 2¾ in.

2698
Bath Salts and Cover
Height 7¼ in.

2698
Large Cologne and Cover
Height 6½ in.

2698
Large Puff and Cover
Height 3½ in.

SATIN FRUIT LINE

2699
Apple and Cover
Height 5⅞ in.

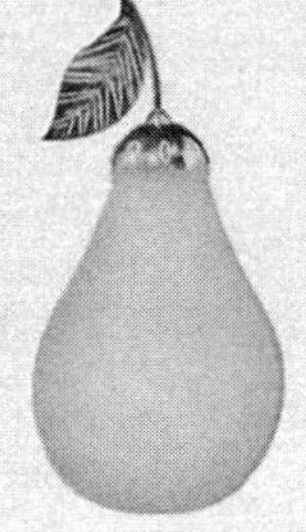

2699
Pear
Height 7⅝ in.

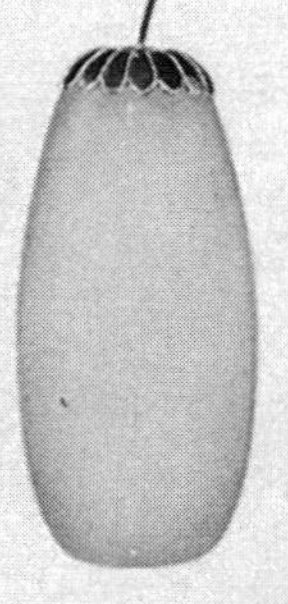

2699
Melon
Height 8 in.

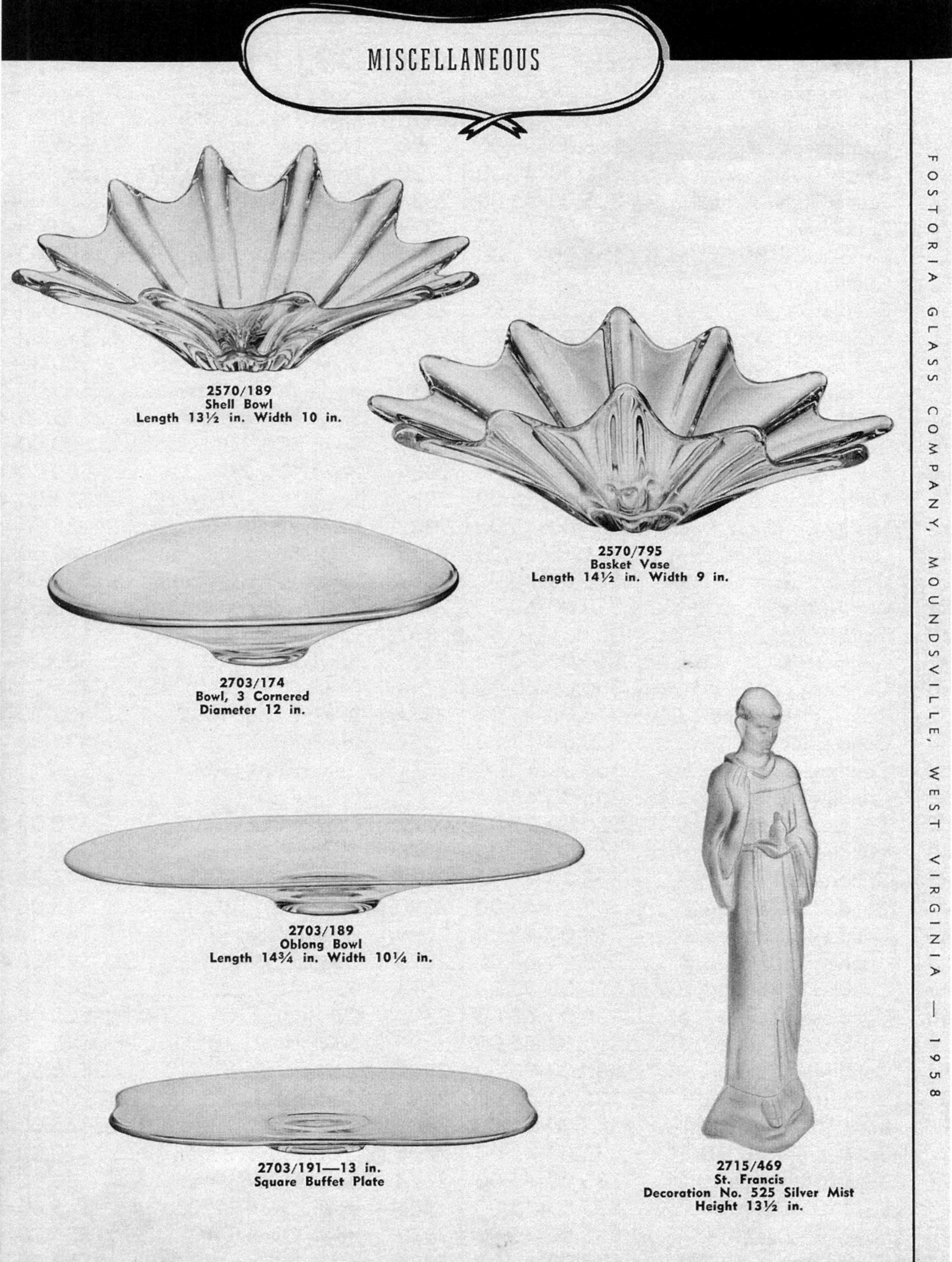

MISCELLANEOUS

2570/189
Shell Bowl
Length 13½ in. Width 10 in.

2570/795
Basket Vase
Length 14½ in. Width 9 in.

2703/174
Bowl, 3 Cornered
Diameter 12 in.

2703/189
Oblong Bowl
Length 14¾ in. Width 10¼ in.

2703/191—13 in.
Square Buffet Plate

2715/469
St. Francis
Decoration No. 525 Silver Mist
Height 13½ in.

FOSTORIA GLASS COMPANY, MOUNDSVILLE, WEST VIRGINIA — 1958

Price Guide

BOWLS & CANDLESTICKS

Suggested prices are for Crystal. Add 50% for Color.

17	Candlestick	$45.00–55.00
18	Candlestick	$45.00–55.00
19	Saucer Candle	$30.00–40.00
140	Saucer Candle, Hndl.	$35.00–45.00
737	Candlestick	$40.00–50.00
1064	Candlestick, 8"	$65.00–75.00
1192	Candlestick, 10½"	$85.00–95.00
1204	Candlestick, 8"	$50.00–60.00
1218	Candlestick, 8"	$50.00–60.00
1485	Candlestick, Cut, 8", 9½"	$75.00–85.00
1485	Candlestick, Dec., 11", 11½"	$90.00–100.00
1490	Candlestick, 8"	$60.00–70.00
1490	Candlestick, Etched, 8", 15"	$80.00–135.00
1513	Saucer Candle, Florence	$35.00–45.00
1540	Candlestick, 8½"	$45.00–55.00
1612	Candlestick, 5"	$30.00–40.00
1639	Candlestick, 8"	$50.00–60.00
1640	Lustre, 11½"	$100.00–110.00
1801	Candlestick, 8"	$60.00–70.00
1856	Candlestick, 8"	$50.00–60.00
1962	Candlestick, 2-Hndl., 9"	$75.00–85.00
1963	Candlestick, 9"	$60.00–70.00
1964	Candlestick, 9"	$60.00–70.00
1965	Candlestick, 8"	$55.00–65.00
1965	Candlestick, Etched, 8"	$80.00–90.00
2108	Candlestick, 8½"	$50.00–60.00
2183	Cabarette, 12"	$35.00–45.00
2244	Candlestick, Etched, 6"	$55.00–65.00
2244	Candlestick, Etched, 8"	$80.00–90.00
2245	Candlestick, Etched, 6"	$55.00–65.00
2245	Candlestick, Etched, 8¼"	$80.00–90.00
2268	Candlestick, Etched, 6"	$55.00–65.00
2269	Candlestick, Etched, 6"	$55.00–65.00
2275	Candlestick, Etched, 9½"	$80.00–90.00
2287	Lunch Tray, Ctr. Hndl.	$35.00–45.00
2297	Bowl "A", Deep/Shallow	$35.00–45.00
2297	Bowl "B", Deep, 10½"	$35.00–45.00
2297	Bowl "C", Deep, 10½"	$35.00–45.00
2297	Bowl "D", Deep/Shallow	$35.00–45.00
2297	Bowl "E", Deep, 12"	$35.00–45.00
2297	Candlestick	$35.00–45.00
2315	Bowl, Ftd., "A", 10½"	$40.00–50.00
2315	Bowl, Ftd. "B", 11½"	$35.00–45.00
2315	Bowl, Ftd. "C", 10½"	$40.00–50.00
2315	Bowl, Ftd. "D", 8¾"	$35.00–45.00
2320	Nap, "A", 11"	$35.00–45.00
2320	Nap, "B", w/Base, 10"	$50.00–60.00
2324	Bowl, Ftd., 10"	$55.00–65.00
2324	Candlestick, 4", 6"	$30.00–50.00
2324	Candlestick, Etched, 9"	$70.00–80.00
2324	Urn, Small	$45.00–55.00
2329	Bowl/Centerpiece, 11"	$50.00–60.00
2331	Lustre, 9"	$80.00–90.00
2333	Bowl, Ftd., 11"	$50.00–60.00
2339	Bowl, "A", w/Base	$55.00–65.00
2339	Bowl, "B", w/Base	$55.00–65.00
2339	Bowl, "C", 10", 10½"	$30.00–45.00
2339	Bowl, "D", 7"	$30.00–40.00
2339	Bowl, "E", w/Base	$55.00–65.00
2342	Bowl, 8-Sided	$35.00–45.00
2342	Bowl, Salad, 8-Sided	$40.00–50.00
2352	Candlestick, Calla Lily	$25.00–35.00
2362	Bowl/Comport, 11"	$40.00–50.00
2362	Candlestick, 9"	$50.00–60.00
2364	Bowl, Flared, 12"	$30.00–40.00
2364	Bowl, Fruit, 13"	$35.00–45.00
2364	Bowl, Salad, 10½"	$35.00–45.00
2364	Lily Pond, 12"	$35.00–45.00
2371	Centerpiece, Oval, Spiral Optic	$45.00–55.00
2372	Candle Block	$20.00–25.00
2378	Ice Bucket, Spiral Optic	$50.00–60.00
2383	Candle, Trindle, 3-Lt.	$45.00–55.00
2390	Bowl, Ftd., 12"	$55.00–65.00
2390	Centerpiece, 11"	$45.00–55.00
2390	Candle, 3"	$25.00–35.00
2394	Bowl, 12"	$45.00–55.00
2394	Candlestick, 2"	$20.00–25.00
2395	Bowl, Hndl., 10"	$45.00–55.00
2395	Candlestick, 3"	$25.00–30.00
2395	Candlestick, 5"	$30.00–35.00
2402	Bowl, 11"	$45.00–55.00
2404	Candlestick, 2"	$20.00–25.00
2424	Bowl, Flared, 9"	$30.00–40.00
2426	Bowl, Oval, 12"	$45.00–55.00
2432	Bowl, Oval, 11"	$35.00–45.00
2434	Bowl, 13"	$50.00–60.00
2441	Bowl, 12"	$45.00–55.00

2443	Bowl, Oval, 8½"	$25.00–35.00
2443	Candlestick, 4"	$35.00–45.00
2445	Bowl, 8½"	$35.00–45.00
2449	Candlestick, 6"	$35.00–45.00
2453	Lustre, 7½"	$75.00–85.00
2455	Bowl, 11"	$45.00–55.00
2455	Candlestick, 6"	$35.00–45.00
2458	Bowl, Flared, 3-Toed, 11½"	$45.00–55.00
2466	Candlestick, 3"	$25.00–35.00
2466	Plateau	$50.00–60.00
2470	Bowl, Ftd., 7", 10½"	$30.00–55.00
2470	Candlestick, 5½"	$35.00–45.00
2472	Candlestick, Duo, 4⅞"	$50.00–60.00
2480	Bowl, 2-Hndl.	$45.00–55.00
2481	Bowl, Oblong, 11"	$45.00–55.00
2481	Candlestick, 5"	$35.00–45.00
2527	Candelabra, 2-Lt., Nocturne	$105.00–110.00
2533	Bowl, Hndl., 9"	$45.00–55.00
2533	Candlestick, Duo	$35.00–45.00
2535	Bowl, Cupped, 7"	$35.00–45.00
2535	Bowl, Flared, 9"	$40.00–50.00
2535	Bowl, Hndl., 9"	$40.00–50.00
2535	Candle, 5½"	$30.00–40.00
2536	Bowl, Hndl., 9"	$40.00–50.00
2545	Lustre, Flame, 7½"	$70.00–80.00
2550	Candle Lamp, 8½"	$75.00–85.00
2563	Bowl, Viking	$55.00–65.00
2563	Candlestick, Viking	$45.00–55.00
2570	Bowl, 9", 11½"	$40.00–55.00
2574	Candlestick, Duo, 5¼"	$55.00–65.00
2594	Bowl, Hndl., 10"	$45.00–55.00
2594	Candlestick, Trindle, 8"	$65.00–75.00
2596	Bowl, Oblong, 11"	$40.00–50.00
2596	Bowl, Square, 7½"	$25.00–35.00
2596	Candlestick, 5"	$45.00–55.00
2598	Bowl, Oval, 11"	$45.00–55.00
2598	Candlestick, Duo, 7½"	$60.00–70.00
2600	Bowl, Ftd., Acanthus	$85.00–95.00
2600	Candle, Trindle, Acanthus	$155.00–175.00
2601	Bowl, Oval, Lyre	$65.00–75.00
2601	Candle, Duo, Lyre	$85.00–95.00
2634	Floating Garden	$40.00–50.00
2634	Mermaid	$145.00–165.00
2634	Mermaid w/Bowl	$185.00–205.00
2635	Madonna	$70.00–80.00
2636	Book End, Plume	$75.00–85.00
2636	Candlestick, Plume	$75.00–85.00
2636	Candlestick, Plume Duo	$95.00–105.00
2639	Bowl, Oval	$40.00–50.00
2639	Bowl, Ivy, 11"	$50.00–60.00
2639	Candlestick, Duo, Ivy	$85.00–95.00
2640	Candleholder, 6-Lt.	$125.00–145.00
2640	Garden Center, 8-Pc.	$175.00–195.00
2640	Lily Pond, 14"	$40.00–50.00
2651	Bowl, Hndl., 11"	$45.00–55.00
2652	Bowl, Hndl., 13½"	$50.00–60.00
2652	Candlestick, Trindle	$55.00–65.00
2653	Candlestick, Trindle, Baroque	$55.00–65.00
2655	Candelabra, 4-Lt.	$150.00–170.00
2655	Candlestick, 4-Lt. w/Prisms	$185.00–205.00
2667	Bowl, Ftd., 7", 9¼"	$30.00–45.00
2667	Candlestick, 2½", 6"	$20.00–40.00
2667	Comport, Ftd., 6"	$20.00–30.00
2668	Candlestick, 2½"	$15.00–20.00
2668	Hurricane Lamp, 11¾"	$45.00–55.00
4113	Candlestick, 6"	$25.00–35.00
6023	Bowl, Ftd., Blown	$50.00–60.00
6023	Candlestick, Duo, 5½"	$35.00–45.00

BROCADES

Suggested prices are for Color and/or Iridized Pieces

2276	Vanity	$240.00–260.00
2287	Tray, Lunch, Hndl.	$85.00–95.00
2292	Vase, Ftd., 8"	$85.00–95.00
2297	Bowl "A", Deep/Shallow, 12"	$85.00–95.00
2297	Bowl "C", Deep, 10½"	$75.00–85.00
2297	Bowl "E", Deep, 12½"	$85.00–95.00
2298	Candle, St. Clair	$65.00–75.00
2298	Clock, St. Clair	$200.00–220.00
2309	Flower Block, 3¾"	$25.00–35.00
2314	Candlestick, 4"	$55.00–65.00
2315	Bowl "C", Ftd., 10½"	$75.00–85.00
2322	Cologne, Stopper	$145.00–165.00
2324	Candlestick, 4"	$50.00–60.00
2327	Comport, 7"	$75.00–85.00
2329	Centerpiece, 11", 13"	$85.00–105.00
2331	Candy Box, Cov., 3-Part	$95.00–115.00
2339	Bowl, "D", 7¼"	$75.00–85.00
2342	Bowl, 12"	$85.00–95.00
2342	Tray, Lunch, Hndl.	$85.00–95.00
2350	Comport, 8"	$85.00–95.00
2359	Puff, Cov.	$95.00–115.00
2362	Bowl, 12"	$85.00–95.00

2362 Candlestick, 3" $55.00–65.00
2362 Comport, 11" $95.00–105.00
2369 Vase, Ftd., 7" $85.00–95.00
2371 Centerpiece, Oval, 13" ..$110.00–130.00
2371 Flower Holder, Oval $50.00–60.00
2372 Candlestick, 2" $40.00–50.00
2378 Ice Bucket, Gold Hndl., Tongs $115.00–135.00
2380 Confection, Cov. $110.00–130.00
4100 Vase, Optic, 8" $90.00–100.00
4103 Vase, Optic, 5" $70.00–80.00

CANDELABRA

Suggested Prices are for Crystal. Add 50% for Color or Decoration.

1 Candelabra, 4-Lt., 19" ...$450.00–550.00
13 Candelabra, 4-Lt., Pink Holders $300.00–400.00
13 Candelabra, 5-Lt., Pink Holders $450.00–550.00
13 Candelabra, 6-Lt., Pink Holders $450.00–550.00
16 Candelabra, 5-Lt., 20" ...$400.00–500.00
16 Candelabra, 6-Lt., 20" ...$450.00–550.00
22 Candelabra, 2-Lt., 20" ...$300.00–350.00
23 Candelabra, 3-Lt., 22" ...$350.00–400.00
25 Candelabra, 5-Lt., 24" ...$400.00–500.00

CANDY BOXES & JARS

Suggested Prices are for Color. Deduct 50% for Crystal.

2219 Candy Jar, Cov., Ftd.,½ lb. .$70.00–80.00
2331 Candy Box, Cov., 3-Part $65.00–75.00
2250 Candy Jar, Cov., Ftd.,½ lb. .$70.00–80.00
2380 Confection, Cov., Spiral Optic $70.00–80.00
2380 Confection, Cov. $65.00–75.00
2394 Candy Jar, Cov., 3-Toed $65.00–75.00
2395 Confection, Cov., Oval, Ftd.$80.00–90.00
2413 Urn, Cov., Ftd. $90.00–110.00
4095 Candy Jar, Cov., Ftd., Spiral Optic $75.00–85.00
5084 Candy Jar, Cov., Ftd. $70.00–80.00

CARVINGS

Suggested Prices are for Crystal. Add 50% for 19th Hole and Special Carvings.

315 Bowl, 7", 9" $50.00–60.00
892 Stemware: Goblet, Claret ...$25.00–30.00
892 Champagne, Low Sherbet ..$20.00–25.00
892 Cocktail, Oyster Cocktail $20.00–25.00
892 Wine $30.00–35.00
892 Tumbler, Ftd., 5 oz., 12 oz. ..$25.00–30.00
1769 Finger Bowl $15.00–20.00
1895 Vase (1895½) $75.00–85.00
2306 Ash Tray, 2¾", 3", 3½", 4" ..$15.00–25.00
2324 Candlestick, 3½", 6" $30.00–45.00
2337 Plate, 7", 8" $15.00–20.00
2364 Bowl, Flared, 12" $65.00–75.00
2364 Bowl, Fruit, 13" $65.00–75.00
2364 Bowl, Lily Pond, 12" $65.00–75.00
2364 Bowl, Salad, 10½" $50.00–60.00
2364 Cheese & Cracker $65.00–75.00
2364 Mayonnaise, 3-Pc. $40.00–50.00
2364 Plate, Torte, 14", 16" $65.00–85.00
2364 Tray, Lunch, Hndl., 11¼" $55.00–65.00
2391 Cigarette Box, Cov. $55.00–65.00
2419 Ash Tray, Sq. 4" $20.00–25.00
2419 Cake Plate, 2-Hndl. $55.00–65.00
2424 Bowl, Flared, 9½" $45.00–55.00
2424 Bowl, Fruit, 11½" $50.00–60.00
2424 Bowl, Reg., 8" $45.00–55.00
2424 Candlestick, 3½" $25.00–35.00
2424 Urn, Ftd., 6½", 7½" $55.00–65.00
2427 Ashtray, Oblong, 3½" $20.00–25.00
2427 Cigarette Box, Cov. $45.00–55.00
2516 Ash Tray, 5" $25.00–30.00
2545 Lamp, Colonial Candle, 7" .$85.00–95.00
2550 Ash Tray, 3¼" $20.00–25.00
2567 Vase, Ftd., 7½" $65.00–75.00
2568 Vase, Ftd., 9" $75.00–85.00
2577 Vase, 6" $45.00–55.00
2577 Vase, 15" $110.00–130.00
2577 Vase, Tapered, 8½" $75.00–85.00
2577 Vase, Wide, 5½" $50.00–60.00
2591 Vase, 15" $110.00–130.00
2596 Ash Tray, 4", Sq. $20.00–25.00
2596 Bowl, 7½", 11" $45.00–60.00
2596 Candlestick, 5", 5½" $30.00–40.00
2596 Cigarette Box, Cov., 4" $45.00–55.00
2612 Vase, 13" $90.00–110.00
2618 Ashtray, Oblong, 4½" $20.00–25.00
2618 Ashtray, Sq. 4" $20.00–25.00
2618 Cigarette, Cov., 5½" $45.00–55.00
2619 Vase, 6", 7½", 9½" $65.00–85.00
4116 Ball, 5" $80.00–90.00
4125 Vase, 11" (4125½) $50.00–60.00
4126 Vase, Ftd., 11" (4126½) $55.00–65.00

4128 Vase, 5" (4128½) $45.00–55.00
4132 Ice Bowl $50.00–60.00
4132 Vase/Ice Bowl, 5", 6", 7½" $50.00–60.00
4132 Vase, 8" (4132½) $70.00–80.00
4132 Decanter, Stopper $95.00–115.00
4132 Tumbler: 5 oz., 7½ oz., 9 oz. $20.00–25.00
4132 Tumbler: 1½ oz., 12 oz., 14 oz. $30.00–35.00
4139 Tumbler: 1¾ oz., 14 oz., 16 oz. $30.00–35.00
4139 Tumbler: 5, 7, 9, 10 , and 12 oz. $20.00–25.00
4143 Vase, Ftd., 6", 7½" $65.00–75.00
4146 Tumbler/Cordial, 1 oz. $30.00–35.00
4146 Tumbler, 4 oz., 9 oz. $20.00–25.00
4148 Ash Tray, Indv., 2½" $15.00–20.00
4148 Cigarette Holder, 2¼" $25.00–35.00
5100 Vase, Ftd., 10" $75.00–85.00
6023 Candle, Duo, 5½" $40.00–50.00

CLOCK SETS

Suggested Prices are for Color.

2063 Candle, Hndl. $30.00–40.00
2276 Vanity, Brocade $240.00–260.00
2276 Vanity, Dec. $190.00–210.00
2283 Plate, 6", 7" $13.00–18.00
2283 Plate, 8", 9" $20.00–30.00
2283 Plate, 11", 13" $25.00–35.00
2289 Vanity, Dec. $190.00–260.00
2297 Candle, 7" $50.00–60.00
2298 Candle, St. Clair, 3½", Dec. $45.00–55.00
2298 Clock, St. Clair, Dec. $180.00–200.00
2299 Candle, 5", St. Alexis, Dec. $55.00–65.00
2299 Clock, St. Alexis, Dec. $180.00–200.00
2306 Smokers Set $30.00–40.00
2352 Candle, Calla Lily $45.00–55.00

DECORATIONS

AUTUMN GLOW (IRIDESCENT)

869 Cocktail, 3 oz. $20.00–25.00
869 Cordial, 1 oz. $30.00–35.00
869 Finger Bowl (766)................$10.00–15.00
869 Fruit, 5½ oz. $10.00–15.00
869 Goblet, 9 oz. $20.00–25.00
869 Ice Tea, Hndl., 12 oz. $20.00–25.00
869 Oyster Cocktail (837) $20.00–25.00
869 Parfait, 6 oz. $25.00–30.00
869 Saucer Champagne, 5½ oz. .$20.00–25.00
869 Wine, 2¾ oz. $25.00–30.00
869 Tumbler, Table, 5 oz., 8 oz. $20.00–25.00
869 Tumbler, 2 oz., 12 oz. $25.00–30.00
1236 Jug, 6-Pt. $150.00–175.00
2283 Plate, 6", 7", 8" $10.00–20.00

BURNISHED GOLD HIGHLIGHTS, Dec. 623
HIGHLIGHTED BLUE SPRAY, Dec. 631
MARDI GRAS, Dec. 627

2513 Candy Jar, Cov., Grape Leaf..$45.00–55.00
2519 Cologne, Stopper, 5½" $45.00–55.00
2519 Puff, Cov., 4½" $45.00–55.00
2618 Cigarette, Cov., 5½" $25.00–45.00
2619 Vase, 6" $45.00–55.00
2619 Vase, 9½" $55.00–65.00
2666 Comport, 6⅞" $30.00–40.00
2666 Ribbon Bowl, 2¾" $30.00–40.00
2666 Sweetmeat, 6¾" $30.00–40.00
2666 Tid-Bit, 7½" $30.00–40.00
2677 Ash Tray, 4¾" $20.00–25.00
4116 Vase, 6" $45.00–55.00

CLUB DESIGN A, B, C, Decoration
POLKA DOT Decoration
SATURN Decoration

Add 50% for Polka Dot Decoration

2297 Bowl, Deep "A" $85.00–95.00
2324 Candlestick, 4" $25.00–35.00
2350 Ash Tray, Lg. $25.00–35.00
2350 Cream, Ftd. $20.00–25.00
2350 Cream Soup $25.00–35.00
2350 Cup, Ftd. $20.00–25.00
2350 Cup, After Dinner $20.00–30.00
2350 Plate, 6", 7" $10.00–20.00
2350 Plate, 9" $30.00–40.00
2350 Saucer, Reg., After Dinner $5.00–10.00
2350 Sugar, Ftd. $20.00–25.00
2373 Window Vase, Cov., Lg. .$175.00–195.00
2373 Window Vase, Cov., Sm. $145.00–165.00
2375 Cake Plate, 10" $50.00–60.00
2375 Lemon Dish $30.00–40.00
2387 Vase, 8" $75.00–85.00
2400 Comport $55.00–65.00
2404 Vase, 6" $55.00–65.00
2409 Vase, 7½" $65.00–75.00
2419 Plate, 6", 7" $10.00–20.00
2419 Plate, 8" $20.00–25.00
2419 Saucer, Reg., After Dinner $5.00–10.00
2421 Vase, 10½" $85.00–95.00

2427 Cigarette Box, Cov. $45.00–55.00
2430 Bowl, 11" $60.00–70.00
2430 Jelly, 7" $35.00–45.00
2430 Candy Jar, Cov., ½ lb. $75.00–85.00
2430 Mint, 5½" $35.00–45.00
2430 Vase, 8" $75.00–85.00
4020 Cocktail, Goblet $25.00–30.00
4020 Decanter, Stopper, Ftd. $110.00–130.00
4020 Jug, Ftd. $145.00–165.00
4020 Sherbet, 4 oz., 7 oz. $20.00–25.00
4020 Tumbler, 5, 10, 13, and 16 oz. $20.00–30.00
4020 Whiskey, 2 oz. $25.00–35.00
4021 Finger Bowl $15.00–20.00
4105 Vase, 8" $75.00–85.00
4120 Cocktail, Goblet $25.00–30.00
4120 Cream, Ftd. $20.00–25.00
4120 Jug, Ftd. $145.00–165.00
4120 Sherbet, 5 oz., 7 oz. $20.00–25.00
4120 Sugar, Ftd. $20.00–25.00
4120 Tumbler, 5, 10, 13, and 16 oz. $20.00–30.00
4120 Whiskey, 2 oz. $25.00–35.00
4121 Finger Bowl (4021) $15.00–20.00

EBONY WITH GOLD LINES Dec.
2297 Bowl "A", Deep $35.00–45.00
2324 Candlestick, 4" $20.00–30.00
2350 Ash Tray, Lg. $18.00–23.00
2350 Cream, Ftd. $20.00–25.00
2350 Cream Soup $20.00–25.00
2350 Cup & Saucer, After Dinner. $25.00–30.00
2350 Plate, 6", 7" $13.00–18.00
2350 Plate, 9" $30.00–40.00
2350 Sugar, Ftd. $20.00–25.00
2373 Window Vase, Lg., Sm. ..$135.00–175.00
2375 Cake Plate, 10" $30.00–40.00
2375 Lemon Dish $20.00–30.00
2387 Vase, 8" $75.00–85.00
2400 Comport, 6" $45.00–55.00
2404 Vase, 6" $55.00–65.00
2409 Vase, 7½" $65.00–75.00
2419 Plate, 6", 7", 8" $13.00–23.00
2419 Saucer, After Dinner Saucer ..$5.00–10.00
2421 Vase, 10½" $85.00–95.00
2427 Cigarette Box, Cov. $40.00–50.00
2430 Bowl, 11" $45.00–55.00
2430 Candy Jar, Cov. $65.00–75.00
2430 Jelly $25.00–35.00
2430 Mint $25.00–35.00
2430 Vase, 8" $75.00–85.00
4105 Vase, 8" $75.00–85.00

ONYX LUSTRE (IRIDESCENT) Dec.
1681 Wall Vase $145.00–155.00
2269 Candle, 6" $85.00–95.00
2276 Vanity $220.00–250.00
2283 Plate, Cupped, 13" $80.00–90.00
2297 Bowl "A", Shallow, 10" $90.00–100.00
2297 Bowl, "A", Deep 12" $110.00–120.00
2324 Candle, 4" $75.00–85.00
2327 Compote, 7" $85.00–95.00
2329 Bowl/Centerpiece, 11", 13" $110.00–130.00
2331 Candy Box, Cov., 3-Part. $110.00–120.00
2367 Bulb Bowl, 7", 8" $85.00–95.00

SPANISH LUSTRE (IRIDESCENT) Dec.
877 Claret, 10 oz. $25.00–30.00
877 Cocktail, 3½ oz. $20.00–25.00
877 Cordial, ¾ oz. $30.00–35.00
877 Goblet, 10 oz. $20.00–25.00
877 Grapefruit w/Liner $25.00–35.00
877 Oyster Cocktail, Ftd., 4½ oz. $20.00–25.00
877 Parfait, Ftd., 5½ oz. $25.00–30.00
877 Sherbet, High, Low, 6 oz. ...$20.00–25.00
877 Tumbler, Ftd., 5 oz., 9 oz. ..$20.00–25.00
877 Tumbler, Ftd., 2½ oz., 12 oz. $25.00–30.00
877 Wine, 2¾ oz. $30.00–35.00
2283 Plate, 6", 7", 8" $10.00–20.00
5100 Jug, 7-Pt. $150.00–175.00

CUT DINNERWARE, STEMWARE & TUMBLERS

Suggested Prices are for Crystal. Add 50% for Color.

1769 Bowl, Finger 4⅛" $15.00–20.00
2315 Bowl, Ftd., "A", 10½" $30.00–40.00
2324 Candle, 4" $20.00–25.00
2337 Plate, 6", 7", 8" $10.00–20.00
2350 Bowl, Baked Apple, 6" $15.00–20.00
2350 Bowl, Fruit $10.00–15.00
2350 Bowl, Soup $15.00–20.00
2350 Celery, 11" $25.00–35.00
2350 Cream, Ftd., 7 oz. $20.00–25.00
2350 Cream Soup $20.00–25.00

2350 Cup & Saucer $20.00–25.00
2350 Cup, After Dinner $18.00–23.00
2350 Pickle, 8" $20.00–25.00
2350 Plate, 9" $35.00–40.00
2350 Sugar, Ftd. $20.00–25.00
2364 Ash Tray, Indv. $10.00–15.00
2364 Bowl, Baked Apple, 6" $15.00–20.00
2364 Bowl, Flared, 12" $30.00–40.00
2364 Bowl, Fruit, 5" $10.00–15.00
2364 Bowl, Fruit, 13" $40.00–50.00
2364 Bowl, Salad, 9", 10½" $35.00–45.00
2364 Bowl, Soup, 8" $15.00–20.00
2364 Candle, 6" $25.00–35.00
2364 Cheese & Cracker $40.00–50.00
2364 Cigarette Holder, Blown, 2" $13.00–18.00
2364 Comport, 8" $35.00–45.00
2364 Lily Pond, 12" $35.00–45.00
2364 Mayonnaise, Plate, Ladle....$45.00–55.00
2364 Plate, Sandwich, 11" $30.00–40.00
2364 Plate, Torte, 14", 16" $55.00–65.00
2364 Relish, 2-Part, 2-Hndl., 6½" $25.00–35.00
2364 Relish, 3-Part, 2-Hndl., 10" .$35.00–45.00
2364 Shaker, Glass Top, 2¼", 3¼" $20.00–30.00
2364 Tray, Lunch, Ctr. Hndl. $35.00–40.00
2369 Vase, 9" $85.00–95.00
2378 Ice Bucket $65.00–75.00
2394 Bowl, 3-Toed $45.00–55.00
2394 Candlestick, 2" $20.00–30.00
2400 Comport, 6" $30.00–40.00
2419 Plate, Sq., 6", 7", 8" $10.00–20.00
2419 Saucer, After Dinner..............$4.00–9.00
2424 Bowl, Flared, 9½" $35.00–45.00
2424 Bowl, Fruit 11½" $40.00–50.00
2424 Bowl, Reg., 8" $35.00–45.00
2424 Candlestick, 3½"..............$20.00–30.00
2424 Urn, 6½", 7½"..................$55.00–65.00
2519 Vase, Grnd. Btm., 6", 7½" $25.00–45.00
2519 Vase, Grnd. Btm., 9½" $45.00–55.00
2560 Bon Bon, 7¼" $20.00–30.00
2560 Bowl, Crimped, 11½" $45.00–55.00
2560 Bowl, 2-Hndl., 11" $45.00–55.00
2560 Bowl, Crimped, 11½" $35.00–45.00
2560 Candlestick, 4", 4½" $25.00–35.00
2560 Candle, Duo $45.00–55.00
2560 Celery, 11" $30.00–40.00
2560 Cream, Ftd. $20.00–25.00
2560 Cream, Indv., 4 oz. $15.00–20.00
2560 Mayonnaise, Plate, Ladle....$25.00–45.00
2560 Olive, 6¾" $15.00–25.00
2560 Pickle, 8¾" $25.00–35.00
2560 Relish, 3-Part, 2-Hndl., 10" .$30.00–40.00
2560 Sugar, Ftd. $20.00–25.00
2560 Sugar, Indv. $15.00–20.00
2560 Sweetmeat, 2-Hndl. $20.00–25.00
2560 Tray, Lunch, Ctr. Hndl. $35.00–45.00
2567 Vase, Ftd., 7½", 8½" $65.00–85.00
2574 Cream, Ftd., 7 oz. $20.00–25.00
2574 Plate, 7", 8" $13.00–18.00
2574 Plate, Torte, 14" $40.00–50.00
2574 Relish, 3-Part, 2-Hndl., 10" .$30.00–40.00
2574 Sugar, Ftd. $20.00–25.00
2577 Vase, 6" $55.00–65.00
2577 Vase, Tapered, 8½" $70.00–80.00
2596 Bowl, Oblong, 11" $45.00–55.00
2596 Bowl, Sq., 7½" $30.00–40.00
2596 Candlestick, 5" $25.00–35.00
2619 Vase, 6½", 7½" $45.00–60.00
2619 Vase, 9½" $50.00–60.00
2666 Bon Bon, 6⅞" $20.00–25.00
2666 Bowl, Oval, 8¼" $30.00–40.00
2666 Bowl, Salad $30.00–40.00
2666 Butter, Cov., 7" $30.00–40.00
2666 Candle, Flora, 6" $20.00–30.00
2666 Cream $20.00–25.00
2666 Cream, Indv. $15.00–20.00
2666 Cup & Saucer $20.00–25.00
2666 Mayonnaise, Plate, Ladle....$35.00–45.00
2666 Pitcher, 1-Qt., 6⅞".............$60.00–70.00
2666 Plate, Canape, 7⅜" $15.00–20.00
2666 Plate, Snack, 10" $20.00–25.00
2666 Plate/Server, Torte, 14"......$50.00–60.00
2666 Relish/Server, 6⅜", 7⅜" $25.00–35.00
2666 Relish/Server, 9¾", 10¾" ..$35.00–45.00
2666 Shaker, Lg., 3¼" $20.00–25.00
2666 Sugar $20.00–25.00
2666 Sugar, Indv. $15.00–20.00
2666 Tray for Cream, Sugar, Indv.$20.00–25.00
2685 Salver, Ftd., 12¼" $65.00–75.00
4100 Vase, 8" $55.00–65.00
4103 Vase, 4" $40.00–50.00
4121 Finger Bowl $20.00–25.00
4126 Vase, Ftd., 11" (4126½) ...$80.00–90.00
4132 Vase, 8" (4132½) $70.00–80.00
4143 Vase, Ftd., 6", 7½" (4143½)..........................$60.00–75.00
6011 Jug, Ftd. $175.00–195.00
6023 Bowl, Ftd., 9"...................$70.00–80.00

6023 Candlestick, Duo $45.00–55.00
6030 Comport, 5" $45.00–55.00

Stems & Tumblers

— Brandy, 1 oz. $30.00–35.00
— Claret/Rhine Wine, 3, 3½, 4, 4¼, 4½, 4¾ oz. $30.00–35.00
— Creme De Menthe, 2 oz. $30.00–35.00
— Cocktail, 3, 3¼, 3½, 4, 4½, 4¾ oz. $20.00–25.00
— Cordial, ¾ , 1, 1¼, 1½ oz. .$30.00–35.00
— Goblet, 9, 10, 10½, 11, 11½, 15¾ oz. $25.00–35.00
— Goblet, Low, 9 oz., 10 oz. .$20.00–25.00
— Oyster Cocktail, 4, 4¼ , 4¾ oz. $20.00–25.00
— Sherbet/Champagne, 5½, 6, 6½, 7, 7½, 9 oz. $20.00–25.00
— Sherbet, Low, 4½, 5½, 6 oz. $20.00–25.00
— Sherry, 2 oz. $30.00–35.00
— Tumbler, 7, 7¼, 10, 12 oz. $25.00–30.00
— Tumbler, 5¼, 5½, 6 oz. $20.00–25.00
— Tumbler/Ice Tea, Ftd., 10, 12, 12¼, 13, 14, 16 oz. $25.00–30.00
— Tumbler, Ftd. 5, 5¼ , 5½, 6 oz. $25.00–30.00
— Tumbler, Water, Ftd., 9 oz. .$25.00–30.00
— Tumbler, Whiskey, Ftd., 20 oz. $25.00–30.00
— Wine, 3 oz. $25.00–30.00

ETCHED DINNERWARE, STEMWARE & TUMBLERS

Suggested Prices are for Crystal. Add 50% for Color.

160½ Water Bottle $80.00–90.00
300 Decanter, Stopper, 1-Qt. ...$90.00–100.00
303 Jug, 7½ oz. $25.00–35.00
303 Jug-7, Optic $80.00–90.00
318 Jug $80.00–90.00
766 Finger Bowl $15.00–20.00
858 Custard, 7 oz. $20.00–25.00
858 Finger Bowl $15.00–20.00
869 Finger Bowl $15.00–20.00
945 Grapefruit w/Liner $50.00–60.00
1236 Jug-6 ....$150.00–175.00
1465 Oil, Stopper, 5 oz. $75.00–85.00
1697 Bedroom Set $85.00–95.00
1736 Finger Bowl Plate $8.00–13.00
1769 Finger Bowl $15.00–20.00
1848 Plate, Sandwich, 9" $30.00–40.00
1851 Cream $30.00–35.00
1851 Sugar $30.00–35.00
1968 Marmalade, Cov. $70.00–80.00
2083 Salad Dressing, Stopper, 7 oz. $80.00–90.00
2138 Mayonnaise, Plate, Ladle $45.00–55.00
2267 Bowl, Ftd. $45.00–55.00
2283 Plate, 6", 7", 8" $10.00–20.00
2287 Tray, Lunch, Ctr., Hndl. $45.00–55.00
2315 Bowl, Ftd., 10½" $70.00–80.00
2315 Cream, Cast Foot $25.00–30.00
2315 Grapefruit/Mayonnaise, Ftd. $45.00–55.00
2315 Sugar, Cast Foot $25.00–30.00
2324 Bowl, Flared, Ftd., 10" ...$90.00–100.00
2324 Candlestick, 4", 6" $20.00–30.00
2327 Comport, 7" $60.00–70.00
2331 Candy Box, Cov., 3-Part .$100.00–120.00
2332 Plate, Cream Soup, 7" $10.00–15.00
2337 Plate, 6", 7", 8" $10.00–20.00
2337 Plate, 9", 10½" $25.00–36.00
2350 Bowl, Baker, 9" $70.00–80.00
2350 Bowl, Fruit, 5" $18.00–23.00
2350 Bowl/Nappy, 8" $70.00–80.00
2350 Bowl, Salad, 10" $80.00–90.00
2350 Bouillon, 2-Hndl. $20.00–25.00
2350 Butter, Cov., Rd. $135.00–155.00
2350 Celery, 11" $30.00–40.00
2350 Cereal, 6" $20.00–25.00
2350 Comport, 8" $50.00–60.00
2350 Cream, Ftd. $20.00–25.00
2350 Cream Soup, 2-Hndl. $20.00–25.00
2350 Cup & Saucer $20.00–25.00
2350 Cup & Saucer, After Dinner. $30.00–40.00
2350 Pickle, 9" $25.00–35.00
2350 Plate, 6", 7" $10.00–15.00
2350 Plate, Bouillon/Cream Soup ..$8.00–13.00
2350 Plate, Salad, 8" $15.00–20.00
2350 Plate, Soup $15.00–20.00
2350 Plate, Dinner, 9" $30.00–40.00
2350 Platter, 10½" $50.00–60.00
2350 Relish, 3-Part $35.00–45.00
2350 Sauce Boat w/Plate $85.00–95.00
2350 Soup, 7" $20.00–30.00
2350 Sugar, Ftd. $20.00–25.00
2364 Ash Tray, Indv. $8.00–13.00
2364 Bowl, Baked Apple, 6", 8" .$20.00–30.00
2364 Bowl, Fruit, 13" $60.00–70.00

2364	Bowl, Flared, 12"	$60.00–70.00
2364	Bowl, Salad, 9", 10½"	$55.00–70.00
2364	Candle, Trindle	$75.00–85.00
2364	Candy Jar, Cov., Blown, 4"	$75.00–85.00
2364	Celery, 11"	$30.00–40.00
2364	Cheese & Cracker	$50.00–60.00
2364	Cigarette Holder, Blown, 2"	$20.00–25.00
2364	Comport, 8"	$60.00–70.00
2364	Lily Pond, 12"	$50.00–60.00
2364	Mayonnaise, Plate, Ladle	$45.00–55.00
2364	Plate, Crescent Salad, 7½"	$25.00–35.00
2364	Pickle, 8"	$25.00–35.00
2364	Plate, Sandwich, 11"	$40.00–50.00
2364	Plate, Torte, 14", 16"	$70.00–90.00
2364	Relish, 2-Part, 2-Hndl.	$25.00–35.00
2364	Relish, 3-Part, 2-Hndl.	$35.00–45.00
2364	Shaker, 2¼", 2⅝"	$20.00–25.00
2364	Soup, 8"	$25.00–30.00
2364	Tray, Lunch, Ctr. Hndl.	$55.00–65.00
2367	Bowl, Ftd., 7"	$55.00–65.00
2368	Cheese & Cracker	$50.00–60.00
2369	Vase, Ftd., 9"	$85.00–95.00
2375	Bon Bon, 2-Hndl.	$20.00–25.00
2375	Bowl, Baker, 9"	$70.00–80.00
2375	Bowl, Flared, 12"	$90.00–100.00
2375	Bowl, Fruit, 5"	$18.00–23.00
2375	Bowl/Centerpiece, Rolled Edge	$90.00–100.00
2375	Bouillon, 2-Hndl.	$20.00–25.00
2375	Candle, 3"	$25.00–35.00
2375	Candle, Rolled Edge	$25.00–35.00
2375	Cereal, 6"	$20.00–25.00
2375	Cheese & Cracker	$50.00–60.00
2375	Comport, 7"	$60.00–70.00
2375	Cream, Ftd.	$20.00–25.00
2375	Cream Soup, 2-Hndl.	$20.00–25.00
2375	Cup, Ftd., & Saucer	$20.00–25.00
2375	Cup & Saucer, After Dinner	$30.00–40.00
2375	Ice Bucket, Metal Hndl.	$80.00–90.00
2375	Lemon Dish, 2-Hndl.	$20.00–25.00
2375	Mayonnaise, Plate, Ladle	$50.00–60.00
2375	Oil, Stopper, Ftd.	$100.00–120.00
2375	Plate, 6", 7", 8"	$10.00–20.00
2375	Plate, 9", 10"	$35.00–45.00
2375	Plate, Bouillon, Cream Soup	$8.00–13.00
2375	Plate, Cake, 2-Hndl., 10"	$45.00–55.00
2375	Platter, Oval, 12"	$65.00–75.00
2375	Relish, 2-Part, 8½"	$25.00–35.00
2375	Sauce Boat & Tray	$85.00–95.00
2375	Shaker, Ftd., 3½"	$35.00–45.00
2375	Soup, 7"	$25.00–30.00
2375	Sugar, Ftd.	$20.00–25.00
2375	Sugar, Cov., Ftd.	$50.00–60.00
2375	Sweetmeat, 2-Hndl.	$20.00–25.00
2375	Tray, Ctr. Hndl., 11"	$55.00–65.00
2375	Whip Cream, Hndl., w/Ladle	$40.00–50.00
2378	Ice Bucket	$75.00–85.00
2394	Bowl, 3-Toed, 12"	$60.00–70.00
2394	Candlestick, 3-Toed	$20.00–30.00
2394	Candy, Cov., 1 lb.	$75.00–85.00
2400	Comport, 6"	$50.00–60.00
2419	Plate, 6", 7"	$8.00–13.00
2419	Relish, 5-Part, 13¼"	$75.00–85.00
2419	Saucer, After Dinner Saucer	$7.00–10.00
2430	Bowl, 11"	$50.00–60.00
2430	Candlestick, 2"	$25.00–30.00
2430	Candy, Cov., ½-lb.	$65.00–75.00
2430	Jelly, 7"	$25.00–35.00
2430	Mint, 5½"	$20.00–30.00
2430	Vase, 3¾"	$45.00–55.00
2430	Vase, 8"	$65.00–75.00
2440	Celery, 11½"	$35.00–45.00
2440	Cream, Ftd.	$20.00–25.00
2440	Cup & Saucer	$20.00–25.00
2440	Pickle, 8½"	$25.00–35.00
2440	Plate, Cake, 2-Hndl.	$45.00–55.00
2440	Plate, Dinner	$35.00–45.00
2440	Relish, 3-Part, 3-Hndl.	$35.00–45.00
2440	Sugar, Ftd.	$20.00–25.00
2470	Bowl, "Hugh", 10½"	$75.00–85.00
2470	Vase, Ftd., "Hugh", 10"	$85.00–95.00
2472	Candlestick, Duo, 5"	$80.00–90.00
2482	Candlestick, Trindle, 6¾"	$110.00–130.00
2484	Bowl, 2-Hndl., 10"	$70.00–80.00
2492	Nappy, 1-Hndl., Reg.	$25.00–30.00
2496	Bon Bon, 3-Toed	$25.00–35.00
2496	Bowl, Flared, 12"	$60.00–70.00
2496	Bowl, Nut, 3-Toed, Cupped	$30.00–40.00
2496	Bowl, 2-Hndl., 4-Toed, 10½"	$70.00–80.00
2496	Bowl/Serving, 2-Hndl., 8½"	$45.00–55.00
2496	Candlestick, 4", 5½"	$25.00–40.00
2496	Candlestick, Duo, 4½"	$55.00–65.00
2496	Candlestick, Trindle, 6"	$110.00–130.00
2496	Candy Box, Cov., 3-Part	$85.00–95.00
2496	Celery, 11"	$40.00–50.00

2496 Cheese & Cracker $50.00–60.00
2496 Cup & Saucer $20.00–25.00
2496 Ice Bucket, Metal Hndl. $80.00–90.00
2496 Jelly, Cov., Stemmed $65.00–75.00
2496 Mayonnaise, 2-Part, 2-Hndl. $35.00–45.00
2496 Mayonnaise, Plate, Ladle....$45.00–50.00
2496 Nappy, 1-Hndl, Flared $25.00–30.00
2496 Nappy, 1-Hndl., Reg..........$25.00–30.00
2496 Nappy, 1-Hndl, Sq., 4" $25.00–30.00
2496 Nappy, 3-Corner, 4⅝" $25.00–30.00
2496 Pickle, 8"..........................$25.00–35.00
2496 Plate, 6", 7" $10.00–15.00
2496 Plate, 8", 9" $20.00–35.00
2496 Plate, Cake, 2-Hndl, 10" ..$45.00–55.00
2496 Plate, Torte, 14" $70.00–80.00
2496 Relish, 2-Part, 2-Hndl., Sq...$25.00–35.00
2496 Relish, 3-Part, 2-Hndl., 10" .$50.00–60.00
2496 Relish, 4-Part, 2-Hndl., 10" .$50.00–60.00
2496 Sauce Dish, 2-Hndl., Oblong $30.00–40.00
2496 Shaker, 2¾" $25.00–35.00
2496 Sugar, Ftd., 3½"...............$20.00–25.00
2496 Sugar, Indv., 2⅞" $15.00–20.00
2496 Sweetmeat, 2-Hndl, Sq.......$20.00–25.00
2496 Tid Bit, 3-Toed, 8¼" $25.00–35.00
2496 Tray, Ctr. Hndl., Lunch $55.00–65.00
2496 Tray for Cream, Sugar, Indv. $20.00–25.00
2496 Tray, Oval, 2-Hndl., 8".......$25.00–35.00
2496 Tray, Torte, 14" $70.00–80.00
2510 Candelabra, 2-Lt., 16 Prism..........................$175.00–195.00
2545 Bowl, Flame, Oval, 12½"...$75.00–85.00
2545 Candlestick, Flame, 4½" $35.00–45.00
2545 Candlestick, Flame, Duo $75.00–85.00
2545 Candelabra, Flame, 2-Lt. $145.00–165.00
2545 Lunch Tray, Flame, Hndl......$65.00–75.00
2545 Lustre, Flame, 7½" $75.00–85.00
2545 Vase, Flame, 10"...............$75.00–85.00
2560 Bowl, Cereal, 6" $15.00–20.00
2560 Bowl, Crimped, 10", 11½" $45.00–60.00
2560 Bowl, Flared, 12" $60.00–70.00
2560 Bowl, Fruit, 5"..................$10.00–15.00
2560 Bowl, Fruit, 13"................$55.00–65.00
2560 Bowl, Hndl., 11" $50.00–60.00
2560 Bowl, Salad, Deep, 10" $50.00–60.00
2560 Candlestick, 4", 4½" $25.00–35.00
2560 Candlestick, Duo $55.00–65.00
2560 Celery, 13"......................$30.00–40.00
2560 Cheese & Cracker $50.00–60.00
2560 Comport, 6" $50.00–60.00
2560 Cream, Ftd., 7 oz. $20.00–25.00
2560 Cream, Indv., Ftd...............$15.00–20.00
2560 Cup & Saucer $20.00–25.00
2560 Ice Bucket, Metal Hndl. $80.00–90.00
2560 Mayonnaise, Plate, Ladle....$45.00–55.00
2560 Mayonnaise, 2-Part, Ladle ..$45.00–55.00
2560 Oil, Stopper, 3 oz. $70.00–80.00
2560 Olive, 5¾", 6" $20.00–30.00
2560 Pickle, 8¾" $25.00–35.00
2560 Plate, 6", 7" $10.00–15.00
2560 Plate, 8", 9" $20.00–35.00
2560 Relish, 2-Part, 2-Hndl..........$25.00–35.00
2560 Relish, 3-Part, 2-Hndl..........$35.00–45.00
2560 Relish, 4-Part, 10" $45.00–55.00
2560 Relish, 5-Part, 13¼"...........$50.00–60.00
2560 Shaker, Ftd., 2⅞" $35.00–45.00
2560 Sugar, Ftd., 3½"................$20.00–25.00
2560 Sugar, Ftd., Indv. $15.00–20.00
2560 Tray for Cream, Sugar, Indv. $20.00–25.00
2567 Vase, Ftd., 7½" $60.00–70.00
2568 Vase, Ftd., 9"....................$70.00–80.00
2574 Bon Bon, 5"......................$20.00–25.00
2574 Bowl, Flared, 12"..............$55.00–65.00
2574 Bowl, Fruit, 13"................$55.00–65.00
2574 Bowl, Serving, 2-Hndl., 8½"...............................$30.00–40.00
2574 Bowl, 2-Hndl., 9½"............$45.00–55.00
2574 Candlestick, 4", 6" $25.00–35.00
2574 Celery, 10½"....................$30.00–40.00
2574 Comport, 5" $45.00–55.00
2574 Cream, Ftd., 6½ oz. $20.00–25.00
2574 Cream, Ftd., Indv...............$15.00–20.00
2574 Cup & Saucer $20.00–25.00
2574 Ice Tub, 6½" $45.00–55.00
2574 Lemon, 6½" $20.00–25.00
2574 Mayonnaise, Plate, Ladle....$45.00–55.00
2574 Oil, Stopper, 4½ oz...........$70.00–80.00
2574 Olive, 6" $20.00–25.00
2574 Pickle, 8"..........................$25.00–35.00
2574 Plate, 8" $15.00–20.00
2574 Plate, Cake, 2-Hndl............$45.00–55.00
2574 Plate, Torte, 14" $65.00–75.00
2574 Relish, 3-Part.....................$20.00–40.00
2574 Shaker, 2⅝" $25.00–35.00
2574 Sugar, Ftd.........................$20.00–25.00
2574 Sugar, Ftd., Indv. $15.00–20.00

2574	Sweetmeat, 5¼"	$20.00–30.00
2574	Tray, Muffin, Hndl, 8"	$25.00–35.00
2574	Whip Cream, 5"	$20.00–30.00
2586	Syrup, Sani-Cut	$85.00–95.00
2594	Bowl, Hndl., 10"	$75.00–85.00
2594	Candlestick, 5½"	$25.00–35.00
2594	Candlestick, Trindle	$85.00–105.00
2596	Bowl, Oblong, 11"	$75.00–85.00
2596	Candlestick, 5"	$25.00–35.00
2614	Vase, 10"	$100.00–120.00
2619	Vase, 6", 7", 9"	$65.00–95.00
2630	Bowl, Flared, 8"	$35.00–45.00
2630	Bowl/Serving Dish, 2-Hndl.	$35.00–45.00
2630	Bowl, Snack	$25.00–35.00
2630	Bowl, 2-Hndl.	$40.00–50.00
2630	Bowl, Utility, 2-Hndl.	$40.00–50.00
2630	Butter, Cov., 1 lb.	$45.00–55.00
2630	Candy Jar, Cov., 7"	$60.00–70.00
2630	Cheese & Cracker	$50.00–60.00
2630	Comport, 4⅜"	$45.00–55.00
2630	Cream, Ftd.	$20.00–25.00
2630	Cream, Ftd., Indv.	$15.00–20.00
2630	Cup & Saucer	$20.00–25.00
2630	Ice Bucket, Hndl.	$80.00–90.00
2630	Jug, Ice, 3-Pt.	$90.00–100.00
2630	Mayonnaise, 2-Part	$40.00–50.00
2630	Mustard, Cov.	$55.00–65.00
2630	Pickle, 8¾"	$25.00–35.00
2630	Pitcher, Cereal, Ftd.	$75.00–85.00
2630	Plate, 6", 7"	$10.00–15.00
2630	Plate, 8", 9", 10½"	$20.00–35.00
2630	Plate, Cake, 2-Hndl.	$45.00–55.00
2630	Plate, Torte, 14", 16"	$70.00–90.00
2630	Relish, 2-Part	$25.00–35.00
2630	Relish, 3-Part	$35.00–45.00
2630	Salver, Ftd., 12¼"	$65.00–75.00
2630	Shaker	$25.00–35.00
2630	Sugar, Ftd.	$20.00–25.00
2630	Sugar, Ftd., Indv.	$15.00–20.00
2630	Tid-Bit, 3-Pc.	$65.00–75.00
2630	Tray, Ctr., Hndl.	$55.00–65.00
2630	Tray for Cream, Sugar, Indv.	$20.00–25.00
2630	Tray, Snack, 10½"	$30.00–40.00
2630	Tray, Torte, 14", 16"	$70.00–90.00
2630	Vase, 2-Hndl., 7½"	$65.00–75.00
2630	Vase, Bud, 6"	$25.00–45.00
2630	Vase, Oval, 8½"	$45.00–55.00
2657	Vase, Ftd., 10½"	$70.00–80.00
2660	Vase, Flip, 8"	$75.00–85.00
2666	Bowl, Oval, 8¼"	$35.00–45.00
2666	Butter Pat, 3½"	$8.00–13.00
2666	Candle, Flora, 6"	$25.00–35.00
2666	Celery, 9"	$25.00–35.00
2666	Cream, 3½"	$20.00–25.00
2666	Cream, Indv.	$15.00–20.00
2666	Cup & Saucer	$20.00–25.00
2666	Pickle, 7¼"	$25.00–35.00
2666	Pitcher, 1-Pt.	$55.00–65.00
2666	Pitcher, 3-Pt.	$65.00–75.00
2666	Pitcher, 1-Qt.	$75.00–85.00
2666	Plate, 7"	$10.00–15.00
2666	Plate, 10"	$30.00–40.00
2666	Plate/Serving/Torte, 14"	$65.00–75.00
2666	Plate, Snack	$25.00–35.00
2666	Relish, 2-Part	$25.00–35.00
2666	Relish, 3-Part	$30.00–40.00
2666	Shaker, Lg., 3¼"	$20.00–25.00
2666	Sugar, 2⅝"	$20.00–25.00
2666	Sugar, Indv.	$15.00–20.00
2666	Tray for Cream, Sugar, Indv.	$20.00–25.00
4021	Finger Bowl	$15.00–20.00
4095	Finger Bowl	$15.00–20.00
4095	Jug, Ftd.	$165.00–195.00
4095	Nappy, Cov.	$70.00–80.00
4100	Vase, 8"	$70.00–80.00
4103	Vase, 4"	$60.00–70.00
4121	Finger Bowl	$15.00–20.00
4121	Vase, 5"	$60.00–70.00
4126	Vase, Ftd., 11"	$70.00–80.00
4128	Vase, 5"	$60.00–70.00
4132	Vase/Ice Bowl	$60.00–70.00
4132	Vase, Ftd., 6", 7½"	$65.00–85.00
4143	Vase, Ftd., 6", 7½"	$60.00–80.00
5000	Jug, Ftd.	$165.00–195.00
5000	Shaker, Ftd.	$40.00–50.00
5082	Grapefruit (5082½)	$45.00–55.00
5092	Vase, Bud, Ftd., 8"	$65.00–75.00
5100	Shaker, Ftd., Sm.	$20.00–30.00
5100	Vase, 10"	$85.00–95.00
6011	Jug, Ftd., 53 oz.	$165.00–195.00
6021	Vase, Bud, Ftd., 6"	$60.00–70.00
6023	Bowl, Ftd.	$85.00–95.00
6023	Candlestick, Duo	$55.00–65.00
6023	Comport, 5"	$50.00–60.00
6030	Comport, 6"	$45.00–55.00

Stems & Tumblers

—	Brandy, 1 oz.	$35.00–40.00

—	Champagne, 5, 5½, 6, 6½, 7, 7¼ oz.	$20.00–25.00
—	Claret, 4 oz., 4½ oz.	$30.00–35.00
—	Claret/Hollow Stem, 6 oz.	$30.00–35.00
—	Cocktail, 2½, 3, 3½, 3¾, 4, 4½, 5½ oz.	$20.00–25.00
—	Cordial, ¾ oz., 1 oz., 1¼ oz.	$35.00–40.00
—	Goblet, 9, 9½, 9¾, 10, 11, 11¼ oz.	$25.00–30.00
—	Goblet, Low, 9 oz., 10 oz.	$25.00–30.00
—	Oyster Cocktail, 4½, 5½ oz.	$20.00–25.00
—	Parfait, 5, 5½, 6, 6¾ oz.	$30.00–35.00
—	Sherbet, Low, 5, 5½, 6, 6½, 7, 7¼ oz.	$20.00–25.00
—	Sherbet, High, 5, 5½, 6, 7 oz.	$20.00–25.00
—	Sherry, 2 oz.	$35.00–40.00
—	Tumbler, 4, 5, 7, 7½, 8, 9 oz.	$25.00–30.00
—	Tumbler 3 oz., 12 oz., 14 oz.	$30.00–35.00
—	Tumbler, Ftd., 2, 2½, 3, 3½ oz.	$25.00–30.00
—	Tumbler, Ftd., 4, 5, 5¼, 5½ oz.	$25.00–30.00
—	Tumbler, Ftd., 9 oz., 10 oz.	$25.00–30.00
—	Tumbler, Ftd., 12, 13, 14, 15, 16 oz.	$30.00–35.00
—	Whiskey, 1½ oz.	$30.00–35.00
—	Wine, 2¾, 3, 3½, 4 oz.	$30.00–35.00

NEEDLE ETCHED DINNERWARE, STEMWARE & TUMBLERS

Suggested Prices are for Crystal.

300	Jug-7	$85.00–95.00
303	Jug-7	$85.00–95.00
312	Oil, Stopper	$50.00–60.00
315	Cream	$20.00–25.00
315	Sugar, Cov.	$35.00–45.00
318	Jug-7	$85.00–95.00
869	Finger Bowl w/Plate	$25.00–35.00
2133	Cream	$25.00–35.00
2133	Sugar	$25.00–35.00
2270	Jug, Cov.	$95.00–115.00
2283	Plate, 6", 7"	$10.00–15.00

Stems & Tumblers

Brandy, 1 oz.	$25.00–30.00
Claret, 4 oz.	$25.00–30.00
Cocktail, 3 oz., 3½ oz.	$20.00–25.00
Cocktail, Oyster, 4½ oz.	$10.00–15.00
Cordial, ¾ oz.	$30.00–25.00
Goblet	$20.00–25.00
Grapefruit w/Liner	$30.00–40.00
Hock, 13"	$80.00–90.00
Parfait, 5½ oz.	$10.00–15.00
Roemer, 13", 14"	$80.00–90.00
Sherbets, 5½ oz., 6 oz.	$15.00–20.00
Sherry	$25.00–30.00
Tumbler, Ftd., 2½ oz.	$25.00–30.00
Tumbler, Ftd., 5, 9, 12 oz.	$20.00–25.00
Tumbler, Table, 5 oz.	$20.00–25.00
Wine, 2½ oz., 2¾ oz.	$25.00–30.00

DINNERWARE, PRESSED

Suggested Prices Are For Crystal Unless Noted.

ALEXIS PATTERN

1630	Tumbler, 3⅞"	$40.00–50.00

AMERICAN PATTERN

2056	Bowl, Oval, 11¾"	$65.00–75.00
2056	Bowl, 3-Toed, 10½"	$50.00–70.00
2056	Bowl, Fruit, Ftd., 16"	$250.00–300.00
2056	Bowl, Fruit/Tom & Jerry	$200.00–250.00
2056	Bowl, Fruit, Shallow, 13"	$65.00–75.00
2056	Bitters Bottle w/Tube	$65.00–75.00
2056	Butter, Cov.,¼ lb.	$35.00–45.00
2056	Candelabra, 2-Lt., 16 Prisms	$175.00–195.00
2056	Candle, 7"	$95.00–110.00
2056	Candlestick, 3"	$28.00–33.00
2056	Candlestick, 6"	$50.00–60.00
2056	Candlestick, Duo, 6½"	$110.00–120.00
2056	Candle Lamp, 8½"	$150.00–175.00
2056	Candle, Twin, 4⅜"	$65.00–75.00
2056	Centerpiece, 9½", 11"	$75.00–90.00
2056	Centerpiece, 15"	$155.00–165.00
2056	Chiffonier	$875.00–975.00
2056	Cocktail, Ftd., 3 oz.	$20.00–25.00
2056	Cocktail, Old Fashioned, 6 oz.	$23.00–28.00
2056	Cocktail, Oyster, 4½ oz.	$18.00–23.00
2056	Cologne, Stopper, 8 oz.	$75.00–85.00
2056	Cordial Bottle, Stopper, 9 oz.	$95.00–115.00
2056	Cream, Tea	$18.00–23.00

2056	Custard/Punch Cup	$8.00–13.00
2056	Decanter, Stopper, 24 oz.	$85.00–95.00
2056	Dessert, Ftd., 4½ oz.	$13.00–18.00
2056	Flower Box, 5¾"	$18.00–23.00
2056	Floating Garden, 10", 11½"	$60.00–80.00
2056	Glove Box, Cov., 9½"	$525.00–575.00
2056	Goblet, 10 oz.	$18.00–23.00
2056	Goblet, Low, 9 oz.	$15.00–20.00
2056	Hair Pin, Cov., 3½"	$300.00–350.00
2056	Hair Receiver, Cov., 3"	$350.00–400.00
2056	Handkerchief Box, Cov., 5½"	$375.00–450.00
2056	Hurricane Lamp, 2-Pc.	$225.00–275.00
2056	Ice Dish w/Liner	$40.00–50.00
2056	Ice Tea, Flared, 12 oz.	$30.00–35.00
2056	Ice Tea, Ftd., 12 oz.	$23.00–28.00
2056	Jewel Box, Cov., 5¼"	$550.00–625.00
2056	Liner: Crab, Fruit, Tomato	$12.00–18.00
2056	Mug, Beer	$60.00–70.00
2056	Mug, Tom & Jerry	$45.00–55.00
2056	Pomade, Cov., Sq., 2"	$300.00–350.00
2056	Pretzel Jar, Cov., 8⅞"	$135.00–145.00
2056	Puff, Cov., Rd., 2⅞"	$300.00–350.00
2056	Puff, Cov., Sq., 3"	$300.00–350.00
2056	Punch Bowl, High Ft., 14"	$300.00–350.00
2056	Punch Bowl, Low Ft., 18"	$350.00–400.00
2056	Relish, 4-Part, 9"	$70.00–80.00
2056	Sherbet, Ftd., Flared, 4½, 5 oz.	$13.00–18.00
2056	Sherbet, Ftd., Reg., 4½, 5 oz.	$13.00–18.00
2056	Sani-Cut Server, 5¼"	$75.00–95.00
2056	Sugar, Tea	$18.00–23.00
2056	Sundae, Ftd., 6 oz.	$20.00–25.00
2056	Table Tumbler, Flared, 8 oz.	$30.00–35.00
2056	Topper, Ash Tray, 2⅛"	$25.00–30.00
2056	Topper/Hat, 4"	$35.00–45.00
2056	Tray, Center Hndl.	$55.00–65.00
2056	Tray, Oblong, 10½"	$75.00–85.00
2056	Tray, Pin, Oblong, 5"	$125.00–145.00
2056	Tray, Pin, Oval, 6"	$85.00–95.00
2056	Tumbler, Flared, 8 oz., 12 oz.	$30.00–35.00
2056	Tumbler, Ftd., 5 oz., 9 oz.	$23.00–28.00
2056	Tumbler, Reg., 5, 8, 12 oz.	$30.00–35.00
2056	Urn, Ftd., Sq., 6", 7½"	$55.00–75.00
2056	Vase, Ftd., Bud, 6"	$28.00–33.00
2056	Vase, 8"	$75.00–85.00
2056	Vegetable Dish, 2-Part, 10"	$30.00–40.00
2056	Whiskey, 2 oz.	$30.00–35.00
2056	Wine, 2½ oz.	$23.00–28.00

BAROQUE PATTERN

2484	Bowl, 2-Hndl., 10"	$40.00–50.00
2484	Candelabra, 2-Lt., w/16 Prisms	$95.00–115.00
2484	Candelabra, 3-Lt., w/24 Prisms	$125.00–145.00
2484	Lustre w/8 Prisms, 7¾"	$65.00–75.00
2484	Vase, 7"	$55.00–65.00
2496	Ash Tray, Oblong, 3¾"	$8.00–13.00
2496	Bon Bon, 3-Toed, 7⅜"	$20.00–25.00
2496	Bowl, Flared, 12"	$35.00–45.00
2496	Bowl, Fruit, 5"	$8.00–13.00
2496	Bowl, Punch, Ftd., 1½-Gal.	$300.00–350.00
2496	Bowl, Rolled Edge, 11"	$35.00–45.00
2496	Bowl, Rose, 3½"	$25.00–35.00
2496	Bowl, Salad, 10½"	$40.00–50.00
2496	Bowl, Serving Dish, 2-Hndl., 8½"	$30.00–40.00
2496	Bowl/Veg. Dish, 8⅛"	$30.00–40.00
2496	Candlestick, 4"	$25.00–30.00
2496	Candlestick, 5½"	$30.00–40.00
2496	Candlestick, Duo, 4½"	$45.00–55.00
2496	Candlestick, Trindle, 6"	$55.00–65.00
2496	Candy Box, Cov., 3-Part	$45.00–55.00
2496	Celery, 11"	$30.00–40.00
2496	Cheese & Cracker	$40.00–50.00
2496	Cigarette Box, Cov., 5½"	$25.00–35.00
2496	Cocktail, Ftd., 3½ oz.	$20.00–25.00
2496	Comport, Stemmed, 5½"	$25.00–35.00
2496	Comport, Tall, 6½"	$30.00–40.00
2496	Cream, Ftd., 7 oz., 7½ oz.	$20.00–25.00
2496	Cream, Ftd., Indv., 4 oz.	$15.00–20.00
2496	Cream Soup & Plate	$55.00–65.00
2496	Cup, Ftd. & Saucer	$20.00–25.00
2496	Cup, Punch, 6 oz.	$15.00–20.00
2496	Goblet, 9 oz., 6¾"	$20.00–25.00
2496	Ice Bucket w/Metal Hndl.	$55.00–65.00
2496	Ice Jug, 3-Pt., 7"	$75.00–85.00
2496	Jelly, Cov., Stemmed, 7½"	$50.00–60.00
2496	Jug, 3-Pt., 6½"	$75.00–85.00
2496	Mayonnaise, 2-Part, 2-Hndl.	$25.00–30.00
2496	Mayonnaise, Plate, Ladle	$35.00–45.00
2496	Mint, 1-Hndl., Sq., 4"	$20.00–25.00
2496	Mustard, Cov., Ftd.	$40.00–50.00

2496 Nappy, 1-Hndl., Flared, 5" .$20.00–25.00
2496 Nappy, 1-Hndl., Reg., 4⅜" .$20.00–25.00
2496 Nappy, 1-Hndl., Sq., 4" $20.00–25.00
2496 Nappy, 3-Cornered, 4⅝" ...$20.00–25.00
2496 Nut Bowl, 3-Toed, Cupped .$20.00–25.00
2496 Oil, Stopper, 3½ oz. $75.00–85.00
2496 Old Fashioned Cocktail, 6½ oz. $20.00–25.00
2496 Pickle, 8" $25.00–30.00
2496 Plate, 6", 7" $10.00–15.00
2496 Plate, 8", 9" $20.00–30.00
2496 Plate, Cake, 2-Hndl. $35.00–45.00
2496 Plate, Torte, 14" $40.00–50.00
2496 Platter, Oval, 12" $40.00–50.00
2496 Relish, 2-Part, 2-Hndl., Sq. ..$25.00–30.00
2496 Relish, 3-Part, 2-Hndl., 10" .$30.00–40.00
2496 Relish, 4-Part, 2-Hndl., 10" .$30.00–40.00
2496 Sauce Dish, 2-Hndl., 6½" ...$25.00–35.00
2496 Shaker, 2", 2¾" $25.00–30.00
2496 Sherbet, 5 oz. $10.00–15.00
2496 Sugar, Ftd., 3½" $20.00–25.00
2496 Sugar, Ftd., Indv. $15.00–20.00
2496 Sweetmeat, 2-Hndl., Sq. $20.00–25.00
2496 Tid Bit, 3-Toed, 8¼" $20.00–25.00
2496 Tray, 2-Hndl., Oblong, 7" ...$20.00–25.00
2496 Tray, 2-Hndl., 6½" $20.00–25.00
2496 Tumbler, 5 oz., 9 oz., 14 oz. .$25.00–35.00
2496 Tumbler, Ftd., 9 oz., 12 oz. $20.00–30.00
2496 Vase, 8" $45.00–55.00

BEDFORD PATTERN

1000 Bottle, Bitters $40.00–50.00
1000 Claret $20.00–25.00
1000 Cream, Indv. $20.00–25.00
1000 Goblet $20.00–25.00
1000 Jug, Claret $125.00–135.00
1000 Jug, Stopper, Hndl. $95.00–105.00
1000 Shaker, Sugar $55.00–60.00
1000 Sugar, Cov., Indv. $30.00–35.00
1000 Tumbler, Whiskey $18.00–23.00
1000 Wine $25.00–30.00

BRILLIANT PATTERN

1001 Berry, 8", 7" $65.00–75.00
1001 Butter, Cov. $55.00–65.00
1001 Cream $25.00–30.00
1001 Nappy, 4½", 4" $15.00–23.00
1001 Spoon $45.00–50.00
1001 Sugar, Cov. $40.00–45.00

CARMEN PATTERN

575 Bowl, Berry, 9" $65.00–75.00
575 Comport, Ftd., 9" $75.00–85.00
575 Cream $40.00–50.00
575 Oil, Stopper $75.00–85.00
575 Spooner $60.00–70.00
575 Sugar, Cov. $75.00–85.00

CENTURY PATTERN

2630 Bon Bon, 3-Toed $30.00–35.00
2630 Bowl, Salad, 8½" $55.00–65.00
2630 Bowl, Salad, 10½" $65.00–75.00
2630 Candy Jar, Cov., Ftd. $55.00–60.00
2630 Cheese & Cracker $45.00–55.00
2630 Cocktail, 3½ oz. $20.00–25.00
2630 Goblet, 10½ oz. $20.00–25.00
2630 Ice Bucket $65.00–75.00
2630 Mayonnaise, Plate, Ladle $40.00–50.00
2630 Mustard, Cov., w/Spoon $40.00–45.00
2630 Nappy, 1-Hndl., 4½" $20.00–25.00
2630 Oyster Cocktail, 4½ oz. $15.00–20.00
2630 Pitcher, Cereal, Pt. $60.00–70.00
2630 Pitcher, Ice Jug, 3-Pt. $80.00–90.00
2630 Plate, Cracker, 11" $30.00–35.00
2630 Plate, Torte, 14" $75.00–85.00
2630 Salver, Ftd., 12¼" $75.00–85.00
2630 Sherbet, 5½ oz. $13.00–18.00
2630 Tid Bit, 3-Toed $30.00–35.00
2630 Tid Bit, 3-Pc. $45.00–55.00
2630 Tricorne, 3-Toed $30.00–35.00
2630 Tray, Muffin, 2-Hndl. $40.00–50.00
2630 Tray, Utility, 2-Hndl. $40.00–50.00
2630 Tumbler, Ftd., 12 oz. $20.00–25.00
2630 Tumbler, Ftd., 5 oz. $18.00–23.00
2630 Vase, Bud $23.00–28.00
2630 Vase, 2-Hndl., 7½ oz. $65.00–75.00
2630 Vase, Oval, 8½" $50.00–55.00
2630 Wine, 3½ oz. $20.00–25.00

COIN PATTERN

1372 Ash Tray, 10" $25.00–30.00
1372 Ash Tray, Rd., 7½" $20.00–25.00
1372 Ash Tray, Oblong, 4" $12.00–18.00
1372 Bowl, 8", Color $35.00–45.00
1372 Bowl, Oval, 9", Color $40.00–50.00
1372 Candleholder, 4½" $20.00–30.00
1372 Candy Box, Cov., Color $55.00–65.00
1372 Candy Jar, Cov., 6$\frac{5}{16}$" $45.00–55.00
1372 Cigarette Box, Cov. $30.00–40.00

1372 Cream $20.00–25.00
1372 Decanter, Stopper $85.00–95.00
1372 Ice Tea/Highball $25.00–30.00
1372 Jelly $20.00–25.00
1372 Juice/Old Fashion $25.00–30.00
1372 Nappy, 4½" $20.00–25.00
1372 Nappy, Hndl., 5⅜" $20.00–25.00
1372 Pitcher, Ice, 1-Qt., Color .$125.00–135.00
1372 Sugar, Cov. $30.00–35.00
1372 Vase, Ftd., Bud $28.00–33.00
1372 Water/Scotch & Soda $30.00–35.00
1372 Wedding Bowl, Cov., Color .$85.00–95.00

COIN (GOLD) PATTERN, DEC.

1372 Candy Jar, Cov., 6⁵⁄₁₆" $50.00–60.00
1372 Cigarette Box, Cov. $30.00–40.00
1372 Decanter, Stopper $90.00–110.00
1372 Wedding Bowl, Cov., 8³⁄₁₆" $80.00–90.00

COLONIAL (TEA ROOM) PATTERN

2222 Bowl, Finger w/Plate $20.00–25.00
2222 Cocktail, Fruit $12.00–15.00
2222 Cream, Indv. $12.00–15.00
2222 Goblet $15.00–20.00
2222 Oil, 4 oz., 6 oz. $30.00–45.00
2222 Shaker (713½) $12.00–15.00
2222 Sherbet, Low, 4½ oz., 3 oz.$12.00–15.00
2222 Tumbler, Ice Tea, 14 oz. $15.00–20.00
2222 Tumbler, Table, 8 oz. $12.00–18.00

COLONY (CASCADE-QUEEN ANNE) PATTERN

Suggested Prices are for Crystal.

1 Banquet Lamp, 15" $350.00–375.00
1 Candelabra, 3-Lt. w/Vase $450.00–500.00
2 Banquet Lamp, 18" $300.00–350.00
4 Lustre w/10 Prisms, 9¾" $85.00–95.00
5 Candle, Hndl. $35.00–45.00
6 Candle w/Ribbon $50.00–60.00
112 Candle, 9½", 9¾" $50.00–60.00
112 Goblet, 8 oz. $30.00–40.00
112 Jug, Ftd., 3-Pt. $85.00–95.00
112 Ink, Cov. w/Tray, 1¾" $90.00–100.00
112 Ink, Cov. #3 ....$45.00–55.00
112 Salt, Indv., Sq $15.00–20.00
112 Shaker, Squat $15.00–25.00
112 Shaker (112½) $15.00–25.00
112 Sponge Cup, 3" $20.00–30.00
112 Tumbler, Table, 8½ oz. $25.00–35.00
112 Water Bottle (112½) $100.00–120.00
121 Bobache $15.00–20.00
161 Candle, 6½" $45.00–55.00
161 Water Bottle, Tumbler (Carafe) $125.00–145.00
175 Shaker (175½) $15.00–25.00
1103 Lustre w/10 Prisms, 14½" $150.00–170.00
1103 Shoe Plate, Stand, 17" ...$300.00–350.00
1103 Shoe Plate Stand, 24", 25" $400.00–450.00
2412 Almond, Ftd., 1⅜" $15.00–25.00
2412 Ash Tray, Indv., Sq., 3", Rim .$13.00–18.00
2412 Ash Tray, Sm., Sq., 3½", Rim.$13.00–18.00
2412 Ash Tray, Lg., Sq., 4½", Rim..$13.00–18.00
2412 Ash Tray, Rd., 3", 4½" $15.00–20.00
2412 Ash Tray, Rd., 6" $15.00–20.00
2412 Bon Bon, 2-Hndl., 5" $15.00–25.00
2412 Bon Bon, 3-Toed, 7" $20.00–30.00
2412 Bon Bon, Ftd., Stemmed $20.00–30.00
2412 Bowl, Cupped, 8" $65.00–75.00
2412 Bowl/Comport, Ftd., 11" ...$85.00–95.00
2412 Bowl, Ftd., Oval $50.00–60.00
2412 Bowl/Comport, Ftd., Low, 9" .$85.00–95.00
2412 Bowl/Comport, Ftd., Low, 10½" $85.00–95.00
2412 Bowl, Ftd., High $95.00–105.00
2412 Bowl/Comport, Ftd., High, 10½" $95.00–105.00
2412 Bowl, Finger, 2" $20.00–30.00
2412 Bowl, Flared, 11" $50.00–60.00
2412 Bowl, Fruit, 10½" $50.00–60.00
2412 Bowl, Fruit, 14" $75.00–85.00
2412 Bowl, Ftd., 11" $75.00–85.00
2412 Bowl, Punch, 2-Gal. $145.00–165.00
2412 Bowl, Rolled Edge, 9" $40.00–50.00
2412 Bowl, Salad, 9¾" $45.00–55.00
2412 Butter, Cov.,¼ lb. $35.00–45.00
2412 Candelabra, 2-Lt. w/Prisms, 6¼" $75.00–85.00
2412 Candle, Queen Anne, 9" ...$85.00–95.00
2412 Candlestick, 3" $23.00–28.00
2412 Candlestick, 7" $45.00–55.00
2412 Candlestick, Duo, 6¼" $55.00–65.00
2412 Candy Box, Cov., Rd. $55.00–65.00
2412 Celery, 10½", Rim $65.00–75.00
2412 Celery, 11½" $35.00–45.00
2412 Centerpiece, 11" $85.00–95.00

No.	Item	Price
2412	Centerpiece, Rolled Edge, 13"	$50.00–60.00
2412	Cheese, 5¼"	$20.00–30.00
2412	Cheese & Cracker, 2-Pc.	$50.00–60.00
2412	Cigarette Box, Cov., Rim	$55.00–65.00
2412	Cocktail, 3½ oz.	$13.00–18.00
2412	Comport, Cov. Low, Rim Pattern	$55.00–65.00
2412	Comport, Low, 4"	$25.00–35.00
2412	Comport, Cov., Low, 6⅜"	$35.00–45.00
2412	Cream, Ftd., 3⅞", 7 oz.	$20.00–25.00
2412	Cream, Ftd., Indv., 4¼ oz.	$15.00–20.00
2412	Cream Soup, Ftd., 2-Hndl.	$35.00–45.00
2412	Cup, Ftd., & Saucer	$20.00–25.00
2412	Goblet, 9 oz.	$15.00–20.00
2412	Ice Bowl	$80.00–90.00
2412	Ice Bowl, 4", Rim Pattern	$85.00–95.00
2412	Ice Cream, Sq., 5½"	$25.00–35.00
2412	Ice Lip Jug, Blown, 2-Qt.	$95.00–105.00
2412	Ice Jug, Ftd., 3-Pt.	$85.00–95.00
2412	Jelly, Cov., Ftd., Stemmed	$50.00–60.00
2412	Lemon, 2-Hndl., 6½"	$20.00–25.00
2412	Lily Pond, 9", 10"	$50.00–60.00
2412	Lily Pond, 13"	$55.00–65.00
2412	Lustre, w/3 Prisms, 6"	$50.00–60.00
2412	Lustre, w/8 Prisms, 7½"	$75.00–85.00
2412	Mayonnaise, Plate, Ladle	$45.00–55.00
2412	Mayonnaise, Plate, Ladle, Rim Pattern	$75.00–85.00
2412	Muffin Tray, 2-Hndl., 9¾"	$40.00–50.00
2412	Nappy, Rd., 4½", 5"	$20.00–30.00
2412	Nut Bowl, 3-Toed, 5⅝"	$20.00–25.00
2412	Oil, Stopper, 4 oz.	$50.00–60.00
2412	Olive, 6½", Rim Pattern	$50.00–60.00
2412	Olive, 7"	$20.00–30.00
2412	Oyster Cocktail, 4 oz.	$15.00–20.00
2412	Pickle, 8", Rim Pattern	$50.00–60.00
2412	Pickle, 9½"	$35.00–45.00
2412	Pitcher, Cereal, Ftd.	$75.00–85.00
2412	Plate, Bread & Butter	$7.00–12.00
2412	Plate, Salad	$13.00–18.00
2412	Plate, Dinner	$30.00–40.00
2412	Plate, Cake, 2-Hndl.	$40.00–50.00
2412	Plate, Cracker	$30.00–40.00
2412	Plate, Mayonnaise, 6¾"	$10.00–15.00
2412	Plate, Torte, 13"	$40.00–50.00
2412	Plate, Torte, Turned Up Edge, 15"	$80.00–90.00
2412	Plate, Torte, 18"	$95.00–115.00
2412	Platter, Oval, 12½"	$55.00–65.00
2412	Relish, 2-Part, 7¼", Rim Pattern	$65.00–75.00
2412	Relish, 2-Hndl., 2-Part, 7"	$25.00–35.00
2412	Relish, 3-Part, 10", Rim Pattern	$75.00–85.00
2412	Relish, 2-Hndl, 3-Part, 10½"	$30.00–40.00
2412	Salver, Ftd., 12"	$75.00–85.00
2412	Serving Dish, 2-Hndl., 8½"	$30.00–40.00
2412	Shaker, 2¾"	$20.00–25.00
2412	Shaker, Indv., 1⅞"	$20.00–25.00
2412	Sherbet, 5 oz.	$15.00–20.00
2412	Sugar, Ftd., 3⅜"	$20.00–25.00
2412	Sugar, Ftd., Indv.	$15.00–20.00
2412	Sweetmeat, 2-Hndl., 5"	$20.00–25.00
2412	Tid Bit, Ftd., 7"	$25.00–35.00
2412	Tid Bit, 3-Toed, 7½"	$20.00–25.00
2412	Tray, Indv., 2-Hndl., for Shakers	$13.00–18.00
2412	Tray, Indv., 6¾", Rim Pattern	$25.00–35.00
2412	Tray, Lunch, Ctr. Hndl., 11½"	$45.00–55.00
2412	Tricorne, 3-Toed, 7"	$30.00–40.00
2412	Tumbler, Ftd., 5 oz.	$23.00–28.00
2412	Tumbler, Ftd., 12 oz.	$28.00–33.00
2412	Tumbler, 5 oz., 9 oz.	$25.00–30.00
2412	Tumbler, 12 oz.	$30.00–35.00
2412	Urn, Ftd., 6⅝"	$55.00–65.00
2412	Urn, Cov., 9" All Over Pattern	$80.00–100.00
2412	Urn, Cov., 9", Rim Pattern	$125.00–145.00
2412	Vase, 12", 14"	$85.00–105.00
2412	Vase, Bud, Ftd., Flared, 6"	$20.00–30.00
2412	Vase, Cornucopia, Ftd., 9¼"	$100.00–120.00
2412	Vase, Ftd., Cupped, 7"	$55.00–65.00
2412	Vase, Ftd., Flared, 7½"	$55.00–65.00
2412	Vegetable Dish/Bowl, Oval	$40.00–50.00
2412	Vegetable Dish, Oval, 2-Part	$40.00–50.00
2412	Whip Cream, 2-Hndl, 4¾"	$25.00–35.00
2412	Wine, 3¼ oz.	$28.00–33.00
—	Banquet Lamp, Quoizel Shade	$400.00–500.00
—	Banquet Lamp, Peg Font	$375.00–425.00

CONTOUR PATTERN

No.	Item	Price
2666	Butter, Cov., Oblong	$23.00–28.00
2666	Butter Pat	$5.00–10.00
2666	Cream	$15.00–20.00

2666 Cream, Indv. $13.00–18.00
2666 Cup & Saucer $15.00–20.00
2666 Oil, Stopper.....................$35.00–45.00
2666 Pitcher, Sauce $30.00–40.00
2666 Pitcher, Sauce, Plate..........$35.00–45.00
2666 Plate, 7" $8.00–13.00
2666 Plate, 10" $20.00–30.00
2666 Plate, Oval, 8⅜" $18.00–23.00
2666 Plate, Party w/Cup $20.00–30.00
2666 Plate, Serving, 14" $35.00–45.00
2666 Relish, 2-Part....................$18.00–23.00
2666 Relish, 3-Part....................$23.00–28.00
2666 Shaker, 2¾" $15.00–20.00
2666 Sugar.............................$15.00–20.00
2666 Sugar, Indv. $13.00–18.00
2666 Tray for Cream, Sugar, Indv.$13.00–18.00

CORONET PATTERN

2560 Bowl/Serving Dish, 2-Hndl. $25.00–35.00
2560 Candlestick, 4" $20.00–25.00
2560 Candlestick, Duo $30.00–40.00
2560 Plate, Cake, 2-Hndl...........$30.00–40.00
2560 Tray, Ctr. Hndl., Lunch $35.00–45.00
2560 Tray, Muffin, 2-Hndl. $30.00–40.00
2560 Vase, Hndl, 6" $30.00–40.00
2560 Vase, Pansy, 3¾" $25.00–35.00

DECORATOR PATTERN

2691 Ash Tray, Indv. $5.00–10.00
2691 Cigarette Holder, 2½"..........$5.00–10.00
2691 Creamer, 3¼"....................$8.00–13.00
2691 Cup & Saucer $13.00–18.00
2691 Cup & Saucer, Demitasse ...$15.00–20.00
2691 Dessert Bowl, 4⅞" $8.00–13.00
2691 Plate, 7" $8.00–13.00
2691 Preserve, Hndl., 4" $10.00–15.00
2691 Sauce Bowl, Plate, Ladle.....$20.00–25.00
2691 Server, 2-Part, 6⅜" $15.00–20.00
2691 Server, 3-Part, 9¾" $20.00–25.00
2691 Shaker, 3" $10.00–15.00
2691 Soup, 4¾"........................$10.00–15.00
2691 Sugar, Cov., 3¼" $15.00–20.00
2691 Tray for Cream Sugar.........$10.00–15.00

FAIRFAX PATTERN

2375 Ashtray $10.00–15.00
2375 Bon Bon, 2-Hndl. $18.00–23.00
2375 Bowl/Dessert, Lg., 2-Hndl...$20.00–30.00
2375 Candle, 3" $18.00–23.00
2375 Centerpiece, 11" w/Block,
Color...............................$85.00–95.00
2375 Cream, Tea $13.00–18.00
2375 Cream, Whipped, 2-Hndl...$20.00–25.00
2375 Lemon Dish, Color $20.00–30.00
2375 Oil, Ftd., Stopper..............$70.00–80.00
2375 Plate, Cake, 2-Hndl., Color.$35.00–45.00
2375 Plate, Cracker w/Ftd.
Cheese...........................$30.00–40.00
2375 Shaker, Ftd., Ebony............$45.00–55.00
2375 Sugar, Tea $13.00–18.00
2375 Sweetmeat, 2-Hndl. $20.00–25.00

FAIRMONT PATTERN

2718 Dessert/Bowl $10.00–15.00
2718 Goblet, Blue.....................$20.00–25.00
2718 Ice Tea, 13 oz., Blue $23.00–28.00
2718 Juice, 5 oz. $13.00–18.00
2718 Plate, 8" $10.00–15.00
2718 Sherbet, Blue....................$13.00–18.00

GOV. BRADFORD PATTERN

1229 Cracker Jar, Silver Lid.........$85.00–95.00
1229 Sugar, Silver Lid $55.00–65.00
1229 Syrup, Silver Hndl. $75.00–85.00
1229 Syrup, Swelled Silver Top ...$75.00–85.00

HERMITAGE PATTERN

2449 Ash Tray, Indv., Topaz $10.00–15.00
2449 Ash Tray, Set, Topaz $45.00–55.00
2449 Bowl, Cereal, 6" $10.00–15.00
2449 Bowl, Finger, 4½", Amber ..$13.00–18.00
2449 Bowl, Flared, 10" $30.00–40.00
2449 Bowl, Fruit, 5" $10.00–15.00
2449 Claret, 4 oz., Topaz..........$25.00–30.00
2449 Cocktail, Ftd., 4 oz. $10.00–15.00
2449 Cocktail, Fruit, Ftd. $10.00–15.00
2449 Cocktail, Old Fashion, 6 oz.$13.00–18.00
2449 Cream, Ftd. $15.00–20.00
2449 Cup, Ftd. & Saucer, Topaz..$20.00–25.00
2449 Dish, Ice, w/Liner, Plate,
Topaz.............................$55.00–65.00
2449 Goblet............................$15.00–20.00
2449 Ice Tea, Ftd., 12 oz., Amber.$20.00–25.00
2449 Plate, Salad $10.00–15.00
2449 Relish, 3-Part $20.00–30.00
2449 Salad, Coup, 6½", 7½",
Topaz.............................$25.00–35.00
2449 Sugar, Ftd........................$15.00–20.00
2449 Sherbet, High, Low $10.00–15.00

2449 Tumbler, 2 oz., 13 oz., Topaz $25.00–30.00
2449 Tumbler, 5 oz., 9 oz. $15.00–20.00
2449 Tumbler, Ftd., 5 oz., 9 oz. $15.00–20.00
2449 Vase, Ftd., 6", Azure $65.00–75.00

HOLIDAY PATTERN

2643 Coaster, 4" $10.00–15.00
2643 Cocktail, 4 oz. $10.00–15.00
2643 Cocktail Mixer, 20 oz., 30 oz. $30.00–50.00
2643 Decanter, Stopper, 24 oz. $30.00–40.00
2643 Old Fashioned Cocktail, 6 oz. $10.00–15.00
2643 Double Old Fashioned Cocktail, 12 oz. $20.00–25.00
2643 Highball, 12 oz. $20.00–25.00
2643 Ice Bowl, 5" $15.00–20.00
2643 Scotch & Soda, 9 oz. $15.00–20.00
2643 Whiskey, 1½ oz. $18.00–23.00

HORIZON PATTERN

2650 Cream, 3½", Color $20.00–25.00
2650 Cup & Saucer, Color $20.00–25.00
2650 Plate, Dinner, 10", Color $25.00–35.00
2650 Plate, Salad, 7" $10.00–15.00
2650 Plate, Sandwich, 11", Color $25.00–35.00
2650 Plate, Torte, 14", Color $45.00–55.00
2650 Platter, Oval, 12", Color $35.00–45.00
2650 Sugar, 3⅛", Color $20.00–25.00
5650 Dessert/Finger Bowl $15.00–20.00
5650 Ice Tea/Highball, Color $25.00–30.00
5650 Juice/Cocktail $15.00–20.00
5650 Sherbet/Old Fashioned $15.00–20.00
5650 Water/Scotch & Soda, Color $20.00–25.00

"HUGH" PATTERN

2470 Bon Bon, 2-Hndl., Wisteria $40.00–50.00
2470 Bowl, 12", Wisteria $90.00–100.00
2470 Candlestick, 5½", Wisteria $85.00–95.00
2470 Comport, Low, Wisteria $65.00–75.00
2470 Lemon Dish, Wisteria $45.00–55.00
2470 Plate, Cake, 10" Wisteria $75.00–85.00
2470 Relish, 3-Part, Wisteria $65.00–75.00
2470 Relish, 4-Part, Wisteria $85.00–95.00
2470 Service Dish, 9", Wisteria $75.00–85.00
2470 Sweetmeat, Wisteria $45.00–55.00
2470 Tray for Cream, Sugar, Wisteria $35.00–45.00

JAMESTOWN PATTERN

2719 Bowl, Salad, 10" $45.00–55.00
2719 Bowl/Serving, 2-Hndl. $35.00–45.00
2719 Butter, Cov., Oblong $30.00–40.00
2719 Celery, 9¼" $25.00–35.00
2719 Cream, Ftd., 4" $18.00–23.00
2719 Dessert/Bowl, 4½" $10.00–15.00
2719 Goblet, 9½ oz. $18.00–23.00
2719 Ice Tea, Ftd., 11 oz. $18.00–23.00
2719 Jelly, Cov., 6⅛" $25.00–35.00
2719 Jug, Ice, 3-Pt., Color $90.00–115.00
2719 Juice, Ftd., 5 oz., Color $18.00–23.00
2719 Pickle, 8⅜" $20.00–25.00
2719 Plate, Cake, 2-Hndl. $30.00–40.00
2719 Plate, Salad, 8", Color $18.00–23.00
2719 Plate, Torte, 14", Color $75.00–85.00
2719 Relish, 2-Part $20.00–25.00
2719 Salver, Cake Stand, 10", Color $85.00–95.00
2719 Sauce Dish, Cov., Color $30.00–40.00
2719 Shaker, 3½" $18.00–23.00
2719 Sherbet, 6½ oz. $10.00–15.00
2719 Sugar, Ftd., 3½" $18.00–23.00
2719 Tray, Muffin, 2-Hndl. $25.00–35.00
2719 Tumbler, 9 oz., 12 oz. $15.00–20.00
2719 Wine, 4 oz., Color $30.00–35.00

LAFAYETTE PATTERN

2440 Bowl, Cereal, Fruit $8.00–13.00
2440 Celery, 11½" $25.00–30.00
2440 Cream, Ftd. $18.00–23.00
2440 Cup & Saucer, Wisteria $45.00–55.00
2440 Mayonnaise, 2-Hndl., 2-Part $20.00–25.00
2440 Olive, 6½", Wisteria $35.00–45.00
2440 Pickle, 8½" $20.00–25.00
2440 Plate, Cake, 2-Hndl. $25.00–35.00
2440 Plate, Salad $8.00–13.00
2440 Relish, 2-Hndl., 2-Part, Topaz $25.00–35.00
2440 Relish, 3-Hndl., 3-Part $25.00–30.00
2440 Sauce Dish, 2-Hndl., Burgundy $35.00–45.00
2440 Sugar, Ftd. $18.00–23.00
2440 Torte Plate, 13", Empire Green $75.00–85.00

MAYFAIR PATTERN

2419 Ash Tray, Wisteria $25.00–35.00
2419 Creamer, Tea, Ftd., Ebony $25.00–35.00
2419 Cup, Ftd., & Saucer, Color $20.00–25.00

2419 Plate, Salad, Topaz $13.00–18.00
2419 Relish, 4-Part, 8½" $20.00–30.00
2419 Relish, 5-Part, Topaz $45.00–55.00
2419 Shaker, 2⅞", Color $25.00–30.00
2419 Sugar, Tea, Ftd. $13.00–18.00
2419 Syrup, Cov., w/Saucer, Topaz $85.00–95.00

MOONSTONE PATTERN

2882 Goblet, 10 oz., Color $15.00–20.00

MYRIAD PATTERN

2592 Bon Bon, 2-Hndl. $18.00–23.00
2592 Bowl, Oblong, 11" $35.00–45.00
2592 Candlestick, Duo, 6½" $30.00–40.00
2592 Jelly, 2-Hndl. $18.00–23.00
2592 Lemon, 2-Hndl. $18.00–23.00
2592 Sweetmeat, 2-Hndl. $18.00–23.00
2592 Vase, Oval, 7" $30.00–40.00
2592 Whip Cream, 2-Hndl. $18.00–23.00

PRISCILLA PATTERN

2321 Bouillon, Color $18.00–23.00
2321 Cream $13.00–18.00
2321 Cream Soup, Color $20.00–25.00
2321 Custard, Ftd., Hndl., Color..$20.00–25.00
2321 Goblet,Color $20.00–25.00
2321 Jug, Color $85.00–105.00
2321 Saucer Champagne $13.00–18.00
2321 Sugar $13.00–18.00
2321 Tumbler, Ftd., Hndl., Color..$25.00–30.00

PIONEER PATTERN

2350 Baker, 9", 10", Color $55.00–75.00
2350 Celery, 11" $20.00–30.00
2350 Comport, 8" $25.00–35.00
2350 Cream Soup, Ftd., w/Plate .$25.00–30.00
2350 Cup, Ftd., & Saucer, Color .$20.00–25.00
2350 Egg Cup, Ftd $15.00–20.00
2350 Grapefruit w/Cry. Liner $25.00–30.00
2350 Pickle, 8" $18.00–23.00

ROBIN HOOD PATTERN

603 Butter, Cov. $55.00–65.00
603 Can, Nickel Top $85.00–95.00
603 Cream $20.00–30.00
603 Jug, 3-Pt. $75.00–95.00
603 Pickle $30.00–40.00
603 Shaker, Salt $20.00–30.00
603 Spoon $55.00–65.00
603 Sugar, Cov. $45.00–55.00
603 Tumbler $30.00–40.00

ROSBY PATTERN

1704 Cracker Jar, Cov. $85.00–95.00
1704 Jug. ½-Gal. $65.00–75.00
1704 Oil, Stopper, 6 oz. $65.00–75.00
1704 Pickle Jar, Cov. $75.00–85.00
1704 Shaker, Glass Top $20.00–25.00
1704 Shaker, Tall, Glass Top $20.00–25.00
1704 Syrup Ewer, Lg. $75.00–85.00
1704 Tumbler $23.00–28.00

RADIANCE

2700 Beverage, 10 oz., 5¾" $10.00–15.00
2700 Buffet Plate, 14" $30.00–40.00
2700 Cereal/Dessert, 5½" $5.00–10.00
2700 Cream, 3¼" $8.00–13.00
2700 Cup & Saucer $8.00–13.00
2700 Juice, 5½ oz. $8.00–13.00
2700 Plate, Dinner, 10" $15.00–20.00
2700 Plate, Salad/Dessert, 7" $5.00–10.00
2700 Platter, 15" $45.00–55.00
2700 Salad Bowl, 12" $30.00–40.00
2700 Sauce Bowl, Plate, Ladle..... $20.00–30.00
2700 Server, 3-Part, 12⅝" $20.00–30.00
2700 Serving Dish, 11" $20.00–30.00
2700 Shaker, 2½" $8.00–13.00
2700 Sherbet, 6 oz. $8.00–13.00
2700 Sugar, 2¾" $8.00–13.00

SEASCAPE PATTERN

2685 Bowl, Salad, 10", Color $85.00–95.00
2685 Cream, 3⅜", Color $25.00–35.00
2685 Cream, Indv., Color $20.00–25.00
2685 Mayonnaise, 3-Pc., Color ... $65.00–75.00
2685 Plate, Buffet, 14", Color ... $95.00–105.00
2685 Preserve, Hndl., Color $35.00–45.00
2685 Relish, 2-Part, Color $45.00–55.00
2685 Relish, 3-Part, Color $55.00–65.00
2685 Sugar, Color $25.00–35.00
2685 Sugar, Indv., Color $20.00–25.00
2685 Tray, Indv., Color $20.00–30.00

SONATA PATTERN

2364 Baked Apple, 6" $13.00–18.00
2364 Bowl, Fruit $8.00–13.00
2364 Celery, 11" $20.00–30.00

2364 Comport, 8" $25.00–35.00
2364 Pickle, 8" $20.00–30.00
2364 Relish, 2-Hndl., 2-Part.........$20.00–30.00
2364 Relish, 2-Hndl., 3-Part.........$25.00–35.00
2364 Shaker, 2¼" $18.00–23.00
2364 Tray, Ctr. Hndl., Lunch........$30.00–40.00

SUNRAY PATTERN

2510 Almond, Ftd. $15.00–20.00
2510 Ash Tray, Indv., Rd. $5.00–10.00
2510 Ash Tray, Sq., 3" $5.00–10.00
2510 Bon Bon, 3-Toed $15.00–20.00
2510 Bowl, 2-Hndl., 10" $40.00–50.00
2510 Butter/Cheese, Cov. $35.00–45.00
2510 Candlestick, 3" $20.00–30.00
2510 Candlestick, 5½" $30.00–40.00
2510 Candlestick, Duo $55.00–65.00
2510 Cigarette Cov. $35.00–45.00
2510 Cigarette Box, Cov. $25.00–35.00
2510 Claret, 4½ oz. $20.00–25.00
2510 Coaster $8.00–13.00
2510 Cocktail, Fruit, 3½ oz. $13.00–18.00
2510 Cocktail, Ftd., 4 oz. $15.00–20.00
2510 Comport, 5" $20.00–30.00
2510 Decanter, Stopper, Oblong$85.00–105.00
2510 Goblet, 9 oz. $18.00–23.00
2510 Ice Bucket $40.00–50.00
2510 Jug, 2-Qt., 8½" $75.00–85.00
2510 Jug, Ice, 2-Qt. $75.00–85.00
2510 Mayonnaise, Plate, Ladle....$40.00–50.00
2510 Mustard, Cov., Spoon $45.00–55.00
2510 Nappy, 1-Hndl., Flared $15.00–20.00
2510 Nappy, 1-Hndl., Reg. $15.00–20.00
2510 Nappy, 1-Hndl., Sq. $15.00–20.00
2510 Nappy, 1-Hndl., 3-Corner...$15.00–20.00
2510 Oil, Stopper, 3 oz. $45.00–55.00
2510 Plate, Sandwich, 12" $35.00–45.00
2510 Plate, Sandwich, 16" $75.00–85.00
2510 Plate, Torte, 11" $30.00–40.00
2510 Plate, Torte, 15" $55.00–65.00
2510 Relish, 2-Hndl., 2-Part.........$25.00–35.00
2510 Relish, 2-Hndl., 4-Part.........$35.00–45.00
2510 Relish, 3-Hndl., 3-Part.........$35.00–45.00
2510 Salt Dip $13.00–18.00
2510 Shaker, 4" $20.00–30.00
2510 Shaker, Indv. $18.00–23.00
2510 Sherbet, Low $10.00–15.00
2510 Sweetmeat, 2-Hndl., 2-Part .$25.00–35.00
2510 Tray, Condiment $25.00–35.00
2510 Tray, Oblong, 10½" $45.00–55.00
2510 Tumbler, 6 oz., 9 oz. $18.00–23.00
2510 Tumbler, 2 oz., 5 oz., 13 oz. $23.00–28.00
2510 Tumbler, Ftd., 9 oz. $18.00–23.00
2510 Tumbler, Ftd., 5 oz., 13 oz. $23.00–28.00
2510 Vase, 7" $35.00–45.00
2510 Vase, Sq., Ftd., 9" $55.00–65.00
2510 Vase/Rose Bowl $30.00–40.00
2510 Whiskey, 2 oz. $25.00–30.00

WEDDING BELLS PATTERN

789 Butter, Cov., Dec. $85.00–95.00
789 Celery, Tall, Dec. $85.00–95.00
789 Cream, Dec. $30.00–40.00
789 Custard, Hndl., Dec. $20.00–25.00
789 Decanter, Stopper, 1-Qt., Dec. $165.00–185.00
789 Jug, ½-Gal., Dec. $145.00–165.00
789 Nappy/Dessert, Dec. $20.00–30.00
789 Punch Bowl w/Ft., Dec. ..$350.00–380.00
789 Punch Cup, Hndl., Dec. $20.00–25.00
789 Shaker, Dec. $25.00–35.00
789 Spooner, Dec. $65.00–75.00
789 Sugar, Cov., Dec. $60.00–70.00
789 Syrup, Dec. $90.00–110.00
789 Tankard Jug, ½-Gal., Dec. $150.00–170.00
789 Toothpick, Dec. $65.00–85.00
789 Tumbler, Dec. $45.00–55.00
789 Vinegar, Stopper, Dec. $95.00–105.00
789 Water Bottle, 1-Qt., Dec. $85.00–95.00
789 Wine, Dec. $45.00–55.00
789 Whiskey, Dec. $30.00–40.00

WISTAR PATTERN

2620 Celery, 9½" $20.00–30.00
2620 Cream, Ftd. $20.00–25.00
2620 Goblet, Silver Mist $25.00–30.00
2620 Mayonnaise, Plate, Ladle....$45.00–55.00
2620 Nappy, 1-Hndl., Flared $18.00–23.00
2620 Nappy, 1-Hndl., Reg. $18.00–23.00
2620 Nappy, 1-Hndl., Sq. $18.00–23.00
2620 Nappy, 1-Hndl., 3-Corner...$18.00–23.00
2620 Plate, 7", Dec. w/Stain $15.00–20.00
2620 Sherbet, High, 6 oz. $13.00–18.00
2620 Sugar, Ftd. $20.00–25.00
2620 Tumbler, 5 oz., 12 oz. $18.00–28.00

EBONY GLASS ITEMS

2288 Tut Vase, 8½" $75.00–85.00
2402 Bowl, 9" $55.00–65.00
2402 Candlestick $25.00–30.00
2404 Vase, 6" $85.00–95.00
2409 Vase, 7½" $85.00–95.00
2428 Bowl, Rd., 7" $40.00–50.00
2428 Vase, 6", 9" $45.00–65.00
2428 Vase, 13" $75.00–85.00
2430 Bowl, 11" $75.00–85.00
2430 Candlestick, 2" $30.00–35.00
2430 Candy Jar, Cov., 5¾" $75.00–85.00
2453 Lustre, 7½" $95.00–105.00
2467 Vase, Ftd., 7½" $75.00–85.00
2496 Smoker Set, 5-Pc...............$75.00–85.00
2538 Place Card Holder $25.00–30.00
2545 Candle "Flame", 2" $30.00–35.00
2545 Candle Lamp, "Flame" $80.00–90.00
2567 Vase, Cry., Top, 7½" $75.00–85.00
2592 Ash Tray, Oblong $25.00–30.00
2592 Cigarette Box, Cov., 6" $65.00–75.00
2618 Cigarette Box, Cov., 5½" .$55.00–65.00
2629 Chanticleer, 10¾" $300.00–350.00
2636 Plume Book End................$80.00–90.00
2638 Candlestick, 4½"..............$45.00–55.00
2666 Bowl, Oval, 8¼" $55.00–65.00
2666 Bowl, Salad, 9", 11" $60.00–80.00
2666 Flora Candle, 6" $30.00–35.00
2666 Mayonnaise, 3-Pc. $45.00–55.00
2666 Salad Set w/Cry. Plate.......$65.00–75.00
2667 Ash Tray, 5", 7", 9"...........$20.00–35.00
2667 Candlestick, 2½"..............$25.00–30.00
2667 Cigarette Holder, 2¾"........$25.00–30.00
2668 Candlestick, 2½"..............$30.00–35.00
2668 Hurricane Lamp, 11¾".......$85.00–95.00

GARDEN CENTER ITEMS

Suggested Prices are for Color.

834 Pitcher, Jenny Lind (70).....$90.00–105.00
1121 Comport, 5¾" (389).........$25.00–35.00
2364 Bowl, Lily Pond, 9" (197) ...$30.00–40.00
2364 Bowl, Lily Pond, 12" (251) .$45.00–55.00
2577 Vase, 8½" (792) $30.00–40.00
2596 Bowl, Shallow, 11" (215)...$35.00–45.00
2638 Bowl, 10½" (220) $40.00–50.00
2666 Bowl, 8¼" (189) $30.00–40.00
2692 Bowl, Fruit, Ftd. (234) $40.00–50.00
2692 Urn, Hndl., 6" (760) $45.00–55.00
2692 Urn, Hndl., 12" (828) $75.00–85.00
2693 Franklin Urn, Cov., 8½" (162) $75.00–85.00
2703 Bowl, Oblong, 14¾" (189) .$50.00–60.00
2724 Goblet Vase, 7½" (779).....$30.00–40.00
2725 Urn, Hndl., 4⅜" (761) $30.00–40.00
4152 Vase/Bowl, 3⅞" (751).......$20.00–30.00
4166 Bowl, Ftd., 5" (151)...........$35.00–45.00
4166 Bowl, Ftd., 9" (199)...........$35.00–45.00
4166 Vase, Bud, 6" (757)...........$20.00–30.00

LAMP & LAMP PARTS

Suggested Prices are for Crystal unless noted.
Add 50% for Color.

— Bobache..........................$13.00–18.00
— Candle Lamp Chimney $30.00–40.00
— Candle Lamp Pot $10.00–15.00
— Colonial Princess, 20"....$600.00–700.00
— Lamp Post Night Lamp w/Shade......................$350.00–400.00
— Screw-In Holder.................$20.00–25.00
17 Banquet Lamp, 19".......$300.00–350.00
21 Princess Lamp, 20" $350.00–450.00
25 Banquet Lamp, 19".......$300.00–350.00
25½ Banquet Lamp, 19", Etched.........................$450.00–500.00
26 Candle Lamp with Shade....$75.00–85.00
26 Candle Lamp without Shade$55.00–65.00
26 Candle Lamp Base without Peg $18.00–23.00
26–1 Candle Lamp Base with Peg$18.00–23.00
122 Bobache..........................$15.00–20.00
179 Lamp, 9¾", 10¾" $70.00–90.00
183 Peg Fount, Victoria Pattern $95.00–115.00
183 Fount, Burner, Chimney, Victoria $125.00–145.00
183 Fairy Lamp, Victoria, Rose Shade $200.00–250.00
188 Bobache..........................$15.00–20.00
191 Squat Lamp, Ftd. $65.00–75.00
191 Squat Lamp......................$60.00–70.00
191B Lamp...............................$60.00–70.00
200 Lamp, Hndl., Ftd., 6½".......$65.00–75.00
200 Lamp, 9½", 10¼", 11"....$80.00–100.00
410 Spring Socket Peg $30.00–40.00
609 Filler Fount $30.00–40.00
734 Sewing Lamp "Priscilla with Flower" $200.00–225.00
803 Fount, Hndl. $40.00–50.00
920 Filler Fount $30.00–40.00

1272 Sewing Lamp, Engvd. Chimney....................$135.00–155.00
1273 Sewing Lamp, Engraved Chimney....................$115.00–135.00
1490 Candle Lamp w/Shade, 13½" $225.00–250.00
1550 Lamp, 9½", 10" $70.00–90.00
1592 Lamp, Ftd., Hndl....................$75.00–85.00
1639 Candle Lamp Complete, 13½" $225.00–250.00
1834 Tulip Lamp, 10"....................$85.00–95.00
2063 Saucer Candle, Hndl., 2 3/16" ..$25.00–35.00
2325 Lg. Electric Boudoir Lamp, Ebony $135.00–155.00
2325 Sm. Electric Boudoir Lamp, Ebony $125.00–145.00
4024 Lamp, Victoria Pattern, Color $275.00–300.00
5056 Lamp, Daisy Etched $175.00–200.00

MILK GLASS

Suggested Prices are for White Milk Glass. Add 50% for Color.

600 Vase, Cupped, 6½" (767) ..$40.00–50.00
824 Tray for Comb, Brush, 11½" ..$40.00–50.00
826 Tray, Pin, 6"....................$25.00–35.00
827 Cologne, Stopper, 10¾" $65.00–75.00
828 Pin Box, Cov., 5"....................$35.00–45.00
829 Puff Box, Cov., 3 1/18" $35.00–45.00
830 Pomade, Cov., 2⅛" $35.00–45.00
831 Handkerchief Box, Cov., 5¼"....................$55.00–65.00
832 Glove Box, Cov., 10⅜"......$70.00–80.00
833 Jewel Box, Cov., 6" $45.00–55.00
834 Pitcher, 8¼"....................$90.00–105.00
835 Tumbler, 4½" $25.00–30.00
1121 Compote, 6¾" (388) $45.00–55.00
1121 Compote, 5¾" (389) $25.00–35.00
1200 Rose Bowl, 4" (146) $25.00–35.00
1200 Bowl, Crimped, 3½" (155) .$20.00–30.00
1200 Spoon Holder, 4¼" (677)...$20.00–30.00
1200 Celery Vase, Swung (792)..$30.00–40.00
1229 Bud Vase, 6"....................$15.00–25.00
1229 Candy Jar, Cov., 6½" $25.00–35.00
1229 Spoon Holder, 3⅞"............$20.00–30.00
1229 Vase, Swung, 10" $35.00–45.00
1229 Toothpick, 2¼"....................$20.00–30.00
1300 Planters Vase, 4¼" (751)....$20.00–30.00
1300 Rose Bowl, 5" (149) $25.00–35.00
1704 Butter, Cov. $50.00–60.00
1704 Cracker Jar, Cov., 8¾".......$75.00–85.00
1704 Cream, 4½" $20.00–25.00
1704 Jug, Ice, ½-Gal. $75.00–85.00
1704 Ice Tea Tumbler, 10½ oz. ...$23.00–28.00
1704 Jelly, 3- Corner, 3⅛" $25.00–30.00
1704 Jelly, Oblong, 4" $25.00–30.00
1704 Jelly, Sq., 3¼"....................$25.00–30.00
1704 Nappy, 3-Corner $20.00–25.00
1704 Nappy, Sq. $20.00–25.00
1704 Oil, Stopper, 6 oz. $50.00–60.00
1704 Pickle Jar, Cov., 4¾"..........$65.00–75.00
1704 Punch Bowl, Stand, 14" .$225.00–275.00
1704 Punch Cup, 5½ oz.............$20.00–25.00
1704 Shaker, 3" $18.00–23.00
1704 Sugar, Cov., 6⅞" $35.00–45.00
1704 Water Tumbler, 7 oz. $20.00–25.00
1886 Pin Box, Cov. (281) $35.00–45.00
1886 Pin Tray (544) $25.00–35.00
1886 Puff Box, Cov. (580) $35.00–45.00
2056 Ash Tray/Topper, 2⅛", 2½"..$20.00–30.00
2056 Topper/Vase, 3", 4" $35.00–45.00
2056 Vase, Ftd., 6", 8½"...........$30.00–40.00
2056 Vase, Ftd., Sq., 9" $45.00–55.00
2056 Wedding Bowl, Cov., 8" $85.00–95.00
2183 Bowl, Shallow, 12"...........$50.00–60.00
2183 Bowl, Sq., 9" $50.00–60.00
2183 Candleholder, 2¾"............$20.00–30.00
2183 Hurricane Lamp w/Chimney .$45.00–55.00
2412 Butter, Cov., 7½" $35.00–45.00
2412 Candy Box, Cov., Colony Pattern $40.00–50.00
2412 Comport, Cov., 6⅜" $45.00–55.00
2493 Tavern Beer Mug $35.00–45.00
2513 Bowl, Crimped (155) $20.00–30.00
2513 Candy Jar, Cov., 6" $35.00–45.00
2519 Floral Cologne, Stopper $45.00–55.00
2519 Floral Puff, Cov. $40.00–50.00
2521 Bird $20.00–25.00
2589 Deer Standing, 4⅜"...........$50.00–60.00
2589 Deer, Lying, 2½" $45.00–55.00
2595 Sleigh, 3", 4¼"....................$20.00–35.00
2595 Sleigh, 6" $30.00–40.00
2620 Basket/Bowl, 11½" $45.00–55.00
2620 Bowl, Cupped, 8½"...........$40.00–50.00
2620 Bowl, Flared Bowl, 10½" ...$40.00–50.00
2620 Bowl, Fruit, 10¾" $40.00–50.00
2620 Candlestick, 3" $20.00–25.00
2620 Cream, 4" $20.00–25.00

2620	Goblet, 9 oz.	$20.00–30.00
2620	Ice Tea Tumbler, 12 oz.	$20.00–30.00
2620	Lamp, Hurricane w/Chimney	$45.00–55.00
2620	Juice Tumbler, 5 oz.	$20.00–25.00
2620	Nappy, 3-Corner, 4½"	$18.00–23.00
2620	Nappy, Sq., 4"	$18.00–23.00
2620	Plate, 8"	$23.00–28.00
2620	Plate, Fruits Dec., 523	$25.00–35.00
2620	Sherbet, 4"	$18.00–23.00
2620	Sugar, 3¾"	$20.00–25.00
2675	Ash Tray, 3½"	$13.00–18.00
2675	Bowl, Cov., Ftd., 10"	$50.00–60.00
2675	Candleholder, 1½"	$20.00–25.00
2675	Candleholder, 6"	$25.00–35.00
2675	Cigarette Box, Cov., 6⅜"	$25.00–35.00
2675	Cream, Ftd., 3⅝"	$20.00–25.00
2675	Cup & Saucer	$20.00–25.00
2675	Egg Cup, 4½"	$20.00–25.00
2675	Egg Plate, 12"	$45.00–55.00
2675	Ftd. Buffet Plate, 12½"	$45.00–55.00
2675	Lamp, Hurricane w/Shade	$55.00–65.00
2675	Nappy, 6"	$18.00–23.00
2675	Nappy, Cupped, 5⅜"	$18.00–23.00
2675	Nappy, Oblong, 5"	$18.00–23.00
2675	Nappy, Sq., 6"	$18.00–23.00
2675	Plate, 9"	$20.00–30.00
2675	Preserve, Cov., Ftd.	$45.00–55.00
2675	Shaker, 3½"	$18.00–23.00
2675	Shallow Bowl, Ftd., 10"	$40.00–50.00
2675	Sugar, Cov., Ftd.	$30.00–40.00
2675	Tray, 7"	$20.00–25.00
2675	Tumbler, Ftd., 9 oz.	$20.00–30.00
2675	Urn, Cov., Ftd., 8"	$55.00–65.00
2676	Hen on Nest, Dec.	$45.00–55.00
2678	Banana Bowl, Ftd., 10¾"	$75.00–85.00
2678	Bowl, Fruit, Ftd., 10"	$65.00–75.00
2678	Bowl, Fruit, Shallow, 10½"	$50.00–60.00
2678	Salver, Ftd., 11¼"	$75.00–85.00
2679	Puff, Cov., 4⅝"	$35.00–45.00
2680	Stagecoach, Cov., 5⅜"	$75.00–85.00
2682	Fish Nappy, 9½"	$20.00–30.00
2693	Urn, Cov., Ftd., 8½"	$65.00–75.00
2694	Ash Tray, 7", 9"	$20.00–30.00
2694	Bowl/Banana Stand, 7"	$65.00–75.00
2694	Candleholder, Duo, 5¼"	$45.00–55.00
2694	Compote, Belled, 8"	$55.00–65.00
2694	Compote, Sq., 9½"	$65.00–75.00
2694	Comport, Cov., Flared	$75.00–85.00
2694	Dripcut Syrup, 5⅕"	$45.00–55.00
2694	Lace Bowl, 7"	$55.00–65.00
2694	Marmalade, Cov., w/Spoon	$30.00–40.00
2694	Mustard, Cov., w/Spoon	$25.00–35.00
2694	Oil & Stopper, 5 oz.	$45.00–55.00
2694	Pepper Mill, 6¼"	$30.00–40.00
2694	Salt Shaker, 5½"	$25.00–30.00
2694	Salver, 13½"	$55.00–65.00
2694	Spoon Holder, Cov., 7½"	$50.00–60.00
2700	Basket, Pansy (743)	$20.00–30.00
2700	Bowl, Violet (747)	$20.00–30.00
2710	Butter, Cov., (300)	$40.00–50.00
2710	Cream/Sugar Tray, Indv. (686)	$55.00–65.00
2710	Nappy, 3-Corner (501)	$20.00–25.00
2710	Nappy, Sq., (502)	$20.00–25.00
2711	Candy, Cov., Ftd., 5¾" (676)	$30.00–40.00
2711	Cream, Ftd., 4¼" (680)	$20.00–25.00
2711	Planter, Ftd., 3½" (677)	$20.00–30.00
2711	Sugar, Ftd., 3⅜" (679)	$20.00–25.00
2712	Bowl, Berry, Ftd., 8" (179)	$55.00–65.00
2712	Bowl, Berry/Dessert (499)	$20.00–25.00
2712	Bowl, Cupped, Ftd., (180)	$45.00–55.00
2712	Bowl, Shallow, 6½" (355)	$45.00–55.00
2712	Candy, Cov., 6¼" (354)	$50.00–60.00
2712	Flora Candle (311)	$20.00–30.00
2712	Jelly, Ftd., 2¼" (592)	$20.00–30.00
2712	Nappy, Oblong (450)	$25.00–30.00
2712	Nappy, 3-Corner (452)	$25.00–30.00
2712	Plate, 8" (550)	$20.00–30.00
2712	Sugar, Cream & Tray, Indv. (686)	$60.00–70.00
2712	Vase, Bud, Ftd., 8" (799)	$25.00–35.00
2713	Bowl, Berry, 8" (179)	$45.00–55.00
2713	Bowl, Crimped, 8" (180)	$45.00–55.00
2713	Butter, Cov., ½ lb. (300)	$45.00–55.00
2713	Candleholder, 4" (315)	$25.00–35.00
2713	Candy Jar, Cov., 6³⁄₁₆" (347)	$45.00–55.00
2713	Dessert/Berry, 4½" (499)	$20.00–25.00
2713	Goblet, 11 oz. (2)	$20.00–25.00
2713	Ice Tea, Ftd., 13 oz. (63)	$20.00–30.00
2713	Leaf Candleholder (311)	$25.00–35.00
2713	Leaf Tray (720)	$25.00–35.00
2713	Nappy, Crimped, 4" (500)	$25.00–30.00
2713	Nappy, Sq., 4" (502)	$25.00–30.00
2713	Planter, 3½" (348)	$20.00–30.00
2713	Plate, 8" (550)	$20.00–25.00

2713 Shaker, 3½" (653)............$20.00–25.00
2713 Sherbet, 7½ oz. (11) $20.00–25.00
2713 Sugar, Cream & Tray, Indv..$60.00–70.00
2713 Tray, Bread, 11" (385).......$50.00–60.00
2713 Wedding Bowl, Cov. (162).$65.00–75.00
2714 Crocus Pot, Cov., 8½"........$60.00–70.00
2720 Trivet, 7¼" (718)..............$30.00–40.00

BLOWN STEMWARE & TUMBLERS

Suggested Prices are for Crystal. Add 100% for Burgundy, Regal Blue, Ruby, and Wisteria. Add 50% for Empire Green and other Colors.

Brandy, 1 oz....................$28.00–33.00
Claret Wine, 3, 3½, 3¾, 4, 4½ oz............................$23.00–28.00
Cocktail, 3, 3¼, 3½, 3¾, 4 oz...............................$23.00–28.00
Cordial, ¾ oz., 1 oz., 1½ oz............................$28.00–33.00
Creme de Menthe, 2 oz. $28.00–33.00
Goblet, 9 oz., 10 oz., 10½ oz..........................$20.00–25.00
Liquor Cocktail, 2½, 3, 3½, 4 oz..............................$18.00–23.00
Oyster Cocktail, Ftd., 3¾, 4, 4½, 4¾, 5, 5½ oz. $18.00–23.00
Parfait, 5½ oz., 6 oz. $23.00–28.00
Saucer Champagne/Sherbet, 5½, 6½, 7 oz. $18.00–23.00
Sherbet, Low, 5, 5½, 6 oz..$18.00–23.00
Sherry, 2 oz.....................$28.00–33.00
Tumbler, Ftd., 2½ oz. $28.00–33.00
Tumbler, Ftd., 8 oz., 9 oz. ..$15.00–20.00
Tumbler, 12 , 13, 14 oz.....$20.00–25.00
Tumbler, Juice, Ftd., 5 oz., 5½ oz............................$18.00–23.00
Tumbler, Whiskey, Ftd., 1½ oz............................$28.00–33.00
Wine, 2½, 2¾, 3, 3¼, 3½ oz............................$25.00–30.00

TUMBLERS, BLOWN

Suggested Prices are for Color. Patterns: Catalina, Congo, Horizon, Humpty Dumpty, Inca, Karnak, Tara

Beverage.........................$30.00–35.00
Cordial...........................$25.00–30.00
Dessert/Finger Bowl $20.00–25.00
Ice Tea/Cooler/Highball $30.00–35.00
Juice/Cocktail $20.00–25.00
Plate, 7⅜" $18.00–23.00
Sherbet/Old Fashioned......$20.00–25.00
Water/Scotch & Soda........$20.00–25.00

Patterns: Homespun, Needlepoint

Ice Tea/Highball, 15 oz. $35.00–40.00
Juice/Old Fashioned, 9 oz. $30.00–35.00
Water/Scotch & Soda, 11½ oz. $30.00–35.00

VANITY DRESSER ITEMS

Suggested Prices are for Crystal unless noted. Add 50% for Color.

482 Cologne, Stopper, 8 oz. $50.00–60.00
605 Cologne, Stopper, 8 oz. $50.00–60.00
1666 Puff, Cov., Etch 221 ....$65.00–75.00
2118 Cologne, Stopper, Cut 138.$65.00–75.00
2135 Puff, Cov., Cut 112 ....$70.00–80.00
2242 Cologne, Stopper, Engrvd. 14 ....$65.00–75.00
2243 Cologne, Stopper, Engrvd. "B" $65.00–75.00
2243 Cologne, Stopper, Etch 253$65.00–75.00
2276 Vanity, Cut 174, Color ...$190.00–210.00
2286 Comb & Brush Tray, Ebony .$85.00–95.00
2289 Vanity, Engrvd., Color $190.00–210.00

VASES

Suggested Prices are for Undecorated Crystal unless noted. Add 50% for Color.

184 Vase, Pressed, 9" $35.00–45.00
184 Vase, Pressed, 11", 14" $60.00–70.00
195 Vase, Pressed, 5" $20.00–30.00
272 Vase, Pressed, 5½"...........$20.00–30.00
300 Vase, Etched, 12".............$85.00–95.00
466 Vase, Pressed, 5", 7" $25.00–35.00
600 Vase, Ftd., Brazilian Pattern, 11"................................$55.00–65.00
725 Vase, Priscilla, Plain $50.00–60.00
725 Vase, Priscilla, Etched.........$75.00–85.00
736 Vase, Iris, Plain.................$50.00–60.00
736 Vase, Iris, Etched $75.00–85.00
760 Vase, Ftd., Dec. 7¼", 12" ..$65.00–95.00
761 Vase, Ftd., Cut, 10" $80.00–90.00
762 Vase, Ftd., Etched, Cut, 8"..$80.00–90.00
763 Vase, Ftd., Etched, Cut, 8", 9"................................$80.00–100.00
764 Vase, Ftd., Etched, Cut, 9"................................$90.00–100.00

912	Vase, Blown, 9"	$55.00–65.00
914	Vase, Blown, 11½"	$40.00–50.00
946	Vase, 7", Opal	$35.00–45.00
950	Vase, Opal, 9"	$55.00–65.00
989	Vase, Opal, 10"	$60.00–70.00
990	Vase, Opal, 12"	$75.00–85.00
1120	Vase, Loop Optic, 12", 15", Color	$95.00–125.00
1150	Vase, Opal, 15"	$110.00–130.00
1154	Vase, Opal, 5"	$45.00–55.00
1155	Vase, Opal, 6"	$45.00–55.00
1229	Vase, 3½", 6", Frisco Pattern	$15.00–30.00
1229	Vase, 13", Frisco Pattern	$45.00–55.00
1231	Vase, 10"	$35.00–45.00
1299	Vase, 14", 17"	$65.00–85.00
1300	Vase, 8", 14", Light	$40.00–65.00
1300	Vase, 12", Heavy	$40.00–50.00
1312	Vase, 14"	$55.00–65.00
1479	Vase, 6", Color	$50.00–60.00
1605	Vase, Nasturtium, Sherwood, 9"	$50.00–60.00
1663	Vase, 9", 16"	$50.00–80.00
1681	Wall Vase, 8", Color	$85.00–95.00
1752	Vase, Snake Optic, 13", Color	$95.00–110.00
1798	Vase, Ftd., Etched, Cut, 9"	$85.00–95.00
1799	Vase, Ftd., Etched, 7¼"	$75.00–85.00
1895	Vase, Heavy, Sham, 10"	$45.00–55.00
1948	Vase, Ftd., 5½", Dec.	$55.00–65.00
1948	Vase, Ftd., 8", 10", 12½", Dec.	$70.00–95.00
2072	Vase, Blown, Engrvd., 12"	$55.00–65.00
2072	Vase, Blown, Engrvd., #16, 10"	$50.00–60.00
2081	Vase, Blown, Engrvd., #17, 12"	$75.00–85.00
2109	Vase, Pressed, 9½"	$45.00–55.00
2128	Vase, 7½", 10"	$45.00–65.00
2209	Vase, Cry., Etched, 9"	$75.00–85.00
2210	Vase, Cry., Etched, 10", 10½"	$80.00–90.00
2210	Vase, Satin Pearl, 10", 10½"	$95.00–105.00
2211	Vase, Cry., Etched, 10"	$80.00–90.00
2211	Vase, Satin Pearl, 10"	$95.00–105.00
2212	Vase, Cry., Etched, 10"	$80.00–90.00
2212	Vase, Satin Pearl, 10"	$95.00–105.00
2218	Vase, Sweetpea, 3-Ftd., Color	$75.00–85.00
2292	Vase, Ftd., Spiral Optic, 8"	$50.00–60.00
2360	Vase, Hndl., 8", 10", Color	$85.00–105.00
2367	Bulb Bowl, 7", 8", Color	$35.00–45.00
2369	Vase, Ftd., Optic, 7", 9", Color	$85.00–95.00
2387	Vase, "Flutes", 8", Color	$85.00–95.00
2387	Vase, Heavy, 8"	$45.00–55.00
2387	Vase, Bubbles, 8"	$60.00–70.00
2404	Vase, "Nautilus", 6", 8", Color	$75.00–95.00
2408	Vase, 8"	$45.00–55.00
2409	Vase, 7½"	$40.00–50.00
2417	Vase, 8"	$35.00–45.00
2421	Vase, 10½"	$65.00–75.00
2425	Vase, 8"	$45.00–55.00
2428	Vase, "Narrow Reeds", 7½"	$35.00–45.00
2428	Vase, 10", 13", Color	$75.00–95.00
2431	Wall Vase, Color	$85.00–95.00
2454	Vase, Tri-Pod, 8", Ebony	$75.00–85.00
2467	Vase, Ftd., 2-Hndl., 7½"	$30.00–40.00
2468	Vase, Rib Optic, Color	$30.00–40.00
2470	Vase, "Hugh", Ftd., 8", Color	$80.00–90.00
2470	Vase, "Hugh", Ftd., 10", 11½"	$65.00–75.00
2503	Vase, Hndl., 8", Color	$85.00–95.00
2522	Vase, Silver Mist, 8"	$55.00–65.00
2523	Vase, Silver Mist, 6½"	$45.00–55.00
2545	Vase, Flame, Ftd., 10", 12", Color	$70.00–90.00
2567	Vase, Ftd., Hvy., 6", 7½", 8½"	$40.00–60.00
2568	Vase, Ftd., Hvy., 9"	$50.00–60.00
2569	Vase, Ftd., Hvy., 9"	$50.00–60.00
2570	Vase, Flared, Hvy., 6¾"	$40.00–50.00
2570	Vase, Reg., Hvy., 7"	$40.00–50.00
2577	Vase, Sham, 15"	$85.00–95.00
2577	Vase, Bubble, 6", Color	$90.00–100.00
2577	Vase, 6"	$40.00–50.00
2577	Vase, Bubble, Wide, 5½", Color	$90.00–100.00
2577	Vase, Hammered, Wide, 5½"	$55.00–65.00
2577	Vase, Hammered, 6", Color	$90.00–100.00
2577	Vase, Wide, 5½"	$40.00–50.00

2577 Vase, Tapered, Hvy., 8½" ...$45.00–55.00
2579 Vase/Cornucopia, Acanthus, 6" ...$70.00–80.00
2591 Vase, 8½", 11½" ...$45.00–65.00
2591 Vase, 15" ...$85.00–95.00
2591 Vase, Hvy., 15" ...$85.00–95.00
2600 Vase, Acanthus, 7" ...$75.00–85.00
2611 Vase, 14" ...$50.00–60.00
2612 Vase, Sham Btm., 13" ...$40.00–50.00
2614 Vase, 10" ...$40.00–50.00
2619 Vase, Grnd. Btm., 6", 7½" .$20.00–30.00
2619 Vase, Grnd. Btm., 9½" ...$40.00–50.00
2654 Vase, Ftd., 9½" ...$50.00–60.00
2656 Vase, Honeycomb Ft., 10" ..$60.00–70.00
2657 Vase, Etched, 10½" ...$85.00–95.00
2658 Vase, Ftd., 10½" ...$40.00–50.00
2660 Vase, Flip, 8" ...$25.00–35.00
2972 Bouquet Holder, 12" ...$45.00–55.00
4095 Vase, Ftd., Spiral Optic, 7", 8" ...$45.00–55.00
4095 Vase, Ftd., Spiral Optic, 9", 10" ...$65.00–75.00
4100 Vase, Loop Optic, 6", 8", 10", 12" ...$40.00–75.00
4100 Vase, Bubbles, 6", 8", Color ...$90.00–110.00
4100 Vase, Hammered, 6", 8", Color ...$90.00–110.00
4100 Vase, Optic, 10", 12", Color ...$70.00–90.00
4100 Vase, Optic, 6", 8", Color ..$50.00–70.00
4100 Vase, Etched Snowflakes, Color ...$125.00–135.00
4103 Vase, Bubbles, 3", 4", 5", Color ...$75.00–85.00
4103 Vase, Ribbed, Hvy., 5" ...$35.00–45.00
4103 Vase, Optic, 3", 4", 5", 6".$25.00–40.00
4105 Vase, Reg. Optic, 5" ...$35.00–45.00
4105 Vase, Loop Optic, 10", Color ...$75.00–85.00
4105 Vase, Reg. Optic, 8", Color..$75.00–85.00
4116 Ball Vase, Bubbles, 4", 5", 6" ...$80.00–90.00
4116 Ball Vase, Hammered, 4", 5", 6" Color ...$80.00–90.00
4116 Ball Vase, Ribbed, Hvy. ...$40.00–50.00
4121 Vase, Plain, 5" ...$15.00–25.00
4121 Vase, Reg. Optic, 5", Color.$55.00–65.00
4121 Vase, Bubbles, 5", Color ...$80.00–90.00
4121 Vase, Hammered, 4½", 5", Color ...$80.00–90.00
4121 Vase, Hammered, 4½", 5" .$50.00–65.00
4123 Vase, Pansy, 3¼", Color ...$25.00–35.00
4124 Vase, Bubbles, 4½", Color .$80.00–90.00
4124 Vase, Hammered, 4½", Color ...$80.00–90.00
4124 Vase, Optic, 4½", Color ...$45.00–55.00
4125 Vase, Bubbles, 7", Color $110.00–120.00
4126 Vase, Ftd., Hvy., 11" ...$45.00–55.00
4128 Vase, Rib Optic, 5", Color ..$55.00–65.00
4128 Vase, Hvy., 5" ...$30.00–40.00
4128 Vase, Bubbles, 5" ...$50.00–60.00
4128 Vase, Bubbles, 5", 6", Color ...$90.00–100.00
4130 Vase, Violet, 3⅝", Color ...$25.00–35.00
4132 Vase, Hvy., 8" ...$45.00–55.00
4132 Vase/Ice Bowl, Bubbles, 5", Color ...$80.00–90.00
4133 Vase, Loop Optic, Blown, 4", Color ...$60.00–70.00
4134 Vase, Loop Optic, Blown, 6", Color ...$60.00–70.00
4137 Vase, Plain, 3¾", Color ...$25.00–35.00
4138 Vase, Plain, 3½", Color ...$25.00–35.00
4143 Vase, Hvy., Ftd., 7½" ...$40.00–50.00
4143 Vase, Ftd., 6", 7½" ...$30.00–40.00
4143 Vase, Hvy., Ftd., 6" ...$40.00–50.00
4144 Vase, Violet/Pansy, 3" ...$10.00–20.00
4145 Vase, Violet/Pansy, 3" ...$10.00–20.00
5085 Vase, Ftd., Spiral Optic ...$45.00–55.00
5086 Vase, Ftd., Spiral Optic, Color ...$55.00–65.00
5087 Vase, Ftd., Spiral Optic, 8".$45.00–55.00
5088 Vase, Bud, Ftd., Ribbed, 5", 8", Color ...$35.00–65.00
5092 Vase, Bud, Ftd., 8", Regal Blue ...$85.00–95.00
5100 Vase, Plain, Optic, Ftd., 10", Color ...$75.00–85.00
5300 Vase, Bud, Ftd., 7" ...$25.00–35.00
5301 Vase, Bud, Ftd., 8" ...$30.00–40.00
6021 Vase, Bud, Ftd., 6", 9" ...$25.00–40.00

MISCELLANEOUS

Prices are for Crystal unless noted. Add 50% for Color.

14 Ink, Cov. ...$30.00–40.00
16 Sponge Cup ...$15.00–20.00

24	Candelabra, 4-Lt. (341)	$350.00–400.00
25	Candelabra, 5-Lt. (342)	$400.00–450.00
93	Salt Dip	$10.00–15.00
95	Salt Dip	$10.00–15.00
97	Cruet/Vinegar, 6 oz.	$65.00–75.00
114	Egg Cup, Ftd.	$15.00–20.00
127	Tumbler, Hndl., 8 oz.	$20.00–25.00
135	Jug, Silver Deposit	$250.00–300.00
136	Shaker	$20.00–25.00
137	Shaker	$20.00–25.00
140	Bowl, Orange	$30.00–40.00
152	Cruet/Vinegar, 6 oz.	$65.00–75.00
160	Water Bottle, Blown	$45.00–55.00
162	Jug, 3-Pt.	$70.00–80.00
175	Cruet/Vinegar, 4½ oz.	$45.00–55.00
187	Oil, Pressed, 4 oz.	$45.00–55.00
193	Shaker #1, Flemish	$20.00–25.00
300	Cruet, Cut Clover Pattern	$65.00–75.00
300	Jug (300½)	$65.00–75.00
300	Pitcher, Etched	$110.00–125.00
300	Tumbler, Etched	$20.00–25.00
302	Pitcher, Etched	$110.00–125.00
302	Tumbler, Etched	$20.00–25.00
305	Water Bottle	$55.00–65.00
308	Ink, Stopper, Various Sizes	$30.00–40.00
315	Bitters Bottle	$30.00–40.00
317	Jug, Cut Neck	$60.00–70.00
329	Jug, Blown, 2-Qt.	$65.00–75.00
402	Tantalus Set, Valkyrie Pattern	$300.00–350.00
417	Syrup, Silver Top	$55.00–65.00
444	Custard Cup, Czarina Pattern	$300.00–350.00
456	Horseradish w/Spoon	$75.00–85.00
459	Berry Bowl, 9"	$60.00–70.00
465	Salt Dip	$15.00–20.00
476	Bitters Bottle	$40.00–50.00
479	Water Bottle, Blown	$40.00–50.00
486	Safety Ink	$20.00–25.00
493	Boston Measuring Cup	$30.00–35.00
551	Butter, Cov.	$40.00–50.00
551	Cream	$25.00–30.00
576	Cup, Custard, Edgewood Pattern	$10.00–15.00
581	Water Bottle, 1-Qt.	$55.00–65.00
582	Mucilage Cup w/Brush	$40.00–50.00
583	Soap Dish, Opal	$25.00–35.00
584	Sherbet, Ftd.	$10.00–15.00
584	Sherbet, Ftd., Hndl.	$10.00–15.00
585	Salt Dip	$10.00–15.00
597	Molasses Can, Dec., 16 oz.	$85.00–95.00
598	Molasses Can, 15 oz.	$85.00–95.00
601	Butter, Cov., Diana Pattern	$45.00–55.00
601	Spoon, Diana Pattern	$50.00–55.00
675	Shaker, Edgewood Pattern	$20.00–25.00
675	Syrup, 8 oz., Edgewood Pattern	$85.00–95.00
675	Vinegar, Edgewood Pattern	$55.00–65.00
676	Shaker, Sm., Priscilla Pattern	$20.00–25.00
691	Shaker	$20.00–25.00
726	Syrup Can	$65.00–75.00
728	Shaker	$20.00–25.00
740	Berry Bowl, 9"	$55.00–65.00
794	Nappy, 4½"	$10.00–15.00
795	Vinegar	$45.00–55.00
820	Tumbler, Etch 203	$20.00–30.00
826	Pin Tray, Dec. (826½)	$30.00–40.00
828	Tumbler, Pressed, Dec.	$15.00–20.00
828	Hair Pin Box, Dec. (828½)	$45.00–55.00
829	Puff Pin Box, Dec. (829½)	$30.00–40.00
830	Pomade Box, Dec. (830½)	$45.00–55.00
831	Handkerchief, Dec. (831½)	$50.00–60.00
832	Glove Box, Dec. (832½)	$70.00–80.00
900	Jelly Glass	$7.00–10.00
910	Jug, Blown, 2-Qt.	$65.00–75.00
920	Filler Fount	$30.00–40.00
921	Syrup, Glass Lip, 16 oz.	$85.00–95.00
952	Jug, 3-Pt.	$70.00–80.00
953	Jug, 3-Pt.	$65.00–75.00
954	Berry/Pickle Dish	$30.00–40.00
963	Bottle, Stopper, Glass Spoon	$70.00–80.00
972	Berry Bowl, 8"	$45.00–55.00
982	Jelly Glass, ½-Pt.	$8.00–13.00
1002	Vase, 20", Color (834)	$135.00–145.00
1062	Shaker	$20.00–25.00
1063	Tumbler, Pressed	$20.00–25.00
1132	Bottle, Stopper, Glass Spoon	$75.00–85.00
1166	Jug, Panel "A"	$85.00–95.00
1166	Jug, Panel "D"	$85.00–95.00
1229	Vase, Bud, 6", Color (757)	$25.00–35.00
1269	Sherbet, Ftd.	$15.00–20.00
1333	Decanter, Qt., Sydney Pattern	$85.00–95.00
1445	Water Bottle, Blown, 40 oz.	$45.00–55.00
1461	Bowl/Nappy, 4½"	$15.00–20.00
1497	Bowl/Comport, 8"	$50.00–60.00
1515	Crushed Ice, Plate, Lucere Pattern	$55.00–65.00

1515	Bowl, 10", Color (208)	$75.00–85.00
1515	Bowl, 15", Color (270)	$85.00–95.00
1515	Centerpiece, 16", Color (279)	$85.00–95.00
1515	Candle Vase, 10", Color (311)	$55.00–65.00
1515	Epergne, Lg., 2-Pc., Color (364)	$155.00–165.00
1515	Vase, 11", Color (827)	$65.00–75.00
1549	Jug. 3-Pt.	$70.00–80.00
1549	Jug, 1-Qt.	$75.00–85.00
1611	Shaker	$20.00–25.00
1626	Cream, Indv.	$20.00–25.00
1626	Sugar, Indv.	$20.00–25.00
1678	Bar Bottle, 12 oz.	$30.00–40.00
1697	Bathroom Set, Etched	$85.00–95.00
1712	Sugar Lid	$8.00–13.00
1723	Sundae/Sherbet, Ftd., 6 oz.	$25.00–30.00
1738	Show Window Stand, 10½"	$170.00–180.00
1738	Show Window Stand, 13", 16"	$200.00–240.00
1739	Shoe Plate Stand, 13"	$180.00–200.00
1739	Shoe Plate Stand, 15", 18"	$220.00–240.00
1743	Jug, Cov., 5-Pt.	$50.00–60.00
1743	Jug, Cov., 7-Pt.	$60.00–70.00
1751	Cream, Indv., w/Plate	$40.00–50.00
1760	Jug, Blown	$55.00–65.00
1762	Butter, Cov., 1-lb.	$50.00–60.00
1793	Jug, Optic, 75 oz.	$60.00–70.00
1800	Safety Ink	$20.00–25.00
1810	Jug, Cov.	$85.00–95.00
1857	Hotel Cream	$25.00–35.00
1857	Hotel Sugar	$25.00–35.00
1861	Jelly	$25.00–35.00
1869	Oil, 6½ oz.	$40.00–50.00
1874	Oil, Pressed, 4 oz.	$30.00–40.00
1904	Bon Bon, Cov., Etched 221	$75.00–85.00
1913	Salt, Indv.	$7.00–10.00
1913	Sherry, 2 oz., Flemish Pattern	$15.00–30.00
1918	Cherry Jar, Stopper	$75.00–85.00
1918	Olive Jar, Stopper, 7"	$65.00–75.00
1918	Rock & Rye, Stopper, 30 oz.	$95.00–105.00
1918	Straw Jar, Cov., Sm. 6¼"	$75.00–85.00
1918	Straw Jar, Cov., Optic	$175.00–200.00
1931	Cream, Cov., 3¼"	$30.00–40.00
1931	Sugar, Cov., 2¾"	$30.00–40.00
1981	Shoe Rest, 3¼"	$85.00–95.00
1981	Shoe Rest, 3⅞"	$85.00–95.00
1990	Tumbler, 8½ oz.	$20.00–25.00
2000	Tray, Condiment w/Salts	$65.00–75.00
2056	Shrimp Bowl, American Pattern	$300.00–350.00
2077	Muffin Cover, 6"	$30.00–40.00
2098	Pie Cover, 10½"	$55.00–65.00
2106	Ash Tray, Vogue Pattern	$20.00–25.00
2106	Coaster, 3⅜"	$5.00–10.00
2106	Sugar Server, Vogue Pattern	$70.00–80.00
2111	Shaker	$8.00–13.00
2128	Shaker	$15.00–20.00
2183	Bowl, 7", Color (168)	$45.00–55.00
2183	Candle, Flora, Color (311)	$40.00–50.00
2183	Flower Float, 10", Color (415)	$55.00–65.00
2222	Salt, Ftd., Colonial Pattern	$10.00–15.00
2228	Candy Jar, Cov., Cut 143	$80.00–90.00
2272	Coaster, 4¼"	$5.00–10.00
2283	Plate, Ice Tea, 4", 5"	$5.00–10.00
2283	Plate, Bread/Butter/Finger	$5.00–10.00
2283	Plate for Bowl/Sherbet, 6"	$5.00–10.00
2283	Plate, 7", 8"	$8.00–13.00
2283	Plate, Sandwich, 9"	$13.00–18.00
2283	Plate, Sandwich, 10"	$13.00–18.00
2283	Plate, Service, 11", 12"	$15.00–20.00
2283	Plate, Service, 13"	$20.00–25.00
2283	Plate, Service, Deep, 11", 12", 13"	$18.00–23.00
2290	Plate, Salad, Deep, 7", 8"	$8.00–13.00
2290	Plate, Salad, Deep, 13"	$20.00–25.00
2321	Mah Jongg	$25.00–30.00
2327	Comport, 7"	$40.00–50.00
2337	Plate, 6", 7"	$8.00–13.00
2337	Plate, 8", 9"	$13.00–18.00
2348	Plate, "Laurel Ribbed", 8"	$13.00–18.00
2350	Cup, Ftd., Pioneer Pattern	$8.00–13.00
2350	Cup, After Dinner, Pioneer Pattern	$8.00–13.00
2364	Plate, 16"	$35.00–45.00
2374	Nut, Indv., Ftd.	$8.00–13.00
2375	Salad Dressing Bottle	$40.00–50.00
2376	Plate, Grill, 10", Fairfax Patt.	$18.00–23.00
2378	Ice Bucket, Drainer, Tongs	$45.00–55.00
2400	Comport	$40.00–50.00
2419	Cigarette, Cov.	$25.00–35.00
2419	Plate, 6"	$5.00–10.00
2419	Plate, 9"	$25.00–30.00

2419 Saucer $4.00–7.00
2419 Saucer, After Dinner..............$5.00–8.00
2442 Coaster, 4" $5.00–10.00
2443 Ice Tub, 2-Hndl. $30.00–40.00
2451 Crab Meat Liner $8.00–13.00
2451 Ice Bowl/Dish, Blown...........$8.00–13.00
2451 Ice/Fruit Bowl, Blown...........$8.00–13.00
2451 Plate/Ice Dish, 7" $8.00–13.00
2451 Tomato Juice, 5 oz...............$8.00–13.00
2456 Candy Jar, Cov., ½-lb. $30.00–40.00
2464 Jug, Ice Lip, 45 oz. $40.00–50.00
2464 Tumbler, Optic.....................$8.00–13.00
2479 Crab Liner, Fruit Liner, 4 oz...$8.00–13.00
2479 Tomato Juice Liner, 5 oz. $8.00–13.00
2493 Beer Mug, Tavern Scene.....$35.00–45.00
2512 Glass Fruits, Color $25.00–35.00
2513 Salt/Almond $8.00–13.00
2518 Cocktail Shaker w/Gold, Color...........................$135.00–155.00
2518 Cologne, Stopper $30.00–40.00
2518 Decanter, Qt., Color $115.00–135.00
2519 Cologne, Stopper, Silver Mist $40.00–50.00
2519 Puff, Cov., Silver Mist $35.00–45.00
2520 Ash Tray, 4½" $10.00–15.00
2525 Cocktail Shaker, Color ...$125.00–135.00
2525 Decanter, Stopper, Color $125.00–135.00
2528 Cocktail Tray.....................$20.00–30.00
2531 Pelican $75.00–85.00
2531 Polar Bear $75.00–85.00
2531 Seal.................................$75.00–85.00
2541 Snack Plate, Sq. $10.00–15.00
2561 Bath Bottle, Stopper $65.00–75.00
2562 Bath Bottle, Stopper w/Gold .$65.00–75.00
2562 Bath Bottle, Stopper, Silver Mist $75.00–85.00
2564 Horse Book End................$50.00–60.00
2570 Shell Bowl (189)................$40.00–50.00
2570 Plate, 17", Color (575) ..$165.00–185.00
2570 Basket/Vase (795).............$40.00–50.00
2580 Elephant Book End.........$125.00–145.00
2585 Eagle Book End............$165.00–185.00
2589 Colt $50.00–60.00
2589 Deer $50.00–60.00
2593 Salt, Indv. $8.00–13.00
2594 Candlestick, Trindle, 8" $45.00–55.00
2595 Nut Dish, "Sleigh", 3"........$15.00–20.00
2595 "Sleigh", 4¼" $23.00–28.00
2595 "Sleigh", 6" $25.00–30.00
2601 Lyre Book End $125.00–145.00
2608 Ash Tray, Rd., 4¼" $8.00–13.00
2615 Owl Book End, 7½".......$140.00–160.00
2616 Box, Cov., Oval $30.00–40.00
2626 Chinese Lotus, Silver Mist..$250.00–275.00
2626 Chinese Lute, Silver Mist .$250.00–275.00
2635 Madonna, 10", Crystal $55.00–65.00
2635 Madonna, 10", Silver Mist .$75.00–85.00
2635 Madonna Base.................$30.00–40.00
2661 Buffet Set, 3-Pc. $75.00–85.00
2661 Sauce Dish, Cov., 5¼" $20.00–30.00
2662 Buffet Set, 3-Pc. $55.00–65.00
2662 Sauce Dish, Cov., 5¼" $20.00–30.00
2663 Buffet Set, 3-Pc. $55.00–65.00
2664 Server, 4-Part, 12½" $25.00–35.00
2665 Plate, Sq., 7", 8" $13.00–18.00
2675 Egg Plate, Oval, 12" $25.00–35.00
2697 Bowl w/Wood, Flared $30.00–40.00
2697 Bowl w/Wood, Floating $30.00–40.00
2697 Bowl w/Wood, Salad $30.00–40.00
2698 Bath Salts, Cov. $20.00–30.00
2698 Cologne, Cov., 5¼" $20.00–25.00
2698 Cologne, Cov., 6½" $20.00–25.00
2698 Puff, Cov., 2¾", 3½" $20.00–30.00
2699 Apple, Cov., Satin $40.00–50.00
2699 Melon, 8".........................$35.00–45.00
2699 Pear, 7⅝" 35.00–45.00
2703 Bowl, 3-Corner (174).........$35.00–45.00
2703 Bowl, Oblong (189) $35.00–45.00
2703 Plate, Buffet (191) $40.00–50.00
2705 Bowl, 6½" $10.00–15.00
2706 Bowl/Salad/Punch, w/Wood $40.00–50.00
2706 Punch Cup $5.00–10.00
2707 Candleholder, 6¾", 8", 9½" $25.00–45.00
2708 Candleholder, 8"..............$25.00–35.00
2708 Candleholder, Duo $35.00–45.00
2708 Comport, Shallow.............$25.00–35.00
2708 Comport, Deep $25.00–35.00
2715 St. Francis, Silver Mist $85.00–95.00
2720 Basket, 12", Color (126) $60.00–70.00
2720 Bowl, Crinkle, Color (168)..$25.00–35.00
2720 Florette, Sq., Color (170)....$30.00–40.00
2720 Bowl, Star, 8½", Color (191) $50.00–60.00
2722 Vase, Peg, 8", Color (312) .$25.00–35.00
2722 Trindle Candle Arm, Color (334)..............................$40.00–50.00

2722	Table Charm #1, Color (364)	$145.00–165.00
2722	Table Charm #2, Color (364)	$155.00–175.00
2722	Table Charm #3, Color (364)	$130.00–150.00
2722	Table Charm #4, Color (364)	$145.00–165.00
2722	Flora Candle, 3", Color (460)	$25.00–35.00
2723	Epergne (364)	$85.00–95.00
2726	Candleholder, Color (311)	$25.00–35.00
2727	Bowl, Hanky, 6", Color (152)	$30.00–40.00
2727	Bowl, Sq., 6", Color (155)	$30.00–40.00
2727	Bowl, Sq., 9", Color (202)	$50.00–60.00
2727	Bowl, Shallow, 11", Color (231)	$55.00–65.00
2727	Bowl, Crimped, 11", Color (239)	$55.00–65.00
2727	Plate, 8", Color (550)	$25.00–35.00
2727	Plate, 11", Color (557)	$55.00–65.00
2728	Vase, Hndl., Color (751)	$40.00–50.00
2728	Pitcher/Vase, 9", Color (807)	$60.00–70.00
2728	Vase, Winged, 11", Color (827)	$70.00–80.00
2729	Bon Bon, 7", Color (135)	$30.00–40.00
2729	Bowl, Oval, 10", Color (540)	$45.00–55.00
2730	Centerpiece, Oval, Color (255)	$50.00–60.00
2730	Candle, 6" Color (319)	$30.00–40.00
2730	Epergne, 2-Pc., Color (364)	$95.00–105.00
4024	Bowl, Ftd., Victorian Pattern	$55.00–65.00
4024	Goblet, Silver Mist, Victorian Pattern	$25.00–35.00
4095	Jug, Ftd., 8½", 9½"	$70.00–80.00
4095	Jug, Ftd., 10¾"	$80.00–90.00
4095	Salt, Ftd., Optic	$8.00–13.00
4095	Salt, Ftd., Colored Ft.	$15.00–20.00
4116	Bubble Ball, 4", 5", Color	$30.00–40.00
4116	Bubble Ball, 6", 7", Color	$45.00–55.00
4116	Bubble Ball, 8", 9", Color	$60.00–70.00
4116	Bubble Ball, 4", 5", Decorated	$80.00–90.00
4116	Bubble Ball, 6", 7", Decorated	$100.00–120.00
4117	Bubble Candy Jar, Cov., Color	$125.00–145.00
4118	Jug, 60 oz.	$40.00–50.00
4118	Tumbler, 5"	$15.00–20.00
4129	Bubble Ball, 2½", Color	$30.00–40.00
4147	Jam Pot, Cov.	$20.00–30.00
4147	Tray, 7½"	$15.00–20.00
4152	Bowl, Snack, 3⅞"	$18.00–23.00
4168	Tumbler, 10½ oz.	$8.00–13.00
4169	Cocktail Mixer, Blown	$45.00–55.00
4171	Bowl w/Wood Stand, 10¼"	$30.00–40.00
5066	Schoeppen, Optic, 7 oz.	$25.00–35.00
5100	Shaker, Ftd., Glass Top	$20.00–25.00
5298	Comport, 6"	$40.00–50.00
5299	Comport 6"	$40.00–50.00
6030	Comport, 5", Astrid Pattern	$20.00–30.00
—	Baby Rabbit, 1¼"	$30.00–40.00
—	Cat, 2¾"	$30.00–40.00
—	Castor Set, Opal	$100.00–120.00
—	Cheese, Cov., Plate, Cut B	$60.00–70.00
—	Dipper w/Wood	$40.00–50.00
—	Dolphin, 4¾"	$85.00–95.00
—	Duckling, Head Back	$30.00–40.00
—	Duckling, Head Down	$30.00–40.00
—	Duckling, Walking	$30.00–40.00
—	Frog, 1⅞"	$30.00–40.00
—	Fruit Jar Filler	$20.00–30.00
—	Lady Bug, 1¼"	$30.00–40.00
—	Mama Duck, 4"	$40.00–50.00
—	Mama Rabbit, 2⅛"	$30.00–40.00
—	Owl, 2¾"	$30.00–40.00
—	Stork, 2"	$30.00–40.00
—	Straw Jar, Cov., Optic	$175.00–200.00
—	Squirrel, Running	$30.00–40.00
—	Squirrel, Sitting	$30.00–40.00
—	Toothpick (Hat)	$20.00–30.00

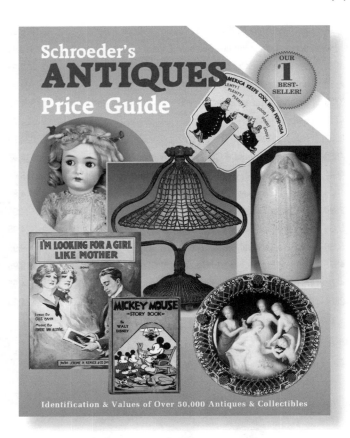